Group Psychotherapy with Addicted Populations

About the Author

Philip J. Flores, PhD, is a clinical psychologist who, for the last 10 years, has worked extensively in the area of addictive diseases. He is a member of the American Group Psychotherapy Association, the Georgia Association of Specialists in Group Work and the Atlanta Group Psychotherapy Society. He has taught Advanced Group Psychotherapy for a number of universities and private hospitals and was a former member of the Arizona Group Psychotherapy Society before moving to Atlanta, Georgia in 1982. He has trained extensively in group psychotherapy with numerous institutes of which Bob and Mary Goulding of the Western Institute of Group and Family Therapy, Irv and Miriam Polster of the Gestalt Training Center, La Jolla and Elaine Goldman of the Western Institute of Psychodrama are the most notable. Dr. Flores has also received a Certificate of Training in Group Psychotherapy from the University of Arizona Health Services Center. Prior to getting his PhD, he worked for a number of years as an alcoholism counselor. He has worked with addictive populations in both outpatient and inpatient settings in Ohio and Arizona before joining the Psychiatric Consultants Group of Atlanta and the Family Outpatient Counseling and Addictive Services (FOCAS), a treatment program which specializes in the outpatient treatment of addiction.

Dr. Flores has published numerous articles on addiction and this is his first book on group therapy. He has maintained a private practice which includes a very active caseload of individuals who have either been married to alcoholics or grown up in an alcoholic home. Dr. Flores continues to lead several adult children of alcoholic therapy groups on a weekly basis.

Group Psychotherapy with Addicted Populations

Philip J. Flores, PhD

The Haworth Press
New York • London

Group Psychotherapy with Addicted Populations is Volume 1 of the Haworth Series in Addictions Treatment.

The Haworth Press, Inc., 12 West 32 Street, New York, NY 10001
EUROSPAN/Haworth, 3 Henrietta Street, London, WC2E 8LU England

Library of Congress Cataloging-in-Publication Data

Flores, Philip J.
    Group psychotherapy with addicted populations.

    Includes bibliographies and index.
    1. Alcoholism — Treatment. 2. Group psychotherapy. 3. Substance abuse — Treatment.
I. Title [DNLM: WM 270 F634h]
RC565.F568   1988   616.86'06   87-7596
ISBN 0-86656-664-3
ISBN 0-86656-757-7 (pbk.)

CONTENTS

Preface

This is a book about addiction and its treatment. However, were that to be the total extent of its author's aim, it would not generate the excitement I think it will stimulate in those who read it carefully. More specifically, this is a book that not only addresses the important topic of addiction, it also outlines sound recommendations for the treatment of addiction within a group therapy setting. In fact, the book presents convincing evidence why group therapy should be the treatment of choice for addiction. It then succinctly outlines how this can be best accomplished within a group therapy setting. And, since group therapy and alcoholism are subjects very dear to me for very different reasons, I am excited to see a book which blends these topics into a smoothly convergent theme.

Alcoholism, the addiction of which I am most familiar, is often called a disease of denial, not only for the alcoholic, but for those who come in contact, professionally and personally, with the alcoholic. If someone is suffering from alcoholism, it is highly unlikely that the person's alcoholism will be diagnosed by a physician, psychologist, or other helping professional. If their alcoholism is diagnosed, the chances unfortunately are poor that the alcoholic will receive an appropriate referral for treatment. Too often, the alcoholic is only admonished to cut down on his drinking and told to straighten himself up and get his life together. If he even is referred to a psychotherapist, the focus of therapy often will be directed towards determining the nature of his "real problem." The message is clearly given that if he were to get at the core of his psychological conflict he could be "cured" and taught to drink normally once again.

To try and cure an alcoholic so they can drink socially and normally is a grave mistake. I know that Eric Berne and Claude Stiener, two very respected associates of mine, believed that an alcoholic could be cured, but I disagree with both of them. I do agree, however, that an alcoholic's life scripts and the games they play, as defined in Transactional Analysis theory are often important parts in the alcoholic's personality and contribute to the progression of the disease. However, alcoholism is the disease in which chemical dependency and physical addiction result in a condition that leaves the alcoholic with an inability to drink normally. The alcoholic's denial must be broken through first and they must come to learn and accept the undeniable fact that they cannot drink normally because they suffer from a disease called alcoholism.

My writing about alcoholism as a condition in which the person "can't" drink normally may seem surprising to those readers who are familiar with my work, my books, and my theoretical development of Redecision Therapy. Those of you who have participated in workshops at Mount Madonna with Mary and I or have attended any of the many seminars and workshops we regularly give throughout the world, know that I am a person who staunchly believes that the "power is in the patient." There are not many "can'ts" that I acknowledge or recognize as legitimate. For I believe that we too often give up our freedom and responsibility to others too quickly because of early messages we have been given and early decisions we have made as children. The result is that we end up relinquishing the power and excitement in our lives for the safety and security of the past. "Can'ts" for me are usually "won'ts." People who overly utilize words like "can't," "need," and "try," lead me to be very cautious of their motivation in therapy. I consequently watch for how they might try to manipulate and con me. I tell them to turn their can'ts into won'ts, their needs into wants, and get them to realize their "try's" are a relinquishing of their potency and power as an exciting, responsible individual. However, I believe alcoholics "can't" drink and this is one very important exception to the verbal games that most people play in therapy. The realization that "I can't drink" and the alcoholic's denial, must be dealt with directly if they are to progress in treatment.

The recognition of "can't" for an alcoholic is essential to their recovery because the alcoholic suffers from a biological abnormality which prevents him from drinking in a socially appropriate manner. Countless studies have clearly demonstrated that genetics play a crucial factor in the onset of the illness since it has been found that alcoholism definitely runs in families. Children born of alcoholic parents, and then separated from them after their birth and raised in totally different environments, have a much higher chance of developing alcoholism than children born of nonalcoholic parents. Recent biological research is uncovering numerous possibilities which exist between genetics, biochemical abnormalities and alcoholism.

The personality of the addicted individual, their genetic makeup, constitutional resistances to the illness, and many environmental variables (along with untold numerous other influences) can cause the illness to appear in an unending variety of forms. Because of the great variability of the illness and the frequent uninformed, naive status of the observer, addiction is frequently unrecognized for what it is and misdiagnosed and left untreated. The course of the illness at times can be variable, as is its onset. However, the course of addiction is usually a very gradual and progressive one in which undetectable changes in personality are easily attributed to other causes and influences besides the use of a chemical substance. The changes usually result in inexplicable deviations of long-established values and social behavior. The individual's ability to achieve in his personal life or occupational pursuit is frequently impaired, resulting in frustration, anger and irritation. Unfortunately, the effects of addiction are often only detectable at autopsy when multiple effects to the heart, brain, and liver are finally diagnosed.

Because of the progressive and insidious nature of alcoholism, the recognition of the disease and the breakdown of denial is essential as Alcoholics Anonymous readily recognizes. The first three steps of the AA program readily address this issue (1. We admitted we were powerless over alcohol — that our lives had become unmanageable. 2. We came to believe that a Power greater than ourselves could restore us to sanity. 3. We made a decision to turn our will and our lives over to the care of God as we understood Him.) And, as I have stated elsewhere, I believe the second and third steps are really Redecisions (as defined by Redecision Therapy) because they require an act of faith from the alcoholic's Free Child. Promoting and encouraging the alcoholic's Redecision not to drink ("I can't drink") is the most important therapeutic event that can be achieved in treatment. The power of the group to confront the alcoholic's denial and to reinforce their Redecision not to drink is why group therapy is such an important component to the recovery process.

This book addresses both of these very critical therapeutic issues in the treatment of addiction. First, it places alcoholism within the realm of a disease paradigm and defines the importance of requiring the alcoholic to maintain his sobriety if he is to obtain any change in his destructive life script. Secondly, its author outlines how the attainment of sobriety and the maintenance of the Redecision that, "I can't drink" is to be achieved within a group therapy setting. The Redecision to not drink ("I can't drink because I am an alcoholic") is one that requires careful monitoring because the pull of the alcoholic's physical and psychological dependency is so strong and pervasive.

Group therapy can be an exciting adventure and I believe, as AA does, that people have the capacity to change. People (not only alcoholics) can change if they are helped by the therapist to cure themselves. Mary and I strive to teach our patients how they have deadened themselves, made themselves depressed, phobic or anxious, while giving them the encouragement and permission to enjoy life instead. For the drinking alcoholic, this is impossible to obtain unless they first stop drinking and remain free of chemical use.

The alcoholic's Redecision to not drink is a new journey, which is both exciting and frightening. This movement can be sustained and encouraged through the feelings of identification, support and belonging, which are generated in the therapy group and AA. Because alcoholics early in their recovery need support, group therapy and AA can meet their dependency needs while allowing them to regulate and set their own pace and involvement in their recovery. During the early stages of recovery, alcoholics usually find it easier to place themselves in a dependent position among others with whom they can identify and feel comfortable. Ultimately, the alcoholic must come to assume responsibility for their own sobriety without dependency on others; but the group can provide the structure for this until they decide they are ready to move through this transitional period. A point this book makes repeatedly is that recovery is a time-dependent process in which the initial stages of treatment are different from the later stages of treatment. After the breakdown of denial and abstinence is obtained, a therapy group can be used to deal with the array of emotions which usually accompany the first few months of abstinence.

In the later stages of the recovery process the author outlines how the group can be utilized to examine the ways that life scripts and games help maintain the alcoholic's psychological dependence on alcohol. This book correctly examines the many ways that unaltered, untreated, and unexamined psychological factors can lead to a relapse. The alcoholic's life script may not be a factor in all cases, but its associated games, cons, and repetitive patterns, can lead to a re-emergence of denial and return to the addictive use of chemicals.

Unfortunately, many therapists hold the erroneous assumption that if alcoholics only knew how to express their feelings better, they could be cured. I have said before that I have yet to see a cure coming from just the facilitation of the expression of feelings. Those familiar with my work with Gestalt Therapy and my association with Fritz Perls and Jim Simkin, know that I am not one to shy away from the expression of feelings. However, the cessation of alcohol intake must be obtained first. Then the alcoholic must come to acknowledge the severity of his problems (which requires a Free Child Redecision). Finally, a sound group therapeutic format must be established which allows the alteration of disruptive life scripts, the confrontation of gains and the strokes for positive change.

All of these sound principles of treatment have been carefully outlined in this book. I hope all of you that read it find it helpful in your understanding of addiction and useful in your treatment of the chemically dependent patient. Because this book outlines how addiction can be treated within a group therapy session, I find it invaluable for those who are either unknowledgeable about addiction or uninformed about group therapy. Both of these important subjects are brought together in a complementary and concise fashion.

Robert Goulding, MD
Distinguished Fellow
American Group Psychotherapy Association
Co-Director of Western Institute
of Group and Family Therapy
Past President
American Academy of Psychotherapists

Chapter 1

An Introduction
to Group Psychotherapy
and Addiction

There is an increasing demand for both degreed and non-degreed professionals within the addiction treatment field to lead groups. One of the most frequently cited reasons for employing group psychotherapy in the treatment of addiction is the factor of economy. Group psychotherapy is an effective way for a relatively small number of treatment personnel to handle a large number of addicted patients. Certainly, the cost effectiveness of group psychotherapy is one reason for its popularity, but there are far more important reasons for utilizing groups. These reasons have to do with the nature of the disease of addiction itself and the nature of the addicted patient entering treatment. Frequently cited advantages for treating alcoholics and addicts in group include, but are not limited to such factors as, peer support and peer pressure, the opportunity for the chemically dependent individual to learn that he or she is not alone and unique in their own personal hell, and to have the opportunity to learn about themselves and identify with others by interacting interpersonally with them on a meaningful and emotional level.

There are important reasons why group psychotherapy is frequently the treatment of choice even if the person is not addicted. These reasons, while not specific to the chemically dependent individual, also have important implications for their treatment. Agazarian and Peters (1982) view group therapy as having advantages over individual therapy when a person's symptoms are most clearly expressed in interpersonal terms. If the individual has difficulty in dealing with other people, and especially if the person is unaware how his or her own behavior and attitude contributes to this difficulty, group psychotherapy should be the treatment of choice. Group therapy works effectively in these cases because the individual's inappropriate behavior and attitudes that give them the most difficulty will begin to emerge within the group. Many of the same critical interpersonal behaviors may not emerge in one-to-one therapy because of transference distortions and the therapist's position of neutrality. In individual therapy, the therapist can only hear the patient's version of their interpersonal difficulties. Usually, even though the therapist may suspect that this presentation is inaccurate because of the person's distortions, denial, confusion and intellectualization, the therapist remains at a disadvantage because he does not actually view the real event. These issues will have more of an opportunity to come alive in the group setting, free of the patient's distortions and defensive operations. Agazarian and Peters add,

> Ego-syntonic pathology can be detached from its state of personal acceptability much more easily under the pressure and with the support, of a group. Merely hearing others discuss similar behaviors as problems, or seeing how self-destructive these behaviors are for group members, creates doubts, causes self-examination, and confronts the patients in a very gradual and effective way. (p. 186, 1982)

SPECIFIC IMPLICATIONS OF GROUP THERAPY WITH ALCOHOLICS

However, the answer to the intricate question regarding the effectiveness of group psychotherapy for addicts and alcoholics must be asked and answered more precisely. Why indeed is group psychotherapy such an effective mode of treatment for alcoholics and addicts? Part of the answer lies within the typical defensive style of the addicted individual. This is a characterological style which involves the defensive posture commonly referred to as denial. Alcoholism is in fact, frequently cited as a disease of denial. However, the chemically dependent individual usually presents with a much more complex set of defenses and the group leader must have a clear understanding of each group member's defensive process if he intends to help them benefit from treatment. John Wallace (1978) addresses this important issue in an informative essay on the alcoholic's defensive style and refers to these characterological defensive features as the alcoholic's preferred defense system. Evidence will be presented in the following chapters outlining the way group treatment helps break through the alcoholic's preferred defense system and his wall of denial. The characteristics of the alcoholic's preferred defense system and its implications for treatment will be dealt with in more detail in Chapters Three and Four. For now, it is important to note that the theme of group psychotherapy and the advantages which group poses for the confrontation and the altering of the addict's and alcoholic's defensive style will be a theme which will be addressed throughout this entire book.

Despite the special considerations which have to be evaluated when treating the addicted patient, there are other important advantages to group psychotherapy and these advantages are not limited exclusively to the addicted population. Within group psychotherapy there is a phenomenon surrounding its curative process that cannot be explained exclusively from a psychological perspective or put in a concise psychological framework. Nevertheless, Chapter Thirteen will deal primarily with the psychological aspects of the curative process in group and will examine the ways group plays an intricate part in the healing, treatment and arrestment of addiction. But there are other important reasons why groups are so effective in producing change in an individual's life and one way of understanding the significance of this impact is to view group psychotherapy from an anthropological perspective. Jerome Frank, for instance, has written an excellent book (1962) in which he creatively draws parallels between healing rituals in primitive cultures and how similar rituals in the practice of modern Western medicine play an equally intricate part in the principles of cure and healing which exist in our present day society. Exploring the ramifications of healing from a cultural perspective, Frank convincingly argues that the group provides a much more powerful curative force because it alleviates the isolation and the demoralization which, for Frank, is the central issue for individuals seeking psychiatric help in our society. Speaking from an anthropological perspective, Frank sees many advantages and benefits of group psychotherapy over individual therapy. The role that culture and society play in addiction and its subsequent treatment is a topic beyond the scope of this book. However, it is important to note at this point that the chemically dependent individual responds more favorably to group because the cultural and societal forces which contribute to addiction can be used in turn by the group to heal and treat the very deficits it has created.

Consequently, as Frank succinctly outlines, the group offers its members many advantages over individual treatment. The empirical research on the effectiveness of group psychotherapy is equivocal, however. Cahn (1970), for instance, found in a national survey that group psychotherapy is a widely preferred method in alcoholism treatment programs. Matakas et al. agree (1978) when he expresses similar sentiments in his view that group psychotherapy is currently viewed as dogma in the treatment of alcoholism and drug abuse even though there is little empirical research to support its popularity. Pattison (1979) feels that there has not been enough empirical research to support the popularity of group psychotherapy as a method of choice for alcoholism and drug abuse. What is lacking, he suggests, is a clear differentiation of the types of group methods which can be selectively used for specific therapeutic goals with different types of patients. Pattison suggests (1979) that this is not to indicate that group psychotherapy is not useful, but rather that there exists a need to construct specific guidelines for group psychotherapy.

Kanas (1982) on the other hand, cites clinical research, both anecdotal and empirical, which has generally been enthusiastic on the effectiveness of group psychotherapy with addicted patients. Furthermore, group psychotherapy has a long history as a significant, if not major, therapeutic modality in the treatment of alcoholism (Stein & Friedman, 1972). Many studies have shown that the treatment of choice for addiction, in most instances, is group psychotherapy. In some cases, the estimation is that the recovery rate is two to three times higher than for patients who only receive individual psychotherapy (Kanas, 1982; Yalom et al., 1978). In a review of the treatment outcome literature on group psychotherapy and addiction, Kanas found most studies supporting the claims made in the anecdotal literature regarding the effectiveness of group psychotherapy as a treatment modality.

However, despite the preference for the use of group psychotherapy as mode of treatment for addiction and its apparent effectiveness, the trend toward group psychotherapy has been hindered by the popular misconception that group psychotherapy with addicted patients does not require specially qualified leaders because groups can take care of themselves. In order for group treatment to fulfill its potential, it requires a special understanding of group process, group dynamics and experience in leading groups. Too often, therapists trained only in individual therapy or experienced with nonaddicted patients, are thrust into a group psychotherapy leadership role. Similarly, many alcohol counselors knowledgeable about addiction and the disease process because of their own addiction, are often placed in the role as a group leader without the benefit of formal training in group psychotherapy. Because group psychotherapy, as it should be applied, is difficult and because addicted patients pose special and unique problems for the group leader, group psychotherapy with this population requires a number of specifically trained skills. Many groups led by untrained or poorly trained leaders do not fulfill their potential or may even have negative effects on a patient's recovery.

Clearly, a need exists for training and educating potential group therapists who are and will be leading groups composed primarily of chemically dependent individuals. This is necessary because working with chemically dependent individuals within a group setting poses numerous difficulties for most group psychotherapists. It matters little whether the group therapist is a recovering addict or alcoholic themselves, or if they have followed the more traditional course of academically based training. In either case, the problem is usually related to two contributing factors. Either there has been a lack of effective group psychotherapy training opportunities for these group therapists or they have been taught a model of group psychotherapy which is inadequate for patients who are chemically dependent.

Unfortunately, most contemporary approaches to group psychotherapy have not taken into consideration special characteristics of the chemically dependent patient and the special problems these patients pose for the group leader. Consequently, group leaders have often desired more direction, better training and more practical suggestions for effectively leading groups composed of addicted patients. Compounding this difficulty is the well-known fact that group therapy is usually a very integral part of an alcoholic's and addict's treatment in both inpatient and outpatient settings. Subsequently, group leaders have frequently found themselves thrown into a "sink or swim" situation. Most have been able to respond creatively by adapting skills they have acquired for individual psychotherapy. However, what often gets passed off as group psychotherapy is usually little more than individual therapy within a group setting. Individual therapy, whether done in a dyad or in a group, is not group psychotherapy. Therapists will also find that principles which work well for individuals are totally inappropriate for group psychotherapy. Beyond this, the rich potential for self-understanding, psychological growth, emotional healing and true intimacy which exists only in a group setting is left unfulfilled. A group leader must be familiar and sensitive to the basic issues which manifest in group psychotherapy or else they will find themselves in waters which are filled with treacherous undercurrents.

Many group therapists have responded to this situation by utilizing procedures they have intuitively adopted from the program of Alcoholics Anonymous. This is not to say that the principles of Alcoholics Anonymous are inadequate. To the contrary, recovery from addiction for most individuals is often impossible without the utilization of the principles of the AA program. This is why most successful treatment programs in this country require that AA attendance be a mandatory part of the treatment process. However, AA is not group psychotherapy and the two different treatment modalities should not be confused. On the other hand, group psychotherapy is not Alcoholics Anonymous and group psychotherapy should never be intended to be a substitute for the AA program. Both Alcoholics Anonymous and group psychotherapy provide important complementary components to the recovery process and in the hands of a skilled clinician, group psychotherapy can be a very important tool in the treatment process. Alcoholics Anonymous will keep the chemically dependent individual sober and teach interpersonal skills and develop the spiritual self while the group can speed along that process as well as giving them an opportunity to understand and explore the emotional conflicts that are secondary to their addiction.

Even though group psychotherapy is an important therapeutic modality in most contemporary inpatient and outpatient addictive treatment programs, the model upon which it is based has been, for the most part, derived from the practice of outpatient psychotherapy with nonaddicted patients. However, the theoretical and practical considerations underlying outpatient group psychotherapy with a nonaddictive population is not always applicable to individuals suffering from chemical dependency. Even Yalom (1975) suggested that alcoholics and character disorders be omitted from group psychotherapy because they are inappropriate candidates for this mode of treatment. Consequently, currently accepted principles of group psychotherapy need to be altered in order to meet the realities and necessities of treating the addicted patient. This problem is further complicated by the fact that most addicted patients, as well as staff members, often become confused about the different types of group treatment modalities. For instance, Alcoholics Anonymous groups,

"Step-work" groups, discussion groups, educational groups, after-care groups and support groups are just a few of the variety of group treatment modalities which many patients are exposed to during their treatment process. It is not surprising that patients often become confused about the principles of group psychotherapy and that the staff fails to appreciate the significance of the impact that group psychotherapy can make on an individual's recovery. It is also important to take into consideration the time factor involved in an individual's recovery. What a group leader does in group psychotherapy with patients in an inpatient setting in a hospital during the first few days of recovery will be dramatically different from what that same group therapist would do with the same recovering person who has six months of sobriety in an aftercare group.

Therefore, the purpose of this chapter as well as this book is to examine and present a systematic model of group psychotherapy as described and practiced by the leading theorists in the field of group psychotherapy and addiction (Yalom, 1975; Brown & Yalom, 1977; Wallace, 1978). This book is an attempt to define proven strategies and articulate suggestions for improving the treatment of the chemically dependent patient by providing a cognitive understanding of the special problems that chemically dependent individuals bring to group psychotherapy. Although group psychotherapy has long been an essential component of treatment programs, group orientations vary enormously from one setting to another. Nevertheless, most professionals who work with alcoholics and addicts on a sustained basis agree that group therapy offers the chemically dependent individual unique opportunities to 1. share and to identify with others who are going through similar problems; 2. to understand their own attitudes about addiction and their defenses against giving up alcohol and drugs by confronting similar attitudes and defenses in others; and 3. to learn to communicate needs and feelings more directly. Furthermore, the group's ability to provide support, structure, and reinforcement for abstinence makes it a powerful catalyst in the recovery process. In measures of time, efficacy and recovery, group psychotherapy generally succeeds where individual treatment modalities frequently fail.

As a group psychotherapist, consultant and trainer for the past ten years, I have had the opportunity to work with and supervise numerous therapy groups in both inpatient and outpatient settings in both the public and private sector. I have been currently involved in an ongoing project aimed at adapting the principles of group psycho-

therapy to addictive populations. The importance of such an endeavor can hardly be underestimated in view of two simultaneously
occurring, although not necessarily related trends in modern addiction treatment. The first is the greater utilization of recovering people themselves as a source of professional treatment personnel. The
second is a trend for most treatment programs to include group psychotherapy as an essential component of the treatment effort. Unfortunately, most professionals have not received adequate training
in either group therapy or addiction during their academic careers.
Certainly, most of them have not been exposed to the principles of
group psychotherapy with an addictive population. It therefore becomes necessary to define a set of theories and practices which are
specialized to meet the needs of the addicted patient in group psychotherapy.

THE DISEASE CONCEPT
AND GROUP PSYCHOTHERAPY

As a group therapist, if you believe that addiction is a disease, it
will affect the way you approach treatment and conduct your psychotherapy groups with addicted patients. The disease model requires that you view alcoholism and addiction as a primary illness
that cannot be cured, only arrested. Furthermore, the disease model
requires viewing addiction to alcohol and drugs much like one
views many chronic illnesses—be it heart disease or diabetes for
example. Since chronic diseases are those prone to relapse, it requires a constant monitoring of the afflicted individual's lifestyle
and alteration of their behavioral habits in order to reduce the risk of
relapse. Accepting addiction as a disease means viewing this condition as a physiological illness and not a secondary sign or symptom
of some underlying mental or emotional disorder. Group psychotherapy from this perspective is aimed not at uncovering psychological pathology, but geared towards identification of the defenses and
characterological deficits that prevent compliance to abstinence and
recovery. The inability to deal with uncomfortable feelings and affect triggered by interpersonal conflict is an equally important component of the recovery process. Group psychotherapy should be
used to enhance adherence to the principles of Alcoholics Anonymous while allowing a closer examination of the difficulties the

recovering person has with their interpersonal relationships. It is rare to find a chemically dependent individual who hasn't relapsed because of the strong affect that has been stirred up secondary to interpersonal conflict.

Furthermore, the disease model requires accepting the chemically dependent individual's metabolic and physiological response to ethyl alcohol as entirely different from that of the non-chemically dependent individual. There is a vast amount of evidence on both the brain and liver, endorphin and receptor sites, permeability of nerve cell membranes, specific hereditary electroencephalograph patterns, metabolic differences, and hereditary studies that control for parental alcoholic environment in several ways which all substantiate the scientific basis for accepting addiction as a disease. Thus, there is little question that the history, symptoms and signs of addiction form a recognizable pattern. Individuals who become dependent on alcohol and drugs will deteriorate in all areas of life — physical, mental, emotional, moral and spiritual. The well-known, total destructiveness of addiction need not be repeated. Attitudes, individual responsibility and public recognition are crucial factors that must be recognized before addiction can be treated effectively. The reason that it is important to recognize the title of disease for the addicted individual is to remove the stigma often accompanying this disease and legitimize its treatment. Finally, the disease concept establishes addiction as the primary illness and not a symptom that must be controlled, altered or modified.

The debate on whether alcoholism and addiction are truly diseases is a common one. Opponents of the disease concept argue that alcoholism does not truly fit the criteria of a disease because, unlike the diabetic for instance, the alcoholic makes an active choice (i.e., to drink or not to drink) to inflict the disease upon themselves while the diabetic does not. Nor does the diabetic derive pleasure from that choice. Furthermore, they would argue, addicts and alcoholics choose to pursue their drug use because they derive pleasure and satisfaction from its use and it is their pursuit of pleasure that leads them to become "sick." However, as Donald Goodwin cogently argues (1980), few opponents of the disease concept have difficulty accepting syphilis and gonorrhea as diseases and these maladies parallel addiction in their etiology. All are derived from a choice to pursue a pleasurable activity which results in the individual suffering an infliction primarily because of their exposure to an external foreign agent and dangerous substance which would have not entered the person's physiological system had it not been at that individual's own volition to do so.

In fact, lifestyles and the affliction associated with improper habits and incongruent with good long-range health is far more a contributing factor to the disease than is usually acknowledged. The crucial aspects of lifestyle and disease has emerged largely because a revolution in the healthcare requirements of the American people has emerged within the last 75 years. This revolution is one in which the medical profession itself is just coming to grips, and a problem which Western industrial societies are just beginning to recognize. The revolution in question is that the morbidity and mortality rates of Americans are no longer related to the infectious diseases prevalent at the turn of the century. Instead, the diseases that are most prevalent today are those related to chronic disorders associated with our lifestyles. Influenza, pneumonia, tuberculosis, gastroenteritis, and diphtheria have been replaced by heart disease, cerebrovascular disease, respiratory disease, various cancers and alcoholism — all of which are part of product of how we live and behave. How much we drink and eat, whether or not we smoke, how we deal with daily stress and how much we exercise are the most important contributing factors to a person's health and their susceptibility to contract a disease. In one sense, the most serious medical problems which plague the majority of individuals today are not ultimately medical problems at all; they are behavioral problems requiring the alteration of characteristic response patterns to and thus are directly related to lifestyles and attitudes toward lifestyles (Stachnik, 1980).

Accepting addiction as a disease also has other important implications for treatment because the disease concept usually implies that abstinence is the only treatment of choice for the addicted individual. Currently, there exists a hotly debated controversy surrounding the issues of controlled drinking versus abstinence (Martlett, 1983; Sobell & Sobell, 1973; Pendery et al., 1982). While the intensity of this debate is fueled by strong personal beliefs and passionate professional territoriality, it has relatively little clinical effect outside the arena of academia and those few treatment programs which utilize aversion and behavioral therapy. The majority of clinicians and treatment programs in this country know by their experience, what Alcoholics Anonymous has always known; abstinence is the only treatment alternative for the addict and alcoholic. Yet the controversy has far more implications than being an academic debate because as every person who is either addicted or has worked with chemically dependent individuals on a sustained basis knows, there is nothing more that an alcoholic or addict wants to hear and believe than the statement that they can learn to control their alcohol and drug use in a socially accepted manner. Put ten alcoholics in a room and tell them that research shows that one out of ten can return to normal drinking and each one will believe that they are the one special case. As Wallace (1985) demonstrated in an informal survey of 160 alcoholics currently in treatment, all 160 had in the past tried controlled drinking and failed. Considering that these 160 failures may not be as unfortunate as the ones who fatally succumbed to their disease, the controversy takes on an added sense of urgency. This is especially true in light of the evidence which suggests that abstinence has few, if any, detrimental effects for a person even if that person is "only" an abuser and not "really addicted." To the contrary, abstinence usually leads to increased health and satisfaction with one's life. One is therefore left with the decision of whether the risk of answering this question of whether to drink or not drink is worth the probable cost to the person struggling with their disease.

The controlled drinking controversy is also complicated by the differences in diagnostic criteria which many professionals use when they are conducting controlled drinking research. An individual diagnosed as an alcoholic in one study might not fit the criteria for an alcoholic in another study. Certainly, many individuals defined as alcoholic by Alcoholics Anonymous would fail to be diagnosed as such by someone using the DSM III criteria (APA, 1980). What many professionals fail to appreciate is that the DSM III criteria for alcoholism is not better than AA's, it is just different.

Curtis Barrett sums up this controversy nicely when he writes:

> To illustrate how very diverse diagnostic or intake criteria might be these days, it is instructive to contrast those used by the DSM III criteria (American Psychiatric Association, 1980), with those used by the venerable self-help group, Alcoholics Anonymous. In DSM III one is first struck by the fact that 'alcoholism' is not listed as a mental disorder. However, careful reading reveals the statement that 'Alcohol Dependence has been called alcoholism' (American Psychiatric Association, 1980, p. 169). To diagnose Alcohol Dependence

the following are required: (a) either a pattern of pathological alcohol use or impairment in social or occupational functioning due to alcohol use, and (b) either tolerance or withdrawal. The distinction between alcoholism and alcohol abuse boils down to whether one finds tolerance or withdrawal. Thus, a person with a history of blackouts, binges, failure to control excessive drinking, loss of job and legal difficulties (e.g., driving while intoxicated), may not be diagnosed as being alcoholic/alcohol dependent if one uses DSM III criteria. (p. 19, 1985)

AA, as always, avoids such controversy and true to its tradition "keeps it simple." AA members are told to diagnose themselves. Another's diagnosis of someone else's alcoholism is held secondary to that individual's diagnosis of himself. AA members are alcoholic if they say they are alcoholic. AA does provide the literature and the information necessary if the person so desires it. But, the self-attribution of alcoholic is the cornerstone of the AA program.

Barrett (1985) adds,

In a chapter on "How it works" (AA World Service, 1939, p. 58) one reads that a person who wants what AA has should consider taking certain steps that are "suggested as a program of recovery." The first of these is: "We admitted we were powerless over alcohol — that our lives had become unmanageable." If the person wants further help in self-diagnosis there is material that will permit a sort of matching operation that is not too different from that followed in the DSM III. (p. 19, 1985)

Sobriety is clearly the goal of AA. However, AA is a program of recovery which addresses the difficult adjustments which are necessary if one is to remain alcohol and drug free. "AA does not teach us how to handle our drinking . . . It teaches us how to handle our sobriety" (AA World Service, 1939, p. 554). AA does not rule out the possibility that the alcoholic may return to controlled drinking, but that it is a goal that cannot be achieved if a person is a true alcoholic. Thus, AA recognizes that those alcoholics who return to controlled drinking were mis-diagnosed.

Considering these criteria problems, it is conceivable that a competent researcher utilizing the DSM III criteria for alcohol dependence, would fail to define an individual whom AA sees as alcoholic; even if this person so defined themselves as one. Such difficulties help explain why the controlled drinking studies have resulted in such controversial and contradictory conclusions.

Those whose interest in alcoholism is only passing or purely academic fail to understand the significance of this criteria problem. For the alcoholic, struggling with their disease, it is literally a matter of life and death. Wallace (1978) for instance, sees the ideological base of AA providing a crucial component in the sober alcoholic's recovery process. In fact, he contends that the alcoholic needs AA's somewhat biased view of reality. "The alcoholic can ill afford the dispassionate, disinterested, and indeed, almost casual play upon words and ideas of the inquiring academic intellectual" (1975, p. 7).

Wallace feels strongly that the alcoholic recognizes intuitively the need for a stable and enduring belief system if he is to stay sober. Wallace has more difficulty in comprehending and discerning the equally biased view or reality of the academician. His contention is that:

> Hidden neatly beneath the rhetoric of science and scientism are the actualities of dreadfully inadequate personality measuring instruments, inappropriate sampling procedures, inadequate measuring operations, improper choice of variables for study, grossly violated statistical assumptions, data gathering, recording and analyzing errors, and so on and so forth. Is it any wonder then that the most outstanding quality of most academic research is now you see it, now you don't? Are we really amazed to find sober alcoholics clinging to their belief systems like drowning poets to their metaphors in a sea of confusion? (1975, p. 7)

Wallace also recognizes the importance of helping an individual achieve a self-attribution of alcoholic and, hence, an explanatory system for their behavior. Treatment from this standpoint is very much the teaching of an "exotic belief" whose true value of actually describing what has occurred to the individual because of their alcoholism is held as irrelevant. Its true value is determined by the fact it 1. helps explain the past in a way that gives hope for the future; 2. allows the alcoholic to cope with their guilt, anxiety, remorse and confusion and; 3. provides them with a specific behavior (staying sober and working the 12 steps of the program) that will change their life in a desired direction. As Wallace says, the alcoholic has a lifetime of sobriety in which to recognize the fact that not all of his personal and social difficulties are the result of his alcoholism. But, he can come to this realization after he has gotten the alcohol and drugs out of his system and has steered his life in the desired direction. As Martin Buber (1964) recognizes, a person in a crisis needs direction; it is only after sobriety has been maintained, can they start to investigate some of the deeper psychological issues in their life.

Recent neuropsychological research has shed some light on the importance of providing alcoholics and addicts a clear structured program which they must follow during their first months of abstinence. New members into the AA program have been told not to make any major decisions during the first year of recovery. They are instructed not to analyze the program. They are told, AA works because it works! Go to ninety meetings in ninety days. Take the body and the mind will follow. Each of these suggestions are based on AA's intuitive understanding that alcoholics, during the early stages of abstinence, are incapable of thinking clearly and do not possess the intellectual capabilities necessary for rational, intelligent decisions. The AA program provides them with twelve clear steps which they must follow. New members are told to "keep it simple." After they finish the 1st step, they are told to complete the 2nd step and then proceed on to the 3rd step and so on.

On neuropsychological tests sensitive to abstract reasoning, flexible thinking, fluid intelligence and new learning, alcoholics and addicts consistently score in the brain impaired range (see Chapter 8). Their verbal intelligence and old learning remains very much intact. Consequently, they will often appear unimpaired to the unsuspecting observer. Their level of impairment is usually not permanent and does not involve cortical structural damage. Rather, their brain dysfunction is of a diffuse nature, usually the result of an alcohol-induced encephalopathy exacerbated by nutritional and vitamin deficiencies. Most alcoholics experience "spontaneous recovery" from the loss of cortical functioning if they remain alcohol and drug free and improve their vitamin and nutritional intake. This recovery of cognitive functioning is gradual and steady. The greatest improvement is usually experienced in the first few months with total recovery achieved with one to two years of abstinence.

Considering the implications from this research, the structure and direction which AA provides at the beginning of the alcoholic's recovery is vital. However, there is another important aspect of the AA program which many professionals fail to appreciate. AA provides the newly recovering alcoholic with hope and inspiration. Jerome Frank would say AA helps combat the alcoholic's demoralization. Yalom would speak of the instillation of hope and the necessity of "vital lies" in our life. This is very close to what Wallace prescribes when he suggests teaching the alcoholic an "exotic belief." AA works because it does not overlook the significance of belief and inspiration in an individual's life. AA utilizes these principles because of its utility and practicality. AA's heritage is closely tied to William James. It is James' philosophy of pragmatism which influenced Bill Wilson, the early architect of the AA program. Truth for James was determined by its utility. If something worked, it was true! AA members are told by Father Martin, "AA works because it works!" The utility of teaching the alcoholic to believe in the principles of AA determines its usefulness and its truth.

An illustration from the Buddhist religious tradition might help clarify the importance of vital lies, instillation of hope and exotic beliefs in the treatment of addiction. The concept of "useful illusions" is a central one in the Buddhist religion. The Buddhist monk and religious teacher realized the importance of mobilizing an individual's faith and hope during the early stages of doubt and confusion in their life. It is "useful" to create an "illusion" which may allow the individual disciple to grasp an important principle of life which they might not otherwise be ready to accept in the early stage of their journey to self-understanding.

J. Hutchinson (1969) sums up the Buddhist position when he describes the aim of the Noble Eightfold Path.

> What was the content of this experience? Buddha's answer resembled a physician's terse diagnosis and prescription of therapy for a disease. Buddhist tradition has communicated Buddha's truth in the form of the Four Noble Truths and the Noble Eightfold Path. The first two of the Four Truths may be termed diagnosis and the third and fourth, therapy. The first asserts that all existence is misery, or *dukkha*, and the second that misery is rooted in ignorant craving, or *trishna*. The third truth asserts that misery may be abolished by abolishing igno-

rant craving, and the fourth truth asserts that this can be done by the Noble Eightfold Path. Thus as one Buddhist writer puts it, Buddha "had found the sovereign remedy for all the major ills of mankind."

Central to the Buddhist teaching is the "blowing out" of the flame of passion. Often confused with annihilation or death, the aim of the Buddha was to get the disciple to extinguish the "ignorant cravings" which produced misery. Much like the Buddhist disciple, the alcoholic must "surrender" what he thinks will make him happy (drinking) and come to recognize that it is his misconception of happiness (ignorant craving) that causes his suffering. The breaking of this cycle is enhanced by useful illusions.

The Buddhist disciple would approach the Buddhist monk with the question of the meaning of life and the desire to experience Nirvana. The disciple was told to meditate and practiced the eight-fold path to enlightenment which included right action and right thinking. After six months of meditation, the disciple again visited the teacher for instructions as he had not yet reached enlightenment. Two years later, the disciple again asked for a meeting with his teacher complaining that he had done all that he had been instructed to do and had not yet reached Nirvana. The student tried to remain accepting as he was told that he must be patient and continue to practice the eight-fold path to enlightenment. Finally, after five years of dutiful meditation and practice, the student could no longer contain his frustration and finally confronted the Buddhist monk with his anger saying, "I have done all that you have told me! I practiced the eight-fold path to enlightenment! I have meditated daily and practiced the principles of right thinking and right action! I have done all these things and I have not reached Nirvana!" To this, the Buddhist monk answered with love and understanding, "My son there is no Nirvana, but because of your meditation and practice of the eight-fold path, you are better off, aren't you?"

Much like the Buddhist disciple, the recovering alcoholic who has worked the twelve-step program of recovery is better off. Their life which was a shambles is now in order. Their health, both psychologically and physically, is usually restored. Now, after five years of sobriety, they can realize that all their problems were not totally caused by their alcoholism. They have not reached enlightenment, but they are better off than they were when they were drinking or using drugs.

This is the significant issue which the controlled drinking advocates clearly miss. Why even bother to teach an alcoholic to drink normally? Alcoholics Anonymous, as advocated by its founder Bill Wilson, was far more interested in the alcoholic's lifestyle and their distorted bankrupt philosophy of life. While drinking and abstinence is of crucial importance to the program, it is only the first step in the Twelve Steps of Recovery. An often-unnoticed fact is that the first step of the AA program is the only step that explicitly mentions drinking. The rest of the eleven steps are there for the alcoholic to use as a guide to change their lifestyle and the bankruptcy of their values. Such a viewpoint leads one to wonder why training alcoholics in controlled drinking is so attractive. It is such a paltry goal and misses the boat completely.

As McCrady (1985) writes,

> People who earn an alcoholism diagnosis have worked hard for it—they have consumed enormous quantities of ethanol and have created terrible personal pain in their lives because of their alcohol consumption. Why, then, continue to attempt to drink and risk the pain over and over? Instead of trying to help alcoholics drink, therapists might better view such a desire to drink as an "irrational belief". Psychologists' burgeoning knowledge of cognitive behavior modification could then be used to help alcoholics challenge the irrational belief that C_2H_5OH is so important that it cannot be totally eliminated from their lives. (p. 370)

Furthermore, if the controlled drinking advocates wanted to demonstrate that alcoholics can drink with control for a time, then it would only confirm what most people familiar with Alcoholics Anonymous have known for a long time. Alcoholics often drink with control for years before they either quit or die. They also have usually been able to control their consumption for weeks at a time, even months. Yet, it is the emotional suffering and the bankruptcy of their lives that needs to be changed and treated. Most alcoholics would admit that control only spoils their drinking. Many ask why would I only want to have one beer? Within this viewpoint, control is not a desirable goal for those addicted because control actually inhibits the freedom that alcoholics most strongly want to pursue. Control is a problem for every addicted individual, not the solution. As Stewart (1985) writes,

Alcoholics in trouble suffer more from the use of control than its loss. A truly free alcoholic is not concerned with maintaining control. He or she is much more interested in ongoing freedom. The alcoholic in control, fearing its loss, is not a good example of enjoyable sobriety . . . Abstinence is one condition of enduring freedom for the alcoholic. Most alcoholics who have been sober for years would support that belief, but one is not sober on abstinence alone. There is a creative discipline in sobriety that is not present in mere abstinence for its own sake. Abstinence for itself, by willpower, is a control, but abstinence and devotion to sobriety is a disciplined act of love. (p. 373-374)

What appears reasonable as a possible solution to this controversy is to ask that the patients themselves weigh the risks and benefits of abstinence-oriented and controlled drinking treatments. However, since an addict or alcoholic, especially one in the throngs of their addiction, is usually incapable of making such an important and rational decision, the risks associated with abstinence-oriented therapy are not as great since those who do choose to be abstinent are not as likely to be harmed by their abstinence. Why not develop a partnership between Alcoholics Anonymous and professionally oriented treatment approaches and combine the two different sets of knowledge and expertise? By doing so, the chances are greater for developing an innovative treatment model that will help more alcoholics and addicts, rather than continue the destructive territorial fighting that is currently occurring. This is precisely the aim of this book and will be a constant theme that runs throughout its presented alternatives to the successful treatment of the chemically dependent individual.

Alcoholics Anonymous has often been criticized and called ideological, as though professionals did not also adhere to ideologies. Chapter Six will be devoted particularly to examining the ideologies of both Alcoholics Anonymous and professionals. The ways that their ideological differences influence or hinder mutual cooperation between them will be explored in more detail. Criticism of Alcoholics Anonymous often focuses on its ideological and religious overtones with the implication that AA puts pressure on its members to accept the AA belief system and that this pressure harms them in some way. Tournier (1979), for instance, criticized AA's effectiveness because he felt that it was a treatment method that had never been scientifically established and that the fellowship's ideology dominated the treatment field which resulted in a situation which limited new ideas. Jones (1970) also criticized the AA program as an "acceptance of totalitarian ideology" (p. 195). Unfortunately, these types of attacks are short-sighted and reflect ill-informed beliefs about the treatment philosophy of Alcoholics Anonymous. Professionals unfamiliar with the fellowship of Alcoholics Anonymous would better serve the treatment of chemically dependent individuals if they were to direct their energies toward understanding the ideological differences which exist between themselves and the AA program. If they were to gain a more accurate understanding of AA, they would find that the disparity between their position and AA's is actually not that great. Professionals may actually learn a great deal more about psychotherapy and treatment, not only for the addicted individual, but for the person who does not suffer from an addiction problem. In short, we professionals may learn that the fellowship of Alcoholics Anonymous has much to teach us about psychotherapy and treatment. It is within the realm of group psychotherapy that these two opposing views can best be merged into a supportive approach to therapy. The results from the marriage of the two principles of Alcoholics Anonymous and group psychotherapy could be an exciting and extremely complementary enterprise.

REFERENCES

AA World Services, Inc. (1939). *Alcoholics Anonymous* (3rd ed.). New York: Author.

American Psychiatric Association (1980). *Diagnostic & statistical manual of mental disorders* (3rd ed.). Washington, D. C.: Author.

Agazarian, Y. & Peters, R. (1981). *The visible and invisible group*. London: Routledge & Kegan Paul.

Barrett, C. L. (1985). Who are the alcoholics? Where are the devils? *Bulletin of the Society of Psychologists in Addictive Behaviors*, *4*(1), 17-28.

Brown S. & Yalom, I. (1977). Interactional group therapy with alcoholic patients. *Journal of Studies on Alcohol*, *38*, 426-456.

Buber, M. (1964). In M. Friedman (Ed.), *The worlds of existentialism*. New York: Random House.

Cahn, S. (1970). *The treatment of alcoholics: An evaluative study*. New York: Oxford University Press.

Frank, J. (1962). *Persuasion and healing*. New York: Schriker Books.

Goodwin, D. (1979). Alcoholism and heredity. A review and hypothesis. *Archives of General Psychiatry*, *36*, 57-61.

Hutchinson, J. A. (1969). *Paths of Faith*. New York: McGraw-Hill.

Jones, R. K. (1970). Sectarian characteristics of Alcoholics Anonymous. *Sociology*, *4*, 181-195.

Kanas, N. (1982). Alcoholism and group psychotherapy. In E. M. Pattison & E. Kaufman (Eds.), *Encyclopedic handbook of alcoholism* (pp. 1011-1021). New York: Gardner Press.

Martlatt, G. A. (1983). The controlled drinking controversy: A commentary. *American Psychologist, 38,* 1097-1111.

Matakas, F., Koester, H. & Leidner, B. (1978). Which treatment for which alcoholic? A review. *Psychiatrische Praxis, 5,* 143-153.

McCrady, B. S. (1985). Comments on the controlled drinking controversy. *American Psychologist,* March, 370-371.

Pattison, E. M. (1979). The selection of treatment modalities for the alcoholic patient. In J. H. Mandelson & N. K. Mello (Eds.), *The diagnosis and treatment of alcoholism.* New York: McGraw-Hill.

Pendery, M. L., Mattyman, I. M. & West, L. J. (1982). Controlled drinking by alcoholics? New findings and a reevaluation of a major affirmative study. *Science, 217,* 169-174.

Sobell, M. B. & Sobell, L. C. (1973). Individualized behavior therapy for alcoholics. *Behavior Therapy, 4,* 49-72.

Stachnik, T. J. (1980). Priorities for psychology in medical education and health care delivery. *American Psychologist, 35*(1), 8-15.

Stewart, D. A. (1985). Control or freedom? *American Psychologist,* March, 373-374.

Stien, A. & Friedman. (1972). Group therapy with alcoholics. In H. I. Kaplem & B. J. Sadock (Eds.), *Comprehensive group psychotherapy.* Baltimore: Williams & Wilkins.

Tournier, R. E. (1979). Alcoholics Anonymous as treatment and as ideology. *Journal of Studies on Alcohol, 40,* 230-239.

Wallace, J. (1975). *Tactical and strategic use of the preferred defense structure of the recovering alcoholic.* National Council on Alcoholism.

Wallace, J. (1978). Working with the preferred defense structure of the recovering alcoholic. In S. Zimberg, J. Wallace & S. Blume (Eds.), *Practical approaches to alcoholism psychotherapy* (pp. 19-29). New York: Plenum Press.

Wallace, J. (1985). Comments on the controlled drinking controversy. *American Psychologist,* March.

Yalom, I. D., Block, S., Bond, G., Zimmerman, E. & Quall, B. (1978). Alcoholics in interactional group therapy: An outcome study. *Archives of General Psychiatry, 35,* 419-425.

Yalom, I. D. (1975). *The theory and practice of group psychotherapy* (2nd ed.). New York: Basic Books.

Chapter 2

Different Models
of Group Psychotherapy

Abraham Maslow is attributed as once saying "If the only tool you have is a hammer, every problem you see will look like a nail." Maslow's satirical, but cogent statement, summarizes precisely the potential dilemma of adapting wholeheartedly and unquestioningly any one single theory of treatment and "cure" for addiction. Looking at addiction only from the disease perspective, for example, can lead an unsuspecting observer to see only the nail (i.e., the disease of addiction) which has to be pounded into place by the only tool available (i.e., Alcoholics Anonymous, for instance). Certainly, AA is not the only organization which has certain members that are myopically limited because of their tunnel vision. Group psychotherapy, as well as most formal schools (i.e., the psychodynamic, Rogerian, Gestalt, etc.) of psychotherapy have more than their share of adherents who believe their way is the only right way to treat patients who suffer from addiction. Unfortunately, such factionalism is short-sighted and limits the number of options available for utilizing different tools in the treatment of addiction.

Certainly, many members of AA have more of a foundation for their enthusiastic stance since nothing argues louder than success. AA members have also "earned the right" to be suspicious of "ignorant professionals" who have often misdiagnosed and offered poor treatment in many of their own individual cases. For example, alcoholics frequently report a personal downward spiral as they were advised "to cut down on their drinking" while the professional sought to get at the "real core" of their problem. One only has to attend a few AA meetings to hear the horror stories told by many of its members. In fact, AA would have never come into existence if it had not been for the failure of the professional healthcare system to offer the kind of help alcoholics desperately needed. AA, as a social phenomenon, is an example of how a certain portion of an inflicted population banded together in a unity of help because society's sanctioned mode of treatment was inadequate. Yet, Bill Wilson himself—the founder of AA—had no doubts about the mutual cooperation of AA and professional help in his own treatment and recovery from alcoholism. He twice returned to long-term individual psychotherapy with his friend and advocate, psychiatrist, Harry Tieboult.

This chapter will focus not so much on the necessity of AA and professionals banding together in the spirit of mutual cooperation, as it will be directed towards providing a systematic model for treating the chemically dependent individual within a group setting. Group psychotherapy, as it is taught and practiced today, suffers from its own form of factionalism. Adherents of different group psychotherapy models frequently attest to the superiority of their particular approach to group treatment. Each model of group psychotherapy has something unique to offer to certain populations and in the hands of a skilled clinician, these different models can provide a powerful therapeutic experience for its group members. However, a model has to be matched with the needs of the particular population being treated and the goals of treatment also have an important influence on the model that is chosen. If group psychotherapy is to be a powerful adjunct in the treatment of addiction, a number of important questions have to be asked and ultimately answered. For example, the particular stage of a person's recovery and abstinence should have a tremendous influence on the goals of the group leader. A group made up of individuals with two to three days of sobriety is far different from a group of individuals with one to two years of sobriety. Secondly, what is the aim of the group? More specifically, is abstinence from alcohol and drugs the goal of treatment and how can this be enhanced in a group psychotherapy setting? The aim of this chapter is not to advocate one approach to group psychotherapy over the other as much as it is to discern which model best meets the needs for the chemically dependent individual in that individual's stage of recovery. Each particular model of group psychotherapy to be presented here requires that the group leader analyze certain aspects of the group or group members' behavior differently.

Different ways of analyzing groups have a tremendous impact on what the leader observes and ultimately responds to in a group. This in turn is influenced by the basic task which the group hopes to accomplish and subsequently effects the different levels of intervention which a group leader chooses to make. These are decisions a group leader has to make before members are placed in a group setting. These crucial aspects of group psychotherapy will be discussed in relation to the most common and popular approaches to group psychotherapy. Each particular model available to the potential leader will be critiqued in relation to the special difficulties these different models pose for the group leader who is leading a group where members are suffering with an addiction problem.

DIFFERENT MODELS
OF GROUP PSYCHOTHERAPY

Successful group psychotherapy, whether it be with chemically dependent members or non-addicted members, requires that two conditions be adhered to and maintained. First, the group's task and structure should fit and be matched with the members' needs. If the leader and the treating institution adhere to the disease model, abstinence must be the goal and the group task should be structured to accomplish this end. Secondly, the leader's decision and technique should be adapted so that there is a match to the overall task or purpose to the group. Unfortunately, group goals are often vague or confusing with not enough emphasis on a systematic plan for accomplishing these goals. Leaders and members often tend to view groups in terms of techniques (i.e., communication exercises, hot seat, etc.) or theoretical orientation (psychodynamic, Gestalt, etc.) rather than terms of a goal or a task to be accomplished. Techniques and theories can become secret rituals rather than tools for the accomplishment of the tasks which are the specified purpose of the group. In the same vein, a variety of group approaches which emerge to serve special purposes, as in AA and group psychotherapy, are often seen as competing enterprises rather than different modes for achieving similar ends.

Singer et al. (1975) has outlined a heuristic "cognitive map" of the group psychotherapy field which categorizes group events in terms of two basic parameters: 1. The task system of the group event, and 2. Psychological levels of the systems involved in that task. This cognitive map will be presented here in an adapted form in order to give the potential group leader a better understanding of the alternatives available in their approach to conducting a group with chemically dependent individuals. Group events for Singer lie somewhere on a hypothetical continuum which has learning at one end and psychological change at the other. Despite the dangers of oversimplification, group members involved in such a presentation can be thought of as being placed in small groups for two primary reasons. They either are gathered together to learn some new information or to change some aspect of their behavior.[1]

Learning, within Singer's context, is defined as that which occurs within an individual's experience which results in a cognitive or perceptual change. Anyone reading this chapter is hopefully attaining a cognitive change as a result of their learning new information. Psychological change is defined in the sense of altered coping capacity, personality structure alteration, or response repertoire expansion. Psychological change from this perspective is usually associated with an experiential component of the group event with less emphasis on the alteration of a member's cognitive set. Every gathering of group members within a group is usually geared towards one of these two components. A particular orientation of the group and its leader plays an important determining factor in the amount of emphasis that will be placed on learning or on change in a particular group. Certainly, learning and change are not mutually exclusive and indeed often mediate each other. Yet, in any particular group psychotherapy setting, there should be an implicit, if not explicit, priority which determines which task should be an implicit, if not explicit, priority which determines which task (i.e., learning or change), shall be pursued at the expense of the other. Within a group psychotherapy setting with chemically dependent members, if one considers the possible consequence of continual alcohol consumption for many practicing alcoholics, change must take priority over learning, at least during the early stages of treatment. Therefore, tasks within a group psychotherapy setting can be defined along a three point continuum: 1. change, 2. learning and change, 3. learning. (See Figure I.)

PSYCHOLOGICAL LEVELS OF INTERVENTION

A group leader has at his or her disposal a number of viable options on how to analyze and intervene in a group psychotherapy setting. The relevant levels of psychological intervention can gener-

---

[1]One could argue that members also join groups for support and entertainment (in the sense that one experiences the joy and tragedy of life). While neither of these reasons are primary to group psychotherapy, they should never be excluded from the group experience since each plays an important role in a group and its member's treatment.

FIGURE I

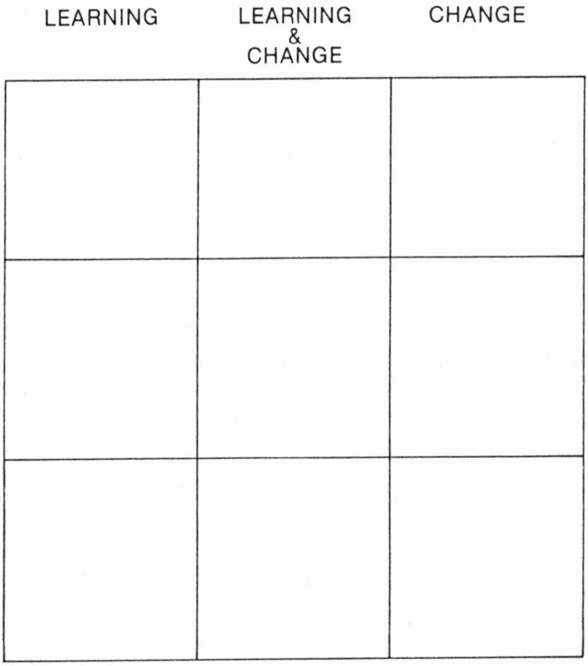

LEARNING	LEARNING & CHANGE	CHANGE

Source: Singer, et al (1975)

ally be placed within three broad, yet distinct categories. First, the group leader can choose to intervene on a group process level (i.e., what is the particular group event and dynamics that have led to the current set of responses for a particular member or members within the group setting at this particular moment). Secondly, the group leader has the choice of focusing on the interpersonal process within the group (i.e., what is the particular interaction occurring between certain members of the group? Why does one member react in a supportive fashion with most of the other group members, only to respond in an attacking manner with another member who presents himself within a similar set of circumstances). Thirdly, the group leader can decide to focus on the intrapersonal process with each particular member (i.e., how does each member defend, react and deal with their anxiety, anger and stress). Each process is a system conceptually different from, but related to the others. Since behavior is multi-determined, any event occurring within a group can be understood as a product of processes occurring on all levels simultaneously. Consider the following example of a first session of a group of newly recovering alcoholics.

> Early in the group meeting, Sam, a rather boisterous and provocative individual who has a long and rather complicated drinking history starts the group by wanting to discuss his anger and difficulty trusting a roommate with whom he shares an apartment. His primary complaint centers around his lack of trust because of his roommate's constant use of drugs. Sam, himself, does not use drugs and is presently struggling to decide whether he should stop drinking or cut down on his consumption of alcohol despite repeated failures at controlled drinking over the last few years. His repeated relapses have resulted in a recent divorce. Group members are divided in their reaction to Sam's presentation; most support him and express concern about his present dilemma. However, Sharon, a quiet and anxious woman struggling with her addiction to prescription tranquilizers, strongly objects to Sam's lack of trust in his roommate and becomes uncharacteristically vehement in her attack upon him.

On the group level, this transaction can be viewed a number of ways. Certainly, the question of trust, which Sam has focused on in his relationship with his roommate, is one issue that the entire group may want to address directly. This is especially true since the group is composed entirely of new members and each person is likely to feel unsure about the level of alliance, support and safety within the group setting. Picking the issue of trust and treating it as an outside phenomenon may be the group member's way of avoiding the intensity of the issue in the here and now. The group's flight from dealing directly with their feelings surrounding their lack of trust in the group leader and its members could also be a displacement of the general uneasiness which each member feels because of the new and unfamiliar group setting.

On the interpersonal level, there may be a triggering of old resentments between members, or more correctly, the transference figures certain members represent to each other. Sharon's strong response to Sam actually reflects her own anger about not being trusted by her husband and other important individuals in her life. Her anger is fueled by Sam's lack of understanding for his roommate's drug problem. She strongly identifies with his roommate's dilemma because she feels she has been judged unjustly by others, because of her addiction to prescription drugs. This is a situation which is made even more intolerable to her because she trusted and now feels betrayed by the physician who had prescribed the tranquilizers for her.

Sam's provocative style, coupled with his lack of tolerance for another's problems and his own insistent denial that he is an alcoholic may trigger Sharon's memories and intolerance of her own father's denial about his alcoholism while continuing to criticize her mother for her lack of trust in him.

On an interpersonal level, like all of us, the two members in question have long-standing anxieties, conflicts, fantasies, defenses and compensations surrounding themselves which they brought with them into group. Sam in particular may be deflecting the focus from his own difficulty with recovery and abstinence by getting the other members to deal with his roommate's problems, while at the same time giving the appearance of being actively involved with the group on a personal level. At the same time, Sam gets to hook the group into an endless debate around defining whether his roommate is an addict, a crucial issue which Sam needs to address and answer about himself. Sam's provocative and evasive defensive style needs to be understood, explored and ultimately confronted in a therapeutic manner. A full understanding of this group session would require data on all three levels. Only then would there be enough information to explain why this behavior became salient to these members in this group at this particular time. However, before these issues are decided, the group leader must return to the first important question. What is the goal of this group?

To help answer this question, the group leader now has within his or her conceptual map a choice of interventions based on the possible task and goal available to him or her.

In relation to a learning task or insight oriented group, the three levels (i.e., group level, intrapersonal level and interpersonal level) refers to the process or system which is the object of study (see Figure II). The group leader chooses which of the three will best serve the interests and needs of the group members. Are the group members there primarily to understand themselves better and how can this best be accomplished? Within the context of change, the

FIGURE II

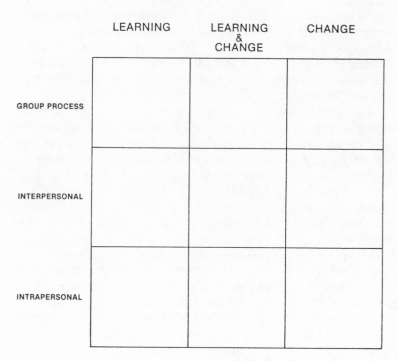

	LEARNING	LEARNING & CHANGE	CHANGE
GROUP PROCESS			
INTERPERSONAL			
INTRAPERSONAL			

Source: Singer, et al (1975)

concept levels refers to those processes utilized as the vehicle for intervention to produce change. For example, peer group pressure (group level), a therapeutic relationship with the leader and group members (interpersonal level) and interpretations and confrontations of defensive structures (intrapersonal level) are all possible ways of altering a chemically dependent individual's behavior.

Most models of group psychotherapy offered to the public in general and individuals suffering from chemical dependency in particular can be included within the following four categories: 1. Process oriented psychodynamic group; 2. Individually oriented growth and personal change groups; 3. Interpersonally oriented groups, and 4. Focus criteria change groups. These four types of groups will be described further and will be systematized in the following Figures III through VIII. Although devised on the basis of Singer's et al.

(1975) informal observations of tasks and structure in different possible group events, the "cognitive maps" presented here are simplified, but consonant with the empirical analytical observations of Lomranz et al. (1972) upon which Singer and his cohorts built their schema. Of course, this cognitive map is overly simplified and there are many group events which defy categorization and do not fit neatly within this typology. Despite the shortcomings of such a typological classification, the presentation and force fit of the different approaches of group psychotherapy will hopefully provide the beginning group leader with a better understanding of the possible options available to him or her in their treatment of addiction within a group setting.

GROUP PROCESS IN
PSYCHODYNAMICALLY ORIENTED GROUPS

Group process learning groups are best exemplified by the Tavistock type (see Figure III) small group or study group (Bion, 1961; Rice, 1965). In a strict Tavistock approach to groups, group process learning events have a unitary learning task which focuses on group level performance, particularly those surrounding authority issues and covert processes. Secondary emphasis, if any at all, is placed on interpersonal phenomenon.

Interpretation and intervention are focused on the here and now phenomena occurring within the group as a system and rigorous observation of time, role and task boundaries are the prime leader techniques. Emphasis is placed on authority relationships and reactions to leadership by group members. Feelings in groups are usually focused first on the group leader and then eventually on the other group members. Such groups are usually difficult to lead and many Tavistock leaders will admit that a strict Tavistock group is not a psychotherapy group and should never be intended as such (Kline, 1983). Tavistock groups will teach members how they respond to authority and react to stressful ambiguous situations. Any recovering alcoholic or active member of AA can answer those questions unequivocally. The chemically dependent person usually has extreme difficulty in both areas of their life. Consequently, such a group approach with newly recovering alcoholics and addicts will only add to their problems rather than give them any help in addressing their abstinence.

FIGURE III

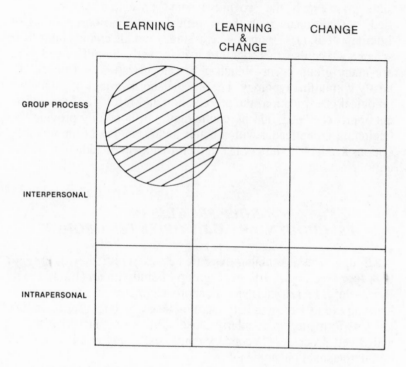

LEARNING   LEARNING   CHANGE
          & CHANGE

GROUP PROCESS

INTERPERSONAL

INTRAPERSONAL

 1) Psychodynamic, Group
Process, & Tavistock Group
as a Whole Focus

Source: Singer, et al (1975)

However, even within the defined area of psychodynamic process oriented group psychotherapy, there exists a wide range of diversity. A student of process oriented group psychotherapy will soon learn that the way Wilfred Bion (1961) — one leading psychodynamic theorist — teaches group psychotherapy is far different from other recognized authorities like Alexander Wolf and Ernest Schwartz (1962). These theorists, in turn, are far different in their approach to psychodynamic group psychotherapy than the brand of psychodynamic group process that is exemplified by Helen Durkin (1964) and Hariette Glatzer (1969).

However, before one can understand the subtleties and differences between these different approaches to group psychotherapy, one must be aware that the foundation of each of their approaches to group psychotherapy is built upon Freudian psychodynamic theory. Sigmund Freud's (1921) contribution to group psychology cannot be ignored. Every major school of group psychotherapy has been directly or indirectly influenced by Freudian thought. Fritz Perls in Gestalt, Eric Berne in Transactional Analysis, Alfred Moreno in Psychodrama, Harry Stack Sullivan with his interpersonal theory of personality and its subsequent influence on Irvin Yalom, as well as every psychodynamic process oriented group psychotherapist from Wilford Bion to Alexander Wolf have had the foundations of their approach to group psychotherapy firmly set in Freudian psychology.

Before venturing to describe the similarities and differences between these particular schools of group psychotherapy, a cursory examination of Freud's early writings on group psychotherapy are in order. Freud's notion of regression in groups is paramount to understanding the dynamics which occur within any group setting and reflect his most important contribution to group psychology. Freud held an overwhelming bias that the group or herd instinct is mindless, primitive and ultimately destructive. Group members will repeatedly, although often unconsciously, try to determine how they are to survive in a newly formed group setting. Therefore, individuals in a strange group setting will be forced to deal with primitive emotions like aggression, fear, anger and anxiety because they are caught in a regressive response to a basic survival situation. Freud, more than anyone else before him, defended the individual against the compelling forces of the herd instinct and perceived each individual as being at battle with the pressures of society to conform to the norms of the group. The conflict is always between the individual — which Freud defended — and society or the herd instinct, which Freud abhorred. Freud saw the group as a source of contagious reduction of mentality which resulted in each member denying their individuality when placed within a group setting. Group members have a thirst for obedience, a need to conform and depend upon a strong group leader. Each person within the group will thus succumb to these unconscious pressures and project their ego ideal onto the group leader. The group ideal is subsequently personified in the group leader and this is, in turn, substituted for the ego ideal of each person in the group. There is a need for the group to make the leader bigger than life. While group members want their leader to be greater than he or she actually is, because this belief insures them protection, they want simultaneously to dethrone and destroy their leader. Each member's ambivalence is related to the more primitive stages of their development and is reflected in Freud's myth of the primal horde (i.e., where the brothers form a blood bond after the killing of the father). Group members will then attempt to create a mythical hero who will hopefully accomplish the task of becoming bigger than life in the belief that this will protect them from the guilt and anxiety which accompanies their individuality and is usually associated with the responsibility which follows free choice. All life, for Freud, is a struggle with the ambivalence brought upon by the individual's dualistic view of wanting to fight authority and their desire to succumb to the safety usually associated in identifying with the group mind. Each member's denial of their individuality leads eventually to personal pathology and is seen as a by-product of the collective forces of the herd instinct and society's pressures to conform.

The primary importance of Freud's contribution to group psychotherapy lies within the realm of the significance he places upon importance of regression in groups. Regression is a phenomenon that is primary to any group setting. If the group leader fails to acknowledge the importance of regression and is subsequent relation to safety and trust with individuals who are chemically dependent, there is little chance that the group experience will be helpful in their treatment. The significance of trust, safety, and cohesion in a group setting will be discussed at length in Chapter Fourteen when Yalom's curative factors are explored in relation to group psychotherapy with addicts and alcoholics. For now, the different theoretical perspectives within psychodynamically oriented groups will be explored.

Wilfred Bion (1961), in his approach to group psychotherapy, ignores the individual in the group and goes as far as to advocate that if the leader addresses individual problems within the group setting, the leader is colluding with the group members in their attempt to avoid group work by allowing the members to shift the focus from the primary group issues. Within Bion's framework, when individuals are brought together in a group setting, they regress into a group mind. Bion prefers to view the group as an aggregate of individuals in a state of regression. The group members will attempt to resist emergence of psychotic or neurotic residuals by employing three basic assumptions (i.e., fight-flight, dependency, and pairing). These assumptions will be explored in more detail in Chapter 12. For now, it is enough to say that Bion views these assumptions as a form of group resistance which needs to be interpreted and ultimately addressed. The individual can not be treated in group and the only appropriate target for treatment, from Bion's perspective, is the commonly shared anxiety of the group and the defenses erected against this anxiety.

In sharp contrast to Bion's position, Wolf and Schwartz (1962) view the group and group process as a metaphor, an illusion which does not exist. Wolf has satirically commented that the group leader must always remember that individuals come for treatment, not groups. To this, he adds the penetrating criticism that "group dynamics never cured anybody." For a group leader to address interpretations to the group only adds to and helps create the illusion of group consciousness. Wolf cautions the group leader against reinforcing such a belief because groups try to make all members alike. Groups coerce each member to regress or behave like the most dominant member within a group. The group ego is a mystique, an artifact resulting from group conformity, pressures and identification. This tendency of producing group consciousness, according to Wolf and Schwartz, must be challenged, as it reinforces an illusion, encourages regression and compliance while minimizing the individuation of group members. Instead, the focus in group should be on the members' separateness, individuality and transference distortions. Because the group setting allows individual conflicts to manifest in relation to other group members, the group leader has more material to work with than he or she would in an individual psychotherapy setting. Individual therapy within a group setting reduces a transference intensity which exists within an individual setting, allowing the individual to profit more from treatment.

Durkin and Glatzer, in turn, advocate a combination of the intrapersonal and the group process focus in their orientation toward group psychotherapy. Durkin and Glatzer's roots are set in the British School of Ego Psychology and they view the analyzing of ego traits and defenses within a group setting as the primary task of the group leader. Within their schema, they focus on the developmental assessment of the ego in the belief that analysis should be directed towards the maladaptive compromises that the ego has had to make in order to survive in a stressful and dysfunctional situation. Psychopathology is part of an ongoing process of the ego's effort to cope and it is within the member's transference distortions that these maladaptive efforts most readily appear. The group allows for more sources of transference distortions and the leader has a readily accessible laboratory to see how individual members act out their pathology rather than just have them talk about it in an abstract manner. The purpose of group, according to Durkin and Glatzer, is to analyze these transference resistances and show each member how their past continues to impact on their present functioning.

The group setting also allows a group leader to deal more effectively with the defenses that are ego-dystonic. Ego-dystonic defenses differ from ego-systonic defenses in that the latter represent a defensive posture that is more ingrained and characterological in nature. Such a defensive stance usually causes the individual little overt concern. In contrast, individuals with ego-dystonic defenses experience much more dysphoria, overt anxiety, symptom formation and phobias. Consequently, ego-dystonic individuals are more likely to seek help because their defensive posture leads them to more discomfort, forcing them to be more aware of their difficulties. In contrast, individuals with ego-systonic defenses experience little difficulty within themselves; but it is their defensive style (i.e., passive-aggressiveness, acting out, addiction, etc.) which causes others more difficulties and frequently leads such individuals to be sent to or brought into treatment by disgruntled, unhappy and exhausted significant others in their lives. A group setting, through the transference distortions and confrontation of other members, allows ego-systonic defenses to become more dystonic, thus prompting the individual to become more motivated for change. Why else would such an individual want to change if they have little discomfort in their coping style and it is others who are having the problem because of their difficulty in dealing with them?

The group, within Durkin and Glatzer's model also allows the leader more opportunities to avoid both negative and positive transference distortions. An overly compliant, passive-aggressive individual who experiences positive transference to his therapist during individual therapy is more likely to cover over and hide feelings of anger. Group members are more likely to be accessible targets for such an individual's anger. Support and understanding of group members needs are also more easily met since other group members are more likely than a group leader to compromise themselves in their relationship with each other.

INDIVIDUALLY ORIENTED CHANGE GROUPS

Groups conducted from an individual change format have as their primary task the goal of producing change in the individual's behavior whether it be reduction in suffering, increased awareness or increased capacity for freer, more creative functioning. While this format reflects a wide range and array of technical and theoretical approaches to group psychotherapy including Redecision Psychotherapy (Goulding & Goulding, 1979), Psychodrama (e.g., Moreno, 1971), Gestalt (e.g., Perls, 1969) and Bio-Energetic (e.g., Lowen, 1969), a vehicle for change in all of these approaches is an intrapsychic focus coupled with group leader intervention. The group is regarded as an aggregate of individuals and the leader essentially works with one group member at a time, doing individual therapy within a group setting (i. e., hot seat), while the rest of the group members function vicariously as observers, contributors, alter-egos and "significant others." Group process, with the exception of peer support, supportive culture or the provision of multiple transference figures are typically viewed as a distraction or a constraint upon the treatment and are not actively utilized in the work. Emphasis is placed on change with insight or learning sometimes viewed as a hindrance or obstacle to change. The stereotypic prototype of this model is the Perlsian-led Gestalt psychotherapy group where members take turns working in the "hot seat" with the group leader. Intellectualization, insight and learning are viewed in Perlsian language as "mind fucking" or "elephant shit." Group members are encouraged to experience, increase their awareness or "lose their mind and come to their senses." Change is the focus of each session and little emphasis is placed on understanding in the usual sense. While not all Gestalt therapy is Perlsian in nature, this overly stereotypic presentation of Gestalt is only used as an illustration and does little justice to other Gestalt therapists like Erv and Miriam Polster who infrequently, if ever, used the classical empty chair technique in their groups or limit their options while doing psychotherapy by following such rigid procedures. Chapter 10 will focus on the personal characteristics of the group leader and how these characteristics effect successful treatment. For now, it is important to mention that the rigid parameters presented here in the descriptive account of different models of group psychotherapy have little application when groups are led by master therapists like the Gouldings or Polsters. However, before one can allow themselves to creatively break the rules of a particular model, one must understand what those rules and parameters are. (See Figure IV.)

Group therapy from the individually oriented change perspective is sometimes referred to as therapy for normals. Emphasis is placed

FIGURE IV

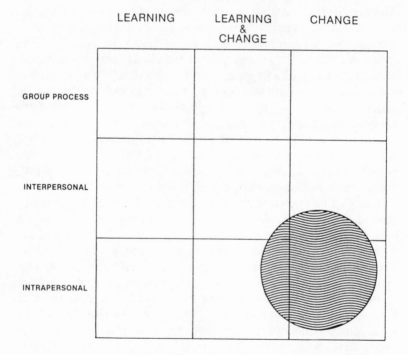

 2) Gestalt, Psychodrama, Redecision Group Therapy

Source: Singer, et al (1975)

on personal growth and increasing awareness. The leader in this type of group, unlike the passive, blank-screen leader typically found in psychodynamic learning oriented groups, is very active; often providing structured experiences, exercises, encountering and fantasy trips. The format frequently provides an intense emotional experience for selected members and because of the intensity of the affect generated in such groups, they are prone to have a far greater occurrence of casualties (i.e., people who get worse as the result of group treatment). Casualties in relation to group leadership style will be discussed in more detail in Chapter 10. For now, it is enough to say that members who enter group with unrealistically high expectations or goals that are couched in vague terms like "increased growth and awareness" are group members that are most likely to be hurt or made worse by the group experience.

Focus Criteria Groups

Focus change groups are specifically designed to change or eliminate group member's self-destructive or undesirable target behavior as is the case with addiction, be it smoking, alcohol, food or drugs. (See Figure V.) Typically, such groups are historically highly confronted and encountering in style. Emphasis is placed on altering and changing behavior with little importance initially placed on learning. AA members, for instance, are told "AA works because it works! Go to 90 meetings in 90 days, take your body and your mind will follow." Such slogans help reinforce the belief that change is prioritized over learning. Singer et al. (1975) submit their interpretation of the focus criteria groups in the following manner:

> All of the target behaviors are addictive in nature; each has become a way of avoiding anxiety, despair, depression, meaninglessness, or powerlessness, and each has been psychologically reinforcing in addition to any physical dependence. The programs in which these events are nearly always embedded (e.g., Phoenix House, Weight Watchers) and their leaders first utilize rituals of entry, such as confession and humiliation, to promote a powerful identification with the program and the group. The substitute dependency makes withdrawal from the target behavior possible. Leaders foster group pressure, supportive sanctions — not interpretations or didactic transferences — help members stay abstinent after the initial with-

drawal. . . . Focused Criteria Group leaders make it appear
that intrapersonal and interpersonal processes are key vehicles
for change, closer inspection suggests to us that group process — covertly utilized — are the primary change inducers. (p.
146, Singer et al., 1975)

While Singer and his co-authors failed to specifically include Alcoholics Anonymous within their focus criteria group format, many

FIGURE V

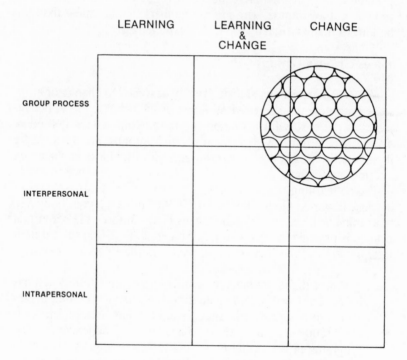

	LEARNING	LEARNING & CHANGE	CHANGE
GROUP PROCESS			
INTERPERSONAL			
INTRAPERSONAL			

 3) Behavior Management,
Overeaters Anonymous,
Smoking Cessation, Etc.

Source: Singer, et al (1975)

of the characteristics of this type of group occur within AA. However, on the other hand, it is fortunate that they exclude AA from this category because while their description of the format is an accurate one, it fails to accurately describe the significance of the twelve steps of the AA program. AA's twelve steps offer a unique learning component to the group process which is the real secret of the program's success. As any recovering alcoholic would readily acknowledge, just going to AA meetings will not guarantee the alcoholic long-lasting sobriety. That only comes from working the twelve steps of the AA program. Another question which has to be answered about AA and other self-help groups concerns the issue of treatment effectiveness. If the AA program is able to offer such groups to its chemically dependent members, why does AA need professionally led groups? If this is the limit of the group experience which professionals have to offer, the answer is that AA does not need professional help. But, a point that must be repeatedly made is that AA is not group psychotherapy and group psychotherapy should never be intended to be a substitute for AA. Group psychotherapy, by itself, usually will not keep an alcoholic sober or an addict clean. The program of Alcoholics Anonymous and Narcotics Anonymous can accomplish this task much more effectively. What group psychotherapy has to offer the chemically dependent individual is an understanding of the intrapersonal and interpersonal conflicts which may lead to a relapse. Group psychotherapy can also speed up the recovery process and reinforce the steps of the AA program for those individuals who have difficulty understanding, accepting and working the Twelve Steps of Recovery in the AA program.

This task can best be accomplished by utilizing the last model presented within Singer's typology.

Interpersonal Learning and Change Groups

The interpersonal learning groups have the roots and now classical sensitivity training or T-groups. Currently, these group approaches have been refined under a Singer label of interactional group psychotherapy; most commonly associated with the work of Irvin Yalom (1985). (See Figure VI.) The stated aim of this approach is to help group members learn and understand the effect which their behavior has on others and in turn how others' behavior affects them. Feelings and emotional expressions are explored in

FIGURE VI

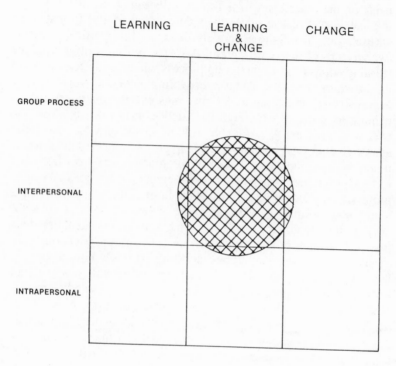

4) Interactional Group
   Psychotherapy, T-group,
   Yalom's Model

Source: Singer, et al (1975)

the belief that they play a substantial part in motives, communication and behavior. Thus, the primary learning task in the T-groups is the focus these groups place on the interpersonal interaction which occurs in groups.

Yalom, for one, has added variants to this approach by utilizing behavioral unfreezing as another way to foster subsidiary change in a group member's behavior. The leader's task is to be a role model giving feedback without making evaluations of the group member's behavior. Experiences are validated through the group leader's direction, allowing individuals within the group to get a consensus from the other group members enabling them to learn how their behavior and actions affect others. Yalom views learning and change as inseparable occurrences, arguing that neither can occur without the other.

Yalom's views on change and learning take on added significance when dealing with the chemically dependent individual. Any group leader, who has had contact with Alcoholics Anonymous on a sustained basis knows that a chemically dependent person can drink themselves to death while they explore and learn all about the reasons why they are drinking. An approach which focuses only on insight, self-understanding and learning will usually have little long-lasting beneficial effect on the chemically dependent individual during the early phase of their treatment and recovery. The pitfalls of a total learning approach to treatment can be demonstrated by the following case study.

> Donna, a 41-year-old, divorcee, has been in and out of psychotherapy for the last 15 years. She has never remained in therapy longer than a year and a half (three different times) and has never been out of therapy longer than nine months. She usually picks psychotherapists who place an inordinate amount of emphasis on understanding and insight, usually terminating treatment when she is either challenged to change her behavior or emotionally aroused by the therapist. At cocktail parties, she can readily and accurately tell her acquaintances the reason she has difficulties in relationships with men and why her failure with her own children is similar to her parents' failure with her. Yet, she does not change! She continues to repeat the perpetual self-destructive and self-defeating interpersonal style that has plagued her since adolescence while being capable of explaining and understanding the reasons that compel her to act as she does. Since her defense system is composed primarily of the defenses of intellectualization, rationalization and isolation of affect, her continual involvement with psychotherapists who only feed her defensive style, helps her not to change and prevents her from looking at the feelings associated with her difficulties.

Of course, a group leader operating at the other extreme of the spectrum, can suffer the same limiting effects of a treatment approach which stresses only change, the expression of feelings and discourages insight. Group "groupies" who are "into discovering themselves" are often prone to manipulate the group therapy situation to their advantage. Mary Goulding, herself, a gifted group psychotherapist, is well aware of the "games" that many group members can be involved in and warns the unsuspecting group leader to be cautious in their application of an intervention that is only experiential. Mary Goulding tells a story of one such a woman who had participated in one of her groups (1980).

> A woman entering a weekend marathon group, started the group telling about her grief in relation to her now deceased mother. The woman quickly plunged into an empty chair dialogue with her departed mother, crying tearfully, and eventually expressing an abrupt explosion of anger at her mother for dying and leaving her alone. By this time, most of the members in the group were in tears themselves or at least very strongly affected by the woman's moving exchange with her mother. As she was encouraged by the group leader to complete her "work" with the deceased mother, the woman tearfully said "and this is the last time I will say goodbye to you, mother." To this the group leader quickly asked "the last time?" "Oh yes!" the woman exclaimed, "I said goodbye to my dead mother in California with Fritz Perls in 1960, in 1972 with Erv and Miriam Polster while they were both in Cleveland and with another therapist in New York!"

This vignette illustrates some of the dangers which may befall an unsuspecting group leader who is too readily taken in by a group member who is all too willing to express affect that is strong and easily accessible. However, a more prevalent danger in working with chemically dependent individuals in a group setting is a possibility of the group member being overstimulated and flooded emotionally by a group leader who employs a format which only encourages the expression of affect. This has certainly been the case on a number of occasions where I have had an opportunity to direct and participate in a psychodrama group at a Veterans Administration Hospital inpatient unit for chemically dependent veterans.

> Mike, a 32-year-old, single, Caucasian male had "volunteered" to be a protagonist in a psychodrama group that met once each week during the patient's stay on the inpatient drug dependence unit. Mike, a quiet and somewhat shy man began talking about his girlfriend who had died in an automobile

accident which had resulted from Mike's inability to negotiate a turn in the road while he was driving her car. His difficulty in controlling the automobile was due to the fact that he was heavily intoxicated at the time he was driving. A powerful and explosive psychodrama scene was enacted with auxiliary alteregos played by supporting members in the group. In the final scene, Mike tearfully and painfully enacted pulling his dead girlfriend from the automobile desperately trying to evoke some response from her lifeless body by shouting and begging for her forgiveness. At the close of the group session, the two co-therapists and many of the group members congratulated the director of the psychodrama for the powerful and masterful direction he had given Mike during this very dramatic encounter. Unfortunately, it was learned the next morning upon arriving on the unit, that Mike had left the hospital A.M.A. (against medical advice) during the previous evening.

Undoubtedly, the stirring and flooding of intense feelings associated with the long repressed experience had proved too threatening and overwhelming for Mike. I saw this scenario repeated too often at the unit. The consequences were not always the same every time, but occurred with enough consistency to warrant my judging that the risk of over-stimulating a patient was not worth the infrequent benefits of such an approach to group psychotherapy with a chemically dependent population. Research conducted within the last few years (Beutler et al., in press) had supported my clinical experience.

A more recent experience with a similar situation in a different group format produced far better results.

Martha, a 31-year-old, recovering alcoholic with three years sobriety had entered an outpatient psychotherapy group because of her difficulty dealing with a recent loss (divorce from her husband) in her life. Early in the session of the group, Martha spoke briefly about her present feelings surrounding her husband's divorce being quite similar to her feelings regarding the loss of a friend who had died in an automobile accident that occurred while Martha was driving intoxicated. The therapist's decision at this time was to focus on the feelings stirred up by the divorce and not pursue the feelings surrounding the death of her friend. This decision was made because Martha was still relatively new to the group and the group leader was not sure of the support she might receive from the group members as well as the amount of ego-strength she now possessed because of the acute state of her present stressful marital situation. The group leader also wanted more time to carefully assess the extent of her capacity to deal effectively with such a traumatic experience as well as give her time to gain more trust and cohesion with the other group members. Approximately six months later, she once again mentioned the incident in passing. The group leader, at this time, decided to pursue it in more detail. As she unfolded her story of guilt and eventual suicidal contemplation because of her friend's death, the other group members were encouraged to respond to her sharing of her story. Since the group had been conducted within an interactional format, her fears of condemnation from the other group members were explored and eventually discovered to be unfounded. The other members support and sharing of their acceptance of her, despite what she had felt was an unforgivable incident in her life, was very cleansing and releasing for this woman. She returned to the group the next week with a noted improvement in affect, speaking of the dramatic change in herself, adding that she felt "as if a weight had been lifted off my chest."

The difference in the therapeutic outcome between Mike and Martha's illustrations reflect important decisions that a group leader must make in their choice of the group format when embarking upon a psychotherapy group with addicts and alcoholics. While one approach could be far more dramatic and initially more impressive, as in the psychodrama group, the other approach, while less exciting, produces change and learning in a steady, controlled and effective fashion. This is the primary reason why the rest of this book will be addressed to outlining and articulating the interactional group model as the preferred mode of treatment for the chemically dependent individual. Yalom's particular brand of interactional group psychotherapy is the model which best serves the tasks and goals which must be established if group psychotherapy is to be an effective tool in the treatment of addictions. While there are modifications which must be made in Yalom's model, it is important to understand the basics of the approach before alterations of the models are implemented by the group leader. Chapter 3 will be directed towards describing Yalom's approach to group psychotherapy. Before completing this chapter, a final conceptual map (Figure VII) will be presented to permit the potential group leader to see that

FIGURE VII

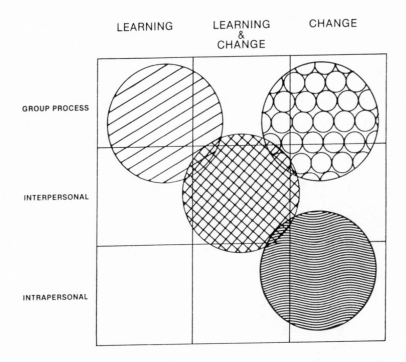

	LEARNING	LEARNING & CHANGE	CHANGE
GROUP PROCESS			
INTERPERSONAL			
INTRAPERSONAL			

 1) Psychodynamic, Group Process, & Tavistock Group as a Whole Focus

 2) Gestalt, Psychodrama, Redecision Group Therapy

3) Behavior Management, Overeaters Anonymous, Smoking Cessation, Etc.

 4) Interactional Group Psychotherapy, T-group, Yalom's Model

Source: Singer, et al (1975)

46   *Philip J. Flores*

the options they have before them are dependent upon the tasks, goals and focus of interventions they wish to make in order to insure that their particular group members' needs are met in the most beneficial and productive manner.

REFERENCES

Beulter, L., Frank, M., Scheiber, S., Calvert, S. & Gaines, J. (in press). Comparative effects of group therapies in a short-term inpatient setting: An experience with deterioration effects. *Psychiatry.*

Bion, W. R. (1961). *Experiences in groups.* New York: Basic Books.

Durkin, H. E. (1964). *The group in depth.* New York: International Universities Press.

Freud, S. (1950, 1921). Group psychology and the analysis of the ego. *Complete psychological works of Sigmund Freud.* London: Hogarth Press.

Glatzer, H. T. (1969). Working through in analytic group psychotherapy. *International Journal of Group Psychotherapy, 19,* 292-306.

Goulding, M. Personal Communication. Western Institute for Group and Family Therapy, July, 1980.

Goulding, R. & Goulding, M. (1979). *Changing lives through redecision therapy.* New York: Brunner/Mazel.

Kline, E. B. (1983). *Personal communication.* Cincinnati: U. of Cinn. Press.

Lomranz, J., Lakin, M. & Schiffman, H. (1972). Variants of sensitivity training an encounter: Diversity or fragmentation? *Journal of Applied Behavioral Science, 8,* 399-420.

Lowen, A. (1969). Bio-energetic group therapy. In H. Rouitenbech (Ed.), *Group therapy today* (pp. 279-290). New York: Atherton.

Moreno, J. L. (1971). Psychodrama. In H. Kaplan & B. Sadock (Eds.), *Comprehensive group psychotherapy.* Baltimore: Williams and Wilkins.

Perls, F. (1969). *Gestalt therapy verbatim.* Lafayette, Calif: Real People Press.

Rice, A. K. (1965). *Learning for leadership.* London: Tavistock Publ.

Singer, D. L., Astrachan, B. M., Gould, L. J. & Klein, E. B. (1975). Boundary management in psychological work with groups. *Journal of Applied Behavioral Science, 11*(2), 137-176.

Wolfe, A. & Schwartz, E. K. (1962). *Psychoanalysis in groups.* New York: Grune & Stratton.

Yalom, I. (1985). *The theory and practice of group psychotherapy.* New York: Basic Books.

Chapter 3

Interactional
Group Psychotherapy

Irving Yalom has written two excellent texts on group psychotherapy. The first, published in 1970 (the second edition came out
in 1975 and the third edition in 1985), deals primarily with the
application of outpatient group psychotherapy to a non-addicted
population. The second text deals almost exclusively with the application of inpatient group psychotherapy with psychotic patients primarily in an acute hospital setting (1982). Since it is Yalom's first
text that provides the theoretical underpinnings for his approach to
group psychotherapy, this chapter will concentrate on his contribution to group psychotherapy as it is outlined for an outpatient setting
in his 1970 text. However, even this text devotes relatively little
space and time to Yalom's theoretical rationale for conducting a
group in his prescribed manner. Many group psychotherapists,
while acknowledging that Yalom's 1975 text provides the reader
with the best practical "nuts and bolts" directions available for conducting an interactional group, criticize him at the same time for
being atheoretical and ignoring the philosophical foundations for his
approach to group psychotherapy.

This criticism is unfounded if one makes the effort to trace
Yalom's link with Harry Stack Sullivan's theory of interpersonal
psychiatry. A clear understanding of Sullivan's basic tenets will
shed much light on the reasons why Yalom advocates that a group
be led in the manner he describes. Jerome Frank's influence is also
paramount in Yalom's approach to group psychotherapy; although
Yalom, to my knowledge, has never acknowledged this relationship
in print except in a passing or cursory fashion. One only has to read
through Yalom's list of curative factors in group (i.e., Installation
of Hope, Altruism, Universality and Existential Factors, etc.) and
see Jerome Frank's (1961) thesis concerning the anthropological
aspect of persuasion and healing heavily influencing Yalom's recommendations. Later in this chapter, an interpretation of Yalom's

theoretical foundations and the ways Sullivan and Frank's work reflects and influences Yalom's approach to group psychotherapy will be presented. First, however, Yalom's description of the "basic plumbing" of group psychotherapy and the basic task of the group leader will be explored. The material presented here is not intended to be original and is only a condensed presentation of Yalom's own work in chapters five (there are two chapter fives in his second edition) of his 1975 text. The interested reader is suggested to explore this chapter in more detail if they wish to go to the original source of the information presented here.

YALOM'S BASIC TASKS

A group leader essentially has three major tasks within Yalom's model of group psychotherapy. These tasks are:

1. Insure the physical survival of the group.
2. Build a group culture and establish therapeutic norms.
3. Teach and model for the group members the "here and now" work in the group setting.

The task of insuring the physical survival of the group involves those efforts which go into establishing and maintaining a group. It is usually easier to predict which members will drop out of treatment than it is to predict which members will succeed and benefit from group psychotherapy. Yalom urges that the group leader spend more time preparing members for groups than in perfect casting. The issue of the management of the boundaries of the group and preparing the members for group will be dealt with more thoroughly in Chapter 14. This current chapter will be devoted primarily to describing Yalom's recommendations for the other two major tasks of the group leader and how the accomplishment of these tasks instills a major influence on the essential success or failure of a psychotherapy group for the chemically dependent individual.

BUILDING A GROUP CULTURE
AND ESTABLISHING THERAPEUTIC NORMS

Once a group is a physical reality, the group leader must turn his energy to shaping the group norms and group culture into a therapeutic social system. This will in turn set in motion the curative factors (see Chapter 13) which for Yalom are crucial to the group's effectiveness. Unlike any other kind of group setting, the group members must feel free to comment on the immediate feelings they experience towards each member and leader in the group. In order for this type of atmosphere to manifest, the group leader must steer the group members in the direction of establishing six essential group norms. They are:

1. Honesty and spontaneity must be encouraged and sanctioned.
2. A high level of involvement with all group members must be insured.
3. Self-disclosure of each member must be established in an atmosphere of what Yalom describes as "reciprocal vulnerability."
4. The desire for self-understanding must be instilled and encouraged in each group member.
5. Nonjudgmental acceptance of other group members' shortcomings, personal failings and individual indiscretions must be established.
6. Dissatisfaction with the self must be experienced and a desire to change the behavior which is related to this satisfaction must be encouraged.

Most group leaders would agree these are desirable norms to establish and maintain. But the question which ultimately has to be asked is how are these tasks to be accomplished? The answer is a simple one that is found within the realm of behavioral modification and reinforcement theory. A group leader must:

A. Establish and reinforce norms that are healthy and functional.
B. Avoid, ignore and extinguish norms that are unhealthy and dysfunctional.

The therapist, within Yalom's perspective, is to build an atmosphere and climate for change. The group leader is an engineer and the group is a laboratory for the investigation and understanding of the interpersonal difficulties that each particular member brings to the group. Only when the group culture is just right, can the group be used as a vehicle for changing each member's maladaptive behavior.

The therapist has at his disposal, two readily available tools or methods for shaping the norms of the groups. First, the therapist is a technical expert, who hopefully has a better understanding of the dynamics and development of behavior, both maladaptive and adaptive. With the benefit of his or her professional training, the therapist has more access to pertinent information which will help him or her readily identify pathological behavior and determine what is healthy adaptive behavior. Secondly, the group leader, because of the special options available to him within a psychotherapy group, has the advantage of operating as a "model setting participant."

TECHNICAL EXPERT

What does Yalom mean when he refers to the leader as technical expert? The leader of a group is automatically assigned certain characteristics by the group members because of the already established role which the leader possesses in the group. For example, with many group members, this role may be the benevolent guardian and for others, this role may be seen as the authoritarian autocrat. While many forms of group psychotherapy (i.e., Tavistock) are primarily interested in the group members' transference reactions to the assigned characteristics of the group leader, Yalom is most interested in the interaction of group members and the building of a therapeutic group culture. Consequently, Yalom advocates that the group leader use the weight of his authority and experience towards the establishment of the norms that are necessary for a highly functioning therapeutic group. Transference and transference distortions towards the leader will always emerge and these distortions can be explored later when it is more advantageous for the leader to do so. While these transference distortions are judged by Yalom to be of therapeutic importance, they are secondary to the establishment of a proper group climate and the assurance that group members not be forced into a regressed posture too early in group.

Yalom therefore suggests that the group leader use his assigned role as technical expert to convince the group members to interact with each other rather than direct their energies towards interacting with the leader. One way Yalom convinces members to behave is by appealing to their reason. This is primarily accomplished by the preparatory first session which each individual is required to attend before they are placed in group (see Chapter 13).

However, even with the best of instructions and detailed preparation, the group members will continue to direct their attention and energy toward the group leader. Yalom therefore suggests far more subtle reinforcing techniques to combat this difficulty. For example, the group leader can compliment members in the group who volunteer comments to other group members. Just a simple comment like "good feedback" gives the other group members a clear message that interaction and feedback between group members is a norm in the group that is actively encouraged. The group leader can also become more direct about his or her desire for the group member interaction by repeatedly asking why the group members do not direct their comments to each other while in group. A group leader can also wonder aloud why comments are being directed only towards him and ask the group in a general way why they refuse to speak to each other. Refusing to answer questions, either directly or indirectly, are other means of accomplishing the establishment of group member interaction. Nonverbal behavior is another valuable tool which often encourages members to speak directly with each other. For example, the group leader can shift his or her body away from a group member who is only speaking directly to the leader and thus give the clear message that the leader is not interested in a leader-centered group. Transferring a member's gaze from his or her own eyes to another member in the group frequently results in the eye contact being established between the two members, thereby encouraging dialogue between them instead of limiting the exchange between the leader and a group member. The group leader, thus has as his or her task, the responsibility of teaching the group to interact with each other rather than just with the leader. This is a task that is not accomplished easily and requires that the leader use his assigned role of technical expert to repeatedly give the group and its members the message in many different ways, both direct and indirect. Only by the leader's constant effort to teach the members that they must direct their energies towards each other can the climate be set for running group psychotherapy within Yalom's described and recommended fashion.

THE MODEL SETTING PARTICIPANT

As Yalom suggests, the leader shapes norms, not only through explicit or implicit social engineering, but through the example the leader sets with his own interpersonal group behavior. It is from this perspective, the position of the therapist in the therapeutic setting, that the role of the group therapist is most radically different from the role of therapist in individual therapy. Yalom's description of the group leader as a model-setting participant raises some very important issues regarding the issue of the leader's neutrality and transparency about their own feelings, attitudes and behavior while engaged in a therapeutic relationship with group members in a group setting. In order for a therapy group to fulfill its potential, it requires that the group discard the social norms which dictate most interpersonal interactions. For example, we are frequently taught as youngsters to be polite and not mention anything which might offend another individual, even if the topic or behavior is blatantly obvious to all concerned. Successful group psychotherapy requires the members try new behavior and take risks in their interaction with group members. The best way for this to be accomplished in group is for the members to observe the group leader's behavior and on some level internalize and model this behavior. Consequently, what the leader says is not as important as what the leader does. Or as frequently reported in Alcoholics Anonymous, "You must learn to walk your talk." AA members, for example, are keenly aware of those participants in the AA program who talk a "good program," but do not follow through (walk) with what they say should be done or what they say they will do. In a similar way, how the leader deals with their own anxiety, anger, and frustration is a clear message how these emotions will be dealt with in the group by its members. In short, as Marshall McCluhan frequently stated, "The medium is the message."

What the leader does and his or her presence as a person in group is far more important than what the leader says. An example will help illustrate this point. Martin Buber (1958), a Jewish theologian and existential philosopher has written exclusively about the Jewish mystical movement of the Hasidim. In the Orthodox Jewish tradition for example, it is believed, as it is in most orthodox disciplines, that only those ordained and chosen are allowed to interpret the scriptures. Within the orthodox teaching, individuals go to see the religious leader for advice, guidance, or the answers to their particular problem. Much like traditional medical care and orthodox views in psychotherapy, the patient went to his doctor for the diagnosis, interpretation, or advice on how to change or alleviate his suffering. This was not the case with the Hasidic movement. Nor is this the case with Alcoholics Anonymous or the Humanistic, Third

Force movement which emerged during the sixties as a reaction to orthodox forms of psychotherapy. This change in perspective reflects a common position of both the modern day religious revisionists and the contemporary forms of psychotherapy. The central issue is the difference between the traditional authoritarian view of the interpretations of the scriptures and the reformation movement which required the active participant of the disciple who was encouraged to discover God or Truth for himself. The Gnostic Movement of early Christianity which advocated the disciple find truth for himself is another example of the shift in perspective. A popular song during the 1960's, by John Prine, captured the spirit of that era with the lyrics "Move to the country, buy me a house, learn about Jesus by myself" which encouraged a personal responsibility in the search for personal understanding rather than relying on blind faith. The personal interpretation of spiritual truth is also exemplified in Alcoholics Anonymous in its reaction of traditional medicine and authoritative forms of psychotherapy in the treatment of addiction. This is the message that Martin Buber sought to give his readers in his interpretations of the Hasidic teachings. Within the Hasidic tradition, for example, the religious leader—the Zaddik—taught by example rather than by exhortation. Nothing is esoteric from this perspective. Everything is simple and each person of faith can grasp the simplicity of the teaching for themselves. The Zaddik was not a scholar or seat of religious reason and wisdom. Much like the model-setting participant which Yalom writes about in his text, the relationship is the crucial factor. The personality of the teacher takes the place of the doctrine! He is the teaching! As a disciple of the Zaddik said, "I did not go to my Zaddik to learn Torah from him, but to watch him tie his bootlaces."

How much and what of themselves the leader chooses to share must be carefully determined, however. When Yalom writes of the group leader's transparency, he is not suggesting that the leader bare all and "let it all hang out." Such an all or nothing approach is certainly doomed to failure and is usually destructive to the group and its members. Honesty for honesty's sake is a burlesque! A group leader must temper how much of himself he reveals and weigh that decision in respect to how honesty and transparency on his part will benefit or hinder the group. Group members must learn this basic premise about honesty and the group leader should be cautious in allowing members to hide behind truth in their destructive attacks on other group members. "I'm just being honest" is never a good excuse for viciously attacking or inflicting pain upon another. As Ernest Kurtz (1983) says, "Honesty with bad intent, is worse than a lie." The group leader must learn to balance their honesty with responsibility. Consequently, the decision on how transparent a leader will be while conducting his group should be determined exclusively by the evaluation of whether his sharing of this information will help or hinder the group and its members. The group leader must never forget that the group is not there for the leader to use for their own benefit or therapy. The question which always has to be asked by the group leader before they honestly reveal themselves is whether the group and its members will be helped by the leader's openness at this moment. An illustration will help clarify this point.

> Bill, a recovering alcoholic with three years of sobriety revealed to the group early in his fourth meeting that he had sexually molested his six-year-old daughter while in the midst of an alcoholic blackout three years prior. Bill had not intended to reveal this information to the group, and its revelation had been prompted by another member talking openly and honestly about their guilt over past deeds they had regretted doing while intoxicated. Bill's revelation to the group hit like a bomb shell and it was obvious by his own withdrawal and presentation that he had gotten carried away by his feelings and had opened up more of himself to the group than he had intended. Some of the group members, themselves children of alcoholic parents who had been sexually abused when they were youngsters, were especially stunned by a mixture of anger and embarrassment which was stirred in them by Bill's confession. As it became more apparent that the group was lost in their confusion about a way to respond to Bill, the leader, rather than let them struggle needlessly with their uncomfortableness decided to share her own feelings about Bill's revelation. The leader stated, "Bill, I've been touched by your willingness to share such embarrassing and painful information with the group. It clearly indicates you have grown to trust the others in here to be willing to risk as much as you have. I know for myself, it brings up a mixture of feelings regarding my own father's molestation of me. I don't know if I would have been able to show the courage you have in sharing this, but I'm glad you took the risk." Quickly following this

feedback from the group leader, other group members began to share similar feelings with Bill, helping him work through and resolve a great deal of guilt and self-condemnation he had been harboring for years. This incident also gave a clear message to the group and its other members. The deepest and most feared secret could be shared in this group and they would not be condemned, judged or rejected. By choosing to respond as she did, the group leader avoided a possible disastrous situation in group which could have been destructive to Bill as well as destructive to the group's therapeutic climate.

Once the group's positive acceptance of Bill's sharing of his secret was experienced by him and the other group members, the group leader could now steer the group to explore the more negative reactions in a structured and guided fashion. After the group had integrated this experience and reached a positive resolution, the group leader could give the group more freedom and less direction in exploring its reactions if a similar situation should occur again in the future. The group, because of the leader's decision to take an active and directive role in the shaping of a positive norm, did not have to struggle needlessly through a difficult developmental phase before it was stable and cohesive enough to do so.

The leader must also model non-judgmental acceptance and appreciation of each member's individual strengths and weaknesses. An appropriate interpretation or confrontation after the group has developed cohesion might be totally destructive and devastating to the group which is still in the early stages of development. For example, the leader does not want to give the message that it is unsafe to reveal secrets in the group. This certainly could have been the case with Bill when he spoke about his sexual molestation of his daughter. A group member, after a period of prolonged silence in the group, may choose to finally reveal a secret. The leader has a choice in the type of response he may make. He may respond with a statement that may be interpreted as "Why haven't you told us this before?" In contrast, the leader has the option of producing a totally different effect if he should respond instead with a statement that says, "It appears you now trust the group enough to share this with us." The message to the group members in the first instance is more likely to evoke a response in which he fears, "Oh hell, I'm sitting on a secret and if I tell it now, I'll get jumped on. I had better keep quiet." In the second instance, the group has learned it is safe to talk about any subject in the group and they can do this when they are ready, without having to fear condemnation or retribution from the leader or the other group members.

INTERPERSONAL HONESTY AND SPONTANEITY

The group leader also has the task of modeling interpersonal honesty and spontaneity. This is essential unless the leader wishes to run the risk of having a group that is leader-centered and one-dimensional (all loving or all angry). However, honesty and spontaneity must be balanced with responsibility. Yalom utilizes Victor Frankl's comments on the social problems of the United States to illustrate this point when he suggested that the Statue of Liberty on the East Coast should be balanced by the Statue of Responsibility on the West Coast. The freedom of honesty and spontaneity becomes possible in a therapy group only when it is tempered by a sense of responsibility. The group leader must always weigh his decisions in group on a narrow ridge which balances between complete spontaneous honesty on the one end and controlled structured responsibility on the other end. Martin Buber, whose writings have had significant influence on Carl Rogers and countless other theorists, has written extensively about the narrow ridge which exists between the exact, structured world of science and the chaotic, inexact world of religion and spirituality. Buber's writing reflects not only his belief that the psychotherapist must be an authentic person in his or her own right, but a person who lives in the "holy insecurity" of knowing there are not absolutes in the world. Buber's concept of the narrow ridge is the key to understanding the edifice upon which his philosophy of the I-Thou relationship stands. It is through this position of denying absolutes that Buber sought to express his personal view on understanding and knowledge.

> I have occasionally described my standpoint to my friends as the "narrow ridge." I wanted by this to express that I did not rest on the broad upland of a system that includes a series of sure statements about the absolute, but on a narrow, rocky ridge between the gulfs where there is no sureness of expressible knowledge but the certainty of meeting that remains, undisclosed. (Buber, 1955, p. 184)

For Buber, the narrow ridge represented the balance between the chaos of uncertainty and the exactness of certainty based on the belief of absolute knowledge. Buber saw difficulties in each extreme position. Believing that one has absolute knowledge leads to dogma, grandiosity and a loss of spirituality. Believing in the other extreme leads to chaos, nihilism, and hedonism. Understanding Buber's narrow ridge opens the door to interpreting his concepts of the I-Thou relationship, the abyss, and the "holy insecurity" of his existential philosophy. It also robs the group leader of the comfortableness which comes when one has pat formulas and concise answers to his patient's problems and dilemmas.

As a practicing psychotherapist and a person who spends the majority of my professional time with patients in individual and group psychotherapy, I am constantly forced to come to grips with this struggle each day in my life as I anticipate the arrival of my next appointment. I always feel the anxiety, some days greater than others of the anticipation of the meeting with the individual. What will be demanded of me this day? Will I respond as another person to the call of this person? I struggle in my conflict with my desire to control the therapy hour; to provide answers, pat formulas and concise information because I fear what may be demanded of a person when he takes the risk of meeting another person in the uniqueness and the uncertainty of the situation. I know I would find comfort in these formulations, but I realize that I must walk Buber's narrow ridge between spontaneity and control. I must assure myself and confirm myself anew of the faith in the meeting of two souls and allow the dialogue between us to take its course.

Psychotherapy, as it should be practiced, demands much, perhaps more in some cases than the therapist can give in that situation. The demand upon the group leader is such that few individuals may attempt to venture into the world of sick souls with their whole being as Buber so aptly illustrates in this statement.

> In certain cases, a therapist is terrified by what he is doing because he begins to suspect that something entirely other is demanded of him. Something incompatible with the economics of his profession, dangerously threatening, indeed, to his regulated practice of it. What is demanded of him is that he draw the particular case out of the correct methodological objectification and himself step forth out of the role of profes-

sional superiority, achieved and guaranteed by long training and practice, into the elementary situation between one who calls and one who is called. The abyss does not call to his confidently functioning security of action, but to the abyss, that is to the self of the doctor, that selfhood that is hidden under the structures erected through training and practice, that is itself encompassed by chaos, itself familiar with demons, but is graced with the humble power of wrestling and over-coming, and is ready to wrestle and overcome thus ever anew. Through his hearing of this call erupts in the most exposed of the intellectual professions, the crisis of its paradox. In a deci-sive hour together with the patient entrusted to and trusting in him, he has left the closed room of psychological treatment in which the analyst rules by means of a systematic and method-ological superiority and has stepped forward with him into the air of the world where self is exposed to self. (Buber, 1963)

Such a stance on the part of the group leader requires they relin-quish their need to be perceived as perfect. The group leader must be willing to accept and admit his or her fallibility. A couple of examples might illustrate this position more clearly.

It is the fourth meeting of a psychotherapy training group and one group member confronts the group leader accusing him of being controlling, dominating and remaining aloof during the previous group meetings. This is the first confrontation of the group leader and there is a moment of stunned silence while the rest of the group members sit on the edge of their chairs waiting to see how the group leader will respond to this attack. The group leader chooses quickly to ask if this is the same way the young woman viewed and responded to her father. The group member, caught by surprise and somewhat relieved for the opportunity to diffuse the conflict between her and the group leader, quickly acknowledged this was true and began, at the leader's encouragement, to explore her feelings towards her father and their relationship. While the group leader's in-terpretation was a correct one, for these were qualities her fa-ther possessed, the group member was also accurate in her perception of the group leader since he was indeed aloof and controlling. It was more in the service of his own needs and fears that the group leader quickly moved the group member to explore her past relationship with her father. It allowed the group leader to take the heat off himself, while promoting the attitude of his own infallibility. Rather than retreat so quickly into the there and then with this young woman, the group leader would have been of more therapeutic help to his group and this woman if he had allowed her full access to her feelings and perceptions of him. After these feelings were explored completely in the here and now, the group leader could have then guided her to understand why she had such a strong reaction to someone who possessed such traits, especially if that person was an authority figure.

By adapting such here and now strategy, the group leader would be giving the group members the message that he is not perfect, that he does possess traits that are not always completely admirable while demonstrating that he could accept such shortcomings in himself and was willing to acknowledge them to another without fear or defensiveness. The group member would subsequently learn a powerful message. They do not have to be infallible and they, as well as others, can have certain faults without it affecting their capacity to have a happy and meaningful relationship with another person. They can also learn that the leader can be confronted and that confrontation could be resolved in a constructive manner.

Another example of a group leader's acceptance of his own infallibility and its subsequent positive effect on the group process is illustrated by a Gestalt group which was led by Erv Polster.

Once while I was in a training group he was conducting, Erv had become embroiled around a group member's difficulty reaching a decision regarding a marriage proposal he was reluctant to make to his girlfriend. Erv, operating from a Gestalt framework, had guided this man to list all the reasons he had for marrying this woman. After being repeatedly encouraged to understand better why he was refusing to marry her, the group member finally responded to Erv that he felt Erv was behaving like a Jewish mother who was trying to marry him off to this woman. Erv, somewhat stunned by his remark, stopped and asked why the man felt this way; whereupon the group member proceeded to outline all of Erv's encouraging statements. Erv, after a moment of contemplation, laughed and said, "You know you're right!" The work was promptly completed and the group laughed along with Erv in admiration for a man who could admit he was wrong and change his thinking when given evidence which illustrated the incorrectness of his position. This was a valuable learning experience for all the group members.

ESTABLISHMENT OF THE GROUP NORMS

Now that the question of how the group leader goes about establishing the group norms has been addressed, the group leader must come to recognize which norms he or she wishes to establish.

First and foremost is the establishment of the norm of the self-monitoring group. If this is not addressed, the group will become leader-centered, dependent and passive. The group leader must channel his energies towards steering the group to reflect on and evaluate itself. Yalom gives an example on how the group leader might respond after the group has struggled with a half hour of superficial chatter or been monopolized by a group member who has rambled on in a nonproductive fashion.

Yalom suggests that the group leader direct the group to reflect on itself by posing questions to its members regarding their passivity. For example, the group leader could say, "I see a half hour has gone by and how has the group gone today? Are each of you satisfied with its direction and content? If not, why haven't you said anything? What could you have done differently? What stopped you from taking action? How do you rate the group so far today on a scale from one to ten? How would you rate your own participation on the same scale? What could have caused a higher rating or what is it you could have done yourself to get the rating higher?"

Each question and statement posed here would have prompted the group and its members to examine itself. The aim of each of these questions is to shift the evaluation function from the leader to the group.

The Norm of Self-Disclosure

While self-disclosure is crucial to the development of a healthy functioning group, the group leader must allow the group members to set their own pace. However, the group leader must at the same time encourage others in the group to talk about themselves. The group only goes as far and as deep as its most guarded and defended member. Each member in the group will self-disclose up to a point, and then wait on the other members to join them in the atmosphere of "reciprocal vulnerability." The most guarded member of a group, usually holding back because of his fears of the other members' possible reaction to his sharing, will have to be gently encouraged to talk about his secret sooner or later when he is ready. He must be told, however, the longer he waits the more difficult the sharing will become. The big secret, and every group has at least one member who has at least one big secret, is like a spider web with the secret at the hub and all conversations resembling threads that may run to that hub. The more the group member fears revealing the big secret, the more restricted he will be in their conversation about other subjects because he will fear this conversation may connect to the thread which leads to the hub at the center of the web where his big secret lies.

Yalom reminds his readers that the group is not a forced confessional and that members should never be coerced into revealing their big secret. Most members fear the reaction of the group and their catastrophic fears and beliefs should be explored before they reveal or self-disclose. This can be accomplished by a very simple, yet effective technique, which Yalom calls, Metadisclosures—disclosures about the disclosure. For example, the group member may suddenly freeze up after talking freely for a time in group and may even openly say that this is a subject he cannot talk about any further. The group leader, rather than forcing the issue or retreating to submissiveness can ask the group member the nature of their catastrophic fear if they were to disclose. "What do you fear will happen if you were to talk about this subject with the group? Who do you fear will react the strongest and who do you believe will be the most accepting? What is the worst thing that could happen if you did share this information with the group?" All of these questions are geared to get the group member to explore their resistance. In Gestalt terminology, this is defined as going with the resistance and is frequently the essence of Gestalt therapy. The group member is encouraged to explore the fears, both rational and irrational, surrounding their reluctance to self-disclose. The group can go even further with the theme of metadisclosures by asking the group member how they feel about not being able to talk about this subject with the group and if the group member's feelings of isolation are painful or familiar. The issue of their feelings surrounding these fears becomes the focus of the work with the group member and is usually much more important and meaningful than the very secret itself they feared to disclose. In fact, the group leader must be cautious in their exploration of the group member's resistance to self-disclosure as it would be a damaging norm to establish in the group if the group member were seduced into a premature self-disclosure. The safety and trust in the group might be seriously damaged if the group leader gave lip service to the group member's right to protect themselves from premature self-disclosure and then proceeded to seduce members into revealing themselves before they were ready to share their secrets.

Metadisclosures can also be used after a person has revealed their secret or disclosed parts of himself in group. A group leader can ask the group member what is was like sharing that secret with the group. A group member can also be guided to explore their fears with each particular member in the group, allowing them to modify their catastrophic belief system and realize they are not as terrible or as loathsome as they believed. As a group leader, I would respond to a group member who has self-disclosed for the first time by reinforcing the risks they have taken and encourage them to verify the invalidity of their expected fears. For example, I might say,

> Mary, you have taken an important risk today by sharing this information with the group and I am happy to see you now trust us enough to share such a painful experience. I know you fear condemnation from the other members because your parents were so critical and demeaning of you. I would like you to remember the responses you have heard from the other group members today and understand they do not think less of you because of what you have said. To the contrary, if you looked around at their faces, you will see more caring and understanding than was there previously in the group before you shared this information. Your fear of rejection and self-disclosure has led you to build a wall around yourself which has resulted in you keeping others away, creating the very rejection and criticism you feared the most.

Yalom's concern is more with the process of disclosure rather than the content of the disclosure. His model is much more focused on the working through of previously inhibiting fears and the evolving climate of acceptance and feelings in the group. This is the key to Yalom's model. The climate and atmosphere takes precedence over the interventions, confrontations and exploration of the members' resistance and expressions of feelings.

Once a disclosure has been forthcoming, a member should never be punished for disclosing. Most importantly, do not permit dirty fighting in the group between its members. Frequently, in the heat of a confrontation, another member may use material which is sensitive to that person in their attack on that person. For instance, in the case of Bill who had revealed to the group his molestation of his daughter while he was in an alcoholic blackout, a group member may have used that material against him during a confrontation and shouted, "What right have you to criticize me, at least I never molested my children!" At this point the leader must "stop action"! Interrupt the conflict quickly and say, "Something important has just happened in group." Ask the offended member about his or her feelings and ask the other members whether they have had similar experiences of having their disclosures used later in a punitive manner against them. Encourage other members of the group to talk about their own reactions to the conflict between the two individuals. Point out to the group how this attack will make it difficult for others to reveal themselves. Explore how this conflict will affect the group and its willingness to be open and honest in the future. It is the leader's task at this time to insure that the group realize that self-disclosure will be honored in the group and that the leader will take precautions to prevent the punitive use of previously disclosed material. Dirty fighting will not be allowed in the group.

This is important for many reasons. Individuals usually fear being authentic and real. Most people, especially alcoholics and addicts, don't want to take an authentic stance in life because of their fear of rejection or dislike. It's all right if you reject me or dislike me because of what you think I am. But if I am real and you get to know me and then you still reject me, this is much more frightening and painful. Consequently, we all use what Bednar (1985) calls impression management in our interactions with others. We try to decide what will get us approval and act in that way. The difficulty with such an artificial approach to life is summed up best by Kurt Vonnegut's statement, "You have to be careful what you pretend to be, because you may wake up someday and discover that's what you are."

In group, the task is to get people to risk being real with each other so they can learn they can be loved and accepted for what or who they are rather than what they do or how they act. This allows them to reverse their introject (You won't like me if you really knew me because I'm bad). A group which encourages honest self-disclosure and is accepting of that self-disclosure permits individuals to understand the way their introjects interfere with their ability to be nurtured and enjoyed by others. Group members will learn eventually how they shut themselves off from meaningful relationships and the ways their negative self-images lead to continued poor choices of lovers and friends. They also learn through this awareness how they contribute to their difficulties. Being authentic with others will lead to a corrective emotional experience which will allow them to create a true sense of self and enhance their self-esteem. Group conducted from this perspective allows reparative work on the person's sense of self. The aim of treatment is to get at the individual's internal messages, self-evaluations and the ways they condemn themselves. If they are encouraged to be more genuine in group, they will begin to feel less deceptive, less false and will eventually take an authentic stand in life. At this juncture, they will learn the crucial message, "I am worth something if I am real."

Procedural Norms and Anti-Therapeutic Norms

Optimally, the more unstructured, unrehearsed and freely interacting the group remains the more effective the group will be. However, the group leader has to be cautious in determining how unstructured and unrehearsed the group is to be. If he is not active and directive enough, the group can degenerate into a number of anti-therapeutic norms. Such norms can be easily established and are often difficult to extinguish if left unattended for too long. Some of the more common and troublesome anti-therapeutic norms that can be established by a group are identified by Yalom and listed below.

A. *Take turns format.* The group will devote the entire meeting sequentially to each particular member. The first person to speak will, for instance, become the focus of the entire session. Groups can have enormous difficulty shifting the focus from one member to the next. This can become especially troublesome for two reasons. First, it enhances premature self-disclosure. The group member elected to be the focus of the group session will succumb more and more to the mounting group pressure leading the overwhelmed member to reveal more of himself or herself than they had been prepared to share. The person can be emotionally raped. The second danger is that it will enhance the other group member's anxiety as they realize their turn in group will be due next. The anxiety and fear of the hot seat may become so great that the member may drop out of group rather than face their turn next week.

B. *One-topic format.* The group can establish a pattern of devoting the entire session to the first issue or topic presented. An unspoken rule against changing the subject matter may be established with sanctions being erected without the open acknowledgement of such sanctions.

C. *Can you top this format.* A norm can be established in the group where members will only reveal or self-disclose if the material is more personal and emotionally charged than the last member's disclosure. The group can develop what Yalom describes as a "spiraling orgy of self-disclosure." The group must learn that the subtle, often unobvious pattern of their behavior is a far more potent source of conflict for them than the "spilling of their guts on the group floor."

D. *The group can become so tightly knit that it can become hostile to new members.* If the leader is not careful, the bringing of new members into the group can result in conflict resulting in the new members being excluded from the group acceptance. Preparing the group for new members is a task that must be addressed cautiously. Chapter Eleven will address the pitfalls which have to be avoided when bringing new members into group.

E. *Leader-centered group.* The group can become unchallenging of the group leader. Their needs can become subservient to those of the leader and the group will become leader-centered and dependent.

F. *One-side experience.* The group can become so one dimensional, all loving or all attacking. Real intimacy will be avoided and the group can establish norms which do not permit the full range and expression of feelings and thoughts.

IMPORTANCE OF GROUP

The more important the members consider the group, the more effective the group will become in their treatment. The group leader must appreciate the importance of this position and reinforce this belief in whatever way the leader can. For a group to survive, it requires two elements: 1. structure or purpose and 2. commitment. The group leader must define the structure and purpose of the group before it starts. Once the group sessions are in progress, the group leader must give its members the message that the group is the most important event in their lives. The group leader accomplishes this by being punctual and informs them well in advance his concern at being absent from one of the group sessions. The leader constantly addresses other members' absences, requiring them to let the group know well in advance the reasons why they are not going to be present for a meeting. If the leader is thinking about the group between sessions, it behooves him to speak about these thoughts with the group members. This sharing of thoughts between sessions helps instill a sense of continuity between the sessions. Encouraging this continuity helps the group work through issues from one meeting to the next. The group leader should aim to make connections whenever he can in group. For instance, if one group member presents an issue in group which is similar to that presented by another group member, the leader might say, "This sounds very much like what John was working on two weeks ago in group." Noticing the withdrawal or change in affect of a group member can be helpful if this is traced to some previous interaction in the group. For instance, the group leader might comment to a withdrawn member, "I've noticed, Mary, you've been quiet in group since you and Joan had the disagreement two weeks ago."

Members as Agents of Help

As Yalom advocates, the group functions best when members appreciate the valuable help they can provide one another. The group must learn to diminish its reliance on the leader as the only source of help. Reinforce whenever possible the mutual helpfulness of its members. Encouraging comments which group members have found helpful can be easily elicited by the simple question, "You've gotten a lot of feedback on this issue, Bob, what has been the most helpful?" If a member wonders out loud in group if they are too selfish, respond by asking, "Ken, there are many people who know you well in here, why don't you ask them?"

These norms, once established, have to be constantly maintained. This requires the monitoring of behavior which may undermine these norms. For instance, one group member may respond to another with this statement, "Joe, you have no right to say that to him, you're worse than he is." The leader should intervene quickly at this point saying, "That's not my experience of you, Joe; while we all may have similar problems, your comments are usually helpful." Ask the other group members at this time about their perceptions of Joe. Is it true that he is helpful or destructive? Once this matter is settled, the group leader can address his comments towards the attacking group member. "It seems the rest of the group perceives Joe differently. Is there something else regarding your feelings towards Joe?"

Yalom defines the role of the group leader as being active and directive. His suggestions are not the nonjudgmental mirroring or clarifying comments typically associated with the tasks of the therapist in individual therapy. The importance of the norm setting in group takes precedent over the other aspects of the group leader's role within Yalom's model. It is vital that the group leader establish, maintain and develop the norms which will allow the therapeutic process to unfold in group. Once these norms are set, the group leader can turn to the third basic task of the therapist which is defined by Yalom as the activation and process illumination of the here and now.

THE HERE AND NOW ACTIVATION AND PROCESS ILLUMINATION

What is the task of the group leader from this perspective? The group leader must insure that the group members focus their attention on their immediate feelings and thoughts towards the other group members, the group leader, and the group itself as a whole. The immediate events in the group take precedent over the events in the past or the current life of each member outside of the group. The events in the here and now within the group become the primary focus of the group leader.

Why does Yalom advocate such an approach and what are the advantages of a here and now focus? Such a therapeutic stance will facilitate the development and stark emergence of each member's social microcosm. As a group leader, you will not have to prompt members to talk about their interpersonal conflicts, doubts or fears. These issues will all emerge within their interactions with the leader and the other members of the group. The person who alienates others will alienate his fellow members in group. The individual who is taken advantage of by others will allow themselves to be taken advantage of by others in the group. Those members who cannot handle anger will experience this difficulty in group when anger is expressed. The idiosyncratic psychological Achilles heel of each individual group member will emerge for all to see in their demonstration of their behavior in the here and now of the group process. The group, from this viewpoint, is a laboratory, a social microcosm where each particular member will act out in the here and now (rather than talk about it in the there and then) their particular idiosyncratic conflicts.

Once the group leader is aware of the what and the why of each member's conflicts in the group, he or she must set in motion the curative group process. How is this task to be accomplished? The group leader's approach must be ahistoric. He or she must deemphasize what has happened outside the group and each member's past individual experiences. The here and now is the power cell of the group and it is comprised of two layers. 1. Content—the current feelings experienced by group and its members; 2. Process—the reflective examination and clarification or process illumination of what has occurred sequentially. Consequently, Yalom's model requires two steps. First, the content of the experience must be understood. The experience of the immediate occurrence of events must be realized and recognized by the group and its members. Secondly, the sequential process of events must be understood. The group must reflect back upon itself and understand the process of its own transactions. The group, therefore, must transcend the pure content of its experience and reflect back on the process which led to that event. Process, for example, examines the reasons Joe responded to Mary and not Bill at this particular time in this particular manner. Why does Lucille pick only the men to respond to when there is a question to be asked and why does she not respond to the members of the group who are the most helpful? Why does Sharon make such a broad general statement like, "I trust everyone" at the time when Sandra is taking about her fears of being judged? These questions exemplify the process illumination which Yalom encourages the group leader to constantly monitor. Adherence to this posture is justified on the basis that psychopathology is ubiquitous in interpersonal interactions. A single interpersonal transaction is representative of a larger pattern of behavior. It gives the group leader a peek at the whole.

The understanding of the here and now requires the self-reflective loop. Within this illustration, the group reflects back on the content of the here and now experience. It is largely the group leader's task to steer the group to the self-reflective loop so that it can understand the process (or the what and why) of a particular experience. (See Figure I.) The group becomes aware of this process by the leader's commentary on the process. Consequently, it is the leader's responsibility to make process commentary so this potential can be actualized.

Process commentary, in turn, requires understanding the metacommunicational aspects of a particular message. As Yalom writes,

> Metacommunication refers to communication about the communication. Compare for example, "Close the window!" "Wouldn't you like to close the window? You must be cold?" "I'm cold, would you please close the window?" "Why is this window open?" Each of these statements contains a great deal more than a simple request or command, each conveys a metacommunication — a message about the nature of the relationship between two interacting individuals. (pp. 122–123, 1975)

The group leader is forced to understand why this group member is making this statement to this person at this time in this manner. Process concerns itself with the how and why of an interpersonal communication. Yalom gives some excellent examples of process illumination in his text. For instance, Yalom reports a student asks a question of the lecturer, "What was the date of Freud's death?" After the lecturer replied 1939, the student said, "No, it was 1938." As Yalom says, a question ain't a question if you already know the answer. Why did the student ask a question to which he already knew the answer? Presumably to either demonstrate his knowledge or embarrass the lecturer. Process illumination in group involves the same principle. The leader must constantly monitor the sequence of such transactions, noting to whom and when they are directed.

Yalom gives another example:

> Early in the course of a group therapy meeting, Burt, a tenacious, bulldog faced, intense student, exclaimed to the group in general and to Rose (an unsophisticated astrologically inclined cosmetologist) in particular, "Parenthood is degrading!" This provocative statement elicited considerable response from the group, all of whom possessed parents and many of whom were parents, and the ensuing donnybrook consumed the remainder of the group session. (p. 123, 1975)

FIGURE I

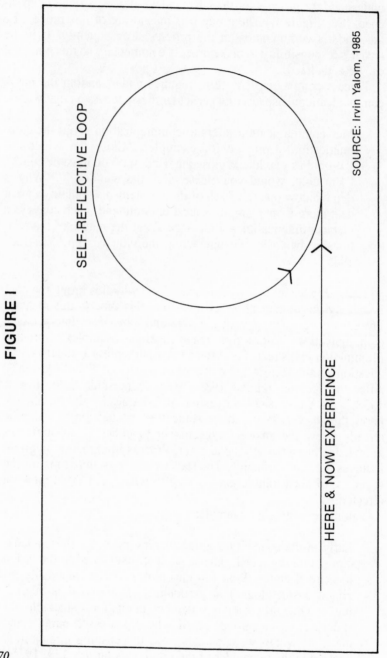

SELF-REFLECTIVE LOOP

HERE & NOW EXPERIENCE

SOURCE: Irvin Yalom, 1985

Examined only on the content level, the members engaged Burt in a debate about parenthood. Examined from a process level, this interaction is rich in inferences about Burt and his transactions with the group and its members. The group leader can ask himself a number of questions about the process of this transaction. 1. Why was Burt's message actually directed at Rose who is more emotional, nonintellectual and has many children? 2. Why is Burt so intolerant of nonintellectuals? 3. Why did Burt attack Rose so indirectly? and, 4. Why did Burt provoke the group and set himself up for a universal attack?

As Yalom suggests, any of these observations could be correct as each represent an aspect of Burt which must be explored and examined in the course of therapy.

Therapists' Techniques for the Here and Now

The process illumination can only occur if the group leader keeps the focus of the group in the here and now. This can be a difficult task as the group, in numerous and subtle ways, will always attempt to shift the focus away from the immediate into the there and then. Whenever an issue regarding an outside event of the group is raised in the group, the group leader must question what way this issue may be related to the unspoken and often unconscious stirrings of the group and its members. The group leader must ask himself or herself how this material applies to the present and how can this event come alive in the here and now.

An example will help illustrate this point:

> In the first meeting of a psychotherapy training group, Tom begins the group by requesting some help from the group members regarding his difficulty with his roommate. Tom proceeds to talk in detail about his lack of trust with his friend and his fear of speaking openly with his roommate about the issues that have led to his distrust. The group first responds by giving Tom advice and eventually relating their own difficulties with friends who have failed them in the past after they had entrusted them with sensitive information. The group leader at this point commented about the importance of the issue of trust and asked the group if this was a fear they shared in regards to the group and the members in the group. The group quickly shifted its focus from the there and then issue of

trust and began to explore their feelings of trust in the here and now with each other. A rich discussion entailed which resulted in a deepening of the interchange between the members of the group and their fears of others' reactions if they were to trust them with the open and honest expression of their deepest fears and feelings. Once this topic of trust shifted to the here and now, it consumed the remainder of the group session. Before ending the meeting, the group leader asked Tom if his problem with the roommate had been properly addressed. Tom admitted that his roommate wasn't really the issue and he realized that his concerns were actually with the group.

Tom's revelation illustrates an important principle of psychotherapy. The question which the group leader has to constantly ask himself is why, out of all the material that the patient can talk about, has he chosen the particular topic that he has at this particular time. There has been a myriad of important events in the individual's life since the last group session. Why, out of all of the events in the last week, had Tom chosen the issue of trust and his fear of talking openly about his distrust? While Tom was not conscious of the reasons he picked the topic of his friend, unconsciously the material had been triggered by the similar atmosphere of fear and distrust in the group. This issue, trust with his roommate and trust in the group, were parallel concerns in Tom's life. The group triggered in Tom an emotion which was associated with his roommate. He picked the topic which was most salient to his consciousness, but was secondary to the real current issues in the here and now. The group leader must learn to keep a third ear to such parallel talk. Drawing parallels between events which the individual chooses to bring up for discussion in the here and now will allow the group leader to gain a peek at the possible unconscious material which lies repressed below the surface.

Fundamental to this therapeutic technique is the recognition of the importance of unconscious factors in all forms of communication. This position holds that an extremely important component of emotional dysfunction exists entirely outside the awareness of the individual, finding expression only in disguised or encoded form. At the heart of this approach is an understanding of the individual's unconscious communications—his or her encoded or disguised messages. It is therefore essential for the group leader to appreciate and be capable of fully applying the kind of listening process which allows the group members' unconscious expressions to be properly decoded and understood for their most significant meanings. Ronald Langs (1976) has outlined an intricate model which he calls the listening process or the communicative approach. Langs encourages the therapist to differentiate between the manifest content and latent content of the individual's message. The manifest content is the surface aspect of the individual's associations. Such communication is direct, immediate, and self-evident in what the person says and means. The latent content is that which is not self-evident within the surface contents of the person's message, but is contained in a disguised or encoded theme. The group leader's task is to decode this latent message and make it manifest. Since the material is often presented in a disguised form (i.e., Tom's concern with his trust of his roommate), the group leader has to listen for the individual's derivatives. Derivative is a term originally coined by Freud and is used to imply that the manifest content (i.e., Tom's distrust of his roommate) is derived from the latent image (Tom's fear and distrust of the group).

Therapists and group leaders have difficulty working with and decoding derivative expressions for a number of reasons. 1. Most people prefer to work with that which is self-evident, directly on the surface, and relatively easy to manipulate. 2. It is a human tendency to treat the indirect — anything that cannot be seen directly, touched, immediately understood, and readily manipulated — as though it were nonexistent. The idea that surface material contains latent meanings and impressions not immediately discernible are concepts alien to many therapists. 3. Perhaps most importantly, individual's derivative associations often contain highly emotionally charged and compelling encoded perceptions of the therapist's errors, personal difficulties and failings.

Even the most skilled therapist can fall prey to their own unconscious avoidance of these derivatives because they may contain confrontive and critical content. An excellent example of such an instance involves a skilled group psychotherapist who was presenting a national training workshop to a large contingent of nurses in a rural community setting. The trainer possessed excellent credentials from a highly respected psychoanalytic institute and had a thriving practice in which group psychotherapy was an integral part of her practice. The all-day workshop was split into two segments. The first part contained an excellent didactic presentation of psychodynamic group theory and the second half involved a demonstration experiential group composed of volunteers from the audience. It was during the experiential component of the presentation that the group trainer succumbed to his unconscious efforts to avoid derivative associations because of their highly charged emotional content. The group resisted his efforts to get them to move from the opening theme which concerned their anger, frustration and alienation with orthodox and fundamental religion. Since the majority of nurses attending the conference were from small, rural towns in the South, they had more than their share of experiences with fundamental religious beliefs which were impractical and unapplicable for their lives.

What the group trainer failed to appreciate was the effect his excellent didactic presentation has on his audience. His emphasis on Freud, psychodynamic theory, and long-term psychotherapy with its associated emphasis on making the unconscious conscious had evoked similar feelings of frustration which they felt in relation to their experience with the fundamental religious teachings in their life. Their inability to apply such fundamental principles of religion in a practical way in their own lives was the manifest content of their message to the trainer. The derivatives of this message was triggered by their latent, unconscious feelings of frustration related to the impracticality of applying Freudian principles of long-term psychotherapy to short-term treatment facilities with patients who were not particularly psychologically minded and lived in small, rural towns in the Deep South. As an observer sitting safely in the audience, I had little problem decoding the group's message to the trainer. Yet, he, himself a very competent group therapist, was unable to hear the frustration being expressed latently because it evoked his own unconscious fears of attack and criticism.

Derivatives can be interpreted and deciphered in many ways. A group leader need not wait for a person to speak before drawing a hypothesis about their personality organization and possible behavior. Since all behavior is determined, derivatives and latent content are present in many forms. For example, a fellow colleague, interviewing a prospective group member noted upon meeting the woman for the first appointment that she had been working rigorously on a large book of crossword puzzles while in the waiting room. She was so preoccupied with the book, which she had nearly completed, that she had not noticed the therapist had entered the room to invite her into his office. She was so intensely motivated in her crossword puzzle that he had to speak her name twice before she was able to respond to his call. As they walked together towards his office, the therapist commented to himself, "I wonder if this woman is into word games." The therapist was proved right as the patient spent the majority of the therapy hour in a rambling discourse of her ideas and thoughts, hiding her feelings behind a rigid defensive structure of intellectualization, rationalization and isolation of affect.

Here and Now Activation: Techniques

More important than mastering any technique, the group leader must fully understand the strategy and theoretical foundations upon which all effective technique must rest. The group leader must discipline himself to think predominantly in the here and now. He or she must move the focus from the outside to the inside and from the general to the specific. Each topic presented must prompt the group leader to ask the question: "How can I relate this to the group?" "How can I make this come alive in the here and now?" Such a focus is the power cell of Yalom's model. It is the theoretical strategem which is the heart of his approach to group psychotherapy. If Yalom's strategy is followed, the group leader will not have to worry about repetitive, boring and monotonous group sessions. Group members will not put the group leader and their fellow members to sleep with abstract ramblings in the there and then about events which occurred six months to six years ago. Their histories, difficulties and patterns of behavior will come alive in the here and now. Once the right atmosphere is established, the group leader will have a dynamic and alive laboratory for the exploration of human interactions and transactions. Keeping the here and now activation alive can be accomplished in a variety of ways. One method for fulfilling this task requires that the group leader take all "there and then" comments concerning individuals or events outside of the group and shift these issues into the "here and now"; exploring the ways these comments might relate to members presently in the group. For instance, a patient might begin to talk about a past hostile confrontation with their father. He could be asked, "Who here in group might evoke similar feelings in you?" Since the presenting complaint concerns a father, the group leader should be cautious for possible transference issues. Such a statement may also reflect the group member's attitude toward the group leader. Another group member might complain of her domineering sister, admitting there are many things she would like to tell her, but which she holds back because of her fear of the sister's reprisal. Turning this woman's "there and then" concerns into the "here and now," she could easily be asked if she has held back saying certain things to the members of the group because of similar fears of reprisals and if she would be willing to share some of these feelings with them today. A group member may comment that he has become aware that his tendency to stereotype people has caused him numerous difficulties in his relationships in the past. Instead of exploring how these difficulties have manifested in the "there and then," the group leader could ask him if he would be willing to tell the group members the way he has stereotyped each of them. Not only would such an intervention activate the interaction between the group members in the here and now, it would give each member some important feedback upon their perceived effect on another group member.

If a group has degenerated into cocktail party chatter and one group member commented that he doesn't think the group is taking its purpose seriously, the group leader could ask the individual if he would be willing to identify those members who do and those members who don't take the group seriously. Someone may complain that the group is too nice and everyone avoids conflicts. Asking the group member to identify the "leaders of the peace and tact movement in group" will activate the group into a rich source of interaction. Sometimes, even something as simple as asking one member to use "I statements" and speak directly to the other member can turn a dull, lifeless monologue into an exciting, alive dialogue.

Each of these illustrations suggest various ways a group leader can move the group into a here and now activation. In all of the examples, the leader had the option of asking a group member to respond to the group or another group member in either a provocative or supportive manner. Asking a group member to identify the most friendly, least threatening, most supportive or involved member will certainly require a different type of risk and invoke a different type of response than if a group member were asked to identify the most angry, least supportive, most uncaring or uninvolved person in the group. Depending upon the group leader's decision and his line of inquiry, he can either build a group culture that is supportive or a group culture that is confrontive. Since both positions are required for a highly functioning therapy group, the leader does not want to sacrifice one position for the other. However, his decision should be guided by the group's stage of development. If the group had not yet developed trust and cohesion, it would not be stage appropriate to ask members to risk provocative confrontations. Stage-consistent interventions would require the group leader to encourage members to respond to the rest of the group in a way that would reduce regression and hostility. Later, after group trust and cohesion has been established, the leader could prompt the group members to risk more provocative positions when it is less likely to disrupt or threaten the group's existence.

Group leaders should also be aware that the neat, exact world of theory and purity of technique often fails to thrive in the harsh world of reality. Most addicted patients have never read Irvin Yalom and don't understand they are supposed to respond in the "right way" to the group leader's noble efforts to help them see the error of their ways. Therefore, the group leader should be prepared to expect a claim of equality whenever he asks a group member to identify another group member as a possible source of interpersonal stimulus. Statements like, "I trust everyone in the group the same. I like everyone here in the group equally" — are never true. Don't ever believe it! No one in a psychotherapy group feels the same about everyone else. Each person in group is different and triggers a whole array of responses from the other members. Careful exploration of group member's responses to these differences are powerful sources of self-understanding and personal growth. While the group leader should never believe such claims of equality, neither should he always actively confront such a position. Rather than raise the group members' resistance, the group leader should encourage the member to explore their reactions to particular group members. This can be accomplished by gentle prodding. "Sure, I know you trust everyone in group; but if you had to pick someone you trusted more than others, who might that be? Would you be willing to take a few seconds and look around at each person's face and see who might trigger this feeling within you?" Such encouragement is not intrusive and most members will have feelings brought to their awareness by looking into the eyes and faces of their fellow group members. On those rare occasions when a person is so defended or resistant that they cannot or will not respond to such a suggestion, ask them how they felt doing the exercise. Ask the other group members to respond with their own feelings in regards to the exercise. Almost always, this will bring forth a rich source of material from the other group members. Some may respond in disbelief that someone could feel absolutely the same about everyone. Others may respond in empathy to the anxiety such an exercise would trigger in them if they were required to take such a risk.

Sometimes, a group leader can choose to "just" encourage an isolated group member to make some genuine contact with another person in group. True intimacy and relatedness can be a powerful curative experience for individuals who have led their lives in false, contrived and unauthentic interactions. "Healing through meeting" is a phrase coined by Martin Buber to emphasize the importance of true authentic dialogue in a person's life. Buber has written extensively about our need for human relatedness. Each of us possesses a primal need to be heard and listened to by another. Often it is enough just to know our cry has been heard and we are not alone in our isolation and suffering. In many cases, an individual's cry cannot be answered and, at these times, a response is not required or necessary. Buber described this phenomena of the human condition as a cry that wants to be heard, but not answered. An example will help illustrate this position.

Mary had sat quietly in group for more than three months, responding only to give support or encouragement to the other group members. Recently, she had begun to ask the group for advice concerning "my many problems." She was married to an alcoholic and had joined the group because she had become increasingly despondent over her husband's repeated failures to maintain sobriety for any length of time. Their six-year marriage had been marked by vacillating periods of multiple job losses, DUI arrests and public humiliations intertwined with periodic episodes of relative success and stability which only lasted long enough to instill in her a false sense of hope that maybe this time, things would be different. As Mary talked about her isolation and despondency, the group began to respond to her as they usually did — namely to give advice endlessly. Mary's passivity and despondency usually evoked such responses in others and prevented her from mobilizing her own resources when confronted with difficulties which required important decisions. Stopping the group's feedback, the group leader asked Mary if she would be willing to look around the room and pick out one person whom she felt best understood her situation or her feelings at this moment. The group leader had chosen to intervene because he did not want the group to shift into their typical "let's give Mary advice and tell her what to do" mode. Rather, the leader hoped to have Mary connect with one person who might truly understand her position and her pain. After some initial claims that she felt everyone in the group understood her equally, Mary finally chose Sally, a woman who had refrained from giving her advice. Sally had been empathically connected with Mary because she had experienced a similar situation in her life. Sally proceeded to describe her own feelings at this moment, relating how difficult it was for her to make decisions which often resulted in her feeling immobilized. As Sally shared more of her own difficulties, Mary began to acknowledge more of herself talking about her rage at her husband and her need to take a stand with him. Mary's experience of herself was deepened by her identification with Sally which was made possible because Sally had understood and really heard Mary in a way that Mary had not experienced before.

Empathic understanding between group members and helping individuals connect with each other is one of the group leader's primary goals during the early stages of a newly developing group. The leader need not always ask group members to respond to each other in such a direct fashion. This can be accomplished by simply watching other group members' nonverbal responses and reactions as someone else is speaking in group. A knowing look, eye contact, a nodding head or a subtle change of expression are clues that someone in group has empathically connected with another. The group leader has to just give permission or encouragement that this empathy be shared. Such a stance helps cohesion be developed in group and one must always remember that unless cohesion is established, none of the other curative factors in group can be set in motion. Cohesion is enhanced as group members learn to share, relate, and feed each other in a caring way. Martin Buber illustrates the importance of people feeding each other in a story about the Baal Shem Tov, the first Zaddich of the Hasidic mystical tradition.

When the Baal Shem Tov was a young rabbi, he prayed that God would someday show him the difference between heaven and hell. Shortly after his prayers, he had a dream one evening as he slept in which God ushered him into a large room where a group of starving people circled a great round table. Although there was an enormously large bowl of delicious, nourishing, warm stew in the middle of the table, all those who sat around the table were depleted, undernourished and emaciated. So large was the table that the bowl of food remained more than an arms length away from each of them. Even though long wooden spoons were tied to each of their hands, which allowed each of these individuals to reach the food at the center of the table, the length of the spoon prevented them from reaching their own mouths. In spite of an abundance of food and nourishment in the room, each was suffering from starvation. The young rabbi was deeply saddened by such a sorrowful sight. Starving people, all who could see, smell and reach the food with their spoons, were unable to feed themselves and get the nourishment they desperately needed and craved. This is hell, God sadly told the young rabbi. God then proceeded to take the young rabbi to another room. Here, the scene appeared much the same as the first. A great round table with an abundance of food and people sitting around a circular table with giant spoons tied to their hands. Only here, instead of sadness and starvation, each person was well-nourished, healthy, happy and well-fed. The room was alive with merriment, laughter and happiness. Although the spoons were still too long to allow this group to feed themselves, they could easily reach across the table to feed each other. This is heaven, God said to the young rabbi, and the difference is that here people feed each other instead of trying to feed themselves in isolation.

So it is with group psychotherapy. Group members are encouraged and permitted to feed each other. None has to sit in isolation suffering from emotional malnourishment. The group leader has many ways he can encourage members "feeding" and interacting with each other. Each of the previous examples are only a few of the possible activating techniques available to the group leader. But it is important to remember, the techniques presented are only intended to illuminate the underlying principle of Yalom's format for group psychotherapy and are not intended to be ends in themselves. Rather, such techniques are to be used judiciously in the leader's efforts to establish a group culture which is curative and alive. As Yalom says:

> Remember that sheer acceleration of interaction is not the purpose of these techniques; if the therapist moves too quickly,

using gimmicks to make interactions, emotional expression and self-disclosure too easy, he misses the whole point. Resistance, fear, guardedness, distrust, in short everything which impedes the development of satisfying interpersonal relations must be permitted expression. The goal is not to create a slick-functioning, streamlined social organization, but instead one which functions well enough and engenders sufficient trust for the unfolding of each member's social microcosm. Working through the resistances to change is the key to the production of change. Thus, the therapist does not want to go around obstacles but through them. (Yalom, 1975, p. 140)

INTERPERSONAL THEORY OF BEHAVIOR

After the group leader has steered the group into the here and now focus, he must now direct his energies toward the goal of helping each member understand their behavior and the impact they have on others. Yalom outlines a systematic approach for understanding the process of personal impact in group and how each group member's interpersonal process within the group will reflect their general behavior and problems outside of group. By exploring in detail this interpersonal process, Yalom aims to answer the question of how process illumination of the here and now interaction leads to change. Before presenting Yalom's outline, it would be important for the group leader to understand the theoretical foundation upon which Yalom's group edifice stands.

Although Yalom does not formally identify himself as a Sullivanian, he does acknowledge the importance of interpersonal learning in groups. He repeatedly draws reference to Harry Stack Sullivan and suggests presenting a brief explanation of Sullivan's interpersonal theory of psychiatry to every patient before they are placed in group. Therefore, understanding Sullivan's key concepts will provide the reader with a better understanding of Yalom and his approach to group psychotherapy.

SULLIVAN'S INTERPERSONAL THEORY OF PSYCHIATRY

Obviously, a comprehensive explanation of Sullivan and his interpersonal theory of psychiatry is beyond the scope of this chapter. The interested reader should go to Yalom (1975) and his recom-

mended references for understanding Sullivan. In order to understand the importance of Sullivan's influence on Yalom, it is only
necessary to appreciate the four basic tenets of Sullivan's theory.
Sullivan contends:

1. Personality is almost entirely a product of a person's interaction with others.
2. As human beings, our need to be closely related to others is
basic.
3. As a young, developing child, we seek the approval of others
and avoid their disapproval.
4. Eventually, the concept of the self (self-dynamism) is developed based on our perceived approval or disapproval by others.

If one fully understands the significance of these four basic principles of Sullivanian theory, one can appreciate the basic aim of
Yalom's approach to group psychotherapy. If we are a product, for
better or for worse, of our interactions with others, what better way
to understand our strengths and weaknesses than to go to the source
of our behavior — our interactions with others. However, to just observe our interactions with others misses the significance of the potential for change which exists within a psychotherapy group.
Yalom utilizes three other principles of Sullivan's theory in his attempt to mobilize the group to bring about change in an individual's
life. These three key concepts are:

1. *Parataxic Distortions*. We all possess a proclivity to destroy
our perceptions of others. Here Sullivan refers to our tendency to
relate to others, not on the basis of the realistic aspects of another,
but on our perceived distortion of interpersonal reality. These distortions are determined and influenced by our interpersonal needs.

2. *Self-Fulfilling Prophecy*. In Sullivan's language, our interpersonal distortions tend to be self-perpetuating and lead to a self-fulfilled prophecy. For instance, an individual who possesses a concept of his self (self-dynamism) as derogatory and inadequate may,
through selective inattention, incorrectly perceive others as harsh
and rejecting. More importantly, the person may gradually develop
traits and attitudes like defensiveness or servility which actually
lead others to relate to him as he expects.

3. *Consensual Validation*. This concept refers to Sullivan's emphasis on the importance of peer relationships in an individual's

psychological development. As children we develop "chum relationships" which causes us to examine and compare our perceptions with others with whom we identify. Through these comparisons, we become aware that our friends or chums often see things differently than we or our family. Perceptions which were distorted become invalidated. As Sullivan says, "Parataxic distortions are modified primarily through consensual validation." If Mary perceives Jim as attacking and hostile while the rest of the group perceives him as supportive and kind, Mary will be forced to come to terms with her distortions of Jim. Perceptions which are not validated by the consensus of others lead to internal psychological shifts.

Understanding these three concepts helps explain Yalom's goal and purpose of group. As Sullivan advocated, the aim of psychiatry is the study of the process that goes on between people. Symptomatology becomes translated into interpersonal behavior and the group leader observes and treats the interpersonal problems accordingly. From this view, a mental disorder is not statically embedded in the person. Instead, psychopathology is considered to be anchored in a dysfunctional system and interaction. These dysfunctional interactions are perpetuated by distortions within that system. Each person carries his or her script and plays their own assigned role based on their invalidated perceptual distortions of themselves and others. This script is constantly re-enacted within the larger framework of our personal relationships with others in our life. We become unwitting actors in a play in which we do not understand the plot. From this perspective, the freedom of appropriate interchanges pertaining to reciprocal impressions, feelings, and observations within the context of the group situation becomes the medium from which awareness, validation, and change becomes possible. The goal or cure of treatment thus becomes the modifying and altering of these interpersonal distortions thus enabling the person to experience a more satisfying life based on the mutual realistic aspects of their interpersonal relationships. This is achieved for Sullivan when the person's sense of self is expanded to the point that he or she is known and perceived by others in the same manner that they perceive or know themselves. Or in Rogerian terms, there is congruence between their sense of self, their behavior and how others perceive them. For instance, a person who perceives himself as loving and caring, but acts hostilely and aggressively towards others while being perceived by others as aloof and unsupportive is in a distinct state of incongruence. Consensual validation from the group brings these three aspects of a person's life: 1. their sense of self, 2. their behavior, and 3. their impression and effect upon others, in sharp contrast. Such a focus will allow them to see the lack of alignment and congruence in their life.

Operating from this theoretical context, the group leader is encouraged by Yalom to follow a complex task which consists of several stages.

1. Each member must recognize what he or she is doing with other people.
2. Then, they must appreciate the impact of their behavior on others.
3. They must, in turn, understand how their behavior influences others in their opinion of them.
4. Eventually, they must decide whether they are satisfied with this interpersonal style.
5. Inevitably, if they decide to change, they must exercise their will to change.
6. Finally, the group and its leader must help the member solidify this change and generalize it to the outside.

Each of these stages that Yalom outlines must be facilitated by the specific cognitive input from the group leader. Eventually, Yalom feels the group must take over the leader's role as the only person responsible for the process observations of individual behavior in the here and now of the group interaction. This is an important role that the group must adopt because it is the series of process comments that allows the group member to change. The group leader can help initiate this process of changing by escorting the group through this sequence.

1. *Here is what your behavior is like.* Through feedback and, later, through self-observation, the patient learns to see himself as others see him.
2. *Here is how your behavior makes others feel.* Members learn about the impact of their behavior on the feelings of other members.
3. *Here is how your behavior influences the opinions others have of you.* Members learn that, as a result of their behavior, others value them, dislike them, find them unpleasant, respect them, avoid them, etc.

4. *Here is how your behavior influences your opinion of yourself.*
Building on the information gathered in the first three steps,
patients formulate self-evaluations; they make judgments
about their self-worth and their lovability. (Recall Sullivan's
aphorism that the self-concept is largely constructed from reflected self-appraisals.) (Yalom, pp. 154-155)

Each of the basic premises which Yalom outlines can be a powerful stimulant to change. Knowing and understanding, as Yalom indicates, are often not enough to produce change. Consequently,
Yalom's four premises address what his later writings (1980) comes
to identify as the key issues in his approach to existential psychotherapy. These four premises parallel Yalom's four ultimate concerns which form the foundation of his existential position — Responsibility, Death, Isolation and Meaningfulness. As Yalom
(1975) writes,

> The therapist's goal is to guide the patient to a point where
> he accepts one, several, or all of the following basic premises:
>
> 1. Only I can change the world I have created for myself.
> 2. There is no danger in change.
> 3. To attain what I really want, I must change.
> 4. I can change, I am potent (p. 157).

RESPONSIBILITY – ONLY I CAN CHANGE
THE WORLD I HAVE CREATED FOR MYSELF

Each person who enters a group starts off on equal ground with
all the other members of the group. Each person is in one sense
given a clean slate or as Yalom writes, "each person is born together in the group." Each member shapes his or her own position,
destiny and life space in group. "Each in the deepest sense of the
concept is 'responsible' for this space and for the sequence of events
which will occur to him in the group" (p. 153). If the group leader
does his job correctly and builds the appropriate group culture, each
group member will learn their new life space within the group is
safe and predictable. Since the group is a place which allows the
learning and trying of new behavior, the group member will eventually come to realize that it is not because he can't change, that he
continues to suffer, but that it is because he will not change. With
this understanding, the group member is forced to realize he is re-

sponsible for what happens to him. If he is to change, only he can accomplish this task for himself.

Death — There is No Danger in Change

Psychopathology, from Yalom's existential position, is rooted in the failure of an individual transcending their death anxiety. Even if the person understands he is responsible for his position in the world, he will frequently fail to make the decisions necessary for change. The obstacle to this change is fear; fear that one may fail. This is an inferred position which Yalom defines as "You behave as if you feel there were considerable danger that would befall you if you were to change. You fear to act otherwise lest some calamity befall you." The group leader's task is to detoxify the discomfort in the belief that change is dangerous. We fear change and responsibility. We continue to engage in self-defeating behavioral patterns even though we may be aware of its dysfunctional nature because our anxiety cements us rigidly in our position. This is the very theme of Eric Fromm's classic book, *Escape From Freedom*. It is essential that the group member explore the fantasies of calamity which he expects to befall him if he should change. As the unrealistic aspects of these expectations are desensitized, he will be able to proceed at small increments to change and, more importantly, learn that there is no danger in change.

Isolation — To Attain What I Really Want, I Must Change

The group leader must understand the payoff or secondary gain that an individual obtains from continuing to engage in behavior that is counter to his best interests. Usually, such conflicts between the way a person behaves and the way they want to be is the result of conflicting desires that cannot be satisfied simultaneously. Such a conflict is frequently the result of infantile needs that get played out on an unconscious level because of the terrifying fears associated with the dread of isolation and adulthood. Yalom writes,

> Another explanatory approach which many therapists take to deal with the paradox that patients persist in behaving counter to their best interests is to consider the payoffs of their present behavior. Though the behavior of the patient sabotages many of his mature needs and goals, at the same time it satisfies

another set of needs and goals. In other words, the patient has conflicting motivations which cannot be simultaneously satisfied. For example, a patient may wish to be able to establish mature heterosexual relationships, but at another, often unconscious, level he may wish to be nurtured, to be cradled endlessly, to assuage castration anxiety by a maternal identification, or, to use another vocabulary, to be sheltered from the terrifying freedom of adulthood.

Obviously, he cannot satisfy both sets of wishes: he cannot establish an adult heterosexual relationship with a woman if he also says (and much more loudly), "Take care of me, protect me, nurse me, let me be a part of you."

The therapist attempts to clarify this for the patient. "Your behavior makes sense if we assume that you wish to satisfy the deeper, more primitive, more infantile need." He tries to help the patient to understand the nature of his conflicting desires, to choose between them, to relinquish those which cannot be fulfilled except at enormous cost to his integrity and autonomy. Once the patient realizes what he "really" wants (as an adult) and that his behavior is designed to fulfill opposing growth-retarding needs, he gradually concludes that "to attain what I really want, I must change." (p. 159-160, Yalom, 1975)

Relationships, whether they be with a group, the group leader, or another person of significance, have a tendency to produce an emergence of infantile expectations and needs. Dependency, the wish to be loved and coddled, as well as the infantile fears of abandonment and rejection, are heightened in any close interpersonal relationship. Those infantile needs and frustrations which have become problematic for the individual become unique characteristics of their personality. This unique set of infantile needs will manifest in the group as they would in any significant relationship. The group leader's task is to force the group member to modify his need by understanding that such needs are infantile wishes that are no longer useful in their adult life. The person must instead learn to tolerate in awareness the tension occasioned by these unfulfilled needs.

Hans Strupp (1978) sums up this position precisely when he writes, (the patient) must take action to satisfy it, abandon it, or modify it. What the therapist no longer permits him (the patient) to do is to use the relationship with a significant person for the purpose of expressing his need in symbolic or disguised ways. The therapist says in effect: If you want me to coddle you, baby you, protect you, love you, you must experience the feelings associated with these expectations in my presence and as directed toward me. This is predictably painful but cannot be helped. Once you have undergone this painful experience, you may realize that your expectations were (a) anachronistic — that is, they may have been reasonable in childhood but no longer useful; (b) unrealistic — that is, as a mature independent adult I cannot possibly coddle you, and, if I did you would be appalled by it and reject it or; (c) based on gross misperceptions of the current situations as well as that prevailing in your childhood, we must understand these distortions. What I will not allow you to do is to act as if you did not have these expectations of me while at the same time expecting me to fulfill them. This is what Freud meant when he said that a conflict must be raised to awareness and fought out on that level. (p. 15)

What Strupp and Yalom are addressing is the conflict that all of us experience in all of our interpersonal relationships. It is important for the group leader to understand that the gratification of these infantile needs is ultimately unproductive for the person. Once they get what they think they want (based on unrecognized, unfulfilled, infantile wishes) they will reject it because it does not fit within their self-definition of the healthy functioning that is expected of a mature, independent adult.

Meaninglessness — I Can Change, I Am Potent

Only when the individual understands the true context of his behavior will he be able to develop a sense of personal mastery and meaning in his life. Understanding the meaning of our behavior moves us from a position of being driven by frightening, unknown forces to a position of control and mastery. We are the rider instead of the ridden. To offer an explanation ("a because") of their behavior allows an individual to attain the true existential position of authenticity. It also allows the person to develop a system by which they can order the events in their lives in a coherent and predictable pattern. Life has meaning for them. They are as they are now because of events in their life which helped shape their perceptions of the world.

As Scott Rutan says, "Our patients come to us with solutions, not problems" (Rutan, 1983). As group leaders, we must not lose sight of the fact that what we see as therapists is a child's normal and even at times creative adaptation to a maladaptive situation. As Sullivanian theory indicates, a child is shaped by their interpersonal environment and interaction with others in their life. If there is a conflict between the growth inclinations of the child and the interpersonal demands of the parents, growth will be compromised for security. Robert and Mary Goulding (1979) share similar sentiments in Redecision Therapy. We all make early decisions on how we are to survive in our world based on the information we have available to us at the time. Unfortunately, children are often forced to make early decisions based on erroneous information before they are cognitively and emotionally capable of such decisions. They hold on to these decisions unconsciously even after the circumstances which led to their position have changed. For example, "If I tell you how I truly feel you will reject me. So if I am to survive with you mother, I will have to act as I think you want me to act." Helping a person understand his position in life and how he came to hold this position will give him a sense of mastery and meaning in his life. He will not be bound to the past and will have the freedom to change in the future. As one group member announced, "I didn't like myself because I used to think I was to blame because of the way I was. Now that I understand why I am this way, I now feel I deserve more from my life."

Such an existential stance in group is summarized by Yalom's statement on will.

> The concept of will provides us with a useful construct in understanding the procedure of process illumination. The interpretive remarks of the therapist can all be viewed in terms of how they bear on the patient's will. The most common and simplistic therapeutic approach is an exhortative one. "Your behavior is, as you yourself now know, counter to your best interests. You are not satisfied, this is not what you want for yourself. Damn it, change!" The expectation that the patient will change is simply an extension of the moral philosophical

belief that if man knows the good (i.e., what, in the deepest sense, is in his best interest), he will act accordingly. In the words of Aquinas: "Man, insofar as he acts willfully, acts according to some imagined good." And, indeed, for some individuals this knowledge and this exhortation is sufficient to produce therapeutic change. To be sure, this is often the case for individuals who change as a result of some short-term experiential group. However, patients with significant and well-entrenched psychopathology generally need much more. (1975. p. 157)

EXAMPLES OF YALOM'S HERE AND NOW FOCUS

Some clinical examples will help illustrate Yalom's suggestions for the sequence of process comments which lead the group member to change.

An experiential training group consisting of eight masters-level counselors at an inpatient alcohol and drug treatment unit met weekly for ten sessions. The first session was dominated by three members. Chuck, a hostile, confrontive, recovering addict with over five years of sobriety spoke angrily about the hospital and the general incompetence of his program director. He spent much of the group time ruminating about whether he should return to school because he saw little hope for the situation changing. Betty, a hysterical recovering addict and nurse with four years of sobriety spoke endlessly about her fears surrounding her participation in the training group. She felt overwhelmed by others and feared they would find out how really unstable she was. Shirley, a psychiatric nurse who was clinical director on the ward, spent the remainder of the group time reassuring Betty and calming Chuck. Her responses were exclusively supportive and she had assigned herself the task of assuring the group that things would somehow work out okay. Shirley also devoted some of the group time expressing her concern about Ann, an MSW on the unit who was unable to attend the first group session because of an unexpected emergency at home. Shirley went to great lengths to assure the group that Ann would be there next week. At the start of the second group session, Ann was indeed present, but remained quiet and withdrawn during the didactic lecture portion of the day. This part of the training group was geared towards presenting theory and the trainees were encouraged to ask questions about the experiential portion of group which was conducted at a different time. After the didactic presentation was completed, the group proceeded to the group room where the experiential portion of the group was to be held. Midway through the group session, Ann suddenly arose from her slumber and began to attack the group leader and the group members, demanding to know "What are the group norms in this group?" Her outburst caught the group by surprise and interrupted Betty, who again was in the midst of hysterically sharing with the group her fears of overwhelming others. The rest of the group responded in an uproar with Chuck leading one half of the group in an attack on Ann and Shirley leading the other half in their attempts to be understanding and supporting of Ann.

By now, the group leader has a vast amount of data accumulated in his observance of Ann, Betty, Chuck and Shirley. There are a number of important questions that he can start asking himself before he can lead the group members through Yalom's sequence of process illumination.

1. *The Group Member Must Recognize What He or She is Doing with Others in the Group.*

Does Ann realize how she is excluding and distancing herself from the rest of the group? Is Shirley aware of her tendency to rescue and take care of others in the group? Betty is overwhelming others with both her premature self-disclosure and her demands not to be rejected by the group members. Does she realize her constant pouring forth of such strong feelings so prematurely creates the very impact on others that she fears most? Chuck seems oblivious to the impact that his anger has on others. Is he aware that the only feeling he can show is anger?

2. *They Must Appreciate the Impact of Their Behavior on Others.*

Ann must come to realize how she affects others with her sudden demands and criticisms. Does Chuck realize that, other than Betty, the rest of the group turns away from him and does not respond to his constant show of anger? Is Shirley aware that her readiness to support everyone leads some individuals to constantly take from her and give very little in return? Betty needs to realize her hysterical presentation leads others to treat her in a patronizing manner.

3. *They Must Understand the Influence Their Behavior Has Upon Others' Opinion of Them.*

Ann must come to realize that her sudden outburst of anger leads others to avoid her and perceive her as an angry woman who can't be trusted. Chuck needs to be aware that his constant show of anger results in others viewing him as a critical and uncaring person. Betty must learn that her fears create the very impression she wishes to avoid. Others do see her as easily overwhelmed and question her stability. Shirley doesn't understand why everyone comes to her with their problems and why they are reluctant to give her the same support she gives them. She doesn't realize her tendency to take care of others leaves her one-dimensional in their eyes. They see her as a giver and someone who doesn't want to take.

4. *They Must Decide Whether They are Satisfied with Their Interpersonal Style.*

Is Ann satisfied with being excluded by others? Is Chuck comfortable with his "angry man against the world routine?" Does Shirley want to shed her image as a rescuer? Is Betty gaining something by appearing unstable and easily overwhelmed? Often, the answers to such questions are not as obvious as one is led to believe. Yalom cautions the group leader to be aware of the difference between primary task, secondary gratification, and the dynamic tension between the two.

The primary task defines the reason the person entered group or sought help. The wish symptom relief, be it freedom from suffering or improvement in relationships. However, as Yalom points out, the individual's presentation in group is rarely this simple and it will usually become more complicated as the group continues. Usually, the primary task changes considerably after the person enters group because of the secondary gratification which arises in group.

Yalom describes this dilemma,

> in each instance the patient has given priority not to the primary task but to some secondary gratification arising in the group; a relationship with another member, an image which he wishes to project, a group role in which he is the most sexually desirous, most influential, most wise, most superior. (1975, p. 147)

The group leader must constantly ask himself if the group members' behavioral presentation is a conflict between the primary task and the secondary gratification of the group. Is Betty's hysteria a way of getting group attention and support? Does her style of relating prevent her from assuming unwanted tasks of responsibility? Does Chuck like to portray the angry man routine because it is an image that he wishes to foster in order to protect himself from others seeing the weak and frightened side of himself? Is Ann's attack on the group really an attack on the group leader? Is her attack a misguided attempt to demonstrate to the group that she is skilled in group therapy and that she wishes to let them know she understands group norms? Members frequently join groups so they learn the skills necessary to "out mental health" others. Is this part of her secondary gain?

5. *Now, They Must Exercise Their Will to Change.*

Yalom, in his book on Existential Psychotherapy, cites a Japanese proverb which states, "To know and not to act, is not to know at all" (p. 286, 1980). This proverb illustrates the importance of members putting into action the insight and understanding they gain through psychotherapy. As Yalom suggests, if the group member fails to act on this new-found knowledge, it will do him little practical good. The group leader must know how to utilize the group to facilitate change and action. Bob and Mary Goulding's (1979) unique perspective on psychotherapy can be of assistance in getting the reluctant member to change. Bob Goulding views psychotherapy in many ways as a chess match between the patient and group leader. There is a part of the patient that wants to get better and part that wants to defeat the therapist. It is this part that the therapist must combat and "win over" if change is to be initiated. Goulding cautions the group leader to be aware of the "first con" that the group member presents. The "first con" is usually presented by the group member in the form that their language takes and it is represented in such key words as "try, need, and can't." Needs are wants and can'ts are don'ts in Goulding's perspective. He requires the group member to change the verbal presentation of their problem with the substitution of the words like won't for can't and want for need. Such a substitution magnifies the patient's resistance and minimizes their helplessness. They must realize they don't change because they are unwilling to risk the change. Try is also viewed as an indication of helplessness and resistance. Members in Bob Goulding's group soon learn that the mention of the word try will result in appearance of the famous "try bell." Bob keeps a cow bell tucked within easy reach of his chair. Upon mentioning the word try, Bob will ring his bell with vigor and delight. Through this medium, the group members become acutely aware of their reluctance to "try" and change their behavior.

An example of a beginning group of inpatient alcoholics meeting for the first time illustrates this dilemma.

> In anger at the staff's insistence that he start attending Alcoholics Anonymous meetings, one group member spoke about his dissatisfaction with the organization. Despite the fact that he had relapsed repeatedly and this was his second hospitalization for his alcoholism, this man could not understand why he was required to attend AA meetings. In a forced and dramatic presentation of his desperation, he pleaded his case by stating, "I've been trying to find an AA meeting I like, but I can't, and I don't think I need it." Encouraged to change his statement to, "I won't find an AA meeting and I don't want one," he became more aware of his passive resistance to these requirements and realized that his relapses were due to his unwillingness to change rather than the result of the failure of the staff, the hospital, AA, or some compelling force in the universe.

6. *Help Them Solidify Change and Generalize to the Outside.*
The group leader must also be cognizant of the magnitude of the power of reinforcement which exists within the group. When a group member changes some aspect of his behavior, no matter how trivial or small, this change should be acknowledged by the group. Bob and Mary Goulding frequently led the group in cheers and applause when a group member reports even an insignificant change in their lives. The group which only spends its time on dredging up pain, anger, and resentment is missing a crucial part of its curative process and is not fulfilling its potential as a powerful change agent in a person's life. Laughter and encouragement only lubricate the curative process. Laughter and encouragement used creatively in the group can be a powerful force in helping a person put their insight into action.

Through the process of illumination, the group members will gradually deepen their awareness of their behavior and the impact which their behavior has on others. They will also learn the consequences they suffer because of the impact they have on others. Yalom outlines the sequence of process illumination in four steps.

1. *Here is what your behavior is like:*

    A. Every time someone shares feelings in here you:

        1. rescue them
        2. laugh or make a joke
        3. get angry (i.e., When someone doesn't agree with what you say, your jaws tighten, you clench your fist, you glare and your voice gets louder).

2. *Here is how your behavior affects my feelings about you:*

    A. I get annoyed at you for always rescuing.
    B. I get hurt that you laugh at my feelings.
    C. I become frightened and I don't want to share my thoughts or feelings honestly with you.

3. *Here is how your behavior influences my opinion of you:*

    A. I don't think you're really sincere because you have to take care of everyone.
    B. I don't trust you and your laughter.
    C. I think you must really be an uncaring SOB and I don't want anything to do with you.

4. *Here is how your behavior influences your opinion of yourself:*

    A. The very reason you came to group was because you were dissatisfied and angry with yourself because you didn't have any friends or a satisfying long-lasting relationship. You viewed yourself as someone who must be unlovable and despised the fact you were alienating everyone around you. Do you want to continue this behavior that is causing you so much difficulty and, most importantly, are you willing to change?

Yalom's model for group psychotherapy brings the members painstakingly through each of these sequences. The group member must realize what his behavior is like and how this ultimately leads to his dissatisfaction with himself and his life. Yalom's model can be summarized as a sequence of change based on fourteen basic assumptions.

1. All of us are influenced and shaped by our interpersonal relationships and we all share our own interpersonal world based on our early relationships.
2. Group psychotherapy can provide a corrective emotional experience of the distorted or disrupted interpersonal relationship which occurred early in our lives.
3. Group psychotherapy acts as a social microcosm of our interpersonal world.
4. Group psychotherapy is a vehicle for the study of interpersonal relationships.
5. Through the process of consensual validation and self-observation, group members become aware of the parataxic distortions involved in their interpersonal relationships.
6. Via feedback from the group leader and other group members, each person can learn to appreciate the impact of his own behavior in regards to how others think and feel about him and how this influences his own opinion of himself.
7. Given this increased awareness, the person learns they are responsible for the reality, not the fantasy, of their interpersonal relationships.
8. Given this kind of responsibility, the person learns that they alone can alter or change their own behavior.
9. Most importantly, such awareness is positively correlated with the amount of affect (feelings) experienced by the individual. Adversely, the more intellectual this experience, the less the learning and the less the correlation with change.
10. Change is a direct function of motivation, involvement in the group, the rigidity of the interpersonal character structure and interpersonal style. Consequently, the more motivated, more involved, and less rigid the person, the more chance there will be for change in their behavior.
11. Such changes in group may initiate changes in other interpersonal relationships. The amount of such change is dependent on the amount of self-analysis and feedback which the person receives from other members in the group.
12. The irrational fears connected with change will be overcome and such changes will not result in the basic fears of loss of individuality, death, abandonment, and engulfment.
13. Over time, the social microcosm of the group results in out-

side behavior becoming honestly present within group and the new learned behavior will be exported eventually to the outside world. The behavior within the group and outside of the group becomes more congruent.

14. Eventually, an adaptive procedure develops internally, first within the group and then eventually generates to the world outside of the group. Group members practice their new learned group behavior outside of the group and return to the group with this experience and change in their behavior over time. Distortions begin to be diminished. One's capacity for developing healthy relationships increases. Eventually, a person's anxiety decreases and their self-esteem increases to the point that they feel freer to be themselves. The increased positive response of other group members to the exposure of themselves leads to an increase in self-esteem and confidence in one's self. A cycle of exposure of one's true self, risk taking and increased self-esteem eventually leads to a more autonomous and conflict-free individual.

CRITIQUE OF YALOM

Before ending this chapter on Yalom and his recommendations for conducting group psychotherapy, I hope the reader will understand that I am carefully presenting the most important factors of group psychotherapy according to Yalom. There are numerous other theorists and schools of group psychotherapy which offer equally excellent rationales and descriptions for conducting group treatment. I have chosen to present Yalom because I, like many others, feel that he provides the most sound and solid rationale for conducting a practical, pragmatic form of group treatment. This is especially important when providing group treatment to an addicted population. Yet, there are important factors of group psychotherapy that Yalom neglects in his presentation. Three of these factors have to do with long-term treatment and will be listed below.

1. The concept of resistance. While Yalom recognizes resistance in the here and now, he does not present its broader implications. Resistance will be dealt with in Chapter 12.
2. Transference is not attended to with the thoroughness it deserves. This will be presented in Chapter 11.

3. Not enough attention is paid to unconscious conflicts and the concept of "working through." This will be discussed in Chapter 14.

Despite Yalom's few shortcomings, his model needs to be explored and understood. This is especially true for the novice or beginning group therapist. Whenever I think in terms of creative group therapists, I immediately conjure up memories of the great masters . . . Erv Polster, Bob Goulding, Louis Ormont, Fritz Perls, and Carl Whitaker. Each is known for going beyond the norm, or the accepted, to create and develop revolutionary forms of group treatment. Yet, before they became masters in their own right, each was first a student of fundamentals.

This is a rule which certainly applies to all creative forms of art. Picasso, for instance, is well-known for his work of abstract, cubist art and his ability to break the fundamental rules in a creative fashion made him immortal. But a walk through the Picasso museum in Spain will reveal that his earlier sketches and paintings emphasized realism. His earlier work clearly demonstrates that Picasso had an acute mastery of traditional art, emphasizing detail, form, composition, contrast and expression. His work demonstrates the axiom for innovation and creativity. You have to know the rules, before you know how to break them. This is the same with the group leader. Before he or she can break the rules of group, he or she must know what these rules are. This is why it is so crucial for a group leader to be well-grounded in one model or approach to group treatment. Once this model is established, the group leader is then free to break the rules in a creative fashion. Yalom's model, more than any other model allows the group leader more freedom, because it teaches sound practical principles for group treatment.

REFERENCES

Bechnar, R. Personal Communication. Lecture given at Twenty-Second Annual Psych. Institute on Group Behavior and Group Leadership, Oct., 1985. Helen, Georgia.
Buber, M. (1955). *The life of dialogue* (M. Friedman, Trans.). London: Routledge.
Buber, M. (1958). *Hasidism and modern man* (M. Friedman, Trans.). Horizon Press.
Buber, M. (1963). *Pointing the way* (M. Friedman, Trans.). New York: Harper Torchbooks.
Frank, J. (1962). *Persuasion and healing*. New York: Schriken Books.
Goulding, R. L. & Goulding, M. M. (1979). *Changing lives through redecision therapy*. New York: Brunner/Mazel Publishers.
Kurtz, E. Personal Communication. Atlanta, Georgia, Feb., 1983. Conference for National Association of Alcohol and Drug Abuse Counselors.

Langs, R. (1976). *The bipersonal field*. New York: Jason Aronson.
Rutan, S. Personal Communication. American Group Psychotherapy Association Conference in Toronto, Canada, Feb., 1983.
Strupp, H. H. (1978). A reformation of the dynamics of the therapist's contribution. In A. German & A. Rozier (Eds.), *The therapist's contribution to effective psychotherapy: An empirical assessment*. Elmsford, N. Y.: Pergamon Press.
Yalom, I. (1975). *The theory and practice of group psychotherapy*. (2nd ed.). New York: Basic Books.
Yalom, I. (1980). *Existential psychotherapy*. New York: Basic Books.
Yalom, I. (1982). *Inpatient group psychotherapy*. New York: Basic Books.
Yalom, I. (1985). *The theory and practice of group psychotherapy*. (3rd ed.). New York: Basic Books.

Chapter 4

Modifications of Yalom's Interactional Model

Alcoholism and alcohol related problems are currently occupying a significant but most often unrecognized portion of psychotherapy and mental health practice. Per capita consumption rates of alcohol have steadily increased in recent years from 1.97 gallons in 1948, 1.98 gallons in 1958, 2.45 gallons in 1968, to 2.82 gallons in 1978 (Coffey, 1980). This in conjunction with recent estimates (Lansing, 1979) by an independent research foundation which suggests a similar increase in the number of alcoholics from 2.8 million in 1945 to 4.4 million in 1960, 5.3 million in 1970, 9.3 million in 1974, and 11.2 million in 1978 provides additional evidence that the incidence of alcoholism is increasing (Glasscote, 1967; Moore, 1971) at a faster rate than the population. However, much work remains to be done in identifying and treating these individuals as suggested by a survey of state hospitals in 1964 which showed only 3.3 percent of daily census were recognized alcoholics, even though the surveyors estimated that alcoholics probably constituted about 30 percent of admissions (Moore & Buchanan, 1966). A more recent survey revealed that while 23 percent of a random sample of psychotherapy patients seen in a large metropolitan mental health center were suffering either from addictive problems or from emotional problems substantially exacerbated by alcohol, only 3.5 percent of these were so identified by their own therapist (Cummings, 1979).

While diagnosis and treatment of the alcoholic patient presents some unique problems to the psychotherapist, there are many treatment issues in alcoholism which parallel broader current concerns

This article originally appeared in *Group*, Vol. 6, #1, in 1982. Reprinted with permission from Brunner/Mazel.

with the effectiveness of psychotherapy more generally (Bergin, 1971; Fishe et al., 1970; Lubosky et al., 1975; Pattison, 1966). These concerns can be distilled and categorized into three general areas: 1. What are the treatment strategies and techniques most suitable for dealing with the alcoholic patient? 2. What are the personality characteristics of the alcoholic patient that lend themselves to successful treatment? 3. Which treatment modalities and strategies should be matched with these particular characteristics if treatment effectiveness is to be enhanced?

This problematic situation is compounded by the lack of agreement in alcohol treatment strategies for alcoholic populations. Wallace (1975, 1976) feels that most therapy for alcoholics is a grab bag of tricks, slogans, and techniques which were developed for purposes other than alcohol treatment and none have taken into account the attributed characteristics and common situational elements of the alcoholic and the alcoholic career.

Historically, the alcoholic patient has been widely viewed as a poor treatment risk who makes only limited use of therapeutic efforts on his behalf (Hartocollis, 1964; Szasz, 1966) and there is substantial opinion that it is frustrating to the psychotherapist who sees techniques that work well with, for example, neurotics, frequently fail along with alcoholics. Yalom (1974) described them as poor candidates for intensive group psychotherapy, although he later modified his stance on this opinion (Brown & Yalom, 1977). Moore (1973) sees the alcoholic patient in psychotherapy as presenting certain difficulties that distinguish him from other patients.

Pattison (1973) suggests that a comprehensive alcoholism treatment program requires a careful development of treatment facilities and methods which match the perceptions, styles and needs of subpopulations of alcoholics. He further states that if this match is not made the treatment program will be relatively unsuccessful, and if there is a good match then the probability of success is increased.

Matakas et al. (1978) reports some important conclusions from their reviews of the treatment outcome literature. Some of their most important findings are: "The one year recovery rate is very close to the five year ratio because most of the recidivism occurs in the first year after therapy. Despite relatively large dropout rates, outpatient therapy is basically no less successful than inpatient forms of therapy. The outcome rates for conditioning therapy mentioned in the literature are not entirely convincing. These latter treatments are reported to be especially suitable for extroverted patients and those showing clear psychopathological signs. In contrast, analytic group therapy is especially to be recommended in the case of patients who are verbally competent and "field dependent." The usefulness of drug therapy appears doubtful and such treatment should be employed only supportively when the patient has good social relationships (Matakas et al., 1978).

Baekeland et al. (1975) has reported that each of the common procedures for rehabilitating alcoholics has had approximately the same degree of success. The success rates — including spontaneous remissions — lie between 40 and 50 percent. The research of recent year has, in addition, shown that most therapeutic procedures are more or less equally effective (Matakas, F. et al., 1978). Thus the problem is not one of selecting the decisive therapy (i.e., behavioral vs. drug vs. insight, etc.) for alcoholics; rather it is one of determining whether there exists different indications for the individual forms of therapy as Matakas et al. (1978) recommends.

TREATMENT STRATEGIES

While there has been a substantial effort to describe and articulate strategies and techniques for alcoholism intervention (Brown & Yalom, 1977; Cummings, 1979; Wallace, 1978) there have been virtually no studies which have compared these approaches. Moreover, generalization from treatments applied to nonalcoholics is unwarranted since it is widely recognized that alcoholics pose new and unique problems for the therapist (Fehr, 1976; Yalom, 1974; Wallace, 1976; Szasz, 1966). This problematic situation is compounded by the fact that there is a paucity of good research addressing the identification of key differential factors predicting success for different treatment approaches (Stinson et al., 1979).

As Adamson et al. (1974) suggests, such characteristics may lie in individual personality and motivational variables but much work remains to clearly delineate their nature. Emrick (1974) in a review of 384 alcoholism treatment studies, concluded that while treatment of some kind is superior to no treatment, differences in treatment methods did not significantly affect long-term outcome. His findings are collaborated by Stinson et al. (1979) who reports that "peer oriented incare" (Alcoholics Anonymous) treatment approaches improve recovery. These results are consistent with Strupp and Hadley's (1979) findings which suggest that non-specific factors in psychotherapy (i.e., therapist characteristics) may be more important than specific factors (i.e., techniques) in determining successful treatment outcome.

The research findings take on added ramifications when considering the high degree of success that a peer-oriented self-help approach like Alcoholics Anonymous (A.A.) has demonstrated in alcoholism treatment (Emrick et al., 1977). This raises the question of what part, if any, professional-oriented systems have in alcoholism treatment when considering the fact that peer-oriented programs like A.A. provide a simpler, more successful and less expensive form of alcoholism treatment (Stinson et al., 1979).

Considering the implications resulting from these recent research findings it may be beneficial to examine more closely the possible symbiotic relationship between professional and peer-oriented treatment systems for alcoholism treatment. Wallace (1978), Yalom (1977) and Cummings (1979) all suggest that a close working relationship between the two will improve success in treatment. Add to this speculation the large number of alcoholics who have not responded well to the peer-oriented system of A.A. (Emrick et al., 1977) and one sees the possibility that each approach has something to compliment the other as far as successful treatment outcomes are concerned. This conclusion is at least partially confirmed by research (e.g., Belasco, 1971; Davies et al., 1956; Dubourg, 1969). However, these results need to be questioned and further research conducted because of the methodological difficulties adumbrated by Emrick et al. (1977).

Among the methodological problems encountered by research in this area are the frequent failures to establish the reliability and validity of obtained data and the frequent absence of pre-affiliation data for comparison with outcome. However, the most striking weakness of previous efforts is that researchers typically assess the effects of treatment only on self-selected A.A. participants, thus confounding A.A. participation with client variables (i.e., perhaps self-selected A.A. members are more motivated to stop drinking).

Currently group therapy is considered to be "dogma" in the treatment of alcoholism, although there is a lack of adequately based clinical investigations regarding its effectiveness. Smart et al. (1969) reports that at least in the United States, group therapy on the whole has been preponderantly employed for patients of the upper-middle-class and seldom for those of the lower-middle-class.

Even though group psychotherapy is an important therapeutic modality in most contemporary addictive treatment programs, the model upon which it is based has been for the most part derived from the practice of outpatient psychotherapy with non-addictive patients. However, the theoretical and practical considerations underlying outpatient group psychotherapy with a non-addictive population is not always applicable to individuals suffering from chemical dependency. Consequently, currently-accepted principles of group psychotherapy need to be altered in order to meet the realities and necessities of treating the addicted patient.

Too often, therapists with experience only in individual therapy or experience only with non-addictive patients are thrust into a group psychotherapy leadership role. Because group psychotherapy is difficult and requires a number of special skills, many groups led by untrained or poorly trained leaders do not fulfill their potential or may have negative effects on the patient's recovery. Clearly, a need exists for educating potential group therapists who are and will be leading groups composed of chemically-dependent individuals.

RECOMMENDATIONS FOR GROUP PSYCHOTHERAPY

Group psychotherapy should be linked as clearly as possible to theory and concepts. In treating alcoholics and addicts, a group psychotherapy model based on Yalom's (1974) interactional style should be employed. This approach should follow as closely as possible the guidelines laid down by Brown and Yalom's (1977) study with alcoholics in an interaction group setting.

The particular strategy for group therapy should also follow the recommendations of treatment as a time-dependent process as described by Wallace (1978). Further consideration should be given to the tactics outlined by Cummings (1979) in his description of exclusion therapy which requires abstinence as the primary goal of treatment. This interactional group model should be contrasted with a group established and run on the guidelines of Alcoholics Anonymous and described both by Emrick et al. (1977) and Alibrandi (1978).

Protocol

A brief description of the protocol for the group psychotherapy treatment strategy will be described below.

The early stages of therapy should be patterned after Cummings' description of "exclusion therapy" (1979). Essentially this approach requires that the issue of drug usage be approached first and the client excluded from therapy unless he/she agrees to the goals of abstinence. Alcohol addiction should therefore be the primary focus during the early stages of treatment.

During the first two months of treatment, much of the group's time would be spent on the education of the disease concept of alcoholism and the development of what Yalom describes as group cohesiveness (1974). The group at this point would provide support and structure as Wallace recommends (1978). Gradually the shift should be initiated to move the group from a support model to an interactional model as described by Yalom (1974). During this time directive and active leadership required at this early stage (Wallace, 1979) should shift to allow the group members to take a more active and responsible role in the group process.

In most cases the entire first six months of treatment would be spent on "just" maintaining sobriety with little or no active encouragement of personality modification (Wallace, 1978). As Brown and Yalom (1977) suggest, group members during this period will not be encouraged to take a look at themselves beyond a rather shallow and superficial level. In one sense the strategy requires that all therapeutic interventions occur at a slower pace (Brown & Yalom, 1977; Wallace, 1978). Dynamics will not be explored in great detail until nine to twelve months of sobriety have been established (Brown & Yalom, 1977).

Much of the time throughout treatment should be spent on confronting the alcoholic's denial system (Wallace, 1978; Cummings, 1979). A heavy focus should be directed towards getting the alcoholic to make a gradual recognition of his/her buried feelings. Usually, feeling of extreme guilt would be best dealt with by providing an overall simplistic cognitive structure of their illness (Wallace, 1978). The strategies which Wallace (1976) describes should be utilized to deal with the alcoholics' "preferred defense structure."

Alcoholism treatment within this perspective should be viewed as a "time dependent" process as described by Wallace (1978) and collaborated by Brown and Yalom (1977). Essentially this means that a particular therapeutic intervention for a recently drinking alcoholic may be entirely inappropriate for one who has managed to achieve several years of sobriety.

Wallace's recommendations for a therapy specific to alcoholism are as follows:

1. Alcoholics can be described in terms of preferred defense structure. This preferred defense structure (PDS) need not be cast in negative terms. In fact, it need not be construed at all in terms of the classical language of defense mechanisms. The alcoholic's PDS can be thought of as a collection of skills or abilities—tactics and strategies, if you will—for achieving one's ends.
2. Therapy with alcoholics as it is currently practiced too often attempts to remove the alcoholic PDS instead of utilizing it effectively to facilitate the achievement of abstinence. Therapeutic efforts that confront the alcoholic PDS prematurely and too heavily will increase rather than reduce the probability of further drinking.
3. Recovery programs successful in producing abstinence, such as Alcoholics Anonymous, partially owe their success to the intuitive recognition of the fact that the alcoholic PDS is to be protected and capitalized upon rather than confronted and radically altered.
4. Paradoxically, the very same defenses that the alcoholic used to maintain his drinking can be used effectively to achieve abstinence.
5. Equally paradoxically, the very same defenses that enabled the alcoholic to drink, as well as achieve abstinence, must ultimately be removed if long-term sobriety is to be maintained. However, in many cases such growth must take place over periods of time ranging from two to five years of abstinence.

Core Treatment Program

It is important to follow Pattison's recommendations and determine the population characteristics of the alcoholics to be treated if these difficulties are to be minimized. Moore (1973, p. 224) describes the typical alcoholic as "employed, or at least partially financially solvent patient, lower-middle-class and up, not necessarily very psychologically minded, not grossly psychopathic, but more likely an 'essential' or 'reactive' alcoholic. He or she may show considerable depression, is not significantly brain damaged, is more or less voluntary, probably still has or has just been separated from a family treatment, is covered by private funds or health insurance or is provided in a public clinic. In other words, I am talking about the bulk of our alcoholic population. While the public inebriate may attract a large part of our attention, he constitutes only an estimated three to five percent of the alcoholic population'' (NIAAA Pub. Alcohol and Health, 1971).

Next, it would be important to determine if there are any personality characteristics shared by the population described. Attempts at identifying personality variables consistently related to alcoholism have historically resulted in ambiguous and contradictory findings. Much evidence indicates that there are various personality types among alcoholics (Pattison, 1966; English, J., 1975). In spite of negative conclusions reached in their reviews, researchers have generally not concluded that the search for an alcoholic personality should be abandoned (Barnes, 1979). Wallace (1978) points out that the strength of a belief in something called an alcoholic personality is a direct function of the degree of involvement with alcoholics on a sustained basis. He defends his argument on the basis of A.A. intuitive knowledge derived from years of successful treatment of alcoholism. Thus, in the fellowship of A.A., persons are said to be alcoholic in personality whether they are drinking or not, and the alcoholic personality can return at any time in the form of a "dry drunk." Further A.A. recognizes the fact that many heavy drinkers are not necessarily alcoholic (A.A. Publications, 1960). On the other hand, Wallace feels that the concept of the alcoholic personality has not fared well among those whose acquaintance with alcoholics is merely passing or entirely academic.

Evidence suggesting shared post alcoholic characteristics have significant implications for treatment. In a recent and extensive review of literature, Barnes (1979) suggests that it may be useful to break the concept of alcoholic personality into two different descriptions — a post-alcoholic personality and a pre-alcoholic personality (Barnes, 1979). There is a vast amount of evidence as presented by Barnes to suggest that there are a number of different personality measurements which can readily differentiate post-alcoholics from neurotics, psychotics, non-alcoholics (MMPI, Field-Dependence, Internal-External, and the Eysenck Personality Inventory). While post-alcoholic personality measures are generally conclusive, those on pre-alcoholic identification have been found on only one longitudinal study conducted with the MacAndrew scale of the MMPI (Hoffman, Kammier & Loper, 1974). This pattern of findings suggests that the process of alcoholism itself may produce some changes that are common to all alcoholics (e.g., Wallace, 1978). What is significant to our purpose is the awareness of significant homogeneity among post-alcoholic personalities. Wallace (1978) agrees when he says that "It is more fruitful to think of the many commonalities apparent among alcoholics as common outcomes of alcoholism rather than as antecedent conditions." Further this seems to indicate strongly that alcoholics may be a rather homogeneous group as a result of their disease.

Therefore, the purpose of this chapter is to examine and present a systematic model of group psychotherapy as described and practiced by the leading theorists in the field of group psychotherapy and addiction (Brown & Yalom, 1975; Wallace, 1978). This is an attempt to define proven strategies which will match these identified characteristics and articulate suggestions for improving the treatment of the chemically-dependent patient by providing cognitive understanding of the special problems that chemically-dependent individuals bring to group psychotherapy. Although group therapy has long been an essential component of treatment programs, group orientations vary enormously from one setting to another. Nevertheless, professionals seem to agree that group therapy offers the chemically dependent individual unique opportunities to: 1. Share and to identify with others who are going through similar problems; 2. To understand their own attitudes about addiction and their defenses against giving up alcohol and drugs by confronting similar attitudes and defenses in others; and 3. To learn to communicate needs and feelings more directly. Furthermore, the group's ability to provide support, structure and reinforcement for abstinence makes it a powerful catalyst in the recovery process. In measures of time, efficacy and recovery, group therapy generally succeeds where individual treatment modalities frequently fail.

THE ALCOHOLIC PERSONALITY

While misconceptions about the addictive personality are legion, recent evidence now suggests that the experience of addiction itself may induce characteristics common to most addictive individuals.

While most of the research on addiction has been focused on alcoholism, it is recognized that many alcoholics have a history of cross addiction and poly-drug abuse. Consequently, for purposes of brevity, the reader is asked to equate the two. The literature review which follows suggests that there is little evidence for a pre-alcoholic personality; however, there is strong evidence for shared, post-alcoholic characteristics that have significant implications for treatment.

In working with addictive individuals in a group setting, the therapist is faced with the task of applying general rules of psychotherapy to a specific and somewhat homogeneous population.

The early psychoanalytic literature (Hoffman et al., 1974; Kinney, 1975) has suggested that the alcoholic personality is often a result of fixation at the oral stage of development. Poor impulse control, inability to delay gratification and abnormal dependency needs are seen as a result of some trauma at the oralsexual stage of development. As an adult, such an individual is likely to engage heavily in such oral activities as eating, drinking, smoking and talking (Fancher, 1973).

Recent research findings have generally supported these psychoanalytic explanations. Minnesota Multiphasic Personality Inventory (MMPI) profiles consistently identify alcoholics as immature, self-centered and frequently having difficulties with societal mores and authority figures. The MMPI is easily the preferred and most frequently used of the personality assessments with alcoholics. Sutterland, Schroeden and Tordella (1950) found only two studies containing data from the MMPI which did not include any specific results. Hoffman (1976) points out that between 1943 and 1963, there were 37 references concerning the MMPI and alcoholism. Since 1964 and 1973 there have been a total of 118 references. The total number of studies quoted on alcoholism exceed by nearly twice those for any other diagnostic categories (e.g., depressive state or schizophrenic reactions). Most research has shown rather conclusively that the MMPI appears to be a very sensitive instrument for measuring in terms of its clinical scales are useful in predicting treatment outcomes.

MMPI

Most studies have concentrated on the attempt to assess the existence of a composite alcoholic from the 13 regular MMPI scales.

These studies consistently show an elevation (T-score often above 70) on a scale of 4 (Pd) in both inpatient (Button, 1956; Chang et al., 1973; Hill et al., 1962; Rohan, 1972; Rohan et al., 1969; Wilkinson et al., 1971) and outpatient populations (Chang et al., 1973; Goss & Morosko, 1969; Rosen, 1960). Other findings suggest that scale 2 (D) also often exceeds T-value of 70 (Goss & Morosko, 1969; Rohan, 1972; Rohan et al., 1969; Rosen, 1960; Wilkinson et al., 1971) or represent a relative profile peak secondary to scale 4 (Hill et al., 1962; Rosen, 1960). A third commonly reported elevated scale is 7 (Pt), which, like scale studies consistently show an elevation (T-score often above 70) on scale 4 (Pd) in both inpatient (Button, 1956; Chang et al., 1973; Hill et al., 1962; Rohan, 1972; Rohan et al., 1969; Wilkinson et al., 1971) and outpatient population (Chang et al., 1973; Goss & Morosko, 1969; Rosen, 1960). Other findings suggest that scale 2 (D) also often exceeds T-value of 70 (Goss & Morosko, 1969; Rohan, 1972; Rohan et al., 1969; Rosen, 1960; Wilkinson et al., 1971) or represent a relative profile peak secondary to scale 4 (Hill et al., 1962; Rosen, 1960). A third commonly reported elevated scale is 7 (Pt.), which like scale 2, sometimes exceeds 70 (Rosen, 1960; Wilkinson et al., 1971) and often is relatively elevated though below 70. The literature therefore suggests that a composite profile pattern for alcoholics is usually a 4-2 or 4-2-7.

Consideration of these typical MMPI personality composites supports a clinical impression of the alcoholic as immature, impulsive, unreliable, and having little concern for societal mores and values. According to Dahlstrom, Welsh and Dahlstrom (1972), "the major features of this personality pattern include a repeated and flagrant disregard for social customs and mores, an inability to profit from punishing experiences as shown in repeated difficulties in relation to others, particularly in sexual and affectional display" (p. 195).

Gross and Carpenter (1971) agree when they stated that alcoholics manifest "such observable characteristics as dependency, denial, depression, superficial sociability, low tolerance for frustration, and impulsivity" (p. 375).

Further evidence by Tarter and Sugerman (1976) define alcoholics as possessing personality features which manifest in an "absence of impulse control, combined with aggressiveness, anti-social symptoms, authority conflict, and gregariousness" (p. 352). Huber and Danahy (1975) reported elevations on the Pd and Ma scales and described alcoholics "as basically impulsive, immature, and irresponsible even though superficially they seem lively and charming" (p. 1235).

Krammier et al. (1973) described the combination of scale elevations in their study as "neurotic patterns of self-centered, immature, dependent, resentful, irresponsible kind of person who has been unable to face reality" (p. 398). Tarter and Sugerman (1976) also supported the dependency issue when they reported that the shift in frequency of elevations of the Pd, D, Sc, and Ma scales "suggest that they may be indicators of dependency problems."

Except for the dependency issues the descriptions of the above-mentioned studies paints a picture of a typical clinical psychopath or sociopath. However, there seems to be one important distinction as illustrated by Button (1956), who stated, "The primary peak on the Pd scale and the secondary peak at D, superimposed upon a relatively 'neurotic' (as opposed to psychotic) profile almost in themselves tell the story of how the alcoholic sees himself; as an unhappy, tense, bitter person who somehow feels responsible for the many evidences of aggression and hostility he sees about him" (p. 271). Button goes on to quote Buhler and Lefever (1947) in pointing out a very important distinction. "Differing from the psychopath, the alcoholic escapes with a bad conscience." This position is also supported by Apfeldorf (1978) who suggested that the high scorer on the MacAndrew MMPI subscale is "bold, uninhibited, self-confident, and mixes well with others." Apfeldorf tells of carousing, gambling, playing hooky, and generally cutting up, yet the alcoholic answers show that he "is drawn to religion and uses repression, faith and inspiration to hold his impulses in check." This analysis suggests that the personality of the alcoholic is composed of many factors or components, including a lively or ready sociability, antisocial attitudes, religiosity, and guilt. Apfeldorf felt it might be fruitful to attempt to accumulate an expanded item pool to explore MacAndrew's study and other profile composites of the MMPI because the picture painted by these contents analyses have a striking similarity to issues of import to A.A. Superficially, self-centeredness, poor impulse control, and guilt are all of central importance to the A.A. treatment approach (A.A. Publication, 1955).

Constructing a consensus of a personality profile based on the aforementioned studies with the MMPI, we are left with the picture of an alcoholic as someone who is self-centered, immature, gregarious, frequently charming in a superficial manner, and expressing all the behavior typically associated with the sociopathic personality save for the tremendous guilt feelings which surface during his sober moments. Thume's (1977) interpretation of A.A. from a phenomenological viewpoint describes the alcoholic's central problem as his inability to relate to anyone or a higher power in any way other than a superficial manner.

Most of the recent studies in the area of personality assessments related to alcoholism have focused on the isolated measure and differentiation between alcoholics and non-alcoholics (Tarter & Sugerman, 1976; Donovan & O'Leary, 1975). In accounting for the consistent findings that alcoholics are more dependent or external than other groups, research generally supports the predisposition rather than the consequence hypothesis. Essentially the latter hypothesis views field-dependence and externality as a consequence of drinking while the former hypothesis suggests that field dependence and externality are predisposing factors. Little research has been conducted to determine if there has been any suggestion of change over time. Researchers have generally been satisfied to accept the conclusion that alcoholics may stop drinking but their cognitive functioning and basic personality will undoubtedly stay the same.

An initial study by Danahy (1977) suggests that this may not be the case. If Alcoholics Anonymous' criteria for recovery is accepted, that is, if an alcoholic must make some change in himself before he can stop drinking, the expected corollary would suggest that alcohol consumption ceases along with some personality or cognitive change. One plausible explanation for the growing interest due to these research findings is that there is strong evidence that there is a relationship between control, dependency, and alcoholism. Dependency conflicts and cognitive styles could lead to, or be a result of, an exaggerated need to be in control as a consequence of conflicts in dependency needs. A corollary to this theory suggests that a change in alcohol consumption should result in changes on measures of dependency and control orientations (Danahy, 1977).

As a result of such plausible interpretations, a number of different measures for this general theoretical framework have been utilized in a wide range of empirical research. As Tarter and Sugerman (1976) report, field dependence has been studied more in alcoholism than in any other area of psychology. They further state that it has been studied in alcoholism to the virtual exclusion of other cognitive styles.

FIELD DEPENDENCE

Review of the work of Witkin and his colleagues (Witkin & Oltmen, 1967) summarizes evidence which shows that individuals apply consistent and stable styles of cognitive organization across both perceptual and physiological characteristics. In Witkin's research the emphasis is upon the approach an individual brings to his experience; that is, his lifestyle. Witkin then derived a battery of tests devised to measure the degree of field dependence vs. field independence.

There is some controversy in the interpretation of field dependence as a separate entity from field-independence. This may be the result of the lack of consistency of the measurement application and the use of different field dependent tests. The Rod and Frame, the Body Adjustment, and Embedded Figures Tests all involve the use of different apparatus in its applications. Tarter and Sugerman (1976) have presented convincing arguments explaining how difference in administration procedures between different investigators applying similar tests can have significant effects on the interpretations of the results. Regardless of (and sometimes in spite of) the vast amount of methodological differences and application inconsistency, there exists an enormous amount of evidence suggesting alcoholics as a heterogenous group show a high degree of field dependence (Witkin, Karp, Goodenough, 1959; Neale, 1968).

Field dependence is undoubtedly a recognizable and measurable trait in alcoholic individuals. The controversy remains in interpreting these results. The decision whether field dependence is a cause or result of alcoholism may be a moot question. Some studies have shown a significant decline in field dependence among alcoholic patients (Chess, 1969; Smith & Layden, 1972; McWilliams, Brown, Minard, 1975). Contrary findings by Jacobson, Pisan, Berenbaum (1975) and Karp (1965) suggest that there is no significant change. However, methodological questions concerning the latter studies seem to indicate a consensus of change in alcoholics from field dependence to field independence shortly after treatment. However, interpretation of the findings which suggest that alcoholics report a decrease in field dependence as a result of treatment suggests that the result may be due to the immediate changes reflecting a recompensation of brain functions. Temporarily impaired by excess alcohol consumption, cognitive functioning could change dramatically. Change in psychological measures should be examined in this light rather than be interpreted as having any relevance to the question of long term stability of field dependence in alcoholics.

EXTERNAL VS. INTERNAL CONTROL
OR LOCUS OF CONTROL

A review of the literature by Rohsenow and O'Leary (1976) reveals twenty-four published studies which specifically deal with control orientation in alcoholic populations in the period covering 1970-1975. However, they only cite one study in the area published prior to 1970. They suggest there may be a link between control orientation and psychotherapy strategies which would account for this recent upsurge in interest in relation to alcoholism.

Three major hypotheses were found to exist concerning locus of control of alcoholics and non-alcoholics controls. Earlier studies have suggested that alcoholics would have an external locus of control because of their inability to control drinking or to cope effectively (Butts and Chotlos, 1973). In contrast, research by Goss and Morosko (1970) found results indicating that alcoholics have an internal locus of control. On the other hand, Gozali and Sloan (1971) conclude that alcoholics have exaggerated internal locus of control. Further research in these areas have tended to show equivocal results. But as Rohsenow and O'Leary point out, better designed studies either tend to find no difference in the I-E scale or that alcoholics are more internally oriented.

External-internal locus of control studies seem to be troubled with the same methodological and controversial issues which involve field dependence and field independence. More recent studies investigating the degree of control after treatment have consistently shown a shift to internal control (Costello & Manders, 1974). However, even this area is not without its conflicting results as Marlatt (1975) indicates. It may be that a drinking binge which led alcoholics to be hospitalized caused them to be more externally oriented temporarily, while they felt out of control. Sobering up may have just returned their scores to their normal levels.

Several different measures of locus of control have been used in these studies. The different characteristics of each probably provide part of the explanation concerning the conflicting result. Rotter's (1966) IE scale which consists of twenty-nine items in a forced-choice format, has generally been recognized as the most consistent and reliable assessment used. Another factor leading to confusion in interpreting results is apparently due to the fact that an IE score designated as internal on some studies is designated as external in others.

A second factor adding to the confusion has to do with the different definitions of alcoholism. The particular definition of alcoholism is rarely specified and what may be an alcoholic in one study is not in another study (Horn & Manders, 1970).

Rotter's IE scale, like Witkin's measure of field dependence and field independence, has resulted in the same type of conflicting evidence regarding the similarities and differences of cognitive styles in alcoholics. However, both have shown that there have been some consistent similarities. Their research conclusions have indicated a more negative treatment prognosis for external and field dependent alcoholics (Rohsenow & O'Leary, 1976; Tarter & Sugerman, 1976). Further similarities between internal and field independent individuals show a pattern of higher intelligence for internals and qualitative difference in abstraction, problem solving, cognition in general, for field dependent individuals (Tarter & Sugerman, 1976).

Although there has been some confusion in determining whether alcoholics are externally or internally oriented there have been several possible explanations advanced to explain some of the unexpected findings of an internal orientation among alcoholics. Goss and Morosko (1970) suggested two possible implications regarding the problem of alcoholism. One is that alcoholics not only believe that they could control their drinking, but they may also have learned that they have a readily available method to control their moods as well.

Oziel et al. (1972) suggests that the passive-aggressive drinking and social behavior seen among alcoholics is the reaction of internally controlled individuals to resist manipulation by others who want them to stop drinking. Distegano et al. (1972) questioned the common assumption that internal control is necessarily a good thing. He suggests that perhaps a "happy medium" between the low scores of alcoholics and the high scores of their general psychiatric population might be a better indication of psychological health. In view of the IE findings, Gozali and Sloan (1971) suggest that perhaps psychotherapy for alcoholics ought to be oriented more toward shifting control orientation from internal to external. This is what A.A. has always tried to do. The A.A. program stresses the admission of "powerlessness over alcohol" and giving up control to a "higher power." While this program cannot, of course, be said to have been proven right by the findings from the IE scale, it is possible that A.A. emphasizes a feature of the alcoholic personality which has therapeutic significance.

Another focus of studies of alcoholics with the IE scale is the relationship of this test to the MMPI. Two of the studies discussed previously have reported numerous significant correlations between the IE scale and the MMPI (Goss & Morosko, 1970; Lottman et al., 1973). However, Gozali and Sloan failed to find any significant correlations in their sample and the reason for these discrepancies is unknown. Goss and Morosko and Lottman reported many similarities in their data. In both studies, significant positive correlations were found between scores on the IE scale and MMPI scale F, 1, 2, 7, and 8, and significant negative correlations between the IE scale and scale K. In addition Goss and Morosko reported a significant positive correlation for scale 0 and Lottman et al. for scale 3. Keeping in mind that higher scores on the IE are indicative of feelings of greater external control, it seems that there is a significant association between external scores and increases in the very MMPI scales which were shown to vary greatly among alcoholics as a function of treatment status. One of the primary points of the first section of this review was that the "neurotic" scales of the MMPI (scales 1, 2, 3, and 7) were related to situational stress, while scale 4 scores were constantly high. This suggests that internal-external orientation may shift along with the fluctuation in psychological distress discussed previously, or that internal control may be more a surface characteristic than a stable trait. However, as Danahy notes (1977) this thesis has yet to be tested with pre- and post-treatment data.

VALUES AND DEPENDENCE
IN ALCOHOLISM TREATMENT

Addictive behavior and difficulties in interpersonal relations (Szasz, 1966) can be assumed to leave traces in an individual's value system. If therapy is to be successful, it may surely be manifested as changes or rearrangements of value priorities. Pokeach (1973) presents convincing evidences that values do exist as stable entities, can be easily assessed, are tantamount in influencing a person's attitudes and behavior, and can be easily changed by effective psychotherapy.

Research has suggested the possibility that religious or spiritual aspects of the "Higher Power" concept to Alcoholics Anonymous may augment the recovery process. Jacobson and Ritter (1977) administered the Purpose in Life (PIL) test and the Allport-Vernon-Lindsey Study of Values (SOV) to a group of alcoholics in a thirty-day treatment program. They reported a significant change in scores when administered soon after admission and repeated again before discharge. They reported that contrary to expectation, significant correlations were found between scores from the second PIL Test and the Religious and Aesthetic scales of the SOV.

Similar studies dealing with self-actualization indicate that external locus of control-field dependency, and a trend toward self-actualization are contrary to each other (Szura & Vermillion, 1975).

Although the evidence and research findings are far from being conclusive, there seems to be a trend indicating that possibly, an alcoholic should as a result of treatment, shift to a more internal and independent locus of control. If this is indeed true, a shift toward self-actualization may also be expected.

Little research evidence has been gathered considering the relationship of values and alcoholism treatment although Emrick (1977) feels it is an important consideration in determining the matching of professional and peer-oriented care systems with alcoholics. Martini's (1978) study is one of the few exceptions which looks at patient-therapist congruence in alcoholism treatment.

In previous research she (Martini, 1978) and others (Townsend, 1978) worked with Beutler (1979) and found that similarity of "Terminal Values" (Rokeach, 1973) was predictive of both the maintenance of the therapeutic relationship and the quality of outcome.

TREATMENT ISSUES

Homogeneity vs. Heterogeneity

Thus, alcoholics and addicts may be a rather homogeneous group as a result of their disease. As Yalom points out, the likelihood of homogeneity within the group can be a detriment to the growth process. Heterogeneity for conflict areas and homogeneity for ego strength are two factors important for group composition (Yalom, 1975). Yalom feels that "homogeneous groups jell more quickly to become more cohesive, to offer more immediate support to the group members, to have better attendance, less conflict, and to provide more rapid symptomatic relief" (p. 261). This is often the situation that the therapist will find with an alcoholism recovery group. It would be wise to encourage the group to rally around the homogeneous problem of alcoholism at the beginning of therapy and use this shared concern to its greatest advantage. The group often consists of patients from different occupations and interests who at first share only their common conflict with alcohol consumption. Later as abstinence becomes less, and growth more, of an issue, the therapist will often find that the group has a very diverse set of problems resulting from drinking. The therapist should also utilize *this* advantage to its fullest.

Passivity and Field Dependence

The work of Witkin et al. (1959), Rotter (1966) and Blane (1968) all point to the general consensus of alcoholics being more cognitively and psychologically dependent than non-alcoholics. This was also borne out in Brown and Yalom's study (1977). They found that dependency or counterdependency was expressed behaviorally but that the alcoholic would emphatically deny all dependency. This observation is especially interesting in light of Donovan and O'Leary's (1975) research on Rotter's internal-external differentiation in alcoholics. Their results showed that alcoholics were either more external or internal that non-alcoholics.

Research applying Witkin and Oltman's (1967) field-dependency/field-independency theory has shown rather conclusively that alcoholics are more field dependent than non-alcoholics (Tarter & Sugerman, 1976). Brown and Yalom (1977) discovered similar patterns in their study. They interpreted this phenomenon as occurring because alcoholics were incapable of fully experiencing themselves from within. Many of their group members based their behaviors on external clues. "For example, they scan their environment, looking to others for direction, trying to determine what others expect. Through self-deception they convert these outside signals into a sense that they have actively made a choice. Yet, much of their behavior is not choiceful. They cannot turn their gaze inward to ask themselves what they want and then act accordingly" (p. 488).

Fehr (1976) considers these styles of alcoholics to manifest in passive-dependent behavior. Schiff and Schiff (1971) discuss the difficulties involved in treating patients with significant passive behaviors. The major treatment hurdle is the frequency with which passive patients discount and deny their problems. Typically, when they do recognize the existence of a problem, they will fail to see its significance in their lives. Even if they do recognize its significance, passive dependent patients will often compound their situations by denying the solvability of their difficulties, leaving little hope for anything better in their lives.

According to Fehr (1976), alcoholics will rarely be able to recognize their real reasons for drinking, and even more often will not view the excessive alcohol consumption as the significant problem in their lives. Rather than viewing alcoholics as people who do not want to stop drinking, it is better to conceptualize them as people who do not realize the possibility of alternate lifestyles. In contrast, neurotic patients frequently have identified their major difficulties before they even enter group therapy. Usually they are self-referrals interested in making some change in their behavior. As Fehr points out, the therapist in this situation is more of a consultant, whose job it is to listen and guide the client. The therapist usually attempts to limit his/her input and is likely to err in the direction of too much intervention. This is in contrast to work with the alcoholic, where the therapeutic error is more likely to be in the direction of too little intervention. The more directive and active the therapist, the more effective (Fehr, 1976; Johnson, 1969; Wallace, 1975).

Alcoholics in group therapy tend to support each other's passivity (Fehr, 1967). The group rallies around the subject of alcoholism, its causes and cures, endlessly debating the merits of Alcoholics Anonymous, and covers many issues extraneous to the task at hand. Group members are notorious for their tendency to focus on themselves and each other as alcoholics rather than persons, thereby limiting the amount of genuine interaction among themselves. As such, there is relatively little in the early exchanges between group members that can be considered therapeutically productive (Fehr, 1976). It is important to realize that conventional group psychotherapy procedures, where the emphasis is on the interaction between group members, should not be employed during the early phases of treatment because of their relative ineffectiveness with passive, dependent alcoholics. Such group procedures should be introduced, however, into the treatment plan as the members mature in their ability to function within the group.

TIME FACTORS

The intelligent treatment of the recovering alcoholic must be viewed in terms of a long timespan. A particular therapeutic intervention for a neurotic may be entirely inappropriate for a recently drinking alcoholic and even for one who has managed to achieve several years of sobriety. Yalom asserts that even most non-alcoholic patients require approximately 12 to 24 months to undergo substantial change, although it is possible to resolve a crisis in briefer periods of time. It is best to interpret the immediate problem of alcoholic drinking as a crisis which must be dealt with first. AA and most alcoholism-directed therapeutic systems recognize that the first year of treatment is crisis oriented and that it is not wise to push change too early in the recovery process (AA, 1960; Chambers & Wallace, 1978; Johnson, 1969).

The therapist may find that in some cases the entire first year of treatment may be spent on "just" maintaining sobriety, with little or no active encouragement of personality modification. Brown and Yalom (1977) address the importance of the time perspective in alcoholism treatment: "The therapist's patience and hope provide reassurance to patients who have frustrated and been abandoned by many would-be helpers. Continuing, unwavering commitment is required of the therapist; it is not the best setting for therapists who need immediate gratification of their needs to be healers" (p. 437).

In one sense, the therapist must recognize that in dealing with the alcoholic client all therapeutic interventions occur at a slower pace. The therapist must move cautiously realizing, on one hand, that conflict and anxiety are necessary for change, but on the other hand, that too much anxiety and conflict will frequently push the alcoholic to cope with this situation by drinking. Yalom recognizes that, although alcoholics often desire change, they realize that they have so much to lose if they resume drinking that they will often resist engagement in the therapy process.

STRUCTURE

Another factor influencing this general reluctance to change has been described by Brown and Yalom (1977) as the rigid defense system of the typical alcoholic. "Members could recognize in one another the tendency to assume rigid positions which they labeled as black and white or all or nothing viewpoints." It is often the case that the alcoholic will exhibit a strong preference for certainty. Judgments of people, events, and situations are often extreme. Wallace (1978) agrees: "Perceived alternatives are few, consisting largely of yes-no, black-white, dichotomized categories. It is in this sense that the thinking is said to be all or nothing in character" (p. 23).

Because of this Wallace feels that alcoholics prefer large amounts of structure and events to proceed in a predictable and structured manner. Meetings of AA, for example, are among the most structured of social encounters. As Wallace (1977) illustrated, a meeting in Southern California begins with a reading of Chapter Five of the book, *Alcoholics Anonymous*. "Hence, for example, an alcoholic from Anaheim, sober for 10 years, attending three meetings of AA a week, has heard the same thing read 1560 times!" (p. 23, 1939). Brown and Yalom (1977) likewise suggest that it is important that the therapist provide a support system on which patients can rely. "Thus, it was vitally important that members be assured that the group was ongoing and would always meet at the appointed time" (p. 442). This simple factor underscores the importance of the long-term therapy experience. Shorter group experiences, Yalom feels, cannot provide the necessary stable, continuous community needed for recovery.

THE DENIAL SYSTEM

Alcoholics can be best described in terms of their preferred defense structure which includes the predominantly used mechanisms of denial, rationalization, projection, intellectualization and minimization (Wallace, 1975). Typically, this results in a group consisting mostly of alcoholics who have no idea of what they are feeling and subsequently are operating from a distorted view of what is really happening to them. In accounting for alcoholic's apparent lack of understanding of the relationship between their drinking and their troubles, professionals conclude that alcoholics are using denial. Alcoholism is considered by many to constitute "a disease of denial" (AA, 1939; Tiebout, 1953; Wallace, 1978). Rather than become angered with alcoholics' blatant refusal to acknowledge what they are feeling, the therapist must recognize that this is the very problem which must be reconciled slowly with supportive and patient understanding.

The most difficult task in alcoholism therapy is to lessen denial and encourage self-awareness and disclosure, while simultaneously keeping anxiety at a minimum. This means that the therapist must be content with a gradually deepening self-awareness rather than demanding sudden, dramatic breakthroughs. As Yalom (1975) clearly illustrates, "pipedreams" or "vital lies" are often essential to personal and social integrity (p. 216). He warns that they should not be taken lightly or impulsively stripped away in the service of honesty. Above honesty, the therapist has a responsibility to his patients and their tasks, which clearly should override any tendency to utilize techniques or confront for confrontation's sake. Moreover, the therapist must insure a therapeutic context in which high levels of support are available as the client uncovers aspects of self and discloses these to others. Alcoholism therapy is best described as consisting of important choices and decisions in light of too much blame or too little responsibility, too much guilt or too much sociopathology, too much anger or too much compliance, too much denial or too much self-disclosure (Wallace, 1975).

Psychotherapy within this context differs from conventional treatment in that the therapist must constantly weigh each intervention since too rapid or too much confrontation may result in alcoholic behavior. This situation must be tempered with gentle probing and the realization that, if changes do not occur, alcoholic behavior cannot be far behind. This theme will permeate the entire treatment process but ideally should become less of a concern the longer sobriety is maintained.

Therapy with alcoholics, as it is currently practiced, too often attempts to remove the alcoholic's preferred defense system instead of utilizing it to facilitate the achievement of abstinence. Therapeutic efforts that confront the alcoholic's preferred defense system prematurely will increase rather than reduce the probability of further drinking. Paradoxically, the same defenses that the alcoholic uses to maintain his or her drinking can be used effectively to achieve abstinence (Wallace, 1977). Equally paradoxically, the very same defenses that enable the alcoholic to drink and to achieve abstinence, must ultimately be removed if long-term sobriety is to be maintained. However, in many cases such growth takes place over periods of time ranging from two to five years of abstinence (AA, 1955; Wallace, 1977).

Wallace (1978) also recognizes that part of the value of placing the alcoholic's behavior within an alcoholism paradigm is the necessity of placing the alcoholic's experience within some cognitive structure. Helping the client to achieve a self-attribution of "alcoholic" and, hence, an explanatory system for his/her behaviors is a central role of the therapist. Psychotherapy with the client at this point is very much the teaching of an "exotic belief" whose true value of actually describing what has occurred because of the alcoholism is held irrelevant. Its true value is that it enables the client to 1. explain past behavior in a way that gives hope for the future and 2. cope with guilt, anxiety, remorse and confusion. It also 3. provides the client with a specific behavior (staying sober) that will change his/her life in a desired direction. The therapist must remember that the recovering alcoholic has a lifetime of sobriety in which to recognize the fact that not all of his/her personal and social difficulties can be attributed to alcoholism. The sober member of AA needs an ideological base and belief system to reduce anxiety and confusion. As Buber (1960) recognizes, a person in a crisis needs direction; it is only later that the necessary personality changes can and must be facilitated if sobriety is to be maintained (Wallace, 1978).

ALCOHOLICS ANONYMOUS
AND GROUP PSYCHOTHERAPY

Is a dual affiliation in both AA and group psychotherapy possible? Recent strategies have been developed addressing this issue. The leading theorists in the field all suggest alternatives, based on years of clinical experience, which indicate that a close working relationship with Alcoholics Anonymous will enhance treatment success (Brown & Yalom, 1977; Cummings, 1979; Wallace, 1975, 1978). Cummings (1979) for instance, in his description of "exclusing therapy," outlines tactics compatible with AA which require abstinence as the primary goal of treatment.

Alcoholics need enormous support to attain and maintain abstinence. Brown and Yalom (1977) were concerned that an interactional group (in which conflict as well as acceptance is necessary) would not be able to provide the total support needed for the recovery process, but resolved this problem by encouraging group members to obtain other help, if necessary, from Alcoholics Anonymous. However, they feared that the dual affiliation might hinder progress in the interactional group. At first there was some dissonance between the two as they had to bridge the gap between AA and some alcoholics' stereotype of "ignorant professionals." This was resolved by pointing out to group members that AA and the therapy group serve very different, but equally necessary, functions in their recovery. There are things that AA can give the members that the group can't and vice versa. The issue of dependency provides an excellent example. AA, by nature of its format, tends to gratify dependency needs. New members are encouraged to rely on AA, on the other members, and on a "Higher Power" to remain abstinent. The therapy group, on the other hand, satisfies dependency needs only enough to keep the patient in therapy.

While AA and professionally oriented therapy groups are both designed to be active treatment regimens geared to facilitate recovery and abstinence from alcohol and drugs, a critical difference exists between the two. Therapy groups are specifically oriented to a global symptom reduction through the specific use of behavioral and psychological prescriptions and techniques, while AA is regimented towards addressing one specific component of recovery (i.e., abstinence).

The core content in the professionally oriented therapy group should attempt to facilitate increased gradual introspection and compliance through the use of group confrontation, discussion and education. In contrast, AA will be almost entirely supportive fostering a degree of dependence on the acceptance of a specific and limited treatment approach focused entirely on compliance and abstinence from alcohol.

Treatment Characteristics

In order to gain a more comprehensive overview of the content of each treatment group, a projected list of similarities and differences between the two treatment groups is presented. Common and divergent elements are listed below:

DIVERGENT ELEMENTS

Alcoholics Anonymous	*Professional-Oriented Therapy Groups*
1. Treatment goal focuses specifically on abstinence.	1. Treatment goals are determined by the Goal Attainment Scale (GAS) which requires social,

Alcoholics Anonymous	*Professional-Oriented Therapy Groups*
	psychological, physical, and drinking related behavior be examined and evaluated.
2. Emphasis on the "how" of abstinence and recovery.	2. More emphasis on the "why" of abstinence and recovery.
3. Opening of group with readings of the AA "Big Book" and the Twelve Steps of Recovery.	3. Development of group cohesiveness and traditional group processes.
4. Structured use of life histories dealing specifically with personal history of alcoholism and recovery.	4. Verbal reports of general progress without notation and rigid format.
5. Didactic format by group leaders to impart AA principles.	5. Mobilization of group support and feedback.
6. Emphasis on the traditional twelve steps of the AA program with less emphasis on feelings and emotions.	6. More emphasis on group discussion of feelings and emotions.
7. More democratic group leadership with members taking a more active role in the group discussion.	7. More traditional role of group leader in the group process.
8. Group discussion focused on ways to remain abstinent.	8. More confrontation and exploration of resistance.

COMMON ELEMENTS

1. Group discussion.
2. Correct misconceptions about alcoholism.

3. Impart information on alcoholism and need for compliance.
4. Formulation of treatment issues.
5. Group support at beginning.
6. Aim to reduce patient complaints and behavior that interfere with alcohol abstinence.
7. Attempt to involve and change family environment.
8. Search for continuing causes of abstinence difficulties.

These specific treatment procedures should be developed and monitored in their application throughout the course of treatment in order to insure that both treatments offered (professional vs. AA) are clinically meaningful and discriminately different. In this way maximal benefit can be realized by the contrasting types of therapy with alcoholics and addicts.

Ideally, a solid, continuing membership in AA frees members to participate fully in the therapy group. AA can serve as a support system which helps the group members with their concerns about alcohol and also allows them to tolerate the frustrations of the therapy process. In fact, active membership should be encouraged, but the therapist must also be willing and able to counter misconceptions, prejudices, and distortions of fact about AA.

Wallace (1978) contends that attendance at AA meetings is, in effect, a behavioral change program in that it advocates practical methods of achieving and maintaining sobriety. "Positive reinforcement (social recognition and status for staying sober), social modeling (the accessibility of role models and their behaviors for learning how to stay sober), desensitization (anxiety and guilt reduction through sharing of common experience, laughter and general merriment over past alcoholic behaviors, and a general atmosphere of social acceptance), and cognitive behavioral change (cognitive restructuring of self, behavior, and alcoholism) are aspects of AA that are most congruent with modern versions of behavior therapy" (p. 102).

Drinking and Relapse

The futility of attempting to apply psychotherapy to someone drugged on alcohol was clearly illustrated in the Brown and Yalom study (1977). Although they never clearly resolved or fully addressed this issue, it was apparent that it caused them extreme difficulty. Beyond the detrimental effects of the drop-out rate, the intoxicated patients proved to be most damaging to the group process. In each case (15 times during the 2-1/2 year study), the intoxicated member stayed for the entire meeting and dominated the session. The drunk captured and held the group's attention in ways which were impossible to ignore. "Members were especially frustrated by the knowledge that the meeting would rapidly vaporize, since the drinking member rarely retained much of the meeting afterward. Members felt the power of alcohol and an overwhelming feeling of futility about the session" (p. 438).

Part of this difficulty can be explained by a failure of the therapists to recognize that the primary issue which must be dealt with in any treatment of alcoholism is the issue of alcohol consumption itself (AA, 1955; Wallace, 1975). All too frequently, psychotherapists continue to hold the archaic notion that alcoholism is a symptom of some underlying pathology. It is difficult to understand why otherwise intelligent psychotherapists will continue to try to apply a mode of treatment (psychotherapy) built upon a rational foundation to an individual who is drugged into an altered state of consciousness. Research has shown rather conclusively that learning which takes place during a drug-induced state of consciousness will not generalize to undrugged states (Fischer, 1976). A substantial part of all psychotherapy is the unlearning of old, self-defeating behaviors and the learning of more adaptive behaviors. This process is seriously impaired if a member is intoxicated, because change often requires insight, cognitive realignment and an emotional catharsis. Central to any therapy with alcoholics is the requirement of abstinence from alcohol (AA, 1939; Madsen, 1974; Wallace, 1978).

Yalom acknowledged the fact that active drinking generally drew normal positive working forces in the group to a halt. Occasionally, he was able to process and integrate the incident into a form of therapeutic benefit through the use of videotape replay. Sometimes, by utilizing this medium, he was able dramatically to illustrate afterwards, when the group member was sober, how repulsive and self-defeating his or her intoxicated behavior actually appeared to the rest of the group. In each case, Yalom illustrated ways in which therapeutic gain could be derived from what may have seemed at the time the most discouraging therapeutic mishap. This should be the case with any instance of alcoholic relapse. Brown and Yalom (1977) mistakenly claim that AA "nonetheless considers a slip to be an unmitigated catastrophe: a slip is written in indelible ink in the AA member's personal story, differentiating him from those members who have maintained continuous abstinence" (p. 433). On the contrary, AA recognizes a slip as an inevitable process in some alcoholics' recovery (AA, 1955). Rather than looking upon it as a catastrophe, relapse should be approached as a learning experience that indicates that the alcoholic is obviously doing something wrong. The task of the group and the therapist at this point is to explore circumstances which may have led to the drinking. Over-confidence, passivity or old patterns of resentment and anger are common themes which may help other members realize that they too may be committing these same mistakes. Often such a relapse in group can be an extremely beneficial experience for the rest of the members as a whole.

All of the factors enumerated in this chapter indicate that the preferred mode of treatment for alcoholism is group psychotherapy. The group's ability to provide support, structure and reinforcement for abstinence make it a powerful catalyst in the recovery process. In measures of time, efficacy and recovery, group psychotherapy generally succeeds where other treatment modalities frequently fail. Brown and Yalom's study helps support the little published fact, which AA and most successful alcoholism treatment facilities know: the group can serve as a powerful change agent in the alcoholic's recovery process.

REFERENCES

AA World Services, Inc. (1939). *Alcoholics Anonymous*. New York: Author.

AA World Services, Inc. (1955). *The story of how many thousands of men and women have recovered from alcoholism*. New York: Author.

AA World Services, Inc. (1960). *Is A.A. for you?* AA Grapevine. New York: Author.

Adamson, J. D., Fostakowsky, R. T. & Shelik, F. S. (1974). Measures associated with outcome at one year follow-up of male alcoholics. *British Journal of Addiction, 69*, 325-327.

Alibrandi, L. A. (1978). The folk psychotherapy of Alcoholics Anonymous. In *Practical approaches to psychotherapy*. New York: New York Press.

Apfeldorf, M. (1978). Alcoholism scales of the MMPI contributions and future directions. *International Journal of Addictions, 13*, 17-53

Backland, F. L., Lundwal, L. & Kissan, B. (1975). Methods for the treatment of chronic alcoholism. A critical appraisal. In R. J. Gibbins, Y. Irael, H. Kalant, R. E. Popham, W. Schmidt & R. G. Smart (Eds.), *Research advances in alcohol and drug problems* (Vol. 2). New York: Wiley.

Barnes, G. E. (1979). The alcoholic personality. *Quarterly Journal of Studies on Alcohol, 40*, 571-634.

Battle, C. C., Imber, S. D., Hoch, R., Stone, A. R., Nash, E. P. & Frank, J. D. (1966). Target complaints as criteria of improvement. *American Journal of Psychotherapy, 20*, 184-192.

Belasco, J. A. (1971). The criterion question revisited. *British Journal of Addiction, 66*, 39-44.

Bergin, A. E. (1971). The evaluation of therapeutic outcomes. In A. E. Bergin & S. L.

Garfield (Eds.), *Handbook of psychotherapy and behavior change: An empirical analysis*. New York: Wiley.

Bergin, A. E. & Lambert, M. J. (1978). The evaluation of therapeutic outcomes. In S. L. Garfield and A. E. Bergin (Eds.), *Handbook of psychotherapy and behavior change*. 2nd ed. (pp. 139-190). New York: Wiley.

Bergin, A. E. & Strupp, H. H. (1972). *Changing frontiers in the science of psychotherapy*. Chicago: Aldine-Atagrton.

Beutler, L. E. (1979). Individual, group and family therapy modes: Patient therapy value compatibility and treatment effectiveness. *Journal of Counseling and Psychotherapy*, 43-59.

Blane, H. T. (1968). *The personality of the alcoholic: Guises of dependency*. New York: Harper and Row.

Blashfield, R. K. (1980). Propositions regarding the use of cluster analysis in clinical research. *Journal of Consulting and Clinical Psychology*, 48(4), 456-459.

Brown, S. & Yalom, I. (1977). Interaction group therapy with alcoholics. *Quarterly Journal of Studies on Alcohol*, 38, 426-456.

Buber, M. (1960). *I and thou*. New York: Charles Scribners Sons.

Buhler, C. & Lefever, D. W. (1956). A Rorschach study on the psychological characteristics of alcoholics. *Quarterly Journal of Studies on Alcohol*, 17, 163-281.

Button, A. D. (1956). A study of alcoholics with the MMPI. *Quarterly Journal of Studies on Alcohol*, 17, 163-281.

Butts, S. & Chotlos, J. A. (1973). A comparison of alcoholics and non-alcoholics on perceived locus of control. *Quarterly Journal of Studies on Alcohol*, 34, 1327-1332.

Carr, J. E. (1970). Differentiation similarity of patient and therapist and the outcome of psychotherapy. *Journal of Abnormal Psychology*, 76, 361-369.

Chaftez, M. E. (1959). Practical and theoretical considerations in the psychotherapy of alcoholics. *Quarterly Journal of Studies on Alcohol*, 20, 281-291.

Chaftez, M. E., Blane, H. T. & Hill, M. J. (1970). *Frontiers of alcoholism*. New York: Science Hours.

Chang, A. F., Caldwell, A. B. & Moss, T. (1973). Stability of personality traits in alcoholics during and after treatment as measured by the MMPI. A one-year follow-up study. Proceedings 81st Annual Convention, APA, 387-388.

Chess, J. E. (1970). Differentiation similarity of patient and therapist and the outcome of psychotherapy. *Journal of Abnormal Psychology*, 76, 361-369.

Coffey, T. F. (1980). Sobering statistics. *Alcoholism. The National Magazine*, 1(1).

Costello, R. M. & Manders, K. R. (1974). Locus of control and alcoholism. *British Journal of Addiction*, 69. 11-17.

Cummings. (1979). Turning bread into stones. *American Psychologist*, 34(12), 1119-1129.

Dahany, S. A. (1977). The effects of assertive training with inpatient alcoholics on measures of assertive behavior, self-esteem, field-dependence. Dissertation, University of Arizona.

Dahlstrom, W. G., Welsch, G. S. & Dahlstrom, L. E. (1972). *An MMPI handbook Volume I: Clinical interpretation*. Minneapolis: University of Minn. Press.

Davies, D. L., Shepherd, M. & Myers, E. (1956). The two-years prognosis of 50 alcoholics after treatment in hospital. *Quarterly Journal of Studies on Alcohol*, 17, 485-502.

Decourcy P. & Duerfeldt, P. H. (1973). The impact of number and types of models on claims success rate and mood of adult alcoholics. *Journal of Genetic Psychology*, 122, 63-79.

Dichter, M., Driscoll, G. Z., Ottenberg, D. J. & Rosen. (1969). A marathon therapy with alcoholics. *Quarterly Journal of Studies on Alcohol*, 64, 155-163.

Disterfano, N., Pryer, L. W. & Garrison, J. L. (1972). Internal external control among alcoholics. *Journal of Clinical Psychology*, 28, 36-37.

Donovan, D. M. & O'Leary, M. R. (1975). Comparison of perceived and experienced control among alcoholics and nonalcoholics. *Journal of Abnormal Psychology*, 84.

Dubourg, G. O. (1969). After care for alcoholics — a follow-up study. *British Journal of Addiction*, 64, 155-163.

Emrick, C. D. (1974). A review of psychological oriented treatment of alcoholism. *Quarterly Journal of Studies on Alcohol, 35*, 523-549.

Emrick, C. D. (1973). Psychological treatment of alcoholism: an analytic review. Unpublished doctoral dissertation, Columbia University.

Emrick, C. D., Lassen, C. L. & Edwards, M. T. (1977). Nonprofessional peers as therapeutic agents in effective psychotherapies. In G. E. German & A. Rozin (Eds.), *The therapist contribution to effective psychotherapy: An empirical assessment*. Elmsford, N.Y.: Pergamon Press.

English, J. (1975). Personality differences in alcohol treatment. *Quarterly Journal of Studies on Alcohol, 36*, 52-61.

Esser, P. H. (1970). Conjoint family therapy with alcoholics — a new approach. *British Journal of Addiction, 64*, 279-286.

Fancher, R. E. (1973). *Psychoanalytical psychology, the development of Freud's thought*. New York: Norton.

Fehr, D. (1976). Psychotherapy: Integration of individual and group methods. In Tarter & Sugerman (Eds.), *Alcoholism: An interdisciplinary approach*. Reading, Mass: Addison-Wesley.

Fischer, R. (1976). On creative psychotic & ecstatic states. In L. Allen & D. Jaffe (Eds.), Consciousness as role 7 knowledge. *Readings in abnormal psychology. Contemporary Perspectives*. New York: Harper & Row.

Fiske et al. (1970). Planning of research on effectiveness of psychotherapy. *Archives of General Psychiatry, 22*, 22-32.

Frank, J. D., Hoehn-Saric, R., Imber, S. D., Liberman, B. L. & Stone, A. R. (1978). *Effective ingredients of successful psychotherapy*. New York: Brunner Mazel.

Glasscote, R. M. (1967). The treatment of alcoholism. Washington, D.C.: The Joint Information Service of American Psychiatric Association and the National Association for Mental Health, 1967.

Goss, A. & Morosko, T. E. (1969). Alcoholism and clinical symptoms. *Journal of Abnormal Psychology*. 682-684.

Goss, A. & Morosko, T. E. Relation between a dimension of internal-external control and the MMPI with alcoholic population. *Journal of Consulting Clinical Psychologist, 34*, 189-192.

Gozali, J. & Sloan, J. (1971). Control orientation as a personality dimension among alcoholics. *Quarterly Journal of Studies on Alcohol, 32*, 159-161.

Gross, W. F. & Carpenter, L. L. (1971). Alcoholic personality: Reality or fiction. *Psychological Reports, 28*, 375-378.

Hartocollis, P. (1964). Some phenomenological aspects of the alcoholic condition. *Psychiatry, 27*, 345-348.

Hartocollis, P. & Shaefer, D. (1963). Group psychotherapy with alcoholics: A critical review. *Psychiatric Digest, 29*, 15-22.

Hayman, M. (1965). Treatment of alcoholism in private practice with a disulfiram-oriented program. *Quarterly Journal of Studies on Alcohol, 26*, 460-467.

Hill, H. E., Haertyen, C. A. & Davis, H. (1962). An MMPI factor analytic study of alcoholics, narcotic addicts, and criminals. *Quarterly Journal of Studies on Alcohol, 23*, 411-431.

Hoffman, H., Loper, R. G. & Kammeier, M. L. (1974). Identifying future alcoholics with MMPI alcoholism scales. *Quarterly Journal of Studies on Alcohol, 35*, 490-498.

Hoffman, H. (1976). Personality measurement for the evaluation and prediction of alcoholism. In R. E. Tarter & A. A. Sugerman, *Alcoholism*. Reading, Mass: Addison Wesley.

Horn, J. L. & Manders, K. R. (1970). Locus of control and alcoholism. *Quarterly Journal of Studies on Alcohol, 31*, 633-658.

Huber, N. A. & Danahy, S. (1975). Use of the MMPI predicting completion and evaluating changes in a long-term alcoholism treatment program. *Quarterly Journal of Studies on Alcohol, 36*, 1230-1237.

Jacobson, G. R., Pisani, V. D. & Berenbaum, H. (1975). Temporal stability of field-dependence among hospital alcoholics. *Journal of Abnormal Psychology, 36*, 387-394.
Jacobson, G. R. & Ritter, D. P. (1977). Purpose in life and personal values among adult alcoholics. *Journal of Clinical Psychology, 33*, 314.
Johnson, V. E. (1969). *I'll quit tomorrow*. New York: Holt, Rinehart & Winston.
Karp, S. A. & Pardes, H. (1965). Psychological differentiation in obese women. *Psychosomatic Medicine, 27*, 238-244.
Katkin, E. S., Risk, R. T. & Spielberger, C. D. (1966). The effects of experimenter status and subject awareness on verbal conditioning. *Journal of Experimental Research in Personality, 1*, 153-160.
Katz, M. M. & Lyerly, S. B. (1963). Methods for measuring adjustment & social behavior in the community: I Rationale, description, discriminate validity and scale development. *Psychological Reports* (13) (Monograph Supplement 4-V13): 503-555.
Kinney, J. (1975). *Loosening the grip*. Dept. of Psychiatry. Dartmouth Medical School.
Krammier, M. L., Hoffman, H. & Loper, R. G. (1973). Personality characteristics of alcoholics as college freshmen and at the time of treatment. *Quarterly Journal of Studies on Alcohol, 34*, 390-399.
Krueger, D. E. (1971). Operant group therapy with delinquent boys using therapist's versus peer's reinforcement. *Dissertation Abstracts International, 31*(11-13), 6877-6878.
Lansing, M. (1979). The american drinking scene in the bottom line. *American Business Men's Research Foundation, 1*(1).
Lottman, T. J., Davis, W. & Gustofson, R. C. (1973). MMPI correlate with locus of control in a psychiatric population. *Journal of Personality Assessment, 37*, 78-82.
Luborsky, L., Singer, B. & Luborsky, L. (1975). Comparative studies of psychotherapies. *Archives of General Psychiatry, 32*, 995-1006.
Madsen, W. (1974). *The American Alcoholic*. Springfield, IL: Charles C. Thomas.
Margolis, M., Krystal, H. & Siegel, S. (1964). Psychotherapy with alcoholic offenders. *Quarterly Journal of Studies on Alcohol, 25*, 85-99.
Martini, J. L. (1978). Patient therapist value congruence and rating of client improvement. *Counseling and Values, 23*, 25-32.
Matakas, F., Koester, H. & Leidner, B. (1978). Which treatment for which alcoholics? A review. *Psychiatrische Praxis, 5*, 143-152.
McLachlam, J. C. (1974). Therapy strategies, personality orientation and recovery from alcoholism. *Canadian Psychiatric Association Journal, 19*, 25-30.
McWilliams, J., Brown, C. C. & Minard, J. G. (1975). Field-dependence and self-actualization in alcoholics. *Quarterly Journal of Studies on Alcohol, 36*, 387-394.
Meeks, D. E. & Kelly, C. (1970). Family therapy with the families of recovery alcoholics. *Quarterly Journal of Studies on Alcohol, 31*, 399-413.
Meichenbaum, D. H. (1971). Examination of models' characteristics in reducing avoidance behavior. *Journal of Personality and Social Psychology, 17*, 298-307.
Moore, R. A. (1971). The prevalence of alcoholism in a community general hospital. *American Journal Psychiatry, 128*, 1083-1085.
Moore, R. A. (1973). *Psychotherapeutics of alcoholism*. Proceedings of the 2nd Annual Alcoholism Conference of NIAAA. Pub #73-9083.
Moore, R. A. & Buchanan, T. K. (1966). State hospitals and alcoholism: A nation-wide survey of treatment techniques and results. *Quarterly Journal of Studies on Alcohol, 27*, 459-468.
Mullen, H. & Sanguiliano, I. (1966). *Alcoholism: Group psychotherapy and rehabilitation*. Springfield, IL: Charles C. Thomas.
National Institute on Alcohol Abuse and Alcoholism. (1962). *Alcohol and alcoholism: Problems, programs and progress*. Washington, D. C.: U.S. Government Printing Office.
Neal, C. R. (1963). An investigation of perception of visual space among alcoholics. Doctoral Dissertation, University of Utah (University Microfilms, No. 63).
Noble, E. P. (Ed.) (1978). Department of Health, Education & Welfare Publication Alcohol and Health, 3rd Special Report to U.S. Congress on Alcohol & Health (No. ADM 78-569).

Oziel, L. J., Obitz, F. W. & Kerpon, M. (1972). General & specific perceived locus of control in alcoholics. *Psychological Reports, 30,* 957-958.
Pattison, E. M. (1966). A critique of alcoholism treatment concepts: With special reference to abstinence. *Quarterly Journal of Studies on Alcohol, 27,* 49-71.
Pattison, E. M. (1973). Criteria in treatment evaluation. Proceedings of 2nd Annual Alcoholism Conference on the National Institute of Alcohol Abuse and Alcoholism. Department of Health, Education and Welfare Pub. #73-9083.
Rohan, W. P., Tatre, R. L. & Rotman, S. R. (1960). MMPI changes in alcoholics during hospitalization. *Quarterly Journal of Studies on Alcohol, 21,* 253-266.
Rohan, W. P., Tatre, R. L. & Rotman, S. R. (1972). MMPI changes in hospitalized alcoholics: A second study. *Quarterly Journal of Studies on Alcohol, 33,* 65-76.
Rohsenow, D. J. & O'Leary, M. R. (1978). Locus of control research on alcoholic population. *International Journal of the Addictions, 13,* 55-78.
Rokeach, M. (1973). *The nature of human values.* New York: New York Press.
Rosen, A. (1960). A comparative study of alcoholics and psychiatric patients with the MMPI. *Quarterly Journal of Studies on Alcohol, 21,* 253-266.
Rotter, J. B. (1966). Generalized expectancies for internal vs. external control. *Psychological Monographs, 80,* 1-28.
Schiff, A. & Schiff, J. L. (1971). Passivity. *Transactional Analysis Journal, 1,* 71-77.
Scott, E. M. (1961). The technique of psychotherapy with alcoholics. *Quarterly Journal of Studies on Alcohol, 22,* 69-80.
Smart, R. T., Schmidt, W. & Moss, M. K. (1969). Social class as a determinant of the types and duration of therapy received by alcoholics. *International Journal of Addictions, 4,* 543-556.
Smith, J. W. & Layden, T. A. (1975). Changes in psychological performance and blood chemistry in alcoholics during and after hospital treatment. *Quarterly Journal of Studies on Alcohol, 36,* 387-394.
Sobey, F. (1970). *The nonprofessional revolution in mental health.* New York: Columbia University Press.
Spitzer, R. L., Endicott, J., Fleiss, J. B. & Cohen, J. (1970). The psychiatric status schedule. A technique for evaluation psychopathology and impairment in role functioning. *Archives of General Psychiatry, 23,* 41-55.
Stienier, C. M. (1969). The alcoholic game. *Quarterly Journal of Studies on Alcohol, 30,* 920-938.
Stinson, D., Smith, W., Arnidjaya, I. & Kaplan, J. (1979). System of care and treatment outcomes for alcoholic patients. *Archives of General Psychiatry, 36,* 535-539.
Strupp, H. H. & Hadly, S. (1979). Specific vs. nonspecific factors in psychotherapy: A controlled study of outcome. *Archives of General Psychiatry, 36,* 1125-1136.
Sutherland, E. H., Schroeder, H. C. & Tordella, C. L. (1950). Personality traits and the alcoholic. *Quarterly Journal of Studies on Alcohol, 11,* 547-561.
Szasz, T. S. (1966). Alcoholism: A socioethnical perspective. *Western Medicine, 7,* 15-21.
Szura, J. P. & Vermillion, M. E. (1975). Effects of defensiveness and self-actualization of a Herzberg replication. *Journal of Vocational Behavior, 2,* 181-187.
Tarter, R. E. & Sugerman, A. A. (1976). *Alcoholism.* Reading, Mass: Addison-Wesley.
Thune, C. E. (1977). Alcoholism and the archetypath: A phenomenological perspective on Alcoholics Anonymous. *Quarterly Journal of Studies on Alcohol, 38,* 75-86.
Tiebout, H. M. (1953). The act of surrender in the therapeutic process. *Quarterly Journal of Studies on Alcohol, 14,* 58-68.
Townsend, P. C. (1978). Value orientations and initial commitment to behavioral and client-centered therapies. *Counseling & Values, 23,* 49-51.
Wallace, J. M. (1977). In N. J. Estes & M. E. Heinemann (Eds.), *Alcoholism, development, consequences, and interventions.* St. Louis: C. V. Mosby Co.
Wallace, J. (1978). *Practical approaches to alcoholism psychotherapy.* New York: Plenum Press.
Wallace, J. (1975). Working with the preferred defense system of recovering alcoholics. *National Council on Alcoholism,* 19-29, New York.

Philip J. Flores

Wilkinson, A. E., Prado, W. M., Williams, W. O. & Schmidt, F. E. (1971). Psychological test characteristics and length of stay in alcoholism treatment. *Quarterly Journal of Studies on Alcohol, 32,* 60-65.

Witkin, H. A., Karp, S. A. & Goodenough, D. R. (1959). Dependence in alcoholics, *Quarterly Journal of Studies on Alcohol, 20,* 493-504.

Witken, H. A. & Oltman, P. K. (1967). Cognitive styles. *International Journal of Neurology, 6,* 119-137.

Yalom, I. D. (1975). *The theory and practice of group psychotherapy* (2nd ed.). New York: Basic Books.

Zupnick, S. M. (1970). The effects of varying degree of peer models performance. *Dissertation Abstracts International, 31,* (6-B), 3719.

Chapter 5

Alcoholism, Addiction, and Psychodynamic Theories of Addiction

(History up to p. 138)

Within the last thirty years, there have been vast and important changes in the field of addiction. Foremost among these changes has been the legitimization of the treatment of alcoholism and drug dependence. In the past alcoholism was judged by many to be a symptom of a more serious core problem. Now, the disease concept has stood this view completely on its head. Depression, anxiety, sociopathy, and character pathology are all now viewed as symptoms, the result, instead of the cause of addiction. Addiction specialists have discovered that if they treat the alcoholism and the drug dependence, these symptoms often vanish or at least greatly diminish. It has taken someone of George Vaillant's stature (a Harvard psychiatrist) before many professionals outside of the AA community listened or paid serious attention to such an argument. Vaillant is saying what AA has known for years. "Thus, the etiological hypothesis that viewed alcoholism primarily as a symptom of psychological instability may be an illusion based on retrospective study" (1982, p. 494). Or put another way, "Prospective studies are gradually teaching psychiatrists the astonishing fact that most of psychopathology seen in the alcoholic is the result, not the cause of alcohol abuse. Put differently, alcoholism is the horse, not the cart, of mental illness" (1983, p. 317).

Not only has the treatment of addiction been legitimized, addiction has finally become recognized as a significant and major health problem. Treatment for addiction used to be available only through Alcoholics Anonymous or an occasional obscure hospital in some distant part of the country. Now, almost every major hospital in every major city in this country has an inpatient or outpatient program established for the treatment of alcoholism and drug depen-

135

dence. It would be tempting to apply the same solipsistic argument
that is often presented about alcoholism — namely that alcoholism is
caused by depression and character pathology — and lay the addiction problem on the hospitals for creating such an epidemic. Unfortunately, it is all too evident that the upsurge of addiction treatment
facilities in this country is the result, not the cause, of the increased
number of individuals suffering from drug-and-alcohol-related
problems. The increase in recognition of drug and alcohol related
problems is also a direct result of the increase in alcohol and drug
use in our present day society. The most important precipitating
factor in drug addiction is the degree of availability and access to a
particular drug. Thus, no matter how great the cultural attitudinal
tolerance for addictive practices is, or how strong individual personality predispositions are, nobody can become addicted to drugs
without access to them. Thirty years ago, we just had to contend
with the alcoholic and the treatment of alcoholism. The picture used
to be clear and simple; stop drinking and go to AA meetings. Now,
it is rare to find an alcoholic, especially someone in their youth,
who hasn't also abused and used numerous other drugs in their
drinking history. Certainly, the recent onset of increased drug use in
our culture has complicated the diagnostic and treatment picture.

Numerous institutions and organizations have utilized Alcoholics
Anonymous and its Twelve Steps program in an attempt to adapt to
this complicated situation. AA's integrity has been maintained
while the emergence of countless other disorders have prompted the
adaptation of the Twelve Steps of the AA program to fit the dynamics of the multiple specific addictions that have developed over
the last few years. Narcotics Anonymous, Cocaine Anonymous,
Gamblers Anonymous, Over-Eaters Anonymous, multiple eating
disorders (i.e., bulimia, anorexia), and even Emotions Anonymous
have applied the principles of the Twelve Step program to their
different maladies with generally successful results. What is it that
these diverse conditions have in common that lead them to derive
benefit from the Twelve Step program and the fellowship of AA?

Certainly, many of the curative factors (Universality, Installation
of Hope, Cohesiveness, etc.) which Yalom identifies (see Chapter
Fourteen) may be operating in the group treatment format which the
AA program employs. The argument could also be presented that
the principles of AA (i.e., honesty, personal evaluation, removal of
character defects, the helping of others, etc.) could be helpful to
anyone who applied these tenets to their life. While this may be

true, such a statement misses the important relationship which exists between different types of addiction and personality variables. It is important to understand the similarities and common characteristics which these addicted individuals share. Those familiar with AA know that many alcoholics stop drinking, rid themselves of their abundant interpersonal problems and turn their life around. Many abstinent alcoholics begin to enjoy life and go on to develop productive, healthy, successful careers and relationships. However, for every success, there is an equal number of individuals who are unable to remain sober and continue to act out their destructive patterns in a similar fashion with other obsessions and addictions. They suffer constant relapses, often end up substituting one problem (cocaine, heroin, marijuana) for another. Many become bulimic, overweight or anorexic. Their eating becomes as compulsive and out of control as their drinking or drug use. They become compulsive workers, gamblers or use sex just as they have used chemicals — to combat the emptiness, boredom and depression that threatens to engulf them. They do not have a healthy sobriety and serenity escapes them. They become what AA terms a "dry drunk." They stop their alcohol use, but their personality characteristics do not change. Even the Big Book of AA recognizes that the AA program may not be for everyone.

> There are such unfortunates. They are not at fault; they seem to have been born that way. They are naturally incapable of grasping and developing a manner of living which demands rigorous honesty. Their chances are less than average. There are those, too, who suffer from grave emotional and mental disorders. (p. 58, AA World Services, 1939)

The questions concerning these individuals who continue to relapse and the reasons for their failures must be answered and understood. It would be tempting to write them off, saying that they are not ready "to get the program" or have not "hit their bottom yet." Father Martin, the lovable leprechaun-like Catholic priest, abhors such an attitude. He is fond of saying, "Of course you are right when you say you can lead a horse to water, but you can't make him drink. But, you can sure make them thirsty!" Father Martin feels strongly that professionals must not take an uninvolved or neutral stance when working with alcoholics and addicts; but rather, you must find ways to increase the addict's and alcoholic's motivation

for treatment. Certainly, one way to increase their thirst for treatment is to provide them with something that is nourishing and fulfilling. This requires an understanding of the special dynamics
involved in the patient who suffers from multiple addictions and
frequently substitutes one disorder for another. Understanding their
condition will allow the professional to treat them in a way that will
address the deficits which lead them to feel unnourished and dissatisfied.

CHARACTER PATHOLOGY AND ADDICTION

This brings us to the purpose of this chapter. Recent advances in
the understanding of addiction has shed some new light on the per-
plexing problem of those "who may be too sick to get the program." Their sickness may be tied into a condition which can be
described by a number of different terms — character pathology, personality disorder, structural deficits or an uncohesive sense of self.
DSM III (APA, 1980) refers to these conditions as personality disorders. Psychiatric and psychoanalytic classifications of personality
disorders are based on the repeated observation that patients who
present symptoms due to maladaptively structured personalities fall
into a small number of fixed groups, separated by similarities in the
collection of personality traits. Furthermore, analytic exploration of
descriptively homogeneous patients reveal broad similarities in basic conflicts and developmental experiences. Although these classifications are intended to discriminate among persons with personality disorders, they offer a useful framework for separating "kinds of
people" in general. Personality disorders are distinguished from
personality types, not by the presence of any definable pathological
trait but by the inappropriate application of that trait in their interpersonal relationships. People with personality disorders tend to see
the unresolved dramas of their earlier experiences lurking in everyday life and react with rigid attempts to combat them in spite of
inner disquiet or contemporary adaptive failure. In fact, the stress
and regressive pull of illness often blurs this distinction between
health and illness, and the general psychiatric classification has
been used along with some of the common descriptive synonyms to
outline the usual range of personality types encountered in psychiatric practice.

Indeed, if an alcoholic or drug addict does have a sociopathic, borderline, or narcissistic personality disorder, this patient is going to present with far more complicated treatment issues than the alcoholic or addict who doesn't suffer from character pathology. The relationship between addiction and character pathology has important implications for treatment. Schuckit has succinctly summarized the etiological possibilities which exist between these two conditions (1973). First, there are those who have character disorders and abuse drugs and alcohol because this is one common symptom of their personality disorder; second, the chemically dependent individual manifests character pathology as a consequence of primary drug and alcohol dependence; or third, there is a common shared factor which leads both to addiction and character disorders.

It is crucial to discern these three different possibilities in treating the addicted individual because what works with an alcoholic with character deficits will not work with a sociopath who is dependent on drugs and alcohol. Vaillant in a study (1983) addressing this question feels that sociopathy and alcoholism have a complex and different multifactoral etiology. He concludes, "as soon as one disorder is present, the second becomes enormously likely" (p. 325). However, he contends that "in pre-morbid personality, the majority of alcoholics may be no different from non-alcoholics. On the other hand, sociopaths are very unhappy people with a poorly developed *sense of self* who seek to alter how they feel by abusing many kinds of drugs" (p. 325).

The understanding of what Vaillant calls "the sense self" and its relationship to character disorders and addiction has reached important heights in the last decades. Two important contributing factors have led to this increase of competent professionals involved in the treatment and understanding of addiction and personality disorders. First, many physicians, psychologists, social workers, counselors, nurses, priests, and ministers have had to seek treatment for their own chemical dependency. They have learned what every addict and alcoholic has had to learn—they've had to stop their chemical use before they were able to make any substantial and long-lasting changes in their life. Grand theories, insight, faith, and understanding have little significant impact on the arrestment and the alleviation of their dependency on alcohol or drugs. Their professional standing and education did not help them. Only Alcoholics Anonymous and the principles of the AA program allowed them to return to the world of the living and relieve them of their symptoms. The second contributing factor has been the serious investigation of alcoholism by a vast number of dedicated professionals who sought to understand this baffling disease the only way it could be realistically appreciated — by working with the chemically dependent individual. Numerous organizations of concerned professionals have emerged within the last decade. The Society of Psychologists In Addictive Behaviors (SPAD), The National Council On Alcoholism (NCA), The National Institute Of Drug Addiction (NIDA), The National Institute of Alcoholism And Alcohol Abuse (NIAAA), The National Association Of Drug And Alcohol Counselors (NADAC), The International Association Of Doctors In Alcoholics Anonymous (IADAA), The American Medical Association (AMA), and The American Medical Association On Alcoholism (AMAA) are but a few of the more prominent organizations that have directed their energy in the last few years towards understanding alcoholism and drug dependency. Many professionals, either because of their own recovery from addiction, their association with colleagues who are recovering or because of involvement in these organizations, are more in touch with the realities of addiction than at any other time in recent history.

CONTRIBUTIONS OF OBJECT RELATIONS THEORY AND SELF-PSYCHOLOGY

Within this change in professional interest in the understanding of alcoholism and drug dependence, there has been an emerging change in individual psychology within the last thirty years which has accumulated in the present day Object Relations Theory of Otto Kernberg (1975) and the Self-Psychology of Heinz Kohut (1977). Recent advances using standardized diagnostic approaches in psychiatry and a shift in psychoanalysis from a drive or instinct theory to a greater emphasis on adaptation and structural theory (ego and the self) have provided new findings and perspectives in explaining the relationship between psychological disturbance, interpersonal dysfunction, alcoholism, and drug dependence. Freud's concept of the private self, an intra-psychic structure which is self-contained and potentially perfectible has been replaced over time by the interpersonal determination of self which is influenced by our relationships with others. The internalized effort to be without short-comings, to put up one's best front as a contained enclosed intra-psychic self (conflict theory) has been exchanged for a view which defines our self as determined by our desires to be with others as oneself, with all its imperfections and its short-comings, while recognizing that others are independent, separate and are not there just to serve our own needs and desires (object-relations theory).

Within this change in perspective, more emphasis has been placed on the effects of interpersonal relationships in determining a person's behavior and personality. Paralleling Martin Buber's anthropological question about what makes man unique, psychoanalysis and psychodynamic theory has arrived at a similar conclusion to that of Buber's. Man is unique because he is defined by his relationships with others. Much like Harry Stack Sullivan's Interpersonal Theory of Psychiatry, this viewpoint holds that we are a product of our relationships with others and that our sense of self is defined by the way we are perceived by others and how we perceive or distort our perception of others. Martin Buber (1955) summarizes this position when he writes,

> The fundamental fact of human existence is neither the individual as such nor the aggregate as such. Each, considered by itself, is a mighty abstraction. The individual is a fact of existence in so far as he steps into a living relation with other individuals. The aggregate is a fact of existence in so far as it is built up of living units of relation. The fundamental fact of human existence is man with man. What is peculiarly characteristic of the human world is above all that something takes place between one being and another the like of which can be found nowhere in nature. Language is only a sign and a means for it, all achievement of the spirit has been incited by it. Man is made man by it; but on its way it does not merely unfold, it also decays and withers away. It is rooted in one being turning to another as another, as this particular other being, in order to communicate with it in a sphere which is common to them but which reaches out beyond the special sphere of each. I call this sphere, which is established with the existence of man as man but which is conceptually still uncomprehended, the sphere of "between". Though being realized in very different degrees, it is a primal category of human reality. This is where the genuine third alternative must begin.
>
> The view which establishes the concept of "between" is to be acquired by no longer localizing the relation between human beings, as is customary, either within individual souls or

in a general world which embraces and determines them, but in actual fact *between* them.

Buber's principle is that the development of this self is merely preparatory for true dialogic existence. We become what we are in order to be able to develop authentic real relationships with others. We therefore remain inauthentic or false until we are able to engage another in true dialogue. Nowhere is this principle more beautifully stated than in his classic description of the I-Thou relationship (1960).

People often confuse the description of the I-Thou with the belief that it describes a mystical union with another in which two separate individuals unite as one. While this is somewhat true, it is not the most significant contribution to the understanding of relationships which this concept describes. Martin Buber was fond of saying an I precedes a Thou and the action takes place between the boundaries. By this, Buber wished to emphasize the importance of understanding one's separateness before entering into an I-Thou relationship. We must first be autonomous and independent before we can fully engage another. If we do not know our boundaries, we can lose ourselves in our relationships and confuse that which is ours with that which is not ours.

This is the theme that Heinz Kohut, Margaret Mahler (1975) and other object relation theorists are now addressing. Coming from a diverse background and a different perspective, their theories, based on empirical observation (Kohut with adults and Mahler with children) are converging on an important and crucial understanding of the human condition. Can I be close to another without losing myself and can I tolerate really being alone? In Kohut's language, how does the individual develop a cohesive self that is authentic and not grandiose or false? We all have basic drive to be loved and respected for what we really are.

This is an important theme in the treatment of addiction. Many alcoholics and addicts feel at their core that they are unworthy or defective in some way. Their chemical use is a way to combat their feelings of worthlessness and contributes to their false-self formation. Their grandiosity and self-centeredness is a defensive facade used to combat their feelings of fragmentation and incompleteness. Our worst fear (addicts and alcoholics don't have a lack of this type of trepidation) is to be rejected and unloved if we are real with another human being. Within this perspective, Martin Buber, the object-relation theorists, and Alcoholics Anonymous all have the same common goals of cure and treatment. The addict and alcoholic has to become real and authentic. They must learn that they will not be rejected or unloved just because of who and what they are. Eventually, they must come to realize it is their behavior and actions which lead them to be rejected and uncared for. Once they realize what it is that they are doing that alienates others, they must change their behavior accordingly. Finally, they must recognize they are separate, alone and responsible for their condition and position in life. It is through this process of awareness and the establishment of healthy relationships that their structural and character deficits can be alleviated.

For better or worse, psychoanalytic and psychodynamic theory is the most influential and comprehensive theory of human psychological development and functioning which has been formulated to date. The change in focus from an intrapsychic model to an interpersonal model is significantly important. Such a shift in perspective has allowed the development of a theory of psychological functioning which explains more completely how similar developmental processes contribute to a wide range of diverse symptomatology. Within this perspective, all addictions (drugs, foods, gambling, sex, etc.) can be seen as relating to a characterological deficit of the self (character defects, poor impulse control, grandiosity, self-centeredness, etc). Such a theory has important implications for the professional working with the chemically dependent individual and can help the group leader make sense out of what was heretofore a seemingly unrelated collage of separated events in the addict's and alcoholic's life.

Kohut summarizes his position with a preface he wrote to a recent NIDA research monograph (1977 pps. vii-ix).

The explanatory power of the new psychology of the self is nowhere as evident as with regard to these four types of psychological disturbance: (1) the narcissistic personality disorders, (2) the perversions, (3) the delinquencies, and (4) the addictions. Why can these seemingly disparate conditions be examined so fruitfully with the aid of the same conceptual framework? Why can all these widely differing and even contrasting symptom pictures be comprehended when seen from the viewpoint of the psychology of the self? How, in other words, are these four conditions related to each other? What do they have in common, despite the fact that they exhibit widely differing, and even contrasting, symptomatologies? The answer to these questions is simple: in all of these disorders the afflicted individual suffers from a central weakness, from a weakness in the core of his personality. He suffers from the consequences of a defect in the self. The symptoms of these disorders, whether comparatively hazy or hidden, or whether more distinct and conspicuous, arise secondarily as an outgrowth of a defect in the self. The manifestations of these disorders become intelligible if we call to mind that they are all attempts — unsuccessful attempts, it must be stressed — to remedy the central defect in the personality.

The narcissistically disturbed individual yearns for praise and approval or for a merger with an idealized supportive other because he cannot sufficiently supply himself with self-approval or with a sense of strength through his own inner resources. The pervert is driven toward sexual enactments with figures or symbols that give him the feeling of being wanted, real, alive or powerful. The delinquent repeats over and over again certain acts through which he demonstrates to himself an escape from the realization that he feels devoid of sustaining self-confidence and of sustaining ideals. And . . . . the addict, finally, craves the drug because the drug seems to him to be capable of curing the central defect in his self. It becomes for him the substitute for a self-object which failed him traumatically at a time when he should still have had the feeling of omnipotently controlling its responses in accordance with his needs as if it were a part of himself. By ingesting the drug he symbolically compels the mirroring self-object to soothe him, to accept him. Or he symbolically compels the idealized self-object to submit to his merging into it and thus to his partaking in its magical power. In either case the ingestion of the drug provides him with the self-esteem which he does not possess.

Through the incorporation of the drug he supplies for himself the feeling of being accepted and thus of being self-confident; or he creates the experience of being merged with a source of power that gives him the feeling of being strong and worthwhile. And all these effects of the drug tend to increase his feeling of being alive, tend to increase his certainty that he exists in this world.

Kohut sees the source of addictions tied into the child's early experiences. However, he makes an important distinction between cause and cure. In the end, Kohut stresses the importance of the child's early relationships in determining both the cause and treatment of addiction.

> It is the tragedy of all these attempts at self-cure that the solutions which they provide are impermanent, that in essence they cannot succeed. . . . Whatever the chemical nature of the substance that is employed, however frequently repeated its consumption, however, cleverly rationalized or mythologized its ingestion with the support from others who are similarly afflicted—no psychic structure is built, the defect in the self remains. It is as if a person with a wide open gastric fistula were trying to still his hunger through eating. He may obtain pleasurable taste sensations by his frantic ingestion of food but, since the food does not enter that part of the digestive system where it is absorbed into the organism, he continues to starve. . . . Thus, in asking the crucial questions concerning the factors in childhood which lead to the addiction-prone personality, we will say that, in the last analysis, and within certain limits, it is less important to determine what the parents do than what they *are*.

If one is to truly understand the implications of object relations theory, one must understand the contributions of three contributing figures: Margaret Mahler (1975), Otto Kernberg (1975) and Henry Kohut (1977). Mahler is most noted for her work with the psychological development of normal children. Kernberg has contributed most to the understanding of borderline personality organization. Kohut is almost exclusively aligned with the understanding and explanation of the narcissistic personality disorder. Each has an important contribution to make in the understanding of the addictive behaviors and all three are not always in complete agreement about specific disturbances. For instance, Kernberg sees many, if not all, narcissistic disorders as having a borderline personality organization. Kohut, on the other hand, views borderline pathology as a result of severe narcissistic injuries caused by an unempathic and uncaring other. What often appears as severe borderline reactions and demands is actually the iatrogenic effects of an unempathic self-

Philip J. Flores

object. Mahler avoids such controversy and insists she is just describing what she observes empirically.

MARGARET MAHLER'S THEORY OF NORMAL DEVELOPMENT

Mahler, after having spent most of her professional career studying severely disturbed children, turned her energies to the investigation of normal children and their mothers at the Masters Children Center in New York. Beginning in 1959, she and her colleagues set up an observation room where groups of children and their mothers could be watched as they interacted with one another, played with toys, or experimented with their opportunities for separation from mother. Children from four months old through four years old were participants with their mothers in the study.

From the mass of data gathered over the years, Mahler began to construct a picture of the normal sequence of stages in the process of becoming a person. In essence, Mahler was studying the phenomena of the psychological birth of the child. Her work was placed in an object-relations point of view which stressed the ego's primary object-seeking qualities. This is in contrast to traditional instinct theory in which objects are sought not primarily because of their relationship potential, but for the purpose of drive reduction. Mahler's work focused on the internalization of interpersonal relationships. She was concerned how interpersonal relations determine intrapsychic structures and how these intrapsychic structures preserve, modify and reactivate past relations. The implications which these internalized relations have in the development of psychic structure and addiction will be explored later in this chapter. First, an overview of Mahler's stages of normal development and a defining of terms important to her theory will be presented.

Ego Psychology and Object Relations Theory

Before one can truly understand Mahler, one must understand her relationship to object-relations theory and Ego psychology. The concept of the ego is an especially confusing one for those familiar only with Alcoholics Anonymous and the way its members apply the term in discussing one's recovery or lack of it. Within AA, ego is commonly used in the popular sense to indicate an individual who is self-centered and has an inflated sense of their self-worth. Freud's original use of the word ego had far different implications and the Ego Psychologists have applied this term in its intended technical meaning to explain that part of the psyche which serves the executive functioning (i.e., reasoning, decisions, defensive operations, etc.) of the personality. Henry Tiebout, an important historic figure from AA's perspective because he was one of the few psychiatrists who was an early supporter of AA and was also a friend and psychotherapist to AA's founder, Bill Wilson, struggled with differentiating the two different definitions that this term carried.

> This popular view of ego, while it may not have scientific foundation, has one decided value: it possesses a meaning and can convey a concept which the average person can grasp. This concept of the inflated ego recognized the common ancestor of a whole series of traits, namely, that they are all manifestations of an underlying feeling state in which personal considerations are first and foremost.
>
> The existence of this ego has long been recognized, but a difficulty in terminology still remains. Part of the difficulty arises from the use of the word ego, in psychiatric and psychological circles, to designate those elements of the psyche which are supposed to rule psychic life. Freud divided mental life into three major subdivisions: the id, the ego and the superego. The first, he stated, contains the feeling life on a deep, instinctual level; the third is occupied by the conscience, whose function is to put brakes on the impulses arising within the id. The ego should act as mediator between the demands of the id and the restraints of the superego, which might be over-zealous and bigoted. Freud's own research was concerned mainly with the activities of the id and the superego. The void he left with respect to the ego is one that his followers are endeavoring to fill, but as yet with no generally accepted conclusions. (1954, p. 4)

Ego-Psychologists, starting with Harry Stack Sullivan (Yalom's unacknowledged mentor) have placed more of an emphasis on the individual's interpersonal relationships. Object-relation theorists have taken the work of the Ego-Psychologist and sought to understand how the individual's external functioning was a representation of their internal perceptions and distortions.

> If, for example, an individual's repertoire of object representa-
> tions is simply and primitively organized and contains a view
> of others either as all-giving or maliciously and sadistically
> withholding (what others have termed need-satisfying object
> relations), then the behavior of others will be selectively per-
> ceived and organized to yield only such behavior as includes
> these two primitive and extreme experiences. In contrast, if
> these internal "images" comprehend many aspects of others,
> including their empathy, intelligence, sense of humor, mo-
> tives, etc., then there is within that person the potential for a
> much more differentiated and subtle experience of others
> (what has been termed object consistency). (p. 300)

If an individual has external difficulties in their relationship with
others, it has been questioned whether these difficulties are related
to their internal mentalistic distortions. Object relations theory is
therefore a mentalistic psychology aimed at answering this question. It is more interested in looking at the inner life of people. The
term object is a technical one which signifies an individual's ability
to carry around an accurate mental representation of another person
in their mind, even when that person is out of sight. This ability to
develop object constancy and have accurate undistorted mental representations of others is an important developmental task that not
everyone is able to obtain. Mahler sought to understand the source
of these distortions and the relationship between developmental arrest and object constancy. Her investigation into these issues lead
her to trace the origin of the ego or the self as it related to the early
maternal relationship. Mahler provides an important view of what
happens to the individual's psyche under the impact of personal
relations in "real life." Kernberg sums up the implications of
Mahler's work when he describes object relations theory.

> What is object-relations theory? In essence, it is the psy-
> choanalytic approach to the internalization of interpersonal re-
> lations, the study of how interpersonal relations determines
> intrapsychic structures, and how these intrapsychic structures
> preserve, modify, and reactivate past internalized relations
> with others in the context of present interpersonal relations.
> Object-relations theory deals with the interactions between the
> internal world of objects (the internalized relations with oth-

ers) and the actual interpersonal relations of the individual. (Kernberg, 1970, p. 1)

Many years earlier, Fyodor Dostoyevsky intuitively grasped and elegantly described this concept.

> You must know that there is nothing higher and stronger and more wholesome and good for life in the future than some good memory, especially a memory of childhood, of home. People talk to you a great deal about your education, but some good sacred memory, preserved from childhood, is perhaps the best education. If a man carries many such memories with him into life, he is safe to the end of his days. And if one has only one good memory left in one's heart, even that may sometime be the means of saving him. Perhaps we may grow wicked later on, may be unstable to refrain from evil, may laugh at men's tears and at those people who say as Kolya did just now: "I want to suffer for all men." We may even jeer spitefully at such people. But however bad we may become — which God forbid — yet, when we recall how we buried Ilusha, how we loved him in his last days, and how we have been talking like friends together, at this stone, the cruelest and most mocking of us — if we do become so — will not dare to laugh inwardly at having been kind and good at this moment! What's more, perhaps, that one memory may keep us from great evil and we will reflect and say: "Yes, I was good and brave and honest then!" (1957)

Freud also alluded to this when he stated, "A man who has been the indisputable favorite of his mother keeps for life the feeling of a conqueror, that confidence of success that often induces real success" (p. 19).

To understand completely the development of internal representations, it is important to grasp the meaning of Mahler's work. It also helps to understand Piaget's research which focused on the stages of cognitive development in children (Piaget, 1954). Piaget parallels Mahler in that he sees object constancy as an important stage in a developmental process. Place a ball in front of a six-month-old child and cover the ball with a blanket and the ball will no longer exist for the infant. Out of sight, out of existence. Pull the blanket away from over the ball and behold, the infant is amazed at the magical appearance of an object that just seconds prior had not existed. Piaget discovered that it is only later in the child's cognitive development that the infant is able to keep a mental representation of the ball even when it is covered by the blanket. The developmentally advanced infant will then search underneath the blanket for the ball knowing that even though the ball is out of sight, it still exists. The principle is the same for infants in their relationships with significant care-givers in their life. The child's ability to realize that mother still exists even though mother is out of the room suggests an important stage of object constancy and, in Erik Erikson's terminology, a stage of basic trust has been achieved.

A couple of examples will help clarify this point.

> Once while a friend was visiting our home, my son and myself were in the living room with this woman as my wife had gone to the kitchen in search of some refreshments. The visitor was an older woman who had been a friend of the family for years. Though uneducated and unsophisticated, she was one of these solid no-nonsense ladies who had been reared in the rural hills of southern Kentucky. My son who was two years old at the time was busy playing on the living room rug and had not noticed my wife's departure into the kitchen. In the process of searching for something in the kitchen, my wife quickly walked into the adjoining garage allowing the screen door to slam behind her. My son, startled briefly by the noise, looked up from his toys, noticed his mother had left the house and quickly returned to his play, unconcerned about her absence. His reaction prompted this very stoic lady to firmly announce "That's a good boy!" Somewhat surprised by the suddenness of her compliment, I thanked her before I asked what had prompted her statement. She replied "He didn't cry when his mother left the room. He's a good boy!"

Unknown to this woman, my son had not reacted in fright because he had developed object constancy. His mother could leave the room and although she was out of sight, she would continue to exist for him because he was developmentally able to carry around a stable mental representation of her in his head.

> Once while working as a psychology intern in a University Hospital outpatient clinic, I was assigned to provide psycho-

therapy to a woman who had a history of multiple psychiatric hospitalizations and numerous different diagnostic labels of which borderline personality disorder was one used most frequently. After approximately ten sessions, the woman gradually began to experience increased anxiety as the time of our weekly session neared its end. She would begin the session without discomfort, only to have her fears mount as she prepared to leave my office. Her anxiety increased to the point that she would feel compelled to call me by the time she had reached the lobby of the hospital seven floors below my office. Each phone call would result in the same expressed concern, "Are you all right, I just became overwhelmed as I rode down the elevator thinking that something terrible had happened to you." Once assured that indeed I was all right and that I was still here, she would quickly compose herself until the next week when she would repeat the same procedure upon leaving my office.

This 35-year-old woman, unlike my two-year-old son, was developmentally arrested and had not obtained object constancy. While my son felt little panic and fear when his mother left his sight because he had successfully negotiated an important developmental stage, this woman was unable to carry a mental representation of me in her head once I was out of sight and consequently became overwhelmed by her fears that an important object in her life had been lost. Her anxiety was triggered by the thought of leaving my presence and increased to the unmanageable point that she had to telephone me to be assured I still existed. A steady and calm assurance from me was enough to quickly soothe her sense of inner turmoil and fragmentation.

These two presentations represent two extreme conditions which may manifest as a result of interference in a child's developmental process. Before one can understand the implications that alcohol and drug use has in relation to an individual's developmental fixation, one must understand the different stages of normal development. Horner (1979) describes this process,

Psychological health and psychopathology can both be understood in terms of the vicissitudes of object relations development and its associated organizing and integrating impact. This developmental sequence begins with the stage of normal

autism at birth and proceeds through the process of attachment
to the stage of normal symbiosis, which is symbolized by the
undifferentiated self-object representation. From this point the
child faces the developmental tasks of the separation-individuation process. This process is subdivided into the subphases
of hatching, the practicing period, and the rapprochement subphase, and it culminates in the achievement of identity and
object constancy. At this point the child, and thus the adult he
will become, has a firm sense of self and differentiated other,
is able to relate to others as whole persons rather than just as
need satisfiers, and can tolerate ambivalence without having to
maintain a split between good and bad object-representations
with its parallel split between good and bad self-representations. He also has the ability to sustain his or her own narcissistic equilibrium or good self-feeling from resources within
the self, which are the outcome of the achievement of libidinal
object constancy that comes about through the transmuting internalization of maternal functions into the self. (Horner,
1979, p. 25)

For those unfamiliar with object-relations terminology, Horner's
statement can be confusing and initially difficult to comprehend.
Mahler's stages of normal development will be thoroughly presented so one can grasp the full implications of Horner's statement.

MAHLER'S STAGES OF NORMAL DEVELOPMENT

Mahler constructed a theoretical picture of the normal stages of
development in the process of the child acquiring object constancy
and thus achieving a formation of a stable self-concept or a cohesive
self. For the process to be completed, it requires two early forerunner phases, normal autism and normal symbiosis, in which the
mother and infant mutually lay the foundation for the child's psychological birth or hatching. Four subsequent stages of the separation individuation process are required and climaxes at or near the
end of the third year of life. (See Figure 1.)

Stage I: Two Forerunner Phases — Attachment

1. Normal Autism - (0-1 month)
2. Normal Symbiosis - (1-4 months)

Stage II: Three Sub-Phases of Separation
Individuation — Hatching

    1. Differentiation (5-9 months)
    2. Practicing (10-15 months)
    3. Rapprochement (15-24 months)

Stage III: Fourth Sub-Phase — Object Constancy

    1. Consolidation of Self & Identity

Stage I: Normal Autism

During the first month of life, the infant is encapsulated in a psychic orbit which serves as a stimulus barrier protecting the child from excessive outside intrusions. In effect, the autistic shell serves as a stimulus barrier and protects the infant against extreme stimulation or excessive environmental demands. The child has a relative disinterest in external reality because the infant's physiological developmental limitations restricts their psychological investment in the environment. This stage of normal autism differs from secondary autism where the child seems from birth unable to utilize their mothers as auxiliary egos; that is, they show no interest in relating to mother, or to any person. Mahler describes the true autistic child as having:

> an obsessive desire for the preservation of sameness; a stereotyped preoccupation with a few inanimate objects or action patterns toward which he shows the only signs of emotional attachment. As a consequence, he shows utter intolerance of any change in his inanimate surroundings . . . The primarily autistic child differs from the organic, as well as from the predominantly symbiotic psychotic child, by his seemingly self-sufficient contentedness — *if only he is left alone*. These autistic children behave like omnipotent magicians if they are permitted to live within, and thus to command, their static and greatly constricted segment of inanimate environment. (Mahler, 1968, p. 68)

Horner (1976) differentiates the early development process of attachment in a normal child from that of the autistic child when she writes,

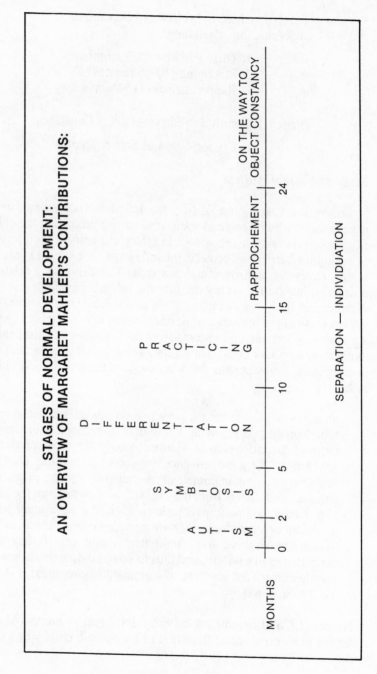

FIGURE I

**STAGES OF NORMAL DEVELOPMENT:
AN OVERVIEW OF MARGARET MAHLER'S CONTRIBUTIONS:**

SEPARATION — INDIVIDUATION

At birth the child is in a state of what Mahler refers to as normal autism. Kohut (1977) who thinks in terms of the evolution of a cohesive self-structure, calls this same period the stage of the fragmented self. Mahler sees constitutional factors operating in childhood autism and comments on the fact that there is no anticipatory posture at nursing, no reaching out gestures, and no specific smiling response. What is lacking is attachment-seeking behavior, and thus the mother/child matrix that fosters ego development is nonexistent. Defensive or compensatory structure (Kohut, 1977) may allow for a higher level of functioning, but their failure would throw the individual back upon the core pathology.

The autistic infant remains fixated at this earliest stage of life and makes no move toward attachment. There is no anticipatory posturing at nursing, no reaching out gestures and no specific smiling responses. What is lacking is attachment-seeking behavior which prevents the establishment of a mother-child matrix that usually fosters the infant's ego development. In situations where the environment is grossly pathological, disrupting the infant's basic organizational process, it is possible to force a retreat into secondary autism, although Mahler recognizes that constitutional factors play a far more important part in this process.

Normal Symbiosis—Attachment

By the second month of life, the infant begins to become dimly aware of the mother as an external object. The infant begins to develop memory traces of the mother's face. The recognition of her face, based on past pleasant experiences, leads to a basic trust that relief of tension will regularly occur in her presence. However, the infant behaves as though he and his mother were a dual unity within a common boundary. From the infant's point of view there are really no boundaries between himself and his mother. They are one. At the height of this joyous period of his life, they are encapsulated in a symbiotic orbit. He cannot really comprehend that he and his mother are separate beings. The infant, through the process of attachment to a primary object, remains encapsulated in a symbiotic orbit. The infant also cannot differentiate between his own tension-reducing efforts and the mother's efforts made on his behalf. During these early months he internalizes his mother and uses her as a

Philip J. Flores

"beacon of orientation," engendering a basic sense of security, safety, and trust. The crude differentiation between object and self, good and bad, pleasure and pain allows the symbiotic child to deal with painful experiences in the only way his limited cognitive defenses permit, by splitting the good and the bad, and projecting the bad outside of the symbiotic partnership. The primitive defensive process of splitting becomes critical in understanding the character pathology present in the adult borderline patient and will be explored in depth later in the chapter.

Crucial to this developmental phase is the infant's ability to attach itself to an external object. Horner describes the ramifications of the infant's inability to bond with another:

> At the most primitive level, failure of attachment may carry with it severe deficits in the early organization of the self. The failure to develop attachment and to achieve a satisfactory symbiosis because of environmental factors, such as institutionalization, may lead to the development of characteristic disturbances such as the inability to keep rules, lack of capacity to experience guilt, and indiscriminate friendliness with an inordinate craving for affection with no ability to make lasting relationships. The "affectionless psychopath" is also characterized by the failure to develop the affectional bond that goes with attachment.
>
> Another form of pathological attachment is attachment through the false-self organization. In this situation the real, core self has remained in a nonattached, non-object-related state. (Horner, 1979, pp. 28-29)

During the first five or six months of life, in the developmentally healthy child, there is innate attachment-seeking behavior to bring about a normal symbiosis. The earliest mental representations of self and object, the undifferentiated self-object representation or schema is characteristic of this stage. There is neither physical nor psychic differentiation. This brings us to the heart of Mahler's developmental work. Important during this time is the mutual selection of cues by mother and infant. Mahler writes:

> We observed that infants present a larger variety of cues to indicate needs, tension, and pleasure. In a complex manner the mother responds selectively to only certain of these clues. (p. 18, 1979)

Mahler points out that this mutual cuing creates the complex pattern that becomes what Lichtenstein (1961) refers to as "the infant's becoming the child of his particular mother."

Bowlby (1958) emphasizes the degree to which an infant himself plays a part in determining his own environment. Certain kinds of babies who tend to be overreactive or unpredictable make it difficult for the mother to provide good enough mothering. But mother is supposed to have a much larger role than the infant by the end of the first year in the determination of the quantity as well as the quality of the transactions that occur between them.

The failure of attachment carries several deficits in the early organization of the self. There is a delicate and subtle interplay between constitutional and environmental factors which determine how this disturbance will manifest. Mahler and Horner have outlined this process in clear detail and their schema will be briefly outlined.

1. The affectionless psychopath is characterized by the failure to develop the affectional bond that goes with attachment.
2. Disruption of attachment due to separation and loss may lead to a lifelong schizoid detachment. In this case, detachment is used as a defense against frightening impact of object relatedness.
3. Another form of pathological attachment is attachment through the fake-self organization leading to narcissistic personality structure.

Stage II: Separation-Individuation Sub-Phases

1. Differentiation

As strong as the child's yearnings for attachment are, the infant gradually begins to experience even more powerful urges to move away from mother, to separate, and to explore. At four or five months, the infant begins to recognize that the mother who soothes, feeds, and reduces tension is separate. This is the beginning of the "hatching process." Hatching is the start of the infant's psychological birth and marks the beginning of the child's emergence as a separate individual free from the symbiotic attachment to a maternal object.

Failure to negotiate this developmental process results in an adult who becomes disorganized and suffers dissolution of the self when faced with object loss. The individual is unable to differentiate inner experiences from outer experiences leading to confusion regarding what is me and what is not me. In the extreme cases, internal stimuli become confused with external reality resulting in hallucinations and delusions. The enmeshed family, which is a breeding ground for schizophrenia, is an excellent example of the child's failure to separate from the parent's intrusiveness. The mother who sits in the therapist's office with her child and tells her daughter, "It's chilly in here, I feel cold, put on your sweater," is a clear indication of a family system where boundaries are not clearly set and separation of feelings are not individually maintained.

2. Practicing

From approximately ten to fifteen months, the child's focus shifts from the mother to their own autonomous functioning. Locomotion, perception and learning become self-motivated. Ego functioning, reality testing, secondary thought process and frustration tolerance leaves a child with less reliance on external objects and the toddler begins to develop more self-reliance and autonomy. The practicing subphase shifts into high gear when the child begins to walk upright near the ages of 10 to 12 months. Now the child is truly physically independent, free to roam widely and proudly.

> Expanding locomotor capacity during the early practicing subphase widens the child's world; not only does he have a more active role in determining closeness and distance to mother, but the modalities that up to now were used to explore the relatively familiar environment suddenly expose him to a wider segment of reality; there is more to see, more to hear, more to touch. (Mahler et al., 1975, p. 66)

Towards the end of this subphase, the child begins to experience an inflated sense of omnipotence which is augmented by the toddler's feelings of his own magical power. He can stand, walk, climb, jump, and even speak. He truly believes he is the center of the universe! There is no stopping him now! Encouraged by his rapid, often spectacular growth in the last few months, the child is led to believe that the world is truly his oyster. Normal grandiosity and primary narcissism are healthy stage-specific developmental phases in the child's development. However, this inflated, omnipotent representation is the nucleus of the grandiose self which can be manifested as extreme self-centeredness or pathological narcissism in adult life if the child's developmental process is impaired by unavailable, intrusive, or uncaring self-objects.

Horner sees the development of a grandiose self as a result of difficulties experienced at the practicing stage of development. Horner writes:

> This inflated, omnipotent self-object representation is the nucleus of the grandiose self which obtains in cases of pathological narcissism, be it with the borderline patient or with the narcissistic personality disorder. Problems of subsequent development are related to the extent to which significant aspects of self are assimilated into the grandiose self structure and thus not available for conflict-free functioning or are otherwise kept out of the mainstream of normal maturation.
>
> When the autonomous functions are assimilated into a pathological grandiose self-structure, they are not available for achievements in reality that contribute to a healthy, reality-based self-esteem.
>
> The grandiose self may be a manifestation of structural pathology from this point of early development, or it may be recalled as a defense mechanism against the dangers of loss of self-esteem in a more evolved character. (Horner, 1979, p. 32)

Anyone working with alcoholics and addicts knows that self-centeredness and grandiosity are important treatment considerations. The implications which Mahler's research has for the treatment of the alcoholic and addict will be explored at length later in this chapter.

3. Rapprochement

Towards the end of the toddler's practicing subphase, he becomes increasingly aware of his separateness from his mother and her separateness from him. At this time, the child is just beginning to confront the crisis of his second birth. While at the height of his omnipotent grandiosity, the young toddler bolts from his house in all his glory and speeds down the driveway to conquer his world and unexpectedly trips, tumbles forward, and scratches his knee. Suddenly, he is made acutely aware of his vulnerability and powerlessness, and invariably, will face disillusionment. His knee hurts and bleeds. To make matters worse, mother is nowhere in sight. The 18-to-24-month-old child is beginning to experience the rapprochement crisis.

He becomes distressed by the acute awareness of his separateness and helplessness. Frustrations persist in his mind and aggression becomes internalized. His experiences with reality have counteracted his overestimation of omnipotence. His self-esteem starts to be deflated and he is now vulnerable to shame. As he becomes acutely aware of his limitations, he undergoes a cognitive and affective decentering process. This occurs at a time when cognitive, motor, and emotional development bring about an awareness of the self that leads him to realize that causes and events exist outside of himself, independent of his needs and wishes. He suffers a loss of omnipotence and wishes to return to the safety of his mother.

The rapprochement phase becomes a period of contradictions. As the child becomes aware of his separateness, he develops strategies for preventing this awareness and maintaining close contact. Darting away behavior becomes pronounced as the child wishes reunion with the love object, but fears engulfment at the same time. The child's ambivalence about closeness and dependency is equally frustrating for the parent. The child has entered "the terrible twos" that all parents dread and bemoan. As one mother complained,

> I don't know what to do with that little bastard! He used to be happy away from me. Now, he cries for my attention and when I pick him up, he pushes me away. I don't know what he wants!

In developmental terms, the child is trying to assert his separateness and his selfhood. He may not know what he wants when he says "no," but he knows by saying "no" that he is separate from mother. There will be confusion on the mother's part, as she tries to understand the child's frustration during this developmental process. This leads to a re-emergence of the child's difficulty tolerating aggression in himself and others.

Monte summarizes the ramifications which this conflict poses for the child,

> From the viewpoint of ego development, the rapprochement phase may be crucial to the child's ability to internalize con-

flict and to reconcile clashes between an "all good" mother and an "all bad" one. The good mother is the person who has provided all pleasures, all securities, all warmth, and all companionship. In the symbiotic phase, this "good love object" was viewed as a part of self. But now the child's growing psychological sophistication confronts a serious conflict. Mothers unavoidably have their dark sides. Sometimes mother is a need-frustrator, or a pain-inflicter, or an indifferent and distracted caretaker, or, most painful of all her shortcomings, mother is sometimes absent altogether. For the child's newly developing ego, the "good mother" and the "bad mother" cannot be one and the same love object. She, who was once so long ago a part of me, cannot be bad; yet, undeniably, mother is not *always* good. If the good mother and the bad mother *are* one person, then I, too, must harbor some bad within me. That is not possible, for I am all good.

Termed *"splitting"* of the ego, the rapprochement child may employ the defense mechanism of dealing with such contradictory love objects by treating them in all-or-none fashion. Thus, mother cannot be both good and bad simultaneously. There is a good mother, and there is a bad mother. The good mother is the love object that was internalized as part of the child's own narcissistic ego during symbiosis. The bad mother is externalized, projected to the outside world, outside me, where all pain-producing, threatening objects belong. (Monte, 1980, pp. 211-212)

Figure II outlines this development process and the difficulties which may emerge in the defensive operation of splitting.

As described by Kaplan, object constancy involves the emotional acceptance of the idea that we are neither saints nor demons but whole people capable of both love and hate. By being able to unite or integrate such polar feelings the individual confirms his sense of personal wholeness. When object constancy is weak, the only way to protect the good, cherished part of the self from the negative or undesirable aspects of the self is to force or split this off. As a result, it becomes impossible to appreciate the wholeness of the self or another. The person will simply get rid of someone like an unwanted object if the person disappoints him. He will also fail to see the person's history of goodness and will only be able to recall the badness of the latest experience.

FIGURE II

SELF OBJECT DEVELOPMENT

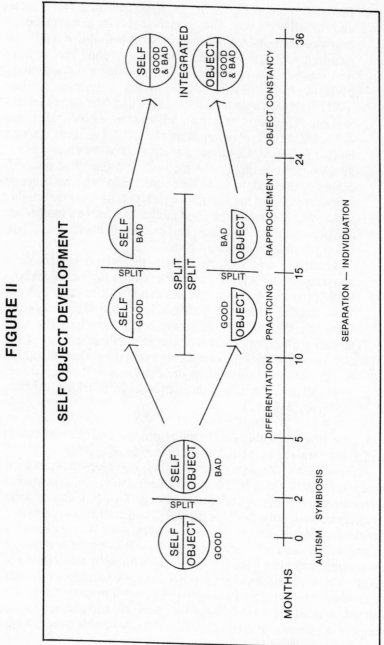

As the child resolves the rapprochement crisis with the help of a "good enough mother," he begins to divest himself of his omnipotence without undue anxiety or shame and integrates goodness and badness into an integrated whole. The child enters the last stage of object constancy, identity integration and the development of a cohesive self.

Mahler writes:

> By the eighteenth month, the junior toddler seems to be at the height of the process of dealing with his continuously experienced physical separateness from the mother. This coincides with his cognitive and perceptual achievement of the permanence of objects, in Piaget's sense. This is the time when his sensorimotor intelligence starts to develop into true representational intelligence, and when the important process of internalization, in Harmann's sense—very gradually, through ego identifications—begins. (Mahler, 1968, p. 21)

Stage III: Object Constancy

Toward the end of the second year, and extending through the third year of life, the child is able to achieve a fair degree of emotional object constancy. Three major tasks are achieved.

1. Internally and mentally, such children are able to maintain an image of mother even when she is not present. This sense of well-being comes from having internalized the good-enough mother and good self-experiences. The child can hold onto these positive images and function as a separate self, even if angry, frustrated, and alone.
2. Separation and Individuation is achieved. Kohut, who thinks in terms of a cohesive self-structure refers to this as a nuclear self is established. Kernberg sees this as a process through which identity integration is attained. Buber describes this as the development of a separate I that is needed before a person is able to engage in an I-Thou relationship. The false self organization or "as if personality" of Winnicott would not prevail. In Satre's language, an authentic self is established.
3. There is an enduring development of psychic structure. The final shift to well-secured separate identity insures the capacity

to regulate one's narcissistic equilibrium from the sources within one's self. In Kohut's language, transmuting internalization is obtained. The individual is able to calm and soothe oneself. He will not have to rely on external self-objects or external sources of gratification (i.e., alcohol, drugs, sex, food, excitement) to ward off painful affective states. Psychic structure has been adequately laid through the assimilation of maternal functions into self-representations. See Figure III.

The following diagram (Figure IV) summarizes the developmental paradigm and is a modification from Horner's earlier presentation (1979).

As presented here, Mahler's research has important implications for understanding the relationship of addiction, development and the establishment of psychic structure. Mahler's work focuses on the developmental and adaptational requirements which a child has to negotiate during their first three years of life. Horner's schema (Figure IV) helps us understand the relationship of this developmental process to psychosis, character disorders and neurosis. Mahler's theory of normal development has been summarized starting with the earliest phases of achieving homeostasis and need satisfying attachment, through subsequent phases of separation, individuation and the capacity for mental representation (i.e., object constancy). Once a child has successfully negotiated these developmental stages, he attains what Kohut calls a cohesive self. Without the attainment of the psychic structure which is laid in the process of developing a cohesive self, there is a much greater risk for both character pathology and addiction.

Khantzian and Treece summarize this position in a statement that directly links structural deficits and addiction. They stress,

> how optimal nurturance from the environment (as primarily represented by the mother) fosters adequate mastery of these phases by the infant, and leads to the development of stable ego structures and capacities to manage drives and object relations. To the extent that the individual is overly deprived or indulged in his/her development, varying degrees of ego impairment occur and drugs then come to substitute and compensate for the developmental defects and impairments. (Khantzian & Treece, 1980, p. 73)

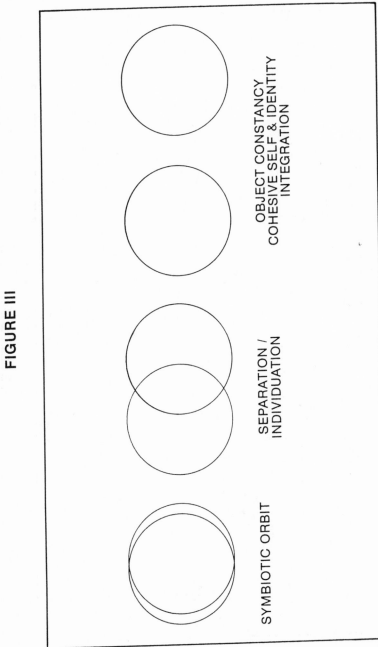

FIGURE III

SYMBIOTIC ORBIT

SEPARATION / INDIVIDUATION

OBJECT CONSTANCY
COHESIVE SELF & IDENTITY
INTEGRATION

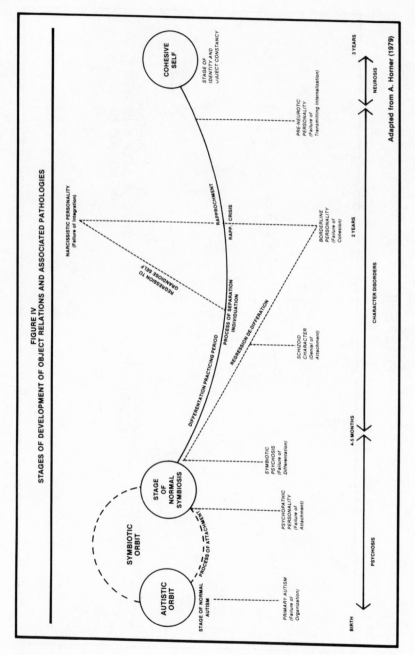

FIGURE IV
STAGES OF DEVELOPMENT OF OBJECT RELATIONS AND ASSOCIATED PATHOLOGIES

COHESIVE SELF

STAGE OF IDENTITY AND OBJECT CONSTANCY

NARCISSISTIC PERSONALITY (Failure of Integration)

RAPPROCHMENT

RAPP. CRISIS

PRE-NEUROTIC PERSONALITY (Failure of Transmitting Internalization)

REGRESSION TO GRANDIOSE SELF

PROCESS OF SEPARATION INDIVIDUATION

DIFFERENTATION PRACTICING PERIOD

REGRESSION DE DIFFERATION

BORDERLINE PERSONALITY (Failure of Cohesion)

SCHIZOID CHARACTER (Denial of Attachment)

STAGE OF NORMAL SYMBIOSIS

SYMBIOTIC ORBIT

SYMBIOTIC PSYCHOSIS (Failure of Differentiation)

PSYCHOPATHIC PERSONALITY (Failure of Attachment)

PROCESS OF ATTACHMENT

AUTISTIC ORBIT

STAGE OF NORMAL AUTISM

PRIMARY AUTISM (Failure of Organization)

BIRTH   PSYCHOSIS   4-5 MONTHS   CHARACTER DISORDERS   2 YEARS   NEUROSIS   3 YEARS

Adapted from A. Horner (1979)

166

Such a position clearly sets drug and alcohol dependence within the range of structural deficits commonly seen in character disorders.

Khantzian sums up this position when he writes,

> Evidence has accumulated over the past two decades documenting a significant relationship between psychopathology and drug dependence. However, the etiologic connection or the relationship between the pathology and addiction has been less clear. Recent advances using standardized diagnostic approaches in psychiatry and a shift in psychoanalysis from a drive or instinct theory to a greater emphasis on adaptation, development and structural (ego and self) factors have provided new findings and perspectives in explaining the relationship between the psychological disturbances, dysfunction and the misuse of drugs.
>
> Although heavy reliance on drugs clearly produces psychological dysfunction and even psychiatric disorders, psychiatric and psychodynamic findings also suggest that substance abusers are predisposed to become dependent on drugs because they suffer with psychiatric disturbances and painful affect states. Their distress and suffering is the consequence of defects in ego and self capacities which leaves such people ill-equipped to regulate and modulate feelings, self-esteem, relationships and behavior. (Khantzian, 1985, p. 1)

Considering the implications which this position advocates, it would be important to investigate Kohut's and Kernberg's descriptions of the narcissistic and borderline personality disorders.

BORDERLINE PERSONALITY ORGANIZATION AND PATHOLOGICAL NARCISSISM

The belief that typical personality traits establish themselves before the development of addiction is not universally accepted. However, Hartocollis (1980) presents evidence that these personality traits will be observed in formerly addicted patients after prolonged abstinence from alcohol, especially if these individuals have not received psychoanalytic treatment. Hartocollis' position is a clear example of the controversy which exists concerning the question whether character pathology is the result or cause of addiction. In all probability, both positions are correct. Certainly, there are addicted individuals who present with a dual diagnosis of character pathology and addiction. There are also those individuals who present as if they were Narcissistic and Borderline because of the stress placed on their psychological system because of their alcohol or drug use. It will be important for the group leader to make a differential diagnosis because such a distinction has important implications for treatment. However, there are shared treatment recommendations which suggest that the way Kernberg advocates treatment of borderline character pathology is very compatible with the treatment regimen recommended by Alcoholics Anonymous and those familiar with the disease concept approach to treatment. These similarities will be explored later in the chapter.

Hartocollis (1980) sums up his position in the following paragraph which emphasizes the deteriorating effect which alcohol and drugs can have on one's psychological functioning.

> . . . alcoholics may for a long time manage to function in an apparently normal way. Narcissistic character traits, obsessive defenses, and a massive use of denial provide such individuals with a protective shield of self-deception, which isolates them from close personal contact with people whom they depend on but cannot trust. They feel empty and angry inside, very much like people with an "as-if personality," but so far as anyone else is concerned they are pleasant and function adequately. Gradually, however, as the cumulative impact of internal and external frustrations undermines the effectiveness of their protective devices, the level of their functioning begins to suffer. And, wishing to maintain their precarious emotional equilibrium, they resort to increasing amounts of alcohol, which has the power to reinforce denial, even though not performance, which continues to deteriorate, exposing further their borderline pathology. (Hartocollis, 1980, p. 99)

The fact that a person is addicted indicates that his primary defenses have been weakened on one level, yet strengthened on another. Drugs and alcohol become a substitute for a person whose basic mental mechanisms have lost their adaptive power. While drugs and alcohol provide temporary relief from psychic pain, its deteriorating chemical effect on the brain results in the use of more

primitive defensive operations like denial, splitting, projective identification, and grandiosity. Secondary defenses are thereby erected
within the context of the repression produced by alcohol and drug
use resulting in superficial, fragile and maladaptive forms of reaction formation and obsessiveness. These defensive operations are
attempts to shield the individual from the intolerant affects produced by loss of self-worth leaving them susceptible to frequent
narcissistic injuries.

Such a developmental process makes the distinction between a
narcissistic and a borderline disorder difficult. This is made more
problematic in that the distinction between the two conditions is not
always clearly defined in the literature. In fact, a borderline patient
for Kernberg is very likely to be viewed as a narcissistic patient by
Kohut. Kernberg believes that a large portion of narcissistic individuals, if not all of them, share the same borderline personality organization.

Kohut, on the other hand, believes that many patients diagnosed
as borderline, are in actuality suffering from a narcissistic disorder
of the self. The frequently sited behavioral pathology (i.e., rage
responses, splitting, projective identification) of a borderline is the
result of narcissistic injuries induced by the therapist's empathic
failures. Before defining the differences between these two disorders, a case illustration might help clarify the importance of assessing the part alcohol and drugs play in an individual presenting character pathology.

Alice was a 35-year-old Caucasian female who had been in
outpatient treatment at a community mental health center for
over five years. She had "worn out" six different therapists
because of her violent outbursts and demanding provocative
behavior. Diagnosed as a Borderline Personality Disorder,
none of the outpatient staff wanted to carry her on their case
load, so they referred her to an outpatient group in which I
served as a co-therapist. As Alice continued to attend her
weekly group sessions, it became clear that her explosive ti-
rades in group and difficulties outside of group usually followed severe or prolonged drinking episodes. Six months into
treatment, I began to point out these patterns in her behavior.
Initially unreceptive to my observations, she gradually began
to respond more favorably after the other group members began to share similar observations. Unable to deny the consen-

sual observation of the group, Alice succumbed to the opinion that she stop drinking and seek treatment for her alcoholism. After completing a thirty-day outpatient treatment program, she returned to the group and continued to attend meetings at Alcoholics Anonymous. The change in her behavior in group was dramatic. She was able to tolerate other member's disagreement and proved receptive to feedback from others for the first time. Where she had reacted to disagreements by vehemently attacking others, she now was able to see alternative viewpoints. Her behavior change was so apparent that staff members who had treated her previously, began to make appreciatory comments about the potent effectiveness of my treatment and group. Little did they realize that her abstinence from alcohol and her involvement in AA allowed her for the first time to tolerate psychological intervention. Being only a graduate student at the time, I enjoyed the notoriety my success produced and did nothing to discourage the staffs attributing her improvement to my therapeutic skills. In actuality, it was the proper diagnosis of her condition which led to the primary condition (alcoholism) being treated appropriately. Instead of committing the frequent error of futilely trying to combat the affective storms produced by her addiction, I required she stop drinking and used the group to reinforce this requirement.

KERNBERG'S BORDERLINE PATHOLOGY

Both Kohut and Kernberg have elaborated on how disturbances in early child development, especially around nurturance and dependency needs, lead to lack of identity integration and the development of a cohesive self. Although both have indicated that narcissistic and borderline pathology predisposes certain individuals to addiction, neither has systematically explored the relationship to addiction. Before that is attempted, a description of the borderline personality characteristics will be presented.

The DSM III lists criteria for the diagnosis of a borderline personality disorder. If five of these eight features are present, chances are strong that the individual may be suffering from the character pathology which Kernberg describes. It will also be important to discern whether these characteristics are the result of prolonged and excessive alcohol or drug use. Certainly anyone who has worked with alcoholics on a sustained basis will recognize these traits in most, if not all alcoholics, when they are acutely intoxicated. A schema (EASY, P.S.) will be presented to help the group therapist understand these diverse characterological features.

1. *E.* Emptiness and Boredom; especially as these feelings relate to self and the lack of clear values and goals in life.
2. *A.* Affective Instability; especially in relation to mood swings, impulsivity and unpredictability.
3. *A.* Anger; especially in the expression of intense anger and rage responses.
4. *S.* Stable Instability; especially in their interpersonal relationships which are marked by a consistent history of intense, unstable relationships.
5. *S.* Self-Destructive; triggered by p found self-loathing and self-punitive superego development resulting in self-injurious behavior (i.e., suicide attempts, self-inflicted wounds, etc.).
6. *I.* Identity Confusion and Diffusion; a lack of identity integration.
7. *I.* Impulsivity; especially in relation to acting out and alcohol and drug use.
8. *I.* Intolerance of Being Alone;
9. *P.* Psychotic Symptoms; capable of experiencing micro-psychotic episodes from which they will quickly re-compensate.
10. *S.* Superficial Adaptation; ability to relate on a superficial and social level.

Because many of these features and defenses are similar to the lower level defenses and features commonly seen in active alcoholics and addicts, many addicted individuals may be considered borderline, particularly in the way they respond to traditional psychotherapy. Most therapists from an object-relations viewpoint would fail to appreciate the impact that alcohol and drugs place on an addicted individual's behavior and would concentrate on the borderline personality organization in their treatment. Certainly in many cases, these issues have to be addressed. However, the chances of successful intervention are enhanced if abstinence can be obtained.

Kernberg has specific suggestions for the treatment of borderline pathology that are significantly important because his approach does not conflict with that of AA's. Specifically, Kernberg recommends supportive psychotherapy over insight-oriented psychoanalytic or psychoanalysis. His suggestions are especially germane if they are applied after the alcoholic or addict has stopped their use of chemicals.

KERNBERG'S DESCRIPTION
OF SUPPORTIVE PSYCHOTHERAPY

Kernberg says supportive psychotherapy is preferred with borderline patients because they have such distorted images of others and do not possess a clear identity of their self (identity confusion). Their object relations are extremely poor and they have a tendency to split others into all good and all bad objects. They also cannot handle the regression which is produced by technical neutrality. Consequently, they require an active therapist who is going to confront and clarify their behavior (Kernberg, 1984).

Supportive psychotherapy has been criticized in the past because it has not been clearly defined. Many professionals look upon it as "Hertz rent a friend." Kernberg is well aware of this criticism and has outlined a treatment process which requires three components in its application.

1. Clarification and Confrontation
2. Support-containing both:

   A) Affective components
   B) Cognitive components

3. Environmental intervention

Clarification and Confrontation. Psychotherapy with the borderline patient requires an active therapist who will continually point out contradictions in the patient's behavior; especially differences between what the patient says and what the patient does. Little emphasis should be placed on the patient's past until the reality of the present is firmly established. Confrontation, however, does not mean angrily attacking the borderline patient in a demeaning and critical fashion since this will only narcissistically injure him and evoke primitive feelings of infantile rage. Rather, the contradictions in the patient's behavioral presentation must be clearly and firmly pointed out to him in a noncritical and supportive manner. The observed contradictions have to be kept in the present because these patients have so much difficulty differentiating the past from the present. Before the past can be realistically explored, the present must first be made clear to them. Premature confrontations about the past will only lead to increased defensive distortions because it activates the patient's unresolved anger at injustices done to him in the past and raises fears that he will once again be disliked and rejected. Kernberg gives an excellent example of the detrimental consequences of premature confrontation with a borderline patient.

> In the third session, the patient complained that Kernberg was angry, sadistic and controlling of him. At this juncture, Kernberg pointed out that the patient was describing him in the same terms and perceiving him in the same way that the patient had described his mother, namely as angry, bitter and unloving. "Could it be", Kernberg asked, "that you see me like your mother?" The patient readily agreed and added, "Yes, and it is my bad luck, after having such a mother, I get a psychoanalyst like this who treats me in the same manner." (Kernberg, 1985)

Supportive Psychotherapy. Kernberg's approach to psychotherapy of the borderline patient requires two components. The therapist must respond with both cognitive and emotional support. This does not mean the therapist only gives the patient a pat on the shoulder. Empathy, a key ingredient in a supportive approach should not be confused with sympathy. Empathy, as Kohut describes it, requires being in tune with the patient's feelings, both positive and negative. Affective and emotional support requires praise, encouragement and a sharing of feelings. During the early part of treatment, the borderline patient requires an active therapist who will participate and interact with him. Cognitive support is also crucial. This requires giving the patient advice at times, especially if it is directly asked for. It also means that the therapist will provide information which will help the patient interpret his behavior and reality. However, Kernberg cautions against taking over too much control and evoking too much idealizing transferences. It is in this area of cognitive and emotional support that the group and AA provides an essential component to the patient's treatment with less risk of compromising the therapist's position and therapeutic relationship.

Environmental Intervention. Kernberg advocates that the therapist must actively intervene in the patient's life both inside and outside of the therapy hour. Outside intervention requires that the therapist talk with the family, school or work if necessary. Support systems (group, AA, etc.) must be established and encouraged. Kernberg believes this is crucial because the patient could be destroying their life outside of the therapy hour while the therapist methodically and painstakingly seeks to understand the patient. While this understanding of the patient is a necessary and often slow process, it should not be accomplished at the cost of the patient's outside life just because the therapist does not want to compromise his stance of technical neutrality. Requiring the borderline patient to attend AA meetings, calling his employer and insuring that he gets to work on time are important steps in the treatment process that will allow the person to survive as he gradually comes to understand himself and the meaning of his behavior.

Intervention is also required within the therapy hour. Acting out, both inside and outside the group session must be curtailed. This requires limit setting, confrontation and clarification. Transference distortions must be identified and examined. It is crucial that the patient be helped to understand the destructive ways he behaves with the group members or the group leader that are parallel to the way he behaves with others outside of the group. Consensual validation from the group can be a critical component of recovery. However, Kernberg warns that external reality in the present must be clarified first before the past is explored. Kernberg gives an excellent example of intervention within the therapy hour.

> Kernberg described a patient who would smoke during the therapy hour, flick his ashes on the carpet and toss his cigarettes across the room in utter defiance of Kernberg's interpretations about his behavior. The man would agree with Kernberg's interpretations and respond with a big smile on his face, "Yes, I see how this is my way of showing disrespect for you and yes I agree this is very similar to my feelings towards my father." However, the patient's behavior did not change and he continued to toss his cigarettes across the room. The pleasure the man obtained from acting out was self-gratifying and consequently greater than his motivation to change. Finally, Kernberg told him he would stop the therapy sessions if the man continued to flick his cigarette and ashes on the floor of

his office. At the announcement, the man promptly flicked his cigarette across the room. Kernberg stood up and asked the man to leave his office. The patient refused and Kernberg threatened to call security if he did not leave within twenty minutes because another patient was due at that time. The patient became enraged and told Kernberg "This is not behavior suited for a psychoanalysis". Kernberg stood his ground and the patient left his office. The next session there was an affect storm in which the patient promptly tossed another cigarette across the room. Kernberg again required him to leave the office. The next session the patient did not toss his cigarette, but angrily attacked Kernberg for treating him in such a cruel and sadistic fashion. Kernberg explored the implications of this man's behavior in the subsequent sessions. Kernberg pointed out to the patient how he had provoked him to act in such a manner. In essence, the patient was told, "You are angry and cruel with me. You deny that you are angry and cruel; treat me in a way that prompts me to be angry and cruel with you. Then you accuse me of the very behavior you deny in yourself." In essence, the patient's projective identification was interpreted. During this process, the patient remained reluctant to discuss the ramifications of his behavior. Kernberg had to repeatedly insist that their interaction be examined. Objections were continually put forth in a manner that would have resulted in compliance without understanding. "Look, I've stopped throwing my cigarettes across the room! Why do you insist on beating a dead horse", was an objection that would have prevented this individual from understanding fully how his behavior had affected others. (Kernberg, 1983)

The key for Kernberg is the insistence that such an exchange be completely examined before it is dropped. Clarification needs to be completed or else the patient's experience would not have been integrated. In this case, this patient would have only perceived his interchange with Kernberg as another example of how people dislike him and treat him in angry and sadistic ways. Interpersonal distortions and object relations would not have been altered unless Kernberg had insisted on its examination and understanding.

Treatment from this perspective involves three key steps:

1. Clarification of their behavior. "This is what you are doing

with me." Confront their distortions in a supportive, firm and caring manner.

2. After they are completely aware of what they have done, gain consensual validation from the group and point out how they do this with others. Give them support, both cognitive and emotionally.

3. Encourage them to act differently with others outside of the therapy hour.

NARCISSISTIC PERSONALITY DISORDER

Narcissism is frequently misunderstood by others as excessive self-absorption and self-love. In actuality, it represents an individual's attempt to create an external self-presentation which is exciting, important and recognized because they lack a firm sense of who they are internally. Woody Allen's movie, *Zelig*, is a clear example of an individual who lacks a solid core of identity and consequently succumbs to social and peer pressures for conformity. Zelig is a chameleon. In the film, he not only acts and thinks accordingly with those whom he is around, but actually begins to change his outward physical appearance to match theirs. In the company of obese individuals, he begins to balloon out in his appearance. With blacks, his skin begins to darken and in the presence of orientals, his eyes become slanted. Zelig's life and his survival depends on his imitating and getting approval from those around him. While the movie can be viewed as a metaphor about social pressures towards conformity and loss of autonomy, the character of Zelig is an example of a severe personality disorder. More specifically, he represents the category of individuals commonly referred to as Narcissistic Personality Disorders.

In order to understand such character pathology from a more objective perspective, the examination of the diagnostic criteria for such patients is in order. The DSM III lists eight features commonly present in the narcissistic personality disorder. It is important to note that while these characteristics are commonly seen features, they do not grasp the complexity of narcissism as Kohut describes.

1. Grandiose Sense of Self-Importance; which often vacillates with strong feelings of unworthiness.
2. Preoccupation With Unlimited Sense of Power and Self; espe-

cially in relation to youth, appearance, beauty and success. Needs to be seen with the right person and is fraught with envy.
3. Exhibitionistic Need for constant attention; desires admiration and recognition.
4. Cool Indifference or rage and humiliation in response to criticism.
5. Feelings of Entitlement; expectations of others without reciprocity.
6. Exploitation of Others; without regard for personal integrity or rights of others.
7. Alternation from overidealization to devaluation of others.
8. Lack of Empathy; insensitive and unable to recognize how others feel.

Certainly, narcissism from this perspective is a pathological condition. Such individuals not only suffer enormous difficulties in their relationships with others and society at large, but they are usually intensely driven people who are deeply unsatisfied with themselves. However, Kohut views narcissism as having a much more complex set of dynamics. Narcissism, as defined by Kohut, is a compensatory structure established by the individual because of the deprivation they suffered as children. Narcissism is in many ways a self-preservative force responsible for helping the child compensate for the continued narcissistic injuries suffered in a frustrating world and dysfunctional family system. Furthermore, it becomes an internal regulating system which allows the child to adapt to an environment which is too insensitive to his struggle to recover from his lost sense of omnipotence. Kohut's view of narcissism therefore defines it as a driving force responsible for the establishment of the self, the enhancement of self-esteem, and the guardian for preserving the integrity of the self-concept. A major task of this force is to find meaning and give value to one's life.

Kohut goes farther than the DSM III in his description of the implications of narcissism for all of mankind. Kohut warns us that we all struggle with issues of narcissism. Not only do addicts and alcoholics have to guard against their tendency to be self-centered, grandiose and easily offended, but we all have a propensity to believe we are the center of the universe. In this capacity, we can delude ourselves into believing we are special and unique while refusing to acknowledge our own mediocrity and limitness. This is a theme which will be explored at length in Chapter 6 when the philosophical and psychological roots of Alcoholics Anonymous are investigated. For now, it will be enough to recognize that Kohut's explanation of addiction is important because it has a significant contribution to make in the treatment of chemical dependency and that it is a model which is in many ways highly compatible with AA. Kohut is attempting to get us to look at our self-centeredness and how our refusal to accept limitations in our lives not only leads to addiction, but to numerous other social, spiritual, and psychological difficulties.

Beyond the Ego: Kohut's Self-Theory

Heinz Kohut's work with patients whose central disturbance involved feelings of emptiness and depression is in many ways an extension of Margaret Mahler's observations concerning the roots of individuality in a child's development. Kohut found the need to extend psychoanalytic theory beyond its present concept of the ego so the patient's narcissistic vulnerability could be understood in terms of the patient's inadequately formed or damaged sense of self. Like Mahler, Kohut emphasizes the critical importance of the mother in permitting the development of internal mental structures for self-control and the eventual emergence of healthy individuality and separateness. Kohut emphasized that a child's nuclear-self is formed during infancy and embodies the fundamental self-esteem, ideals and ambitions of the child. The relationship with the mother allows the various agencies, drives and conflicts of the mental apparatus to become unified into an integrated sense of self. However, the formation of the nuclear self does not take place in relation to overt praise and rebuke. Rather, it is the empathic, nonverbal, intuitive responsiveness of the mother to the child's needs and the atmosphere she creates to validate healthy strivings that integrates or fragments the nuclear-self.

The nuclear-self is bipolar, organized around the two anchor points of ideals and ambitions. In his final book (Kohut, 1984), Kohut included a third constituent of the self, which involves the maturation of the alter ego or twinship needs (see Figure V).

To understand Kohut's contribution to the treatment of addiction and narcissism, it is important to understand some of his key concepts. Important contributions by others (i.e., Winnicott, Kernberg, Mahler, etc.) will also be presented.

FIGURE V

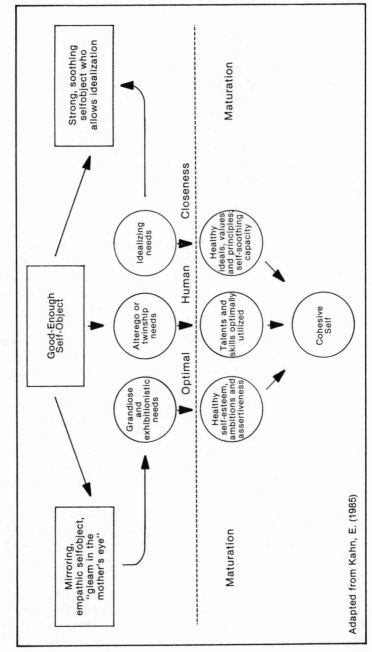

Adapted from Kahn, E. (1985)

DEFINITION OF TERMS

Self-Object: Self-objects are mental representations of others which we experience as part of ourself. Expected control over them is closer to the sense of control which a mature adult would expect to have over his body and mind. In archaic forms this control is expected to extend to others as if they were part of the self. There are two kinds of self-objects, mirroring and idealizing.

Mirroring Self-Object: Are objects who respond to and confirm the child's innate sense of vigor, greatness, and perfection. It is the gleam in the mother's eye as she is empathically in tune with the child's achievements. It is from this pole which emanates the child's basic strivings for power and success. Good-enough mothering results in the satisfaction of the child's healthy grandiose and exhibitionistic strivings. If these needs are adequately fulfilled, the child develops a healthy self-esteem with an appropriate sense of assertiveness and ambitions. Failure of the self-object to optimally gratify the child's mirror-hungry needs results in an individual who needs constant admiration, confirmation and recognition from others because they are empty and cannot give this to themselves.

Idealizing Self-Object: Are objects with whom a child can merge as an image of calmness, infallibility and omnipotence. If the child is presented with a strong, soothing self-object who allows idealization, he develops a capacity for healthy ideals, values and principles. The child internalizes the calming soothing qualities of the self-object and transmuting internalization is achieved. In contrast, the child who does not have an idealizing self-object available is forever attempting to achieve a union with an idealized object, since in view of their specific structural defect (the insufficient idealization of their superego), their narcissistic equilibrium is safeguarded only through constant admiration, investment and merger with a powerful other or ideal.

Empathy: The mode of gathering data which allows the therapist to get a look at the inner mentalistic life of people. Empathy is not just a useful way by which to gain access to the inner life of man, it is an attempt to experience the other's feelings, wishes, hopes and fears via vicarious introspection. The essence of psychotherapy lies in the therapist's protracted empathic immersion into the observed, for the purpose of data gathering and explanation. Only after the other's experience is understood via vicarious introspection can it be explained. Scientific rigor is then employed in order to fit the observed and experienced data into a context of broader meaning and significance.

Optimal Frustration: The amount of anxiety, stress, or frustration an infant can tolerate without detrimental effects on their ego, self, and development. Optimal frustration promotes growth and the development of psychic structure. Healthy personality development takes place under conditions of frustration that is not too long nor too intense. Just as too much or too little frustration in a given period can be an obstacle in a child's personality development, too little or too much frustration during psychotherapy can be an obstacle in the treatment experience.

Alter Ego of Twinship Merger: A firm self, resulting from the optimal interactions between the child and his self-objects is made up of this third constituent in relation to the first pole from which emanates the basic strivings for power and success and the second pole that harbors the basic idealized goals. The core of the child's personality is determined by the tension arc in the intermediate area of basic talents and skills which is established between ambitions and ideals. This sector consists of the need of the self just to be alike and with another person, a human among humans. Failure of the self-object during the child's development will result in the individual being unable to feel part of a larger whole. It will keep them alienated from their fellow man and will prevent them from utilizing their talents and skills in a constructive manner.

Self-Object Transference: This refers to the revival of insufficiently responded to childhood self-object needs in treatment and interpersonal relationships. 1. Mirror-hungry personalities thirst for self-objects whose confirming and admiring responses will nourish their famished self. 2. Ideal-hungry personalities are forever in search of others whom they can admire for their prestige, power, beauty, intelligence or moral stature. 3. Alter-ego personalities need a relationship with a self-object that by conforming to the self's appearance, opinions, and values confirms the existence and reality of their self.

Transmitting Internalization: It is in the matrix of a self-object environment that has responsive-empathic self-objects that a specific process of psychological structure formation is formed. The nuclear self of the child is laid via the process of transmuting internalization. Structure building cannot occur without a previous stage in which the child's mirroring and idealizing needs have been responded to efficiently. Structure is laid in the consequence of minor, non-traumatic failures in the responses of mirroring and the idealized self-objects. These failures lead to a gradual replacement of the self-objects and their functions by the child's self and its functions. Self-regulating and self-soothing become internalized. It is the failure of transmuting internalization that leads the individual to seek externally (i.e., food, sex, drugs, others, etc.) what they can't provide internally.

False Self: In the event that the integrity of the child's nuclear self is threatened, defensive or compensatory structures or a false self-organization may be established to prevent the self from further narcissistic injury. Such individuals develop an "as-if personality," frequently bolstered by a grandiose self which hides their "true self" from further fragmentation. Such a defensive process prevents them from nourishing their deflated sense of self because each success is attributed to the way they "acted" rather than the way the "really are." Consequently, they feel like "an imposter" (i.e., imposter syndrome) who will eventually be discovered and exposed for what they really are.

The false self is a defensive function designed to hide and protect the true self. The false self accomplishes this by complying with environmental demands along five categories (Winnicott, 1965):

1. At one extreme: the false self sets itself up as real and it is this that observers tend to think is the real person.
2. Less extreme: the false self defends the true self. The true self is acknowledged as a potential and is allowed a secret life.
3. The false self has as its main concern a search for conditions which will make it possible for the true self to come into its own.
4. The false self is built on identifications and can take on chameleon-like properties.
5. The false self is presented by the whole organization of polite and well-mannered social constraints.

Good-Enough Mothering: A term coined by Winnicott to describe the adaptative functioning of the mother which allows the child to lay down psychic structure as the result of optimal frustration. The good-enough mother doesn't gratify completely or traumatically frustrate the growing infant. Instead, she gradually diminishes her intuitive understanding for the sake of the child's furthering development and growing ability to tolerate frustration.

Application for Therapy — Corrective Emotional Expression

Refueling: During the practicing subphase, the infant forays away from the mother; but as the child becomes fatigued, depleted or anxious, the child seeks to establish emotional contact with the self-object. The good-enough mother will allow emotional "refueling" without engulfing the child or pushing the child away in a rejecting fashion.

Splitting: As the infant begins to enter into the separation-individuation subphase, the symbiotic unit becomes split into four sets of images — good self, good object, bad self, bad object. The purpose of this split is to preserve the good images long enough for the infant to tolerate the awareness that "all good" and "all bad" images are the same person. The child is able to tolerate the realization that the "good mother" who feeds them is the "bad mother" who punishes them when they are bad. The developmentally arrested child, in order to protect himself against the overwhelming anxiety produced by his inability to tolerate his mother as both good and bad, will split his feelings into all-or-nothing or black-and-white images. Thus, mother cannot be both good and bad simultaneously. The child either internalizes and introjects the bad object into himself (i.e., I am bad, mother is good) or idealizes mother and projects the bad image onto the world (i.e., It is bad out there, I am good).

As a defense, Kernberg introduced the term and defined it as an active defensive separation of the "all good" images from "all bad" images. Such a defensive process results in the individual being unable to keep a mental representation of an object as being capable of both good and bad images. Objects are idealized either as "all good" when gratifying or devalued as "all bad" when withholding. (See Figure II.)

Projective Identification: A primitive defensive operation found in borderline personality structure. The purpose of the projection is to get rid of all bad internalized images by placing it on others out there. Consequently, the outside externalized objects are perceived as bad (i.e., angry, threatening). An effort is then put forth by the person to control these externalized objects to prevent them from treating the person the way they fear they will be treated (i.e., attacked and control). Paradoxically, because of their suspicious defensive behavior, these individuals induce the very behavior in the others which they most dislike. They subsequently empathize and identify with this anger and feel confirmed in their belief that the objects out there are indeed bad (i.e., controlling and angry). Their suspicions become a self-fulfilled prophecy.

A couple of examples will help clarify this important defensive process.

> A thirty-three-year-old cocaine addict became acutely intoxicated on cocaine and began to have fears that the people (police and the army) were after him. He proceeded to run down the street hiding behind mail boxes and telephone booths. Others, alarmed by his defensive suspicious and angry behavior, notified police who began to pursue him. Upon perceiving police chasing after him, this individual's fears of being attacked and followed by others were confirmed. He consequently lashed out and attacked the police officers justified in his beliefs that they were out to get him for no good reason.
>
> Ralph, a forty-two-year-old, recovering alcoholic with five years sobriety was referred by his employer because of his constant arguments with employees at work. He performed his job more than satisfactorily; but because he created such distress in the office, he was about to be fired despite an excellent work record. After four group sessions, Ralph began to bitterly complain about the group leader's inadequacies. He insisted the group leader was not helping him and that the prices he charged for group sessions were outrageous and unfair. After the fifth session, he accused the group leader of looking at him in a disparaging way before he had entered the group session last week. He also accused him of reacting much more favorably to all the other group members and that the group leader seemed to have a special dislike for him. Since this was completely untrue, the group leader explored this incident at length, eventually pointing out to him the way Ralph was treating him was exactly the way he was treating all others in his life — namely, he would attribute to others (projection), qualities (anger, annoyance, criticism) which he possessed. He would then deny that he was treating them in this way and accuse others of behaving in ways which were actually his own behavior (projective identification). The group leader was able to validate his observations by gaining a consensual validation from the group. Ralph, through feedback from the other group members, was able to realize an important defensive process that has led to many interpersonal difficulties in his life.

Transitional Object: Winnicott's concept which defines the infant's first recognition and choice of a possession that is "not-me." The possession is usually a blanket, a toy or a teddy bear. The object usually soothes and facilitates the infant's recognition of separateness and soothes the child in the transition of becoming self-sufficient.

SELF-PSYCHOLOGY, NARCISSISM AND GROUP PSYCHOTHERAPY

Self-psychology has special relevance to group psychotherapy because of a number of important reasons. Some of the more significant contributing factors will be explored in the following pages. The most important contribution of group is that it allows the full impact of one's relations to peers to be examined and experienced. It is through the relationship with one's peers that the concept of the self can be modified. Horwitz (1984) has addressed the importance of peer influence in group and has identified three group functions which modify and influence one's concept of the self.

1. Mirroring in group.
2. Peer relationships, particularly partnering.
3. Sense of belonging.

The Mirrored Self: Group therapy can be thought of as a hall of mirrors. Not to be confused with Kohut's concept of mirroring, Horwitz described this function to include both the responses one receives from others (feedback) and the reactions to others that the person transmits to them. The importance of group is that it allows the individual to learn how he or she reacts to others. First the person gets feedback on how he or she is perceived and secondly, the person learns if he is able to react appropriately to others. Can he feel empathy? Does he project, distort and affect others in ways that he does not wish to or intend? Group, from this perspective provides an important integrative effect for the individual allowing him or her to own and recognize previously disavowed parts of the self.

Horwitz writes:

> The importance of mirroring may be understood in terms of the objective of all psychotherapies to integrate into a harmonious whole the diverse, conflicted, and repressed parts of the

self, which the individual has tried to keep hidden from himself and others. The unintegrated self-representations are part of a dynamic unconscious that, nevertheless, influence an individual's character style, contribute to symptoms, and modify overt behavior. They determine one's sense of cohesiveness and self-esteem as well as feelings of acceptability and genuineness. The dual mirroring functions in a group are prime factors in uncovering and exposing those hidden parts of the self, which ideally in treatment should be brought into the light of day and ultimately integrated into a more unified self. (1984, p. 530)

Peer Relatedness or Partnering: Peer transference has long been unrecognized or viewed as secondary to therapist transference. Horwitz sees peer transference and peer relationships as an important part of an individual's developmental process. Developmentally, peer relationships and the desire for partnering reflects an important step in separating parental ties and expectations. Partnering reflects a healthy wish to have an equal relationship with another. Separation and individuation once obtained indicate that the person is ready for a mature reciprocal relationship that is not built on neurotic, sado-masochistic, dependent or narcissistic features. Therapy groups have the special feature of permitting experimentation with nonexploitive and nonneurotic relationships as a prelude to applying new learned behavior to the "real world."

Sense of Belonging: The importance of one's relationship to others and its impact on one's sense of self has always been recognized as a very crucial part of treatment. While some viewed the relationship which a patient establishes with the therapist as more important than insight, not all agree that this stance has justified the importance that it has been given. Finding a person who unconditionally accepts the darker and less pleasant sides of one's personality while remaining interested and committed to the relationship has important therapeutic ramifications. This effect is often referred to as the "corrective emotional experience." Group psychotherapy allows the member to identify with others without losing their self. "A sense of belonging not only enhances and strengthens a sense of self through various supportive experiences, but it becomes a vehicle for uncovering the repressed and hidden selves" (Horwitz, 1984, p. 336). The group becomes a holding environment which cushions narcissistic injuries allowing the individual to continue to expose his weakness to others and himself. Feelings of being accepted and valued despite his exposure of the "bad-parts" of himself lead to internalization and desired change in the self.

Group dynamics, whether in a therapy group or AA, can be powerful and influential. Rapprochement as "the need to belong" goes on throughout life. The social implications are important. In order for members to remain an individual within a group, this requires a certain permanence and resistance of the differentiated self. Group life therefore is at the center of the "average expectable environment." For free participation within the group one needs assurance of the integrity of their individuality, just as for the rapprochement crisis experienced earlier in life, one needs to have accomplished separation-individuation. "For such integrity," Rangell (1982) writes, "one needs integration or synthesis of all psychic structures, and of inner and outer, of one's past, present, and future" (p. 887). Integration is the key. A person who has a sense of a cohesive self and others, good or bad, love and hate, will be able to belong without losing the self. Not only does this have important implications for recovery, it has important ramifications for one's integration into society and the establishment of healthy interpersonal relationships with others.

ADDICTION, OBJECT-RELATIONS, AND PSYCHODYNAMICS

Kohut's Self-Psychology has been extensively described because of the important influence his work has on the relationship between object relations theory and addiction. However, Kohut's work has been extended by others. Some of the more important contributors will be explored. Khantzian for one has attempted to link object relations theory to addiction.

> This chapter is an attempt to advance a contemporary psychoanalytic perspective that considers who the psychiatric disorders and psychopathology associated with addiction are psychodynamically related to and the result of vulnerabilities in ego and self structures that leave alcoholics and addicts ill-suited to regulate and manage their behavior, feelings (affects), and inner states of well-being involving self-comfort and self-esteem. As a result, alcoholics resort to the use of

alcohol both as manifestations of such disturbance and as attempts to cope and compensate for them. (Khantzian, 1982, p. 582)

Khantzian is close to summarizing a position which he, Krystal (1982), and Wurmser (1978) have taken in their attempt to advance Kohut's theory of structural deficits in relation to addiction. Instead of the disease of addiction being defined completely as a physical/ biochemical abnormality, they are suggesting that deficits in psychic structure is the disease. People prone to addiction have not had the empathic nurturing self-objects necessary to develop transmuting internalization. Consequently, they are left without the resources to calm and soothe themselves during times of stress. Such individuals frequently feel empty and depleted inside. As many alcoholics and addicts announce, "I usually feel as if I were a quart low." Only when they drank alcohol did they feel normal. Because these people lack the internal structure necessary to combat their nauseous sense of fragmentation, anxiety and failing self-esteem, they are drawn to external sources (i.e., alcohol, drugs, sex, excitement, food, etc.) in their attempts to self-soothe and self-calm (i.e., transmuting internalization).

Kohut writes,

Individuals whose nascent selves have been insufficiently responded to will use any available stimuli to create a pseudo-excitement in order to ward off the painful feeling of deadness that tends to overtake them. . . . Adults have at their disposal an even wider armamentarium of self-stimulation — in particular, in the sexual sphere, addictive promiscuous activities and various perversions, and in the non-sexual sphere, such activities as gambling, drug and alcohol induced excitement, and a lifestyle characterized by hypersociability. If the analyst is able to penetrate beneath the defensive facade presented by these activities, he will invariably find empty depression. (Kohut & Wolfe, 1978, p. 418)

In Kohut's view, the individual's inability to obtain self-soothing via transmuting internalization, is the reason they attempt to relieve these tensions by the use of alcohol and drugs. It is the alcoholic's and addict's inability to calm and soothe themselves which leads them to look for others to do for them what they are unable to do for themselves. Since their self-object needs and desires are distorted, they inevitably are continually disappointed in their relationships and the attainment of their goals. Seeking from the outside what can only be furnished from the inside leads to constant frustration and despair. Most alcoholic's and addict's lives are dominated by a deficiency in which they experience themselves as being empty and deprived. They believe if only another would supply them with this deprived "refueling," they could become whole and complete. They are inevitably disappointed, because as mature adults, they can no longer tolerate to have these infantile needs satisfied in infantile ways. Consequently, they constantly battle to deny their sense of neediness. They become counter-dependent and perceive others as rejecting and withholding. "If you loved me, you wouldn't disappoint me. Since I am disappointed, you don't love me." Their use of splitting, projective identification and fear of closeness makes it impossible for them to obtain any satisfying relationships. They become resentful, disappointed people who do not understand the part they play in this process. Alcohol and drugs becomes their sole mistress and their only friend.

The chemically dependent individual's difficulties are also exacerbated by failures in psychic structures responsible for containing regulating behavior and affects. Areas of vulnerability in ego and self-functioning include disturbances in self-care, affect regulation, dependency, alexithymia, anhedonia and affect regression produced by a narcissistic crisis.

Self-Care: Alcoholics and addicts are notorious for their self-destructive behavior. They essentially lack the inability to take care of themselves and protect themselves from self-defeating actions. Because the chemically dependent individual suffers with a deficient or underdeveloped ego capacity for modulating their feelings, they are often unable to tell when they are tired, sick, hungry, anxious or depressed. Such disturbances in self-care also leads the individual to fail to be aware, cautious, worried or frightened enough to resist or avoid behavior which is injurious or damaging. Because they are poorly prepared to properly evaluate the consequences of risky or self-damaging behavior, they are constantly placing themselves in destructive and painful circumstances. Khantzian (1982) sees this inability for self-care as developmentally determined. Writing about Mahler and other developmental theorists, he contends, "They emphasize the importance developmentally of optimal parental nurturances and protection early in children's development for the establishment of this function, and how extremes of deprivation or indulgence have devastating consequences for the development of this capacity" (p. 589).

Affect Regulation: Whereas self-care limitations prevents the addict and alcoholic from guarding against continual self-defeating and dangerous behavior, they also suffer from deficits in ego functioning which interferes in their ability to use their feelings as guides or signals in managing and protecting against the instability and chaos of one's internal emotional life. Alcoholics and addicts have a disturbance in the regulation of affect which manifests as "an inability to identify and verbalize feelings, an intolerance or incapacity for anxiety and depression, an inability to modulate feelings, activation and initiate problems, and extreme manifestions of affect, such as hypomania, phobic-anxious states, panic and lability" (Khantzian, 1982, p. 590).

If development is undisturbed, feelings act as guides or signals for regulating one's behavior. Because alcoholics and addicts suffer from developmental arrest, they usually fail to differentiate or progress in the development of understanding their feelings. Consequently, they are unable to use feelings as signals or guides.

"That is, they suffer an ego defect in their stimulus barrier whereby they are either unable to identify affects, or their feelings are unbearable or overwhelming. As a result, denial or the effects of alcohol are used to ward off overwhelming feeling states in circumstances that would not be traumatic for other people (Khantzian, 1982, p. 591). Such individuals are then unable to soothe or comfort the self when distressed and become dependent upon an external agent to do so.

Dependency and the Self: The defect in the self leads to failures in ego-ideal formation. In Kohut's schema, alcoholics and addicts have not adequately internalized the admired and admiring, encouraging, valued and idealized qualities of their parents. As a result, they lack self-worth and suffer from chronic feelings of poor self-esteem. As a consequence of their inability to accurately evaluate themselves and judge their relationships, they greatly depend on others as sources outside themselves for approval and confirmation. Outside activities and the use and dependence on others are attempts by alcoholics and addicts to feel good about themselves because they are almost totally unable to achieve this for themselves from within.

Kernberg stresses how the rigid and primitive defenses of these individuals lead to repression and dissociation of parts of the self. Alcohol and drugs can be viewed as an attempt to refuel the grandiose self and activate the all-good self and object images while denying the all-bad internalized objects. Krystal (1982) has suggested that because of these defensive operations, alcoholics and addicts are unable to experience their aggressive and loving feelings unless they drink or use drugs. Chemical use thereby allows a brief and tolerable enjoyment of such feelings.

Alexithymia: Alexithymia has been identified as a characteristic pattern indicating an inability to name and use one's emotions. The alcoholic's and addict's inability to verbalize feelings leads to the somatization of affect responses. This results in them being confronted with sensations rather than feelings. Such physiological sensations are therefore not useful as signals, but remain painful and overwhelming. Such painful affective states call attention to the uncomfortableness rather than to the "story behind the feelings." Such individuals are marked by their striking inability to articulate their most painful, bothersome and important feelings. Many, if not all of their feelings are translated into somatic complaints about physical discomfort and craving. Alcohol and drugs are then used to block the affect, preventing the individual from interpreting and attending to the signal. Krystal (1982) sees this as also contributing to "a diminution in the capacity for drive-oriented fantasy. Thinking becomes operative, mundane and boring. The capacity for empathy with development of utilizable transference is seriously diminished" (p. 614). In short, alcoholics and addicts lose the capacity to enjoy themselves or others unless they are drinking or using drugs.

Anhedonia: Many alcoholics and addicts do not possess the capacity to experience joy, pleasure or happiness. Drugs are virtually the only way they can obtain gratification and relief from distressful affective states. Krystal (1982) views this as a consequence of infantile traumatization resulting in a "doomsday" orientation, involving a constant dreaded expectation of the return of the unbearable traumatic state. Such individuals will then keep themselves very active and busy for they fear slowing down, lest their expected catastrophe should occur. Krystal (1982) writes about the importance of this in treatment,

> there is hardly any knowledge about how to help the patients to cultivate their capacity for pleasure and joy. This problem is

an especially serious one in dealing with the alcoholic professional, such as the alcoholic physician. These individuals tend to present a combination of severe compulsiveness, "work addiction", and anhedonia underlying their problem drinking. The drug is often used to maintain a severe machine-like self-control regime. Many of these patients maintain for a long time a very high degree of success in their professional and business careers. Their "superb" adjustment to reality is actually part of the "operative" life style. (p. 615)

Affect Regression: Wurmser (1978) has constructed a heptad of specificity in compulsive drug use. The cycle of the addictive process involves seven steps and is always initiated by a significant acute narcissistic crisis (i.e., disappointment in self or a love object). This is experienced as an unbearable blow to self-respect which plunges the individual into a regressive spin. In succession, the individual experiences:

1. There is a sudden plummeting of self-esteem triggered by a "big letdown" from an expectation that may be justified, but usually greatly exaggerated.
2. The narcissistic injury produces an affect regression which cannot be articulated into words. The feeling is an uncontrollable, intense sense of rage, shame or despair. Affect defenses are broken down and inadequate to contain internal feelings.
3. The affect disappears and a vague, but unbearable tension remains. There may be a longing, a frantic search for excitement and relief. As a result of integrative dysfunction, there is an increasing dependence on externalization (i.e., drugs, excitement to self-soothe). Splitting occurs between observing and acting. More troublesome feelings are suppressed, massively denied and disavowed. The individual fails to appreciate and interpret what he has experienced and perceived.
4. This development leads to desire for action, a seeking for an external concrete solution to the denied internal conflict. Aggression, excitement and drugs (external objects) are acted upon so the individual can direct his affect outward away from internal uncomfortableness.
5. Aggression can now be dealt with by externalization. However, it is usually directed against the self (shame, humiliation) as well as being directed against others (violating social

limits, transgressing boundaries). The reassertion of power by externalization requires the use of archaic forms of aggression.
6. Splitting of the superego occurs. As Wurmser writes, "The drowning man has commonly little regard for questions of integrity." Trustworthiness, reliability and honesty are utterly irrelevant because despair has taken over. While commitments to others are acknowledged, they are treated with little importance.
7. The final point is enormous pleasure and gratification. The acute narcissistic crisis is temporarily resolved and the demand for the restoration of this blissful condition creates an extraordinarily demanding, unrealistic attitude on the part of the individual which predisposes him to severe disappointment and thus to an increased narcissistic vulnerability. This cycle is then completed and he is returned to the starting point of what Wurmser calls the "vicious cycle." The patient is back where he started with a much lower level of self-esteem and vulnerability.

TREATMENT OF INTERNAL STRUCTURAL DEFICITS

Krystal (1982) disagrees with Kohut's view that the alcoholic's inability to obtain self-soothing gratification can be cured by treatment through the process of "transmuting internalization." In many ways, the fellowship of AA allows this to occur. Krystal disagrees that the alcoholic's and addict's difficulty is related to a deficiency in the self structure. Krystal views this problem due to "an inhibition resulting from a mistaken attribution of these functions to the object rather than the self-representation" (p. 611). Krystal believes these individuals see themselves as victims of childhood deprivation and expect the therapist to supply them with the missing love in the belief that all will be good and well if this is done. Krystal sees the addict and alcoholics stance as one which is, "If you love me, you will make me feel good, therefore, as long as everything is not perfect and I do not feel blissful, you do not love me." He also adds that "these patients have terrible resentments about their past, and demand that the therapist roll back the reel of their lives and fix everything retroactively" (p. 611).

Krystal is correct in his assessment of their demands and expectations; but what he fails to appreciate is the reality of their experienced deprivation. These needs haven't been met by a supportive empathic self-object. This is what drives them to search for what is unavailable and to constantly confirm their view that the world is rejecting and unfair. Krystal believes that this condition is an illusion; supposedly something that these individuals fabricate. Such a stance does not correlate with Mahler's developmental theory which is essentially a deprivation model. Granted that alcoholics and addicts distort objects in their world and perceive others as unempathic and ungratifying. This is precisely why therapists who take a nongratifying, nondirective stance provoke such anger and rage in the chemically dependent individual. Such a unempathic stance on the part of the therapist rekindles painful memories of archaic self-objects who have failed them in the past.

Krystal is also correct in pointing out that their expectations are unrealistic and can never be fulfilled or gratified. This is exactly the realization that the chemically dependent person must come to accept. They must admit their search is futile and then they must surrender to this realization. In AA terms they hit bottom. They must then accept the fact that no one can give to them what they want and that they alone are responsible for accomplishing the arduous task of structure building via internalization of the twelve steps of the AA program. This is why AA and group psychotherapy works while individual therapy frequently fails. AA and the group becomes a substitute self-object or transitional object which allows the recovering individual to identify and internalize those aspects which he is lacking structurally. Self-object distortions, triggered by too much identification and expectation of one individual, are minimized and the person is given enough time and distance to diffuse the transference distortions. In AA language, "We can do what I couldn't accomplish alone."

Krystal fails to understand the complete ramifications of a child's early experience. When the parents' behavior is rejecting, angry or persecutory, the child, because he is unable to give up the external object since he needs his parent for survival, cannot change his outer reality because he is too helpless and dependent. He consequently handles the frustration and disappointment by internalizing the love-hated parent. This is done in an attempt by the child to master and control the object in his inner psychic world. This love-hate relationship is repressed and retained as an introject, a psychological representation of the child's inner world. It is the emotional relationship between the self and the external object that is internalized, not the feelings as such. The introjects become part of the structure of the personality.

The earlier in life this splitting and introjection occurs, the more painful and frustrating the external world becomes. For instance, an alcoholic is likely to see others as either all good or all bad. When the all good objects inevitably disappoint him, he feels enraged at again being deprived. He is either forced to perceive them as all bad to preserve his all good introject or feel that he is all bad and undeserving of the good object. He may have a strong yearning for merger with the good object only to feel trapped and engulfed when he gets close leading him to break away. Individuals are perceived only in terms of the alcoholic's introjects or denied split off traits. Relationships in the outer reality are not only unconsciously interpreted in light of the alcoholic's inner world, resulting in distorted expectations, but the alcoholic engages in an unconscious attempt to force and change close relationships into fitting the internal role models.

If a parent was demeaning and critical, the individual will force others in their external world to change into a critical demeaning object so that their external reality fits their internal world. The relationship takes on the form of a third entity and becomes introjected. The child grows up demeaned and criticized. As an adult, he demeans and criticizes himself. In his relationship, he perceives others as demeaning and critical, eventually forcing them to fit his internal experience of them.

TREATMENT OF INTROJECTS

As Kohut has pointed out, the building of psychic structure occurs as infant and parent misunderstand one another's signals and try again to come to a better understanding of each other. The concepts of good enough mothering and optimal frustration play an important part in the therapist's stance during treatment. It is when the therapist and patient struggle to overcome the obstacles to their relationship and their misunderstanding that maturation takes place and psychic structure is laid. While the most rapid and fundamental features of structuralization take place in the early years of life, development is a process which continues throughout life. The therapeutic task is to walk the line between optimal frustration on the one hand and optimal anxiety on the other hand with just enough gratification provided to keep the chemically dependent individual from leaving treatment.

Because alcoholics and addicts cannot tolerate technical neutrality, they require a therapist who is active, alive and who will gratify them on some level. They must be made aware that the therapist cares. However, complete support and gratification will not lead to internalization, correction of introjects and structure building. It requires empathic understanding first and then conveyance of that understanding to the patient. This requires a therapist and group leader who will face misunderstandings and see that conflicts are resolved. As Basch says "It is only unexamined errors that have catastrophic consequences" (1980, p. 101).

Individual therapy usually has little success with alcoholics and addicts. The one-to-one traditional setting evokes too many transference distortions and frequently results in the therapist being frustrated and defeated. Individual therapy, at least during the beginning of recovery, is too threatening for the addict or alcoholic. They cannot tolerate the stimulation of their dependent yearnings, nor can they handle the hostility that will inevitably surface and threaten the continuity of the relationships. Nevertheless, the alcoholic and addict must establish a capacity to relate to others on a meaningful level. He must be helped to achieve an appropriate dependent relationship without the crippling interference of his own hostility and fear of closeness. Only under the sway of his wish to please others and be with others can he identify and achieve a more stable internalized set of values patterned after the model set by those trying to help him.

How can this potential for healthy relationships be internalized? The group approach and Alcoholics Anonymous is effective for a number of reasons. First by virtue of the number of group and AA members, it dilutes the intensity of feelings which otherwise inundates the one-to-one setting. Thus, the alcoholic or addict can spread his attachments to several people. The group offers the alcoholic and addict a way of dealing with the intense hostility and ambivalence in his relationships by supplying him with a number of figures upon whom he can depend or direct his anger. His fear of closeness, hostility and dependence is therefore not as severely threatened. Thus, the structure of the group and its relationship to AA permit maintenance of the splitting defense as long as needed.

Of similar impact is the response of the group leader, who, by his firm yet non-hostile ability to absorb anger, can lay the foundation for later identifications.

The group and AA can also provide an alternative to the alcoholics and addict's lifestyle in the bars and on the streets. This is an alternative which can supply the need for a transitional object and, thereby, pave the way for the development of a more stable and adequate sense of object constancy. The constant availability of the group and the AA program provides a soothing function for the chemically dependent individual at the moment of crisis whenever it should occur.

This is where the group and the AA program can become the opportune agent of change in the chemically dependent individual's life. Much as the scrap of blanket or teddy bear serves the infant, the group and AA program allows the individual to begin the strenuous business of movement towards autonomy and separation. The group can become the transitional object for the addict and alcoholic who is seeking to emancipate himself from his symbiotic tie to his drugs and alcohol as well as his self-object.

Kosseff (1979) outlines the transitional qualities of the group in this process of internalization.

1. The group is a tangible representation of the relationship between the patient and the therapist. However, the patient is protected from the intensity of the dependency on the therapist because it is transferred to the group.
2. The group carries a degree of separation from the therapist and allows the patient a combination of support and freedom which the dyadic relationship didn't provide.
3. The group is a bulwark against too great feelings of frustration and fear of punishment if he should function autonomously. The group offers its support of other members as an alternative to dependence on one object.
4. The group provides a "space between" the therapist and patient and allows an area of freedom for the patient to fill creatively. He can use the group as he chooses, relaxing or tightening up his relationship with the therapist and splitting his transferential identification as he needs.
5. The group serves as a convoy in the patient's efforts to deal with his internalized bad objects.

6. The group as a "good-enough, facilitating environment" substitutes for and also denies the possibility of being controlled by or controlling the therapist.

7. As the patient gives up his internal distortions of the therapist, with the help of the group, he becomes more able to differentiate reality from distortion. Boundaries between group leader and patient become firmer.

8. The group as transitional object promotes the emergence of the real self and facilitates the mastery of the self as the patient experiments with objects in a new way. Giving and receiving empathy, reassurance, understanding and self assertion in group leads to freeing of impulses and capacity for greater closeness emerges.

In summary, the group's value as a transitional object is in its facilitation of the identification process. It helps the alcoholic and addict 1. shift from a set of internalized split-images of self to a more unitary representation of self by identification with other group members; 2. shift from the part object seen as if it were the whole object (the therapist seen solely as bad object); 3. shift the fears of being engulfed by the group leader to a gradual recognition through other group members that this cannot happen because the group leader is not that powerful and because they, by sharing the leader with the patient, interferes with the patient's longing for fusion. Kosseff (1979) sums up this process when he writes:

> The group helps the patient let go of primitive idealizations of the therapist and his omnipotence by pointing out both the reality and the shortcomings of the therapist. As the patient is able to face these less positive attitudes toward the therapist, he is able "to change places" with him and see himself in a more worthwhile light. Where the patient in individual treatment would tend to overlook differences between his view of the therapist and the reality of the therapist, the other group members jar the patient's efforts at continuing pathological identification with the therapist or themselves and force him to acknowledge, and ultimately accept, his differences from others. Where the therapist's relative silence in individual treatment may tend to foster such pathological identification, visible group behavior and interaction force objective recognition of differences. What had been a sealed-off, dead-end identifi-

cation with the therapist, a giving up of the real object and a substitution of an internalized, possibly idealized object, along with a giving up of the real potentialities of the self in favor of a false compliant self, now gives way to a recognition of the self as good and different from others. As the danger of fusion and immolation with the therapist subsides, the patient develops the hope and possibility of separation and true individuation. (1979, p. 237)

Often after the alcoholic has completed treatment, he will want to return for visits, especially when anxious. This is where the lifelong availability of the AA program provides an even clearer illustration of this transitional function. Many individuals have difficulty weaning themselves from the AA program and are likely to seek continual contact with it. They gain continual confidence from the AA activities which win approval of the AA community. In this way, the unfolding of a sense of self-approval, defined as object constancy, can be discerned. What was not completed in childhood may take place later on as the program itself gradually acquires a maternal function, first as a transitional object and later, after internalizing some of the values of the program, as the source of object constancy.

The alcoholic's reliance on AA is often judges with concern and suspiciousness by professionals. Some critics of AA express fear that the addict and alcoholic may become too dependent on the program. A common suggestion is to get the individual prepared to "face the world as it really is." From the point of view of the addict's and alcoholic's inner life, the emergence of such dependent behavior signals an important change in a positive direction. It is unfortunate that so many professionals view it as a negative turn of events. It is fortunate that the alcoholic becomes "hooked" on the people in the AA program. Such an occurrence is often the first evidence of the alcoholic's ability to engage in one-to-one relationships which allows him to accept his need for help and to find new people with whom he can identify. This process takes time. Such individuals do ultimately win a healthy independence.

Closely related to this principle of healthy dependence on others is the maturation of narcissism as Kohut defines it. The alcoholic and addict is narcissistically oriented. His reliance on his grandiose self is manifested within the fabric of values expressed by the drug and alcohol subculture. Thus, there is a need for a principal of treatment that will interfere with the narcissistic fixations of the alcoholic and addict, those which perpetuate lowered self-esteem. There is also a need for a principle of treatment which will facilitate the maturation of healthy narcissism. Thus treatment should foster an idealized attachment to a program which allows an individual's narcissistic needs to be met in a healthy fashion. It is helpful if the alcoholic and addict admires the values expressed in the philosophy of the program in which he participates. A useful illustration is AA since its values are so often enthusiastically held and so frequently represent a direct confrontation with the tenets held by the drug and alcohol subcultures. The alcoholic and addict by idealizing the values of his group or AA program not only becomes less enamored by drinking and drug use, but is tempted to allow some dependence upon those he idealizes. Since these new objects of admiration are more dependable and far more empathic than his drinking or drug using friends and earlier parental figures, the alcoholic and addict is more willing to risk relying on another human being. It is within this climate that a sense of hope can be generated, a beginning faith that personal change is possible and with the help of new objects for identification, a more adaptive patterning of relationships can emerge.

REFERENCES

AA World Services, Inc. (1939). *Alcoholics Anonymous* (3rd ed.). New York: Author.

American Psychiatric Association. (1980). *Diagnostic & statistical manual of mental disorders* (3rd ed.). Washington, D.C.: Author.

Basch, M. F. (1980). *Doing psychotherapy*. New York: Basic Books.

Bowlby, J. (1958). The nature of the child's tie to the mother. *International Journal of Psychoanalysis*, *39*, 350-373.

Buber, M. (1955). *Between man and man*. Boston: Beacon Press.

Buber, M. (1960). *I and thou*. New York: Schriber & Sons.

Dostoyevsky, F. (1957). *The brothers Karamazov*. New York: Basic Books.

Hartocollis, P. & Hartocollis, C. (1980). Alcoholism, borderline & narcissistic disorders: A psychoanalytic overview. In W. Fann, I. Karacan, A. Porkory & R. S. Williams (Eds.), *Phenomenology & treatment of alcoholism* (pp. 93-110). New York: Medical & Scientific Books.

Hatcher, R. L. & Krohn, A. (1980). Level of object representation and capacity for intensive psychotherapy in neurotics & borderlines. In J. S. Kuawer, H. D. Lerner, P. M. Lerner & A. Sugerman (Eds.), *Borderline phenomena & the Rorschach test* (pp. 299-320). New York: International University Press.

Horner, A. (1976). Oscillating patterns of object relations and borderline patient. *International Review of Psycho-Analysis*, 479-482.

Horner, A. (1979). *Object relations and the developing ego in therapy*. New York: Aronson.

Horwitz, L. (1984). The self in groups. *International Journal of Group Psychotherapy*, *34*(4), 519-540.

Kahn, E. (1985). Heinz Kohut & Carl Rogers: A timely comparison. *American Psychologist*, *40*(8), 893-904.

Kernberg, O. (1970). *New developments in psychoanalytic object-relations theory*. Topeka: Menninger Foundation.

Kernberg, O. (1975). *Borderline conditions & pathological narcissism*. New York: Aronson Press.

Kernberg, O. (1983). The borderline patient. *Psychiatry (Audio Digest)*, *12*, No. 16.

Khantzian, E. J. (1982). Psychopathology, psychodynamics & alcoholism. In M. E. Pattison & E. Kaufman (Eds.), *Encyclopedia of alcoholism* (pp. 581-597). New York: Gardner Press.

Khantzian, E. J. (1985). On the psychological predisposition for opiate & stimulant dependence. *Psychiatry Letter*, *3*(1),

Khantzian, E. J. & Treece, C. J. (1980). Psychodynamics of drug dependence: An overview. In Psychodynamics of Drug Dependence. NIDA Research Monograph 12, Washington, D.C.: Department of HEW.

Kohut, H. (1977). Preface in *Psychodynamics of drug dependence*. NIDA Research Monograph 12. Washington D. C.: U.S. Department of H.E.W.

Kohut, H. (1977). *The restoration of the self*. New York: International University Press.

Kohut, H. (1984). *How does analysis cure?* Chicago: University of Chicago Press.

Kohut, H. & Wolfe, E. S. (1978). The disorders of the self and their treatment: An outline. *International Journal of Psychoanalysis*. *60*, 413-425.

Kosseff, J. W. (1975). The leader using object-relations theory. In Z. A. Liff (Ed.), *The leader in group* (pp. 212-242. New York: Jason Aronson.

Krystal, H. (1982). Character disorders: Characterological specificity and the alcoholic. In M. E. Pattison & E. Kaufman (Eds.), *Encyclopedia of alcoholism* (pp. 607-617). New York: Gardner Press.

Lichtenstein, H. (1961). Identity & sexuality: A study of their interrelationship in man. *Journal of American Psychoanalytic Association*, *9*, 179-260.

Mahler, M. S. (1968). *On human symbiosis and the vicissitude of individuation*. New York: International University Press.

Mahler, M. S. (1979). *This selected papers of Margaret Mahler, Volumes I and II*. New York: Jason Aronson.

Mahler, M. S., Pine, F. & Bergman, A. (1975). *The psychological birth of the human infant*. New York: Basic Books.

Monte, C. F. (1980). *Beneath the mask. An introduction to theories of personality* (2nd ed.). New York: Rinehart & Winston.

Piaget, J. (1954). *The construction of reality in the child*. New York: Basic Books.

Rangell, L. (1982). The self in psychoanalytic theory. *Journal of American Psychoanalytic Association*, *30*(4), 863-891.

Schuckit, M. A. (1973). Alcoholism & sociopathy. Diagnostic confusion. *Quarterly Journal of Studies on Alcohol*, *34*, 157-164.

Tiebout, H. (1954). The ego factors in surrender in alcoholism. *Quarterly Journal of Studies on Alcohol*, *15*, 610-621.

Vaillant, G. (1983). The natural history of male alcoholism. Is alcoholism the cart or horse to sociopathy? *British Journal of Addiction*, *78*, 317-326.

Vaillant, G. & Milofsky, E. (1982). The etiology of alcoholism, A prospective viewpoint. *American Psychologist*, *37*(5), 494-503.

Winnicott, D. (1965). *The maturation process & the facilitating environment*. New York: International University Press.

Wurmser, L. (1978). *The hidden dimension: Psychodynamics in compulsive drug use*. New York: Jason Aronson.

Chapter 6

Alcoholics Anonymous
and Group Psychotherapy

As far as many professionals are concerned, Alcoholics Anonymous is a much maligned, beleaguered and misunderstood organization. A great many of AA's critics who write despairingly of the organization, do so without the benefit of attending AA meetings or making themselves familiar with its workings on more than a passing, superficial, or purely analytic level. They fail to understand the subtleties of the AA program and often erroneously attribute qualities and characteristics to the organization that are one-dimensional, misleading and even border on slanderous. AA has been called by some a cult, a religion, ideological, unscientific, unempirical, and totalitarian (i.e., Jones, 1970; Tournier, 1979; Marlatt, 1983). Its members are said to be coerced into a regressive dependency which fosters servitude, compliance and the surrendering of individual control to a higher power. Nothing could be farther from the truth. Such a stance completely misses the point of AA. Fortunately, there are many professionals who have a much less narrow view of AA (i.e., Kurtz, 1982; Bateson, 1973; Barrett, 1983; Thune, 1977).

Until recently, the relationship between professionals and self-help groups like AA was predominately one of mutual disregard and distrust, with the possibility of constructive interaction receiving scant consideration. At least part of this polarization stemmed from the fact that members of AA, before finding acceptance, help and constructive change as a result of their involvement in the program, had unsuccessfully sought help from professionals. Many professionals on the other hand, have found that trying to work with alcoholics along traditional lines was both frustrating and unrewarding. Both groups were equally dissatisfied in their interactions with each other. AA members for instance viewed professionals as incompetent, uncaring and distant. Professionals, on the other hand, saw alcoholics as unmotivated, manipulative, and untreatable.

However, within the last decade or so, various developments have brought many professionals and loyal AA members closer together. It has been a common assumption that peer or mutual-help groups have always had grassroots rather than professional origins. However, as Lieberman and Borman (1979) have noted, there has, in fact, been appreciable professional input in the formation and encouragement of several self-help groups. This is the case with Alcoholics Anonymous if one take the time to pursue the historical roots of the Twelve Step Program. Alcoholics Anonymous' chief architect, Bill Wilson, had read William James' classic text, *The Varieties of Religious Experience* (1902) extensively and James' philosophical position of Pragmatism is a theme which runs throughout Alcoholics Anonymous' program of recovery. Wilson also had extensive correspondence with Carl Jung and Jung's influence is strongly reflected in the spiritual emphasis of the program. Kurtz (1982) also notes that there are "profound parallels that exist between the AA insight and the animus of existential philosophy" (p. 38-39). AA's philosophical and theoretical roots are diverse and they run deeply. The source of AA's influence will be explored in more detail later in the chapter. First, it is important to understand why AA has remained so misunderstood by countless professionals when the organization's sole purpose is to help suffering alcoholics and remain free of controversy (the fifth and tenth tradition of The Twelve Traditions).

While many dedicated professionals are aware or fast becoming aware of the importance of understanding and working closely with self-help groups like AA, there are countless other professionals who have little desire or motivation to understand, much less learn from these organizations. Lieberman and Borman (1979) point out that those professional contributors who work most closely with self-help groups share a distinguishing characteristic of having become disenchanted with the dominant orthodoxes of their respective fields of specialization in the treatment of addiction. Thus, professionals who have worked with alcoholics and addicts on a sustained basis have learned that more traditional, orthodox methods of treatment have been insufficient in their treatment. Therefore, the first form of "training" which has induced professionals to become interested in self-help groups like AA has been professional defection from their prescribed ideological frameworks. Professionals in a refractory frame of mind were, in short, looking for better ways to help alcoholics at a time when alcoholics were trying to find ways of helping themselves.

A related consideration is that many professionals have had to look for a way to get better help for themselves through AA because, in many cases, their own professional specialties had failed them. There are many physicians, psychiatrists, and psychologists who are members and staunch supporters of AA for the reason that it, alone, has provided successful help in the treatment of their own addiction. As Kurtz writes (1982), "It is time to take Alcoholics Anonymous seriously" (p. 30). However, AA should not be understood only for its therapeutic success and social significance, it needs to be appreciated for its unique intellectual significance. AA is not given the intellectual respectability it deserves for a number of reasons. Kurtz for one sees this lack of appreciation tied to our culture's rejection of all existential philosophies that stress limitation and personal responsibility.

> AA is not generally accorded intellectual respectability because its core insistences on essential limitation and on mutuality as preferable to objectivity reveal it to be a counter enlightenment phenomenon antithetical to the central assumptions of self-styled "modernity". (p. 38)

Thune (1977) expresses similar sentiments, but feels the misunderstanding of AA is due to the program's nonpositivist, quasirevivalistic, and transcendentalistic emphasis.

> It is no accident that the therapeutic program of Alcoholics Anonymous challenges the conventional medical, psychological, and sociological concepts of causation and that it ignores the findings and questions of specialists in these fields. Its roots lie less in the sciences than in such non-positivist, quasirevivalistic, transcendental efforts of the Oxford Group Movement. To attempt to understand AA on an analytic and positivist model obscures its uniqueness. (p. 75)

To properly understand AA, one must investigate AA from a number of different perspectives. Its history and philosophical roots must be appreciated. An understanding of its pragmatic "workings" needs to be integrated with the existential, psychological, and religious contributions of many gifted and dedicated professionals (James, Kurtz, Wallace, Thune, & Bateson). Lastly, the familiar misconceptions about AA must be corrected and the programs true position in the treatment of alcoholism must be interpreted within the context that will allow professionals to understand its significance to treatment of all types of disorders. In short, AA can offer some important principles of treatment that are applicable to psychotherapy, both individual and group, for patients who are not addicted.

THE SELF-HELP MOVEMENT

Several forces have contributed to the self-help movement of which AA is the earliest and best known. One factor is America's pluralistic ethnology; Americans are joiners who frequently seek a social identity through group affiliation (Dumont, 1974). The limited numbers of available professionals who could offer help have also contributed to the self-help movement. During the 1930s, when AA was formed, there were far less professionals available than there are now. Psychotherapy was also limited almost exclusively to individual therapy. Those professionals who were available continued to emphasize one-to-one therapy and underutilized the therapeutic potential of groups, peer influence, and consequently failed to reach as many people as they would have if they had worked more with groups. Thus, professionals failed to meet the demands for service because they were too few in number and they did not utilize the most efficient and appropriate therapeutic strategies available for the disorders presented to them.

Even if the supply of professionals had been ample and these professionals had utilized the most efficient approaches to the kinds of problems dealt with in self-help groups, such groups would have continued to flourish for a number of other reasons. Two of the most important reasons are that self-help groups are free and inexpensive and peer influence is powerful.

This is especially true if the peer shares a similar problem. Identification, support, and sharing of common concerns are powerful curative forces. It hasn't been until recently, that professionals have come to understand the power of groups to maximize therapeutic gain. AA has intuitively recognized what Yalom and others are starting to take advantage of in an organized fashion. Peers are frequently more influential than professionals in producing behavior change.

Psychological theory and research supports the clinical opinion that peers are a source of important influences. Peers have enormous influence on individuals during their childhood and adolescence (Muus, 1968; Patterson & Anderson, 1964). Peer influence is especially important in the early socialization of individuals (Hartup, 1970). Festinger (1954) has presented convincing evidence that individuals are most influenced by persons whom they perceive as like themselves. Gartner and Riessman (1984) agree when they write "The strongest influences are those whom the subject sees as like himself. For example, in the statement of the old-timer at the AA meeting that he is an alcoholic, but obviously under control, the new member sees what he or she can become" (p. 21). Emrick (1977) expressed similar sentiments when he wrote "Resocialization may best describe the events and mechanisms occurring in peer-oriented residential treatment centers for drug addicts" (p. 121).

While peers powerfully affect individuals, peer groups do even more so. Research presented by Emrick (1977) points to the influence of groups in providing individuals with social support, social identity, and social reality. Peer groups represent even more influence than groups not made up of peers. By definition, there is more of a basis for similarity in peer groups. In psychotherapy groups with peers, the similarity lies in the problem or issue which was the reason for the person joining the group. Common experiences and attitudes about alcohol and drugs yield more interpersonal attraction than when these commonalities are absent. Homogeneity of group members, as Yalom has clearly demonstrated, leads to more cohesiveness. Homogeneity and cohesiveness in turn yield greater influences of group members as well as greater uniformity of attitudes. Add to this the fact that people learn better and more readily from peers and are more likely to imitate peers, and there is ample evidence why self-help groups like AA are so widespread and flourishing.

ALCOHOLICS ANONYMOUS: ITS HISTORICAL ROOTS

The usual birthdate assigned to AA is 1935, but the program's origin actually began earlier than that and stared with its founder,

Bill Wilson. To understand AA's history, you have to understand William Griffith Wilson. A seemingly hopeless alcoholic who had made and lost two fortunes on Wall Street, Wilson was an intensely inquisitive man who had tried for years to control his drinking and had experienced repeated failures. Pushed to the point of despair and suicide, Wilson was visited by a good friend prior to what was to be Wilson's fourth and final hospitalization for his alcoholism. His friend, Ebby T., a hopeless alcoholic like Wilson, was miraculously sober. The friend revealed to Wilson that he had been led to salvation from his alcoholism after joining the Oxford Group Movement — an evangelically oriented group styled to recapture the pietist insight of primitive Christianity. Ebby T. had joined the Oxford Group Movement at the recommendation of Rowland H., a friend who had been treated by the noted Swiss psychiatrist Carl Jung. This young man, a talented and wealthy financial wizard had attempted virtually every known cure for alcoholism and in desperation traveled to Zurich, Switzerland, to enter analysis with Jung in 1931. Shortly upon his return to the U.S. he promptly relapsed. Rowland H. was subsequently told by Jung that he was "frankly hopeless as far as any further medical and psychiatric treatment was concerned." Jung suggested that the only possible source of hope might be "spiritual or religious experiences — in short a genuine conversion." He was cautioned however "that while such experiences had sometimes brought recovery to alcoholics, they were . . . comparatively rare" (Kurtz, 1979, p. 8-9). As Ebby T. conveyed this story to his friend Bill W., it was presented with a Jungian insight and emphasis. Only later did this event have any significance on Wilson or AA.

Despite Ebby's efforts, Wilson did not remain sober. Wilson, however, did come to share this information with his doctor, William D. Silkworth. It was through the influences of these individuals (Jung, Silkworth, Ebby T.) that a series of events were initiated which would eventually serve as a foundation for the AA program.

In *Alcoholics Anonymous Comes of Age* (1957), Wilson acknowledged the importance to AA of William D. Silkworth, in helping to lay the foundation from which the disease concept of alcoholism was derived. More importantly, it was Silkworth who quoted William James' statement that "transforming spiritual experiences are nearly always founded on calamity and collapses" (James, 1902). In his book, Wilson describes the conversion experience he encountered while being treated for an especially severe case of depression and anxiety following his most recent drinking spree. By all descriptions available he experienced what has been typically described in philosophical and religious literature as a mystical experience (Buber, 1960; Kaufman, 1963; Stace, 1966). Though not frequently articulated, Wilson's recorded descriptions share many of the common properties which are reported in such an experience as they typically appear to transcend historical context and cultural influences. Typically reported is a flash of bright, blinding light followed by periods of euphoria, timelessness, serenity and feelings of oneness with some higher presence. As Wilson wrote, "I now found myself in a new world of consciousness which was suffused by a Presence. One with the universe, a great peace stole over me."

Wilson was almost immediately apprehensive about his "spiritual experience." Had he not been warned by Dr. Silkworth of alcohol-induced brain damage? It was only much later, at an AA convention in 1955, that Wilson set it down in print. He had been reluctant to recount this event for he had discovered that it impaired rather than aided his credibility. There was nothing that he wanted to avoid more than the impression that AA was a bunch of drunks who had gotten sober because they had gotten religion.

When he had had a little time to reflect on this experience, Wilson began to test it. Discussions with his good friend, Dr. Silkworth, assured him that he was not mad, that conversion experiences sometimes were reported by "hopeless alcoholics" who had then been turned around and recovered from their alcoholism. He referred Wilson to William James' *Varieties of Religious Experiences*. In the years that followed, Wilson poured over James' writings. Much of the significance of James' writings was that it allowed for Wilson a generalized discussion of the conversion experience. It was James' theory that spiritual experiences could have a definite objective reality and might totally transform a man's life. Some, but by no means all of these experiences, James believed, came through religious channels. All, however, appeared to have their source in pain and utter hopelessness. Complete "deflation at depth" was the one requirement to make someone ready for a transforming experience. "Deflation at depth," as any recovering alcoholic knows, is captured and expressed in AA terminology as hitting bottom.

Leuba (1896) and Starbuck (1899) — whose writings were frequently cited by James — address the conversion experience with specific clarity. Leuba emphasized this reversal and also pointed out that a second precondition to conversion is self-surrender. In fact, this is the first step of AA's Twelve Step Program. But Wilson was still apprehensive. It wasn't until later that Wilson was able to integrate his experience. Kurtz captures his struggle when he writes about Wilson's understanding of his experience through his reading of William James.

> What Wilson got — or thought he got — from the book was to prove significant to the history of Alcoholics Anonymous:
> . . . Spiritual experiences, James thought, could have objective reality; almost like gifts from the blue, they could transform people. Some were sudden brilliant illuminations: others came on very gradually. Some flowed out of religious channels; others did not. But nearly all had the great common denominators of pain, suffering, calamity. Complete hopelessness and deflation at depth were almost always required to make the recipient ready. The significance of all this burst upon me. *Deflation at depth* — yes, that was *it*. Exactly that had happened to me.
> This was the substance of what Wilson had come to understand; also important was the meaning he found inherent in it, for his moment was — taken together with his "spiritual experience" — the third of the four founding movements of Alcoholics Anonymous. One-half of the core idea — the necessity of spiritual conversion — had passed from Dr. Carl Jung to Rowland. Clothed in Oxford Group practice, it had given rise to its yet separate other half — the simultaneous transmission of deflation and hope by "one alcoholic talking to another" — in the first meeting between Bill and Ebby. Now, under the benign guidance of Dr. Silkworth and the profound thought of William James, the two 'halves,' joined in Wilson's mind to form an as yet only implicitly realized whole. (pp. 20-21)

Wilson came to realize such dramatic shifts in personality are rare but they do happen. Foremost among them are the phenomena of conversion, such as religious conversions exemplified by the reports collected by William James and described in the case histories of Carl Jung. Similarly, Jung told Wilson some cases of traumatic neurosis and relapse occurred after successful therapy and those occurrences represent shifts from health to neurosis.

Likewise, both Martin Heidegger (1962) and Karl Jaspers (1975) wrote extensively about situations which were capable of compelling a person to often make dramatic and drastic changes in their lives. Jaspers described these occurrences as "limit situations"; conditions in which an individual would be confronted with the futility of their present mode or pattern of interacting. Limit situations, as Heidegger describes them, function as a catalyst for the evaluation and confrontation of one's existence. Anguish and despair (Angst) were the necessary emotional components required to compel one to drastically alter one's awareness (Enlschlossenheit) and interaction with the world (Existenz).

Wilson intuitively recognized this phenomena as the crucial component of his recovery. Surrender is therefore the cornerstone of AA's twelve steps to recovery. Surrender usually refers to a state of nonassertion of individuality, of losing oneself in something else, but the difference as Angyal (1965) and AA apply it is momentous. "One submits to the alien and becomes diminished through submission, one surrenders one's isolation to enter a large unit and enlarges one's life" (Angyal, 1965, p. 107).

Years later Wilson began corresponding with Carl Jung. His letters proved to be an important influence in Wilson's development of the AA treatment philosophy. It is important to note that Wilson's insistent drive to understand what he had experienced led him to struggle and resolve the psychological, religious and spiritual aspects of what was later to become known as Alcoholics Anonymous. It was Wilson's desire to interpret and define this experience that later brought him in contact with the Oxford Group Movement.

Wilson wrote, "when the pupil is ready, the teacher appears." Such is the case because Wilson soon became involved with the leader of the Oxford Group Movement. The interchange which resulted was reciprocal and soon the spiritual principles of the Oxford Group were to become the foundation upon which AA operates. 1. Self-examination, 2. Acknowledgment of faults, 3. Restitutions of wrongs done, and above all, 4. Constant work with others. The formulation of AA's basic tenets of character defects, restitution of harm done, and working with others can be directly traced back to Oxford Group Movement, Ralph Waldo Emerson and the influence of the Transcendentalists. The application of these principles would eventually lead to the development of the treatment modality which would soon become unsurpassed in the treatment of alcoholism and drug addiction.

AA – HOW IT WORKS AND HOW IT DOESN'T WORK

Misconceptions about AA are legion. Sometimes it is better to understand the way things don't work, before a true understanding of its actual workings can be comprehended. Common misconceptions about AA will be presented and hopefully corrected. In an attempt to gather a more comprehensive understanding of AA, a number of different perspectives will be presented. AA, of course has its own explanation on how it works and I will attempt to interpret what AA does to treat alcoholism. However, Existential, Psychological and Phenomenological frameworks are equally creditable ways of looking at and understanding AA. Each of these perspectives will be examined. Finally, AA will be explored in relation to its religious, spiritual and ideological significance. A final question will be raised concerning AA's lack of formal scientific principles. Is AA less credible, as some claim, because it is not scientific or empirically derived?

Common Misconceptions of AA

John Wallace (1984) and others have outlined some common misconceptions which professionals hold about AA. They are:

1. AA promulgates a simplistic, naive disease concept of alcoholism.
2. AA ignores psychological etiological factors.
3. AA is a substitute dependency.
4. AA forces members to admit to being an alcoholic.
5. AA rejects controlled drinking on purely ideological beliefs.
6. AA is a religious organization.

AA Promulgates a Simplistic, Naive Disease Concept of Alcoholism

AA's concept of alcoholism as a disease is neither simplistic nor naive. The founders of AA adopted the disease concept based on what they felt was the respectable medical opinion of that time (AA World Services, 1960; Jellinek, 1960). While the original hypotheses that alcoholism was an allergy has never been proven, many of today's leading biologically oriented researchers (i.e., Goodwin) still hold to the disease concept, as does the American Medical Association. AA, in fact, has never accepted alcoholism as just a physiological disease. In the fellowship of AA, members refer to alcoholism as a "four-fold disease" that involves physical, mental, emotional, and spiritual factors. Many members use the disease concept as a metaphor or analog. True to their heritage of William James' Pragmatism, they are more concerned about the effectiveness of utilizing the disease concept rather than engaging in polemics about whether alcoholism fits the right criteria for the true definition of disease.

Another reason many professionals have difficulty understanding AA's use of the disease concept is that they do not properly understand what AA means when AA talks about the "disease of alcoholism." Thune (1977) addresses this confusion when he writes,

> While it is a commonplace that AA has insisted that alcoholism is a disease, what has not been clearly recognized is that it is not taken to be a disease in the conventional sense. For AA has taken the category of disease and, without overt warning, radically redefined it to produce a category remarkably unlike that which exists for conventional medical science. Not only have diagnosis and therapy acquired a fundamentally new meaning and relation, but even the goal of 'therapy' cure, does not exist in the form found in conventional systems. (p. 73)

AA Ignores Psychological Factors

This is a gross misconception. The first step of the AA program is the only step that addresses drinking. The rest of the eleven steps of the Twelve Step Program (see Figure 1) are dedicated almost exclusively to what AA calls "the removal of character defects." AA is commonly referred to by its members as a "program for living." Many people don't understand the purpose of AA and view it as a program geared "to get a person to stop drinking." This is a one-dimensional view of AA. Just to stop drinking is to be dry. AA members do not aim for dryness, they seek sobriety. Critics fail to understand the difference between "being sober" and "being dry." Sobriety for AA is a complex, subtle, and multidimensional occurrence that can only be obtained if a person actively "works the steps of the program." AA members know that to stop drinking is necessary only because it allows the alcoholic to work the other eleven steps. An alcoholic doesn't join AA to stop drinking. Alcoholics don't even join AA to go to meetings. Although both of these occurrences are prerequisites for recovery. Alcoholics attain sobriety only if they work earnestly to remove the defects in character that are such an intricate part of the alcoholic's bankrupt value system and life-style.

FIGURE 1

12 Steps of the AA Program

1. We admitted we were powerless over alcohol — that our lives had become unmanageable.
2. Came to believe that a Power greater than ourselves could restore us to sanity.
3. Made a decision to turn our will and our lives over to the care of God as we understood him.
4. Made a searching fearless moral inventory of ourselves.
5. Admitted to God, to ourselves, and to another human being the exact nature of our wrongs.
6. Were entirely ready to have God remove all these defects in character.
7. Humbly asked Him to remove our shortcomings.
8. Made a list of all persons we had harmed, and became willing to make amends to them all.
9. Made direct amends to such people wherever possible, except when to do so would injure them or others.
10. Continued to take personal inventory and when we were wrong promptly admitted it.
11. Sought through prayer and meditation to improve our conscious contact with God as we understood Him, praying only for knowledge of His will for us and the power to carry that out.
12. Having had a spiritual awakening as the result of these steps, we tried to carry this message to alcoholics, and to practice these principles in all our affairs.

Wallace (1982) defines recovery of the AA member in relation to sobriety.

In AA, members distinguish between being dry and being sober. To be dry and dry alone is perceived by members as, at best, a transitional state on the way to sobriety and, at worst, a miserable, uncomfortable, and undesirable condition. 'Dry but not sober' is a commonly heard description in AA that refers to a person who is not drinking but who has failed to come to grips with important aspects of self that involve values, attitudes, feelings, typical patterns of behavior, and personality factors.

Among AA members, *sobriety* refers to a complex, subtle, and multidimensional state in which aspects of the drinking personality, life-style, and world view are no longer evident. Sobriety is, in effect, a change of consciousness, an altered state or, if you will, an heightened spiritual awareness in which elements of serenity, acceptance, contentment, gratitude, and joyfulness are evident. Words like 'balance,' 'wholeness,' 'fulfillment,' and 'spiritual transformation' are necessary if the AA concept of sobriety is to be grasped and distinguished from mere dryness or abstention alone. (p. 290-291)

AA, as always, encouraged its members to monitor themselves psychologically. Bill Wilson, himself, twice returned to individual psychotherapy after attaining sobriety. Certainly, this demonstrates that at least the founder of AA was committed to the importance of psychological factors in his own recovery. Support of this position is also reflected in the Big Book (1955),

By now the newcomer has probably arrived at the following conclusions: That his character defects, representing instincts gone astray, have been the primary cause of his drinking and his failure at life; that unless he is now willing to work hard at the elimination of the worse of these defects, both sobriety and peace of mind will still elude him; that all the faulty foundation of his life will have to be torn out and built anew on bedrock. (p. 50)

AA Is a Substitute Dependency

This is an especially troublesome criticism since many professionals see anything less than complete autonomy and independence as problematic. Even if one accepted the premise of this argument, it is preferable to have a dependence on an organization that promotes health, sobriety and helping others to a drug that promotes sickness, death and unmeasurable suffering to oneself, family and society. For some reason, many professionals fail to understand how their devotion to their church, tennis club, or professional organization is any less dependent than an AA member's devotion to AA.

Weinbergh expresses similar sentiment when he writes,

> Even if one accepted the premise (which to be consistent would also seem to rule out devotion to an organized religion or to psychiatric cults such as psychoanalysis), the author is hard pressed to consider this argument as reasonable. Since one cannot deny that alcohol dependency is extremely harmful to the individual, his family, and society, whereas AA dependency means sobriety, stability, and helping others as a result of living the program, what is the alleged harm in substituting the latter for the former?

AA members are in fact told, "You did not get sober to go to AA meetings." Dependency is actually discouraged in the program. What often gets passed off as dependency by AA's critics is actually the alcoholic's investment of himself in relationships within the AA fellowship. Often, this is the first time that the AA member has engaged in any type of meaningful human contact while not drinking or intoxicated. Weinbergh stresses the importance of this involvement when he writes:

> The close ties to an accepting group of peers which are generated over time may serve as a powerful incentive to resist the first drink and avoid facing loss of esteem in the group. Finally, AA groups frequently sponsor social events — picnics, dances, etc. — which help foster group involvement and also provide the alcoholic with an atmosphere which combines fun with sobriety, a combination often unknown to him for many years if at all in his adult life. It is of great importance to learn or relearn such an association, because there is little incentive in staying sober if one cannot have any fun in life without drinking.

AA Forces Its Members to Admit Being an Alcoholic

AA's literature is most clear on this point. *The only requirement for membership is a desire to stop drinking* (1955). AA literature specifically outlines the freedom of the individual to interpret and utilize the Twelve Step Program as he or she desires. Diagnosis of the self remains the key to membership. Again, the Big Book of AA spells this out:

> We do not like to pronounce any individual as alcoholic but you can quickly diagnose yourself. Step over to the nearest barroom and try some controlled drinking. Try to drink and stop abruptly. Try it more than once. It will not take long for you to decide, if you are honest with yourself about it. It may be worth a bad case of jitters if you get a full knowledge of your condition. (pp. 31-32)

AA, actually, has no criteria itself for applying the label of alcoholic to its members. AA members do follow some customs in this procedure, however. First, they are told to diagnose themselves. They are alcoholic if they say they are alcoholic. C. Barrett (1985) sums up this process when he writes,

> Alcoholics Anonymous (AA), itself, has no criteria for applying the label "alcoholic" but members of AA do follow some customs. First, AA members clearly diagnose themselves: they are alcoholic if they say they are alcoholic. In a chapter on "How it works" (AA World Service, 1939, p. 58) one reads that a person who wants what AA has should consider taking certain steps that are "suggested as a program of recovery". The first of these is: "We admitted we were powerless over alcohol — that our lives had become unmanageable." If the person wants further help in self-diagnoses there is material that will permit a sort of matching operation that is not too different from that followed in DSM III. One can read: "We alcoholics are men and women who have lost the ability to control our drinking." There are also numerous personal stories or case histories, similar to those presented in psychology and medical textbooks, that one can use. The person may recognize a similar pattern of thought and behavior in himself and decide that, as the saying goes, "the shoe fits". (p. 19)

AA Rejects Controlled Drinking on Ideological Beliefs

AA members certainly have strong opinions about controlled drinking. However, this is not due to their ideological beliefs as much as it is due to their own numerous failures at controlled drinking. As the Big Book passage just quoted states, prospective members are encouraged to try controlled drinking. In fact, I personally have never met one alcoholic out of the thousands of alcoholics I have become acquainted with in AA who hasn't tried controlled drinking and failed. As the Big Book makes clear, the inability to consistently control one's drinking is central to AA's definition of alcoholism. John Wallace (1984) sums up this position best when he writes,

> Of all misconceptions of AA, this one is probably the most dangerous. First, the AA position on controlled drinking did not just appear out of the blue in a burst of ideological inspiration. The AA position grew out of hundreds of thousands of *empirical observations* of the drinking behavior of countless individuals in their natural social ecologies. It is correct to say in this instance that AA ideology grew naturally out of AA empirical observations of hundreds of thousands of individuals. (p. 291-292)

Wallace and others (See Chapter One) have presented convincing evidence that controlled drinking research has not been able to clearly demonstrate that controlled drinking is a viable option if a person is really an alcoholic. Wallace, who has found numerous flaws in many of the controlled drinking studies, writes:

> Second, a careful reading of the more influential pieces of controlled drinking research reveals that formal research on this matter has not been characterized by the care, thoroughness, and precision that one expects of scientific research. In fact, the more widely publicized pieces of formal research concerning controlled drinking have shown numerous serious methodological shortcomings (p. 292).

Since the consequences of encouraging an alcoholic to try controlled drinking can be life threatening, AA discourages it as a treatment option. However, if a person wants to try it, AA will not ostracize them from the program, as some critics seem to think. AA, in fact, welcomes back any member who chooses to return to abstinence. As the Big Book clearly states, "The only requirement for membership is a desire to stop drinking" (1955).

Many critics who see AA as an ideological movement also feel that AA members are fanatical in their support of AA and prejudiced against professionals. In many ways, this criticism is somewhat correct. AA members, because they had failed to receive the help they desired from professionals and have in turn gotten relief from their suffering in AA, are both weary of professionals and extremely supportive of the AA program.

Weinbergh addresses both these issues when he writes:

> Because the most vocal and dogmatic minority are obviously the most visible, one may erroneously generalize to the group as a whole. In fact, most AA members are no more zealous, self-righteous, or hyperverbal than anybody else and are just as quietly going on about the business of living. Naturally, if you *ask* a person who has dramatically changed about their "conversion", whether a formerly fat now thin, a formerly atheist now Catholic, a former Republican now Socialist, or a former drunk now sober, you stand a fairly good chance of hearing a lengthy and enthusiastic oration.
>
> Alcoholics have not been accorded dignity, respect and competent treatment by society as a whole, but professionals entrusted with their care bear a special burden of responsibility for the systematic maltreatment and non-treatment, overt and disguised rejection, that historically has been the rule rather than the exception. Even though the climate appears to be gradually changing as professionals become enlightened, it may be a long time before an alcoholic can be reasonably confident that any given professional understands the illness, accepts its victims, and is competent to participate in its treatment. One additional factor worth noting is that AA, like the enormous number of newer self-help groups proliferating for assorted purposes, is founded on the idea of people helping each other in a mutual fashion, and the strength and success of such groups is most probably related in part to the avoidance of the helper-helpless model of typical professional situations.

AA *Is a Religious Organization*

While spirituality is a critical part of the AA approach to recovery, AA is clearly not a religious program—at least no more so than the way William James and Carl Jung applied spiritual or religious themes in their approach to treatment. However, to the extent that some define religious as a code of conduct or ethics, then AA may be considered as being partly religious in nature. It is true that many AA members are church goers, but there are an equal number who do not participate in any organized forms of religion. For those unfamiliar with AA's approach to spirituality, this may be especially confusing. It is important to remember that God is defined in AA as a higher power. The AA member is left to his own resources in coming to grips with his understanding of God. For many AA members, this understanding takes on a Judeo-Christian concept; but, for many others, it does not. Wallace addresses this issue when he writes:

> Members of AA are not required to accept, practice, or promote any religious belief or concept. Members are *encouraged* to find a "power greater than self," but this external power can be construed in any manner that each individual member chooses. For many AA members, the AA group itself serves as a power greater than self. For others, abstract concepts such as love or truth may serve as higher powers around which a life can be oriented and through which direction can be sought. For still other AA members, a higher power may be construed in terms of historical or legendary figures (e.g., Christ, Buddha, God, Yahweh, and so forth). (p. 299)

Barrett (1984) recognizes that many professionals have difficulty with this issue because they fail to accurately understand AA's purpose and intent. They confuse AA's use of God with the church. They forget or do not know that AA's roots are not tied in any greater extent to traditional forms of religion as it is tied to the empirical sciences and positivism. As Barrett writes,

> This is no small matter since, it may be recalled, the early close association between the Akron AA and the Oxford Group (. . . a spiritual movement that sought to recapture the power of first century Christianity . . .) was ended in the later

1930's. Thus AA is not accurately identified with any religious group or a religious movement. (p. 23-24)

The Big Book also addresses this issue:

The only requirement for membership is a desire to stop drinking. There are no dues or fees for AA membership: we are self-supporting through our own contributions. AA is not allied with any sect, denomination, politics, organization or institution, does not wish to engage in any controversy; neither endorses nor opposes any causes. Our primary purpose is to stay sober and to help other alcoholics achieve sobriety. (AA World Services, Inc., 1953)

Barrett, (writing as a psychologist) also adds, "However, we would be true to our tradition (e.g., following James) in studying AA as a religious experience and social psychology could assist us in studying program ingredients such as modeling, goal setting, self-disclosure, and active participation (e.g., 90 meeting in 90 days)" (p. 22). Such a position is admirable, because it demonstrates there are some professionals who are willing to learn and understand the intricate workings of AA, rather than criticize it because they are either threatened by it or do not understand it. Of more concern, is science's refusal to investigate the relationship it has with religion and quasi-religious organizations like AA. This will be an issue dealt with in more detail later in the chapter. At this point, the different models for explaining why AA works will be presented.

AA – WHY AND HOW IT WORKS: AN INTERPRETATION OF AA

AA describes its organization as "a fellowship of men and women who share their experiences, strength and hope with each other that they may solve their common problem and help others to recovery from alcoholism" and adds that its purpose "is to stay sober and help other alcoholics achieve sobriety." Anonymity is required to avoid the possible stigma of membership and possible ostracism of family and friends. Anonymity also insures confiden-

tiality which permits free and candid discussion of problems and
difficulties.

However, the keystone upon which the Alcoholics Anonymous
philosophy is built remains the recognition and admittance that one
has an uncontrollable drinking problem. The members of Alcoholics Anonymous do not pursue or coddle a malingering prospect.
They make it plain that if he actually wanted to stop drinking they
would anywhere, anytime, reach out to help him. The program will
not work with those who only want to quit, or who want to quit
because they are afraid of losing their families or their jobs. The
effective desire AA states must be based upon enlightened self-in-
terest. The applicant must be fed up with the stark social loneliness
which engulfs the uncontrolled drinker, and he must want to put
some order into his bungled life.

Alcoholics Anonymous is guided by its suggested "Twelve
Steps." Suggested is the word to be emphasized, however, for there
are no musts in AA except those that the member sets up for himself. Basically, AA will demonstrate that alcoholics can be accepted
and loved. The alcoholic who comes to AA for the first time, a
stranger, rejected and lonely, is received as a valued member of the
human race worthy of being salvaged. Listening to members recount life experiences as dismal as his own, and then observing how
they have overcome their drinking problem, the alcoholic is filled
with hope if they could do it, perhaps he can also. He becomes
motivated to try.

The alcoholic learns he must live one day at a time without taking
a drink. By attending AA meetings and verbalizing problems, he
strengthens his resistance to drink and gradually reconstructs his
lifestyle to rid himself of dependency on alcohol. The most crucial
concept involves the alcoholic recognizing himself as an individual
whose illness is an uncontrollable drinking problem, he can accept
the tenet which becomes the foundation of his rehabilitation program: "even one drink is too many."

The alcoholic, due to the nature of his illness, has established an
elaborate denial and rationalization system. These psychological
defenses which prevent the recognition and admittance of his illness
are as much involved and intricately connected with his disease as
alcohol itself is. Vernon Johnson (1969) sums up the dynamics of
this interplay best:

> The primary factor within this primary condition, however,
> is the delusion, or impaired judgment, which keeps the harm-

fully dependent person locked into his self-destructive pattern. It must be met and dealt with first since it blocks his entering any therapeutic process at all. The alcoholic evades or denies outright any need for help whenever he is approached. It must be remembered that he is not in touch with reality. (p. 44)

AA recognizes this need for recognition. It is the first of its Twelve Steps and only when the alcoholic has reached his crisis and at a gut level, has surrendered to some Power greater than himself. The spiritual and religious dynamics at the level of recovery cannot be overstated for an alcoholic must confront himself in his naked existence. The existential overtones to such a crisis is the central psychological factor of the recovery program. The alcoholic is asked simply to exchange the destructive dependence upon alcohol for a constructive Power (Steps 2 and 3). The alcoholic's idea of what that Power may be is not important in AA. The important thing is for the newcomer to recognize that he or she has not been able to manage the part of their life that has been affected by drinking. As the alcoholic surrenders he sees that it is possible for him to risk being himself, and he moves consciously toward deepening his meaningful relationship with others because this will help him recover himself.

Once this gut-level surrender to some spiritual awakening is accepted, the alcoholic must pay a personal cost. The dynamics of forgiveness and restoration are difficult concepts to acknowledge. The wrongs that have been done during the period of illness can never be completely reconciled. It is the process of this reconciliation which involves the monotonous and painstaking road to sobriety. Regardless of what friends and neighbors may think, the alcoholic does not necessarily feel happy to wake up in the morning facing life without a drink. Despite painful hangovers he has experienced previously, these may seem more tolerable than the gnawing fears and vague anxiety he now feels as he anticipates each day's activities.

The cost is one to be paid in psychological pain. The reward is the sense of forgiveness and the vitality of new interpersonal relationships. The goal to stop drinking is not a totally adequate one. A new way of viewing life, a new sense of self-worth and self-respect, and a new appreciation of one's responsibility and relationships with others are vital to sober living. Often a mature religious faith helps provide a new beginning and emotional help for the trying times facing every alcoholic.

Once he has made a moral inventory of himself (4th Step) with the aid of AA, he acknowledges these wrongdoings to his Higher Power and another individual (5th Step), the alcoholic then restores and makes amends to persons he has abused and, in general, cleans up his past as well as he can (Step 9). This catharsis is regarded as important because of the compulsion which a feeling of guilt exerts in the alcoholic obsession. The belief is that personal resentments have a strong influence on the push back to the bottle. Making a list of grudges (Step 8) and resolving not to be stirred by them (Steps 10 and 11) is a prerequisite to sobriety and the helping with other alcoholics (Step 12).

The AA approach is practical and is based on the idea that every problem drinker at one time or another has gone at least twenty-four hours without a drink. So the AA member does not swear off alcohol for life or for any other extended period of time. The alcoholic is made to realize that there is nothing he can do about tomorrow now. AA wants the alcoholic to concentrate on staying sober today during this twenty-four hours. Then when the alcoholic feels the desire to take a drink, it is accepted as simply something that must be dealt with today. They are taught not to worry about tomorrow's craving, but merely concentrate on postponing taking a drink today.

Regular attendance at local meetings plays an important part in the life of sobriety. Group meetings and relationships provide the testing ground for new ways of dealing with one's emotions and with the problems of living. Alcoholics frequently accept confrontation and support from others who struggle with the same problems as they, although they may reject similar responses from physicians, ministers, or other professional persons. AA is one of the most successful approaches to sobriety because it practices these principles. AA has the benefit of comradeship and shared problems coupled with the added asset of emotional objectivity and professional understanding of personality dynamics that others provide.

But the general atmosphere of an AA meeting is one of gaiety and good fellowship. Generally, AA members take their alcoholism seriously, but not themselves. That is another important part of the recovery program.

The Role of the Sponsor

Once the alcoholic has maintained a period of sobriety (usually at least a year), he is ready to embark on Twelfth Step work and possibly begin his informal apprenticeship as a sponsor. While sponsorship usually requires the alcoholic have an extended period of sobriety, Twelfth Step work can be initiated with very little sobriety. Although there are no clear rules in AA regarding sponsors, the more sobriety and more stability the AA member has in his life, the more respect he is attributed within the fellowship. This in turn usually leads to a much greater desire for newcomers in the AA program to seek him out in the hope he would serve as their sponsor. While Twelfth Step work and sponsorship are often intricately connected, one does not necessarily imply the other. In order to avoid confusion around this area, it will be important to understand these concepts thoroughly.

It must be remembered that alcoholics helping other alcoholics is the primary purpose of AA in both the Twelfth Step of the AA program ("Having had a spiritual awakening as the result of these steps, we tried to carry this message to alcoholics, and to practice these principles in all our affairs") (1955, p. 60) and in the Fifth Tradition ("Each group has but one primary purpose – to carry its message to the alcoholic who still suffers") p. 564.

Sponsorship is therefore viewed by many as Twelfth Step work. Madsen (1974) describes the importance of this relationship for the new AA member:

> As soon as possible, the newcomer is expected to pick out an AA sponsor. The newcomer thereby becomes the sponsor's "baby" or "pigeon". . . the close tie between sponsor and pigeon may be brief or last for a lifetime, varying with the dependency needs of the pigeon . . . if identification is made with AA and a sponsor, the newcomer is on the program and his chances for a sober life are excellent. (p. 183)

Emrick (1977) views the Twelfth Step worker and sponsorship in AA as serving two important functions. First, the "Twelfth Stepper" is frequently called upon to act as a crisis worker. Since many alcoholics join the organization during a crisis, the sober member of AA will frequently be called upon to intervene during a particularly stressful time. Twelfth Steppers usually do not insist that the alcoholic admit his alcoholism; but rather seek to develop quick rapport by recounting a brief history of their own alcoholism. If the alcoholic can identify and is responsive to the Twelfth Stepper, he may accompany him to a meeting. Some alcoholics respond to such an approach, some do not.

Secondly, the Twelfth Stepper or sponsor gets involved in an ongoing helping process with either one or numerous new members in the AA program. In this relationship, the sponsor may serve various functions for the sponsoree. He or she may be used by the sponsor as a father-confessor, social companion, psychotherapist, advice giver and, in some cases, vocational and financial advisor. Bateson (1976) describes the Twelfth Step as that "which enjoins aid to other alcoholics as a necessary spiritual exercise without which the member is likely to relapse" (p. 333). Madsen (1974) expresses similar sentiments when he defines Twelfth Step work as "the missionary step, the pledge to help other alcoholics onto the road to sobriety . . . 'Twelfth-stepping' gives a sense of purpose and serves as a constant reminder to the alcoholic of 'where he's been'" (p. 182).

It is Madsen's statement which summarizes the true value of Twelfth-Step Work and sponsorship. Alcoholics stay sober by helping other alcoholics. Alibrandi (1978) writes,

> Another benefit of sponsorship . . . is the reminder of what it used to be like. As he shares his own experiences with the newcomer, he recalls the difficulties alcohol created in his life and the progress he has made in sobriety. This sponsor believes that to forget the disaster of his own drinking is to increase the danger of drinking again. (p. 167)

When an alcoholic acting as a sponsor helps a sponsoree, the helper gains as much as the recipient does in the interaction. Twelve Step Work is based on the unspoken principle which translates into the message that before a person be healed they have to know they can heal another. While such a discovery was serendipitous for AA, it is a very important component of the recovery process. Without it, the alcoholic would never come to realize that he can make a difference and be of importance to someone else. In this capacity, the alcoholic learns he is not so inherently corrupt that he cannot be of value to others. As R. D. Laing (1960) writes, "Frustration becomes despair when a person begins to question his own capacity to mean anything to anyone."

The origin of one drunk staying sober by helping another was stumbled upon by Bill Wilson as he fought to maintain his newfound sobriety while on a business trip in a strange city. He picked up the phone instead of a drink and through that phone call remained sober by trying to help another alcoholic. Alibrandi (1978) describes this event. "The drunken plea, 'Can you help me?' was changed to 'Can I help you?' For the first time, a drunk, the traditional taker found the ability to give. Bill contacted Dr. Bob Smith, a suffering alcoholic and shared the experience of his sobriety after years of drunkenness, and together they founded the AA fellowship" (p. 163).

Wilson's discovery that giving to another alcoholic would keep him sober was the catalyst which made the AA program work. Kurtz demonstrates the paradox involved in this approach when he writes,

> The ability to make a difference is a deeply basic human need; indeed, A.A. founded its fellowship upon this vital need. At A.A.'s very beginning, when co-founders Bill Wilson and Dr. Bob Smith approached the bedside of the alcoholic who was to become "A.A. Number Three," it was their implicit appeal to Bill D.'s need to give that opened his mind and laid the solid foundation for what would become the essential hallmark of the A.A. approach. Wilson and Smith told this first "man on the bed" that they were talking to him for their own sakes far more than for his. Bill D. believed them, and therefore he listened: "All the other people that had talked to me wanted to help *me*, and my pride prevented me from listening to them, and caused only resentment on my part, but I felt as if I would be a real stinker if I did not listen to a couple of fellows for a short time, if that would cure *them*." (p. 59)

It is the paradox of the helper getting more in return when he gives than when he takes which is the foundation of the Twelfth Step work and the AA program. It is not by chance that this portion of the AA program is the twelfth and final step. AA members are strongly encouraged to work the steps of the AA program in sequence. They are told you don't do steps one and two and then jump to step six. Step twelve is to be initiated only after the other eleven steps are completed. AA members are cautious of "two steppers." Two steppers are members who only stop drinking (the first step) and then try to help all other alcoholics (Twelfth Step) before they are mentally, physically and spiritually able or ready. The AA member who is truly ready to do effective Twelfth Step work has undergone a very important psychological and spiritual change. The Twelfth Step is the final step in this process because AA realizes the alcoholic requires constant reminders of where they have been, what they once were and the direction they must travel if they are to maintain a healthy sobriety. Twelfth-Step work also insures a building of self-respect and helps the recovering alcoholic maintain the right kind of values and behavior which are central to serenity and sobriety.

Emrick sums up this process when he writes,

> The personal strength gained by the peer influencer also varies. He finds meaning and purpose for his life and acquires self-respect, status, and prestige by being important to others. He becomes more ethical rather than thinking of himself in an egocentric, narcissistic fashion. He becomes philosophical about failure by stressing that the source of failure of a recipient rests not with him (the peer influencer) but in the battle between the strength of AA and the lure of alcohol. Thus, he acquires the ability to encounter success and failure without drinking. He develops useful mechanisms of defense against the inner forces which have in the past led to drinking. Initially, he utilizes undoing, reaction formation, and counterphobia as he helps others stop drinking. When he matures in AA, sublimation operates more centrally. Finally, in his role as sponsor, he acquires skills for relating closely with others by experiencing emotionally involved relationships with sponsorees. (p. 126, 1977)

AA – HOW IT WORKS:
A PHENOMENOLOGICAL PERSPECTIVE

Carl Thune (1977) has presented a penetrating examination of AA from a phenomenological perspective. Many of his insights will be presented here in relation to George Kelly's phenomenological theory of personality. AA, from Thune's perspective, works because of its emphasis on AA members recounting their life histories at AA meetings. It is through the telling of their life history that they are taught how to interpret their past in a way that gives meaning to the past and hope for the future. Thune, operating from a pure phenomenological framework, holds the position that the past never merely exists for anyone, whether they be alcoholic or not. Instead, the past is interpreted and created through the use of conceptual models. More significantly, "these models become models of and for the creation of the future, a future that is no more automatically 'given' than is the past" (p. 83).

Thune introduces the importance of life histories in AA when he writes,

> In a sense, then, one of the first lessons A.A. must teach new members is that their lives were incoherent and senseless as they knew them. Simultaneously, it must reveal the "correct" understanding and interpretation of the drinking alcoholic's vision of the world before a new member can accept the full benefits of the program — a program which offers a different coherence and meaning in their active alcoholic lives. In other words, according to A.A., not only do drinking alcoholics incorrectly perceive and understand the world, but they cannot even correctly perceive and understand their perceptions and understandings of it. Through therapy they must learn new methods for evaluating them.
>
> More abstractly it is not just a revised and now coherent vision of the world which A.A. offers, but one which has altered the relation between its components. For example, in their life histories members describe the drinking alcoholic's life as he understands it — going steadily "down hill" or "around in circles." As long as drinking continued the future was merely a continuation of the past with the present being but a moment in which that past was re-enacted. (p. 81-82)

The Life History, AA From a Phenomenological Perspective

One of the major tenets of phenomenology is the demonstration that the world and the self, rather than being automatically given in the order of things, are being constantly recreated as an individual proceeds through life. Insight into an individual's life then comes from an analysis of the world as he constructs it; a world in which he must live as he tries to make sense of his experience.

It is suggested by Thune that the nature, meaning and experience of these constructions of the self and the world by an alcoholic are subject to an ongoing process of reconstitution and redefinition, both in the process of his becoming an alcoholic and in the course of any successful treatment and recovery program. Central in this process will be the redefinition of the meaning and experience of alcoholism. Complementing this is the suggestion that alcoholism is better understood as in the terminology of AA, a defective mode of life. The implication is that a treatment regimen directed at reconstitution and redefinition of self and world provides a better way to deal with alcoholism than a model holding it analogous to a physical disease or a bad habit subject to modification. This is AA's claim and lies at the heart of the success that AA has enjoyed.

Like most therapeutic systems, AA faces the twin problems of diagnosis and treatment. However, the program's analysis of these facets of the therapeutic process bears little relation to those of more "orthodox" Western medical systems (Thune, 1977). It is here at the diagnosis and definition of alcoholism that AA parts company with many of the psychological definitions of alcoholism.

Objective diagnosis (an important and necessary component of scientific assessment in psychology) from a source other than the alcoholic himself is held irrelevant to the program. The success or failure of the program depends on whether the individual can diagnose himself as an alcoholic. It is this self-diagnosis that is the essence of AA's twelve steps to recovery (Norris, 1976). To paraphrase Laing (1971), the alcoholic must come to understand that one does not have alcoholism; rather one is alcoholic.

In addition to the "physical allergy" to alcohol suggested by the disease model of alcoholism, the alcoholic is held to possess an alcoholic personality described as immature and self-centered, he is spiritually sick, his naively egotistical and self-centered personality prevent any but the most artificial and superficial relation to others or to a "higher power." Central to the AA process will be the redefinition of the meaning and experience of alcoholism. Complementing this is the suggestion that alcoholism is better understood as in the terminology of AA, a defective mode of life (Madsen, 1974).

Within AA's therapy, the change demanded to eliminate this mental and spiritual disequilibrium, which the program identified as the heart of alcoholism is more than just a shift in understanding of the essence of the self. It requires a sharing with others of one past. From its founding, the life history has been a key element of AA practice and theory. In the life history, the members recount their experience and eventual control of alcoholism. In most cases if the speaker is not a physical derelict at the time of his active alcoholism the attempt is made to demonstrate that he was at least in a derelict frame of mind when drinking. And after accepting the program, many claim to have experienced "personality changes" which accompanies a new understanding of themselves and their world.

The stories surrounding their life histories are typically stereotyped and lead to the conclusion of the proper way to analyze and construct their past. The person's past is the means through which an individual attains control over his alcoholism. Through the stories the alcoholic comes to understand his life as more intelligible; he views it within a different structure and logic than he had previously.

Unlike most medically oriented therapeutic systems, the real problem as AA analyzes it, centers around helping the alcoholic to understand his basic "being" as alcoholic rather than as normal and non-alcoholic. It is AA's emphasis on the spiritually defective mode of being rather than a physical disability that provides the clearest expression of the belief that alcoholism is a defect of being. In many respects, AA invokes a spiritual or religious vocabulary in the absence of perhaps a more accurate but inaccessible philosophical-ontological terminology.

Alcoholism from the program's perspective is a total lifestyle or mode of being and action in the world within which misuse of alcohol is only one component; although be it the most important component. Elimination of drinking is an indispensable first concern, but is just the first step before altering other important aspects of the over-all defective life style. It is not uncommon to hear AA members chide someone who has stopped drinking but still maintains the defective mode of life as being on a dry drunk. The implication is that the alcoholic has given up alcohol but not their self-perceived construction of their self, which is associated with the alcoholic lifestyle.

Whereas society has irrevocably linked alcohol to the alcoholic AA insists upon their separation. As mentioned before, AA will argue that an individual is an alcoholic whether or not he drinks and that his behavior may be that of a typical alcoholic even if he has not had a drink for years. AA is therefore aware that many drinkers, even heavy drinkers are not necessarily alcoholics (1955).

Considering this orientation, it is not surprising that research which claims that alcoholics can be trained to drink socially (Sobell & Sobell, 1973) strikes AA as absurd; since alcoholism from this viewpoint appears as a bad habit subject to correction through education. The chasm which seems to exist between AA and the scientific community evolves around the latter's attempt to place alcoholism in a research paradigm and its insistence on identifying personality variables related to its etiology. This controversy is not easily resolved. Highly qualified researchers have for years been unable to determine whether alcoholism is a physical or mental problem. The outstanding specialists in the field, however, such as Ruth Fox (1973), E. M. Jellinek (1960), and Marty Mann (1973) have all realized that alcoholism embraces cultural, psychological, and physical factors.

While there is a considerable amount of misunderstanding and controversy surrounding AA's approach to alcoholism, there is virtually none of the efficacy of AA as a treatment modality. The literature is replete with substantial evidence which supports the fact that AA really does work (Bourne & Fox, 1973; Baily & Leach, 1965). The crucial question therefore is not whether AA works; but rather why does it work? This answer has long escaped psychologists for a number of reasons. Part of the answer for psychology's lack of understanding may be due to AA's transcendental and non-positivist foundations; variables which do not lend themselves easily to scientific investigation. As Kuhn (1962) suggests, a scientific community can often become a closed system with communication limited to only those with selected membership within that community. Under these conditions it is understandable that professionals have generally been reluctant to leave their accepted scientific paradigm to investigate variables which do not fit nicely and neatly into its accepted and proven methodology.

Kuhn's explanation helps explain the reluctance some professionals may have in their acceptance of AA as a legitimate treatment alternative. In light of Thune's phenomenological explanation of AA, it appears that much of their reluctance is due to their failure to shift paradigms when trying to understand and investigate AA. The problem then is not AA; but theirs due to their failure to expand their cognitive models of explanation so that AA is understood and examined in its proper light. If this shift in perspective is accomplished, one may understand better Thune's conclusions about AA.

> AA's "treatment", then, involves the systematic manipulation of symbolic elements within an individual's life to provide a new vision of that life, and of his world. This provides new coherence, meaning and implications for behavior. While the processes which have been discussed above clearly occurred in the groups investigated, the literature indicates that

similar patterns exist in other AA groups. Indeed, any alcoholism treatment program must successfully demonstrate to the alcoholic that he is an alcoholic, or , more exactly, it must succeed in allowing the alcoholic to demonstrate this fact to himself. This seems possible only if the alcoholic himself can discover a new past to confirm what ultimately must be a self-diagnosis. I suggest that even in systems operating according to principles different from AA's, one of the therapeutic requirements is the presentation of a new model which defines self and world.

These suggestions, however, should not be taken as contradictions of the conclusions reached by other analytic perspectives. Rather, they are intended to provide phenomenological perspective which complements other perspectives such as those offered by medicine, sociology and psychology. It is the summation of these different but clearly complementary perspectives, rather than academic arguments over which is true or which is formally or logically prior, that will lead to a more complete understanding of alcoholism and the mechanisms of therapy. (1977, p. 88)

The Self-Attribution of Alcoholism

Next to the importance which Thune places on the significance of the telling of one's life story at an AA meeting, he views the constant introduction of oneself as an alcoholic as the next most essential component of the recovery program. Each self-proclamation of "I am an alcoholic" is a constant reminder to each AA member that they are just a drink away from being the person they once were. This is a very confusing state of affairs to those whose interest in AA is only passing, superficial or purely academic. They fail to understand the significance of this ritual. In fact, many critics take special issue with AA's insistence that each AA member introduce themselves as an alcoholic. Individuals outside of the AA program interpret this as either degrading to the alcoholic or a constant negative reminder of the person's multiple shortcomings. They fail to understand how such a requirement can lead to anything but continual debasement and loss of self-respect. To the contrary, an AA member who introduces himself as an alcoholic does so proudly for he is conveying an important message to himself each time he stands up and makes such a proclamation. In order to understand the implications for such a self-attribution, it would be important to understand George Kelly's phenomenological theory of personal constructs for it parallels many of Thune's interpretations.

Kelly's (1966) Personal Construct Theory is founded on the model of "man the scientist" and views man as actively engaged in the interpretation and prediction of events in his world. Crucial to understanding both Thune and Kelly's theory of personal constructs is the idea that each personal construct is based upon the simultaneous perception of likeness and difference among objects of its context. There is no such thing as a difference without a likeness being implied, and vice versa. Each construct is therefore, dichotomous or bipolar in nature; and in dealing with an alcoholic, the therapist must frequently go off searching for the submerged poles in the alcoholic's thinking. It is important to understand that in Kelly's system each construct discriminates between two poles, one at each end of its dichotomy.

Consequently, Kelly's personal construct theory helps explain the significance of a person defining themselves as an alcoholic. The self-attribution of alcoholic connotes far more information for the alcoholic in AA than it does to the individual outside the program who defines themselves as someone who once drank too much. The term alcoholic signifies everything (self-centered behavior, negative attitude, corrupt values) that the sober AA member must guard against if they are to maintain a healthy sobriety. By constantly utilizing the self definition of alcoholic, the AA member, within Kelly's perspective, automatically implies the opposite; which is everything a healthy recovering and sober member of AA must attain. Each AA member is thus reminded with each pronouncement of "I am an alcoholic" that they are just a drink away from losing what they have become; which is a person whose values, attitudes, and behavior is the direct opposite of that of an alcoholic.

Bill Wilson had expressed similar sentiments many years before Kelly, when he wrote that within every recovering alcoholic there are two built-in authorities which the outside world could never understand. First, in the life of each AA member there still lurked a very real and ruthless tyrant and that tyrant was represented by booze and all that was associated with it. For this second authority Wilson called it an inner voice. In talking with others he would refer to it as a power, life-force, or any words with which the listener would be comfortable. What Wilson was describing is in Kelly's terms the two opposite poles of the alcoholic's personal construct system. In one sense the recovering alcoholic is everything that the practicing alcoholic is not. This helps explain the confusion often expressed by non-alcoholics in their failure to grasp how it is that one drink can cause an alcoholic to slip back into his old behavior. It is not his behavior that the alcoholic has slipped into, rather it is his personal construct associated with that behavior.

Andreas Angyal (1965), another early supporter of AA's treatment strategy, had presented very similar sentiments to those of Thune and Kelly.

Like Kelly, Angyal viewed the personality as dynamic and capable of operating between two poles of existence. At the one end there is the healthy potential and at the other there is the unhealthy or neurotic character. It was Angyal's opinion that this unhealthy or neurotic pole was best described as a lifestyle or a way of perceiving and interacting with the world. A person's neurotic style would permeate their entire personality and being. Angyal shared the opinion that neurosis was not just a focal emotional disturbance which could be eliminated or cut out as you would cut out a bad spot in an otherwise good apple.

Alcoholism from this perspective is viewed as more than just excessive drinking. This is why AA believes that alcohol consumption cannot be curtailed without addressing and treating the rest of the alcoholic's personality disturbance. The conflict which professionals have with AA's treatment approach presents itself around the issue of the necessity of total abstinence. While many professionals continue to view alcoholism as a focal disturbance and a symptom of some underlying personality characteristic, AA and Angyal see it as the primary issue which must be dealt with first. Abstinence from alcohol is the first step required from breaking the alcoholic style of living. Only after abstinence has been assured can the alcoholic learn to focus on changing his neurotic character.

Within this system, at any given moment, the individual is either healthy or neurotic depending on which system is dominant. AA would agree and would further say that drinking only encourages the neurotic lifestyle to dominate the healthy potential within the alcoholic. As AA recognizes, the alcoholic is isolated spiritually and can only relate to others on a superficial level. He cannot define his self because his being is controlled and clouded by his drinking. His alcoholism makes it impossible to relate to anyone or anything on a meaningful level. Because the fellowship of AA gives the recovering alcoholic an identification with something greater than himself, it permits a shift towards healthy relationships with others.

Angyal agreed with Thune when he suggested that the alcoholic's new definition of himself does not cut him off from his past history, but it changes his perception of his past. This is exactly what Thune says AA accomplishes in its recovery process. This is experienced through the alcoholics telling of their life history. Angyal however addresses two other very significant issues that Thune and Kelly omit. The first is the significance of denial and the second concerns relapse.

Angyal wants to come to grips with the baffling process of denial so common to the alcoholic's recovery. Why is it that the alcoholic is so reluctant to seek treatment? Why does he have to hit bottom before he will ever admit he has a drinking problem? Why is it that everyone else but the alcoholic will know he is an alcoholic, and what is it that blinds him to what everyone else sees so readily? Having to admit that one has been at fault is not a calamity for a self-confident person, but it is for the alcoholic, in whose system compensatory pride is a crucial element and losing face is disastrous. The prospect of giving up the alcoholic lifestyle is experienced as a threat not to life but to the alcoholic's integrity. It is a self-betrayal to be resisted at all costs. Small wonder that when an alcoholic's drinking is threatened, the alcoholic feels that everything is falling to pieces, that he is about to drive into nothingness, that he is dying.

The second issue that Angyal addresses is the recovery process so necessary to AA's treatment approach. This involves two secondary issues. First is the initial recognition of alcoholism and the second revolves around the typical problem of relapse which is a constant concern for any recovering alcoholic. The first step in AA's twelve steps to recovery is the admittance that one is an alcoholic. Angyal writes "To take responsibility to acknowledge, simply and frankly, the part one has played, and is still playing, in all of one's actions and in one's self-destruction. By one admitting this to another, the alcoholic discards his false front and moves beyond the confines of anxious secrecy" (1965, p. 118). This step forward could not have been made without some confidence that the alcoholic can live differently in the future. AA gives them this model. When this has been accomplished, the next step is dealing with the guilt and shame. AA views the resolution of guilt and shame as an intricate part of their recovery process. The necessary components of resolving guilt and shame is in essence paraphrased in the last nine steps of the AA recovery process. Angyal writes, "There is only one way of dealing with guilt—to regret it. This means sorrow for the harm that was done and the constructive actions left undone; for chances that were never taken, for the adventures missed and perhaps no longer possible, for having short-changed those who loved or needed one and tried in vain to come close to be helpful" (p. 136). But more is required than regret in combatting shame. The removal of shame occurs only if the alcoholic gives up the alcoholic life-style, with a strong desire to live in a different way. Shame requires a change in a person's sense of self. This is accomplished more slowly and usually with more difficulty.

The resolution of shame depends on whether or not the alcoholic's insights and struggles will result in lasting changes of real consequences. This depends on whether the alcoholic identifies with the new emerging pattern of health, and redefines himself in terms radically different from the patterns associated with his self-concept. Angyal stresses the importance of this change in an alcoholic's life pattern. "Drawing on the reports of reformed alcoholics one finds that they differ from the short-lived conversions in that the habit was given up not merely because of its specific deterious effects; a broader change of attitudes has rendered the habit uncompatible with the dominant system" (p. 121). The AA member now feels that drinking is inconsistent with his self-definition as a rational and responsible being. As this process unfolds, the detrimental elements of shame diminish.

Angyal also makes an important distinction between the task of getting healthy (sober) and staying healthy (sober). He feels too little emphasis is placed on the latter. AA recognizes the danger of allowing the constructive orientation to get lost inadvertently and unnoticeably. The alcoholic pattern may reinstate itself through a series of small steps, and a long time may pass before the person realizes the change.

Therefore, it is crucial to the alcoholic's recovery process that he avoid his past drinking situations. Through the process of his disease the alcoholic usually has isolated himself from anyone who doesn't drink like he does. Continual contact with people to whom one had been tied in a alcoholic relationship represents a continual threat to new attitudes which may also wear off in routine dealings with people who assume that the patient's new conduct is merely a hypocritical pose.

Angyal suggests that the strongest protection against future relapses is the sense of humility which AA deems essential to the
alcoholic's development when he admits the "bankruptcy" of his
former ways and discards his alcoholic compensations and pre-
tenses. Angyal makes a final point in describing the change necessary before sobriety can be obtained. "It may sound exaggerated or
outright false when a member of Alcoholics Anonymous, who has
not touched a drop of liquor for years, still refers to himself as an
alcoholic. Far from being insincere, this self-evaluation is literally
true and is the best protection against relapses. When an alcoholic
proudly proclaims that he 'has licked the habit for good' the time is
not far off when he will go on a binge" (1965, p. 161).

PRAGMATISM: ITS INFLUENCE ON AA

While it is true that Kelly has repeatedly avoided drawing any
comparisons between his theoretical foundations and the often similar philosophical positions of existentialism, pragmatism, and phenomenology, there are strong similarities nevertheless. But the issue is not one of similarities and difference in subordinate systems,
rather the issue is one of defining the foundation upon which the
rational scientific approach is erected. Jacob Bronowski in defining
the philosophy of science for the 20th century, strongly feels the
key principle to any science is the idea that man and the physical
world are evolving. But this is not surprising, any freshman course
in biology will teach you that. But matter itself evolves. Matter and
life are following the same pattern. This evolution is a process in
which atoms build up into more complex structures. Evolution, as
Bronowski explains, is the climbing of a ladder from the simple to
the complex by steps, each of which is stable in itself.

Bronowski indicates that man's intellectual evolution is also a
process. A dynamic changing view by which man advances slowly
and painstakingly in stages. "Scientific, rational foundations are
laid in man's ascent" (1973) explains Bronowski. Man builds his
theories and knowledge upon these foundations laid by others and
arrives at a temporary stage in his evolution. Knowledge is never
certain and what we define as truth is not a determinate representation of independently existing structure of things, but is rather an
intellectual construction, chosen from alternatives by reason of its

economy and simplicity, which does not literally describe reality, but makes contact with it simply by furnishing instruments for predicting future observations on the basis of present ones.

What Bronowski has described here parallels Kelly's explanations of the therapeutic process and his theoretical foundation. Superordinate constructs are built step-by-step upon the shoulders of subordinate constructs. Therapy itself is a step-by-step process of examining and, if necessary, reconstructing the faulty subordinate constructs. Experience or reality is, within certain limits, what we decide to make it. Why not, as Kelly suggests, construe it as we want it to be. That is, construe it in a manner which will make it more efficient from the standpoint of allowing us to make better predictions in the future and enhance the probability of deriving pleasure from it in the present.

Truth is, in other words, what pays or what works. At least, William James thought so. James anticipated Kelly and many of his ideas when he explained, "A true idea is a projected map of experience to lead one wherever one wants to go." The individual, according to James, verifies truth by experiencing the consequences of an idea. Truth is a means to the achievement of a vital end of an organism. Truth designates ideas which start ideas. Scientific theories, for James, are adopted because they simply work; their consequences are satisfactory.

James himself evolved and, later in his life, came to propose a form of Bergson anti-intellectualism. James gave up his trialistic view of truth in which he felt knowledge was defined and coerced by experience (as in natural science), or coerced by analytic intent of concepts (as in pure science), or free choice as in moral sentiment involved in religious and metaphysical beliefs. James exchanged this view for the one in which an individual judges a belief by its comparison of a whole stock of beliefs (metaphysics, logic, science, etc.). Similar to Kelly, he proposes that the belief which balances itself between these whole sets of beliefs without disturbing the oldest and most honored beliefs was generally accepted as true for its survival value. James felt truth was a projected map of experience and that truth was synonymous with what was useful. Truth is pragmatic!

Of course, James was one of the primary proponents of the philosophical system called pragmatism. One of its chief tenets was that if something ceases to be useful, it will cease to be true. The notion of absolute truth functions as a limit point of investigation rather than any ultimate knowledge. What we expect, we find to be true. What is expedient is truth. Truth fits our needs.

John Dewey is another pragmatist who shared James' sentiments. Like James, Dewey has some arguments which closely parallel many of Kelly's and Thune's propositions about AA. For instance, Dewey criticized the spectator and onlooker aspect of knowledge and claimed that thought was only one mode of action involved in any experience. Dewey's organic theory of knowledge gave the view of man struggling with his world and its environment and that knowledge was derived from this experience of action with the world. Just as AA encourages the recovering alcoholic to get involved with the program so he can expand his horizons of experience or dilate his constructs to pick up new elements, Dewey felt that too many theorists retreat from the world of chance into a safe world of abstract thought.

Certainly, this is an agreement that many members of AA share in their criticism of professionals whose interest in alcoholism is purely academic or passing. Abstractly, their theories sound correct. But, when put to the concrete test of reality, these abstractions frequently fail to materialize. As Dewey says, many professionals are reluctant to leave the safe world of theory and engage alcoholics on a real concrete level because this type of meeting is too demanding. Many professionals compound this problem by confusing the abstract with the concrete or the real. For example, some professionals misinterpret the importance of technical neutrality in their treatment of alcoholics. Abstractly and theoretically, the principle of neutrality insures the therapist be nonjudgmental and accepting of the alcoholic, voicing neither pleasure nor displeasure with their behavior. The intent behind this principle is theoretically sound. It is best for a person to come to their own decisions themselves, free from the influence and judgment of others. Theoretically, this is the way control is internalized. Such a stance also insures against harmful dependency, idealization and compliance. However, on a concrete, experiential, and "real" level, such a stance can be disastrous for an alcoholic. The excessive reliance on abstract concepts often leads many individuals to misinterpret the actual experience. Abstract understanding alone frequently comes at the cost of the experience of the concrete. The separation of the abstract from the concrete is an example of the dualistic-split which permeates Western rational thought.

Dewey, throughout his life, had criticized the dualistic tendency of Western thought. He felt Western philosophy reflected an important and unexamined bias which has been carried over from the legacy of early Greek philosophical influence. "Spectator knowledge," as Dewey criticized was judged superior by Greek philosophers because it differentiated the knowledge obtained by the ruler, through passive contemplation, from the knowledge obtained by the ruled, who were forced to labor as slaves in lowly, practical activity. Consequently, idealism came to be accepted as a higher form of knowledge. Dewey believed this was in actuality a retreat from the unpredictable world of action to the safe world of abstract thought. Therefore, knowledge obtained by the spectator or onlooker was judged by Dewey to be influenced by the fear of becoming involved in a mode of action and a reluctance to engage in the struggle of the experience of the world as it is. Agreeing with Will Durant and the AA philosophy, Dewey believed thought without action was a disease (Durant, 1926).

What AA and Dewey are criticizing is the association of the ego, abstract thought and dilemma of human existence; namely that knowledge is acquired at the cost of the burden of knowing. Buber especially accentuated the importance of differentiating the abstract (I-It) from the concrete (I-Thou). Buber emphasized the essential difference between the direct, mutual meeting, into which one enters with one's whole being and in full presentness, and the indirect non-mutual relationship of subject and object. Buber felt we were in definite danger of losing ourselves in the abstract idealism of our own thought. An abstraction which has spirited Alfred North Whitehead to raise the question concerning the tendency for many to confuse abstract interpretations with concrete occurrence. "The fallacy of misplaced concreteness," warns Whitehead, "is the common misconception of science."

Whitehead has also criticized the scientific logos which have threatened to reduce nature to "a dull affair, soundless, scentless, colorless, merely the hurrying of material endlessly, meaningful." Here Whitehead is not criticizing the scientific method which science employs, but rather its "misplaced concreteness." While Whitehead credits the development of mathematics and abstract thought as "the most original creation of the human spirit," he also warns that the intolerable use of abstraction is a major vice of the intellect and he claims reason is needed in its application. A living science is impossible according to Whitehead and cannot exist unless there is a belief in an order of nature. The "scientific material-ism" of brute fact cannot be applied as reality itself because life is not an abstraction; it is a real event. "The event," Whitehead de-clared, "is the unit of things real." By this he meant that however theoretical systems may change and however empty of content their symbols may be, the essential and enduring facts of life are the concrete happenings, the activities, the events.

Whitehead and James reflect a common principle which lies at the heart of AA's success. AA insistence on "the event"—the real actual meeting of the alcoholic by another alcoholic—insures that the concrete is not lost at the expense of the abstract. This orienta-tion is clear in the oft repeated AA mottos, "Vitalize, Don't Ana-lyze," "Go to Ninety Meetings in Ninety Days," and "Take Your Body and Your Mind Will Follow." Such encouragement reflects James' recommendation that you should act your way into a new way of thinking rather than think your way into a new way of act-ing.

EXISTENTIAL VIEW OF AA

Kurtz makes a convincing argument that AA works because it parallels existential philosophy in a number of important aspects. Kurtz further states that AA has not been credited the recognition it deserves as a movement of unique intellectual significance. When AA is examined in relation to its sources and origins, the program expresses many important existential themes. The first theme of all existential philosophies is the realization of man's limitation of be-ing. The first step of AA ("We admitted we were powerless over alcohol") requires the alcoholic to recognize and admit this essen-tial limitation. Kurtz writes,

> "We admitted that we were powerless over alcohol—that our lives had become unmanageable" (26, p. 59; 27, p. 21-24). AA addresses itself not to alcoholism, but to the alco-holic. The First Step of the AA program focuses upon the alcoholic as one who is essentially limited. The acknowledg-ment "I am an alcoholic" that is inherent in the admission of powerlessness over alcohol accepts as first truth human essen-tial limitation, personal fundamental finitude, at least for the alcoholic. (p. 43)

Powerlessness over alcohol and the acceptance of one's limitation in relation to alcoholism serves as a prototype for the alcoholic facing and accepting other limitations of the human condition. The larger insight of AA is the wholeness of the human condition. The larger insight of AA is the wholeness of limitation, an insight that is required after the alcoholic is able to accept the limitation that he cannot drink alcohol. Kurtz sums up this dilemma when he writes.

> AA borrowed and learned from diverse sources — William James and the Oxford Group, Carl Jung and William Duncan Silkworth. Its own continuing experience also significantly shaped the development of AA's thought. The concepts embodied in both terms of its name best briefly clarify that insight. The alcoholic, in the AA understanding, is one who finds himself in an utterly hopeless situation: obsessively-compulsively addicted to alcohol, he by definition must drink alcohol and so destroy himself. Although alcoholism is conceptualized by AA as by others as "disease" or "malady," the alcoholic does not have alcoholism — he is an "alcoholic." Therefore he cannot do what others, nonalcoholics, do with joyful impunity: non-obsessively-compulsively drink alcohol. Contained in the term 'alcoholic,' then, are the implications of utterly hopeless helplessness and essential personal limitation. (p. 41)

Central to the alcoholic's acceptance of limitation is the recognition that while he is vulnerable, he can only attain sobriety by exposing this vulnerability and accepting this limitation. This is the healing dynamic of AA; a mutual vulnerability openly acknowledged and shared with other alcoholics. Kurtz writes:

> "Not God" means first "You are not God," the message of the AA program . . . The fundamental and first message of Alcoholics Anonymous to its members is that they are not infinite, not absolute, *not* God. Every alcoholic's problem had *first* been, according to this insight, claiming God-like powers, especially that of *control*. But the alcoholic at least, the message insists, is *not* in control, even of himself; and the first step towards recovery from alcoholism must be the admission and *acceptance* of this fact that is so blatantly obvious

to others but so tenaciously denied by the obsessive-compulsive drinker.

But Alcoholics Anonymous is *fellowship* as well as *program*, and thus there is a second side to its message of not-God-ness. Because the alcoholic is not God, not absolute, not infinite, he or she is essentially limited. Yet from this very limitation — from the alcoholic's *acceptance* of personal limitation — arises the beginning of healing and wholeness . . . To be an alcoholic within Alcoholics Anonymous is not only to accept oneself as not God; it implies also affirmation of one's connectedness with other alcoholics . . . The invitation to make such a connection with others and the awareness of the necessity of doing so arise from the alcoholic's very acceptance of limitation. (p. 42)

Another important aspect of the alcoholic's acceptance of the limits of the human condition is the requirement that he understand that he has limited control and limited dependence. He must learn the difference if he is to stay sober. Kurtz writes:

The emphasis on control as limited, as neither absolute nor to be abdicated pervades the AA program. "You can do something, but not everything" runs the constant implicit, and at times explicit, message. AA members are warned against promising "never to drink again." They learn, rather, "not to take the first drink, one day at a time." They are encouraged to attend AA meetings, which they can do, rather than to avoid all contact with alcohol, which they cannot do. The AA sense of limited control is admirably summed up in its famed "Serenity Prayer": "God grant me the serenity to accept the things I cannot change, the courage to change the things I can, and the wisdom to know the difference." (p. 53)

Hitting Bottom: An Existential Viewpoint

Such an acceptance of limitation requires more than an intellectual insight. An individual will only give up his self-centered and perceived absolute control of the world if it is wrenched away from him and ruthlessly exposed with all its false assumptions and deceptive facades. Confronted with such a realization engenders the dread, fear, and trembling of Kierkegaard, the Angst of Heidegger, the angoisse of Sartre, and the abyss of Buber. Borrowing a term from William James (i.e., deflation at depth), AA refers to it as hitting bottom. Carl Jaspers, another existential writer, refers to it as "limit situations." These great philosophers share the common opinion that an emotional upheaval is required before an individual will truly question the core of their existential predicament. Not until this issue is addressed in the stark naked light of existence will an individual want or be able to accept the limitedness of the human condition.

Albert Camus sums up this position most graphically when he challenges his readers to examine the authenticity of their lives. Like Sartre, Camus believes most of us are living our lives in "bad faith," hanging on to illusions because we do not want to face death, terror, and suffering in life. Camus felt that if we were brutally honest with ourselves we would discover there are only two real truths in life. We are going to die and after death, there is nothing. He further states that if we truly answer these questions without hanging on to our refusal to accept limitations in life, we will either kill ourselves or decide for the first time to truly live our lives authentically. We will become what Sartre calls "authentic." We will trivialize the trivial and prioritize the vital. We will no longer deny death and the limitations in life. By denying death, we ultimately deny life because the two are inseparable.

Needless to say, Camus' challenge is one that most individuals, alcoholics as well as non-alcoholics, fear accepting because of the suffering it produces. In most cases, alcoholics pushed to the edge of their psychic abyss because of their alcoholism, have no choice but to address Camus' challenge. They literally must either die or change their life by surrendering to the first step of the AA program. If the alcoholic is able to meet this challenge and integrate this experience, they often lead more meaningful lives. Nietzsche, in his own iconoclastic style, captures this experience graphically when he writes, "That which doesn't kill you will make you stronger."

All philosophy and all the social sciences have to deal with the problem of real human suffering. AA, at least, recognizes suffering as a necessary and a possible positive part of life. Many other treatment modalities have failed to recognize the actual therapeutic aspects of mobilizing a patient's assets at the time of crisis, avoiding the consolidation of symptoms, therefore making them more problematic. The ideal conclusion of suffering and treatment, to take a page from Victor Frankl, is to give the individual a reason for his suffering; or in Logotherapeutic terms, the will-to-meaning, which gives the person's suffering meaning. Once suffering is viewed in a meaningful paradigm, it can serve as a growth process.

AA is addressing a very fundamental principle of treatment. Before a person's resources can be mobilized for therapeutic change, they have to experience a state of personal incongruence. Often, change does not occur unless a person's pain and suffering prompts them to initiate an honest assertion of their condition and behavior. However, suffering has to be integrated into some personal meaningful paradigm. People who suffer for no known reason become defeated, bitter or demoralized.

Victor Frankl's personal experiences during World War II vividly demonstrate this principle with stark realization. A Jewish psychiatrist who was arrested by the Nazis during the war and shipped to one of their most brutal extermination camps, Frankl had little reason to believe he was ever to leave the death camp alive. With each passing day, month, and year, he was repeatedly told by his Nazi guards that Germany was winning the war and he would never be released from prison. Experiencing only unbearable suffering, unmerciful death, and tragic losses around him, Frankl saw many of his fellow prisoners slowly give up and literally lay down and die. Frankl was able to eventually discern who were about to die and who would go on living. Those individuals who could not see any reason for their suffering were more likely to die because their life had ceased to have meaning. Frankl realized that only those who had managed to put their suffering within some meaningful context through their faith, belief, or hope were the ones least destroyed and defeated by their pain and suffering.

In a less dramatic, but very similar fashion, AA members share "the kinship of common suffering." Within this context, recovery from alcoholism requires a person share their suffering with another who understands their experience. As Kurtz defines it, mutuality in AA is triggered by the sharing of common suffering. This, in turn, teaches the alcoholic "that to be fully human is to need others" (p. 55). AA therefore provides the alcoholic with a commonly shared explanation of their suffering. It helps the alcoholic make sense of his affliction by providing him a meaningful paradigm for his experience.

AA is in many ways an educational process which allows suffering to be integrated into a person's life in a meaningful way. However, AA is education of a unique sort. It trains the alcoholic to be more self-aware and more honest with himself. It also teaches him to achieve more adequate control over his primitive impulses and strivings; to be freer in expressing his feelings; to become more tolerant of human limitations and develop the ability to postpone, modify, and even forego gratifications whose demands previously seemed impervious. Through education, the alcoholic learns to accept that there are limits to unbounded joy in life. Like Freud, who once described the goal of psychoanalysis as transforming neurotic misery into ordinary human suffering, the alcoholic is on the road to recovery when he accepts the fact that he is as limited in unbounded happiness as the rest of us.

This is not to imply that happiness and joy are an antithesis to therapy, treatment, and recovery. Rather, the alcoholic must be taught not to suffer for the wrong reasons. Pain and suffering are a part of life. But, so is joy and happiness. As the Buddhist religious doctrine teaches, it is ignorant craving that often produces suffering. This was a point made vivid in James Clavell's novel *Shogun*. After an innocent man had died because of Blackwell's ignorance of Japanese customs, Blackwell stood cursing himself and the world because of his anger at this man's senseless death. Speaking to his Japanese lover, Blackwell exclaimed the world was not right, that things like this should not happen. As he questioned whether he could continue to live with integrity in such a senseless world, his Japanese lover responded to his frustration, anger, and feelings of futility. Speaking from a very traditional Eastern philosophical position, she told him he was angry because of his refusal to accept the world as it was and his insistence on trying to make it into something other than that which was given. Blackwell suffered as he did because he wanted the world to be different and because he wanted it to fit neatly into his self-centered, predetermined set of expectations.

Suffering, from this perspective, is defined as an individual's unwillingness to accept the world as it is and their insistence on making it fit into their own expected image. Thinking of this sort is a form of idolatry in which the alcoholic uses chemicals as a way of fixing the world when the limits they face are found to be unacceptable. Alcohol and drugs become a way of denying unhappiness, suffering and limits. Through the process of their alcoholism, the alcoholic disregards more and more the acceptable or normative pleasures which are usually earned in the areas of achievement, knowledge, friendships, good health, and well-being. Alcohol and drugs reward self-centeredness and hedonistic pleasure. Such an attainment of pleasure is akin to a cheap thrill and comes at a cost of the alcoholic's integrity and self-esteem. Pleasure has to be authentically earned by a subtle and important interplay between values, beliefs, customs, ideas and behavior that causes no harm to others. Alcohol and drugs are thrills cheaply purchased at the price of self-respect. Self-worth and self-esteem are gradually lost because the rules for socially accepted normative ways of attaining pleasure have been altered and compromised. Alcohol-and-drug-induced highs are tricks (pleasure without purpose) played on the brain which comes at the cost of self-esteem.

Treatment from this perspective requires the removal of cheaply purchased thrills and replaces them with authentically earned happiness. Integrity cannot be purchased. It is earned and, once earned, it is the antithesis of shame, disrespect, and neurotic misery.

Ernest Hemingway once defined happiness as getting your money's worth and knowing when you have gotten it. It is important to understand the implications of Hemingway's statement because it has many important implications for the hollowness and loss of self-respect which an alcoholic experiences when happiness is purchased through the use of chemicals. It is important to note that Hemingway does not describe happiness as a bargain — something that you steal or get cheaply. Happiness is earned and comes at a cost. However, as Hemingway carefully adds, you have to know when you have earned it. Happiness purchased cheaply is hollow and leads to little sense of mastery. Essentially, it is unappreciated because it is not earned. Happiness attained without understanding is purchased at the price of self-respect. Schopenhauer expressed similar sentiments when he wrote, "What a person is contributes more to his happiness than what he has." Kant also sums up this position when he wrote, "Morality is not properly the doctrine of how we may make ourselves happy, but how we make ourselves worthy of happiness."

For the recovering alcoholic, the pursuit and understanding of happiness requires a shift in perspective. Unless this shift is made, the alcoholic will either relapse or suffer what AA calls "white knuckle sobriety." Many alcoholics do not make this shift in perspective. Those who attain serenity usually do, however. Serenity is a term commonly acknowledged as a desired aim and is actively pursued by AA members. Although it is often a misunderstood concept, the early Greek philosopher, Epicurus, captured it perfectly.

Epicurus believed that pleasure is the only conceivable, and quite legitimate, end of life and action. "Nature leads every organism to prefer its own good to every other good. We must not avoid pleasures, but we must select them." Epicurus exalts the joys of tranquility rather than those of the senses, he warns against pleasure that excites and disturbs the soul which they should rather quiet and appease. In the end he proposed to seek not pleasure in its usual sense, but *ataraxia* — tranquility, equanimity, repose of mind.

In many ways, existential philosophy is profoundly pessimistic in one sense and optimistic in another. Existentialists generally believe that happiness can only be achieved once the individual gives up the illusion of unlimited happiness.

Ernest Becker (1973) described this situation perfectly when he stated, "I am talking to the cheerful robots. I think the world is full of too many cheerful robots who talk only about joy and the good things. I have considered it my task to talk about the terror and suffering in the world." The terror that Becker talks about is our refusal to deal with suffering and death. We must view these aspects realistically and try not to avoid them by only dwelling on the beautiful things in life. Becker defines this position nicely when he writes, "Joy and hope and trust are things one achieves after one has been through the forlornness." Otto Rank agreed when he wrote, "the dynamic evil is the attempt to make the world other than it is, to make it what it cannot be, a place free from impurity, a place free from death and suffering."

Many existential writers believe that in such a confrontation between the realistic acceptance of the world as it is and the self-centered demands for unlimited gratification, reason would prevail and the individual would choose more realistically between the alternatives — continued unhappy struggles with old patterns of expectations or authentic existence with expanded freedom of choice and responsible expression of drives and wishes. With Socrates, we are urged to "know thyself." In this fashion, AA members are taught to believe that the authentic existence advocated by the AA program holds the key to self-examination, self-knowledge, emancipation, cure, and eventually salvation.

To grow up, the alcoholic must relinquish the paradise of limitless abundance and arrogance. He must learn to renounce, to work, to suffer, postpone gratification, become responsible and above all take an active, responsible part in mastering his fate. AA has set out to undermine the alcoholic's dishonesty with himself. Unlike any other time in his life, the alcoholic must come to understand that self-deception is a pervasive and universal human characteristic. However, unlike the non-alcoholic, the alcoholic cannot afford to deceive himself for self-deception inevitably leads back to a relapse. Alcoholics must be constantly reminded that they can delude themselves into believing they were living their lives independently, whereas, for the most part, their lives were lived for them by alcohol and the forces of which they were not aware, which they did not understand, and over which they had little control.

Honesty, Denial and the Need for Others

The insight of AA and the philosophy of existential thinkers are identical in that both see denial and self-deception as the root of all human evil and the source of all alienation. The reversal of this trend requires the alcoholic to face his need for others with uncompromising honesty. Kurtz sums up this process when he writes,

> According to the insight of AA, because of their essential limitation, human beings have needs. The denial of essential limitation usually manifests itself not directly, but in the denial of need. The alcoholic's denial of need is twofold: his denial of his need for alcohol blends into and intertwines with his denial of his needs for others. Early in the process of alcoholism, the alcoholic denies that it is his unmet, because insatiable, need for others that leads him to seek comfort or excitement in alcohol. "A few drinks" become more important than the people at a party, for example, as alcohol becomes a surer source of satisfaction than human interaction. Later in the process, after a few failures of "I can stop whenever I want to" (denial of the need for alcohol), the denial becomes again of the need for others: "Just let me alone — I can lick this thing by myself." (p. 73)

The concepts of honesty and mutuality which Kurtz advocates are crucial to understanding AA's recovery program. The interaction of both are essential for the healthy functioning of the individual. It is this combination which allows the individual to obtain the harmony necessary to function as an involved participant within the world. As the existentialists suggest, an alcoholic in a state of isolation frequently suffers the manifestations of anxiety and alienation which determine the formation and actualization of the sweeping condition they refer to as an existential crisis. In a similar sense, the alcoholic is not part of the whole, he is uninvolved and has no real freedom to choose.

Of course, these are existential themes. Alienation and the inability or refusal to choose is characteristic of what Sartre calls "acting in bad faith." In a sense, authenticity, which is such a necessary part in an existential definition of health, is impossible for a person who is isolated from the world and himself.

Kurtz describes the struggle for authentic existence to become and to be what one really is as the most significant and meaningful event in any individual's life. This theme is also prevalent in most existential philosophy and existentialist Martin Buber addresses this very issue numerous times in his writings. He criticizes the collectivity of social thought which thickens the distance between men. Collectivity for Buber is the herd instinct or the "crowd" which alienates man thus not allowing for him to meet man in all his uniqueness. Buber, like Angyal, feels that man's guilt lies in not fulfilling and recognizing his own potential and uniqueness. Martin Heidegger is right to say than man experiences a primal guilt due to this situation. Real guilt, according to Heidegger, consists in the fact that "existence is guilty in the ground of its being" and man is guilty in his existence if he does not fulfill himself by becoming what Heidegger calls "the one" (das Man).

Buber anticipated Kurtz when he describes the importance of the I-Thou in determining a necessary state of human development. Like the AA program, Buber's concept of the I-Thou stresses the importance of a person's involvement in something larger than one's self. Of course the supreme I-Thou for Buber is the relationship that occurs when one experiences God on a personal level. However, Buber's I-Thou is more than a relation to God. It is that concrete experience of being in harmony with the universe which is prevalent when one is really there. This meeting can occur whenever the person is open to the experience of true relating; whether it be with another person or some inanimate object. Even obscure meetings are microcosms of the supreme relationship. For Buber, relating to someone or something can be an experience comparable to being in touch with a spiritual power which unites the individual with the order of the cosmos.

Buber's genius was not his formulation of the I-Thou, for that was done by others before him. But, it was Buber alone who placed at the center of a monumental corpus the task of pointing to the essential difference between the direct, mutual meeting, into which one enters with one's whole being and in full presentness, and the indirect non-mutual relationship of subject and object, the I-It.

Like Angyal, Buber recognizes the necessity of autonomy or the ability to relate in the sphere of the I-It. Buber sees this separateness of the I in positive terms because it is the development of this I which allows the eternal Thou to be confronted with all its uniqueness. Therefore the detached I is necessary in Buber's system for a number of reasons. Buber feels that man is more than just a rational animal. Animals for Buber do not need confirmation of their being because an animal is what it is unquestionably. Man, in contrast, needs to have a presence in the being of the "other." Consciousness, therefore, is higher because the element of choice is present. Man now, by his separateness of the I, can meet man as a Thou, in that each is able to recognize the paradox of their uniqueness and their similarity.

The parallel theme with Angyal and Buber is the importance they lay upon a person being autonomous, yet capable of choosing *not* to control in order to become part of the dynamic whole. As Angyal emphatically states, "we are nothing in ourselves. We are a message which comes to life only by being understood and acknowledged by someone." Buber differentiates between the psychologist who clarifies by reference to his own self in self-observation, self-analysis, and experimentation; relating what he knows from literature and observation. Buber's therapist, on the other hand, must enter, completely and in reality, in the act of self-reflection in order to become aware of human wholeness. In other words, he must carry out this act of entry into that unique dimension as an act of his life, without any prepared philosophical security, that is, he must expose himself to all that can meet him when he is really living.

The implications for this in therapy is profound. The person in treatment is usually isolated and if he is to get in touch with that healthy potential in himself, it is necessary to understand his ability to engage in true mutual dialogue. That is why the actual meeting of two individuals can disrupt that spiral of isolation so prevalent in an alcoholic's life. Buber's emphasis in therapy has rested particularly on the healing-through-meeting process that is such an intricate part of true dialogue.

It is important to distinguish between this concept of true dialogue and the misconception of confusing it with the idea of our "self" being determined by another. The so-called mirror self is much more concerned with the intellect, and less with the actual encounter. George Herbert Mead proposed that essential human nature emerges in the process of interaction with others. Selfhood develops with the ability to communicate, and we communicate not only with others but with ourselves through inner dialogue. The mirror metaphor, with its emphasis on communication and the social development of self-consciousness, tells us very little about the life of impulses and feelings. As Dewey says, a living creature is a part of the world, sharing vicissitudes and fortune and making itself secure in its precarious dependence only as it intellectually identifies itself with things about it. Thought is emerged in life processes in which thinking is only a directive force in experience. As AA would agree, the living experience is an intimate participation into the activities of the world. Buber would say that really knowing the other person cannot be accomplished by the idle view of an unconcerned spectator. We must get involved and by doing so we can break that spiral of isolation so prevalent in alcoholism. Buber would suggest that this true meeting is sometimes enough to at least initiate the recovery process.

As Buber suggests, a crucial step in AA is self-transcendence, which involves embracing new relationships with others who are also recognized as essentially limited. Such a shift in perspective requires a recognition that to be fully human is to need others. For the alcoholic, this is no easy task. Kurtz feels this task is made more difficult for the alcoholic because of the deep feelings of shame which accompany their alcoholism. In fact, Kurtz feels AA works because it is a therapy for shame. It will be important to understand Kurtz' description of shame for it has many parallels to Kohut's description of the narcissistic personality disorder. Chapter 5 dealt exclusively with the relationship of object-relations, self-psychology and character pathology to addiction and group psychotherapy. Kohut's description of these issues will not be repeated here, but it would be important for the interested reader to refer to this chapter for there are many important parallels which exist between shame, as Kurtz describes it, and Kohut's description of narcissism.

AA: A Treatment for Shame and Narcissism

Kurtz says there are two different ways of feeling bad. One is guilt and the other is shame. For Kurtz, shame is a much more powerful and primitive emotion. Guilt implies feeling bad for something you've done. It is a violation of rules and its focus is on behavior and actions. I promised to pick you up after work and give you a ride home. I did not follow through with my promise, so I feel bad or guilty for something I've done. Shame is a falling short of a goal and concerns a person's sense of self and unworthiness. Shame strikes at the core of our being. Rather than feeling bad for what I've done, I feel bad for who or what I am. Guilt is repaired by a quantitative effort; redoing or correcting a behavior. Shame can only be repaired by quality; a re-being of what I am and requires a conversion or a new sense of self.

From Kurtz's perspective, treatment for shame is a far more intricate and difficult process. Shame cannot be treated by talking about it. Shame can only be healed through vulnerability. We cannot get in touch with another's pain without getting in touch with our own pain. Therefore, treatment which allows the alcoholic to learn that his own pain is not only not shameful, but allows him to connect and identify with another's shame and pain, teaches him that the sharing of pain can be healing. The alcoholic learns to accept in others those aspects of himself of which he is ashamed. Before a person can be healed, he has to learn he can be accepted as he is by another. This process is initiated by accepting those shameful aspects of the self in another.

Mutuality, thus, becomes the crucial aspect of therapy. This is why AA and group psychotherapy works while individual therapy frequently fails. Both AA and group psychotherapy allows the breaking of the cycle of interpersonal isolation which is central to the establishment of shame. Every alcoholic fears that they will be found out for what they feel they truly are or that they will be looked upon and ignored. To expose one's real self is frightening. What is needed is confirmation from others through a process of reciprocal self-revelation. Embarrassment is the experience of a person exposing and getting in touch with the shameful parts of their hidden true self. When an alcoholic confronts himself, he is made aware of his internal incongruence and his false-self, defensive facade. Under the false-self is fear and shame. Such feelings can only be resolved by the confrontation of this disparity and the continual confirmation from another, affirming that others are accepting of the exposed true self.

Shame involves exposure. It is triggered by a sense of being looked at and caught unexpectedly. Shame is enhanced by the exposure of self to self. Shame thus involves an experience of self being diminished. Typically, the self refuses to see itself. This is the basis of the alcoholic's denial and self-deception. Shame occurs when the self breaks through the false-self, deceptive facade. In therapy, the self must be confronted as feared and seen as it is. For an alcoholic who possesses a tremendous fear of confronting their true-self, such an exposure of self requires courage as much as insight.

Kurtz draws some important parallels between the existential position of inauthenticity and the "false self" of Winnicott (see Chapter 5) and object relations theorists. Kurtz describes how this false self-presentation originates,

> Sometimes, out of that terror, a person will dissimulate in his presentation of himself to others in an effort to quell the pain of separateness by winning approval and acceptance. To the extent that he does so, and succeeds, he will experience a queer, unnamable apprehension, becoming trapped in an uneasy state that he finds both painful and corrupting. (p. 61)

Kurtz sees the fear of exposure of the true self to others as the cause of dishonesty and self-deception. Once this habit of dishonesty has been set, it leads to the alcoholic's corruption.

> Whether from unwillingness or inability to tell the truth about who he is, such an individual knows himself in his heart to be faking. "Not merely is he ashamed of having and harboring a secret, unlovely, illegitimate self. The spiritual burden of not appearing as the person he 'is', or not 'being' the person he appears to be — the extended and deliberate confusion of seeming and being — is by and large intolerable if held in direct view." Despairing of attaining the integrity he craves, the person turns to grasp at its illusion: since he cannot make public his private self, he commands his private self to conform to the public one. This choice beguiles to a loss of truth — not so much "telling" it, but knowing it. (p. 61)

Most individuals, alcoholic and non-alcoholic, are often unaware that they are false, unreal and unauthentic. They know no other existence. They eventually come to believe their false self as real because without this defensive facade they have nothing. Their apprehension is therefore catastrophic when their false-self facade is threatened. They will feel exposed to the shame and the fear of non-being.

It is here at the realm of the construction of the false-self that Kurtz and the existentialists unite with Kohut and self-psychology in explaining the paradox of existence and recovery for the alcoholic. Kohut views narcissism as a defensive facade that is adapted because the true self is either fragmented, weak or uncohesive. To expose this unprotected true self to the world is a threat which must be avoided at all costs. Kurtz refers to this deep sense of worthlessness and embarrassment as shame and states this is a feeling which plagues every alcoholic. The alcoholic, in Kohut's view, is lacking in a cohesive self and constantly seeks confirmation from others or a joining with a powerful other in order to bolster its self-esteem.

From Kohut's perspective, this is why AA is such an effective treatment program. Kohut defines narcissistic disorders as presenting with three types of transference distortions (see Chapter 5). They either are idealizing, mirror-hungry or merger-prone. AA thus provides for them an idealized other (i.e., the AA program, the principles of AA, etc.) or goal that is concrete and attainable. If the alcoholic does what the principles of the AA program ask of him, he will get all the mirroring and confirmation he needs. AA will accept him, no matter what he has done in the past and will always be there for him anytime he desires or needs it in the future. AA is a constant "good enough" mother that serves as a transitional object until the principles of the program are internalized. AA also provides idealized others (sponsors and sober members) with whom the alcoholic can merge. Merger with the idealized other serves as a container for the depleted self of the alcoholic. For those alcoholics whose need for confirmation is insatiable, they will be adored by other AA members as long as they stay sober. Certain members of AA can take on "guru-like" qualities. They are then assured the mirroring upon which they thrive and they will do all that is necessary (sobriety) to ensure this source of confirmation is never lost. At the same time, they will serve as an idealized other for the recovering alcoholic.

However, the danger for Kohut is that the narcissistic individual can come to believe that his false-self is his true-self. He can be deluded by his narcissistic and grandiose fantasies. Kurtz defines this process as the refusal of the alcoholic to accept limitations in his aspirations. The alcoholic not only is caught by his narcissism, but he is further corrupted by his own grandiosity.

It is here that the dilemma of wanting more and being satisfied with less that the alcoholic's struggle parallels that of all human existence. As intelligent creatures, we all have the ability to conceive a state of affairs that does not exist at the present time. Through a vehicle called the mind, we can project into the future a set of circumstances which will set into motion an action that will change the present. Consequently, we can plan, achieve, and create a state of affairs that wouldn't have existed if we hadn't acted. We have the ability to affect others and make things other than they are. Consequently, the more we achieve, the more we believe in our achievements. The more we believe in our achievements, the more we delude ourselves into thinking we are unique, special and unlimited. We become mesmerized by our own sense of our uniqueness and when we do this, we lose the edge that allows us to achieve, create and improve our lives. We come to believe we are gods. We believe we have absolute control and lose the humility and humbleness which keeps us from beguiling ourselves.

Consequently life incorporates a standing paradox. Man is a finite creature on the one side and infinite in his desires on the other side. No matter how we try, we cannot help but be caught up by our own self-centered achievement. Even in the highest flights of altruism, there is bound to be something personal, self-enhancing, and all-too-gratifying. All our achievements come at the cost of deluding our self into believing that we are special. Yet if we didn't aspire for greatness, we would remain ordinary. We are constantly reminded that there is a perfection beyond our grasp. Charles Frankl (1971) sums up this dilemma when he writes:

> No matter how men try, they cannot help but be caught up in local circumstances, a parochial outlook, and a personal, all-too-personal, self. There is bound to be egoism even in their highest flights of altruism; there is bound to be something personal, self-enclosed, and partisan about their thinking even when they believe they are being most objective. And yet despite the fact that men are captives of necessity in this way, they are also free. They cannot hold any point of view which is not relative, or have anything but a limited grasp of perfection. But they can know that there is a perfection beyond their grasp. They can see beyond their own local circumstances, recognize that some other point of view is possible, and believe that there is such a thing as impersonality and objectivity. In short, man is a creature living tensely between two worlds: one is the actual, limited world in which he lives, but

from which he cannot help but feel alienated; the other is an
ideal world for which he longs, but from which he is perma-
nently excluded. To be disappointed idealists is the common
and eternal fate of all men. Man's whole moral life requires
him "to seek after an impossible victory and to adjust himself
to an inevitable defeat." (p. 88)

The source of all our achievements is also the force of our wick-
edness and folly. Frankl's argument suggests that our vices and vir-
tues have the same origins. Consequently, there is a taint in whatever human beings do. Our triumphs tempt us to forget our
weaknesses and every growth in our power leads to increased pride
and dogmatism. However, Frankl feels that if men could not see
beyond the immediate future, they would not be goaded by their
desires that something better is possible, and that none of their subsequent triumphs would be imagined. However, knowledge is acquired at the burden of knowing. Understanding is achieved at the
cost of knowing that death and suffering are a part of life. Such
understanding produces anxiety. This is what separates man from
the animals. This is why man can never achieve the simple happiness which animals experience because animals unlike humans, are
what they are unquestioningly. Frankl describes the existential dilemma which confront every individual and is the source of self-
deception in the alcoholic.

But anxiety is also the source of something else. It is the
source of man's sinfulness. For the pain of anxiety drives men
to try to escape it. They sink into sensuality in the effort to
forget that there is anything beyond the immediate. They lose
themselves in fanaticism in the effort to convince themselves
that they have brought the Absolute to earth. They try to cut
down their aspirations and fall into cynicism, or to inflate their
powers and fall into pride and arrogance. In a word, they try to
identify their own limited and relative powers with the Absolute. And this is the original sin. Sin is the narcosis of the soul;
it is a perennial temptation to which men must inevitably succumb. (p. 89)

Original sin, as Frankl identifies it, is due to man's eating of the
fruit of knowledge. Purposeful thoughts lead man to be banished
from the Garden of Eden where he had shared the simple happiness

of the animals who did not question their existence. It is thinking which creates in man the split between abstract and the concrete. Consciousness causes problems because it imposes a dualism where none really exists. Bateson (1972) describes this conflict in thinking as an error in epistomology left over from the philosophical heritage of Descartes who created this split with his subject-object dualism. Alcoholics try to impose control where there is no possible control. No one can really control themselves because there is no "self" to control. The self is only an abstraction. Bateson sees this as an error in thinking (i.e., symmetry in Bateson's language) and being (i.e., epistomology). The individual becomes caught in an internal battle and alcoholism becomes the battlefield according to Bateson. AA asks the alcoholic to give up the battle and rather than think symetrically, he is urged to approach life in a complimentary fashion. As Bateson says, AA urges the alcoholic to give up the incorrect epistomology and consequently will no longer try to do the impossible, which is to control himself. Rather the alcoholic accepts himself as he is. Kurtz sums up this position when he writes:

> Humane thinkers, those who study human phenomena, existentialist thought reminds, must eschew the imperative of control. Human beings, as human, are neither tools nor mere objects — for what is an "object" but another potential tool? The subject-object dualism that derives from Descartes has immeasurably increased human knowledge and control of things. Applied to persons, however, as the experience of AA within the field of alcoholism testifies, it is not only sadly lacking but tragically destructive. Subject-object dualism, with its demand for "objectivity" regards the attainment of truth as an act of conquest rather than of revelation. The dualistic style and approach thus do violence to humane values. Treating persons as things can only increase alienation. Such an approach thus fuels rather than cures alcoholism. (p. 47)

AA, SCIENCE, AND RELIGION

In many of the different perspectives of AA presented so far in this chapter, it is hoped the reader is left with the impression that many of the differences between AA and the scientific community are related more to semantics than the actual differences which exist

between the two groups. Once one gets past the polemics it is obvious AA and professional treatment have more similarities than differences. Conflicts between ideological approaches to treatment
have been common, not only for alcoholism, but for most traditional forms of knowledge and understanding. An investigation into
the historical background of this conflict will shed some light on the
subject of how values, ideologies, and belief systems impose restrictions on an individual's perception of reality.

Osborne and Baldwin (1982) address this issue in a recent article
when they suggest that much of psychotherapy involves a lateral
shift from one state of illusion to another. They raise some important issues not only for psychotherapists and AA, but for the entire
scientific community at large. As Watzlawick (1976) warned, the
most dangerous delusion of all is "the belief that one's own view of
reality is the only reality (p. xiii). Indeed, as Osborne and Baldwin
suggest, many professional psychotherapists may be caught up with
patients in "the enactment of an illusion which is far broader than
the client's problem" (p. 266). This is a very important issue because while many professionals can easily criticize AA's ideological base, they fail to examine their own perceptual bias with the
same critical scrutiny. Closely tied to this process is the failure to
realize that the conventional distinction between facts and values
may be another illusion reflecting "pseudo-objectivity based upon
intersubjectivity" (p. 267). Or as Bixenstine (1976) contends, facts
cannot be separated from values, but actually reflect a special class
of values. While Osborne and Baldwin wrestle with these important
issues, they limit their discussion primarily to Western psychotherapies and Eastern religious tradition of self-knowledge.

The purpose of this section of the chapter is to broaden the context of this examination so that the investigation is not limited to
Western psychological theory, of which AA's is an intricate part. It
is also intended that professionals who have criticized AA for its
lack of scientific rigor will understand that science is not necessarily
a better way of knowing, it is just different from AA. Hopefully AA
can be accepted for what it does and not be disregarded because it
does not fit neatly into a preconceived set of expectations. While
both the scientific method and AA have made important contributions to our understanding of how we "perceive" alcoholism, an
examination of the principles of the scientific method (with its reliance on empiricism and rationalism) can help us understand how
professionals have discarded other important ways of defining alco-

holism because of their tendency to deceive themselves into believing that their current preferred illusion is the real reality. This is a mistake which many professionals seem to be unaware of in their refusal to accept AA as a credible treatment program.

There have been two great traditional explanations of knowledge that have marched side by side in our brief existence on earth. Historically, religion had provided us with whatever explanations of reality we needed until the Renaissance compelled us to recognize the empirical sciences as the new source of authority on knowledge and ultimate reality. Unfortunately, science's rapid rise to authority has come at the expense of our former traditional methods of knowing. The costs of our acquiescence to science as a source of authority must be constantly examined and monitored, lest we deceive ourselves into believing we are the rider rather than the ridden. Beyond this, the difference between these two traditions — religion and science — may not be as great as we have been led to believe and we may find that their relationship is actually complementary. It will be further suggested that this complement is most apparent in the program of AA.

It is often difficult, if not impossible for scientists to be cognizant of the cultural and societal forces at work which subtly influence their interpretation of reality. We in the scientific community have to constantly examine our own idiosyncratic bias and culturally imposed values lest we hold basic assumptions, which unnoticed, would color our perceptions of reality. As Alfred North Whitehead (1925) warned, it is not the individual's conscious bias and assumptions about his world that prove troublesome, but those which he doesn't know he possesses.

The issue raised here is a crucial one for two important reasons. First, knowledge about our world and the assumptions we make about what we believe we know is one of the primary purposes of science. Fortunately, if nothing else, we have been taught two very important lessons when we turned loose of our early beliefs in scientific absolution. Our intellectual ethnocentrism has been forced to give way to the opinion that there is no certainty in knowledge and things are usually not as they appear to our immediate senses. Therefore, omission of the examination of our own individual bias and our tendency to be mesmerized by our beliefs in our own intellectual superiority can lead to implied assumptions about our existence and reality which would then not be dealt with directly. This is a mistake which science cannot afford to make. The second reason we need to monitor our own values is more important. As Jacob Bronowski (1973) suggests, the intellectual and moral leadership of the twentieth century rests with scientists, and this is both a responsibility and a challenge that has to be met. We must, as Bronowski writes, be ". . . what every strong intellect want to be, . . . a guardian of integrity" (p. 429). In this context, science and scientists can ill afford not to respond to the gravity of the responsibility of the monitoring of its own values and cultural bias. Not only must we guard against our unconscious assumptions of reality, but the seductive qualities of power associated with knowledge.

Sir Francis Bacon once wrote that knowledge was power (Durant, 1926). Bronowski agrees and adds,

> Science is also a source of power that walks close to government and that the state wants to harness. But if science allows itself to go that way, the beliefs of the twentieth century will fall to pieces in cynicism. We shall be left without beliefs, because no beliefs can be built up this century that are not based on science as the recognition of the uniqueness of man, and a pride in his gifts and works. It is not the business of science to inherit the earth but to inherit the moral imagination, because without that man and beliefs and science will perish together. (p. 433)

We must not fall in love with the aristocrat of the intellect and the seductive properties of power and grandiosity which frequently follows the belief that knowledge and certainty are one. Bronowski writes,

> And that is a belief which can only destroy civilization that we know . . . When people believe that they have absolute knowledge, with no test in reality . . . This is when . . . they aspire to the knowledge of gods. We have to cure ourselves of the itch for absolute knowledge and power. (p. 374)

Subrahayam Chandrasekhar, the Nobel-Prize-winning physicist, expressed similar sentiments when he proposed, "I think one could say that a certain modesty toward understanding nature is a precondition to the continued pursuit of science" (p. 73). Chandrasekhar felt compelled to criticize science because of his colleagues' tendencies to develop an overbearing arrogance towards reality after many of them had had great insights and made great discoveries early in their life. Chandrasekhar adds, "Many of the great scientists of the 1920s who made quantum mechanics — Dirac-Heisenberg, Fowler, even Maxwell and Einstein — did not ever equal themselves" (p. 72). Chandrasekhar felt this was so because these men imagined afterwards that because they had succeeded so triumphantly in one area that they believed they must have a special way of looking at science and reality which must therefore be right. "But science doesn't permit that," Chandrasekhar warns. "Nature has shown over and over again that the kind of truths which underline nature transcend the most powerful minds" (p. 72). Unfortunately, Chandrasekhar doesn't think that a scientist would be as likely to show the modesty that Beethoven demonstrated, when at age 47, he reportedly told a friend, "Now I know how to compose." When, Chandrasekhar asks, has there ever been a 47-year-old scientist who announced, "Now I know how to do research" (p. 72).

Chandrasekhar contends that, "When you discuss the works of a great artist or writer, the assumption is that there is a growth from the early period to the middle period to the mature work and the end. The artist's ability is refined through time. It obviously required an enormous effort, an enormous emotional control, to be able to write a play like *King Lear*. Look at the contrast between that and an earlier play, *Romeo and Juliet*. Now why is a scientist unable to refine his mind?" (p. 72).

VALUES AS REPRESENTATIONS OF REALITY

Bronowski and Chandrasekhar are therefore arguing for a science that is not corrupted by the failure of the intellect to realize its limits. Corruption can take many forms, however. Whether it is the quest for salvation and the definition of meaning which religion has usually tried to furnish or our own propensity to retreat into arrogant intellectual certainty, the result remains the same — alienation and self-deception. Bronowski wanted to avoid this dilemma and suggested that while our values frequently are not given or blatantly obvious, the will, upon the proper examination, reflect a purpose and a unity with the cosmos.

Bronowski arrived at this view in the later years of his life when he diverted his interest in physics and mathematics to biology because he felt evolutionary theory best captured the relational aspect of human values to our perceptions of reality. Science, for Bronowski, had shifted from a paradigm which now embraced physics as a model for explaining the universe to a paradigm which now embraced biology and the evolutionary relationship of life and matter. Paralleling Alfred North Whitehead's concept of an organismic universe, Bronowski came to believe that we are evolving much as nature and matter evolve and implied an important relationship existed between our values and evolution.

> Evolution is the climbing of a ladder from simple to the complex by steps, each of which is stable in itself . . . I call it Straified Stability. That is what has brought life by slow steps but constantly up a ladder of increasing complexity—which is the control progress and problem in evolution. And now we know that is true not only of life but of matter. (p. 342)

Thus, Bronowski gradually came to believe our mind reflected similar properties in its makeup. Agreeing with Johnny Von Neumann, Bronowski described that,

> he (Von Newmann) looks at the brain as having a language in which the activities of the different parts of the brain have somehow to be interlocked and made to match so that we devise a plan, a procedure, as a grand overall way of life—what in the humanities we would call a system of values. (p. 433)

Within this context our values and belief systems are not just wish fulfillments as some would have us believe, but a physiological manifestation of a genetically determined reflection of the cosmos. These values, though imposed, are influenced by our volition and serve a pragmatic purpose.

> Our actions as adults, as decision makers, as human beings, are mediated by values, which I interpret as general strategies in which we balance opposing impulses. It is not true that we run our lives by any computer scheme of problem solving. The problems of life are insolvable in this sense. Instead, we shape our conduct by finding principles to guide it. We devise ethical strategies or systems of values to ensure that what is attrac-

tive in the short term is weighed in the balance of the ultimate, long-term satisfaction. (p. 436)

Knowledge as Self-Deception

The examination of values in science is not new. However, a scientist's own idiosyncratic experiences can distort the most objective of explanations and observations. For instance, Kuhn (1962) claims that while many values may be shared by scientists, they will frequently differ in their application of these values. Usually, the judgment of the accuracy of facts is generally stable. However, the judgment of simplicity, consistency, plausibility and so on will often vary greatly from individual to individual. In short, though values are widely shared by scientists and though commitment to them is both deep and constitutive of science, the application of values is sometimes considerably affected by features of individual personality and biography that differentiate the numbers of the group.

Sigmund Freud (1910) succinctly pointed out that the most important goal of psychoanalysis was to make us more self-aware and more honest with ourselves. With Socrates, Freud urged "know thyself." Psychoanalysis, therefore, was built upon the foundations laid before it by the early Greek maxim—"You shall know the Truth and the Truth shall set you free." Above all, Freud set out to undermine our dishonesty with ourselves. Hans Strupp (1972) summed it up by saying,

> Unlike any man before him, Freud identified self-deception as a pervasive and universal human characteristic. Insight into our unconscious motivations through psychoanalysis is meant to pave the road for the kind of mastery and control Freud had in mind. (p. 40)

Unfortunately, Freud's cardinal article of faith becomes the frail human intellect which is to serve as the only reliable guide on this discovery of truth. Alas, as Strupp points out, the intellect of rational thought may be as much an illusion as Freud considered religion to be. Unfortunately, Freud was following the path laid by philosophers before him who believed that human reason was capable of unlocking the secrets of the universe and thus offered man ultimate truth. But as Shestov (1932) warned, these philosophers only succeeded in chaining man to the power of *Ananke* which they slavishly revere as a deity.

> Reason does without commandments, men will love it of themselves unbidden. The theory of knowledge simply signs the praises of reason, but no one has the audacity to question it, and still less dare doubt its sovereign power. (p. 33)

Reason versus Knowledge

The confusion between scientific and religious criteria has been a recurring problem in the philosophy of science. Frank (1961) for one has tersely noted the insistence of researchers to examine value-laden behavior by scientific criteria in isolation rather than immediately involving cultural criteria. As Whitehead convincingly argues, the best way to advance beyond the culturally determined bias of reality is by abstraction. Whitehead credits the development of the science of pure mathematics as "the most original creation of the human spirit" (p. 19).

The more abstract the better, Whitehead argued, for it rids us of all our expectations and prejudices of reality. Mathematics is the mediating process between the abstract and the concrete. So long as you are dealing with pure mathematics, you are in the realm of complete abstraction and to arrive at truth, divorced from bias, you need abstraction to treat objects in their complete uniqueness.

However, Whitehead warns that the intolerable use of abstraction is a major vice of the intellect and claims the judicious use of reason is needed in its application. Here, Whitehead is reacting to the arrogant use of abstraction and is making an Emerson-like distinction between understanding and reason. Emerson viewed reason as a higher form of understanding because it allowed the intuitive feelings of the heart and sentiment to complement the perceptual apprehension of reality (White, 1972). (It is important to remember that Emerson, the Transcendentalists had an important influence on the Oxford Group Movement.) Understanding alone, as Emerson, the Transcendentalists, and eventually the Oxford Group and AA came to realize, is incapable of comprehending the moral unity of our relationship with the cosmos because it is based on the knowledge limited by our five senses and thus presented to us with a distorted perception of reality.

Years prior to Emerson's development of his doctrine of moral sentiment, Kant had "solved" this problem for the Transcendentalists when he tried to show that understanding cannot lead us to any knowledge of what things are in themselves or what we are in ourselves since it cannot penetrate beyond the realms of possible experience. Because objective in this realm are necessarily subject to the principles of causality, man as an empirical object also is subject to the same principles. To escape this predicament, Kant appealed to Practical Reason, or moral consciousness, which assured him that there is a supersensible noumena world consisting of entities that are neither in space nor time and hence not subject to causal influences.

Beyond the restrictions of the distinction between our phenomenal world of existence and the noumena world of reality, Whitehead is suggesting science has compounded its difficulty in empirical observation by being reactionary. Whitehead charges that during the Reformation, science in its rush to debunk the canons of reasoning associated with the dogma of Christianity treated induction of rationalism led science to an obsession with scientific materialism which was narrowly focused only on brute fact. Science, Whitehead accuses, has never shaken off the impress of its historical revolt of the later Renaissance and has remained predominantly an anti-rationalistic movement based upon the naive belief that it is value-free. What reasoning science wanted, it borrowed from Greek rationalism and mathematics. Science, therefore has never cared to justify its meaning.

Science versus Religion

Bergin (1981) for one agrees with Whitehead and argues that science has lost its authority as the dominating source of truth it once was. "The change is both reflected in and stimulated by analysis which reveals science to be an intuitive and a value-laden cultural form." Bergin proposes that a science dominated by mechanistic thought and ethic naturalism has proved insufficient and something more is wanted especially since the spiritual and social failures of many organized religious systems have been followed by the failures of non-religious approaches. Bergin like Bakan (1972) stands in opposition to the worshipping of the scientific method in place of God and condemns the notion of "methodolatry" in science.

Reactive polarization of scientists and philosophers to issues of beliefs and values in science has been a growing problem as it has been for professionals and AA. This situation prompted Max Born once to observe, "There are two objectionable kinds of believers. Those who believe the incredible and those who believe that belief must be discarded in favor of the scientific method" (Bronowski, 1973, p. 364).

However, the distinction between religious and scientific criteria is usually more subtle. Frank (1972), for instance has facetiously drawn a comparison of the Catholic religion and his discipline psychology which he calls the Religion of Mental Health. "The Mental Health movement resembles organized religions in some respects. Science is its theology and is followed by rituals like this conference in which various members of the priesthood read papers to their colleagues, who try to maintain an air of respectful attention. As a devotee of this religion, I would like to point out that, like all religions, it leads its adherents to ignore phenomena that are inconsistent with its cosmology" (1972, p. 242-243).

Whitehead for one is insistent that science meet this challenge and expand its paradigm to include intuition and emotion. Whitehead is thus protesting against the scientific logos and the inhuman attitude of modern science; the mentality which is able to reduce nature to a "dull affair, soundless, scentless, colourless; merely hurrying of material, endlessly, meaninglessly" (Brown, 1959, p. 316). Thus modern science confirms Ferenczi's aphorism, "Pure intelligence is thus a produce of dying, or at least of becoming mentally insensitive and is therefore in principle madness" (Brown, 1959, p. 317). Whitehead agrees and writes, "What is wanted is an appreciation of the infinite variety of vivid values achieved by an organism in its proper environment. When you understand all about the sun and all about the atmosphere and all about the rotation of the earth, you may still miss the radiance of the sunset. There is no substitute for the direct perception of the concrete achievement of a thing in its actuality" (1925, p. 199).

Whitehead is therefore proposing the appreciation of the concrete as a way out of the labyrinth of abstract thought. Unlike Emerson and AA, he does not radically appeal to sentiment only as a higher form of knowledge. However, he does propose a need for the development of a more comprehensive acknowledgement of our relationship with the cosmos — one that avoids the confusion of the concrete with the abstract and draws upon more than what our frail intellect can offer.

Thus, Whitehead is not criticizing the scientific method itself but rather the "fallacy of misplaced concreteness." We are, Whitehead warns, in danger of losing ourself in the abstract idealism of our own thought. We confuse the abstract with the concrete and then judge the abstraction to be real. The "scientific materialism" of "brute fact" cannot be applied as reality itself for external objects exist, not in the sense of "simple location" (just there), but rather in relation. "Scientific investigation," Whitehead warns, "cannot speak of an entity without reference or relationship to the universe as a whole and its relationship to that entity." Whitehead recognizes that science needs a more comprehensive framework in which to apply its discoveries. While science claims it now has no need for philosophy, Whitehead charges it has carried one over from the Greek influence whether science has recognized it or not. "A living science is impossible," Whitehead speculates, "and cannot exist unless there is a belief in an order of nature" (1925, p. 39).

THE SYNTHESIS OF SCIENCE, RELIGION, AND AA

American philosophy, in particular, has been characterized by its response to the challenge of modern science and the scientific method. As Mortin White (1973) illustrates, there is a strong dualistic tendency deeply ingrained in American philosophical thought. This dualism has been manifested as a response of moral sentiment to science's challenges that knowledge is determined by experience or limited to analytical intent of meaning. Ralph Waldo Emerson, Johnathan Edwards, William James, and Charles Pierce have all spearheaded an appeal to some form of emotion, sentiment, or passion as methods of establishing knowledge which are fundamentally different from that associated with the scientific method. As James wrote, "Science can tell us what exists; but to compare the *worths*, both of what exists and of what does not exist, we must consult not science, but what Pascal calls our heart" (p. 192, in White, 1972).

Historically, religion has furnished man with the answers to his questions concerning his cosmos and its origin. But as A. N. Whitehead (1933) illustrates, religion due to its inability to accept change has become stagnant. "In the first place," Whitehead explains, "there has always been a conflict between religion and science. In the second place, both religion and science have always been in a state of continual change. However, for over two centuries religion has been on the defensive and on a weak defensive." In earlier times religion was the most adequate method of explaining reality due to the limitations of knowledge. While science in the last few hundred years has remained what Whitehead terms "adventurous" and adapted itself to intellectual endeavor, thus continuing to grow, religion has not (p. 182, 1925).

Physics in particular has illustrated the far-reaching implications possible whenever a science has been able to unite itself with moral sentiment in its investigation. "Conceptual riddles," as J. Bronowski (1973, p. 363) illustrates, "are solved in Quantum Physics by mathematical formulations only after being solved as mental riddles first. The speculation and arguments surrounding these riddles required, not calculation, but insight, imagination — if you like metaphysics." Max Born indicated his support of this position when he confessed, "I am now convinced that theoretical physics is actual philosophy" (p. 364, in Bronowski, 1973). What he meant was that the new ideas in physics amount to a different view of reality. The world is not a fixed solid array of objects out there, for it cannot be fully separated from our perception of it. It shifts under our gaze, it interacts with us, and the knowledge that it yields has to be interpreted by us.

In trying to distinguish appearance from reality and lay bare the fundamental structure of the universe, science has had to translate the "rabble of the senses." Its highest edifices, Einstein has pointed out, "have been purchased at the price of emptiness of content" (p. 113 in Barnett, 1948).

Thus, gradually, scientists have been forced to abandon the ordinary world of our experience, the world of sense perceptions. In contrast to the edifice that Locke and the rationalists had built in defining knowledge, scientists have arrived at the startling conclusion that since qualities exist only in the mind, the whole objective universe of matter and energy, atoms and stars, does not exist except as a construction of the consciousness, an edifice of conventional symbols shaped by the sense of man. As Barrett writes,

> So paradoxically what the scientist and the philosopher have called the world of appearance — the world of light and color designed by the physiology of human sense organs — is the world in which finite man is incarcerated by his essential nature. And what the scientist called the world of reality — the

colorless, soundless, unpalpable cosmos which lies like an iceberg hidden beneath the plane of man's perception – is a skeleton structure of symbols. (Barrett, 1948, p. 137)

In his brief tenancy on earth, man egocentrically orders events in his mind according to his own feeling of past, present, and future. But except on the reels of one's own consciousness, the universe, the objective world of reality, does not "happen," it simply exists. It can be encompassed in its entire majesty only by a cosmic intellect. While science tells us nothing of the true "nature" of things, it nevertheless succeeds in defining their relationship and depicting the events in which they are involved. "The event," Alfred North Whitehead declared, "is the unit of things real" (p. 198, 1933). By this he meant that however theoretical systems may change and however empty of content their symbols and concepts may be, the essential and enduring facts of life are the happenings, the activities, the events. For example, the principle of uncertainty indicates we cannot actually forecast the actual encounter of electrons. Thus in a sense the electrons are not "real" but merely theoretical symbols. On the other hand the meeting itself is "real" – the event is "real." It is as though the true objective world lies forever half concealed beneath the translucent, plastic dome of man's consciousness and cannot be comprehended by his senses, only experienced by his being.

The principle of uncertainty asserts therefore that it is impossible with any principles now known to science to determine the position and the velocity of any electron at the same time. For by the very act of observing its position its velocity is changed; and conversely, the more accurately its velocity is determined, the more indefinite its position becomes. Quantum physics thus appears to shake two pillars of old science, causality, and determinism. By its admission of margins of uncertainty it yields up the ancient hope that science, given the present state and velocity of every material body in the universe, can forecast the history of the universe for all time. One by-product of this surrender is a new argument for the existence of free will. For as physical events are indeterminate and the future is unpredictable, then perhaps the unknown quantity called "mind" may yet guide man's destiny among infinite uncertainties of a capricious universe.

It is here that Werner Heisenberg's Principle of Uncertainty startles us with its great simplicity. J. Bronowski exclaims it as a "profound idea, one of the great scientific ideas, not only of the twentieth century, but in the history of science" (p. 365, Bronowski, 1973). In one sense, it is a robust principle of the everyday. The fact exists that man cannot observe nature objectively but inescapably takes part in the processes he observes. Heisenberg's Principle which states there can be no physics without an observer seems more and more to be primary among all physical laws. The answers to the mysteries of understanding the human condition seems to be at a point where science and religion meld.

In many ways, Heisenberg's Principle of Uncertainty reflects a fundamental issue in the debate between religion and science. While one (science) is more objective, the other (religion) is more subjective. This shouldn't imply that one method is superior than the other. Rather, both disciplines are similar in that they attempt to understand and interpret reality. Since the scientist cannot help affecting what he observes, it may behoove him to put forth more compassion than he normally would for the more subjective methods of understanding the human condition. If professionals realize that even a "hard science," like physics, can have compatible explanations and interpretations of reality with the more subjective religious disciplines like Zen and Taoism, perhaps they will soften in their objections to these disciplines. In many ways, this is a similar condition which exists with many professionals in their relationship with AA. Certainly, more openness to other disciplines will allow critics to see more clearly the legitimate and important contributions that AA has to offer in the treatment of addiction. However, this is a question begging a listener because the professional treatment community needs AA far more than AA needs professional help.

PSYCHOTHERAPIST: HEALER OR REPAIRMAN?

The way AA perceives and defines addiction is often totally divergent from the way many professionals interpret addiction. This is a theme that has run repeatedly throughout this chapter and brings us to the conclusion and ultimate purpose of this presentation. The comparison of these two different interpretations has more than academic significance because the way a problem is defined ultimately determines how the problem's solution will be approached. Consequently, the comparison of the divergent interpretations of addiction by AA and many professionals has clinical significance. On one side of the ledger is the professional scientist practitioner who represents the objective world of science with its emphasis on rationalism, control and empiricism. At the other end is AA which represents a more religious approach with its emphasis on the subjective world of empathy, faith, intuition and revelation. Each viewpoint has something important to offer. This is not to imply that the scientific approach to treatment is mutually exclusive from AA's approach to treatment. Rather, the group leader has to be aware of these differences so that the integration of these two approaches can be successfully obtained.

Bakan (1972) defines the difference between the two extreme positions that a group leader can take and labels the one as the role of the repairman and the other as the role of the healer. Each has value and merit. Technical competence dominates in the role of the repairman. The repairman's intelligence and dedication to matters of fact allows him to proceed systematically, orderly, efficiently, parsimoniously and economically. The repairman restores to order whatever is out of order in the course of his work. The healer's attributes are different. He has to be able to communicate and understand on a very deep and personal level the cosmological and existential entailment of the person's suffering. In doing this the healer conveys the message that the forces for healing are inherent in the sufferer. The healer must also convey the clear message that the person's suffering is not tied into their sins or inherent badness.

As Bakan defines these roles, they are distinctly different. He does not advocate either be disregarded for other. Rather, he cautions that each has some inherent shortcomings if applied in isolation and warns the therapist about their respective limitations.

> As a healer, one concerns oneself with things that are only limitedly comprehended. Success in these areas makes one feel like a magician. (Freud said this of himself when he began with the cure of certain cases of hysteria.) This is a temptation to be avoided by the healer. A healer should believe in the abiding mystery of what he concerns himself with, but a magician must never believe in 'magic' in the mysterious sense. The magician becomes a failure if he believes the illusions that he creates. A rigid scientism on the other hand, is so impatient with anything short of well-founded belief that it closes off from consideration the realities which have not yet been en-

compassed by science. Both of these are to be avoided. (p. 126)

Bakan sees the danger inherent in any position that becomes too rigid and self-fulfilling. Like Bronowski, he cautions us not to confuse knowledge with certainty. It is Bakan's belief that when we give up the nature of the search for truth and believe we have obtained it, we commit idolatry. Idolatry in the conventional religious sense, Bakan writes, is worship of the means or the method towards the fulfillment of the religious aim. Bakan writes:

> Put simply, engaging in ritual, painting religious pictures, reading religious literature, and such activities are not idolatrous unless they themselves become the *objects* of the worship, rather than the means towards the fulfillment of the religious impulse. Idolatry is the loss of the sense of search, of the sense of freshness of the experience. It is the over quick fixing upon any method or device or concept as the ultimate fulfillment of the religious impulse. Idolatry is allowing the impulse to be bribed by incomplete but immediate satisfaction. The use of religious objects as reminders, as sensory provocation, or the like, of the religious impulse is not idolatrous. What is idolatrous is the frame of mind that allows them to be ultimate. (p. 154)

Bakan sees the idolatrous frame of mind tied in to neurosis. Neurosis, from his perspective, is a rigidity or fixation at a certain stage of development which involves a refusal or inability to respond afresh and anew to novel experiences. It ultimately robs the person of joy and spontaneity in their lives. In many ways, this also describes the alcoholic who is caught and "stuck" in a rigid position refusing to accept the world as it is, and insisting that the world conform and meet him absolutely on his terms. Idolatry, from this perspective, can occur in both a religious and scientific framework because each involves a worship of method and a substitution of method for the wonder of the unknown. Worship of method, or idolatry, can be preferred to the search for the unknown because it is more exact, predictable, and at least initially less anxiety provoking. But as Bakan warns, we must not confuse the method with the aim or the intent of the method. In fact, Bakan points out how the concept of the God of the Judeo-Christian tradition was an act of religious genius because it provided its believers with a God with whom contact was always a bit dubious. Bakan describes the importance of God within this context because it prevents the complete understanding of Him from every being obtained.

> Never could mankind have the sense of closure in contact with this God and yet the contact with this God was always in the realm of possibility, even if it be unknown whether at any time, or for any individual, such contact could be. This is the paradoxical feature of this God, that of possible yet dubious contact, contact always possibly available, and yet in doubt — a God, and I think that this is critical, knowable in the limited region of the expression of his nature (in a piece of the world, a concretization in parts of man, and so forth) but not ultimately knowable. This was a God to be continuously worked toward, a God who was as continuous, as frustrating, and as fulfilling as life itself. The commandment against idolatry was a commandment to believe that complete substantial contact with God could never take place. The substantial contact with God must always be in the nature of a search. One must always be filled with a sense of wonder of what was not yet reached. One must always be yearning toward fulfillment, but fulfillment must be maintained as an ideal. Fulfillment was always away and seeming fulfillment always mythical, at least, and more than likely, idolatrous. The genius of the concept of God so developed inheres in the very fact that a certain lack of completion was always involved. For in this lack of completion is contained the means whereby man can maintain the freshness of experience that experience demands. (p. 156)

Such a stance as Bakan describes is a fitting way to end this chapter on AA. His description portrays accurately the position a therapist and a group leader must take in dealing with an individual in treatment whether that person is addicted or not. We can lose the openness and the freshness of the wonder in our interactions with our patients if we reduce them to objects. When we know exactly what to expect of them and exactly what they need in order to "get well," we are committing idolatry because we are more concerned with our method than the purpose of our intentions. Alcoholism treatment, both in AA and group psychotherapy, must not succumb to the pressure to retreat from the demanding world of actual encounter into the abstract world of methodolatry. Bakan sums up this position when he writes:

> If it were possible to root our idolatrous tendencies in both science and religion, then the singularity of the impulse expressed in both science and religion would emerge with clarity. It is not that religion, as some have maintained, supplies mythical answers until science can provide more valid ones. Rather it is that both religion and science are attempts on the part of mankind to search out the nature of himself and the world in which he lives. But it is search rather than answer which is significant. Indeed, as soon as either the scientist or the theologian allows himself to be fixed upon an answer as though it were the ultimate fulfillment of his impulse, then indeed does he stop being either scientist or theologian and becomes an idolater. (p. 159)

REFERENCES

AA World Services, Inc. (1955). *Alcoholics Anonymous*. New York: Author.
AA World Services, Inc. (1957). *Alcoholics Anonymous comes of age*. New York: Author.
AA World Services, Inc. (1960). *Is AA for you?* New York: Author.
AA World Services, Inc. (1953). *Twelve steps & twelve traditions*. New York: Author.
Alibrandi, L. A. (1978). The folk psychotherapy of Alcoholics Anonymous. In S. Zimbergh, J. Wallace & S. Blume (Eds.), *Practical approaches to alcoholism psychotherapy*. New York: Plenum Press.
Angyal, A. (1965). *Neurosis & treatment: A holistic theory*. New York: Wiley Press.
Bailey, M. B. & Leach, B. (1965). *Alcoholics Anonymous – pathway to recovery: A study of 1,058 members of the AA Fellowship in New York City*. New York: National Council on Alcoholism.
Bakan, A. (1972). *On method*. San Francisco: Jossey Bass.
Barnett, L. (1948). *The universe and Dr. Einstein*. New York: Bantam Books.
Barrett, C. L. (1985). Who are the alcoholics? Who are the devils? *Bulletin of the Society of Psychologists in Addictive Behaviors*, *4*(1), 17-28.
Bateson, G. (1971). The cybernetics of self: A theory of alcoholism. *Psychiatry*, *34*, 1-18.
Bateson, G. (1971). The cybernetics of self: A theory of alcoholism. *Steps to an ecology of mind*. New York: Ballantine Books.
Bergin, A. (1981). Psychotherapy & religious values. *Journal of Clinical Psychology*, *48*(1), 95-105.
Bixenstine, E. (1956). The value-fact antithesis in behavioral science. *Journal of Humanistic Psychology*, *16*, 35-57.
Bourne, P. & Fox, R. (1973). *Alcoholism, progress in research & treatment*. New York: Academic Press.
Bronowski, J. (1973). *The ascent of man*. Boston/Toronto: Little, Brown & Co.
Brown, N. O. (1959). *Life against death*. Wesleyan U. Press.
Buber, M. (1960). *I and thou*. New York: Schuber & Sons.
Chandrasekhar, S. (John Tierney). (1983). Quest for order. *Science*, 69-82.

Dumont, M. P. (1974). Self-help treatment programs. *American Journal of Psychiatry, 131*, 631-635.

Durant, W. (1926). *Story of philosophy*. New York: Simon & Schuster.

Emrick, C. D., Lassen, C. L. & Edwards, M. T. (1977). Nonprofessional peers as therapeutic agents in effective psychotherapies. In G. E. German & A. Rozin (Eds.), *The therapist contribution to effective psychotherapy: An empirical assessment*. Elmsford: Pergamon Press.

Festinger, L. (1954). A theory of social comparison processes. *Human Relations, 7*, 117-140.

Fox, R. (1973). Treatment of the problem drinker by the private practitioner. In P. Bourne & R. Fox (Eds.), *Alcoholism, progress in research & treatment*. New York: Academic Press.

Frankl, C. (1971). *The case for modern man*. Boston: Beacon Press.

Freud, S. (1910). The future prospects of psycho-analytic therapy. *The standard edition of the complete psychological works of S. Freud*, Vol. II (pp. 139-152). London: Hogarth Press.

Frank, J. (1961). *Persuasion and healing*. Baltimore: Johns Hopkins Press.

Frank, J. (1972). *Remarks*, In Chafetz, M. E. (Ed.), Proceedings of the 2nd annual alcoholism conference on NIAAA (pp. 242-244).

Gartner, A. & Riessman, F. (1984). *The self-help revolution*. New York: Human Sciences Press.

Hartup, W. W. (1970). Peer interaction & social organization. In P. H. Mussen (Ed.), *Carmicael's manual of child psychology*, Vol. 2 (3rd Ed.). New York: Wiley.

Heidegger, M. (1962). *Being & time*. (MacQuarrie, J. & Robinson, E., Trans.). New York: Harper & Row (orig. 1927).

James, W. (1902). *The varieties of religious experience*. New York: Longmans.

Jaspers, K. (1975). On my philosophy. In W. Kaufman (Ed.), *Existentialism from Dostoevsky to Sartre*. New York: New American Library (orig. 1941).

Jellinek, E. M. (1960). *The disease concept of alcoholism*. New Haven: Hillhouse Press.

Johnson, V. E. (1969). *I'll quit tomorrow*. New York: Holt, Rinehart & Winston.

Jones, R. K. (1970). Sectarian characteristics of Alcoholics Anonymous. *Sociology*, Oxford, *4*, 181-195.

Kaufmann, W. (1968). *The reception of existentialism in the United States*. Midway, *9*, 97-126.

Kelly, G. (1963). *A theory of personality. The psychology of personal constructs*. New York: W. W. Norton & Co.

Kuhn, T. S. (1962). *The structure of scientific revolution*. Chicago: University of Chicago Press.

Kurtz, E. (1979). *Not God, a history of Alcoholics Anonymous*. Center City, MN: Hazeldon Foundation.

Kurtz, E. (1982). Why AA works. The intellectual significance of Alcoholics Anonymous. *Journal of Studies on Alcohol, 40*, 230-239.

Laing, R. D. (1960). *The divides self: An existential study in sanity & madness*. London: Tavistock Press.

Laing, R. D. (1971). *The self and others* (2nd ed.). Harmondsworth, England: Penguin Books.

Leuba, J. H. (1896). A study in the psychology of religious phenomena. *American Journal of Psychology, 7*, 309-385.

Lieberman, M. A. & Borman, L. D. (1979). *Self help groups for coping and crisis: Origins, members, processes & impact*. San Francisco: Jossey Bass.

Madsen, N. (1974). *The American alcoholic*. Springfield, IL: Charles C. Thomas.

Mann, M. (1973). *The disease concept of alcoholism*. San Francisco: Faces West Production.

Marlatt, G. A. (1983). The controlled drinking controversy: A commentary. *American Psychologist, 38*(10), 1097-1110.

Muus, R. E. (1968). *Theories of adolescence* (2nd ed.). New York: Random House.

Osborne, J. W. & Baldwin, J. R. (1982). From one state of illusion to another? *Psychotherapy: Theory research and practice, 19*(3), 266-275.

Patterson, G. R. & Anderson, D. (1964). Peers as social reinforcers. *Child Development, 35*, 951-960.

Shestov, L. (1932). *On job's balance*. (Coventry & Macartney Trans.). London: Dent & Sons.

Sobell, M. B. & Sobell, L. (1973). Alcoholics treated by individualized behavior therapy: One year treatment outcome. *Behavior Research & Therapy, 11*, 599-618.

Stace, W. (1966). What is mysticism. In P. Struhl & K. Struhl (Eds.), *Philosophy now* (pp. 235-251). New York: Random House.

Starbuck, E. D. (1899). *The psychology of religion*. New York: Scribners.

Strupp, H. H. (1972, June). Freudian analysis today. *Psychology Today*.

Thune, C. E. (1977). Alcoholism and the archetypal past, A phenomenological perspective on Alcoholics Anonymous. *Journal of Studies on Alcohol, 38*(1).

Tournier, R. E. (1979). Alcoholics Anonymous as treatment and as ideology. *Journal of Studies on Alcohol, 40*, 230-239.

Wallace, J. (1984). Myths & misconceptions about Alcoholics Anonymous. *About AA*. New York: AA World Services.

Watzlawick, P. (1978). *The language of change*. New York: Basic Books.

White, M. (1972). *Documents in the history of American philosophy*. New York: Oxford University Press.

White, M. (1973). *Science and sentiment in America*. New York: Oxford University Press.

Whitehead, A. N. (1933). *Adventures of ideas*. New York: The Free Press.

Whitehead, A. N. (1925). *Science and the modern world*. New York: The Free Press.

Chapter 7

The Use of Confrontation
Techniques in Group

Beginning group leaders soon discover that few alcoholics and addicts enter treatment of their own free will. Consequently, when these patients are initially introduced to treatment and group, they usually are under extreme external pressure from either the family, employer, court, or are impelled by serious physical health problems related to their chemical use. The group leader finds that many of his group members are in a severe emotional state characterized by guilt, shame and depression or extremely obstinate and angry because others have forced them to comply with demands that seem to them to be unjust, unfair and punitive. Even if the chemically dependent individual agrees that they need treatment, they usually harbor wishes to be able to drink and use drugs in a safe and normal way. Their compliance to treatment is more motivated by their remorse and wish to avoid further condemnation than it is by their desire to actively learn ways to insure that their treatment will be successful. Thus, the group leader is faced with the difficult task of dealing with resistant patients on two different levels. If his group members are not actively rebellious and resistant to treatment, they usually are working very hard at giving the staff and group leader the impression that they are actively engaged in their recovery and treatment. This presents the group leader with a delicate problem because those group members who are actively resistant are usually easier to treat than those who are passively compliant.

Their facade of forced compliance must be exposed as a manipulation of the treatment process or their recovery will be motivated only by their desire to be free from external distress and pressure. In either case, the patient's postures need to be confronted and altered quickly; usually within 28 days, the length of a normal inpatient program. Unless this is accomplished, the AA program will not be internalized and they will never be able to make the shift to personal responsibility for their recovery and abstinence. Although group psychotherapy can be a significant adjunct to an alcoholic's and addict's treatment, group leaders also discover that few patients are completely willing to do everything necessary to insure the successful treatment of their addiction. Most alcoholics and addicts possess varying levels of motivation to abstain from alcohol and drug use. This is especially true during the early initial stages of treatment when their level of alcohol and drug induced cognitive impairment is most severe and they are more rigid and limited in their ability to explore alternative solutions to old problems. Even when addicts and alcoholics enter treatment completely of their own free will and possess a strong innate desire to stop their use of chemicals, many of these patients will have difficulty doing the things necessary to insure their recovery because of the various degree of character pathology they possess. This condition is also made more severe by the recency of their chemical use, which usually leaves them more rebellious, suspicious and manipulative.

The art of treating addiction is to overcome the enormous denial and resistance, whether it be passive or active, that most alcoholics and addicts possess. Such a stance in treatment raises many important ethical and therapeutic issues. Confrontation, if done too punitively or if motivated by a group leader's counter-transference issues, can severely damage the therapeutic alliance. However, the group leader cannot afford to stand back and take a stance of therapeutic neutrality because time, the severity of the chemically dependent patient's condition, and his lack of motivation interferes with the normal evolution of psychotherapy which usually takes place with most non-addicted patients. Treating the chemically dependent patient requires the group leader make a dramatic shift in focus and utilize techniques with which the group leader usually has little training or experience. Confrontation, intervention, coercion and the use of therapeutic leverage are techniques that can have damaging effects on an individual or a group if they are applied inappropriately and indiscriminantly. Such an approach to treatment is often completely contrary to most contemporary forms of psychotherapy and many group leaders are either uncomfortable with its utilization or do not understand its proper application. Consequently, these methods are frequently misused, ignored or overzealously applied. In some cases, group leaders who are unfamiliar with its proper utilization applied these methods indiscriminantly to all group members with equal intensity all of the time. They fail to realize some alcoholics and addicts require a little of it and some require more. They fail to treat their group members as individuals and these techniques become ends unto themselves. What would be an appropriate confrontation for an alcoholic at the beginning of treatment would be completely destructive for that same alcoholic later in treatment. As Abraham Maslow once said, "If the only tool you have is a hammer, everything starts looking like a nail."

It is important to remember that defensive operations organize the self not only for effective normal functioning, but also to avoid anxiety. Therefore, confrontive techniques used solely as tools to hammer away at the rigid defences of alcoholics and addicts are likely to increase anxiety and thereby precipitate avoidance responses and denial. Withdrawal, avoidance, or placating responses can be triggered by such techniques and will, in turn, reinforce rigid patterns of thought and behavior, thereby increasing resistance to change. Treatment in many cases can be enhanced with a more indirect use of confrontation. Also, any tendencies towards compliance (agreement with the staff and group leader to avoid the anxiety of confrontation) are amplified by direct attacks. Thus, indirect confrontation also decreases the likelihood of passive compliant forms of resistance.

This brings us to the purpose of this chapter. Each of these techniques — coercion, the use of therapeutic leverage, confrontation and intervention — will be explored in an attempt to define the limits of its usefulness and applicability. Usually, if not always, these techniques are much more appropriate during the early part of treatment. They should be utilized either to get the chemically dependent individual to realize the extent of their difficulty in the hope that they will enter treatment or once in treatment help them to truly understand the severe disparity between their actions and feelings. In short, these techniques can help the individual take a more honest look at himself and hopefully recognize that his self-deceptions are a significant contributing factor to the severity of his condition.

SPECIAL PROBLEMS
OF THE ADDICTED PATIENT

The basic thrust of treatment for an addicted patient is to get them to perceive and understand the relationship between their present difficulties in life and their alcohol and drug use. When this is accomplished, the patient must be made to see the advantage of not drinking or doing drugs compared to the problems resulting from the continual use of chemicals. This choice must be weighed by each patient and a personal decision made. However, given to rely on their own resources, most addicts and alcoholics will cling to the belief that they can one day attain normal and healthy use of drugs and alcohol. While most therapists have been taught that it is important not to make decisions for patients and that a therapeutic alliance must never be compromised, at any cost, the group leader must carefully evaluate such a stance when leading a group composed of members who are currently struggling with these decisions in the early stages of their recovery. As Shore states, "Therapists who remain inflexibly supportive while alcoholics continue to kill themselves by drinking need to reconsider the moral repercussions of their position" (Shore, 1981, p. 13).

Alcoholics and addicts consequently present group leaders with new and unique problems in group. Working with this population requires the group leader to evaluate many of his conventional and unquestionable assumptions about treatment. An approach that is very effective with a non-addicted patient might be totally inappropriate for someone who is currently addicted or is in the early stages of his recovery. The group leader must also be aware that many alcoholics and addicts have rather sophisticated defenses and are usually adept at applying these defenses in an effort to defeat the therapist. Unlike neurotics or non-addictive patients, who come to treatment of their own free will and are actively seeking help in the relief of their symptoms, most addicted patients want to convince the group leader and the treatment staff that there has either been a horrible mistake made in their referral for treatment or that they need the staff and group leader to focus on their real problem. This problem is often formulated in the patient's mind as the root cause of their pathological use of chemicals. Secretly, the patient hopes once this root cause is discovered, he will be able to return to the normal use of chemicals. The chemically dependent individual will emphasize this issue, because drinking or drug use is frequently the only pleasure that the patient feels they derive out of life and it is a pleasure that must be protected at all costs. Some frequent examples of the defensive operations which are intricately connected to misconceptions about alcohol which the group leader can expect to have to confront and alter in a group include:

RATIONALIZATION

1. I only drink beer.
2. I only drink on weekends.

3. I can stop any time I want to.
4. I never drink alone.
5. I drink only to be sociable.

DENIAL

6. I may drink too much, but I'm not an alcoholic.
7. I can't be an alcoholic, I'm a woman.
8. Sure I drink, but I never miss work and I have a good job.

PROJECTION

9. You can't imagine the pressure I've been under.
10. I only drink because everyone is against me.
11. I drink because my wife is such a bitch and my boss doesn't appreciate me.
12. I could control my drinking if everyone would leave me alone.
13. Sure I drink, but everybody else does and they have more of a problem than I do.
14. If you had to put up with what I have to put up with, you'd drink too.

MINIMIZATION

15. I've been drinking a little, but only on the weekends.
16. Oh, I can stop drinking anytime, I have several times in the last 10 years.
17. I can control the amount of my drinking anytime I want to.

Each cluster represents examples of different ego defenses. While this list is not intended to be conclusive, it does give a group leader a flavor of what to expect from his group members. Modifying each misconception requires a confrontation from the group leader. It is crucial in the early stages of treatment that the addict or alcoholic realize that it is their defensive operations which are preventing them from recognizing the significant contribution that drugs and alcohol play in their difficulties.

DEFENSE MECHANISMS

The list of common misconceptions about alcohol are basically products of an elaborate set of defense mechanisms. Neo-Freudians were the first to draw the distinction between healthy ego-defenses,

such as sublimation and intellectualization, and unhealthy ego-defenses such as denial and suppression. The group leaders should
understand that repression and ego-defenses are a normal healthy
process and reflect an individual's tendency to selectively forget
negative experiences that may be too painful or uncomfortable. Repression and ego-defenses are utilized by all of us in our attempts to
cope with day-to-day problems. It is only when the degree of repression reaches such proportions as to deny reality that symptoms
of illness are manifested. When ego-defenses are utilized with such
frequency and intensity that reality testing becomes compromised,
the individual must be encouraged to face the inappropriateness of
their defensive position. The importance of confronting these misconceptions are crucial in treating the alcoholic and addict because
inappropriate ego-defenses and repression are the key misconceptions that the group leader must recognize and deal with before any
progress in treatment can be initiated.

Borowitz (1964) hypothesized that the basic psychological effect
of alcohol is to modify ego function, which involves a decrease in
perceptual activity. In fact, an alcoholic and addict are generally
thought to possess a poorly developed ego with inadequate defenses. Vernon Johnson (1973) agrees and he views the alcoholic as
unable to perceive what exactly is happening to him because the
dynamics of the illness are so complicated. Addiction is an intricate
process which involves an interplay of repression, cortical deterioration, and impaired judgement. While it is not important that the
group leader know why a person is an alcoholic or addict in order to
counsel and help him, it is important to have an understanding of
the dynamics involved in the addiction process.

An alcoholic or addict is an individual with a chronic disease
which gets progressively worse. This is important to remember because as the alcoholic and addict's condition deteriorates, his ego
strength weakens and his self-image deteriorates. Guilt, shame and
remorse are factors that frequently cause the alcoholic to set up
elaborate defenses to control these uncomfortable emotions. As the
emotional pain becomes greater, the more rigid his defenses become. Eventually, he becomes a victim of his own psychological
defense mechanisms.

Marty Mann, among others, stressed the importance of straight-
ening out the patient's misconceptions and fallacies about the disease of alcoholism. Alcoholics, Mann felt, share the view of society
that alcoholism is a moral deficiency. Alcoholics and addicts gener-

ally don't view themselves as physically dependent and this is one of the reasons why they make every effort to deny that addiction is their problem. The guilt and remorse they feel because of their drinking and drug use leads them to refuse to acknowledge or accept help. The disease concept convinces them that they are not bad, but rather ill. This relieves their guilt. Any modality of treatment which gets the addict and alcoholic to accept himself as an individual with some worth, will help his recovery. Increased self-esteem and self-worth are important factors in treatment.

Ruth Fox sums up this position when she writes,

> The alcoholic needs to be reassured that alcoholism is truly viewed by the medical profession and other health authorities as an illness, not a moral failing or a wicked self-indulging weakness. The usual immediate result of this assurance is a draining off of the emotions which constrict and distort the alcoholic's self-image and view of the problem, and a release from the enormous guilt feelings which paralyze the patient's ability to take steps toward recovery. (Fox, 1967, p. 54)

Fox's position is consistent with the psychoanalytic belief that when the cause of repression is discovered, the repressed material rapidly emerges into the patient's consciousness. In other words, if the threat is eliminated, it becomes safe for the repressed material to return to awareness. It is at this stage of recovery, that the alcoholic can look at his illness realistically.

The return to consciousness of repressed feelings is a crucial step in the recovery process for a number of reasons. The alcoholic and addict can now become reacquainted with themselves at a more meaningful level. Admittance of one's illness and addiction is a significant first step in AA's Twelve Steps. V. Johnson suggests,

> The effect of this new degree of self-awareness has been to create the need for a reduction of the burden of moral anxiety and guilt which it has brought into conscious focus . . . In some fashion, the alcoholic begins now to see the truth that these defects of character are the signs of his sickness, and that upon their removal, his recovery depends. (Johnson, 1973, p. 116)

Psychoanalytic theory generally supports Johnson's contention that an emotional component to this awareness is a prerequisite for recovery. Nemiah (1961) in a similar fashion concludes,

> The pain is further heightened to an unbearable intensive by the anger that stems from their ambivalence. To protect themselves from pain, they employ abnormal mechanisms of defense: denial of loss leads to a blocking of the process of grief . . . resulting in a variety of somatic complaints, violent self-castigation, and suicide. (Nemiah, 1961, p. 63)

It is through the process of pain and grief that the alcoholic and addict's awareness of their condition is realistically faced and accepted. Only through an emotional catharsis and crisis will the alcoholic and addict finally admit to God and others that his life is hopeless in the face of his chemical use. This is the stage AA recognizes as the surrender to the acknowledgement that the alcoholic is ill. This process cannot be an intellectual awareness alone. It also requires an understanding at an emotional and spiritual level.

For treatment to continue on at this point, it is important that the group leader not be manipulated into trying to perform insight psychotherapy with a patient who continues to drink or use drugs. The group leader must make it clear to the patient that abstinence will have to come first. Even when addiction is accompanied by an underlying psychopathology, the pathological drinking can kill long before its cause is found. Very often abstinence brings about amelioration in most of the conditions previously blamed by the alcoholic and addict as the reasons for his drinking and drug use.

Johnson sees the removal and alleviation of guilt and remorse as an important factor in treatment. This only occurs after abstinence is attained. "Our most startling observation has been that alcoholism cannot exist unless there is a conflict between the values and the behavior of the drinker." Johnson goes on to conclude, "Very simply, the treatment involves a therapy designed to bring the patient back to reality." It is through the group leader's confrontation of repression and denial that the establishment of reality testing takes place with an associated emotional catharsis.

Albrecht (1969) summed up this position when he concluded, "During this phase of heavy drinking, the individual becomes very skillful at using denial, rationalization, and projection to avoid full confrontation with his drinking problem. He denies that he has a problem; he finds a multitude of reasons for his drinking and he blames others for his drinking." Not only is the alcoholic and addict unaware of his highly developed defense system, he is also unaware of the powerful feelings of self-hate buried behind it. His defense systems continue to grow, so that he can survive in the face of his problems. The greater the pain he suffers, the higher and more rigid the defenses become. The alcoholic and addict therefore become more rigid in their defensive processes as time goes by. Consequently, this adds to the group leader's difficulty as he struggles to get the alcoholic and addict to see their situation more realistically. As the alcoholic and addict succumbs more to their rigid defense system, they become more and more out of touch with their feelings. Given these sets of circumstances, the group leader's task during the early stages of treatment becomes clearly defined. He must help the alcoholic and addict to 1. discover themselves and others as feeling persons and 2. to identify the defenses that prevent this discovery.

Getting the alcoholic and addict to recognize their feelings is important because of two factors. First, feelings and spontaneous expressions tend to be much more honest. It is more helpful to be revealing than to be right. A spontaneous expression may release both positive and negative emotions that must be recognized and dealt with. This is the only way the alcoholic's and addict's rigid defense and repression can be altered and reality testing can be restored. Secondly, it is essential to know one's own feelings at a given moment, for it is necessary to sense with equal accuracy the feelings of the other person. If the alcoholic and addict are to return to the world of the "living," they must be able to deal with other people accurately and empathetically.

Because of the chemically dependent individual's addiction, confrontation is often the only way to alter their self-destructive and rigid defenses. However, the way confrontation is utilized is crucial. There are constructive and destructive forms of confrontation. Alcoholics need someone who will call a spade a spade in a realistic fashion without adopting a punitive, moralistic or superior attitude. Confrontations, as Vernon Johnson illustrates, are often mistaken for forms of attacking the individual. Attacking serves only to raise defenses. Confrontation, on the other hand, is defined as a description of the other person made in such a way as is most likely to be received by him. Johnson states that, "We are most useful as confronters when we are not so much trying to change another person as we are trying to help him see himself more accurately."

COERCION

However, before confrontive techniques can be applied in group, it requires the alcoholic and addict seek treatment. In many, if not most, cases, this is the single largest obstacle to treatment. Pretreatment strategies must be established and managed to insure that the reluctant patient is adequately coerced to seek treatment, especially when they are unable or unwilling to see the reality of their condition. Coercion to seek therapy, however, is a controversial issue which manifests itself in many ethical, legal and practical implications. Questions concerning an individual's rights and freedom to refuse treatment even though his behavior may prove to be a menace to himself and society are not easily resolved or answered (Wald, 1974). Aside from the crucial and now popular issues of infringement of rights and invasion of privacy is the problem of the efficacy of forcing someone to seek treatment when cooperativeness and motivation to be treated are absent. It generally has been an axiom in the field of psychotherapy and counseling that a client has to invest a large part of himself in the treatment process if therapy is to be successful (Perls, 1969; Schultz, 1969; Rogers, 1942; Carkhuff, 1969). However, evidence is now mounting that perhaps this is not necessarily true; especially for alcoholics (Bourne & Fox, 1973; Johnson, 1973).

Ruth Fox (1970) announced that it is not necessary to wait for the alcoholic to hit bottom or motivate himself into treatment before taking therapeutic measures. Sterne and Pittman (1965) demonstrated plainly that it is often the psychotherapist or group leader, rather than the addict or alcoholic, that needs the motivating. Chafetz (1968) and his colleagues showed that helping professionals can motivate the reluctant patient to undergo treatment by promptly meeting the patient's obvious dependency needs, by communicating through action concern for the patient's low self-esteem, and by continuity of care. As Alcoholics Anonymous and Al-Anon have consistently illustrated, a new or changed attitude surrounding the problem drinker frequently moves such a patient to seek help of his own volition (Baily, 1965).

Denial

There is now a general consensus among theorists and practitioners in the field of addiction that alcoholics and addicts generally possess especially poor ego defenses (Johnson, 1973; Bourne & Fox, 1973; Jellinek, 1972; Weinberg, 1976).

Rationalization and denial are such frequent components of an alcoholic's and addict's illness that these ego defenses have become synonymous with the addiction process. Most theorists recognize the necessity of identifying its use and stress the importance of breaking through this denial system before successful recovery can be initiated (Hazelton Foundation, Johnson Institute, etc.). Denial is frequently a progressive part of the alcoholic's and addict's illness. It becomes overdeveloped, more rigid, and increasingly difficult to penetrate in its later states until the alcoholic is almost completely out of touch with reality (Jellinek, 1972). A late-stage alcoholic and addict minimize, rationalize and deny any problem with alcohol or drugs, usually projecting the cause of their problems onto others. Guilt, remorse and deteriorating judgement perpetuate the drinking cycle until the alcoholic and addict totally reject any responsibility for their plight (Johnson, 1973). Weinberg (1976) saw the tendency to avoid this issue by family, friends and helping professionals when dealing with the alcoholic and addict in the earlier stage of their illness, as providing the social environment which encourages denial. Until changes in cultural attitudes occur, Weinberg contended, professionals will continue to be frustrated by a stubborn resistance to change.

Other theorists disagree and suggest strategies for effectively dealing with this problem. It is understandable how the alcoholic's and addict's elaborate ego defenses and strong denial system often lead many counselors, judges and other helping professionals to erroneously assume the popular concept that the alcoholic or addict has to hit bottom before he can be helped. Recent evidence suggests that this is not the case (Bourne & Fox, 1973; Johnson, 1973). Fox (1967) contended that no alcoholic will ever consider giving up alcohol until the suffering it causes him is greater than the pleasure it gives him. The general consensus is that the alcoholic and addict must lose something important to them or at least be threatened with such a loss (Bourne & Fox, 1973; Johnson, 1973).

Vernon Johnson (1973) maintained that it is dangerous to wait for an alcoholic or addict to hit bottom. He sees the need to train counselors to recognize an alcoholic's and addict's "cry for help" and "defiant dependence" as components of the treatment process which the counselors can use to their advantage once they are identified. Evidence from industrial programs indicates an induced crisis, by individuals with the authority to confront and back up their accusations, can be an effective alternative to previous modes of treatment.

Employee Assistance Programs

Substantial opinion and research evidence support a strategy of "constructive coercion" (Minovitz, 1973) or "forceful coercion" (Murray, 1973) as a viable alternative for inducing a crisis in an alcoholic's life. Lew (1973), in research conducted on industrial treatment programs, held the view that alcoholics are motivated to change when they are in crisis, and that if they do not have to accept the consequences of their behaviors, they are not likely to be motivated toward recovery. Other research (Lemere, 1958; Gerard, 1962; Tiebout, 1965) indicates that the importance of work-based employee assistant programs lies in the employer's right to bring about a job-related crisis in the alcoholic's or addict's life while he is still on the job. Because of the deteriorating effects of addiction, a written company policy which confronts the individual's poor job performance and attendance, while directly avoiding accusations of his being an alcoholic or addict, is generally successful in inducing treatment. Often job security is the individual's chief vehicle for denial. Once his job security is challenged, his denial begins to crumble.

The strength of the employer and supervisor in confrontation centers in the intrinsic makeup of a supervisory role. Supervisors are trained to be more ready to act and have more power at their disposal than the alcoholic's spouse, friends, clergyman or physician (Wrich, 1974). Previous attempts to use the family as the locus for identifying the developing problem drinker have been unfruitful because of the diffused emotional relationships that characterize family structure and process (HEW Report to Congress, 1974).

Independent research by the NIAAA (1976) indicates that the seventy percent success rate in industrial programs is often unparalleled, even by Alcoholics Anonymous. Most other treatment facilities report success rates which rarely reach above the twenty percent level. This suggests that the highly confrontive nature of industrial programs and A.A. produces an atmosphere which facilitates successful treatment for alcoholics. The court, too, has this power to bring about a crisis through confrontation.

The constructive confrontation strategy makes specific assumptions. Coercion, in some form, is necessary in human behavior (Simmel, 1950). Society provides few clear norms about alcohol and drug use, so developing alcoholics and addicts rarely face consistent sanctions; thus they have few internal controls for managing this behavior (Inkeles, 1968). Enforced cooperation relieves the alcoholic or addict of the burden of developing motivation for himself; the strategy activates and uses existing social controls within the system rather than moving the deviant from the system into a specialized control setting.

Coercion, Attitudes, and Motivation in Treatment

It appears that one of the problems in motivation of the alcoholic or addict to accept treatment is that reluctance on the part of the patient to seek or accept help is psychological in nature. Particularly this is true if the procedure is unknown and possibly threatening. Canter (1969) tested this hypothesis and concluded that it is important to inform alcoholics and addicts about various treatment approaches to enhance their receptivity to treatment. Rossi (1972) reached a similar conclusion and suggested that the motivation of the alcoholic and addict to accept treatment is not only internal, but is related to the characteristics of the social environment and the personalities of the helping professional. Rossi further suggested that the patients motivated to recovery be seen as a multidimensional interaction of the patient, the setting, and the psychotherapist. DeVito's research (1969) results were similarly encouraging and lend credence to the hypothesis of the value of firm external controls in the successful treatment of alcoholics and addicts.

Zax (1961) demonstrated that significant relationships in the counseling process enhance the tendency to remain in treatment longer. Wedel (1965), in a similar study, concluded that the efforts of social workers had great personal significance to some individuals. Wolff (1968) found that few alcoholics and addicts in his study had sufficient ego strength to stop drinking; the motivation had to come from other sources, such as religious faith, group involvement, or family considerations. Sterne and Pittman (1965) examined the concept of motivation to determine to what extent it was crucial to recovery. They concluded that the majority of individuals in the helping professions excessively rely on the belief that client motivation is essential for success in treatment. Failure to accept an alcoholic or addict as a client and the lack of success in treatment are often conveniently explained by the lack of motivation on the client's part. Their findings suggest a need for improvement of professional training. They also concluded that there needs to be systematic research to isolate factors that contribute to the alcoholic's and addict's acceptance of treatment.

While it sometimes is crucial for the legal system or employer to initiate the treatment process through coercion, there is research to indicate that addicts and alcoholics do not need pressures to keep them actively involved in the recovery process (Heilman, 1976). Other research, however, cites the importance of force as an essential part of treatment (Seixas, 1976). Other evidence suggests that individuals coerced into treatment do as well — no more, no less — than those who presumably enter treatment on their own. Bibb's (1970) research concluded with the findings that outpatient treatment as a contingency of probation can yield results comparable with those of voluntary patients, as long as someone other than the therapist polices the terms of the probation.

Typically, these studies show that negative expectancies and attitudes on the part of the psychotherapist and group leaders frequently have an adverse effect on the success rate of the treatment. Effectively dealing with reluctant patients may be the most important overall competency that group leaders and psychotherapists can develop. Involuntary clients may account for the majority of a group leader's or psychotherapist's caseload and failure to learn how to deal adequately with hostility and reluctance on a patient's part may be the single largest contributing factor for failure in treatment (Vriend, 1973). It is true that many professionals have simply not had sufficient training to deal skillfully and easily with reluctant patients (Kennedy, 1977).

It is important to point out that coercion takes many subtle forms and does not necessarily have to be so obvious as that employed and practiced by the employer or court. Unhappy spouses, worried friends, concerned doctors and disgruntled bosses all make up a contingency which often uses subtle pressure to force individuals with many different types of problems into counseling when those individuals do not agree that they have a problem. It is suggested here that the person who seeks psychotherapy completely of his own free will may be more of an exception rather than the rule. Dealing with such patients requires the group leader to know how to utilize his therapeutic leverage to insure maximum benefit from treatment.

THE USE OF THERAPEUTIC LEVERAGE

The group leader must be aware that the alcoholic and addict will not give up their alcohol or drugs until the pain and dysphoria they experience outweighs the pleasure and euphoria they derive from its use. Consequently the alcoholic and addict must be made to see the way alcohol and drugs affects important areas of their lives. The group leader must also learn early in the individual's treatment what is significantly important enough to the addict or alcoholic that continued drinking and drug use might threaten. In some individuals it is their job. In others, it is their spouse, health, family or self-respect. In some cases, it might even be the threat of incarceration. Such knowledge is important since it can be used to encourage and even coerce the individual to utilize the tools of treatment, group or AA. Since alcohol and drug use affects judgement, and in most cases of chronic use causes temporary but severe levels of cognitive impairment, many patients are unable to accurately understand, interpret and perceive the true nature of their condition, much less make clear rational choices concerning decisions which will have profound effects on their life, family, health and job. More will be said about the subtleties of alcohol and drug-induced cognitive impairment in Chapter 8 on inpatient treatment. For now, it is important for the group leader to understand the necessity of utilizing therapeutic leverage to guide the alcoholic and addict through the early stages of their treatment. This is required until the patient is more capable of making rational choices for himself. Getting the patient to agree to try it the group leader's way under threat of loss of wife, job, health or even jail can be tempered by telling the group member that if he doesn't like this way after one year he can then try it his own way.

Group members who are concerned about their physical condition should have frequent laboratory testing and have ready access to a physician. Particularly important are liver functioning tests and neurological examinations. CT scan evidence of cerebralatrophy, though costly and difficult, can be a very important source of therapeutic leverage, particularly with the abundance of recent research evidence demonstrating reversability of this condition if sobriety is maintained. Psychological testing, especially with an emphasis on neuropsychological assessment, can provide similar evidence to the patient at a much reduced cost. Evidence presented from psychological and neuropsychological testing can be even more powerful since it is concrete and concerns specific demonstrable behavior. Showing an alcoholic or addict that their IQ and abstract reasoning scores are markedly low can have a powerful influence on their motivation to abstain from further chemical use, especially if they are cautioned that further chronic use might produce permanent and irreversible brain damage.

If the alcoholic or addict is married, or involved in a significant relationship, the group leader will discover that there are usually multiple difficulties in the marriage or the relationship. In many cases, the spouse has either threatened divorce, is in the process of divorce or separated from the patient. If the marriage or relationship is important to the patient, and especially if the spouse is not also addicted, this can be a source of important therapeutic leverage. The alcoholic or addict's spouse or significant other should be involved in the treatment process. This is especially true if the patient is hospitalized and being treated at a 28 day inpatient program. Involvement in Al-Anon and conjoint therapy sessions will insure that the spouse or significant other does not engage in self-defeating behavior that might threaten the therapeutic leverage. The input from this individual can be helpful to treatment if utilized properly. They can be supportive of the alcoholic and addict and can contribute information and observation which can help strengthen the therapeutic leverage. However, the spouse or significant other must be taught not to make idle threats. They must be encouraged only to threaten separation or divorce if they intend to follow through with such threats. Such a stance by the spouse or significant other can often serve as a powerful motivating force in the chemically dependent person's recovery.

The patient who is suffering job-related difficulties because of their drinking or drug use can be under extreme pressure to remain abstinent. This is especially true if the referral comes from the employer. Under these circumstances, contact with the employer, the EAP representative, or the medical department of the company should be maintained. This, of course, will require that the group leader have a signed consent of release of information. This insures that the group leader is protected legally; but, as importantly, it is a clear therapeutic contract which clearly defines the goals, motives and intentions of the group leader. The purpose of this contract should be presented to this patient not just as a threat to his job but as a clear message that the treatment program is serious about his recovery and expects him to face the consequences of his behavior.

The patient should be told that the specifics of his personal sharing in treatment or group will not be discussed, but only his progress related to his drinking or drug use. This assures the group member that his confidentiality concerning matters unrelated to his progress with abstinence from drugs and alcohol will be maintained. For many alcoholics and addicts, the therapeutic leverage related to their job security and work performance is the most powerful motivating force in their recovery.

A very similar position can be taken with the alcoholic or addict if they are a court referral. This is especially true if the person has two or more convictions for public intoxication or driving while intoxicated (DWI) or driving under the influence (DUI). A therapeutic contract established through the court or a probation officer can serve as a powerful incentive in the individual's recovery. Utilizing a group therapy format for these referrals requires special adaptations of the group format. However, if this adaptation is accomplished successfully, group is the treatment of choice for court referrals. Later in this chapter, such a format will be presented and described in detail because such a format will contain the utilization of all the techniques (i.e., confrontation, intervention, coercion, therapeutic leverage) to be described in this chapter.

Certainly, the use of therapeutic leverage as outlined here raises many important considerations concerning the therapeutic contract. Trust is a crucial factor in all forms of psychotherapy and treatment. In many cases, trust and the therapeutic alliance will be severely compromised because of the nature of the disease of addiction and the circumstances leading to the patient entering group or treatment. There are a couple of ways that the group leader might avoid the pitfalls associated with the use of leverage in treatment. If the patient is in group under the auspices of a treatment facility or hospital, it would be beneficial to have someone else other than the patient's primary therapist or group leader serve as the enforcer to this policy. This will allow the group leader to be able to avoid compromising his therapeutic alliance too severely. However, the group leader should be definite in outlining the limits of the therapeutic contract. He should tell the group member explicitly that he must convey information concerning the patient's progress to the rest of the staff at the hospital. After the patient has completed the initial part of his treatment, the group leader could then establish a new contract with the group and its members. This will be especially important if the group is to be an ongoing, long-term, after-care group. However, it may be difficult, if not impossible, for some individuals to trust their group leader once they have felt coerced or manipulated into treatment, no matter how much it may have helped them. Trust and a therapeutic alliance may be impossible to establish or re-establish in such cases. Referral of the group or individual group members to other group leaders might be in order in these circumstances.

While the utilization of therapeutic leverage may create some difficulties for the group leader, the gains from its application usually outweigh its costs in terms of treatment effectiveness Zimberg (1980) outlines the advantages of such an approach if it is carried out in a well-planned and therapeutic manner.

> When used judiciously, appropriately, nonpunitively and nonjugmentally, therapeutic leverage can be very effective in directing the alcoholic into a more responsive therapeutic status. If used, however, by a therapist with serious countertransference problems, including anger and frustration at the patient, it can destroy the therapeutic relationship. One must be constantly self observing when treating an alcoholic to insure that the therapeutic leverages are designed to facilitate the alcoholic's recovery and not to satisfy one's need for successful treatment or as retaliation and punishment for the alcoholic's provocative behavior. (Zimberg, 1980, p. 112-113)

CONFRONTATION

Before a group leader can effectively apply the use of therapeutic leverage in group, he must understand the intricate interplay between the purpose of an alcoholic's and addict's defenses and the confrontive techniques necessary to alter them. Defenses are always there for a reason. They must not be stripped away too quickly and confronted too severely just for the sake of confrontation. It is a general axiom in psychotherapy that defenses should not be altered until the patient completely understands their purpose and has developed enough ego strength and alternative resources which will allow him to substitute more constructive ways of defending himself from painful affective states. However, the alcoholic or addict can kill himself or completely destroy his support system while the group leader allows him the necessary time it may require for him to figure this out by himself. This is one instance where the group leader has to alter his normal stance of support and unconditional acceptance. Confrontation is one method that the group leader can utilize in dealing with the alcoholic and addict's rigid, self-destructive defensive process. However, the parameters and limits of confrontation must be understood and appreciated first.

In contrast to empathic clarifications and interpretations, both of which are directed at what the patient says and presents to the group leader, confrontations address something that the patient is unaware of or denying. Confrontations are more effective when they are directed towards something that the patient could or should be addressing, but is not because he is either consciously or unconsciously avoiding it. Patients who desribe incidents while omitting feelings, or if their description of the incident is notably similar to previous episodes in their lives, or present a discrepancy between their thoughts, feelings and actions are all prime indications that a confrontation might help them progress past their stuck position.

If confrontations are done properly they will bring new material to the patient's awareness. However, if they are punitive or attacking, they will only raise defenses and increase resistance. In some cases, as with the passive compliant patient, there is some benefit to this tactic because it makes overt what would otherwise be kept covert by the patient, making it obvious that that which is hidden is an essential ingredient and component of effective confrontations. Consequently, the group leader is more effective when he limits his confrontations to observable events that will be obvious to the individual once they are pointed out. If the group leader does not keep his facts straight or misjudges the accuracy of his observations, his confrontations will lose their potency and impact. Confrontations are much more powerful as factual statements and should never be confused with a hypothesis about a patient's motives or behavior.

For instance, a confrontation by a group leader who tells an alcoholic, "I think you are an alcoholic because you drink too much" is offering a subjective opinion that at best suggests a plausible hypothesis about a person's behavior. It is a relative statement open to debate since what may be heavy drinking for one person may be moderate consumption for another. Such a statement is not based on observable facts and it is likely to trigger the confronted individual to counter with his own subjective opinion. However, the group leader can make a much more credible confrontation if he focuses his observations on demonstrable facts. For instance, the group leader in this same instance could have said, "It might be helpful for you to carefully assess the consequences of your drinking realistically. Your wife is divorcing you because she finds you intolerable when you drink. You have two DUI arrests which have cost you a tremendous amount of money because of lawyers' fees and raised insurance premiums. Your boss is threatening to fire you because your work efficiency and attendance has been severely compromised by your weekend binges. This is certainly not normal drinking. Such a pattern of difficulties does suggest that you may be an alcoholic or if your are uncomfortable with that word, someone who has a severe problem with their drinking."

The difference between the two confrontations is obvious. The first can be interpreted as subjectively biased and opinionated. The second deals with observable and undeniable facts. Even though the second statement is highly confrontive, it does not transmit an attitude of anger or disrespect. Confrontations should never come at the expense of a patient's integrity or respect. If done properly, they will not injure the person, although the confrontation may trigger a painful awareness. Group leaders who "blast away" at a patient "for his own good" need to carefully explore alternatives to such a stance. In most instances, they will discover that there are more effective ways to convey the same information without taking anything away from the impact of the message. An example will help clarify this point.

> John, a 31-year-old, poly-drug abuser, had entered treatment because of mounting difficulties and concerns related to his escalating drug and alcohol use. His second wife has just filed for divorce and he was beginning to experience severe physical complications (i.e., memory loss, shakes, D.T.s and convulsions) relating to his drug and alcohol use. Two weeks into a therapy group that met daily, he began to become more and more verbal after sitting quietly and passively while his thinking cleared and physical conditioning stabilized. As he gained strength and sobriety, his typical defensive maneuvers returned. He began to dominate the group meetings with his excessive rambling about extraneous events and circumstances in his life. The group leader carefully determined that this issue needed to be dealt with and corrected because not only was it damaging to the group, it was a defensive maneuver which alienated others from John and was a significant complaint of

his wife. Left to his own resources, it might have taken John months to come to this awareness. At the start of the next session, John started into an elaborate explanation of his sister, describing her as a "big bullshitter" and appeared on the way to a repeat of his performance in the last two meetings. In the middle of his explanation, the group leader interrupted John briefly to say, "John, excuse me a second, but before you go on any further, I would like to ask you a question." John promptly stopped, his curiosity raised by the group leader's inquisitiveness. At this point the group leader gently confronted John with, "I ask this question in all respect John, and hope not to offend you; but does bullshitting run in the family?" John stopped and thought for a second, laughed out loud, and with a smile triggered by the awareness of his behavior said, "Yeah, now that you mention it, I guess that it does." The rest of the group laughed along with John and began to share that they, too, had noticed his tendency to ramble on in a nonproductive manner, but had not wanted to say anything because he had been so quiet for the two previous weeks, and that they feared if they said anything, it might lead him to retreat once again into his shell. Further exchanges among other group members led to the awareness of the manner that he and others often used words to cover over their real feelings. A productive exploration of fears and defenses were examined by the group members during the remainder of the session as a consequence of this confrontation.

In this example, the group leader could have easily confronted John earlier or more directly. A statement like "That's bullshit," would have certainly been more provocative and to the point. However, such a statement would have likely offended John, angered him, and led to his retreat from the group. It could have also set a tone for the group that may have far reaching dire consequences concerning openness, trust, and safety. Also, as this example clearly demonstrates, confrontations need not be made punitively or in anger. A judiciously applied intervention mixed with a touch of humor and irony can be as, if not more, productive than one presented in an overly firm, provocative or dogmatic manner.

The targeted intent of a confrontation needs to be cautiously assessed before it is delivered in a group composed of alcoholics and addicts. Since an alcoholic or addict usually utilizes his defenses as a means of protecting himself against painful affective states related to deep feelings of shame, low self-esteem, and overly intro-punitive self-loathing and hate, confronting these defenses prematurely or inappropriately can be counterproductive to their recovery. The group leader will avoid the dangers associated with a "shot gun type hit everything that moves" approach if they limit their confrontations to the alcoholic's drinking or drinking-related behavior during the early or beginning stage of an individual's treatment. The group leader will keep his feet on more solid theoretical ground if he follows the axioms of treating newly recovering or actively using addicts' and alcoholics' defenses differently. While it is necessary to vigorously confront drug and alcohol use and all defensive operations related to their use, it will prove more beneficial not to confront other defenses while demonstrating empathic understanding and supportive soothing of feelings separate from their drinking or drug-using behavior. Many obvious inconsistencies and rigid defenses in the newly recovering or actively using alcoholic and addict may have to be tolerated by the group leader until the individual is ready to look at these issues more realistically and honestly. This requires that the group leader temper many of his confrontations until he feels more confident that the addict or alcoholic is able to tolerate the confrontation without relapsing and retreating into further alcohol or drug use.

It is a delicate balance between confrontation and support that the group leader must learn to manage when working with this population. Too much support for some individuals will only reinforce continued alcohol and drug use. Premature and inappropriate confrontation, on the other hand, may trigger a relapse or increased defiant resistance for other patients. Unfortunately, inappropriate and poorly timed confrontations do not always come from the group leader. Therefore, it is important that the group leader be adept at handling and managing confrontations between group members. Sometimes an accurate and empathic confrontation from someone else in the group can have a much more dramatic effect on the patient. However, a confrontation from another group member usually has a greater chance of being destructive because it is frequently triggered by anger at the individual. If the group leader can respond quickly when such a confrontation occurs, he can guide the interaction so it is not completely devoid of caring and support. An example will help illustrate this point.

Fred, an immature and arrogantly defiant nineteen year old veteran had been required by the U.S. Army to enter an inpatient drug rehabilitation program in the VA hospital. A few months earlier, he had been given an early discharge on honorable conditions because of repeated disciplinary problems related to his drug use. In the three weeks he had been on the hospital unit, he had remained consistently oppositional, defiant and angry. During the tenth meeting of a daily inpatient group, the group leader noticed Dave, another group member, shaking his head and glaring as Fred continued one of his frequent harangues about the innate badness and unfairness of the staff, the doctors and the entire U.S. Army. At the end of Fred's daily tirade, the group leader quietly asked Dave, who was a rather large, burly, but well-respected and feared, 38 year old Vietnam veteran, what he was feeling as Fred talked. Dave, never one to mince words, replied "Man, I see a bunch of self-pity bullshit!" Since Dave, an IV heroin addict, was widely respected and feared by all of the other veterans on the unit, Fred was somewhat taken aback by his comment. Rather than leave the confrontation set at this point, the group leader asked Dave whom Fred reminded him of. Although initially startled by the question, Dave quickly responded "You sound like me nineteen years ago and, man, if you don't change your attitude, you're going to end up like me — a junkie, or dead or in jail." As the group leader explored Dave's exchange with Fred, it became more apparent that there was a great deal of concern underneath Dave's angry confrontation. Although it was somewhat uncharacteristic for Dave, he proceeded to demonstrate a soft, caring side of himself to Fred and the group. This softened the initial harshness of his confrontation and made it much more palatable for Fred. Such a confrontation would have lost much of its effectiveness if it had come from the group leader or if the confrontation just had been left with Dave's opening statement. Explorations of the reasons behind the confrontation led Fred to an awareness of himself that he had not previously possessed.

Confrontations done in this manner can be effective. But the group leader must remember that a confrontation is not an end in itself. It should be applied strategically and when used in conjunction with other clinical skills and knowledge, it can enhance working with the alcoholic's and addict's denial and resistance to treatment. Confrontation need not always be direct or lacking in warmth and caring. Paradoxical interventions which take advantage of metaphors, humor, irony and the use of counterforce allows the group leader to assume a warm, empathic stance while placing the responsibility for change squarely on the shoulders of the alcoholic and addict — where it belongs — thus lessening the group leader's frustration and making treatment more effective. Sobriety and abstinence are impossible unless the alcoholic and addict are prepared to assume responsibility for that change. Confrontations only work if they are motivational and facilitative in nature. The group leader cannot and should not force or attempt to force the alcoholic or addict to change. In such a power struggle, no one wins. The addict and alcoholic have another excuse to continue their use of chemicals and the group leader only becomes increasingly discouraged and frustrated.

The discussion of confrontation in this chapter has hopefully made clear criticisms and misunderstanding about the nature and appropriate use of confrontation in group psychotherapy. Confrontations, like good interpretations and clarifications, are attempts to make patients aware of behavior of which they had not previously been aware. As they develop more of an accurate and realistic understanding of themselves, the defenses they use and the reasons for these defenses can be examined. When working with the alcoholic or addict, the shift from an accurate awareness of their drinking and drug use to an understanding of their defenses and the reasons underlying the use of these defenses should take months, and in many cases even years. With many alcoholics and addicts, the unconscious motives for their behavior should not be explored until they have enough sobriety and emotional stability in their life to handle this awareness. This is the most significant and important difference that has to be learned by the group leader who is working with addicted patients.

The shift from confrontations which are limited to behavior, attitudes and actions which have a direct influence and connection with maintaining sobriety to a more explorative examination of the unconscious motives behind all defensive operations is a strategic decision that must be carefully assessed for each individual patient. Some will be ready for such a shift in treatment more quickly; others will require much more time. Once the group leader feels that the recovering addict or alcoholic is capable of managing a more explorative form of psychotherapy, he can then transfer him to a more advanced group or shift the focus of the group.

The principle of making the unconscious conscious was originally conceived by Freud. "Where id was, there shall ego be" (Freud, 1933, p. 80) clearly summarizes Freud's position about psychotherapy. The psychotherapist or group leader is to bring to the patient's awareness (ego) what was previously unconscious (id). Yet in no way did Freud intend the making of the unconscious conscious, as the ultimate aim of psychotherapy. In other words, confrontation should never be done for confrontation's sake. Once more in Freud's words, the intention of psychoanalysis is "to strengthen the ego, to make it more independent of the super-ego, to widen its field of perception and enlarge its organization, so that it can appropriate fresh portions of the id" (Freud, 1933, p. 80). In many ways, Freud is suggesting that helping a patient become aware of his unconscious is dependent on the strengthening of his capacity (ego-strength) to tolerate this awareness.

This is an accurate description of the strategic position that a group leader must take in working with an alcoholic or addict in group. It is also important to be aware that increased awareness of unconscious motives should not be expected in itself to result in behavior change. The explicit purpose of confrontation, and eventually interpretation, is to bring thoughts and feelings of which the person is not aware, and over which he has no control, into his awareness, where he can examine them, consider their relationship to other thoughts and feelings and exert some conscious control over the extent to which they influence his behavior. To accomplish this task, the group leader has to learn how to shift his tactics in group from a position of confrontation to interpretation and support.

Another ingredient absolutely vital to the group leader who wants to help alcoholics and addicts work on a more accurate awareness of their unconscious motives is a healthy, informed, unambiguous, and relaxed attitude toward alcohol, drinking, drunkenness, alcoholism, and drugs. The group leaders who work most effectively with alcoholics and addicts are those who have the capacity to share deeply with others and who can relate to them with hope. Certain people seem to have a natural ability to feel deeply with those who hurt emotionally and physically. This capacity for empathy may be cultivated through self-awareness, but it cannot be learned as a technique or a skill.

Still, there are good, sound, basic communication skills that the group leader must be familiar with before he can hope to communicate realistically with the chemically dependent patient. First, certain assumptions must be made before any attempt is made to explain the individual's psychological state at the time of an emotional crisis and physical illness. Emotional disturbances and bodily disorders are often spoken of in terms of cause and effect. This implies the erroneous assumption that man is composed of two fundamentally different substances, mind and body; and that the two in some way reciprocally affect one another. It is the fashion in current thought to sidestep this vexed problem of the dualism of the mind and matter. The assumption psychoanalysis makes is that the basic unit which reacts to stimuli is neither the mind nor the body, but the organism. Neither takes precedence over the other. An emotionally distressing event may precipitate a physical disorder and a physiological disturbance will result in an emotional reaction.

The nature of the communication with the alcoholic and addict must take into consideration the nature of the dilemma and should cover fundamental principles of interviewing techniques. The group leader should pay attention to the affect and style of what the patient says, rather than just the content. Knowing how to listen is an art. R. D. Laing suggests the concept of paralinguistics when consulting a patient. Pay attention to the way it is said, what is left out, bodily mannerisms, facial expressions and the like. Communication with a patient, whether they are addicted or not, should require more than just language. The alcoholic or addict in a highly aroused emotional state may become quite receptive to the group leader's hidden agenda. If the patient realizes that the outcome of his rehabilitation is of concern to the group leader more as a personal affront on his ability as a group leader, rather than one of real, genuine concern for the patient, treatment and recovery may be impaired.

Psychoanalysis operates on two basic principles, repression and suppression. Uses of indirect methods of interviewing not only reveal individual fantasies of significance, but permit one to observe the train of thought. It therefore allows a patient to free associate, that is, to observe and to communicate all the ideas that flow through his consciousness. If the group leader interrupts too frequently, or interjects too many of his own ideas into the flow of associations, that flow may be contaminated and distorted, and may not reveal the underlying motivating factor. In fact, owing to normal reluctance of all of us freely to disclose all of our thoughts and fantasies, true free association is an ideal rarely achieved. Moreover, the observation of where a patient seems to be holding back ideas, to be resisting the unfettered flow of thoughts, provides important information about his whole personality structure.

A group leader has to restrain himself from impatient interrupting, from premature, or from personal reminiscence. He must know when to keep quiet even when the patient is silent—to allow the patient to say what he has to say in his own way, at his own pace. At the same time he must observe the patient's behavior, his movements, his gestures, his tone of voice, the bodily show of his affects—for clues to the regions of emotional conflicts. The group leader must know what to say and when. The content of questions depends on knowing what topics the patient is ready to discuss and the timing depends on knowing when the moment is appropriate for discussing them.

The group leader must also know what not to say. He must know when to give advice and when silence is wisdom. He must sense when the patient is ready for communications; he must also know when to reassure and support the patient to diminish intolerable anxiety, and when to provoke it in order to keep the communication process moving. Too often, it seems that the group leader is too concerned with the rationale of the message he sends the patient and often misses underlying clues that indicate the possible reactions and fears of the individual.

Reviewing reports and research findings, the indication is that treatment programs which stress insight therapy with the alcoholic or addict are not as successful or effective as AA based therapy. Regardless of the treatment modality chosen, communication and psychotherapy should still remain an intricate part of an alcoholic's and addict's rehabilitation process. Sucessful treatment of addiction requires cooperation of persons from many disciplines. Although a cure is never possible, addiction can be arrested and group therapy remains as one of the proven approaches to its treatment. Under the proper management, it can enhance the alcoholic's and addict's recovering process.

INTERVENTION

Conducting group with the alcoholic or addict who remains ambivalent about his abstinence and is reluctant to admit his illness is a problem somewhat unique to alcohol and drug treatment. The recognition that an alcoholic or addict must hit bottom, that they must face that existential crisis in their life, before rehabilitation can actually begin, is a popular maxim in alcohol and drug treatment. The problem of crisis, its recognition, its ramifications and the methods of intervention which must be employed in the treatment approach are all important factors which the group leader must take into consideration. But before the group leader charges into the treatment process, he should be aware of the games and tactics often involved in that treatment process. Steiner acknowledges that the games of an alcoholic are an intricate part of his illness. Steiner postulates that a person chooses a role for himself at an early age and that role may turn him into an alcoholic. He also warns that some forms of treatment may do more harm than good. Steiner (1971) writes:

> The therapist's job is, first and foremost, not to play the "alcoholic game". That is to say, he should not play any of its roles — Persecutor, Rescuer, Patsy, Connection — in order to avoid providing the patient with a payoff from the therapist himself. This is the bare-bones necessity of alcoholism therapy . . . soon as the therapist can see that self-destructive drinking is not the result of a defective ego but a deliberate strategic maneuver to accomplish certain ends, he will be much better able to treat alcoholics. (Steiner, 1971, p. 38)

Although Steiner himself does not recognize the disease model of alcoholism, he nevertheless has good therapeutic advice for the group leader. Foremost among his recommendations is that the group leader take precautions which will prevent him being conned by the alcoholic or addict. While an alcoholic or addict may indeed be physiologically addicted to his drug or ethanol, social learning forces do come into play and life scripts do indeed play an intricate part of the illness itself. If, as Steiner says, the alcoholic or addict is playing out a life script, getting him to identify his problem and admit that his script is destructive and inappropriate is still a key ingredient to successful treatment. For once the addict and alcoholic has faced the conclusion that he is unable to control his drug use and drinking and that it is the cause of his problems, he can choose a new life script.

Choosing remains the crucial point. The alcoholic or addict must take responsibility for his actions and at a gut level choose to change his life. "Every time you try to rescue an alcoholic," V. Johnson warns, "you are delaying useful treatment" (1973). The alcoholic and addict's decision to choose is usually made as a result of a crisis in their life. Johnson goes on to say, "When you examine the lives of those who claim to have had it, you discover that a buildup of crisis has forced them to look at the reality of their condition. The only way back to reality is through crisis." But Johnson warns that it is pointless and dangerous to wait until the alcoholic or addict hits bottom. The crises everybody was trying to help the alcoholic or addict avoid could actually be employed to break through his defenses. Frequently, it requires an act of intervention in order to stop the downward spiral toward death. Vernon Johnson has experimented with alternate useful methods of employing crisis at earlier stages of the disease. The group leader, Johnson says, must be tuned in and aware of the cry for help. "Crises do not have to be invented or created. . . . the problem is to get counselors knowledgeable enough to use them creatively."

"We have learned," Ruth Fox (1967) states, "it is not necessary to wait for the alcoholic to hit bottom or motivate himself into treatment before taking therapeutic measures" (Fox, 1967, p. 39). Recent evidence generally supports Fox's position, but with added emphasis on the importance of the job and court instead of the family in the intervention. V. Johnson agrees, "Under the first principle of intervention, we said that an executive of the next rank up, or the boss, is likely to be the most fundamental person. So the boss instead of a member of the immediate family may set up the confrontation" (Johnson, 1973, p. 98).

The importance of work-based intervention programs lies in the employer's right to bring about a job-related crisis in the addict or alcoholic's life while he is still on the job. Herein lies a potential for truly effective action. Often job security is the individual's chief vehicle for denial. Once his job security is challenged, his denial begins to crumble. More importantly, his denial is challenged before he has lost everything, has more available sources of social support and consequently more reasons for attaining sobriety. It has long been noted that there is a strong relationship between intact marriages, steady employment and continued sobriety. Along these same lines, research has reported that "prognostically, lower-class alcoholics are considered to be the poorest treatment risks" (Schmidt, 1968, p. 103).

Thus, interventions are a way of getting alcoholics and addicts to seek treatment before their alcohol and drug use has caused them irreversible psychological, physiological and social ramifications as well as overwhelming marital, employment and legal consequences. While evidence has been presented concerning the effectiveness of employee assistance programs, the criminal justice system is another source of early identification and intervention. This is particularly true for those individuals who are introduced to the court system as a result of a DUI (Driving Under the Influence) or DWI (Driving While Intoxicated) convictions. The use of intervention with this population requires special considerations of the dynamics involved in this approach. Since there are general principles of intervention which govern its application, a model for its use with DWI offenders will be presented and carefully outlined. First the reasons for this approach with DUI offenders will be presented since it will help explain the theoretical foundation upon which all models of effective intervention stand.

DWI and Intervention

Over the years of working with alcoholics and addicts, experienced professionals began to realize there were many factors which combined to contribute to the negative expectancies and poor attitudes concerning rehabilitation of the alcoholic or addict when these individuals were left to their own resources in deciding whether to seek treatment for their chemical use. Building on evidence gathered from job and family based intervention programs, there were indications that DWI programs could provide an ideal opportunity by which effective treatment and early identification could be initiated. Perhaps most significantly, it was discovered that the great majority of drinking drivers arrested had not been treated previously for an alcohol problem (Scott, 1976). Highway safety programs were seen as another highly effective method for identifying individuals with alcohol and drug problems earlier in the course of their problem drinking and drug use when it is known there is greater opportunity for effective treatment and intervention. The proceedings of the National DWI Conference (1976) concluded with the following recommendations to Congress:

1. Treatment is a supplement to an alcoholic's legal responsibility.
2. Evidence indicates that pressures are needed to keep alcoholics actively involved in their recovery process.
3. Three segments are required for effective treatment; early detection, creation of a crisis, and continual long-term counseling or care.

It has been recognized that the early identification of addiction plays an important and significant part in the chances of successfully treating an identified patient. Due to the nature of the sample of the population which characteristically makes up each DWI class, these classes provide an optimal opportunity for both early identification and intervention in the addiction process. It, therefore, is important to make sure that this identification process is being carried out with optimum effectiveness.

The purpose of early intervention and treatment is only partially completed once an addict or an alcoholic is identified. Getting that identified patient into treatment, when that individual feels he has no problem, remains an area of controversy. The ethical consequences of intervention to seek treatment, when it is documented and obvious that that individual's excessive drinking or drug use will cause further harm to both the patient and society, must be weighed cautiously by both the agency doing the evaluation and the criminal justice system doing the sentencing.

If the use of intervention is to be effective in getting identified alcoholics and addicts into treatment, it must be judiciously applied and followed up by some responsible representative from the court. Allowing this responsibility to fall entirely on the shoulders of the group leader or the agency providing the services only complicates and confuses the issue in a labyrinth of bureaucratic red tape and buck passing. The authority to enforce recommendations lies within the realm of the criminal justice system and it is within this system that the pressure should be applied.

The DWI intervention program should be adapted to take advantage of these circumstances. It is obvious that the DWI program provides an ideal opportunity for early identification and intervention in the alcoholism process. However a program patterned after the solid principles of intervention and group psychotherapy would allow more individual time with each DWI offender. This would provide the group leader with a better opportunity to deal with the alcoholic's and addict's denial system and would also encourage more personal confrontation with group interaction if the group were conducted in a weekend marathon setting.

Principles of Intervention

Early intervention in the treatment of addiction, through the use of confrontive techniques, is designed to help the individual recognize the need for treatment. Intervention is most effective when it consists of a collective, guided effort by the significant others (i.e., spouse, employer, friends, children) in the person's environment so that a crisis is induced through confrontation which will remove or reduce the individual's defensive obstructions to recovery. Twerski (1983) sums up the principles of intervention when he writes:

> To be effective in the intervention, the participants must understand the disease of alcoholism and know its generally inexorable course if untreated. They must also act out of sincere concern for the welfare of the patient; be aware of the risks in confrontation; be adequately prepared to participate in the intervention as a well-orchestrated team if required; and be ready to endure the discomfort of confrontation and of describing sordid behavior to a patient or loved one, and to implement significant changes in their own lives if the subject rejects treatment. (Twerski, 1983, p. 1030)

Twerski draws a distinction between two types of intervention. The first is conducted through conventional medical or psychiatric settings and involves the professional confronting the patient with the gravity of the alcohol or drug problem. The second consists of a collective guided effort which is a more intense mode of intervention that requires the participation of as many people as possible who are significantly involved with the patient. Twerski (1983) meticulously outlines the strategy for both of these approaches and the interested reader should consult this cited article for more information on this procedure. At this point, a description of a third approach which combines elements of the two different processes as outlined by Twerski will be presented. This third approach emphasizes the use of a conventional psychotherapy group format and allows the group leader to adapt to a situation which requires that he deal with a number of reluctant patients who are coerced into treatment by the criminal justice system.

There are six principles of intervention which the group leader must be familiar with if they are to conduct a psychotherapy with reluctant patients who are coerced into treatment for their alcohol or drug abuse.

1. Do not do interventions alone. They must be done in a small group with a supportive co-therapist and treatment team. If the group is conducted under the principles to be described, the

group leader will be able to use the force of group peer pressure as a powerful mode of intervention. Since an actively using alcoholic or addict has little investment in the group leader, the professional has little if any credibility in the intervention process. The group leader's effectiveness is determined by his ability to mobilize the other group members as a source of support in the intervention process.

2. Establish and maintain specific goals for each group session. If the group leader does not structure the group so that each session is gradually more confrontive and addresses a deeper level of the individual's denial, the group process will deteriorate into an aimless exchange limited to war stories, acting out and argumentative complaining. The group leader must remember that group intervention is not therapy. The goals of these sessions are training, identification and intervention. Conventional approaches to conducting the group must be discarded or used more sparingly.

3. Focus on specific data which is obvious, concrete and nondebatable. This is the most important component of the intervention process. The group leader must use the beginning group sessions to gather concrete information about the alcoholic's and addict's chemical use and determine how their use of drugs and alcohol has adversely affected their lives. This data must be gathered in a non-obtrusive manner and delivered back to the individual in a way that will be palatable, undeniable and non-debatable.

4. Create an atmosphere of care and concern. This has to be the first task of the group leader. Confrontations must be used very sparingly until therapeutic atmosphere is created. If this atmosphere is not established, the group will remain argumentative, resistant and defensive. Often, the only thing that will catch an alcoholic or addict off guard is the feeling that the group leader, the treatment team, and the group members care. Most alcoholics and addicts are afraid of highly confrontive behavior. They have their defenses up and ready. They have usually been in control of similar situations for so long and know that they can handle one group leader or counselor.

5. Operate from well-established treatment structure. Allow no loopholes. Determine the agreed-upon treatment modality (i.e., inpatient, outpatient, AA, etc.) they and the other group members will accept if it is established that they are addicted.

Once this is agreed upon, minimize the time between the intervention and their entering into the chosen treatment program.
6. Consequences must be established if they refused to go. In the situations where the intervention is conducted by the employer, it may be a loss of a job. If the intervention is done with the family, it may be a divorce. Interventions conducted with court referred patients usually have to rely on the support of the court system to enforce such consequences. In some cases, it may be probation, jail sentences or fines.

A Group Intervention Format for Court Referred Offenders

Many group leaders find themselves struggling with the difficult task of trying to conduct psychotherapy groups with reluctant patients who do not want to be in a group, but are forced to attend because of an alcohol or drug-related arrest. A format for dealing with DWI offenders who are coerced into group therapy and treatment by the court system will be described. While the specifics of this format will be somewhat limited to DWI offenders, there will be enough generalizability in this format to allow the creative group leader to adapt its principles to fit their particular situation. For instance, in many cases, the court will refer for treatment an individual who is suspected of having an alcohol or drug problem. Often, these individuals only commit crimes while intoxicated or do crime to pay for their drugs. Treatment is often an alternative to jail sentence since it is reasoned that their crime will stop if their alcohol and drug use stops. Conventional therapy, especially supportive individual therapy, is doomed to fail with these individuals. A psychotherapy group conducted in the prescribed manner should be the treatment of choice.

After an individual has been arrested and convicted for a crime (in this case, a DWI), the offender should be offered the option of jail or treatment. Most will choose treatment. This is important because this element of choice, albeit a somewhat compromised one, enhances their receptability to treatment. It is also important that this choice is given after the offender has been convicted because this allows the court leverage for insuring compliance through its use of the probation sentence or plea bargain. If the convicted offender does not follow through with his agreed-upon commitment, he must be aware and assured the court will enforce the alternative consequences to this choice. Such a contract should be clearly stated and defined by the court. The offender must also be made aware of the limitations which this contract imposes on the typical restrictions of therapeutic confidentiality. A signed consent should be obtained and the offender told in no uncertain terms that the treatment staff is bound by this contract to let the court or the probation officer know if this contract is violated. Since such a stance will undoubtedly compromise the therapist-patient alliance, the treatment staff can salvage much of this by assuring the offender that personal information will not be shared with the court. In fact, it is often helpful to agree to show the offender a copy of the correspondence that will be sent to the court and obtain his signature on the letter. This assures the offender that he will be well informed about the information given to the court and re-establishes much of the compromised trust and safety which was lost in the original treatment contract.

In the situation with the DWI offender, he is given the option of spending a weekend in jail or a weekend at a DWI school. Most offenders choose the school and arrive at the program on a Friday evening. Most do not know they are about to enter an intensive weekend marathon experience with alternate times being split between large group lectures and small psychotherapy groups. The small groups are limited to ten members and the marathon setting insures complete abstinence from drugs and separation from typical outside support systems.

The DWI program should not be geared towards treatment and the group leaders should not intend to do psychotherapy during the weekend. Rather, the focus of the program and therapy groups should be on intervention and emphasis should be placed on pretreatment, identification, assessment and diagnosis. The three-day marathon setting can be a very powerful one-time situational experience in the individual's life if it is properly directed. Because of its structure, it will allow the group leader the time and intensity necessary to determine the extent of each offender's involvement with alcohol or drugs. Since it is often impossible for many group leaders to have such an intense treatment program or the support of an entire treatment team behind them, goals, objectives, and even the expectations of such an approach will have to be modified to fit their particular situation.

To reach the objectives of identification, group intervention and treatment recommendation, three goals must be established:

1. Assessment and data collection. One-third to one-half of DWI offenders typically have no significant alcohol or drug problems. Those that do need to be assessed and this assessment must be supported by specific, concrete data which is gathered during the group sessions.
2. Utilize the group dynamics to break through the denial so that the individual can make a connection between their chemical use and the difficulties they experience.
3. Motivate the identified patient to seek treatment.

Group Intervention Format

Group conducted in this prescribed manner should not be confused with group psychotherapy as it is practiced with individuals who seek group therapy of their volition. While many general principles of group process and group dynamics are utilized during the group intervention, the aim of each group session is distinctly different from most other conventional types of psychotherapy, both individual and group. The limitation of time, the dynamics involved in the addiction process and the general resistance of the group members requires the group leader take a very active position in directing the focus of the intervention process. Each group member must be given information about the disease concept and this should be done in a lecture format in a large group setting separate from the small group meetings. The aim of the small group process is to incorporate the presented educational material so that it is relevant to each group member's life. Within this context, the group leader should direct his energies at getting the group members to interact with each other. It is through the interaction of the group members that the group leader will gain the data necessary to confirm each member's possible addiction to alcohol and drugs.

Since most group members do not know what to expect at the start of the first group session, their anxiety and defenses are extremely high. The first session, or in some case the first few sessions, should be directed towards alleviating this anxiety and reducing each member's defensive posture. This is accomplished best by asking each group member to introduce himself, explain the circumstances behind their arrest and their reasons for attending the weekend group meeting. The least guarded members should be encouraged to speak first and the group leader should respond supportively to any display of anger or agitation in the group. Anger must be diffused before the group can move to a freely engaging group interaction. Many members will be outraged (some justly, most unjustly) at either the court, their attorney, the judge, or the police who arrested them. If their anger is supported in a constructive and caring fashion during the first session or sessions, their hostility will begin to give way to reason and occasional displays of humor. Exploring these exchanges with good-natured laughter, which is not laced with hostility, can do a great deal to relieve the tension during the initial stages of a beginning group. When the group has begun to feel more comfortable, the group leader should give the group something to work with by taking away what they think will be the focus on the session. Most alcoholics and addicts will come ready to defend their drinking or drug use. State clearly that you, as the group leader, are not concerned with: A. how they drink or use drugs; B. what they drink or what drugs they use; C. when they drink or use drugs; D. with whom they drink or use drugs; or E. where they drink or do drugs. Such a stance will diffuse their defensiveness and engage them in the evaluation process. Once they have discharged their anger and anxiety, many if not all group members can be persuaded to "Make the most out of the situation now that they are here. You can either remain angry and make this a horrible weekend or you can use it to learn about yourself." At this time, the conducted convincingly, the group leader will be surprised at the number of people, addicted as well as non-addicted, who want to understand how alcohol and drugs play a part in their lives. The appeal is most effective when presented in the following manner:

> People who drink and do drugs fit into two general categories. There are those who can without any problems and there are those who have a physiological or genetic propensity to become addicted or dependent. A hundred million people in this country drink. Ninety million of them are social drinkers. A small percentage, ten percent or ten million, cannot drink socially. If you are part of that minority, we want you to get involved in the group this weekend so you'll have a chance to understand your degree of involvement and how it is affecting your life. We want to encourage you to look at the consequences of your drinking and drug use. We would also like for you to look at your life history, its involvement with chemicals and decide that if you continue to drink or do drugs, whether it

is in your best interest to do so. There are eight critical major life areas we would like you to examine.

1. Self-Esteem (Self-Image)
2. Family relationships
3. Peer relationships
4. Job performance
5. Finances
6. Legal situation
7. Sexual activities
8. Health

Explore each of these areas in relation to your drug or alcohol use. Have any of these areas been adversely affected by your drinking and drug use? If any of these areas have been affected, are you willing to continue to jeopardize them in order to continue to drink or use drugs? It is your decision. Until you decide, however, we would like to encourage you to explore these questions with other members in the group. We are not here to argue with you or try to convince you otherwise. It is your choice. But you have a unique opportunity here in group to get feedback from other group members who may be struggling with the same decision or issues. We just want to hold up a mirror for you. Prove to us and yourself which category of people you fit in with—those who can or those who can't drink or use drugs socially.

If the group leader takes this stance and avoids using the labels of alcoholic or addict, he can often engage and challenge most reluctant group members. Since most alcoholics and addicts suffer from various degrees of grandiosity or narcissism, and feel that they can convince anyone that they do not have an alcohol and drug problem, they will often readily take on such a challenge. They are usually unable to resist the opportunity to point out the way alcohol or drugs are affecting others. Because of their own identification with other alcoholics and addicts, this is a skill with which they are acutely adept. With these two principles operating, the group leader will find that in a very short time he has an actively engaged group on his hands.

Usually at the beginning of the group, the group leader and his co-therapist can expect to be questioned about their drug use. Such questions are inevitable and self-disclosure is essential. If the group leader does not volunteer this information, he can expect to be openly questioned about his own use of alcohol and drugs. Guardedness about this subject or an attempt to retreat into the safety of therapeutic neutrality will not work. The short time duration of the group, its involuntary nature, and because the group leader is asking everyone else to self-disclose about a specific topic, guardedness or evasiveness on his part will only increase the defensiveness of the other group members. On this subject, the group leader must model what he asks others to do. Freely volunteering personal information about drugs and alcohol early in group will enhance the group process. However, the group leader must be totally honest. If he happens to be a recovering alcoholic or addict, this should indeed be shared with the group. If the group leader has in the past abused drugs and does not use drugs now, this information, framed in the proper perspective, can lead members to increase their own self-disclosure about their own drug and alcohol use. If the group leader drinks alcohol and does it in a non-alcoholic fashion, this should not be hidden from the group. Presented in the proper context, it will often enhance self-disclosure. However, if the group leader or his co-therapist uses any drugs, even so-called recreational use of marijuana, this must not be shared. In fact, if a therapist is using drugs of any kind, his position is severely compromised if he is going to work effectively with this population. One must not forget that drug use is illegal. Admitting this to the group conveys a subtle message that laws are for you and not for me. Not only is this position hypocritical, it is dishonest. It would be better for all concerned that if a therapist does use drugs, they refrain from working with all addicted patients. Addicted patients should be referred to another therapist and the therapist should avoid work of any type that is associated with the addiction treatment field.

As the group members become more engaged with each other, cohesiveness will begin to develop. Confrontation up to this point should have been kept to a minimum. Self-disclosures, especially as the different group members begin to share the way alcohol or drugs have affected their lives usually leads to a rapid deepening of feelings. As the group members begin to identify with others around concerns about alcohol and drug use, they can be easily encouraged to gently confront each other. With the proper timing and encouragement, the group leader can usually have the group very responsive to confrontations. It usually takes only a little encouragement to get some group members responding to others in an honest and open fashion. Openness and honesty can be enhanced by first focusing on the least guarded members. The more anxious and guarded members will have to be brought in more slowly. Caution should be used with those members who are reluctant to be open and honest. This only establishes a norm of defensiveness in the group if they are allowed to go first. As the group interaction increases, the group leader can use the more open group members to engage the more guarded ones in the group process. A statement like, "Hey, Joe, do you think that Bill really wants any feedback?", can be a very effective way of engaging even the most reluctant member.

By the end of the third day, group members have usually become intensely honest and open with each other. Before the group ends, ask each member to assess themselves as either being harmfully involved or not harmfully involved with alcohol and drugs. Encourage them to go through the major life areas and determine how the drinking and drug using circumstances in their life relate to the information they have gathered this weekend from the personal issues they have heard shared in group, the lectures and the feedback that they have received from others. Ask them to describe to the group what they feel would be examples of appropriate action for them to take, based on what they heard and discovered about themselves. Then, request that they state why they believe this is true. Upon completing this task, ask that each remaining group member indicate concurrence or disagreement with the stated assessment and plan. Consensus in the group is usually high and this often leads to compliance. In some cases, individuals who have shared very little during the weekend will announce that the group has confirmed what they had long suspected, but feared examining, namely that they are alcoholic. Treatment recommendations are to be delivered at the end of group and individual sessions scheduled to discuss consequences for failures to follow through with agreed-upon treatment goals.

The main goal of the intervention is to help the patient make a choice about his drinking and drug use. They must be able to determine by the end of the weekend the advantages of not drinking and doing drugs compared to the problems in their lives resulting from their drinking and drug use. This choice must be ultimately made by each member of the group. Despite an abundance of evidence to the contrary, some individuals will refuse to see their situation accurately or will fail to take adequate measures to change their self-destructive behavior. The group leader must be aware that he cannot control the behavior of the chemically dependent person, nor can he dictate what that person must do. He can confront, coerce, intervene and use all the therapeutic leverage at his disposal, but the choice of action is determined by the subject. The alcoholic or addict has the choice of keeping or losing his job, going to jail, and preserving or dissolving his family. He also has the option of entering treatment. Hopefully, the techniques described in this chapter will increase the chances of a positive outcome.

REFERENCES

Albrecht, G. L. (1969). The assessment of Fulton County adolescent behavior, knowledge and attitudes in relation to the legal system: A preliminary report. Mimeographed report, Fulton County Juvenile Court. Atlanta, Georgia.
Alexander, F. (1950). *Psychosomatic medicine*. New York: W. W. Norton & Co.
Baily, M. B. (1965). Al-Anon family groups as an aid to wives of alcoholics. *Social Work N.Y.*, *10*, 68-74.
Borowitz, G. H. (1964). Some ego aspects of alcoholism. *British Journal of Medical Psychology*, *37*(3), 257-263.
Bowen, W. T. & Androes, L. (1968). A follow-up study of 79 alcoholic patients. *Menninger Clinic Bulletin*, *32*(1), 26-34.
Brown, R. & Fox, R. (1973). *Alcoholism*. New York: Academic Press.
Canter, F. M. (1969). Motivation for self-confrontation in alcohol patients. *Psychotherapy: Theory, Research & Practice*, *6*(1), 21-23.
Carkhuff, R. (1969). *Helping & human relations, Vol. 2. Practice & research*. New York: Holt, Rinehart & Winston.
Chafetz, M. E. (1968). Research in the alcoholic clinic. *American Journal of Psychiatry*, *124*, 1674-1679.
Devito, R. A. (1969). New dimensions in treatment of alcoholism. *Illinois Medical Journal*, *135*(4), 389-392.
Fox, R. (1958). *Medical clinics of North America*. May, 804.
Fox, R. (1967). Disulfiran as an adjunct in the treatment of alcoholism. In R. Fox (Ed.), *Alcoholism: Behavioral research, therapeutic approaches* (pp. 242-255). New York: Springer Publ.
Franco, S. C. (1960). *Occupational Medicine*, *2*, 157.
Freud, A. (1948). *The ego and mechanisms of defense*. London: Hogarth Press.
Freud, S. (1936). *Inhibition, symptoms and anxiety*. London: Hogarth Press.
Gerard, D. C. (1962). *Troubled employees program*. Center City: Hazeldon.
HEW. (1974). *Alcoholism treatment & rehabilitation*. National Institute on Alcohol Abuse & Alcoholism. Washington: Department of HEW Publications.
HEW. (1976). DHEW publication No. (ADM) 76-272.
Inkeles, A. (1968). *Socialization & society*. Boston: Little Brown & Co.
Jellinek, E. M. (1960). *The disease concept of alcoholism*. New Haven: College & University Press.
Johnson, V. (1973). *I'll quit tomorrow*. New York: Harpter and Row.
Lemere, F. (1958). Alcoholism & the worker. *Quarterly Journal of Studies on Alcohol*, *19*, 428.
Lew, D. (1973). *Realities of alcoholism in industry*. Rockville, MD: NIAAA Publications.
Mann, M. (1973). *The disease concept of alcoholism*. San Francisco: Faces West Productions.

Minovitz. (1973). *Using industrial alcoholism programs as a model for health & welfare agencies*. Rockville, MD: NIAAA Publications.

Mischel, W. (1971). *Personality*. New York: Holt, Rinehart & Winston.

Murray, T. (1973). *The fight to save alcoholic executives*. Rockville, MD: NIAAA Publications.

Nemiah, J. (1961). *Foundations of psychopathology*. New York: Oxford University Press.

Perls, F. (1969). *Gestalt therapy verbatim*. California: Real People Press.

Rogers, C. (1942). *Counseling & psychotherapy*. Boston: Houghton-Mifflin.

Rossi, J. J. (1972). Motivational issues in capturing alcoholism patients into a rehabilitation program. In: *Selected papers from the twenty-third annual meeting of alcohol & drug problems association* (pp. 51-56). Atlanta, Georgia.

Saslow, G. (1969). New views on the alcoholic. *Rehabilitation*, 22-26.

Schertzer, B. & Stone, S. (1974). *Fundamentals of counseling*. Boston: Houghton Mifflin Co.

Schmidt, W. (1968). *Social class and the treatment of alcoholism*. Monograph 7. Toronto: University of Toronto Press.

Schultz, W. (1969). *Joy*. New York: Grove Press.

Scott, M. (1970). In D. Calahan (Ed.), *Problem drinkers*. San Francisco: Jossey-Bass.

Sexias, F. (1976). *Tie in with local council on alcoholism. DWI rehabilitation programs*. Falls Church: AAA Publ. World Services.

Shore, J. J. (1981). Use of paradox in the treatment of alcoholism. *Health and Social Work*.

Simmel, G. (1950). *Sociology of Georg Simmel* (K. Wolff, Trans.). New York: Free Press.

Steiner, C. (1971). *Games alcoholics play*. New York: Grove Press.

Sterne, M. & Pittman, D. (1965). The concept of motivation: A source of institutional & professional blockage in the treatment of alcoholics. *Quarterly Journal of Studies on Alcohol*, *26*, 41-57.

Tiebout, H. M. (1965). *Quarterly Journal of Studies on Alcohol*, *26*, 496.

Twerski, A. J. (1983). Early intervention in alcoholism: Confrontational techniques. *Hospital & Community Psychiatry*. *34*(11), 1027-1030.

Urich, J. (1974). *The employee assistance program*. Center City: Hazeldon.

Wald, P. (1974). *Right of alcoholic & addict prisoners to refuse treatment: Some preliminary perimeters*. Presented at Washington area council on alcohol & drug abuse symposium. Washington, D.C.

Wedel, H. L. (1965). Involving alcoholics in treatment. *Quarterly Journal on Studies on Alcohol*, *26*, 468-479.

Weinberg, J. (1976). *Why do alcoholics deny their problem?* Center City: Hazeldon.

Zax, M. (1961). Demographic characteristics of alcoholic outpatients and the tendency to remain in treatment. *Quarterly Journal of Studies on Alcohol*, *22*, 98-105.

Zimberg, S. (1980). *The clinical management of alcoholism*. New York: Brunner/Mazel.

Chapter 8

Inpatient Group Psychotherapy

The field of alcoholism and drug treatment is a relatively misunderstood and controversial neonate within the psychotherapy realm. In many ways, inpatient group psychotherapy suffers from a very similar lack of understanding and controversy as that which plagues the alcohol and drug treatment fields. As Yalom states, "Despite the fact group therapy has been well established for forty years, many medical directors of acute inpatient wards deeply question the effectiveness of inpatient group psychotherapy and choose not to provide it on their wards" (Yalom, 1983, pp. 24–25). Yalom finds this to be an appalling situation since he can cite an abundance of clinical evidence and research findings which support group therapy's effectiveness in a hospital setting (1983). Despite evidence to the contrary, many inpatient psychiatric units fail to appreciate the significant impact that group therapy can have on a patient's treatment while he is hospitalized. Fortunately, most medical directors of inpatient alcohol and drug treatment units have not committed the same oversight in their assessment of the importance of group therapy in an alcoholic's or addict's treatment. Group therapy is warmly embraced and is a very integral part of most inpatient alcohol and drug treatment programs. Next to the patient's introduction to the disease concept and his required involvement in Alcoholics Anonymous, it is difficult to identify a component of inpatient treatment that is utilized or valued more than group therapy.

However, the goals, structure, and methods for the utilization of group therapy are not always consistent or clearly defined. This is true for both A & D and psychiatric inpatient groups. The confusion surrounding its application is one reason many medical directors fail to appreciate its effectiveness. Contemporary forms of group psychotherapy, adapted from theoretical models derived from work with non-psychotic patients treated in an outpatient setting, do not usually apply to inpatient populations. Inpatient group psychotherapy, with both psychiatric and chemically dependent populations, requires the special circumstances surrounding inpatient treatment be appreciated and taken into consideration before the group leader embarks on the delicate task of treatment. Yalom outlines some important considerations that must be taken into account for effective inpatient group psychotherapy. These will be reviewed later in the chapter. First, it will be important to assess the special characteristics and circumstances surrounding the newly hospitalized alcoholic or drug addict because this defines the limits of the applicability of group psychotherapy for these patients.

Even as controversies concerning the validity and meaning of the "disease concept" remain heated outside the field of addiction treatment, group leaders within the field have attempted to define the disease and structure its treatment to fit a group therapy format. A stage specific framework identifying the predominant problems and the complementary therapeutic techniques through the different phases of inpatient treatment is required in the development of an efficient inpatient group therapy model. While not all alcoholic and drug dependent patients entering treatment require medical detoxification, it is generally the appropriate initial step in hospitalization. A discussion of the criteria utilized in evaluating the need for medical detoxification is beyond the scope of this book. However, it should suffice to say that these patients need to be excluded from group therapy until they are stabilized medically. A familiarity with, and understanding of, the symptoms of progressive withdrawal is essential for the group leader in all phases of alcoholism and drug dependence treatment. Stage specific interventions require an understanding of the differences between an individual who is two days away from detoxification and an individual who is two years sober. Specifically, because all forms of psychotherapy, individual, family and group, rest on the assumption that the person will be rational enough to make decisions based on accurate insight and understanding of himself and his situation, it is impossible to do traditional forms of therapy with addicted patients who are in the early stages of withdrawal. While most therapists would agree with such a position, few fail to understand the significance of an alcoholic's or addict's cognitive impairment six months into their recovery because these symptoms are often very subtle and specific. Because most alcoholics and addicts do not demonstrate significant difficulties in their verbal intelligence, they often "sound better" than they really are. For a group leader to be aware of the subtle differences in someone two, six, or twelve months sober, they must have some awareness and understanding of these cognitive deficits so they can adapt their treatment within group to match the needs and capabilities of the patient. Understanding these cognitive deficits will help the group leader realize why the confrontative techniques (i.e., coercion, leverage, intervention, etc.) described in Chapter 7 are so necessary for addicted patients during the early stage of their treatment.

NEUROPSYCHOLOGICAL IMPAIRMENT

Within the last ten years there has been a vast accumulation of evidence related to the neurological functioning and neuropsychological deficits associated with alcoholism. Recent surveys and reviews of the literature (Wells, 1982; Parsons & Farr, 1981; Grant, 1980; Wilkinson et al., 1981; Ryan & Butters, 1980) reveal that the pattern of impairment associated with chronic alcohol abuse is identifiable and even predictable. Most importantly, the pattern of deficits noted in cortical compromise and cognitive deficiencies have important implications for treatment. Unfortunately, the significant contributions, which neurology and neuropsychology have to offer in the treatment of alcoholism, often goes unnoticed or is not utilized. Even when useful information about treatment is forthcoming, it either remains entirely academic and devoid of clinical application or is obscured in vague, non-descriptive terminology like "organicity." Neurological consequences needs to be articulated and conveyed so that the implications that these identified deficits may have in their clinical applications are practical. It is important to determine how certain patterns of neurological impairment may affect the motivation, abstinence and recovery of the alcoholic patient. Do alcoholics who score in the impaired range of neuropsychological testing and show morphological abnormalities as revealed by neuroradiological studies (CAT Scan) and neuropsychological testing respond differently to treatment? In short, is there a relationship between neurological impairment and treatment outcome? Finally, what special strategies should be adapted and applied to an identified pattern of neurological impairment?

These questions have not been answered unequivocally and replicated research addressing this problem is non-existent except for a

few exceptions (i.e., Wells, 1982; Parsons & Farr, 1981). One purpose of this chapter is to present the evidence available and draw
inferences about their application for treatment. Hopefully, such an
exercise will help bridge the gap between pure research and clinical
applicability of such research findings. Specifically, this chapter
will attempt to delineate the relationship between Wernicke-Korsakoff syndrome, alcoholic encephalopathy and alcohol induced dementia. Each of these conditions will be briefly explored in relation
to the continuum and premature aging theories of alcoholism. What
is the pattern of impairment for each of these conditions and how
might they relate to treatment and recovery? Considering the evidence to be presented here, it is suggested that a highly structured
recovery program like Alcoholics Anonymous owes much of its
success to the very structure and directive strategies inherent in its
intuitive design which serves as a paradigm for recovery.

Gallant (1983) supports the importance of assessing cognitive
functioning when planning treatment strategies for alcoholics and
drug addicts. He writes,

> It is essential to evaluate neuropsychological impairment of
> every alcoholic before initiating any treatment plan. Even mild
> impairment of judgment or cognition can seriously interfere
> with both psychotherapy and the administration of medication
> such as Antabuse, particularly if the impairment is not evident
> to the therapist or the patient. Efforts to correlate impairment
> on simple neuropsychological tests and presence of brain atro-
> phy may offer information on the future course or prognosis of
> the alcohol-induced damage. Such efforts may also show that
> inexpensive and readily available neuropsychological evalua-
> tion measures may be just as helpful as more costly computer-
> ized tomography (CT) for the evaluation and formulation of a
> treatment plan for the alcoholic patient. (Gallant, 1983,
> p. 448)

Most alcoholics' and addicts' hospitalization in an acute state of
intoxication will stabilize after two to seven days of detoxification.
A competent and experienced physician should be able to safely
manage the detoxification period and accurately assess when the
possibility of life-threatening seizures or delirium tremens is diminished enough to allow the patient to safely participate in group therapy and the rest of the treatment program. Many patients will not

suffer the severe symptoms of withdrawal and will be able to benefit from group therapy much more quickly. Table I outlines the possible neurological complications which result from the chronic use of alcohol.

Alcohol and drugs usually produce striking central nervous system dysfunction. Researchers, until recently, have largely ignored the subtle effects that these chemicals have on the brain other than assessing the acute consequences of delirium tremens or long-term chronic effects as manifested in a Korsakoff's syndrome. Wells (1982) sums up this situation when he writes,

> . . . psychiatrists who are interested in organic brain disorders have centered most of their attention either on the consequences of its withdrawal (delirium tremens) or on the thiamine deficiency that so often accompanies its use and gives rise to the Wernicke-Korsakoff syndrome. Only recently have the long-term effects of chronic ethanol abuse per se on central nervous system function and structure begun to attract much attention.
>
> While deterioration of brain function has always been acknowledged in alcoholics, it usually has been attributed to malnourishment, hepatic failure, head trauma—in fact to just about everything but the effects of the alcohol itself. Even though a few doubts persist about whether functional and structural cerebral deterioration can be caused by alcohol abuse alone,[2] there is no question that such a deterioration can be demonstrated in many chronic alcoholics for whom malnourishment, hepatic failure, and head trauma have been reasonably eliminated as possible causes. (Wells, 1982, p. 111)

There had never been any doubt that neuropsychological testing would reveal abnormalities in alcoholics or addicts who were in acute withdrawal or suffering from a Korsakoff's syndrome. However, the application of neuropsychological assessment procedures to individuals without these conditions have revealed consistent findings that often collaborate with computerized cranial tomography (CAT Scan). Wells sums up these findings when he writes,

> The results of these investigations have been remarkably consistent. Tests of over-all intelligence often reveal no signif-

TABLE I

NEUROLOGICAL DISEASES ASSOCIATED WITH ALCOHOL

1. Acute intoxication

2. Alcohol withdrawal syndrome (time of appearance after cessaction of drinking)
   Tremulousness (7-24 Hours)
   Hallucinosis - visual or auditory (12-48 Hours)
   Delerium tremens (36-96 Hours)
   Withdrawal seizures (7-48 Hours)

3. Nutritional diseases of the nervous system
   Polyneuropathy
   Wernicke-Korsakoff Syndrome
   Amblyopia

4. Possible nutritional or toxic effects of alcohol or metabolites
   Alcoholic myopathy
   Cerebellar degeneration

5. Secondary to cirrhosis - Hepatocentral degeneration

icant differences between groups of chronic alcoholics and matched controls, but tests designed to evaluate more discrete neuropsychological functions frequently show abnormalities among alcoholics. Many alcoholics demonstrate defects in short-term memory, performance on complex memory tasks, visual-motor coordination, performance on visual-spatial tasks, abstract reasoning, and psychomotor dexterity. Relative sparing of verbal skills is often observed and long-term memory is preserved. (Wells, 1982, pp. 111–112)

Most of the results from these neuropsychological studies have been derived from data obtained by the Wechsler's Adult Intelligence Scale (WAIS) and the Halstead-Reitan Neuropsychological Battery (HRB). Tables II, III, and IV show the differences in scores on the HRB for alcoholics, psychiatric control patients and brain damaged patients. As demonstrated by these scores, alcoholics generally score worse than control subjects and better than brain damaged subjects. Alcoholics have the most difficulty with tasks (i.e., Category and Trails B) sensitive to abstract reasoning, short term memory, and motor speed. Table V demonstrates the number of studies which substantiate consistent difficulties in these areas for both alcoholics and addicts. Table VI lists the percentages for a number of studies conducted with the HRB which substantiates the consistency of these findings. Table VII provides a similar list of results from studies using the WAIS to demonstrate a clear disparity between performance IQ (new learning) scores and verbal IQ scores (old learning).

The tables (II through VII) presented reflect the results of studies conducted with alcoholics or addicts that were not suffering from Wernicke-Korsakoff syndrome. This is important to remember because it suggests that an alcoholic or addict need not be so severely and obviously impaired as a Korsakoff's patient before their cognitive deficits can be assessed. It also suggests that many, if not all, alcoholics and addicts suffer from subtle deficits in cognitive functioning which may interfere with their ability to process, retain, understand and recall vital information necessary for their recovery. Considering that two of the leading theorists in the area of cognitive impairment in alcoholics suggest that chronic alcohol use may produce either premature aging of the brain (Cermak & Peck, 1982) or that the Korsakoff's syndrome may just be a part of the continuity of this alcohol induced process (Ryan & Butters, 1980), it is important

TABLE II

MEAN SCORES OF ALCOHOLICS (A) AND PSYCHIATRIC (P) AND BRAIN-DAMAGED (BD) PATIENTS ON SUBTESTS OF HALSTEAD-REITAN NEUROPSYCHOLOGICAL BATTERY

	Alcoh.	Psych.	B.D.
Trails, Part A	61.3	39.0	65.0
Trails, Part B	150.0	80.1	183.1
Aphasia Errors	4.7	2.2	6.5
Spatial Relations	2.7	2.0	3.4
Perceptual Errors	8.2	2.8	10.2
Seashore Rhythm Test	6.5	3.6	7.8
Speech Perception Test	9.4	6.1	12.3
Halstead Impairment Index	0.69	0.31	0.83
Average Impairment Index	2.18	1.06	2.47

Source: Parsons & Farr (1981)

TABLE III

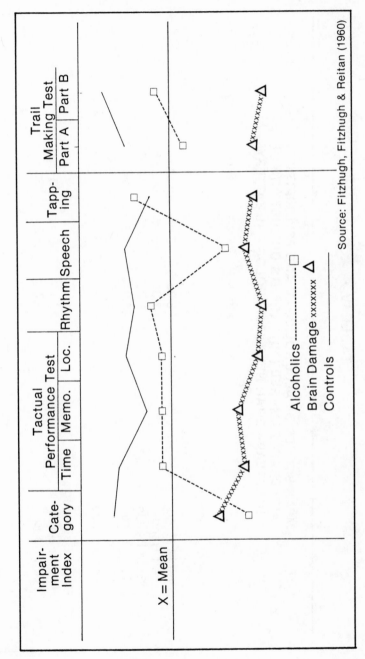

Source: Fitzhugh, Fitzhugh & Reitan (1960)

329

TABLE IV

MEAN SCORES OF ALCOHOLICS (A) AND PSYCHIATRIC (P) AND BRAIN-DAMAGED (BD) PATIENTS ON SUBTESTS OF HALSTEAD-REITAN NEUROPSYCHOLOGICAL BATTERY

	Alcoh.	Psych.	B.D.
Category Test	90.0	51.5	93.7
Tactual Performance Test			
Right Hand	8.96	5.95	9.14
Left Hand	7.64	5.25	8.68
Both Hands	6.33	3.00	7.33
Total Time	22.9	14.2	24.3
Memory	6.75	8.14	4.93
Localization	2.44	4.18	1.70
Finger Oscillation			
Right Hand	38.1	50.0	37.8
Left Hand	36.7	46.2	32.6

Source: Parsons & Farr (1981)

TABLE V

PATTERN OF IMPAIRED HRB SUBTESTS
ACCORDING TO HALSTEAD'S CUTOFF POINTS

	Alcohol		Other Drugs		Other Drugs Excluding Marijuana	
	Ratio of Impaired to Total Studies	%	Ratio of Impaired to Total Studies	%	Ratio of Impaired to Total Studies	%
Category	10-13	77	7-17	41	7-13	54
TPT-Time	9-13	69	4-12	17	2-7	29
TPT-Memory	0-13	0	0-12	0	0-7	0
TPT-Location	9-13	69	2-13	15	2-8	25
Rhythm	2-10	20	4-13	31	4-10	40
Speech Perception	5-9	56	1-9	11	1-7	14
Finger Tapping	6-10	60	5-12	42	5-9	56
Trails B	5-8	63	4-13	31	4-9	44

Source: Parsons & Farr (1981)

331

TABLE VI

IMPAIRMENT PATTERNS ON HRB FOR ALCOHOLICS

HRB	No. of Studies	Impaired	Percent
Category Test	15	13	87
TPT-Time	15	12	80
TPT-Memory	15	3	20
TPT-Location	13	8	62
Rhythm	12	3	25
Speech Perception	10	5	50
Finger Tapping	12	3	25
Trails B	11	8	73

Source: Parsons & Farr (1981)

TABLE VII

IMPAIRMENT PATTERNS ON WECHSLER SCALES AND HRB FOR ALCOHOLICS

Wechsler Scale	No. of Studies	Impaired	Percent
Information	7	2	29
Comprehension	8	2	25
Arithmetic	7	3	43
Similarities	8	1	25
Digit Span	8	1	25
Vocabulary	7	1	14
Digit Symbol	8	6	75
Picture Completion	8	4	50
Block Design	8	8	100
Picture Arrangement	7	5	71
Object Assembly	7	6	86

Source: Parsons & Farr (1981)

to understand the degree of impairment in these patients because it will help the group leader understand the types of deficits commonly seen in less compromised alcoholics.

THE WERNICKE-KORSAKOFF SYNDROME

Tables VIII and IX list the symptoms commonly seen in the Wernicke-Korsakoff syndrome. This is a two stage illness with Wernicke's encephalopathy the early acute phase, and Korsakoff's psychosis, usually the later permanent residual condition. Wernicke's encephalopathy usually responds quickly to proper medical treatment of which thiamine administration during the acute phase of withdrawal is crucial in preventing the structural alternation of portions of the brain which occurs in Korsakoff's psychosis. The Wernicke syndrome is reversible because the symptoms (i.e., ocular abnormalities, confusion, hallucinations, disorientation, etc.) are due to biochemical abnormalities which have stopped short of significant structural damage to the brain. Korsakoff's, on the other hand, is an irreversible condition due to the presence of permanent physical change to brain structure, usually involving the frontal-limbic-diencephalic system. Wernicke's is usually associated with thiamine deficiency and this is why its symptoms are usually alleviated with vitamin B-1 injections. None of the animal studies conducted to date show thiamine deficiency alone leads to irreversible memory problems; a condition limited to Korsakoff's patients. Although most textbooks on neurology accept avitaminosis as a primary cause of Wernicke-Korsakoff syndrome, impressive data exists which shows prolonged alcohol ingestion without malnutrition still results in permanent learning difficulties.

The most severe and noticeable condition in a Wernicke-Korsakoff patient is memory impairment. The patient's long-term memory, as well as their language and IQ functions are usually relatively intact. The true Korsakoff patients suffer from the inability to retain and recall new information (antegrade amnesia) learned after the onset of their illness. These patients' old learning and long term memory are usually unaffected, so they often appear "more together" than they actually are. Their personality becomes more passive and malleable. Because the medial dorsal nucleus of the thalamus, the mamillary bodies in the limbic system and the hippocampus area are all structurally altered, these patients demon-

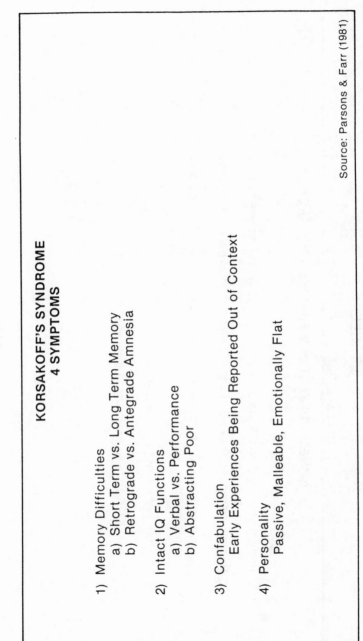

TABLE VIII

KORSAKOFF'S SYNDROME
4 SYMPTOMS

1) Memory Difficulties
   a) Short Term vs. Long Term Memory
   b) Retrograde vs. Antegrade Amnesia

2) Intact IQ Functions
   a) Verbal vs. Performance
   b) Abstracting Poor

3) Confabulation
   Early Experiences Being Reported Out of Context

4) Personality
   Passive, Malleable, Emotionally Flat

Source: Parsons & Farr (1981)

TABLE IX

AMNESIC DEFECT IN WERNICKE-KORSAKOFF'S

1. Immediate and remote memory intact - verbal and non-verbal

2. Recent memory impaired - cognitive deficit, decreased attention

   a) Impaired use of semantic encoding - use associative and acoustic cues normally

   b) More sensitive to proactive interference

   c) Perseveration, inappropriate strategy

strate a marked tendency to perseverate (i.e., keep repeating mistakes) and lack motivation (amotivation syndrome) to change. Since the limbic system alters their affective responses, they fail to care or be upset by situations which would normally alarm others. Consequently they can be very accepting of their physical condition and continued old behavior (i.e., perseveration) despite its continual negative consequences. Their capacity for foresight and planning is extremely poor because their abstract reasoning is compromised. Since they lack the inability to store new information into memory and their retrieval of old stored memories is impaired, they usually confuse old information with new information. This is a condition described as confabulation and is frequently confused with lying. Their damaged hippocampus does not allow them to recall new memories and it is this damaged hippocampus which is judged to be the reason for their increasing experience of blackouts. The normal acquisition and retrieval of information is continually compromised until attempts at recall produce early experiences being reported out of context. Confabulation is usually most pronounced during the acute early stages of Korsakoff's as the patients struggle to hide their difficulties from others. This condition is also exacerbated by personality characteristics that have been learned through the years as they attempt to cover over memory problems. This along with the patient's lack of motivation is inaccurately hypothesized as the reasons for their memory difficulties. It is rare to find this symptom in patients who have had Korsakoff's for a period of five years or longer (Butters & Cermack, 1980). Their condition eventually deteriorates into one of apathy.

Table VIII illustrates the four most common symptoms in Korsakoff's patients. Table X lists evidence gain from post-mortem autopsies on alcoholics and the similar symptoms experienced by patients with lesions in the same areas of the brain as those typically experienced by chronic alcoholics. All this evidence suggests a patient who will be extremely difficult to treat because of difficulties in these five areas.

1. Motivation (Lack of understanding and desire to initiate change)
2. New Learning (Perseveration — repeating of old mistakes)
3. Memory (Inability to learn and retain new information)
4. Affective (Inappropriate display of emotions)
5. Abstraction (Lack of insight and fore planning)

TABLE X

EVIDENCE FOR ANATOMICAL LOCALIZATION

1. Post-mortem Autopsy

2. Symptoms similar to patients with lesions in this area

   a) Withdrawal symptoms (D.T.'s) parallel patients with acute lesions.

   b) Inability to persist with cognitive set (Amotivation).

   c) Spatial perseveration responses.

   d) Poor capability for insight and planning.

3) Personality typically malleable, carefree.

   f) Field dependency problems.

Add to this the fact that most alcoholics still have their verbal IQ skills intact, the therapist is faced with an individual who can talk a "good game," but does not have the ability to plan alternatives or the motivation and the capabilities to carry through with those plans. During a time of crisis, they can only fall back on old ways of coping and this is why the alcoholic continues, as AA says, "to repeat old behaviors and expect different results."

Many of the symptoms seen in a Korsakoff's patient will manifest in an alcoholic, although to a lesser degree. In fact, this is an hypothesis proposed by Butters and Ryan (1980). Certainly, the evidence presented in Tables II through VIII support their contention. There is a unanimous rejection of the notion that alcoholics suffer from a generalized or global intellectual deterioration. Alcoholics, however, have a marked inability to learn new material as demonstrated by their relatively poorer performance on performance IQ tasks (Table VII). Their intact verbal skills leave them adept at hiding these deficits from both themselves and others. Their abstractious reasoning difficulties as demonstrated by their poor Category and Trails B performance (Table VI) suggest they do not possess the ability to think abstractly, creatively and will have a tendency to perseverate (keep repeating old mistakes).

However, there are some very important variables to this condition which the therapist and treatment team must take into consideration when assessing the degree of impairment in an alcoholic. Grant et al. (1980) lists four criteria which must be carefully evaluated.

1. Pre-Morbid Level of Functioning
    A. IQ level prior to their alcoholism.
    B. Age.
    C. Social economic status (SES).
    D. Education.

Each of these factors has an effect on WAIS and HRB measures of cognitive functioning. Higher IQs, lower age, higher SES, and higher education are usually related to better scores on these measures. Higher scores can also indicate that these individuals may have had higher intellectual functioning prior to the onset of their condition and consequently could afford to "lose more" without it effecting them as dramatically.

2. The Duration of Alcohol Consumption

The duration of alcohol consumption has a direct effect on the degree of cortical compromise. The longer the duration of drinking, the more severe the damage.

A. Ten to twelve years usually does little damage to the cortex.

B. Twelve to twenty-five years is the pre-clinical period. Damage during this period is usually reversible if abstinence is maintained.

C. Twenty-five years and over is the clinical period. The chances of permanent impairment to the cortex is maximally increased, even if the person were to remain abstinent.

Table XI summarizes Grant's findings of the relation between poor performance on Category tests (Abstraction, etc.) and age. The older the alcoholic and the longer he drinks, the greater his risk for cortical compromise. His level of cortical impairment is also dramatically effected by the age at which he started his ETOH consumption. A fifty-year-old alcoholic who started drinking at age thirty is likely to be less impaired than a fifty-year-old alcoholic who started drinking at age fifteen if the amount of this daily consumption is equal.

3. Level of Alcohol Consumption

The amount of alcohol consumption is directly related to the level of the alcoholic's impairment. Table XII outlines an important distinction which must be made in assessing the severity of impairment in the alcoholic. A thirty-year-old alcoholic who has been drinking two fifths of hundred proof whiskey a day for ten years is going to be much more impaired than a fifty-year-old alcoholic who drinks two bottles of twenty proof wine a week for twenty years.

4. The Length of Abstinence Since the Time of the Neuropsychological Testing

An alcoholic tested three days into his recovery is going to be much more severely impaired than an alcoholic tested three months or even three weeks into his recovery. In fact, the length of time between the alcoholic's last drink and the date of his neuropsychological testing is the most significant contributing factor to his assessed level of dysfunction.

If neuropsychological testing is to have any practical implications for an alcoholic's treatment and recovery, it will be important to

TABLE XI

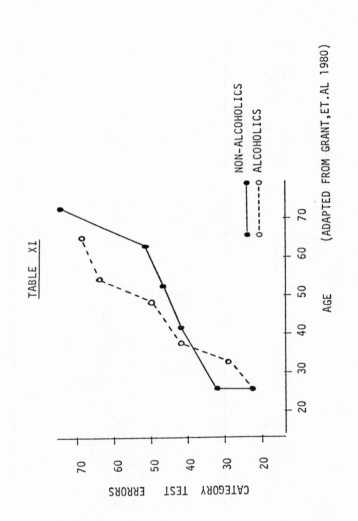

CATEGORY TEST ERRORS

AGE   (ADAPTED FROM GRANT,ET.AL 1980)

NON-ALCOHOLICS ●———●
ALCOHOLICS   ○------○

TABLE <u>XII</u>

PRE-NATAL PERIOD	PRE-EXPOSURE PERIOD	LATENT PERIOD	PRE-CLINICAL PERIOD	CLINICAL PERIOD

C--------B--------A(X)--------A(Y)--------A(Z)--------D

```
C    = Conception
B    = Birth
A(X) = Age of first exposure to drug
A(Y) = Age of first neurological changes due to drug
A(Z) = Age of first signs of dementia
D    = Death
```

(ADAPTED FROM GRANT, ET. AL., 1980)

carefully evaluate the length of abstinence the patient had at the time he was tested. Wells (1982) writes, "the level of impairment on neuropsychological tests, is to some extent, a function of when the subject is tested after he stops drinking; the defects found are generally greater immediately after" (Wells, 1982, p. 112). Most alcoholics do indeed show more impairment early in their recovery. Most studies demonstrate a continual improvement in cortical recovery up to and including one to two years after abstinence is maintained. The level of impairment in alcoholics, other than those alcoholics who suffer from a Korsakoff's syndrome, has been found to be reversible. Alcoholics experience spontaneous recovery from their deficits if abstinence is maintained. They only have to abstain from ETOH consumption to achieve this reversibility. The degree of the recovery in cognitive functioning is greatest during the first few weeks of abstinence. However, the degree of improvement continues on a positive gradient for many more months (Table XIII). Such findings in neuropsychological research lends credible evidence to a very important AA maxim about recovery. Alcoholics are told by AA and their sponsors not to make any major decisions or changes in their life and to "keep it simple" during the first year of their recovery. The neuropsychological research evidence presented here substantiates the wisdom of AA's intuitive understanding and knowledge about alcoholism and its effect on a person's thinking process. As the alcoholic's performance scores on the Category Test and other neuropsychological measures suggests, alcoholics require at least a year before their abstract reasoning capacities return to normal levels of functioning. Consequently, it is best that they refrain from making major life decisions until they've had more time to stabilize cognitively.

This is where the pure research and neuropsychological testing has practical applications for clinical practice. A model of group therapy and treatment pattern after the AA philosophy has important implications for treatment because it is substantiated by recent neuropsychological findings. AA's insistence on abstinence parallels important cortical recovery changes that must be attained and considered before alcohol-induced dementia or encephalopathy can be properly treated. AA's insistence on keeping it simple and outlining concrete, distinct steps to recovery provides the alcoholic with a clear strategy and an achievable plan with measurable goals. This is crucial for individuals suffering from an impaired ability to think abstractively. It gives them what they desperately need at the begin-

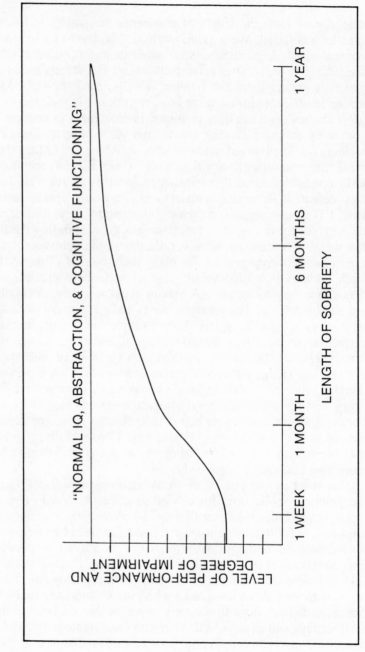

TABLE XIII

"NORMAL IQ, ABSTRACTION, & COGNITIVE FUNCTIONING"

LEVEL OF PERFORMANCE AND DEGREE OF IMPAIRMENT

1 WEEK   1 MONTH   6 MONTHS   1 YEAR

LENGTH OF SOBRIETY

ning of treatment—direction, structure, and guidance. As the alcoholic gradually recovers his lost cognitive functioning, alternative treatment strategies can be implemented once his capacity for new learning, consolidation of information, abstract thought, creative thinking and motivation have all returned to their pre-morbid level of functioning. At this point, now that the alcoholic can now utilize insight, self-understanding and autonomous decision-making, the group leader can then start to employ alternative modes of treatment in his therapy groups. Until the alcoholic reaches this stage however, the group leader must conduct his inpatient psychotherapy groups in a more structured and directive manner.

Now that the special circumstances surrounding the alcoholic's level of cognitive impairment have been explored, it will be important to understand the implications this information has for conducting an effective inpatient therapy group. The treatment objectives of inpatient group therapy need to be adapted to also fit the special circumstances of inpatient hospital treatment. Yalom (1983) has done an excellent job of outlining recommendations for conducting an inpatient therapy group and his suggestions will be presented in detail. However, important as these recommendations are for conducting inpatient groups, they are derived from his work with psychiatric patients. Consequently, these recommendations have to be altered to fit the special circumstances of the chemically dependent patient. These alterations will be explored later in the chapter when they are examined in light of suggestions by Vannicelli (1982) and others.

YALOM'S RECOMMENDATIONS
FOR INPATIENT GROUPS

There are numerous other difficulties confronting the inpatient group leader. He not only has to contend with the resistent patient and the cognitively impaired patient, but he has to also contend with difficulties which are often idiosyncratic to the special circumstances involved in all inpatient treatment. As Yalom writes, " . . . specialized skills are required for effective leadership. Neither individual nor outpatient group therapy training constitute sufficient clinical preparation for the inpatient group therapist. The acute inpatient ward constitutes a radically different clinical setting and requires a radical modification of group therapy technique"

(Yalom, 1983, p. 36). The techniques and tasks of the group therapist outlined in Chapters 3 and 4 of this text have to be modified to
meet the demands of the inpatient setting.

Yalom (1983) lists the different factors which will impinge on the
leader's attempt to conduct an effective inpatient group.

1. There is considerable patient turnover. The average length of
   stay is four to six weeks. There are some patients who only
   stay a few days. There is generally a new patient in the group
   almost every meeting.
2. Some patients attend the group meeting just for a single meeting or two. There is not time to work on termination. Some
   member terminates almost every evening, and a focus on termination would consume all the group time.
3. There is a great heterogeneity of psychopathology: patients
   with neurosis, characterological disturbance, substance
   abuse, adolescent problems, major affective disorders, anorexia nervosa, and sometimes even psychosis, are all present
   in the same group.
4. All the patients are acutely uncomfortable; they strive toward
   resolution of withdrawal or acute despair rather than toward
   personal growth or self-understanding. As soon as a patient is
   out of an acute crisis, he or she often desires to be discharged.
5. There are many unmotivated patients in the group: they may
   by psychologically unsophisticated; they do not want to be
   there; they may not agree that they need therapy; they often
   are not paying for therapy; they may have little curiosity
   about themselves.
6. The therapist has no time to prepare or screen patients.
7. The therapist often has no control over group composition.
8. There is little therapist stability. Many of the therapists have
   rotating schedules and generally cannot attend all of the
   meetings of the group.
9. Patients see their therapist in other roles throughout the day
   on the ward.
10. Group therapy is only one of many therapies in which the
    patient participates; some of these other therapies are with
    some of the same patients in the group and often with the
    same therapist.
11. There is often little sense of cohesion in the group; not

enough time exists for members to learn to care for or trust one another.

12. There is not time for gradual recognition of subtle interpersonal patterns, or for "working through," and no opportunity to focus on transfer of learning to the situation at home. (Yalom, 1983, pp. 50–51)

Considering the difficulties which a group leader will have to adapt to in running an inpatient group, the single most important task of the leader is to establish appropriate and realistic goals which can be attained within the confines of the limits of the situation, time, and patient population on an inpatient unit. Not establishing goals will lead the therapist, the group members and the group to drift aimlessly. However, if the goals are unrealistic or overly ambitious, the group leader will become increasingly disappointed and stamp themselves, or group therapy, as hopelessly ineffective. Goal-setting often involves two different but parallel processes. Explicit goals must be established with each individual member regarding their sobriety and the attainment of the interpersonal tools necessary to insure recovery. Implied goals, based on the group leader's assessment of the needs of the particular individual in relation to the group process, must also be monitored by the group leader. He must carefully determine which particular group member needs to be supported, confronted, encouraged, or left alone during group.

This situation is complicated by the fact that the goals of the therapy group are not always identical to the goals of the hospital or treatment facility. Unfortunately, some medical and program directors are not supportive of group psychotherapy. They fail to appreciate and realize group therapy's potential as a powerful adjunct to a patient's recovery. In some cases, an inpatient unit can be so rigidly invested in AA and the disease concept that they view all forms of psychotherapy as counter-therapeutic to the alcoholic's or addict's recovery. Certainly, group therapy conducted by either over-zealous group leaders who are too provocative and promote too much regression too soon or group leaders who fail to adequately understand the disease concept, thereby neglecting the importance of appreciating the level of cognitive impairment and the need for abstinence before any type of introspective self-understanding can be achieved, can have detrimental effects on a newly hospitalized patient. This is why the goals of the group leader must be realistic and in tune with the goals of the treatment facility. If group is conducted in a prescribed manner that takes careful consideration of the special circumstances of the newly hospitalized patient, the therapy group will not be in conflict with AA and the disease concept. Group can be used to address those areas of the patient's recovery that the disease concept and AA neglect.

The disease concept and AA will be far more effective in helping a patient achieve and maintain sobriety. Since this is the essential first step of a patient's recovery, this goal must be given priority. Group therapy, if it promotes too much anxiety, introspection, or encourages the belief that control of alcohol or drug use is possible, will only interfere with the recovery process. Group psychotherapy is most effective if it achieves two goals. First, by helping the group member avoid and manage stress, it can play a vital role in reducing one's propensity towards relapse. Second, and most importantly, according to Yalom, the primary goal of the inpatient therapy group is to engage the patient in the therapy process. This is a twofold therapeutic process that Yalom refers to as horizontal (the multi-faceted therapy program in the hospital which includes therapy groups, lectures, AA meetings, etc.) and longitudinal (post-hospital course of treatment which includes after care groups, AA meetings, etc.).

The Horizontal Process

Group therapy is most effective during the initial stages of treatment because of its ability to help ameliorate the alcoholic's and addict's isolation, shame, and self-loathing. Through identification with others in the group, the alcoholic and addict learns they are not alone in their wretchedness. They also learn they are not unique in their tendency to become intoxicated and engage in behavior that is offensive and disrespectful to themselves and others. Universality, as a curative process, allows the alcoholic and addict to learn they share a common bond with others whom they come to identify with and care for deeply. Cohesiveness and trust with others in the group who are understanding and accepting of their defects of character leads to a loss of isolation and alienation—two profound circumstances that contribute greatly to their continual drinking and drug use. The disease concept places their difficulties within a concise manageable framework and alleviates their guilt and improves their self-esteem. One to two months of structured abstinence allows them to clear cognitively, emotionally and physically. Often for the first time in years, the alcoholic and addict will feel some hope and have some understanding of their condition and a direction in which to guide their efforts.

The Longitudinal Process

As important as the horizontal process is in the alcoholic's and addict's recovery, their hospitalization and inpatient treatment will be effective only if it is coupled with continual after-care therapy. Outpatient group therapy and continual attendance at AA meetings are two important components to this longitudinal process. Consequently, an important goal of inpatient group psychotherapy is to provide an introduction to group therapy that is relevant, comfortable and effective. Such an experience will increase the likelihood that the hospitalized patient will participate in continual treatment in an after-care group. If the alcoholic and addict learns that talking helps and group can be used to identify major problem areas, continual involvement in an ongoing after-care or outpatient group will be far more attractive to them.

Composition of the Inpatient Groups

Yalom distinguishes between two basic strategies in composing an inpatient therapy group—the team approach and the level approach. The team approach has patients randomly assigned to different groups, usually according to the order of their admission to the hospital. The level approach requires the patient be assigned to a group according to the level of their functioning. More severely ill patients to one group, and higher functioning patients to another group. Both approaches have positive and negative consequences. To get the benefit of both approaches, Yalom advises having a team group every day and a level group every other day. While Yalom is making these suggestions specifically for psychiatric patients, his recommendations have to be altered before they are generalizable to chemically dependent patients. Since most alcoholics and addicts present with similar levels of ego functioning, his recommendations are not as germane for this population. On rare occasions there are those patients who present with far more serious psychiatric difficulties and their symptoms, which were somewhat sedated by their use of alcohol or drugs, become even more severe with abstinence.

Transfer to the psychiatric unit may be required for these patients. Most chemically dependent patients will be able to enter group at the same level and there is usually little need for a lower level and higher level group.

However, Brix (1983) suggests a variation of this two-stage format for chemically dependent inpatients which has some parallels with Yalom's suggestions. His recommendations call for a format which involves a two-stage experience for the patients. The first stage is a leader active group. The second stage emphasizes what Brix calls a "group centered approach." Brix writes,

> As soon as gross effects of toxicity have abated to the point where the patient is lucid and reasonably attentive, he or she enters our so called "A" group, which meets five days weekly in 45 minute sessions. My goal in this group is to orient the patient to the overall treatment program and especially to help the patient to begin to experience what it is to be a member of a therapy group without relying on a topic or exercise-centered format. Because of the wide variability in cognitive functioning among patients at this state of treatment, I remain very flexible in my approach — sometimes serious, sometimes more whimsical, but typically quite active. Following 7–10 days in the "A-group", most of our patients are transferred to our more group-centered "B-group". This transfer is viewed by practically all patients as a status symbol, and a sign of their progress by the staff. (Brix, 1983, pp. 254, 255)

In order for the hospitalized patient to participate successfully in a group-centered group, Brix feels they must first be able to tolerate the frustration and anxiety generated by such a format. Brix writes,

> The format of the psychotherapy groups grows out of a belief that (1) a group-centered group experience, even if only of a few sessions duration, is at least equally valuable, perhaps more valuable, than any other group experience many alcoholic patients can have, but (2) patients profit more from the group if they are prepared for entry by participating first in a more leader-active group. (Brix, 1983, p. 254)

Following seven to ten days in "A" group, Brix transfers these patients to his group-centered "B" group. They are notified a day ahead of their entry with the following message:

For the remainder of your treatment you will be participating in the "B" psychotherapy group. The format of the "B" group assumes one thing about you and that is that you want to better understand yourself and your emotions. It is not unusual for group members at times to be anxious and perplexed as they find they have been momentarily overcome with strong feelings. This is all a part of being a patient in group therapy. To make the most of this for yourself you really have to do only one thing and that is express openly and honestly what you are thinking and feeling about the group and your fellow group members. You are requested to be prepared to remain in the 1-1/2 hour session without interruptions. (Brix, 1983, p. 255)

Such a format with its emphasis on prepared instructions for entry into a therapy group accomplishes two important tasks for the group leader. It allows him to prepare the individual for the psychotherapy groups and it provides the needed structure for conducting such a group. While Brix's suggestions for the "B" group format are questionable because they may provide too little structure for the newly recovering alcoholic or addict; his reasons, however, for the shift from an "A" group to a "B" group approach merit careful consideration because they possess several advantages for treatment. Brix suggests the following advantages to a "B" group format,

As I see it, there are at least four compelling reasons to include a group-centered therapy group in an alcoholism treatment program: (1) this format tends to guard against the therapist's relying excessively on the use of confrontation, (2) the danger of the therapist's interventions being counter-transference based is reduced, (3) there is somewhat greater likelihood that therapeutic use of transference phenomena can occur, and (4) there is greater probability that patients will become therapeutic for one another. (Brix, 1983, p. 256)

Because of the short duration of time, rapid turnover of patients and the other difficulties which Yalom listed, there are too many forces acting against Brix's "group-centered" format; at least the way he describes it in his manuscript (1983). However, his suggestions for the two level approach and the way he implements the shift from "A" to "B" group is highly effective. If a group leader were to follow his recommendation, the "B" group format would be more beneficial if Yalom's strategies were incorporated into its format.

Yalom's Strategies and Techniques of Leadership

Conducting an effective inpatient therapy group along Yalom's recommendations requires the group leader be very active and provide structure for the group. As Yalom says, "There is no place in inpatient group therapy for the passive, inactive therapist. Nor is there a place in inpatient group psychotherapy for the non-directive leader!" (1983, p. 107). The rapid turnover of the patient population and their short duration of stay in the hospital prevents the group leader from operating from the perspective of a more passive, less structured leadership style. The group leader must therefore think of the life of the group to last a single session. This translates to a position where the leader must do as much effective group work as possible for as many patients as possible within the group framework. To accomplish this, the group requires an active and directive leader.

There are four essential tasks of the group leader on the inpatient unit.

1. The group leader must be active, efficient and should not allow the group to waste time.
2. The group leader must establish safety as a priority in group.
3. Supportive group leaders are necessary for inpatient groups.
4. The group leader must be directive and provide structure for the group.

1. *The group leader must be active and efficient.* Internal chaos within the individual requires that the group leader impose externally oriented structure as the first step in helping the individual develop a sense of internal control. Inpatients prefer and respond best to a leader who:

A. Insures equal distribution of time within the group. Nothing is more destructive to group than to allow the rest of the group members to repeatedly suffer through a hyperverbal patient's repetitious and constant complaints.

B. Actively circles group members inviting different individuals to contribute and interact.
C. Actively focuses group attention on topics that are meaningful and relevant.
D. Prevents rambling patients from derailing the group work.
E. Provides a clear direction for the group sessions.

2. *Safety as a priority for inpatient groups.* The group leader must create an atmosphere which is constructive, warm, safe, and trusting. Each group member must experience the group as a place where they will be heard, accepted, and understood. Inpatient group therapy is not the place for destructive confrontation, criticism or the escalation of anger. This does not mean that the group leader should pretend that anger doesn't exist. However, rather than escalate or encourage its expression, the group leader should move in for rapid conflict resolution. Most chemically dependent patients have little experience with the resolution of conflict or the nondestructive expression of anger. Learning that conflict can be resolved constructively without physical injury and harm can be extremely therapeutic for many patients. Often encouraging little annoyances, before it has a chance to build into a rage or tirade can be important to this learning process. If anger is ignited between two members, rather than have them express their anger directly, encourage them to direct it at an issue, policy or even the group leader.

3. *Supportive strategies for the inpatient group leader.* Support in group is more than being nice or friendly. The group leader must balance his support with firmness and predictability. Explain explicitly what is expected of the group and its members. In turn, explain to them the reasons for your actions. A consistent, coherent group procedure will do wonders for providing the support that each group member requires before they will venture to share honestly with the group and its members. To encourage this type of interaction, the group leader must accomplish these tasks:

A. Acknowledge each group member's contribution to group. Members respond positively to a therapist's liking them, valuing them and noticing and reinforcing their positive characteristics.
B. Take each member seriously. Don't discount or minimize their efforts.

C. Discourage self-defeating behavior. Although many group members will be insensitive about their own behavior, they are often very sensitive to others. They will keep alienating others in group without understanding how or why they are doing this. At times, it requires an extreme effort on the group leader's part to pick out the positive aspects of many patient's behavior.

D. Help the other group members to understand the reasons for another's behavior. As Yalom states, "To understand all is to forgive all." The group will often accept another's irritating behavior if they understand the reasons why the person behaves as he does.

E. Identify and emphasize the group member's value to one another. Since most alcoholic and addicts have such strong feelings of self-condemnation, the realization that they are of value to other group members can be extremely therapeutic for them. This is in fact one of the important aspects of Twelfth Step Work in the AA program (see Chapter 6).

F. Do not attack the patient or support one group member at the expense of another. Each member must learn that group is a safe place for them. If confrontation does occur, either from another group member or the group leader, it must be non-destructive and follow along the guidelines outlined in Chapter 6.

G. Give the group member control of the depth of the sharing and openness they may show in group. One reason many group members are reluctant to open up in group is that they fear they may go too far and express or show more of themselves than they had intended. Each member must know they can set their own limits in group in discussing their feelings. Drinking and drug taking behavior should be excluded from these precautions (see Chapter 6). It is extremely important that alcoholics and addicts openly discuss their feelings related to their use of alcohol and drugs. Consequently, any techniques which interfere with this requirement should be used sparingly.

H. Treat each group member with respect and dignity. Don't interpret or expose their non-verbal behavior or their conflicts for its own sake. Only if this behavior is directly related to their alcohol or drug use, should it be openly confronted against their wishes.

4. *Provide direction and structure in group.* A clear structured setting, preferably in a circle without a table in a closed private room with few chances for outside interruptions is crucial. Starting promptly and ending on time provides the group members with clear boundaries. A unit policy that group not be interrupted and that attendance is mandatory instills an added sense of importance to the therapeutic setting.

Yalom suggests a basic blueprint which provides the optimal amount of structure for an inpatient group (see Table XIV). It is Yalom's opinion that the gaining and accepting of a working contract with each group member is vitally important to the effectiveness of an inpatient group. If this is not obtained, the session can degenerate into a rambling confused discourse.

TABLE XIV

YALOM'S BASIC BLUEPRINT FOR AN INPATIENT GROUP

1) Orientation and preparation.   2 to 3 minutes
   (The group leader introduces himself,
   reminds the members of the purpose,
   length, and time of the meeting. If
   there are observers, new members, or
   a new co-therapist, he introduces them
   to the group.)

2) Agenda go-round   10 to 20 minutes
   (Each member formulates a personal
   agenda for the group session.)

3) Work on agendas   60 to 80 minutes
   (The group leader attempts to fill as
   many agendas as possible within the
   group time.)

4) Summary, comment and close of the   2 to 3 minutes
   group.

Agenda Rounds. Yalom's description of agenda rounds is not without precedent. Robert and Mary Goulding operate from a Transactional Analysis (TA) framework in their use of Redecision Therapy in therapy groups (Goulding & Goulding, 1979). The Gouldings require a contract from each group member before they do any work in group. In their one, two, and four-week training groups (see Chapter Nine), they spend the first part of the training period doing contract work. Each member is required to decide what it is they wish to change about themselves in group that day. You do not enter a Gouldings group without a "contract" for your work in group. Group members soon learn that these contracts must be explicit. If a person says they want to "try" to change, Bob Goulding reaches under his chair and begins ringing his famous "try bell." The Gouldings believe you either want to change or you don't. Such a stance prevents what Yalom refers to as the "movie goers" turning up in group. Individuals do not come to the Gouldings group to see what show is playing today.

While Yalom's recommendations are not as stringent as the Gouldings, he accomplishes the same goals. First, the agenda rounds will provide structure, but not too much structure. After all, the group leader does not want a leader-centered group. The aim is to establish a freely interacting group. Too much structure will prevent free interaction between the group members and will encourage the group members to become dependent on the leader for direction and guidance. Too little structure promotes regression and wastes important group time as the members stumble around aimlessly trying to establish some direction for the group. Secondly, the agenda rounds provide some contact with each member, although it may be brief and non-directed. This at least gives the group leader a "reading" of each member's emotional state at the beginning of group. Thirdly, the leaders use of a structured opening to group gives the clear message that activity and participation are expected of each individual. A group member who repeatedly fails to come up with an agenda meeting after meeting needs to be assessed carefully by the group leader.

Group members need to be taught how to utilize the agenda rounds. A basic task of the group leader is to help each member formulate realistic agendas. The structure of the agenda can be very loose or it can be very specific. Yalom suggests the agenda be stated in a way that the individual identify some personal aspect of themselves that can be realistically attained within a single group setting.

Yalom also feels agendas are much more effective when they are channeled into interpersonal themes so they can be worked on in the here and now of the group process. It is not necessary for the group leader to hold to such a rigid format and Yalom's recommendation reflects his bias toward his belief that the group work be kept in the "here and now." When working with alcoholics and addicts, the "there and then" can be as important and have as much significance on their recovery as the "here and now." Consequently, it is recommended that the group leader structure his agenda rounds in a style which Yalom recommends; but the group leader must remain aware that a recently detoxified alcoholic or addict may be capable of little more than following instructions. It may be best not to require them to come up with too elaborate a scheme or plan. In the wisdom of AA, "keeping it simple" may be best for them until they have had more time to stabilize.

For instance, the group leader might start his group off by stating,

> It's time to start group today. I'd like to start with an agenda round. Would each of you introduce yourself, say a little about how you are feeling and if there is anything you would like to talk about in group today. Who wants to go first?

At this point, rather than call on someone to speak first or direct the order of responses from the group members, the group leader should sit quietly. With his opening statement, he has provided enough structure to get the group started and he would be over-controlling if he proceeded to pick members to respond in turn. Usually the members will take up the direction at this point. It is rare for a group to sit in silence for very long with such a structured opening. If the silence goes on for more than five minutes, the group leader should avoid "picking" someone to start. Rather, it would be best to comment on the group's difficulty and wonder aloud why no one wants to start.

The example illustrates that the group leader's opening statement can be short and simple. If there are brand new members in the group on that day or it is the very first meeting of the group, the group leader may want to explain the purpose of the agenda rounds in more detail. For instance, the group leader could add to his opening instructions by saying,

There are no restrictions on your topics in group. You may want to specifically work on some behavior you want to change or you just may want to take some time to report to the group how you are feeling. Sometimes, some group members want feedback from other members. At other times people may have something left over from the previous group that they want to discuss further.

Formulating agendas can be difficult for many patients. One danger inherent in leaving the agenda vague is that the psychotherapy group can itself become vague or turn into a quasi-AA meeting. This is not to imply that AA meetings are bad; just that psychotherapy groups serve a different purpose and that it is the group leader's task to insure that the purpose of the group is fulfilled. This requires that the group leader help the group members formulate their agendas. In one sense, it is the group leader's job to teach the group members how to think in specific and clear terms when it comes to utilizing the therapy group. The group members must come to realize the group is a unique form of treatment which serves distinctly different purposes from that of AA, educational lectures, and discussion groups. This is especially important as the patient begins to stabilize and their thinking clears to the point that they can meet Yalom's criteria for establishing realistic and "do-able" agendas.
Yalom addresses this issue when he writes,

> The formulation of an agenda is not an effortless, automatic task. Patients do not do it easily, and the therapist must devote considerable effort to help them in this task.
> For one thing, the great majority of patients have considerable difficulty understanding precisely *what* the therapist wants and *why*. The task must be explained to patients simply and lucidly. The therapist may give examples of possible agendas and painstakingly help each member shape his or her own. The therapist must also explain to patients *why* he or she wants an agenda by stating the advantages of the agenda format.
> Agenda formation requires three steps and the therapist must escort most patients, especially in their first meeting, through each of the three steps:
> 1. The patient must identify some important personal aspect that he wishes to change. Moreover, the task must be realistic:

that is, the aspect must be amenable to change and appropriate for a therapy group approach.

2. The patient must attempt to shape his or her complaint into interpersonal terms.

3. The patient must transform that interpersonal complaint into one that has here-and-now ramifications. (Yalom, 1983, pp. 216–217)

Usually, most problems with agenda rounds have to do with the group members' tendency to state their agendas in a vague and overly generalized manner. For instance, a group member may give their agenda in the following way. "I'm depressed and I want to stop being depressed." As Yalom states, this is a useless agenda because it is a task that cannot be accomplished in one single meeting. The Gouldings suggest in their contract work that the group member start with small specific behavior changes which can be reasonably and successfully attained. They recommend building slowly on small successes and eventually graduating to more difficult tasks after a person has begun to restore their confidence in their ability to change. Accepting a contract like, "I want to be happy forever" is doomed to failure and a set-up for both the group leader and the group member. In response to the group member who wants to stop being depressed, the group leader could respond in the following manner,

Listen, Jim, I understand that this is a very important agenda for you because your depression has been very painful and incapacitating in the past. However, I wonder how realistic this is for you. You've been depressed for years and I doubt if you could change that in one session. As you've stated before, you can be very impatient and I'm concerned that this may be an example of you wanting too much too soon. One reason for your depression is your isolation. You've complained of not having friends and how this sense of loneliness leads both to your drinking and depression. Would you be willing to look at how you isolate yourself here in group? What is it about yourself that shuts off contact with others, even here in group? I would like to suggest you explore this issue in group as a means to understanding how this may contribute to your depression.

In this example, the group leader has moved the group member from the global to the specific. He has been gentle, but persistent in his efforts to get the group member to make a commitment to focus his agenda so it applies to interpersonal terms in the "here and now."

Examples of good clear agendas include:

1. I'm lonely. I want to change that.
2. I want to communicate with others.
3. I want feedback on how others perceive me.
4. I don't trust easily. I want to change that.

DIFFICULTIES WITH AGENDA ROUNDS

Each of these examples can be easily turned into interpersonal here and now work. Unfortunately, not all group members are so concise and quick to formulate their agenda in such nice and neat packages. The biggest difficulty novice group leaders have with agenda rounds is their inability to contain their agenda round to ten or fifteen minutes. Each agenda, if properly conducted, should only take each member one to two minutes a member. Before they are aware of it, the group leader discovers their entire group session has been consumed by the agenda round, or worse, they've only gotten around to half the group. Frequently, if a group member starts to demonstrate strong affect during their opening agenda statement, the group leader will find it difficult to move beyond that person for fear that this will disrupt or disturb the individual's sharing and openness. A group leader should never allow himself to be tied down to any technique, but most group members will respond to a gentle disruption. For example the group leader might say,

> It's obvious, Mary, that this is a very important and painful topic for you. I'd like to stop you here for a minute and ask that you take some time in group today to talk about this further. I'm going to finish the agenda round first. Would you agree to make a commitment to talk about this when the agenda round is completed?

With this response, the group leader has maintained the integrity of the structure of the group without compromising a particular group member. Further, the group leader has acknowledged the importance of this issue and has gotten a firm commitment from the group member that she will pursue the topic after the agenda round is completed.

THE SPECIAL CIRCUMSTANCES OF INPATIENT THERAPY GROUPS WITHIN THE HOSPITAL

Inpatient treatment involves much more than the proper clinical management of the group, its members, and the group dynamics. Because inpatient therapy groups are conducted in a treatment facility that has many different components to its treatment program and these different components have a vast array of objectives and multiple associated personnel, it requires the therapy group adapt to fit within the total treatment picture. In outpatient groups, the boundary between the group and the outside world is typically distinct and clearly drawn. With inpatient groups, however, these boundaries are not as clear and are more diffuse. The inpatient group is a subsystem within the larger system of the hospital unit and the team approach to treatment. The blurring of boundaries between the group and many other hospital activities can be a source of added difficulty for the group leader. Management of these boundary issues is therefore of extreme importance to successful inpatient group treatment. If this were not the case, this chapter could end here and the group leader would just have to concern himself with the direct clinical issues presented so far. However, the hospital setting and the team approach requires the group leader and the rest of the staff work in concert with each other. If this is not successfully accomplished, the results could be disastrous for the patient. An extreme example of this would be a case where part of the staff requires total abstinence as the goal of treatment while a few others secretly advocated controlled drinking.

Vannicelli (1982) responds to these issues in describing the special difficulties the alcoholics present in group therapy. In order for these difficulties to be managed on the inpatient unit, she recommends six key issues be addressed.

> Our leaders are encouraged, however, to remain mindful throughout of some subtle differences between the defensive styles of alcoholics and neurotics and how these differences influence their relationship to the group. More specifically, we remain sensitive to the fact that alcoholics have well-developed skills for evading limits and for shifting or diffusing the focus. In contrast to working with neurotic patients, whose

more focused anxieties provide motivation and direction for therapeutic work, the intense but diffuse discomfort of alcoholics does not perform these functions. In fact, quite often their diffuse defenses make working in therapy groups quite difficult. Thus, it falls to the leader to provide limits and focus in the group. To do this he needs to be able to intervene without generating more anxiety than necessary — a task which is considerably facilitated when the leader has knowledge of, and feels prepared to handle, the frequent trouble spots in alcoholic groups.

There are six key issues which need advance thought so that the leaders will be prepared to respond in an unchallenging but firm manner. (Vannicelli, 1982, pp. 19–20)

Vannicelli's six key issues are:

1. Group leaders must be prepared to respond to challenges to disclose information about their own drinking and drug abuse.
2. The patients' contract with the group and the group's contract with the hospital.
3. Confusion may occur regarding group expectations when members belong to other kinds of groups (AA, education groups, etc.).
4. Special problems arise concerning confidentiality because of the frequency of communication between the group leader and outsiders (other than staff, other patients, employers, family, etc.).
5. Active outreach by the group leader to provide intervention if needed.
6. Group defensive maneuvers regarding the drinking theme and (for after-care groups) abstinence and its consequences on the group when a member relapses.

LEADER'S TRANSPARENCY ABOUT ALCOHOL AND DRUG USE

Vannicelli warns that the group leader can expect questions about his own alcohol and drug use. Rather than avoid the question or answer it simply without questioning the underlying reasons for it being asked, the group leader needs to explore the motives behind the patient's curiosity. For Vannicelli, this curiosity always translates into the implied concern of "Will you be able to understand or help me?" The answer of course is a double-edged sword. If the group leader doesn't drink or do drugs, the member may wonder how the therapist could possibly understand his condition. If the group leader drinks at times (I will not repeat my stance regarding therapists who use drugs and work with alcoholics or addicts other than to refer to my sentiments in Chapter 7 and advise that they not work with such patients) and admits this to the patient, the group member is also likely to wonder if a person who can drink controllably will be able to be of help to them. A group leader who is recovering himself may be a source of comfort for some members and suspect to others since the therapist is "not a professional, but just another recovering addict like myself."

A better response to such a question might be as follows.

My guess is that you ask because you wonder if I'll be able to help and understand since I have (or don't have) the same problem. Could you say more about your concerns and has there been anyone else in your past who didn't understand?

Transparency about drinking and drug use has important implications for treatment. But, the issue is not limited to this subject. Yalom feels that a group leader should do more self-disclosure in an inpatient group. Many of the restrictions of the therapist's transparency which were outlined in Chapter 3 on outpatient group therapy also applies to inpatient groups. Self-disclosure on the leader's part is most appropriate when it helps facilitate the attainment of therapy goals. Transparency should be used in the service of providing support, acceptance, and encouragement. It is not the task of the group leader to manufacture positive feelings, but to locate and identify such reactions to patients through selective self-disclosure. A patient in need of support and help does not benefit from a group leader who manufactures false feelings or expresses distrust or anger towards the patient.

THE GROUP CONTRACT

In working with inpatient A&D groups, it is helpful to think of the group contract as having three major components. The first regards the issue of abstinence. Certainly, this is a goal that is clearly advocated by AA and is a theme which runs continuously through this book. The second and third components of the contract concern the special circumstances involved in inpatient groups and are derived from recommendations made by Rice and Rutan (1981).

Vannicelli sums up the importance of the group norm of abstinence when she writes,

> The group norm regarding drinking should be made explicit as part of the initial group contract and should indicate that all members will be working toward abstinence and that any difficulties encountered in working toward this goal (in the form of either fears about drinking or actual drinking) will be discussed with the group. The importance of a set of shared norms about what it means to be working on one's drinking problem should not be underestimated. Although there is some disagreement about whether abstinence is the only appropriate goal for alcoholics, mixing patients with divergent goals in the same group poses an almost insurmountable challenge to the integrity of the group. Since the group members do not share a notion of what it means to get better, they find themselves at an impasse in terms of either helping one another to get there or assessing how they are doing. Furthermore, since the wish of nearly every recovering alcoholic is that he may some day be able to drink again, the presence of a member in the group who is acting on this wish may well arouse anxiety that is dealt with by means of unproductive and extreme proselytizing (in support of A.A., abstinence, etc.). (Vannicelli, 1982, p. 29)

Inside and Outside Group Contracts. Rice and Rutan (1981) view the contract as a container for the group boundaries. Having clear and specific boundaries will insure that the members of the inpatient group will profit more from their treatment. The contract will determine who will be in the group and for how long. It also determines how this material is used both inside and outside of the group.

Outside Contract. The outside contract is the contract made between the group leader and the hospital or unit director. Specifically, it has to do with the relationship of the hospital treatment program to the treatment provided by the group. The agreement should include:

1. Group therapy will be congruent with the overall treatment program of the unit or hospital.

2. Group therapy will be recognized as a primary mode of treatment and not given a secondary status to other types of therapies.
3. The group boundaries will be respected by all staff members and patients. Group sessions and time will not be violated either by staff members entering uninvited or patients being called out indiscriminately for other appointments.

Inside Contract. This is the contract made between the group leader and its members.

1. All group members will attend each session, be on time and stay for the entire group.
2. Confidentiality between patients will be honored. Information shared within the group will not be given to patients outside the group by the other group members.
3. Group members will not sub-group. Information shared outside of group among group members in between group sessions must be brought back into group and talked about.

SIMULTANEOUS MEMBERSHIP IN OTHER GROUPS

Recovering alcoholics and addicts are likely to be members in a number of different groups simultaneously. Not only will they attend or interact in AA meetings which are held outside of the hospital, either before, during or after their inpatient treatment, they will attend a vast number of different task-oriented and education groups while in the hospital which will put them in repeated contact with group members in group formats which have distinctly different orientations and objectives from that of the therapy group. This creates two distinctly different, yet very important obstacles which the group leader has to overcome. First, the group leader will discover it will be impossible to prevent group members from having out-of-group contact. Most contemporary forms of outpatient group therapy recommend that out-of-group socializing between group members be discouraged. However, this rule will be difficult to enforce because recovering alcoholics and addicts frequently have a simultaneous dual membership in both AA and the therapy group. Beyond the uncontrollable reality of the situation, it may not be as damaging as many clinicians believe. Certainly, it should not be actively encouraged and the possible hazards resulting from the mixing of therapeutic and social relationships should be carefully discussed and understood. Sexual contact between group members should be explicitly forbidden, of course. However, making all forms of socializing taboo often promotes acting out or forces the members either to hide their planned encounters or keep chance meetings secret from the group. Rather than set up questionable objections to out-of-group socializing, it would be better if the group leader encouraged the group members to agree to always talk with the group about any out of group exchange that may have taken place between group members. Whatever happens between two or more members outside of group should always be shared within the group. Vannicelli sums up this position when she writes,

> It is also common that members of the therapy group may belong to the same A.A. group. Thus, it is impractical (and not desireable) to try to limit group members' activities with one another outside of the group. However, since in a group of alcoholics, as in any group, it is desireable to keep as much of the group energy as possible within the group, patients should be encouraged to discuss with the group any "relevant" content that comes up outside. Although the word "relevant" is somewhat vague, and different patients will surely interpret it in different ways, there should be a shared understanding that if the outside-of-group contact exceeds the usual socializing at A.A. meetings, it should be discussed with the group. It is sometimes helpful to give patients concrete examples. (For instance, if two group members find themselves talking to one another about another member or about what happened in the group; if two or more group members find themselves socializing extensively; or if two patients find themselves having a "special" liaison.) Discussion with patients around these examples should help clarify that important business or relationships that go on outside and are not discussed with the group rob the group as a whole of the opportunity to explore these matters and rob the patients involved of the opportunity to get valuable feedback from other members. Equally important, the outside-of-group business that does not get talked about in group takes on the character of "special secrets", the existence of which runs counter to the group's shared goal of mutual openness and trust. (Vannicelli, 1982, p. 24)

Simultaneous participation in multiple groups that have different prescribed expectations, goals, and ground rules which differ from those of a therapy group can create special problems for the group leader on an inpatient unity. Participation in groups that either have a substantially didactic component to it, like education groups, or a more structural and supportive component like AA groups, are likely to create some confusion for the individual when he enters a more unstructured group therapy setting which offers little didactic information. It will be important for the group leader to clarify the difference between the therapy group and other types of groups they may have to attend while in the hospital. The recommendations of Brix which were cited early in the chapter on the use of "A" and "B" level groups and the pre-group preparation conducted along the guidelines recommended in Chapter 14 are a couple excellent ways this difficulty can be avoided or corrected.

Specifically, the group members should be told about the complementary nature of AA and group. AA is to be used primarily to help them stop drinking. Group therapy is to help them learn new ways of coping and responding in their interpersonal relationships. While these two modalities are not mutually exclusive, they must realize that what is required of them in group is far different than what is required of them in AA. For instance, they can go to AA meetings whenever they want to. In fact, they are often encouraged by "senior" AA members to sit passively and just listen at the beginning of their involvement in AA. Group therapy, on the other hand, requires the group member be there every session and be on time. They must be willing to be actively involved in the group process and realize there will be less structured guidance. Unlike education groups, they must be made aware that the information will not be given to them in a structured format. If the group member does not fully understand that they are required to take a more active and responsible role in the therapy group, they may become confused or irritated leading them to fail to appreciate the full benefits which can be derived from the group therapy experience.

THE SPECIAL PROBLEMS OF CONFIDENTIALITY ON AN INPATIENT UNIT

The rules governing confidentiality and information exchange are more complicated in a therapy group on an inpatient unit. In most contemporary forms of therapy, the patient can be assured that all informations shared by the patient will be kept confidential. This is not the case with inpatient therapy groups. Many if not all chemically dependent patients are referred for treatment either by their employer, family, or court. Consequently, this often requires that the group leader share information with the referral source since divorce, continual employment, or incarceration is often contingent and mitigated by the patient's participation in treatment and group therapy. In addition, the team approach to inpatient treatment requires that all pertinent information about the patient must be shared with the rest of the treatment staff. In order to avoid feelings of betrayal or deception, the group leader must have a clear contract outlining the limits of confidentiality. The group members must be told in advance that an exchange of information will occur. A signed release should also be obtained.

Of course, a signed release is not needed for the exchange of information which occurs between the group leader and the rest of the inpatient treatment staff. However, each group member must explicitly understand that what they share in group will be shared with other members of the treatment team. For instance, they might be instructed in the following manner,

> If the co-leader or I feel that something we learn about you in group is important to your treatment and recovery, we will share this information with the rest of the staff. It is important to understand we are all equally involved in your treatment here at the hospital and it has been our experience that a team approach is the most successful way to treat addiction. Occasionally, we may have to speak to others outside the hospital like your employer, spouse, attorney, or representative from the court. If we do, we will get a signed written release from you and we will avoid, as much as possible, giving them any personal information other than you are or are not participating and progressing in treatment. After we have spoken with any of these individuals, we will let you know with whom we spoke, why, and what we told them.

Information given to outsiders is not the only source of difficulty plaguing group leaders on an inpatient unit. They must also be prepared to deal with the sticky problem of dealing with information which comes from sources outside of group about the member in group. There are two basic rules for dealing with outside information.

1. Make it a policy that the group leader will keep no secrets and that he will determine how the information will be used based on its clinical relevance. He should also make no promises to family members, friends, or employers that will bind him to some potentially damaging collusion with the informant. The group leader may indicate that he may decide not to reveal the source of the information unless it is absolutely necessary. However, the group leader should retain the freedom to make this decision without pre-established restrictions.
2. The group leader should never assume the information is more valid, truthful or reliable than that supplied by the patient.

When given information about a group member, the group leader should first encourage the patient to talk about this issue on his own. Confrontation should only be used as a last resort. For instance, the following vignette illustrates how one group leader dealt with this dilemma.

Arnold, a thirty-four-year-old alcoholic, had entered treatment after physically attacking his wife while he was in the midst of an alcoholic blackout. Since he was much too ashamed to talk about this with the treatment staff or the group, the group leader had to decide how to use the information of physical abuse he had gotten from Arnold's wife during her family assessment interview. As another member in group began to talk about his own difficulties containing his anger while intoxicated, the group leader noticed Arnold's discomfort and said, "It's obvious this brings up some strong and uncomfortable feelings for you, Arnold. I wonder if you share similar feelings of guilt and embarrassment about your anger when you have been intoxicated." This was a mild invitation for Arnold to speak and it was presented to him in a non-threatening or non-judgmental manner. This was enough to help Arnold get through a very difficult issue. If this subject had not been addressed, it would have likely lead Arnold to withdrawal and hide more from himself and the rest of the group during the next four weeks. Since guilt and denial are such contributing factors to relapse, and since the group leader did not have the luxury of waiting weeks, or even months before Arnold felt trusting or safe enough to share this information, it was important to encourage him to open up about this topic. However, the group leader did it in a manner that was not too intrusive and allowed Arnold to maintain his integrity by giving him the opportunity to introduce it himself.

Sometimes, the exchange of information that occurs between a therapist and a patient during a private conversation can be another source of conflict for the group leader. Since most inpatient group leaders see some of their group members individually or in other capacities while they are in the hospital, they may find themselves privileged to information that has not been shared with others on the treatment team. Such a situation can put the group leader in a very compromising situation, especially if he has agreed beforehand to the patient's request to "please keep this information just between the two of us." If the group leader is part of an inpatient treatment team, he must realize that this is one important instance where inpatient treatment differs radically from outpatient treatment. The rules of confidentiality are altered in a team approach to inpatient treatment. The group leader must never allow himself to make a personal commitment of confidentiality to a patient on an inpatient unit. For instance, it may be very flattering to hear your favorite group member say to you in private, "I trust you more than anyone here at the hospital. There is something I just wouldn't tell anyone else because I don't think they would understand. But promise that you'll keep what I'm about to say between the two of us." At this point the group leader should resist his temptation to succumb to such a flattering remark. Instead, it would be better for the group member and the group leader if he were to respond to this request in the following manner.

Wait just a second before you share that with me. I am flattered that you've grown to trust me so much in such a short time and I do want to encourage you to share what you're about to talk about. However, I can't promise I won't share this with other members of the treatment team. Now, I may not. But if I think it's important to your recovery and treatment at the hospital, I may have to let others know for your own good. Understand my concern is what is going to be best for you in the long run.

A patient will rarely object to such a stipulation on the therapist's part. If he were to refuse to share his "secret" after the therapist responded in this manner, it is likely that the patient was either trying to manipulate the therapist or caught up in his own destructive transference distortion. Such a stance by the group leader will keep him from contributing to the patient's primitive projections. Since many alcoholics and addicts suffer from primitive character pathology, they will be prone to split the treatment staff into all good or all bad segments. If the group leader carefully monitors his tendency to agree quickly to such requests, it would prevent him from placing himself in a compromising situation. For instance, what if the patient were to share that he had plans to commit suicide this evening or that he knew another patient had smuggled drugs or alcohol on to the unit. How could the group leader not break his promise of confidentiality in such a situation?

ACTIVE OUTREACH

Inpatient Alcohol and Drug (A & D) treatment has been made more complicated for the group leader because of two co-existing changes in addiction treatment over the last few years. First, many hospitals require their inpatient group leaders conduct after-care groups for those patients who have successfully completed their four to six week inpatient programs. Second, because of financial restrictions, more hospitals are now conducting day treatment programs which provide a treatment format very similar to the inpatient program except the patient is allowed to stay at home in the evening or continue to work during the day. In either case, the group leader must adapt and respond to situations which are somewhat unique to an alcohol and drug addiction population. Specifically, the group leader will be required to do a considerable amount of active outreach work because most of his group members will either have a very short, unstable period of sobriety or they will be without the protective confines of a closed hospital unit. Consequently, the group member's sobriety will be much more tentative and to compensate for this situation, the group leader will be required to do a considerable amount of active intervention, particularly in telephoning and reaching out to delinquent group members. While the group leader of a non-addictive group can afford to slowly explore the reasons why a group member's attendance is irregular or erratic, he cannot take such a leisurely approach with newly recovering addicts and alcoholics. Most contemporary forms of group therapy do not advocate that the group leader actively telephone or question group members if they have missed a therapy group. With a newly recovering alcoholic or addict, such an occurrence or unannounced absence should be interpreted as a warning signal or cry for help. For this reason, instead of waiting for the next session to explore the reasons for the group member's unannounced absence, the group leader must either telephone immediately after group meeting or within the next day. At other times, if a group member has been going through a particularly difficult time and the group member calls to say they are not going to be able to make it to group this evening, the group leader should carefully investigate any possible reasons he might have for avoiding group. Often, with a little prompting or careful questioning, the group member might come to understand his reasons for resisting group and respond to the group leader's concern.

Although, such an active stance by the group leader has advantages in that it may prevent a relapse or bring forth unknown resistances to the patient's consciousness, it does place the group leader in a position which may be perceived as too controlling or parental. To minimize this, utilize the other group members to monitor attendance as much as possible. Focus more on the group member's behavior and conduct all interventions in a nonjudgmental style. Outreach delivered in a concerned manner can do much to help group members see the possible destructive overtones to their resistance and avoidance of group.

Group Members Who Relapse and Come to Group

Because after-care group and day treatment therapy groups operate outside of the protective confines of a closed hospital unit, the group leader is more likely to be faced with the difficult task of dealing with an active group member who relapses. Relapses, as addressed in Chapter 4, can be an important learning experience for the alcoholic or addict if it is properly integrated and understood. The only bad relapse is an unexamined one. Not only would it be beneficial to examine the reasons for the individual group member's relapse, but it would also be a valuable learning experience for the other members of the group. It would help them all identify the different stages of relapse. First, it would be important for the group leader to take a position which most veteran AA members take when dealing with an alcoholic's relapse. Don't let the individual who relapsed describe his experience as a "slip." This implies his return to drinking was due to something that happened to him. As AA says, "if you don't want to have a slip, don't go where it is slippery." AA members prefer to speak of "slips" as "premeditated drunks." Explore with the alcoholic the reasons that lead him to return to his old "slippery ways" and how these patterns can be identified and avoided in the future.

In addressing this problem, Vannicelli lists four common drinking landmarks that can occur within the context of a therapy group.

1. Group members who come to group visibly intoxicated.
2. Group members drinking between sessions and refusing to acknowledge it directly even when confronted.
3. Group members drinking and admitting it, but not wanting to stop.
4. The group member who periodically drinks and continues to endorse the policy of abstinence while the behavior indicates otherwise.

Each situation requires a different strategy for appropriately responding to its unique set of circumstances.

1. Coming to Group Intoxicated

Ask the group member firmly, but politely, to leave the group and return next week. Explain quickly that group members are not allowed in group intoxicated, but that it would be important for them to return to the group. With a more obstinent and difficult individual, ask him politely if he would mind waiting outside. Suggest he have a cup of coffee and cigarette. This might give him a way out that would allow him to save face in front of the other group members. Send the individual to a nearby AA meeting or call a sober member of AA to come in to speak with him. After the intoxicated member leaves, explore in detail the group's reaction to the incident.

2. Suspected Drug or Alcohol Use Without Acknowledgement

If it is not obvious that the group member is intoxicated, but the group leader has information from an outside informant that he is drinking or doing drugs (i.e, wife, etc.), it would be best to gently confront the group member. Often, invitations to speak about such issues are enough to get the individual started. However, if the group member is insistent that he is sober or clean, it is best not to push the issue. It is rare to have an alcoholic or addict who is using or drinking who will continue to attend a therapy group which has a contract of abstinence. If the after-care group or day-hospital has a contractual agreement for periodic random drug screens, this will often eliminate such difficulties.

3. Continual Admitted Drug and Alcohol Use

After a repeated series of relapses the group member needs to be evaluated for further supplemental treatment. If alcohol is the problem, Antabuse (disulfiram) should be prescribed. Inpatient hospitalization also needs to be considered. Supplemental individual therapy or increased AA meetings are other ways of adjusting the patient's treatment. If the member decides he does not want to agree to these requirements or openly acknowledges he wants to continue to drink or do drugs, it should be politely, but firmly, explained to him that group is only for those individuals who want to stop using drugs or alcohol. Tell the member a referral can be made to someone who will be able to see him on an individual basis and that he can return to group at anytime in the future if he should change his mind. Under no conditions should the group leader try to mix an actively using addict or alcoholic in a group with newly recovering members.

Vannicelli stresses the importance of a solid group contract in order to avoid the possible pitfall associated with each of these problem areas. She writes,

Effective handling of the last four issues (simultaneous membership in other groups, communication with outsiders, patients who drink and drinking as a group focus) all require the presence of an explicit treatment contract that clarifies what will be expected of group members (and what they, in turn, can expect). This explicit agreement with the patient ideally will be laid out in a pre-group interview in which each of the ground rules will be stated. The rules should include the following: (1) a statement regarding minimum tenure in the group (e.g., we expect members to make a commitment of at least 3 months); (2) expectations of regular and timely attendance and advance notice when a patient absolutely must be late or away (and an indication whether the patient will be charged or not for missed meetings); (3) need for advance notice to the group if the patient is considering leaving; (4) commitment to abstinence and willingness to talk about fears of drinking or actual slips should they occur; (5) commitment to talk about other important issues in the patient's life that cause difficulty in relating to others or in living life fully; (6) commitment to talk about what is going on in the group itself as a way of better understanding one's own interpersonal dynamics; (7) specifics of the limits regarding outside-of-group contacts between group members (or requirements for bringing back into the group relevant material that comes up outside, or both); and (8) the nature and extent of communications between group leaders and outsiders. (Vannicelli, 1982, pp. 36–37)

SUMMARY RECOMMENDATIONS FOR INPATIENT GROUP THERAPY

Unlike most other forms of contemporary group treatment, inpatient group therapy with alcohol and drug abusing patients involves the simultaneous management of three diverse influences on the patient's treatment process. First, there are the neurological deficits commonly seen with most newly recovering alcoholics and addicts. Second, there are the more typical clinical management issues that confront any group leader who is leading a group on an inpatient unit. As Yalom outlines, these clinical difficulties are made more problematic by the special circumstances surrounding inpatient treatment. Third, because group therapy is a subsystem within a larger hospital system, the group leader must be able to negotiate the common difficulties that arise anytime a subsystem has to exist within a larger supra-system. Specifically, this problem usually manifests itself with the group leader who finds himself as part of a treatment team. The usual principles of a therapy group are compromised by the special dynamics of the team approach to treatment. All three of these diverse influences — neurological impairment, clinical management, the treatment team approach — must be brought together in a united complimentary effort if the group leader is to provide a beneficial treatment experience for his group members. The goals of group and treatment on an inpatient unit need to be adapted to fit these circumstances. Specifically, the therapy group must be a complimentary experience to the patient's overall treatment experience. If the therapy group is at odds with the goals of the rest of the inpatient treatment program, the patient's chance of successful recovery will be greatly diminished. Mueller (1982) identifies and summarizes eight important goals that must be achieved by the patient during his hospitalization.

1. Have the patient identify where alcohol and drugs are in his life in terms of losses suffered due to drinking — (i.e., family, job, monetary, health, self-respect, legal, spiritual).
2. Individually tailor each treatment plan in terms of aiding each patient to identify the individual goals for his treatment.
3. Have the patient realize that being an alcoholic or addict means never being able to drink or use drugs again.
4. Have patient recognize alternatives to drinking and identify what he needs to do to stay sober (i.e., attend AA, outpatient groups, etc.).
5. Whenever possible, involve the patient's social-emotional system in treatment — family, friends, AA sponsor, employer.
6. Provide a treatment experience whereby the patients feels valued by both staff and other patients through interaction, acceptance, and "permission giving" to experience and express feelings.
7. Educate the alcoholic and addict about the disease of alcoholism and addiction.
8. Provide a sober environment in which he can obtain treatment. This will involve both AA and ongoing outpatient groups. Particularly the inpatient group therapy experience will make the patient more receptive to continual outpatient group therapy.

The group leader's task is to lead the group member through these goals. Berger (1983) outlines this sequence when he writes,

> First, the therapist should increase the patient's motivation for sobriety by exploring the deleterious effect alcohol has had on his life, using a here-and-now emphasis, and avoiding the trap of looking with the patient for underlying causes of his drinking. The therapist should gently confront the patient's defenses (such as denial, projection, and grandiosity), and

help him take responsibility for his actions, including the alcoholism. Furthermore, the therapist may have to deal with the patient's fantasy that one day he will be able to return to social drinking.

Second, the therapist must help the patient learn to readjust to life without alcohol. He must learn to fill his time constructively, with alcohol no longer a central part of his life. Simultaneously, the therapist may optimize the alcoholic's chances for sobriety by suggesting family education sessions, encouraging him to attend AA meetings, and judiciously using disulfiram to minimize impulsive drinking. (Berger, 1983, p. 1043)

Through this tailored treatment process, the support systems which have enabled the patient's drinking and drug use must be cut off. Unlike techniques of most contemporary and traditional forms of group therapy, the addict and alcoholic must not be encouraged during the initial stages of treatment to look introspectively within himself for strength or self-understanding. Rather, he should be encouraged by confrontation and life review to look at his failures so that his initial pain is intensified. This requires that the group leader not be conned by tangential discussions of coexisting internal conflicts. The alcoholic and addict must not be allowed to escape from the paradox that his drinking and drug use is the problem. He must instead take responsibility for this. However, he must learn that within himself, there lies no defense against his desire to use or drink. In short, he must learn he cannot drink and use drugs, but that he alone cannot quit drinking and using drugs. This position pressures the alcoholic or addict into hopelessness in himself and his old support systems. He is then asked to accept guidance, help, and control from a source outside of himself. Paradoxically, he is given no alternative. This combats his grandiose self-centeredness and isolation. Eventually, through AA and the therapy group, he must learn that others with whom he can identify are the new source of hope and strength.

REFERENCES

Berger, F. (1983). Alcoholism rehabilitation: A supportive approach. *Hospital and Community Psychiatry, 34*(11), 1040-1043.
Brix, D. J. (1983). Use of a group-centered psychotherapy group with the inpatient treatment

of alcoholism. *Bulletin of the Society of Psychologists in Additive Behaviors*, 2(4), 253-258.
Butlers, N. & Cermack, L. S. (1980). *Alcoholic Korsakoff syndrome: An information-processing approach to amnesia*. New York: Academic Press.
Cermak, L. S. & Peck, E. (1982). Continuum versus premature aging theories of chronic alcoholism. *Alcoholism: Clinical and Experimental Research*, 6(1), 89-95.
Gallant, D. M. (1983). Prediction of cortical atrophy in young alcoholics. *Alcoholism: Clinical & Experimental Research*, 7(4), 448.
Goulding, R. & Goulding, M. (1979). *Changing lives through redecision therapy*. New York: Brunner/Mazel.
Grant, I., Reed, R. & Adams, K. (1980). Alcohol & drug-related brain disorder: Implications for neuropsychological research. *Journal of Clinical Neuropsychology*, 2(4), 321-331.
Mueller, S. R., Sutter, B. H. & Prengaman, T. P. (1982). A short-term intensive treatment program for the alcoholic. *The International Journal of Addictions*, 17(6), 931-943.
Parson, O. A. & Farr, S. P. (1981). The neuropsychology of alcohol & drug use. In S. B. Felskov & T. J. Boll (Eds.), *Handbook of clinical neuropsychology* (pp. 320-365). New York: John Wiley & Sons.
Rice, C. A. & Rutan, J. S. (1981). Boundary maintenance in inpatient therapy groups. *International Journal of Group Psychotherapy*, 31(3), 297-309.
Ryan, C. & Butlers, N. (1980). Further evidence for a continuum of impairment encompassing male alcoholic Korsakoff patients and chronic alcoholic men. *Alcoholism*, 4, 190-198.
Vannicelli, M. (1982). Group psychotherapy with alcoholics, special techniques. *Journal of Studies on Alcohol*, 43(1), 17-37.
Wells, C. (1982). Chronic brain disease: An update on alcoholism, parkinsons disease, and dementia. *Hospital and Community Psychiatry*, 33(2), 111-126.
Wilkenson, D. A. & Carlen, P. L. (1981). Chronic organic brain syndromes associated with alcoholism: Neuropsychological & other aspects. In Y. Israel, F. Glace, H. Kalanet, R. E. Popham, W. Schmidt & R. G. Smart (Eds.), *Research advances in alcohol and drug problems*, Vol. 6. New York: Plenum Press.
Yalom, I. (1983). *Inpatient group psychotherapy*. New York: Basic Books.

Chapter 9

Special Training
for the Group Therapist
and the Relationship
of Persuasion
to Group Psychotherapy

While there are a number of dedicated professionals working in the field of addiction, many have not had the opportunity to get themselves well-trained in group psychotherapy. Consequently, many therapists desire more of an opportunity to enhance their group therapy skills. However, a method for accomplishing this task is not often available or clearly defined. I am reminded of what Robert Goulding once told me. If you want to be a good group therapist, you must do two things. First, you must do a lot of groups. Second, you must work with the "masters." By this he meant, rather than just talking about how to do group, you can learn a great deal more by actually doing groups. Also, you must be careful not to learn bad habits. Training with individuals who are inadequately experienced in the effective group treatment of addiction can lead to greater problems. Robert Goulding is not as concerned with grand theories as he is with conducting effective therapy and producing behavioral change. Like Alcoholics Anonymous, he takes a very pragmatic approach to treatment. If it works—use it!

A comment by Ralph Reitan, the originator of the Halstead-Reitan Neuropsychological Battery, illustrates this point with a specific example.

Some years ago, a resident neurological surgeon at the Indiana University Medical Center volunteered to take a battery of

This article originally appeared in *Journal of Contemporary Psychotherapy*, Vol. 15, #1, Spring 1985. Reprinted with permission from Human Sciences Press.

neuropsychological tests in order to have a better understanding of the types of examinations that might be given to his patients. After taking this extensive battery of psychological tests, that among other things yielded information concerning the differential status of the two cerebral hemispheres, he returned to obtain a brief interpretation of the results . . . The differential level of this man's abilities in these two areas prompted me to offer an initial comment to the effect that the test results indicated that he probably would be much better at telling about an operation after it was over than he would be at actually doing it. The neurosurgeon looked shocked, admitted that this was correct, and confessed that he regularly was the last person to be able to identify any landmarks! The test results, in other words, had definite practical implications with respect to evaluation of the subject. (Reitan & Davison, 1974, p. 20–21)

Like this surgeon, many group therapists are better at talking about how to run a group than they are at actually doing a group. And as Ralph Reitan suggests, the importance of his results had practical implications. The approach to treatment of alcoholics and addicts in group also requires a careful evaluation of the practical implications of the methods to be used. Unfortunately, many myths about groups get passed on to neophyte group therapists by others whose interest in group therapy and addictions is only passing or purely academic. In one sense, this is similar to the criticism which has been directed towards professionals in the alcoholism and addiction field who have only "learned" about theories of addiction while never actually working with recovering individuals on an ongoing basis. While I do not completely believe that a person has to be an addict or an alcoholic in order to help and treat one, I do believe a person has to leave the realm of objectivity and immerse themselves as much as possible in the subjective experience of the other who has sought help.

Like learning how to do group therapy properly, addicts and alcoholics learn to change more by doing rather than talking. Unfortunately, just talking about their addiction has usually contributed to the alcoholic or addict's problem and has added to their intellectual defenses and their denial system. This is why the Alcoholics Anonymous maxim of "Walk Your Talk" is so effective. It requires a recovering individual to "do" rather than just talk. Members of

Alcoholics Anonymous, like most good therapists, are not fooled by what an alcoholic or addict says. Alcoholics and addicts are advised to go to 90 meetings in 90 days. Take your body and your mind will follow they are told. In essence this is the principle William James proposed years ago. If you want to change your belief, act as if you believe and you will soon believe as you act.

As most individuals working with addictions will attest, getting alcoholics and addicts to change is difficult. Coercion, manipulation, confrontation, intervention and persuasion are important and necessary assets in the therapist's repertoire if he or she hopes to work successfully with addicted individuals. While many counselors working in the addictive disease field are familiar with the use of these techniques (i.e., confrontation, intervention, coercion and manipulation), those outside the field of addictions often shudder at the implications of such a treatment approach. However, as Jay Haley (1976) advocates, manipulation is an integral part of human interaction and occurs whether therapists recognize or identify it as such. Haley and others therefore suggest openly identifying and understanding the implications of such an approach rather than applying such principles in ignorance.

All these aspects of addictive treatment — coercion, manipulation, intervention and confrontation — were explored at length in Chapter 7. For now, the relationship of persuasion to treatment and recovery will be examined. This is an important endeavor, because the elements of persuasion play an important part in all forms of psychotherapy. Psychotherapy in fact is viewed by many as a subtle form of interpersonal persuasion (Frank, 1972). However, persuasion or the lack of it in a psychotherapeutic relationship, is not always clearly definable. Most therapists agree that persuasion is influenced by a number of important factors; of which the personal characteristics of the therapist are generally recognized as the most significant. Experience, credibility, training, dedication, values and enthusiasm are attributes usually agreed upon as being important contributors to the therapist's power to persuade. Understandably, psychotherapy conceptualized in this manner raises significant issues of values, ethics, and responsibility in treatment. While not all agree or recognize persuasive influences exist in psychotherapy, many suggest that persuasion is a salient feature of psychotherapy whether or not it is identified. It is important to remember that in all psychotherapy, trouble is apt to follow the ignorant applications of important forces. Further, it is suggested that these persuasive influences cross doctrinal differences and can be augmented by applying them within a group therapy setting when treating alcoholics or addicts. In the hands of a skilled and ethical psychotherapist, these persuasive influences can be enhanced and the group can be a powerful tool in the addict's and alcoholic's recovery process.

More specifically, these issues will be explored in relation to the idea that learning by doing, as in Alcoholics Anonymous, is preferred to learning by talking. This is not only true of recovery from addiction, but it is also true for the training of a group therapist. I will be outlining suggestions for those interested in learning more about group therapy by actually doing and participating in a group therapy training experience. More specifically, I will be examining my own training experience and how these training experiences reflect on my approach to group psychotherapy with addicted individuals.

During the period from May 24, 1980, to June 19, 1981, I attended two different month-long psychotherapy training programs directed respectively by Erv and Miriam Polster and Bob and Mary Goulding. This chapter is an attempt to integrate these two very similar yet paradoxically different training experiences. Beyond this, I am venturing to discern the similarities and the differences in order to critique the theoretical approach and practical applications of these two excellent training programs. All four therapists are excellent theorists, therapists and trainers. My interest was particularly vested in them as individuals and therefore to simplify and to personify my experience, I'll concentrate on their work. It is with them in mind that I shall address my theoretical ramblings and my experiential observations. Although this chapter is written more for my benefit than it is for their's or the reader's, I hope all who read this will be able to profit from its being written.

DESCRIPTION OF THE TRAINING PROGRAM

Both training programs, the Gouldings' Western Institute of Group and Family Therapy in Watsonville, California, and Polsters' Gestalt Training Center in San Diego, were composed of approximately thirty trainees each. Usually, half of the participants were from outside the United States, which helped form a highly cosmopolitan atmosphere at both programs. All participants were engaging in postgraduate training beyond their respective professions which included psychiatry, psychology, social work, nursing, ministry and counseling.

Both programs explicitly accentuated the relationship between concept and practice. Five days a week, from eight to ten hours a day, trainees spent their time in four segments of training.

1. A short time usually each day at lectures listening to theory and application.
2. Doing therapy as therapist, usually with supervision from the Polsters, the Gouldings, or their faculty.
3. Observing therapy and demonstrations by the faculty, including of course the Gouldings and Polsters.
4. Being in therapy as the client, usually focusing on one's own personal issues and personal growth.

The weekends were generally free. Beyond the formal training format, two important factors contributed to the facilitation of a reciprocal learning atmosphere. First, the issue of group cohesion which Yalom (1975) describes as the crucial curative factor in effective group therapy, was constantly developing within the intimate atmospheres created by the arrangements of both of these programs. Second, many of the trainees were excellent therapists in their own right. Therefore, learning was not limited to the faculty's influence alone. Each trainee would frequently explore and share their own personal experiences with each other throughout the month-long training program, thus maximizing both their learning and personal growth.

Before describing the Polsters' and the Gouldings' respective theories, I would like to explore the roots of each of these two approaches.

FOUNDATIONS OF GESTALT
AND REDECISION THERAPY

The Polsters describe Gestalt therapy as a phenomenologically rooted existential psychotherapy. It is phenomenal in that it emphasizes the individual be aware of what he or she is experiencing now. It is existential in that its focus is on responsibility, freedom, and choice. Gestalt therapy started as a revision of classical psychoanalysis (Perls, 1947, 1948; Polster, 1975). It quickly became a whole and autonomous system for integrating wisdom from diverse sources into a unified clinical methodology (Perls, Hefferline & Goodman, 1951). Its popularity had in the past almost singularly been attributed erroneously to Fritz Perls. However, not all Gestalt therapy is Perlsian (Dubin, 1976; Dolliver, 1981). Gestalt therapy has been strongly influenced by others [e.g., Laura Perls (1976), Isadore Fromm, Paul Weisy, Paul Goodman (1951), Erv and Miriam Polster (1976), James Simkin (1974), and Joseph Zinker (1977)] and it is with these others in mind that a very brief explanation of Gestalt's historical roots and influence will be explored.

Gestalt therapy is tied to the Gestalt psychology at the Berlin School of Wertheimer, Kohler, Kohler, and Koffka in that both are forms of phenomenological field theory. The chief characteristic is the total immediate experience, here and now, with introspection usually seen as a source of bias. Experience, in this schema, must be differentiated from assumptions and inferences. Awareness is used to gain basic insight into the basic situation of the field. Intellectualization and rationalization are seen primarily as defenses and resistances which must be observed and explored by the therapist.

Early experimentation in Gestalt psychology indicated there was an inherent tendency of the organism to organize perceptions in an orderly principle and a completed organized configuration was labeled as a complete gestalt. Incomplete gestalts were discovered to persist troublesomely in an individual's memory and later came to be designated as unfinished business. It was postulated that these incompleted gestalts must be re-experienced and completed lest they remain figure and distort present experiences thus interfering with the process of assimilation which is required before a completed experience can become ground.

Change only occurs through heightened experience and anxiety is frequently seen as a signal of the source of discomfort which must be experienced and completed. Neurosis occurs because of impasses which contribute to fixation and distortion of present experiences. Individuals stuck at an impasse remain unaware and doubt their own ability which further stops the spontaneous flow of awareness. Interference with awareness results in a constricted I-boundary which in turn interferes with either a lack of separateness or excessive dependence on the environment. The goal of therapy is frequently to expand I-boundaries and to heighten the fluidity of awareness so that figures succeed one another freely allowing the individual full contact with the environment. I-boundaries are expanded primarily through contact.

The experiment is the key to Gestalt therapy and the attempt is to "work through" the impasse. Since thinking is viewed as a primary defense against assimilation, Gestalt frequently draws on action methods to heighten awareness and increase contact. Fritz Perls expanded on Wilhelm Riech's theory of body armor and character structure, consequently providing Gestalt theorists a rationale for bypassing cognitive defenses through the emphasis on somatic defenses and restrictions. Moreno's psychodramatic techniques served as a prototype for developing action methods like two-chair dialogue, enactment, and directed fantasy which facilitated the increase of awareness necessary for contact thus expanding I-boundaries allowing impasses to be worked through more readily. It must be remembered that the premise of Gestalt therapy is that human nature is organized into patterns and wholes. However, as Friedlander (1976) and Kelly (1955) have demonstrated, every concept implies an opposite; our minds and senses constantly react to dualities in our environment. Gestalt therapy parallels a Hegelian philosophy of thesis, antithesis, and synthesis in its treatment philosophy.

Thus, in summary, Gestalt therapy, like no other therapy before it, outlines and articulates a theory of optimal human functioning. In one sense, it is a belief system which describes how the individual can live fully and free one moment to the next, autonomous and independent.

Gestalt theory and Fritz Perls' influence is also evident in Redecision Therapy. Bob Goulding, half of the team that originated this theoretical approach, spent a great deal of time working with Fritz Perls. The Gouldings have in fact incorporated Gestalt theory (or at least Gestalt techniques) in their Redecision Model. The Gouldings also stress responsibility, freedom, choice and the present. Unlike the pure Gestaltists, they have a strong cognitive component to their therapy. This, the Gouldings inherited from Bob's relationship with Eric Berne. Berne worked to develop a behavioral theory that would help explain the nature of man. Berne was a scientist and he was interested in understanding, predicting, and controlling both behavior and feelings. His approach was primarily cognitive rather than purely psychoanalytical. However, he too was strongly influenced and trained in Freudian psychology. Some claim that his ego states (Parent, Adult, Child) are just a substitute for Freud's Ego, Id, and Superego. However, Transactional Analysis is far more than ego states. It has developed into a sophisticated theory that focuses far more on decision and change than any other theory before it.

Trainees soon learn that the Gouldings are tenacious in their commitment to bring about change. They insist on working in short, 20-minute segments and are convinced people can change in one session. They are radical existentialists in the sense that they insist trainees recognize that they, as well as their perspective clients, are completely responsible for how they think, behave, act and feel. Consequently, each must then learn that they also have the power to bring about change in their life.

The Gouldings operate out of a simple, but effective, model which generally follows three principles of intervention: 1. contract work; 2. impasse clarification work; and 3. redecision work. However, there is much more going on in the Gouldings' therapy approach and the interested reader should examine John McNeel's (1977) excellent analysis of the seven components of Redecision Therapy for a succinct description of a Gouldings' workshop.

When we feel bad, the Gouldings insist we are frequently doing one of three things; we are either in another place, another time, or somewhere else in a fantasy stuck in our "game." The game and fantasy for the Gouldings is tantamount, for without them it is not possible for "rackets" and bad feelings to persist. These racket feelings can frequently be traced to early decisions and it is here that the Gouldings make their most important and unique theoretical contribution. In Transactional Analysis theory, decisions, even forgotten ones, no matter how strongly encouraged by early parental programming, or how necessary for survival through childhood, are ultimately self-determined and to some extent reversible. Each of us, according to this schema, have made necessary early decisions as children in order to survive in the world as we then experienced it. However, while these early decisions served survival purposes at the time they were made, they now remain out of our awareness at a preconscious level and frequently contribute to the present problems we are now experiencing. Hence, erroneous decisions made with inadequate information at a primitive level must be brought into awareness, discarded if necessary and redecisions based on reality and factual data made to replace faulty ones.

The Gouldings' genius is in the pragmatic effectiveness of their model to bring about redecision and changes. The now classical Libermann, Miles and Yalom (1973) treatment effectiveness outcome study clearly illustrates that Bob Goulding was the most effective of all the therapists evaluated in the research project. His effectiveness in part was determined by two factors. First, in the language of Yalom et al., he was identified as a moderate affective stimulator which translates into the statement that he aroused his group members but did not blow them away with his confrontations. Secondly, through his combinative use of cognition (T.A.) and catharsis (Gestalt) he was able to bring together two crucial components for effective change. Insight has been shown not to be enough for behavioral change. Unless there is emotional arousal accompanying this insight, change was usually not experienced. With this as an all too simple foundation for describing Gestalt and Redecision theory, I will now look at the theoretical approaches of the Gouldings and the Polsters.

THEORETICAL DIFFERENCES

It is important for me to note an important contributing factor when I discuss the theoretical differences between the two approaches. Bob Goulding had once pointed out to me that the way Fritz Perls did therapy was far different from the way Fritz wrote about doing therapy. I think this is also true for both the Gouldings (1979) and the Polsters (1973). They both have excellent books which intricately describe what they do in therapy. Both books offer a rich source of practical and theoretical orientation to their respective theoretical approaches. I will not attempt to wade into their territorial waters and try to explain what I think they are attempting to say. Rather, I am going to share my experiences and my interpretations of what I saw them doing in therapy during my all too brief one month training seminars with each of them. I stress a cautionary note indicating that my own perceptual bias is probably coloring what I selectively saw them do at La Jolla and Mount Madonna.

SIMILARITIES OF GESTALT AND REDECISION

Both share two important aspects of group therapy that is usually not emphasized by their training programs, but occurs often subtly and unnoticed. These two factors are: 1. interpersonal learning and 2. group cohesiveness. Both of these curative factors are of such importance that a group cannot function therapeutically without their existence (see Yalom 1974, p. 4). I suspect this is achieved so readily because of the nature of the "patients" and the environmental settings of both programs. Most of their "patients" arrived enthusiastically wanting to move into new stages of intensity and dialogue. They inspire a mutuality among their colleagues which enliven and add spirit to a previously dry professional formula. It is advantageous to be away from one's working world and this insures minimal distraction and a high level of fascination with colleagues in training and with the program itself. As Miriam Polster says (1974), "it is the only game in town and it infects trainees with a zest to learn all they can while they're there."

The Gouldings and Polsters also share an enthusiasm for the good natured kidding of ourselves and our neurotic struggles. Their workshops are spiced with humor. "Laughter doesn't obscure a point," the Polsters write, "often it makes it even clearer and lubricates what might otherwise be a lugubrious passage. This is as true of therapy itself as it is of teaching" (Polsters, 1974).

Therapeutic experiences at these programs are usually profound. There is an element of immediacy present in both of these programs that might not exist if they were not time limited. There is an increased feeling of intensity created by the fact that each "patient" is being viewed by his peers. I suspect this is what Yalom is referring to when he writes about the importance of interpersonal learning that takes place within an interactional group setting. Bob Goulding has often said that he believes a good therapist usually is a good patient. By this I think he meant that good therapists have the capacity to explore their feelings and the limits of their situations in life more readily. They are as creative when examining themselves as they are when examining others. When the chemistry is right (and it frequently is), other group members taking a risk and plunging into themselves can be excitingly moving. When this is coupled with an authenticity of looking at forbidden parts of yourself, the results are often inspiring. These, I believe, are clear examples of what Yalom (1974) often refers to when he describes instillation of hope, universality, imitative behavior, and existential factors as curative factors in group therapy.

Usually the process at these two training programs is somewhat familiar for all students. The issue of safety has to be addressed first in group and dealt with for all members. This involves trust in both the group leaders and the other group members. Once this is obtained, cohesion begins to develop. Most trainees or "patients" then begin to drag skeletons out of their closets and look at issues which have been long buried. These buried issues are usually old issues not completely resolved. The amount of resolution is in direct proportion to authentic affect which emerges with the topic. During the second and third week there is a usual regression to a more primitive and less controlled state. Emotions are laid bare and there is an acute tenderness that is generalizable to all interactions. Feelings, both good and bad, are bubbling upon the surface. Re-enactments of forgotten themes in the students' lives are frequent. If the atmosphere is right, and if the group is safe and supportive, there is a comradeship which develops that is exceedingly touching. The students are usually gradually aware of this regression and are almost always able to laugh at themselves as they discover that they still carry these unresolved scares. It is heartening to know that the pain is usually a little less intense and the drama of their lives becomes a little more significant to them. Usually by the last week they are able to put their lives back in order as they venture to face the real world again. Their cognitive controls and defenses are back in order. But they are a little more integrated and a little more free from their past demons. We all realize at this point that some pains and disappointments in life are never completely resolved. We do learn to accept them. More than anything else, we learn to get back in touch with the feeling of what it is like to be on the other side of the therapeutic enterprise. This allows us to be more able to appreciate the client's struggle as they come to grips with their own fears and pain in life. It is a development of empathy that is very crucial to good therapy.

LANGUAGE AS IT APPLIES
TO GESTALT AND REDECISION

The Gouldings have a much stronger focus on language than do the Polsters. This would be understandable considering Berne's cognitive influence upon the Goudings' model. The Polsters, in contrast, have their roots in Gestalt Theory which generally avoids intellectualization. Like Bandler and Grindler (1976), the Gouldings recognize that language serves as a surface structure of the individual's perceived reality. In contrast, the Polsters recognize that language is important, but they are of the opinion that it is often overdone by what Erv refers to as the technicians who describe themselves as Gestalt purists. Erv criticizes this application because he points out that the dogmatic application of key words like "should," "can't," "try" and "need" often interfere with the therapeutic process. In fact, this did happen to me on one occasion when I was involved as "patient" in a therapy process with one of the trainees. During the session I had gotten in touch with some strong and painful feelings I had experienced as a child. I expressed this to the therapist stating very emotionally that, "it hurts." When the therapist, in a pure technical sense, asked me what "it" meant, I immediately corrected myself and responded in a more proper linguistic and responsible mode stating that, "I hurt." However, the therapist's question interrupted my emotional process and I was jarred into my cognitive state by the inquiry.

I believe that this example illustrates Erv's point about the overemphasis on language. The Polsters emphasize the affective component of the message rather than the content. However, I still agree with the Gouldings' stance on focusing on language, the hidden messages, and the "cons" given in dialogue. After my training experience with the Polsters, I have shifted away from the insistence that language always be properly monitored in therapy. However, I believe the Gouldings with their approach are more likely to avoid what they refer to as "victim roles" being played out in therapy by their "patients."

Erv has stated that he realizes that he is sometimes manipulated by the client. This is a risk he is willing to take because he approaches the client in what he calls an "expansive state." Expansive in the sense of allowing the client the opportunity to experience and become aware of some facet of himself/herself that otherwise might be closed off or lost if Erv chose to focus on the possibility of being manipulated.

I strongly agree with the Gouldings' stance that words like "try," "can't" and "need" result in continual debasement of personal power and lack of recognition of responsibility for one's life. The Gouldings' model addresses these issues much more actively. However, the Gouldings' stance about language bears further examination. Dealing with language alone, as the Gouldings know, does not necessarily result in powerful changes of will and power. A great deal of what occurs in therapy may be compliance and may just be surface structural rearrangements which do not affect deeper issues. The Gouldings are quite aware of this problem and stress constantly that their trainees not be conned by an adaptive child response. Redecisions must be made in a free child ego state.

Yalom (1980) illustrates this point succinctly in his most recent book. Drawing on Faber's (1966) distinction between two different types of will, Yalom criticizes current psychological thought because it places an exaggerated emphasis on conscious will and has failed to fashion a succinct, workable definition of will which adds to the confusion of what will is exactly.

Faber's first realm of the will (and it is here that Yalom feels that Faber has made his most important contribution) is not experienced consciously during an act and must be inferred after an event. Yalom and Faber are suggesting that important choices are not consciously experienced as choices. Most of us are not able to predict the consequences of our choices that we do consciously make and how these choices will bind us to some destiny in our lives. There is, however, a second realm of will that is a conscious component and is experienced during an event. "I do this to get that," if I stop eating I will lose weight, etc. Yalom suggests these two realms of will must be approached differently in therapy. Yalom writes,

> The second realm (conscious) of will is approached through exhortation and appeals to willpower, effort, and determination. The first realm is impervious to these enjoiners and must be approached obliquely. A serious problem occurs when one applies exhortative second realm techniques to first realm activities. For example, I can will knowledge, but not wisdom; going to bed, but not sleeping; eating, but not hunger; meekness, but not humility.

However, I believe Yalom is overlooking a very crucial issue that William James and the pragmatists proposed years ago. James argued that there was no objective truth in the world. Truth, for James, was determined by utility. Truth is what works! James proposed that an individual act himself into a new way of thinking rather than think himself into a new way of acting. Act as you want to believe and you will soon believe how you act. James' influence on Alcoholics Anonymous is well-documented and his pragmatism is the very reason this program enjoys the success it does. A.A. members are told to change their behavior first and that their thinking will follow. Similarly, this is the same principle which operates within the Gouldings' insistence on producing behavioral change. Confucius, in fact, proposed this axiom over two thousand years ago. "I hear and I forget, I see and I remember, I do and I understand."

PHYSICAL CONTACT IN GROUP

The Gouldings are very insistent that no one reinforce a person's pathology in group. This, they frequently point out, occurs when physical contact is made inappropriately. One sure way to reinforce pathology, according to the Gouldings, is to rescue clients by holding, embracing, or stroking them when they are feeling bad, weak or being manipulative. I generally agree that the pendulum concerning touching has swung to the other extreme with the growth of interest in the "touch-feely" group therapy movement that Gestalt therapy usually signifies. The reduction of the taboos against physical contact in therapy was a welcome relief from the stuffy, inhuman atmosphere surrounding ideas of therapy which were prominent before the 1960s. However, the motives and hidden agenda and frequently the "needs" being met are not those of the recipient but those of the therapist or of the group member who does the giving.

A case in point to illustrate this point may be beneficial here. Once, when I was in therapy as an undergraduate and seeing a counselor associated with the university, I had a particularly emotional session concerning my relationship to my deceased mother. I began uncharacteristically sobbing during the session. Before I was able to get more than two good sobs out, the female therapist had jerked me to her bosom with such rapid eagerness that I was shocked out of my feeling state when I found my face buried in her breasts and my sobs suffocated in her motherly like clutches. I was so surprised that she had grabbed me so rapidly that I remembered thinking at the time that she must have leaped over the desk to get where I was sitting.

The Gouldings believe in the importance of allowing persons some time to finish their feelings and not to interrupt the grieving process. They believe that a person may be held if and only when they ask for that type of support and physical contact and touching does not reinforce pathology. Again, this places the power within the individual's own control. I never saw this rule violated at the

Gouldings' because they were so insistent on its recognition. I do believe, as the Gouldings do, that a therapist is able to give support without physically holding a person during an emotionally impacted moment. I also believe that much of the physical contact is less than therapeutic because it involves therapists operating out of their own needs rather than the clients' and this interferes with a healthy, autonomous grieving process.

Erv at times would engage in a type of physical contact which would avoid most of these pitfalls. Erv had a strong dislike for following pat formulas for doing therapy. He felt it took away from the therapist's creativity and helped deaden the excitement in the engagement between two people. This excitement depended on the aliveness and authenticity of contact for its essence and if this was missing, therapy would lack in its effectiveness. Erv would ever so gently place a finger on a person's knee or hand to let them know that he was there and that they were not alone during an emotionally trying moment. He would then embrace only if they asked for physical contact.

PERSONAL CHARACTERISTICS OF THE THERAPIST

In writing about his experiences in therapy with Fritz Perls and Erv Polster, Joseph Zinker (1976) reports he learned from Erv to be aware of the ocean inside of himself, while Fritz switched on his lightning. In this sense, I, too, experienced Erv as an expander. He was like an ocean in that Erv helped me expand my awareness and my experiences. Much like the noted novelist, Jerzey Kozinski (1978), Erv was intent on all the trainees heightening their awareness of the drama in their own personal existence. Much like Erv, Jerzey Kozinski warns about the tendency that we all have to deaden our experience in life. Kozinski says we all have to be aware of our own personal drama as well as the personal drama in others' lives or we are short-changing ourselves and not being true to our existence. We all are playing out our own intense personal drama with the rest of society as a background. Erv was very intent on helping us recognize this fact. Erv's favorite phrase during my month-long workshop was, "now, that is interesting!", with a heavy emphasis on the word "interesting."

Bob, in contrast, was a focuser. He wanted to simplify things and get at the heart of the matter and cut away the bullshit. I suspect Bob has been heavily influenced by his special relationship with Fritz and it is this ability to cut through bullshit like a laser beam, as Zinker describes Perls, that Bob proved most effective. Somehow through this process and my work with Bob I got in touch with my strength and power as a human being. With Erv, I got in touch with my sensitivity as a person.

My personal relationship with both men was similar in many ways but strikingly different in other aspects. Bob was an especially engaging individual. One thing which became clear at Mount Madonna was that Bob genuinely enjoyed people and was a warm, giving individual. He actually did more to establish rapport and a relationship with an individual outside of group than many therapists, I have experienced, have been able to do within a group. Erv, in contrast, tended to be more reserved outside of the therapy session. However, this reservedness always included a boyish shyness that was generally authentic and charming. Yet, there was this inscrutable quality about Erv which kept bringing to mind his uncanny likeness to a Zen master. Both men were enjoyable and engaging. Bob possessed a boisterous and provocative presence, while Erv gave the impression of an all-knowing Buddha.

Erv once commented that his first meeting with Isadora Fromm left him with the feeling that he had been really looked at for the first time in his life. This too was my frequent experience with Erv as I was often enthralled by his piercing yet gentle and inviting gaze. Erv's eyes had a way of sparkling and laughing while he interacted with others. I frequently felt as if I could hide nothing from this man and that he possessed the ability to go wherever I would need to go in order to explore the inner depths of my psyche.

Both of these men had that important quality I'll refer to as charisma. As Jerome Frank (1962) points out, the personal attitude of the healer is often one of the most important qualities which the therapist can have in his repertoire. Likewise, Bergin (1971) among others has presented convincing research evidence which shows that the personal characteristics of the therapist are the most important contributing factors to treatment effectiveness. Frank's thesis of psychotherapy actually being a subtle form of persuasion takes on added significance when looking at the relationship of the personal magnetism of the therapist to the values change in therapy. Beutler (1979) provides evidence for sufficient reason to believe that patients' values, attitudes, and beliefs change in psychotherapy and that to some degree, these changes are associated with the degree to which therapy is successful. However, these values change in a systematic fashion and the successful patient usually takes on the values of his therapist.

Frank (1978) has identified two sources which invoke the patient's expectancy of help. One is the personal magnetism of the healer which is often strengthened by his own belief in what he does. This was clearly evident with both the Gouldings and Polsters. All are exciting people and enthusiastic about their modus operandi and truly believe that they can be of help to anyone. They all are also very charismatic individuals and there is an abundance of clinical evidence that . . . confirms the hypothesis that part of the healing power of all forms of psychotherapy lies in the therapist's ability to mobilize the patient's hope for relief (Frank, 1978). Consequently, part of the success of the Gouldings and Polsters may be attributed to their ability to mobilize the patient's expectation of help. As Frank suggests, the therapist's power is based on the patient's perception of him as a source of help and it tends to increase the greater the patient's distress. This, I believe, is especially important in describing the Gouldings' and Polsters' approaches to psychotherapy. Frank (1962) points out that:

> Another source of the patient's faith is the ideology of the healer or sect, which offers the patient a rationale, however absurd, for making sense of his illness and the treatment procedure, and places the healer in the position of the transmitter or controller of impressive healing forces. In this he is analogous to the shaman. The healer may pose as a scientist who has discovered new and potent scientific principles of healing, thus surrounding himself with the aura that anything labeled scientific inspires in members of members of modern Western societies.

An example may help clarify this point. While being supervised by Mary Goulding, while I was therapist with one of the other trainees at Mount Madonna, I made an intervention and an interpretation concerning a dynamic or game I thought my trainee "patient" was involved in. This was quickly denied and discounted by the trainee as not fitting for him. However, when Mary agreed it did fit for him, he quickly changed his resistant stance and the therapeutic work consequently had a profound effect on him during the rest of the month of training at Mount Madonna.

PEAK EXPERIENCES

The entire aspect of the similarity between religion and psychotherapy was brought home to me very succinctly by the experiences
I had at these two group psychotherapy workshops. It was evident
afterward that there were some striking parallels between their approaches to therapy and certain religious phenomena. I, as many
others who attended the workshop, left feeling very happy and even
spiritually high. What we all shared could be classified as a quasi-
religious experience (i.e., the Gouldings and Polsters had many of
the characteristics commonly attributed to gurus; charismatic, powerful, positive, etc.).

In reflecting back on these group experiences, I realize that an
important part of the Gouldings' and Polsters' effectiveness was in
fact determined by their own belief in their modus operandi. Research has in fact shown that this is frequently the case. Those therapists who are most involved and committed to their particular
mode of treatment apparently instill their own enthusiasm in the
treatment process and frequently infect their patients with this quality. Consequently, accepting and believing in the Gouldings' and
Polsters' respective approaches required taking some of their assumptions on faith and for those that did their mode of therapy was
quite effective.

Both Transactional Analysis and Gestalt theory are sometimes
criticized as being overly simplistic explanations of personality and
do not share the sophistication that say Kelly's Personal Construct
Theory or Freudian Psychology share in describing the intricacies of
the dynamics of personality. It occurred to me that TA, Gestalt, and
even Alcoholics Anonymous may be effective modes of treatment
precisely because of their simplicity and the emotional involvement
of the practitioner. I am not implying that all therapy can be explained by the placebo effect but I am sure that it is an important
part of the treatment process.

For instance, Wallace (1978) recognizes that one value of A.A.
as a treatment modality is that it places the alcoholic's behavior
within an alcoholism paradigm and places the alcoholic's experience within some cognitive structure. Helping the alcoholic achieve
a self-attribution of alcoholic and hence an explanatory system for
his/her behavior is a central role of the therapist. Frank (1962) for
one sees this cognitive component as a very vital part of therapy.

First, they provide a cognitive structure that enables the patient to name his symptoms and fit them into a casual scheme. Since major sources of anxiety are ambiguity and fear of the unknown, this, in itself, can powerfully reduce the patient's anxiety and enhance his self-confidence.

Yalom (1976) agrees when he stresses that both catharsis and insight are very necessary components of change. If you do not obtain both, Yalom doubts whether any significant change can occur.

In truth, psychotherapy with the patient at this point is very much the teaching of what Wallace describes as an "exotic belief," whose true value of actually describing what has occurred because of the alcoholism is held irrelevant. Its true value is determined by its efficacy and the fact that it enables the patient to 1. explain his/her past behavior in a way that gives hope for the future; 2. cope with his guilt, anxiety, remorse and confusion; 3. and provides them with specific behavior (in the case of an alcoholic, staying sober) that will change their life in a desired direction. Wallace has maintained the recovering alcoholic has a lifetime of sobriety in which to gradually recognize the fact that not all of their behavior can be attributed to alcoholism. The sober member of A.A. needs their ideological base and belief because it works by reducing anxiety and confusion. I am suggesting that the theoretical models of the Gouldings and Polsters serve a similar function as A.A. does for the alcoholic.

Yalom (1974) and others address this issue extensively. Each of us hold constructs that are important for our survival. In other words, our defenses are there for a good reason and a sensitive therapist should not rip these away too rapidly. Yalom wrote about the issue of responsibility being salient to honesty. Honesty for honesty's sake is an overly rigid posture that does not guarantee therapeutic gains. "Vital lies," as Yalom describes them, are sometimes essential for survival and it is the prudent therapist who knows when to remove and build up defenses. There is a similar tradition in classical Buddhist doctrine which suggests that "useful illusions" serve similar purposes for the disciple in religious training as it does for the patient in therapy. Each needs hope and the promise that there is an answer. While searching for enlightenment, the Buddhist student will learn when he is ready, that the search was futile since he possessed the answer from the start. As T.S. Eliot wrote:

We shall not cease from exploration and the end of all our exploring will be to arrive where we started and know the place for the first time.

I contend this theme of searching and finding ourselves is parallel to Hesse's story of Siddartha and complements Freud's description of therapy. Freud once described the goal of therapy as transforming neurotic misery into ordinary human suffering or as Strupp puts it: "Therapy terminates when the patient accepts the fact that he is as unhappy as the rest of us." Erv expressed similar sentiments at La Jolla when he said, "We must learn to suffer without too much pain."

The question raised here is one of timing. I believe it is the therapist of the Gouldings' and Polsters' caliber who knows when to encourage, confront, and influence. I don't believe the avoidance of these issues is possible. Frank (1962) agrees that "psychotherapists must be aware of their influence on patients. This cannot be helped. The only question is whether the therapist uses his/her influence consciously or unconsciously." As Modell (1962) says,

It would be well to remember that in all therapy, trouble is apt to follow the ignorant application of important forces.

For example, while working as a "patient" with one of the trainees at La Jolla, I decided to let down my defenses and share some very painful childhood experiences because I trusted the trainee who was the assigned therapist in group that day. However, this trainee's reaction to my strong affect was one of congratulating himself for having provoked me into getting in touch with some very powerful and painful feelings. Never, did he recognize or acknowledge the sense of personal responsibility in me — the patient. I felt raped!

Many years ago Buber wrote, (1964):

Help without mutuality is presumptuousness; it is an attempt to practice magic. The psychotherapist who tries to dominate his patient stifles the growth of his blessing. As soon as the helper is touched by the desire, in however subtle a form to dominate or to enjoy his patient other than a wrong condition needing to be cured, the danger of falsification arises, besides which all quackery appears peripheral.

My experience in this case resulted in my taking a very guarded stance with this trainee throughout the rest of the workshop. I was important to this individual only as a reflection on his ability to practice therapy. I felt he had got me once and that he wouldn't get me again.

Not only is this an illustration of trust in another being manipulated but it demonstrates a violation of one of the canons of existential philosophy. Martin Buber (as well as the Gouldings and Polsters) support the goal for existential therapy of making the patient more aware of his/her own potential for choice and growth because it parallels his early teachings of Hasidism concerning the uniqueness and potentiality which each individual possesses and is responsible to fulfill. The existential psychotherapist's insistence that the patient take an active part in the healing process, thus avoiding making that patient a passive recipient who has something done to him, illustrates an intricate part of the Gouldings' and Polsters' training philosophy.

RESISTANCE IN THERAPY

Both the Polsters and Gouldings have interesting and contrasting ways of looking at resistance in therapy. Bob Goulding views therapy as a chess match and sees the patient as having two warring parts: One that wants to change and the other that wants to defeat the therapist. The therapist's job, according to Bob, is to watch for that first con — the con which indicates that the patient is resistant to change. The Polsters on the other hand feel that defenses are there for a reason. They are not to be discarded too quickly. Rather, they are to be explored for they are rich in therapeutic issues. The exploration of the feelings associated with resistance is the substance of therapy. Erv is fond of saying, "what is, is" and "one thing follows another." This emphasizes his almost Zen-like stance in therapy. His position is one of allowing things to happen and to watch the flow. In either case both the Gouldings and the Polsters are dealing with an important therapeutic issue. The Gouldings blast away, or more often, side-step the resistance in an effort to get past the first con in order to push therapeutic change. The Polsters are more apt to mesmerize the individual with a martial arts-like stance of utilizing the individual's own energies and power to their own advantage. In either case, both are tremendously successful.

There is at least some research evidence which sheds light on this issue. Beutler (1980) has presented some preliminary findings which indicates that those therapists who perceive more dysphoria in patients are more effective in achieving successful treatment outcome. Further, those therapists who perceived the patient as more resistant where also more successful in treatment than those therapists who identified resistance less. Both of these factors have important implications for training and treatment. It may be that those therapists who are more successful in therapy are more sensitive to resistance and the hiding of dysphoria. The Gouldings describe resistance as the first con and insist that the therapist be aware of it. Likewise, many patients try to con their therapist by hiding their dysphoria. I'm confident that the Polsters would be as sensitive to resistance and dysphoria as the Gouldings. The Polsters would more likely deal with the resistance and dysphoria in an exploratory manner.

While the Gouldings and Polsters work out of two distinctly different models, I saw more similarity in their therapy than I saw differences. Research (Frank, 1974) in this area indicates that the type of relationship offered by therapists seems to be determined more by levels of experience than by their theories. One experimental study found that therapists of different schools agreed highly as to the nature of the therapeutic relationship and that experienced practitioners of different schools agree more highly than did junior or senior members of the same persuasion. Further, studies of taped interviews showed that experienced experts of different schools created relationships more similar to each other than novices of the same school. Apparently experience in actual practice overcomes doctrinal differences.

As I suggested earlier, the differences between the Gouldings and Polsters may be greater in theory than in actual clinical application. It is not so much what each does as it is how they do it. All four were able to make interventions work because of their timing and their personalities. For instance, within the mystical Jewish tradition of the Hasidism, the religious leader (Zaddik) was not an impersonal vessel or medium through which great powers operated; nor was he the great scholar and seat of religious reason. Buber (1936), Kopp (1972), Rogers (1972). Rather, as the Zaddik, he first of all would be a person in his own right, one who helped those who trusted him and who was able to help only because they trusted him.

The relationship between the Zaddik and his disciple was the crucial factor in this attempt to give spiritual help, just as the relationship between therapist and patient is crucial. The personality of the teacher takes the place of doctrine. He or she is the teacher. As one student of the Zaddik said: "I did not go to my Zaddik to learn Torah from him, but to watch him tie his bootlaces." Likewise, I learned much from watching the way the Gouldings and Polsters dealt with their own anger, sadness, confusion, and fear in therapy.

I do not want to end this chapter with the impression that Gouldings and Polsters are religious zealots out to convert trainees. Bob, Erv, Miriam, and Mary are all excellent professionals with a deep sense of integrity and commitment to help their respective clients. There is an important point to this chapter I do not want to go unnoticed. Frank (1962) has demonstrated that if there is an absence of trust of confidence in the therapist, little can be accomplished. Complimenting this, Hans Strupp (1981) suggests that the effectiveness of psychotherapy does not depend upon particular kinds of interventions, but rather upon the quality of the therapeutic relationship and the timing of the intervention. This suggests that the distinct humanistic qualities which the Gouldings and Polsters possess enhance their relationships with their participants and their technical skill and experience enhance the timing of their intervention. This is what the Gouldings and Polsters teach so well. Each trainee has the unique opportunity to learn that the marriage of humanism and technology can be a rewarding one.

REFERENCES

Bandler, A. & Grindler, S. (1966). *The structure of magic*. New York: Basic Books.
Bergin, A. B. (1971). The evaluation of therapeutic outcomes. In A. E. Bergin & S. L. Garfield (Eds.), *Handbook of psychotherapy and behavior change: An empirical analysis*. New York: Wiley Press.
Beutler, L. (1979). Values, beliefs, religion, and persuasive influences of psychotherapy. *Psychotherapy, Theory, Research and Practice, 16*(4).
Beutler, L. (1980). *Personal communication*. University of Arizona Health Science Center.
Buber, M. (1936). *I and thou*. New York: Charles Scribner & Sons.
Buber, M. (1964). In M. Friedman (Ed.), *The worlds of existentialism*. New York: Random House.
Dolliver, R. (1981). Some limitations in Perls' gestalt therapy. *Psychotherapy, Theory, Research and Practice, 8*(1), 38–45.
Dublin, J. (1976). Gestalt therapy. Existential-gestalt therapy and/versus 'Perlism.' In E. W. L. Smith (Ed.), *The growing edge of Gestalt therapy*. New York: Brunner/Mazel.
Faber, L. (1966). *The ways of will*. New York: Basic Books.
Frank, J. (1962). *Persuasion and healing*. New York: Schriken Books.
Frank, J. (1978). *Psychotherapy and the human predicament*. New York: Schriken Books.

Friedlander, S. (1976). In Gestalt therapy. Erv & Miriam Polster. In B. Wolman (Ed.), *International encyclopedia of neurology, psychiatry, psychoanalysis and psychology*.

Goulding, M. & Goulding, R. L. (1979). *Changing lives through redecision therapy*. New York: Brunner/Mazel.

Haley, J. (1976). *Problem solving therapy*. San Francisco: Jossey-Bass.

James, W. (1907). *Pragmatism*. New York:

Kelley, G. (1955). The psychotherapy of personal constructs. *Clinical diagnosis and psychotherapy* (Vol. 2). New York: W. W. Norton.

Kopp, S. (1972). *If you meet the Buddha on the road, kill him!* New York: Brunner/Mazel.

Kosinski, J. (1977, December). Horatio Algers of the nightmare. *Psychology Today*, 59–64.

Lieberman, M., Miles, & Yalom, I. (1973). *Encounter groups: First facts*. New York: Basic Books.

McNeel, J. (1977). The seven components of redecision therapy. In G. Barnes (Ed.), *After Eric Berne*.

Modell, W. (1955). *The relief of symptoms*. Philadelphia: Saunders.

Perls, F. (1947). *Ego, hunger, and aggression*. New York: Vantage Books.

Perls, F. (1948). Theory and technique of personality integration. *American Journal of Psychotherapy, 2*(4), 565–586.

Perls, F., Hefferline, R., & Goodman, P. (1951). *Gestalt therapy*. New York: Dell Publishing.

Perls, L. (1976). Comments on the new directions. In E. W. L. Smith (Ed.), *The growing edge of Gestalt therapy*. New York: Brunner/Mazel.

Polster, E. (1975). Techniques and experience in Gestalt therapy. In F. D. Stephenson (Ed.), *Gestalt therapy primer*. Springfield, IL: Charles C Thomas.

Polster, E. & Polster, M. (1973). *Gestalt therapy integrated*. New York: Brunner/Mazel.

Polster, E. & Polster, M. (1976). Therapy without resistance: Gestalt therapy. In A. Burton (Ed.), *What makes behavior change possible?* New York: Brunner/Mazel.

Polster, E. & Polster, M. (1974, Fall). Notes on the training of Gestalt therapy. *Voices*.

Reitan, R. & Davison, L. (1974). *Clinical neuropsychology: Current status and applications*. Washington, D.C.: V. H. Winston & Sons.

Rogers, C. (1951). *Client-centered therapy: Its current practice, implications and theory*. Boston: Houghton Mifflin.

Simkin, J. (1974). *Gestalt therapy mini-lectures*. Willbrae, Calif: Celestial Arts.

Strupp, H. (1981). Toward the refinement of time-limited dynamic psychotherapy. In S. Budman (Ed.), *Forms of brief therapy*. New York: Guilford Press.

Wallace, J. (1978). Critical issues of alcoholism recovery. In S. Zimberg, J. Wallace, & S. Blume (Eds.), *Practical approaches to alcoholism psychotherapy*. New York: Plenum Press.

Yalom, I. (1975). *Theory and practice of group psychotherapy*. New York: Basic Books.

Yalom, I. (1981). *Existential psychotherapy*. New York: Basic Books.

Zinker, J. (1976, Spring). My therapy: Memories, learnings, aspirations. *Voices*, 55–60.

Zinker, J. (1977). *Creative process in Gestalt therapy*. New York: Brunner/Mazel.

Chapter 10

Characteristics
of the Leader

There are many contributing variables which influence successful group therapy. Of all the multiple influences occurring within a group setting, none has more of an impact or importance than the intangible qualities of the group leader. Most importantly, the intangible non-specific qualities which influence successful group therapy have more to do with the type of person the therapist is rather than what it is that the therapist does. This is not meant to imply that specific qualities like techniques, training, and experience have nothing to contribute to successful group therapy. To the contrary, all forms of successful psychotherapy, both individual and group, are impossible without it. However, the specific qualities of the therapist are those qualities which can be taught and learned by the dedicated student. The non-specific contributing factors to successful therapy include such important intangibles like caring, sensitivity, and empathy. Is it possible to teach another to be able to tap into a deep source of ultimate concern and authentic respect for another human being if that quality doesn't exist in the individual before he embarks on the vigorous course of training which is required for any competent professional?

Eric Cassell (1985) in his book, *The Healers Art*, has raised this important question and exhorts the physician and the therapist to retain his role as a healer, that is, as someone who views the patient in a holistic sense without regulating disease as an entity which has an independent existence separate from the individual. Cassell stresses the group leader, therapist and physician be aware of the effect which all forms of disease have on the patient in terms of the feeling of disconnectedness, loss of sense of omniscience, and loss of control it produces. These complications are well known to most seasoned and competent group leaders, but, they are often difficult to convey to the therapist in training. In fact, Cassell asks if it is possible to teach sensitivity? He suggests that it be attempted, despite the ever-increasing stress on techniques, theory, and technology.

Today, alcohol and drug treatment is falling prey to the same difficulties which confront all forms of medical care. More and more emphasis is placed on greater technology, large group practices, multi-million dollar corporate hospital chains with revolving treatment personnel, state and federal bureaucratic dominated treatment policies, and multiple specialties; all factors which tend to oppose a close therapist-patient relationship. Cassell like others before him (i.e., Yalom, Polster, Goulding, Ornstien & Kohut) offers an important reminder of the need to restore or re-establish the necessary human connection between the patient and the person or persons providing the care and treatment if the individual is going to fully benefit from these advances in technology.

VALUES OF THE GROUP LEADER

The values of the group leader are an important integral part of his individuality. While it has been well documented that the therapist's values and his characteristics have an important impact on successful treatment, the research in this area has been limited to non-addictive populations. A brief review of this research will be presented later in the chapter even though the material does not pertain exclusively to group therapy with alcoholics or addicts. Much of this information is generalizable to all forms of treatment and should prove to be helpful for the group leader in working with addicted patients. However, the importance of the therapist's characteristics are made more significant to alcohol and drug abuse treatment because of the special circumstances induced by the dual impact of group therapy and the common characteristics of the addicted patient. First, group therapy is a much more active and interaction mode of treatment than individual therapy. Consequently, the personality of the leader plays a much more significant part in successful treatment than it would in individual therapy. Secondly, the addicted patient requires a leader who is more alive, exciting and active. Before venturing to give a plausible explanation why this may be so, a brief example of this author's experience at a national alcoholism conference with Irvin Yalom and Father Martin will help clarify this point.

Towards the end of the conference, after both Yalom and Father Martin had presented equally excellent but totally divergent all day workshops, the participants and presenters were invited to an "informal" get-together one evening. Father Martin came early and shortly after his arrival had quickly attracted a rather large gathering of individuals who sat around him in an "informal" circle, laughing, joking and exchanging stories with the lovable leprechaun-like priest. Many of the participants at the conference were recovering alcoholics and addicts like Father Martin and they were eager to be in the presence of the priest who had become famous because of his charisma, charm and excitement. Father Martin didn't disappoint them, as it was obvious that he sincerely enjoyed their company and loved exchanging small anecdotes about alcoholism, recovery and spirituality. Yalom arrived a couple hours later and quietly circled the reception hall, often unnoticed by many of the conference participants. Eventually Yalom stopped and talked politely to a few individuals who asked him about some of his more obtuse, yet stimulating, comments about existential psychotherapy. Yalom remained kind and courteous in his responses, but it was apparent that the participants were somewhat uncomfortable in his presence and at times, he was a little awkward in his social interaction with many of them. On numerous other occasions, a small gathering of individuals would point towards the direction of "Yalom's presence," speak softly to each other, look as if they wanted to approach, but would drift off or engage each other in conversation giving the appearance that they thought better of the idea. It was apparent that Yalom was somewhat intimidating to them and unaware of this, he did nothing to discourage their discomfort. After a half an hour or so, Yalom turned to leave. However, he stopped very briefly at the gathering in the corner of the room from which loud billows of laughter would sporadically emerge. He stared somewhat inquisitively at the Catholic priest who was entertaining the gathering with his stories and jokes. He hesitated ever so slightly then departed as quietly as he had entered the room. For one brief moment, I caught glimpses of both men and the different personality styles of each were placed in sharp contrast as they stood there in the same proximity. I wondered which man would be most effective in treating alcoholics and addicts. The kind, quiet, polite man with the piercing intellect or the charismatic, charming, lovable elf with the sparkling eyes and contagious wit. Certainly, each had something equally important to offer. Which would a recovering alcoholic or addict respond best to? At least based on this experience, it was apparent that those characteristics which Father Martin possessed were far more inviting to alcoholics than those which Yalom characterized.

   The divergent personal characteristics which Yalom and Father Martin personified represents an important variable in the treatment of the addicted patient. In many cases, those characteristics which Yalom embodied would be preferable to certain types of patients. Certainly, those individuals who have fears of intrusiveness and need a more insightful approach in their treatment would have difficulties with a Father Martin type therapist. It is a well documented fact that certain patients respond more favorably to certain types of therapists. The therapist-patient match is in fact one of the most significantly influential factors in successful treatment and the research on this will be reviewed later in the chapter. However, one therapist cannot be everything to all patients, no matter how skillful and charismatic a person he may be. There are certain characteristics of a therapist that are more likely to evoke a favorable response in either an alcoholic or addict. Because of the nature of the characterological deficits commonly seen in addicted patients, it is suggested that those characteristics embodied by Father Martin are more likely to produce a positive effect than those characteristics embodied by Yalom.
   Because so many addicts and alcoholics suffer from the characterological deficits commonly seen in Narcissistic and Borderline conditions (see Chapter 5), they constantly have to battle feelings of boredom, deadness and emptiness that threaten to overtake them. One cocaine addict aptly described his need to capture some excitement or "rush" in his life because without it he felt dead or empty.

   You know, doc, how your foot feels when it falls asleep after it is kept in the same position too long so that it cuts off your circulation. You stand up suddenly and your foot feels like it's dead. You have to stomp it on the ground and smack it with your fist so you can start to feel it again. Well, this is how cocaine is for me. Without it I feel dead, like I've got no circulation. Cocaine gives me a smack, a stomp, to help me come alive.

Many therapists don't fully appreciate the impact which their personalities or values will have on an addict or alcoholic who is struggling to identify some viable alternative life style which will allow him to fill up the emptiness or deadness within him. The addict and alcoholic is suspicious of others whom he perceives as dead or empty trying to make him adhere to their values. Most of the dominant values shared by middle class professionals (i.e., delay of gratification, control of impulses, rational thought, hard work, responsibility, etc.) are not the same values or characteristics shared by most alcoholics and addicts. While the professional therapist may look upon the use of alcohol and drugs as an escape, the addict or alcoholic views his alcohol or drug use in a far different light. Unlike the professional who frequently hold the position that drugs and alcohol are for those who cannot cope with reality, the addict sees that reality is for those who cannot cope with drugs. In many ways, the addict or alcoholic views many professionals as dull, dead, or timid people who cannot tolerate excitement within themselves because of their meekness and deadness.

Addicts and alcoholics frequently adhere to values and behavior that are frequently foreign to many professionals who do not suffer from such character defects. Impulsiveness, spontaneity, action and excitement are frequently judged by professionals to be forms of "acting out" which have to be curbed or modified in treatment. To the addict and alcoholic this is a compromise they must avoid at all costs because they view this as a trading of one's soul for a condition that is lifeless, boring and dead. Consequently therapists are dealing with patients who frequently see them as dull and unspontaneous individuals who have sold their soul to "make it" in the world.

This situation can be exacerbated by a therapist who adopts a stance of technical neutrality. An unresponsive therapist stirs up unconscious fears of annihilation and nothingness which are associated with primitive identifications. Transference distortions are heightened and the alcoholic or addict is reminded of the dull, deadened and distant parental figure who tried to shape them to fit their expectations. Resistance is consequently heightened as the alcoholic or addict is forced to deal with the therapist in the same manner as they were forced to deal with their unresponsive parental figures. This is why the addict or alcoholic needs a strong exciting self-object to fill him up or stimulate him like drugs or alcohol does. A passive, unexciting therapist will be perceived as just another bad object who is withholding, dull and lifeless. Addicts are searching for an idealized other who is a model or representation of what they wish they could be. If they can be stimulated interpersonally and can come to identify with those positive aspects of an exciting, alive therapist, they will react more positively to treatment. This is especially important during the initial stages of treatment because it will enhance the establishment of a working alliance. An addict needs someone exciting and alive who will serve as a model for him in his own attempt to combat the emptiness and deadness which threatens to overtake him.

Masterson, writing about the borderline patient, expresses similar sentiments about the importance of the personality characteristics of the therapist. Therapist dynamics that Masterson (1981) thinks interfere with effective therapy are: Passivity, compulsivity, submissiveness and dependency. The passive therapist negates the patient's need to have an active real person who can help the individual distinguish between reality and internal distortions. The submissive therapist will fail to confront the patient leading him to feel that the therapist does not care. The compulsive therapist will be more likely to react angrily at the alcoholic's or addict's anger and acting out since Masterson views the therapist's compulsivity as a defense against his own anger and need to control. Since it is rare to find an addict or alcoholic who will readily comply with the demands of treatment, a therapist who is easily angered or frustrated when the patient doesn't do as he wishes will have a difficult time when working with this population. The therapist who is dependent and needs the patient's approval is in danger of repeating part of the patient's developmental problem. The patient needs to achieve his separation, individuation and autonomy in treatment. He must be free from disapproval, even when he doesn't comply exactly to the pre-established expectations of the therapist. All of these described therapist characteristics will also interfere with the therapist serving as an appropriate role model (external object) which the patient can internalize.

THE THERAPIST AS A PERSON

Erv Polster, Irvin Yalom, Carl Whitaker and numerous other theorists have written extensively about the importance of the therapist as a person in effecting successful change in therapy. Yalom suggests the therapist's personal characteristics are why some interpretations click and why others don't. Change is produced by those interpretations which are made when the relationship is just right. If the patient feels he is controlled, approached in a superior manner, or treated as an object by the therapist, he will not benefit from the interpretation. Any interpretation, even the most eloquent, has little benefit if the patient doesn't hear it. Genuineness, concern, acceptance and empathy take precedence over all technical considerations because it's the relationship which serves as fertile ground for the techniques to take root.

Erv and Miriam Polster feel that the personhood of the therapist is one of the key elements which helps facilitate change in psychotherapy. Most excellent therapists are exciting people. They have access to a wide range of human emotions. They can be tender or tough, serious or funny, courageous, or respectfully cautious. If their patients spend enough time with such people, the Polsters feel it will frequently rub off. Their patients will experience someone who knows how to accept, arouse, tolerate and frustrate. They will eventually learn a respect for what it is like to be a human being who can meet surprise and adventure without hiding characteristics of themselves when they appear.

Carl Whitaker differentiates between three different types of therapists. He identifies each of the types as the Non-Therapist, the Social Therapist and the Professional Depth Therapist. Each serves a very different function in therapy. Whitaker describes their different roles in detail when he writes about their differences.

1. The Non-Therapist

Included in this group would be the professional administrator and the psychiatrist whose relationship to patients is a business one. The nontherapeutic psychiatrist seldom reacts to the child in his patients; he does not really accept them in terms of their potential capacity. His artificial role-playing contributes little to the patient's growth, though it may make significant contributions to their current adjustment. He denies his own patient needs, does not identify with patients in any but the most superficial sense, and has never had any adequate therapy himself. The non-therapist has access to his own fantasy life, but is unable to make that part of his life available to other people. One of the most conspicuous examples in this category is the psychiatrist who has had an incomplete psychotherapeutic experience, and is thereby categorically determined to keep himself from any entangling alliances. (Whitaker, 1953, pp. 135–136)

2. The Social Therapist

In contrast, the Social Therapist forces growth in persons around him. He accepts his own patient needs and his fantasy life. He thereby can identify with patients and their needs and can go with the patient into the symbolic experience of a therapeutic relationship. In the course of this, he accepts their projections upon him, reacts positively to the child in the other person, and carries the person into "therapy," although in ordinary circumstances, not through the *core* phase of therapy. Because he has satisfied his own patient needs, he knows his own limitations and will frequently refer patients who need deeper therapy to a professional therapist. (Whitaker, 1953, p. 136)

3. The Professional Therapist

Like the social therapist, the Professional Depth Therapist has been a patient, and has resolved the major portion of his infantile transference needs. He can identify with his patients in the specific sense of seeing the patient as his child self while he is critically aware of his limitations in the therapeutic sense. As a professional, he learns to separate his therapeutic function from his real life. His motivations have to do with his own efforts at reconstructing his body image, and he thereby accepts the therapist-vector in the patient as a specific dynamic in the therapeutic process. He can take patients through the therapeutic experience, help them constructively with the symbolic relationship and also with their relationship to him as a person. By virtue of his personal motivations in the therapeutic relationship, he goes to sufficient depth with each patient to gain from the therapeutic potential of the patient. In thus being patient to his patient, he strengthens the patient's capacity to become a separate, growing person. (Whitaker, 1953, p. 136)

QUALITIES OF A GROUP LEADER

Martin Grotjohn (1983) has described certain qualities of the group leader which he feels are essential to effective group treatment. The group leader is of central importance in group therapy because group therapy, more than individual therapy, is based on the dynamics of interaction. Grotjohn lists six important qualities of the group leader.

1. Reliability
2. Spontaneity and Responsiveness
3. Trust
4. Firm Identity
5. Humor
6. Fallibility

Reliability. The group leader must be reliable. Group members require a consistent parental figure whose behavior is predictable and understandable. Groups must start and end on time. Group members must learn that the leader will not support them for some behavior one moment and then attack that very same behavior on another moment. Only then will he invite trust and confidence from the group members. This first requires the leader have trust and confidence in himself. This can only be accomplished if the therapist has experienced life in the fullest. He must know fear, anxiety, courage and dependence. He must not be afraid to love and he does not need to be a stranger to anger. The group leader must possess the capacity for what Karl Jaspers calls "unlimited communication" or be what Erv Polster calls "a connoisseur of contact." He must also have the capacity for what Franz Alexander calls "dynamic reasoning"—the ability to see his patients not only in the here and now, but how they became as they are. Group leaders must listen with what Theodore Riek calls "the third ear" if they are to truly understand their patients. However, while the group leader should always strive to understand, he must be able to tolerate the tension of not understanding rather than forcing his explanations or interpretations. As Riek says, "it is better not to understand than to misunderstand."

Spontaneity and Responsiveness. While a therapist in individual therapy has the time to wait, think and speculate, like a slow-moving chess player, the group leader must rely more on his spontaneous responses to the multiple situations and interactions in group. Grotjohn compares the group leader to a conductor of an orchestra. He leads, but he is also a central part of the presentation. The individual therapist is like a critic who sits in the audience and has the advantage of standing up, stopping the music, making a comment and then sitting back down. The group leader on the other hand not only interprets, but does something that shows what or how it is done. This requires the group leader split himself and be both participant and observer to the group.

Trust. This requires the group leader not only possess the ability to trust his fellow man, but that he have basic trust in himself. This means the therapist must have the capacity to tolerate bad experiences and despair in himself and others. However, as Erikson notes, a person cannot develop basic trust by himself. The group leader must know how to develop and protect the trust of the group, for as the leader will discover, the group members will come to trust the group more than they trust the therapist. One aim of the group is to restore the members' belief and trust in their fellow members and themselves. Trust in others reduces narcissistic self-centered preoccupation and teaches members to care about each other.

Firm Identity. The central firmness of the group leader allows the group members to recognize the therapist for what he is — a real person and not only as an imagination of transference. A firm identifical will allow the therapist to have an openness to the group and its members so he can be a parent to one, a friend to another, or a disciplinarian to another. He will be able to be many things to different members, yet he will maintain a firm identity to all. At times, he may be a blank screen in order to invite transference distortions, but simultaneously, he will be able to be real and human enough to develop a working alliance with the group and its members. This requires he be active, but not too active so that he dominates the group or its members.

A firm identity will also help the leader with his own countertransference reactions while at the same time allowing the group to use him for three different transference resolutions.

1. Transference to the leader as a central figure, as in individual therapy.
2. Transference to peers in group, as among siblings in a family.
3. Transference to the group as a whole as a symbolic mother.

Humor. Creative use of humor can help correct transference distortions because it invites the group to look upon him as a real person. Humor must not be used to hide hostility or wound. The group leader must not fight with members for dominance because of his own narcissism or display of brilliance. Humor should be used to support honesty, courage and frankness.

Fallibility. The group leader must be expected to make mistakes. More importantly, he must be allowed to do so. The group leader will learn that he does not lose his position by admitting a mistake. To the contrary, his central position will be confirmed even more by the humanness of his fallibility. The only unforgivable mistake is pulling rank on group members or having the inability to tolerate patients moving slowly in treatment. Working with alcoholics and addicts is not the place for a person who demands immediate success and dramatic results. This was a point explicitly made in Janet Malcolm's book, *In The Freudian Archives* (1984). Malcolm emphasizes that it is the psychotherapist who is able to plod along in a sometimes dreary, slow pace with his patients that is the most successful analyst. Those who only have the sharp, quick intellect, often do not possess the capacity to tolerate their patient's inability to keep pace with them and their discoveries about the patient. Such psychotherapists can become easily frustrated and dissatisfied with the lack of immediate success in treatment.

PSYCHOTHERAPY OUTCOME RESEARCH

While many of the qualities of the therapist which Grotjohn and others describe are certainly admirable, science has taught us that things are not always as they seem to be on the surface. Research has demonstrated that while many of the innate characteristics described by experienced clinicians like Whitaker, Yalom, Polster and others does indeed play a very significant part in successful treatment, the interplay between a therapist's characteristics and successful treatment is a subtle and delicate one. However, before the reader is left with the impression that the possession of these described innate human characteristics are all that is needed for successful treatment, it is important to understand what research has discovered about this factor. A most important discovery was made by Strupp and Hadley (1979) when they concluded that non-specific factors like therapist characteristics were crucial in setting up an initial alliance with a patient, they were not enough to produce successful treatment outcome if long term treatment was required past the first two or three meetings. After the initial meeting, specific factors like technique, training and experience played a more significant part in treatment. Strupp and Hadley discovered that individuals who were not professional therapists, but possessed important innate characteristics like the capacity for caring and warmth could provide immediate relief to many patients during the first couple of sessions if these individuals could demonstrate their ability to understand and empathize to the patient. However, after the initial relationship was established and more specific interventions were required of the non-professional therapist, they were at a loss in determining how to respond. This is where the specific training and skill of the professional therapist are required to move the patient beyond the limits of their presenting condition.

In one of the most thorough and complete reviews of all treatment outcome studies, Bergin (1971) agreed with this position when he concluded that successful psychotherapy is determined in a large part by the characteristics of the therapist. Bergin found that the three most significant contributing factors to successful treatment are (in rank order of importance):

1. The patient's characteristics
2. The therapist's characteristics
3. Technique or theoretical orientation of the therapist

The implications of Bergin's findings suggest that two of the most important contributing factors in successful treatment outcome are beyond the control of universities, training institutes and teaching facilities. As Cassell asked earlier in this chapter, "Is it possible to teach sensitivity?" Certainly, the capacity to care represents a very crucial variable to successful treatment, but it appears that this is something the therapist brings with him to the therapy situation. However, as Whitaker suggested, a therapist may be far more effective if he has had a successful therapy experience himself. This is one good argument for the therapist in training to receive their own therapy before they are turned loose on their patients. Certainly, this suggestion would hold true for group leaders. It would be important for them to have a good group therapy experience before they could be expected to be effective group leaders themselves. Bergin's findings also stress the importance of the patient's contribution to successful treatment. The fact is that many patients are just not suitable for psychotherapy. They are either too disturbed or too resistant to benefit from treatment. The specifics of these patients' characteristics will be explored later in the chapter.

Psychotherapy Update

In recent years, research concerning psychotherapy process and outcome has increased greatly in sophistication and has generated interesting findings with important clinical relevance. The upsurge in treatment outcome research had, in a large part, been stimulated by earlier claims that psychotherapy was found to be no more beneficial than no treatment (Eyzenck, 1952). Greatly improved methods of reviewing and aggregating the vast amount of literature on this subject has demonstrated that much of the early research methodology had been seriously flawed. The most powerful conclusion of this massive review is that psychotherapy works. The average treated patient was found to be as well off as the patient in the 80th percentile of the control groups.

Specific Effects. Another result emerging from this review was a failure to demonstrate that some therapies are better than others. One interpretation of this result is that different psychotherapies, however diverse they may seem in their specific techniques, are really effective by virtue of their shared, or non-specific, ingredients such as the healing ritual which provides hope, reverses demoralization, establishes a helping relationship, and provides the patient with an increased sense of understanding and control over their present situation (Frank, 1963).

The quality of the therapeutic alliance, even when it is measured early in treatment, has been found to be the best and most consistent predictor of outcome. It appears that a good therapeutic relationship between patient and therapist is more important in predicting change than are factors that reside only in the patient or the therapist. Moreover, it appears that the patient is more powerful than the therapist in determining the nature of the therapeutic alliance. However, there is evidence which suggests that part of the success in all forms of psychotherapy may be attributed to the therapist's ability to mobilize the patient's expectation of help. Frank (1963) specifically suggests that the common effective factor in all forms of therapy is the patient's faith in treatment and this factor should be deliberately mobilized in treatment.

Mobilizing a patient's faith in treatment and his expectancy of help is a crucial issue when working with alcoholics and addicts. Treatment approaches like AA which encourage, engage, and promise relief may work better with these patients because they mobilize a patient's expectancy for help. Treatment approaches which are passive, unresponsive, and rely on the alcoholic's or addict's own source of motivation frequently fail because they do not address this crucial issue in treatment.

Frank identifies two important sources which will evoke the patient's expectancy of help. First is the personal magnetism of the healer, which is often strengthened by the healer's faith in what he does. Another source of the patient's faith is the ideology of the healer or sect, which offers the patient a rationale, however absurd, for making sense of his illness and the treatment procedure. Anyone who has attended AA meetings on a regular basis knows by their experience that each of these forces are operating strongly in the AA program.

Frank sees any procedure which places the healer in the position of transmitter or controller of impressive healing forces as enhancing the patient's faith in the treatment process. Whether that position is defined as an enthusiastic recovering alcoholic with many years of happy sobriety or a professional psychotherapist is irrelevant for Frank. Each position is analogous to the shaman in more primitive cultures. In our culture, the healer is ordained as a scientist who has discovered new and potent scientific principles of healing, thus surrounding himself with the aura that anything labeled scientific inspires in members of modern Western societies. Healers in our present day society characteristically back up their pretensions with an elaborate scientific-sounding pattern of theories and diagnostic labels.

Frank further posited that since the success of psychotherapy does not seem to be linked to any particular type of therapy and that the relief of discomfort was the same regardless of the types of treatment utilized, that relief of the patient's suffering may have more to do with the therapist's ability to mobilize the patient's trust, hope, and faith in the treatment process. Furthermore, the type of relationship offered by the therapist seems to be determined more by the level of experience and competence of the therapist than it does by their theoretical orientation. Therapists of different schools all agree that the success of their therapy depends in the first instance on the therapeutic relationship or therapeutic alliance in which the patient accepts some dependence on the therapist, based on the patient's confidence in the therapist's competence and his intentions. However, research demonstrates that experienced practitioners of different schools agree more highly on the nature of this relationship than did junior or senior members of the same theoretical persuasion. There is more of a difference between novice and experienced therapists of one school or methodology than there is between experienced psychotherapists of different disciplines. Apparently, psychotherapy experience modifies methodological differences over time. Studies have demonstrated that experts of different schools create relationships more similar to each other than experts and novices of the same school. Apparently, experience in actual practice overcomes doctrinal differences.

Patients' Characteristics and Contributions to Successful Therapy

Based on the abundance of research evidence gathered over time, the most powerful vehicle for producing significant therapeutic change seems to be an emotionally charged interpersonal relationship. This relationship need not be with a professional therapist, but it does need to be an emotionally charged one with a real person. The effectiveness of this relationship in producing desireable therapeutic change is determined in a large part by the therapist's personality and his skill at managing interpersonal relationships, especially with individuals who have a history of difficulties in this area. Some patients, like severely psychotic individuals, cannot tolerate the closeness of a real interpersonal relationship. Others, who are severely mentally retarded, brain damaged, intoxicated, or suffer from severe character disorders are incapable of forming a true working alliance with a therapist. What a patient brings to psychotherapy, at least as far as their interpersonal skills are concerned, determines in a large part the potential success of a therapeutic encounter. The more the patient has to offer the therapy situation and the less severe their difficulties, the more likely treatment will be successful. Conversely, the more severe the patient's disorder, the less the chance they will benefit from treatment, no matter how skillful and "together" the therapist may be.

Initial Phase of Treatment. The patient's willingness to enter treatment is determined by a number of important factors of which their level of experienced distress is the most influential. The effec-

tiveness of the initial stages of treatment are enhanced by the therapist's ability to mobilize the patient's expectancy for help and this is
influenced in a large part by the patient's ability to possess a favorable expectation from treatment. This requires the patient be able to
accept and respond to symbols of healing. Good responders to psychotherapy expect treatment to help them and are better integrated
socially, and are less mistrustful than poor responders. The ability
for a person to respond favorably is not so much a sign of excessive
gullibility as it is of easy acceptance of others in their socially defined roles. However, the more suggestible the patient and the
greater the experienced distress, the more likely they are to stay in
treatment.

There are a number of important factors which will enhance the
patient's willingness to perceive the therapist as a source of help.
Certainly, the therapist's ability to inspire the patient's confidence
in him as a credible psychotherapist or healer is essential. It should
be understood, however, that there is not a close correspondence
between these inferred attributes as rated by either the therapist himself, external observers, or the patient whom the therapist serves.
The most consistent relationship found between therapeutic outcome and inferred therapist qualities are those derived from the patient's perception of the therapist rather than either from the therapist's perception of himself or the ratings of external observers.

The patient's willingness to continue treatment is in turn dependent to a large part on the patient's personal liking of their therapist.
It has also been found that if the patient perceives the therapist to be
a credible person, there is more of a chance that he will find the
therapist more attractive. The concepts of credibility and attractiveness are not mutually exclusive. Research has demonstrated that
those who are perceived as experts and who engender trust produce
greater influence over attitude and behavior change. Patients are
consequently more accepting of explanations or interpretations
which vary with their own perceptions of the world and belief systems when these interpretations and explanations are presented by
therapist who are perceived as attractive and credible. The acceptance of advice giving is thus dependent on the patient's perceived
estimation of the therapists' competence, skill, anticipated thoroughness, and mutual attractiveness. Like credibility, attractiveness
interacts completely with issues of interpersonal similarity and compatibility.

The patient's perception of this therapist as an interpersonally attractive person facilitates the initial development of perceptions which in turn produce positive outcome. Attractiveness is more important than credibility during the initial stages of therapy and results in the patient's remaining in treatment long enough to develop a therapeutic alliance which is necessary for real change. Credibility which usually includes such qualities as trust, competence and ability are more subtle features of the therapist and have more influence on the patient's gain throughout therapy.

The Therapeutic Process: Therapist's and Patients' Contributions

Therapist's Contribution. The therapist must have the capacity to be empathic. He must be able to experience what the other person is experiencing without losing himself or becoming the other person. However, as Ornstein says, this empathic understanding is useless if the therapist is unable to communicate to the patient what he understands. The therapist who just sits there with his empathic understanding does little good for his patient if he is unable to convey his understanding back to the patient.

The therapist must also be able to listen to what the patient says. More importantly, he must also be able to listen to what the patient doesn't say and leaves out in his conversation. This requires listening with the third ear. Listening is not a passive process. It is an alert activity which is required if the therapist is to be able to make understandable, for himself and the patient, what the patient is experiencing. This in turn helps the patient make sense of his own experience. This is where theory plays an important part in the patient's treatment. The more sound the theory, the more it will give the patient cognitively. A solid framework for understanding will help the patient master his situation more completely.

The therapist must also possess a non-judgmental attitude. He must listen without judging. Freud referred to this as neutrality. However, many therapists have come to confuse neutrality with a non-responsive blank-screen-stance in therapy. Despite Freud's caution, the therapist is more effective if he realizes it is impossible not to form a judgment of the patient. The therapist forms constant opinions on what the patient has to say. But, the therapist must not impose his opinions or judgments on the patient unless this opinion concerns alcoholic drinking and drug use. While it is generally a therapeutic maxim that the therapist not impose his standards on his patients, this stance can be destructive for an alcoholic or addict. In most cases, it is best if the patient discovers his own value system. With alcoholics and addicts, because of their shared characterological deficits and cognitive impairment, they may require an imposed value system like AA until they've had enough time to restore their cognitive functioning to the point that they are able to think clearly and rationally for themselves.

The therapist should also avoid counter-provocative behavior when the patient is hostile. It is important for the therapist to tune into his own feelings and use his counter-transference as a barometer to help him understand his patient better. If this understanding leads to a calculated confrontation with the alcoholic and addict, there is less chance that it will be triggered by the therapist's own unconscious anger.

Patient's Contribution. There are three basic patient contributions that need to be assessed in treatment.

1. The patient usually comes to treatment with anxiety, doubts, and fears. They are often unexpressed. If the patent is a court referral, they'll also present with anger and hostility. Such feelings have to be expressed at the beginning of treatment or the therapist will lose the patient. Repressed feelings increase the likelihood that these feelings will be acted out. Talking, on the other hand, diffuses their intensity.
2. The patient presents with a certain level of psychological development which is the result of his previous experiences. The more troublesome these experiences were at an earlier age, the more difficulty the patient will have. The more difficulty the patient has, the more disturbed they will be and the more difficulty they will have understanding and relating to the therapist. The more disturbed patients will not be able to understand or handle passivity or interpretations. They will require support, calming and soothing from the therapist.
3. Every patient comes to treatment with certain expectations. Many come with what is commonly referred to as the curative fantasy. Their hope is that the therapist will somehow magically remove their discomfort and ills. Many will have a silver-platter attitude. On an unconscious level, they still cling to magical thinking. Much like a small child who believes that if his mother will only kiss his hurt, his pain will go away. For such individuals, their parents are frequently viewed in an un-

realistic, omnipotent fashion. If the child hurts himself, for instance, he will often blame the mother. If he views the therapist like he did his mother, he'll believe on some level that the therapist will be so powerful as to be able to magically cure him.

With alcoholics and addicts suffering from more severe characterological deficits, like borderline patients, the therapist can expect to easily entice their rage and anger. Because they frequently viewed the therapist as magically powerful, they will expect him to remove their hurt and pain. Since he doesn't, they reason that he must have it and is withholding it. Their rage is, in one sense, saying, "Why don't you make me feel better? If you cared, you would give to me so I wouldn't hurt so badly. Since you aren't removing my pain, you must dislike me. Since I've done all you've asked and I still hurt, you must be uncaring and awful because you have treated me so badly."

As distorted and unrealistic the curative fantasy may be, it should not be interfered with too quickly. Often, this belief may be the most salient motivating factor in an individual's continual investment in treatment, abstinence and recovery. This situation was dramatically demonstrated by a newly recovering alcoholic who had little more than one year's sobriety and decided to attend a national conference on alcoholism treatment. A nationally recognized alcoholism treatment expert, who also had nearly fifteen years of sobriety through AA, openly stated that AA doesn't have all the magical answers. He further added that if a person were to just stop drinking, this would not cure him of all of his problems. Abstinence was just the first step in the long and difficult process of recovery. Upon hearing this, the newly recovering alcoholic admitted to the other group members the next week, "That scared the hell out of me. If I would have heard that just one week sooner, I don't think I could have handled it. Thank God, that information wasn't given to me sooner."

The curative fantasy and it's proper utilization in treatment can have an important influence on recovery as demonstrated by the following vignette.

Angie, a thirty-two year old artist and photographer had sought treatment because of an unhappy marriage. Her husband refused to respond to her requests that they seek conjoint

Philip J. Flores

therapy and he had a history of physically abusing her when he became intoxicated. After a few weeks of therapy, it became obvious that she, as well as her husband, was an alcoholic. She promptly responded to the therapist's request that she stop drinking and join AA. After nearly a year of individual therapy and regular AA attendance, she divorced her husband and eventually entered a psychotherapy group at her therapist's suggestion. Six months into the therapy group, in a moment of extreme frustration, she screamed at the other group members and the group leader, "Look, I've done everything you've told me to do and things still aren't perfect. I still get angry and people still hurt me!" The next few sessions following her outbursts were marked by her sharing of deep feelings of sadness and hurt as she struggled with the realization that things were not ever going to be perfect. This was a stance which she had taken early in her life as a child. Her parents, who were brutally critical of her, demanded that she live up to their expectations and only showed her love or affection when she performed perfectly. After more than two months of struggling with this realization, she finally stated to the group and its leader one evening, "I realize that even if things aren't perfect, they are a lot better than I imagined they would ever be. I guess I kind of like this reality thing. But, if I knew it was going to be this hard when I started out, I don't think I would have had the courage to put myself through all this pain. I thought a couple of months ago that I would just go back to my old ways of dealing with things, but I realized that wouldn't work for me either. I think that's why I got so angry. I didn't like where I was and I couldn't go back to where I've been. I felt stuck and cheated by you. Now I realize this place here ain't really so bad."

GROUP PSYCHOTHERAPY RESEARCH

The most extensive controlled research on the effectiveness of group therapy was in part conducted by Yalom (Lieberman, Yalom & Miles in 1973; *Encounter Groups: First Facts*). The research project was complex and, as Yalom states, expensive. The full description of the project will not be explored here. However, one major aim of the study was to investigate the effect of leader technique upon treatment outcome. Eighteen experienced and expert group leaders from ten different ideological (i.e., Gestalt, psychodrama, TA, psychodynamic, etc.) schools were recruited to each run a group which met for a total of thirty hours over a twelve week period. An extensive battery of psychological and personality measures were administered to each member of each group three times: Before the start of the first group, immediately after the twelfth group session was completed, and six months after termination from the group.

Yalom discovered some disturbing results. Two-thirds of all the subjects who participated in the study found it to be an unrewarding experience. In fact, some individuals actually got worse as a result of treatment and were judged by Yalom to be casualties. A casualty is one who, as a result of his group experience, suffered considerable and persistent psychological distress. Since several types of groups had been studied, it was found that the key causative factor of casualties was not the type of group, but rather the individual personal style of the group leader. Leaders with the highest casualty rate were described as "aggressive stimulators" by Yalom. They were intrusive, confrontive and challenging. They also revealed a great deal of themselves and surprisingly were judged by most members to be the most charismatic. Groups that experienced low casualty rates had leaders who were described as "loving" and created an "accepting, trusting climate."

Yalom further discovered that if he analyzed the research data for each group independently, he was left with an equally interesting conclusion. In some groups, almost every member underwent some positive change with no casualties among their group members. In other groups, there were cases where not a single member benefitted from treatment. All were either casualties or were fortunate to remain unchanged. Again, it was discovered that the leadership style was the most important contributing factor to successful treatment. In fact, the group that had the highest success rate was led by a leader who belonged to the same ideological school as the leader who had the lowest success rate and highest number of casualties. The ideological school to which the group leader belonged actually had little to do with the success rate of any of the therapy groups in this study.

Yalom, trying to answer the question of what determines successful group therapy writes,

> The next obvious question—and one very relevant to psychotherapy—is: Which type of leader had the best, and which the worst, results? The T-group leader, the gestalt, the T.A.,

the psychodrama leader, and so on? However, we soon learned that the question posed in this form was not meaningful. The behavior of the leaders when carefully rated by observers varied greatly and did not conform to our pre-group expectations. *The ideological school to which a leader belonged told us little about the actual behavior of that leader.* We found that the behavior of the leader of one school—for example, transactional analysis—resembled the behavior of the other T.A. leader no more closely than that of any of the other seventeen leaders. In other words, the behavior of a leader is not predictable from one's membership in a particular ideological school. Yet the effectiveness of a group was, in large part, a function of its leader's behavior. (p. 501)

Yalom's discovery of the lack of congruence between what a group leader says he does in group and what he actually does in group was made clear in a statement which Bob Goulding made about Fritz Perls. After having worked and trained with Perls for many years, Goulding confessed that the way Perls wrote about doing psychotherapy was often quite different from the ways Perls actually did psychotherapy. Certainly, Yalom's research findings support Goulding's personal observation of one universally recognized expert in group therapy. This observation is made more relevant by the fact that Robert Goulding was one of the eighteen group leaders which participated in the original Liebermann, Yalom and Miles study. It was Goulding who was also the group leader who had the most improved group members with no group therapy casualties and was consequently rated the most effective group leader in this study.

Yalom and his cohorts attempted to determine what it was about Robert Goulding and the other successful group leader that influenced successful treatment outcome. He derived a factor analysis of a large number of leadership variables and categorized them into four basic leadership functions.

1. *Emotional stimulation* (challenging, confronting, activity; intrusive modelling by personal risk-taking and high self disclosure).
2. *Caring* (offering support, affection, praise, protection, warmth, acceptance, genuineness, concern).
3. *Meaning attribution* (explaining, clarifying, interpreting, pro-

viding a cognitive framework for change; translating feelings and experiences into ideas).
4. *Executive function* (setting limits, rules, norms, goals; managing time; pacing, stopping, interceding, suggesting procedures.

These four leadership functions were found to have a powerful relationship to successful treatment outcome (see Figure 1). As Figure 1 illustrates, there was a direct linear relationship between caring, meaning attribution and successful treatment outcome. In other words, a group leader cannot care too much for his group members and he cannot provide for them too much meaning for their confusion or suffering. On the other hand, the group leader who does too much or too little emotional stimulation and too much or too little executive functioning increases the likelihood of having an unsuccessful group. In either of these cases, the leader can either be too passive and not provide the group with enough direction or he can be too provocative, confrontive and the group will become leader-centered and too dependent upon him for direction and leadership.

THE IMPLICATIONS FOR CONDUCTING A SUCCESSFUL THERAPY GROUP

It was through the examination of the individual subjects' ratings of the different leaders that Yalom was given the first indication of any trend in positive success of group participation. The leaders studied ranged from those who were primarily analytic and interpretive, to those who saw the management of group forces as their distinctive function, and to still others who offered instructional, often non-verbal exercises almost exclusively. Some of the leaders believed passionately in love; others just as passionately in hatred. Some leaders depended solely on talk therapy; others used music, lights, and the touch of human bodies. The study found the most effective leaders—the ideal type—were moderate in the amount of stimulation and executive behavior they showed, high in caring, and that they actively utilized meaning attribution. Meaning attribution showed the strongest association with positive outcome.

The nature of the group as a social system was judged by Yalom to be very important. Whether a participant identified with the group, whether he likes it, his role in the group and whether the

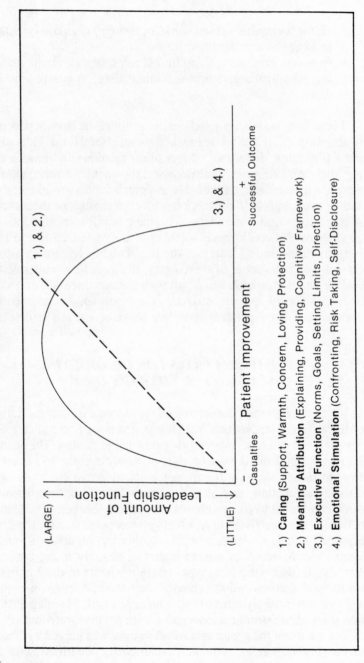

FIGURE I

Amount of
Leadership Function

(LARGE)

(LITTLE)

Patient Improvement

Casualties −

+ Successful Outcome

1.) **Caring** (Support, Warmth, Concern, Loving, Protection)
2.) **Meaning Attribution** (Explaining, Providing, Cognitive Framework)
3.) **Executive Function** (Norms, Goals, Setting Limits, Direction)
4.) **Emotional Stimulation** (Confronting, Risk Taking, Self-Disclosure)

group likes him are all relevant to the outcome. The study further indicated that group members who liked their groups, who participated actively, and who were valued by other group members learned more. All these indications illustrated the leader who instilled norms that favored moderate emotional intensity and confrontation were the most popular.

Contrary to what many encounter group leaders and members seem to believe ("There is no group, only persons") the study indicated very clear evidence that the nature of the group as a social system is important in affecting outcomes. Also contrary to the opinion expressed by some that "the group can comfort, but it can't cure" (Back, 1972). Yalom studies that under the proper leadership, group therapy can have a significant effect on a person's life. Groups in which the leader instills a sense of cohesion functioned better and individual members rated their experience more favorably. The clear indication is that non-authoritative leaders operating in a more democratic manner were reviewed more favorably by members due primarily to the feeling of autonomy on their part when in the group. Many intangibles combine to make up what may be described as a good leader. Bach sums it up best with his definition that "a good sensitivity trainer combines the religious healer's charisma with the scientist's language." Undoubtedly the criticism of psychotherapy groups was mis-directed in that group therapy is not bad but rather it is the leader that is poorly trained or inadequately prepared who must be evaluated with a critical eye.

ALCOHOLISM TREATMENT OUTCOME STUDIES

In a review of the most common procedure for rehabilitating alcoholics, it was concluded that all procedures have approximately the same degree of success (Matakas et al., 1978). The success rates — including spontaneous admission — lie between forty to fifty percent. There were some reported exceptions to these general findings. Some treatment programs treating skid row alcoholics had success rates as low as five percent while some private hospitals utilizing a select patient population reported success rates as high as ninety percent. Overall, the one year recovery rate was found to be very close to the five year rate because most of the recidivism occurs in the first year of therapy. Consequently, like most other psychotherapeutic treatment modalities, alcoholism treatment research has shown that most therapeutic procedures are more or less equally effective. Thus, the problem is not one of selecting the decisive therapy for alcoholics, rather it is one of determining whether there exists different indications for individual forms of therapy.

As Emrick (1973) demonstrated in an extensive review of 478 alcoholism treatment outcome studies, some treatment is better than no treatment. However, Emrick (1979) later noted that some types of behavioral intervention may actually do more harm than help for some patients. Emrick further suggests that research should be directed toward identifying those patients who might be harmed by this type of treatment.

Matakas (1978) in a similar view stated that "the criteria for conditioning therapy mentioned in the literature are not entirely convincing" (p. 2). The usefulness of drug therapy with disulfurim was also reported to be doubtful and it was suggested that it should be employed only supportively with other forms of treatment.

Patient Characteristics Related to Types of Therapy

Inpatient therapy and length of therapy was found to be basically no more successful than outpatient therapy. However, there were some identified characteristics which indicated that one form of treatment may be preferable to another dependent upon the patient's circumstances. Patients with more severe levels of addiction as well as more social and psychological instability were judged to be better candidates for inpatient treatment. On the other hand, patients who have a stable and permanent work relationship that might be compromised by long term inpatient treatment were more likely to benefit from outpatient treatment. This is especially significant since those patients who respond best to treatment are those who have a permanent work situation, intact marriage, and continual family support (Matakas, 1978).

Psychotherapy. Research also demonstrated that group therapy was the treatment of choice, although it was noted that "there is a lack of adequately based clinical investigations regarding its effectiveness" (Matakas, 1978, p. 5). Baekeland et al. (1975) cited some controlled studies that reported results ranging from total abstinence in 15 percent of the cases to significant improvement in 47 percent of the cases. Yalom (1974) described his experience with alcoholic groups as favorable. He determined however that many of the alcoholic groups were extremely nonintrospective, conceptualized their problems concretely (see Chapter Eight of this text), and expected advice or solutions from other members of the group, especially the group leader.

Self-Help Groups. Emrick et al. (1977) noted that AA is more successful than other therapeutic approaches when the alcoholic goal is total abstinence. Emrick also noted there were certain shared characteristics of alcoholics who were more likely to profit from AA treatment. They included a diminished tendency for members to continue to use denial. AA members who possessed social competence, strong identification with their mothers, and a tendency to overutilize rationalization were also likely to benefit from AA attendance. The typical AA member was found to be middle class, had discarded his fellow drinking companions, had a supportive spouse, possessed very strong guilt feelings and passively authoritarian. The most important criteria for success in AA was good ego-strength, long addiction history and a strong motivation to stop alcohol consumption.

Behavioral Therapy. Matakas (1978) reported varying success rates for both classical and aversive conditioning therapies. However, as Emrick et al. (1983) and Wallace et al. (1979) are correct in pointing out, there is much evidence to suggest that this research, like most other research on alcoholism treatment success, is seriously flawed. Since it has been clear from the start that this author's bias leans heavily towards abstinence as the primary goal of treatment and since the effectiveness of "controlled drinking" has not yet been clearly established, the research findings in this area will be limited towards those behavioral strategies which enhance abstinence from alcohol rather than encourage continual alcohol consumption.

Wallace (1978) has written an excellent review for using behavioral techniques in the treatment of the addicted patient. He deliberately avoids the controversial topics of behavioral methods for controlled drinking, aversion conditioning, and systematic contingency-management techniques for similar reasons. Namely, his many years of clinical experience with alcoholics have taught him that these methods do not work. Wallace realizes that most relapses occur within the first year and that the skillful utilization of these techniques can enhance recovery, especially during the first crucial months of abstinence from alcohol. In fact, Wallace sees AA operating within a behavioral change format. He writes,

Attendance at AA meetings is, in effect, a behavioral change in the life of the alcoholic of significant proportions. Going to such meetings alters his typical schedule of activities, enables him to make new friendships, exposes him to a host of social supports and reinforcements, and permits him to gather information about other alcoholics and the disease of alcoholism very directly. In many respects AA itself is a behavioral change. (p. 102)

Characteristics of the Alcoholic

Knauert (1979) in an analysis of the different characteristics of alcoholic patients suggests that it is incorrect to look upon alcoholism as one unitary disorder. He outlines particular alcoholic sub types and raises the question that one of these sub types may be the type of alcoholic who can respond to a "controlled drinking" strategy. Knauert differentiates between two different types of alcoholics; primary and secondary alcoholism. In order to further differentiate these sub types, it is suggested here that primary and secondary alcoholism can be further differentiated into two separate categories under each sub type.

I. *Primary Alcoholism*

    A. Process
    B. Endogenous

II. *Secondary Alcoholism*

    A. Reactive
    B. Compensatory

Primary Alcoholism. The primary alcoholic compromises 70 to 80 percent of the alcoholic population. This is the alcoholic who has all the commonly identified characteristics of alcoholism (i.e., tolerance, physical dependence, compulsive use, etc.). The process alcoholic differs from the endogenous alcoholic in that he has had a period of normal drinking, while the endogenous has not. Usually this period of normal alcohol use varies from five to twenty years. The process alcoholic condition has gradually gotten worse to the point that he can no longer control his drinking and his alcohol consumption, which was once normal, is now clearly pathological.

The endogenous alcoholic appeared to be addicted from the first moment he ever took a drink. He has never established a pattern of normal drinking and such individuals frequently experienced a blackout or became intoxicated the first time they drank. Their response is much more physiological and immediate in nature. Such alcoholics frequently described their first drink in glowing terms. "Looking back now, I knew I was an alcoholic from the very moment I took my first drink. I felt so good. I knew I would never give this up. I still can't understand how people can take only one drink. One drink doesn't do anything for me. Why drink if I can only have one? It doesn't make any sense because I only drink to get drunk or high."

Secondary Alcoholism. This subgroup of alcoholics compromise the remaining 20 to 30 percent of alcoholics. Their drinking is often pathological, but they do not demonstrate many of the associated physical symptoms (blackouts, tolerance, etc.) common to most alcoholics. The compensatory alcoholic frequently has a severe secondary psychiatric problem that is often exacerbated by his alcohol or drug use. These patients are more likely to be polydrug abusers and experience more social difficulties because of their drug and alcohol use. In some cases, compensatory alcoholics' symptoms actually get worse as they are withdrawn from drugs or alcohol. Their drug and alcohol use is frequently a form of self-medication.

Reactive alcoholics represent 5 to 10 percent of the alcoholics. Their drinking or drug use is frequently triggered by outside circumstances like a death, job loss, divorce, or psychological and physical trauma. They have either had a period of normal drinking or did not drink or use drugs before the onset of the adverse stimulus in their life. Their use of chemicals is usually shorter in history and can be traced back to a particular event. Many reactive alcoholics are not truly physically dependent upon alcohol. Consequently, they are usually the most successful candidates for "controlled drinking" strategies.

The evaluation and differential diagnosis of the sub types of alcoholics is crucial. As it has been stated repeatedly in this text, the consequences of advocating controlled drinking for an alcoholic who is not a reactive alcoholic can be life-threatening. The seriousness of weighing the advantages of this approach to treatment must be cautiously made. A continual stance taken in the text is that it is not worth the risk.

CONVERGENCE OF PATIENT
AND THERAPIST CHARACTERISTICS

While psychotherapy research has succeeded in demonstrating that treatment works for most patients, there is not a clear understanding of why some patients profit more from it than other patients. Indeed, the research cited in this chapter clearly suggests that the techniques and the theories to which psychotherapy outcome are usually attributed account for relatively little of the patient's actual change. In contrast, there is an abundance of evidence which suggests that most of the treatment gain is determined by virtue of the patient's coming to perceive the therapist as a competent, trustworthy, accepting and caring individual who is responsive to their presenting difficulties. These perceptions are not dependent upon the therapist's theoretical orientation, training or technique. Nor are these perceptions consistently evident from one patient to another. While it is evident that the characteristics of the patient determine, in a large part, whether they will be able to perceive the favorable qualities of the therapist, it is not clear why some patients click with some therapists and not others. Certainly, the convergence of patient and therapist values and personalities play a large part in the establishment of the therapeutic relationship. There is evidence which suggests that success in both psychotherapy and alcoholism treatment is very much dependent upon the establishment of a good working alliance. The nature of the therapeutic relationship and the working alliance is therefore important to understand if one is to be an effective group leader.

Hans Strupp (1977) has succinctly outlined the process of the establishment of a good working relationship in therapy. The matching of therapists and patient characteristics are determined in a large part by the successful management of the early hours of therapy. Furthermore, a good human relationship is judged by Strupp to be a precondition for the therapist's technical interventions. Strupp writes,

> There is ample evidence that any "good human relationship — i.e., an interaction characterized by understanding, acceptance, respect, trust, empathy, and warmth — is helpful and constructive. If such a relationship is provided by one person (therapist) for another (patient) who is unhappy, demoralized,

defeated, and suffering from the kinds of problems which our society has diagnosed as requiring the services of a specialist in mental health, the outcome will generally be "therapeutic", provided the recipient is able to respond to, or take advantage of, what the therapist has to offer. Some therapists believe that psychotherapy begins precisely at the point where a patient cannot profit from a good human relationship, and the professional is needed specifically by those persons who are chronically unable to seek out and profit from a good human relationship. (1977, p. 9)

Strupp emphasizes repeatedly that it is not the utilization and techniques or the eludication of historical antecedents that produce change in a patient. It is the reliving and modification of historically meaningful patterns that come alive in the here and now of the therapist to patient relationship or group to members interaction that produces change. Understanding is determined by reason and the weight of therapeutic change is not carried by reason but by the emotional relationship between the patient and the group and the group therapist.

Certainly the therapist as a person plays a crucial part in determining how important and effective this relationship will be. A therapist who is just a nice person will fail to provide the entire range of stimulus that the patient will need in treatment. The therapist must be able to challenge, soothe, care, love and fight with the patient if he is to provide the full range of emotional experiences which can potentially come alive in any authentic relationship. The therapist will hopefully have free access to all his passions and will discipline them to achieve his own purposes. Whenever a therapist is kind, altruistic, or generous, it should not be determined by his desire to be nice or thought of as kindly. Rather, his ability to soothe another and be generous should emerge out of the depths of his own self-worth. Nietzsche (1968) captures these sentiments exactly when he writes,

Gracefulness is part of the graciousness of the great-souled. When power becomes gracious and descends into the visible — such descent I call beauty. And there is nobody I want beauty much as from you who are powerful. Let your kindness be your final self-conquest. Of all evil I deem you capable:

therefore I want the good from you. Verily, I have often laughed at the weaklings who thought themselves good because they had no claws. (1968)

In concluding this chapter, there is an important message for the beginning group therapist. It is important, as stated previously, that they learn from the masters and make themselves familiar with the basic principles of group therapy before they embark on developing their own style. Yet, it is important that each group leader not try to be another Yalom, Polster, Goulding or Whitaker. These men are all experts in their own right and each is uniquely different in their approach to group therapy. It is important that the beginning group leader not try to completely emulate another or make himself a carbon copy of a therapist he admires. It is best that each group leader develops and discovers his own style. This principle is clearly demonstrated in Sheldon Kopp's story of the Hassidic religious leader's (the Zaddik) advice to his young disciple.

Thus, the relationship between the Zaddik and his disciple was the crucial factor in this attempt to give spiritual help, just as the relationship between therapist and patient is crucial in its secular equivalent. The personality of the teacher takes the place of doctrine. Even this must be guarded against turning into dogmas. As we read the stories of the many Zaddiks, we see that what best characterized them was their dissimilarity, their startling individuality. This was not always pleasing at first to those people who wanted not only help, but also a model, a way of behaving which they could emulate. And so in one story the followers of Rabbi Zusya asked him, "Rabbi, tell us, why do you teach in this way when Moses taught in another way?" "When I get to the coming world," answered Rabbi Zusya, "there they will not ask me, 'Why were you not more like Moses?' but instead they will ask me, 'Why were you not more like Zusya?'" (1971, p. 36)

REFERENCES

Back, K. W. (1972). Beyond words: The story of sensitivity training and the encounter movement. *Psychology Today*.

Bakeland, F. L., Lundwall, L. & Kissin, B. (1975). methods for the treatment of chronic alcoholism: A critical appraisal. In R. J. Gibbins, Y. Iracl, H. Kalant, R. E. Popham, W.

Schmidt & R. G. Smart (Eds.), *Research advances in alcohol and drug problems* (Vol. 2). New York: Wiley.

Bergin, A. E. (1971). The evaluation of therapeutic outcomes. In A. E. Bergin & S. L. Garfield (Eds.), *Handbook of psychotherapy and Behavioral change* (1st ed.) (pp. 217–270). New York: Wiley.

Cassell, E. J. (1985). *The healers art.* Cambridge, Mass.: MIT Press.

Emrick, C. D. (1974). A review of psychologically oriented treatment of alcoholism. II. The relative effectiveness of different treatment approaches and the effectiveness of treatment versus no treatment. *Quarterly Journal of Studies on Alcohol, 35,* 523–549.

Emrick, C. D. (1979). Perspectives in clinical research: Relative effectiveness of alcohol abuse treatment. *Family and Community Health, 2*(2), 71–88.

Emrick, C. D. & Hansen, J. (1983). Assertions regarding effectiveness of treatment for alcoholism. Fact or fantasy? *American Psychologist, 38*(10), 1078–1088.

Emrick, C. D., Lassen, C. L. & Edwards, M. T. (1977). Nonprofessional peers as therapeutic agent. In A. German & A. Rozin (Eds.), *The therapist's contribution to effective psychotherapy: An empirical assessment.* Elmsford, N.Y.: Pergamon Press.

Eysenck, H. J. (1952). The effects of psychotherapy: An evaluation. *Journal of Consulting Psychology, 16,* 319–324.

Frank, J. D. (1973). *Persuasion and healing* (2nd ed.). Baltimore: Johns Hopkins Press.

Grotjohn, M. (1983). The qualities of the group psychotherapist. In H. I. Kaplan & B. J. Sadock (Eds.), *Comprehensive group psychotherapy* (pp. 294–301). Baltimore: Williams & Wilkins.

Kopp, S. B. (1971). *Guru: Metaphors from a psychotherapist.* Palo Alto: Science & Behavior Books.

Knauert, S. P. (1979). Perspective from a private practice: The differential diagnosis of alcoholism. *Family and Community Health, 2*(2), 1–12.

Lieberman, M., Yalom, I. & Miles, M. (1973). *Encounter Groups: First facts.* New York: Basic Books.

Malcolm, J. (1984). *In the Freud archives.* New York: Alfred Knopf.

Masterson, J. F. (1981). *The narcissistic & borderline disorders.* New York: Brunner/Mazel.

Matakas, F., Koester, H. & Leidner, B. (1978). Which treatment for which alcoholic? A review. (Selected translation of international alcoholism research.) *Psychiatrische Praxis, 5,* 143–152.

Nietzsche, F. (1968). *Basic writings of Nietzsche* (W. Kaufman, Trans.). New York: Modern Library.

Strupp, H. H. & Hadley, S. W. (1979). Specific versus nonspecific factors in psychotherapy: A controlled study of outcome. *Archives of General Psychiatry, 36,* 1125-1136.

Wallace, J. (1978). Behavioral modification methods as adjuncts to psychotherapy: In S. Zimberg & J. Wallace (Eds.), *Practical approaches to alcoholism psychotherapy* (pp. 99-117). New York: Plenum Press.

Wallace, J., Forves, R. & Chalmers, D. K. (1979). Alcoholism Treatment Revisited. *World Health Project, 2*(1), 1-28.

Whitaker & Malone (1953). *The roots of psychotherapy.*

Yalom, I. D. (1974). Group therapy and alcoholism. *Annals of the New York Academy of Sciences, 233,* 85-103.

Yalom, I. (1985). *The theory and practice of group psychotherapy* (3rd ed.). New York: Basic Books.

Chapter 11

Transference in Groups

The concept of transference has long held a central position in psychoanalytic psychotherapy. It was one of Freud's greatest discoveries and it continues to be of central importance in psychoanalysis nearly fifty years after his death. While nearly every therapist worth his salt recognizes the importance of transference in psychotherapy, it has been only in the last few years that transference has been recognized to be an equally important phenomenon in group therapy. In the past, there has been some debate as to whether transference actually occurs in groups. Some critics felt that group therapy watered down transference reactions and neutralized transference distortions. Many theorists felt that transference could only be triggered within the context of free association. Since group interfered with free association, they reasoned that group was a mode of treatment which interfered with its occurrence. While it is true that free association is required for a transference neurosis, it is not necessary for transference phenomena, which is a totally different issue. Yalom even had to go so far as to state the obvious in his attempt to justify his addressing this issue in his 1985 test on group psychotherapy. For instance, he outlines six clear principles for dealing with transference in a therapy group.

1. Transference does occur in therapy groups; indeed, it is omnipresent and radically influences the nature of the group discourse.
2. Without an appreciation of transference and its manifestations, the therapist will often not be able to understand the process of the group.
3. The therapist who ignores transference considerations may seriously misunderstand some transactions and confuse rather than guide the group members; but if you see only the transference aspects of your relationships with members, you fail to relate authentically with them.

4. There are patients whose therapy hinges on the resolution of transference distortion; there are others whose improvement will depend upon interpersonal learning stemming from work not with the therapist but with another member around such issues as competition, exploitation, or sexual and intimacy conflicts; and there are many patients who choose alternate therapeutic pathways in the group and derive their primary benefit from other therapeutic factors.

5. Attitudes toward the therapist are not all transference based; many are reality based, and others are irrational but flow from other sources and irrationality inherent in the dynamics of the group (As Freud knows, not all group phenomena can be explained on the basis of individual psychology).

6. By maintaining flexibility, you may make good therapeutic use of these irrational attitudes towards you, without at the same time neglecting your many other functions in the group. (Yalom 1985, p. 202-203)

If Yalom's principles are followed, the group members will come to discover the extent to which they invest one another with early familiar qualities. Under the group leader's guidance and leadership, the group members should have the opportunity to learn how they project parental and sibling images onto the group leader and the other group members. They will hopefully see how these distortions are determined by their own circumscribed experiences as children and that the investment of others with attributes they do not possess is a result of their own distorted character structure.

DEFINITION OF TRANSFERENCE

There are a number of elaborate definitions of transference. Simply defined, transference involves two separate characteristics:

1. It must be a repetition of the past.
2. It must be inappropriate to the present.

If both of these characteristics do not occur in conjunction, it is unlikely that the phenomena being observed are really transference. For instance, if a group member perceives the group leader as controlling and demanding and the group leader is, in fact, controlling and demanding, this is not transference. In this example, the group member's perception of the therapist is totally appropriate to the present. Further, if the group member has not had a history where he has repeatedly perceived neutral people as demanding and controlling, it is unlikely that they will do so in the present, unless they are given a valid reason for reacting that way currently.

However, if a group member has experienced someone important in the past (i.e., father, mother, sister, brother, etc.) as cold, indifferent, exploitive or unfair, and there is an unrealistic imposing of these attitudes or characteristics on current neutral people in the present, there is a high probability that the person is caught in a transference distortion. Transference makes the other person appear to be what they are not.

For instance, if Mary perceives Burt as an angry, critical man who cares little for the other group members' feelings and the rest of the group members perceive Burt as kindly, caring and gentle, there is obviously some incongruence in Mary's perceptions. She has seven other individuals who perceive Burt in a totally different light. What is it about Mary that leads her to distort Burt in such a way that it defies the reality of the rest of the group members? Mary is an otherwise successful woman, wife, mother and accountant. She makes her living by dealing in accurate perceptions. Mary, who grew up in a home with an overly punitive and critical alcoholic father, is reminded of his presence every time Burt speaks in his own characteristic style. Mary is transferring her own feelings of anger and resentment at her father on to Burt. These are feelings inappropriate to the present, because Burt is actually nothing like her father except in his size and speech.

Levy (1985) writes about this process:

> Psychoanalytic theories of psychopathology are rooted in the idea that the past distorts the present, that past difficulties are continually repeated, and that recovery is based upon uncovering old conflicts and resolving them in such a way that their distorting influence is abolished. The patient can be expected to distort his important adult relationships significantly, in a way that conforms to the structure of his unconscious difficulties, which usually have to do with his conflict-ridden relationships to his parents during the formative years of development. (Levy 1985, p. 94)

Transference, as it occurs within the therapeutic setting, allows the group leader to get a glimpse into the patient's past. Examining the group member's interaction in the group becomes a means of understanding the way the patient's past, recreated in the here and now of the group member transference reactions, interferes with the patient's present relationships. The transference is a means of knowing the past by re-experiencing it in the present. We all possess the tendency to repeat the past by distorting the present and until the patient is aware of his own idiosyncratic distortions, he will be doomed to a repetitive occurrence of these historic events.

Levy stresses the importance of recognizing that these repetitions occur with all individuals:

> Such distortions need not be limited to people with significant psychopathology. All personal interactions are colored by past experiences that shape current expectations and responses. Especially conflictual and unsatisfying relationships with parents and other influential figures from the childhood years have a particularly lasting and distorting influence on people's adult relationships. How can one relate such ubiquitous distortions to the concept of transference in a manner that ensures that the latter term will keep its specific clinical meaning? Transference is the manifestation, within the psychotherapeutic relationship, of the ubiquitous distorting influence of past relationships on current ones, intensified by the regressive forces inherent in the treatment situation and clarified by the therapist's neutrality, relative anonymity, and objectivity in the face of the patient's distorted view of him. (Levy, 1985, p. 94)

Utilizing transference as a means to interpret a person's past can be a valuable tool in therapy. However, like any technique, it can be destructive if used as an end in itself, instead of a means for better understanding the patient. Therapists, if they are not cautious in its application, can hide behind transference interpretations because of their own difficulties in dealing with an emotionally arousing encounter. As Kernberg (1984) warns, transference is usually crystallized around some realistic aspect of the therapist's personality. Like paranoia, there is always an element of truth in it. But, it is a perception that is usually exaggerated and distorted by the observer. If the therapist is not careful, he will fail to appreciate the part they are contributing to the transference distortion.

Scott Rutan (1983) tells a story which captures the essence of this type of predicament:

During a case conference, a medical student was having particular difficulty managing his first psychiatric referral. From the student's description, it was apparent that his patient was a chronic drug abuser and a street-wise borderline character disorder. It was also obvious that she was well aware of the student's nervousness and incompetence. This only infuriated her more. As he proceeded to make one therapeutic blunder after another with this woman, week after week, her narcissistic rage continued to grow in proportion to every narcissistic injury she suffered. Finally, after more than three weeks of being subjected to repeated affective storms with this woman, one senior resident, noting that the medical student was beginning to show some wear and tear as a result of these encounters, kindly offered the suggestion of medication. As this possibility was discussed, the residents and medical students turn to Rutan and ask him what he thought of the idea of medication. Without blinking an eye, Rutan replied, "I think it's a great idea; but for the medical student, not the patient."

Therapists, unattuned to their own countertransference reactions, can attribute qualities to the patient that are inaccurate, distorted or exaggerated. Or, as this case illustrates, they can act out against the patient because of their own internal discomfort or anger.

TRANSFERENCE POSSIBILITIES IN GROUP

Harry Stack Sullivan's influence on Yalom has been outlined in Chapter 3. It is important to repeat briefly here the significance which Sullivan's concept of parataxic distortion has on Yalom's approach to resolving transference distortions in group. Parataxic distortion refers to our proclivity to distort our perceptions of others. These distortions are self-perpetuating and lead to self-fulfilled prophecies. A primary distortion of addicts and alcoholics is that people can't be trusted. They continue to pick as friends and lovers other addicts and alcoholics who are notoriously untrustworthy. Their view of others and the world as untrustworthy is consequently kept consistent. Therefore, they feel justified in keeping others at a distance and not trusting. This is the addicted individual's game. Their pay-off is that they do not have to get too close to someone who is trustworthy, because the underlying fear of every addict and alcoholic is that they will not measure up and will be found to be inadequate and unacceptable by others.

Distortions like this can only be modified by what Sullivan refers to as "consentual validation." For children who are developing psychologically, this requires they compare their perceptions with their peers'. It is the isolated individual who keeps his distortions self-perpetuating. He comes to believe he is unique in his "badness" and that if others truly knew him as he really was, they would reject him. Perceiving others as untrustworthy is a defensive operation which protects him from exposing his true self to others. Group psychotherapy requires each member to address his unconscious fear and modify their distortions through consentual validation. As members in the group begin to understand their transference distortions, they will be forced to look at themselves more realistically and subsequently reveal more of their true selves to the group. Eventually, through the corrective emotional experience, they will come to realize that they can be accepted for who they really are and need not continue to relate to others, based on their early past experiences.

The group leader must remember that transference is an unconscious phenomenon. Group members do not realize that they have it or that they are doing it. Only when they are acting in a way that doesn't make sense to other group members, does the transference distortion have a chance to be exposed for what it is. A group member's reaction or overreaction is usually obvious to others in the group before it is obvious to the person. The reliving of their infantile reaction in the present is needed before this behavior can be changed. Change is subsequently impossible without the person being aware of his transference distortions. The therapy group allows its members to deal with these infantile distortions as an adult now that they have the capacity to more fully understand it. It can be relived in the safety of the group and changed so that old unconscious patterns need not continue to plague them. As one group member exclaimed after an enlightening awareness of her transference distortions, "The great thing about this group is that I can go back and experience what I had to struggle with alone as a child and have all these people here to help me."

While transference occurs in every form of psychotherapy, group therapy expands the transference possibilities. Not only does each group member trigger separate individual transference reactions, there are three distinct transference processes inherent in every group experience that must be differentiated. This involves the vertical, the horizontal and the symbolic (see Figure 1).

1. Leader transference (vertical)
2. Peer transference (horizontal)
3. Group as a whole transference (symbolic mother)

Leader transference. Leader transference usually refers to libidinal distortions related to unresolved oedipal issues. Consequently, power, dependency, success and authority conflicts will manifest around the vertical pole. These are the type of transference issues which most readily emerge in individual therapy. Depending upon the group members' individual early experiences, some will see the group leader as cold and distant; others will perceive the group leader as warm and supportive. Some will be fiercely protective or dependent on the group leader for guidance and direction, while others will be defiantly independent and challenging of the group leader.

Peer transference. Peer transference involves competition issues related to jealousy, envy and cooperation. Group members will often rekindle sibling rivalry issues. Members may frequently remind each other of brothers, sisters, husbands, wives or lovers. At other times, group members will evoke parental transference distortions. It is because the group offers such a diverse source of transference stimulus that it allows more distortions to be experienced and ultimately resolved.

Group as a whole transference. The group as a symbolic mother helps steady the course of therapy. A great part of the group's therapeutic efficiency is based on a preoedipal maternal transference. If the group is a symbolically bad mother, it will stir up primitive feelings of anger and rage. Few alcoholics or addicts can tolerate such feelings and will find the group much too threatening. This is why cohesion, trust and safety are so crucial and important to a beginning therapy group. The group's benevolent tolerance, acceptance and safety may amount to an experience of rebirth and dissolution of the mother-infant symbiosis. The intensity of the individual transference distortions, be they rebellious anger or fears of dependency and engulfment, are diluted by the presence of the other group members. A symbolic good mother will serve as a container for the group members' anxiety and will allow the necessary hold-

FIGURE I

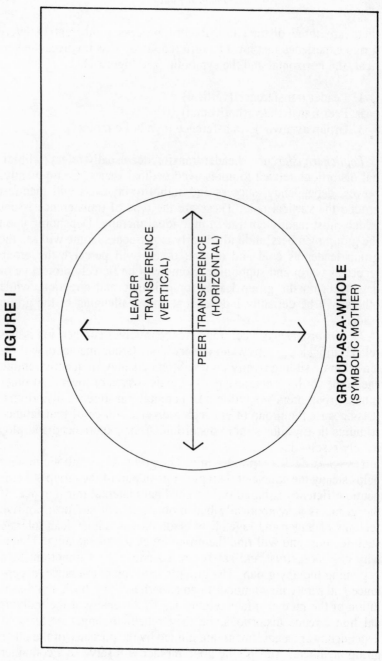

ing environment to be established so that the transference distortions can be addressed and modified.

MODIFICATION OF TRANSFERENCE DISTORTIONS IN GROUPS

Once a proper therapeutic climate has been established, the group leader can turn his energies towards exposing and modifying each group member's transference distortions. The group leader has at his disposal three primary means for accomplishing this task:

1. Interpretation
2. Consentual validation
3. Transparency

Interpretation. Interpretation plays a very special and unique part in psychoanalysis and psychoanalytic group psychotherapy. While every form of psychotherapy has its own means for bringing about change in a person's life, interpretation is the cornerstone upon which information is conveyed in psychoanalytic group psychotherapy. It is a statement made by the group leader that refers to something the patient has said or done in such a way as to identify features of his behavior that he has not been fully aware of. Transference interpretations are intended to expand the patient's awareness of his own personal idiosyncratic distortions of others which occur in group. The harnessing of transference is a key task for the group leader. But, he must not confront or expose transference in an attacking, premature or embarrassing manner. Timing is the key. A poorly-timed interpretation can result in more repression or regression in group. Accuracy is another important factor. With an inaccurate interpretation, the group member will often latch on to the statement as a way of defending himself. An accurate interpretation will trigger deeper associations and deeper feelings. However, accurate interpretations can also evoke strong negative feelings in the patient. Do not expect group members to respond appreciatively to accurate interpretations by saying "Thank you so much, that was really helpful." Accurate interpretations expose the person and are frequently experienced as narcissistic injuries. With an accurate interpretation, the group leader is essentially saying, "Your slip is

showing and I know it." It is often embarrassing to the member
because the group leader has penetrated his defenses and the result
is usually fear, anger or shame.

Consentual validation. Transference distortions are most readily
corrected when members of the group start comparing their perceptions to those of the other group members. This is especially important for alcoholics, addicts and character disorders. Interpretations
rarely work with these patients because of the tendency to overutilize egosyntonic defenses. Their characterological defensive posture protects them too well. They frequently do not experience the
same degree of internal discomfort that neurotics experience, so
they rarely seek therapy on their own. They are usually sent or
brought to therapy by others who find their characterological features disturbing, offensive, and troublesome. These patients are
convinced that it is "others out there" who are the problem. They
would be fine if only they were left alone. Consentual agreement
from the rest of the group members is needed to counter-validate
their distortions before they are able to even entertain the idea that
they might be the reason for their difficulties. Such validation from
peers carries far most impact than it does when it comes from the
group leader.

Transparency. Transference distortions can also be corrected if
the leader is more transparent and reveals more of himself. However, if the leader reveals himself too soon, transference may be
disturbed. Since transference, like free associations and dreams, are
a way to get to a person's unconscious, the premature use of transparency can interfere with a valuable and important source of self-
discovery and awareness. While it is important for the group leader
to use transparency as a way to correct destructive transference distortions, he must carefully evaluate his reasons for revealing more
of himself to the group and its members. Transparency should not
be used by the leader as an excuse to dominate the group or use the
group to gratify his own needs. The group leader should not fight
with members of the group for dominance by narcissistically dis-
playing his brilliance or by showing his superiority in other ways.
The group leader should use his transparency as a means for using
peer relationships in an effective way to exercise therapeutic pressure. He should be able to handle his relationships with the other
group members not with envy or interference, but by carefully re-
specting it. A jealous parent is not a good parent.

TYPES OF TRANSFERENCE IN GROUPS

Transference will reveal itself in many forms. While individual therapy will create a specific type of atmosphere which will lead to the likelihood of particular types of transferences being manifested, group therapy contributes to its own unique influences. The group leader can expect to witness three common types of transference in the therapy group.

1. Displaced transference
2. Acting-out transference
3. Repetition compulsion

Displaced transference. Some theorists believe displaced transference is the kind most likely to manifest itself in a therapy group (Alonso, 1985). Group members will use their history as a way of displacing their resistance. For instance, a group member may say that he is angry with his father, while in actuality, he is very angry at the group leader. His historical material may appear very rich and the group leader will be tempted to chase off in pursuit of his affect, failing to realize that he is the actual source of its manifestation. Group members may also displace their transference reactions onto each other, rather than risk demonstrating such feelings directly to the group leader. In extreme cases, this can result in scape-goating. The group will direct its aggression onto one group member rather than the group leader.

Acting-out transference. Acting-out is a term that is often confused by therapists in its application. Acting-out is usually used to describe aggressive, antisocial behavior that is frequently directed against society. This is too narrow a definition. Acting-out is really a transference phenomenon. Rather than talk about his feelings, a person will discharge them directly instead of utilizing sublimation. If angry, he will miss a session or scream at the group leader. He may also idealize the group leader. When the inevitable disappointment occurs, he will then act on his anger, rather than talk about his feelings of disappointment or frustration.

Acting-out is really a form of communication. While it has been viewed by some as a form of resistance, it is not so much resistance to transference as transference itself, because it carries communicative significance. There has been unwarranted overemphasis on motoric action in defining acting-out. Actually, acting-out involves more than behavior. It involves thinking and processing of information. In this context, acting-out frequently results in the group member's either doing to the group leader what he wishes would be done to them, or what he fears might happen to him. He treats the group leader affectionately because this is what he wants from him, or he attacks him because he fears that the therapist will attack first.

Blanc and Blanc (1973) define acting-out as "behavior motivated by unconscious object-related fantasies repressed by the ego" (p. 101). Kernberg sees acting-out as closely tied to the relationship between the patient and therapist. He writes, "A patient may tend to act toward the therapist rather than reflect feelings about him" (1975, p. 85). Acting-out, in the classical sense, is a discharge of drive tension that is achieved by responding to a present situation as if it were the original situation that first gave rise to the drive. The term transference is employed if the attitude or behavior is in response to certain definite persons. It is called acting-out (proper) if it is done indiscriminantly.

The character structure of a person is an example of a chronic and habitual pattern of acting-out which develops as a result of conflict between instinctual demands and a frustrating outer world. Alcoholics and addicts, because of their propensity to utilize characterological patterns in defending themselves, will overutilize acting-out in therapy. Group therapy, due to the nature of its regressive pull, will enhance acting-out to occur even in those individuals who may not normally employ its use.

Consequently, there is a general agreement among group leaders that acting-out is more likely to occur in a therapy group than in individual therapy. It is also more likely to occur with chemically dependent patients. It is futile to prohibit it. Rather, the group leader must use it as information. The amount of kind of acting-out is dependent not only upon the composition of the group, but also upon the conscious and unconscious attitudes of the group leader.

COMMON TYPES
OF ACTING-OUT TRANSFERENCE

Three common types of characterological acting-out transferences are captured in Kohut's description of the narcissistic transference (1977). They are the idealizing, mirror hungry and merger transferences (see Chapter 5).

Idealizing transference. The origination of idealizing transference is established in the need for the small child to have a secure relationship with a strong parent in order to feel secure and safe. The parent is idealized and perceived as more powerful and stronger than he actually is; as a means for the child to ward off intruding fears of anxiety and environmental threat.

Idealizing can also take on the form of ideas or ideals. Ideals can be goals for the child to pursue and identify within a healthy fashion. A child's source of self-worth is often pushed by his ideas of achievement and recognition. As the child grows older, this culminates in a mature capacity for pride and self-esteem. Self-identity is established and the ability to satisfy the self is internalized. If this process is successfully negotiated, the child will grow to an adult who does not need the constant presence of a strong other or ideological cause to feel secure.

The individual who grows up in an environment that deprives him of the idealized other will constantly search for this throughout his adult life. He will seek strong leaders, just causes, or rigid belief systems in order to feel secure. In the more pathological form, he may fall victim to the charismatic religious leader who provides him with a rigid predictable belief system that will protect him as long as he abides by all the rules. In other cases, such deprived individuals will pursue political systems with authoritarian leaders or, on a less dramatic level, choose a spouse who will be harsh and controlling. Since he will not allow himself to see others as they truly are, he will distort their perceptions in order to only focus on the strengths or the admirable qualities of the other. These are the patients who idealize their therapist and see them as all-wonderful. They only feel secure in the therapist's presence. In order to defend themselves against their need to see their leaders as strong, they will not allow themselves to see faults in others upon whom they must depend.

Yalom (1985) gives an excellent example of such an idealizing transference in a passage from Tolstoy's classic novel, *War and Peace*. The protagonist, Rostov, finds himself overwhelmed emotionally when thrust into the present of his idealized leader, the Tsar.

He was entirely absorbed in the feeling of happiness at the Tsar's being near. His nearness alone made up to him by itself, he felt, for the loss of the whole day. He was happy, as a lover is happy when the moment of the longed-for meeting has come. Not daring to look around from the front line, by an ecstatic instance without looking around, he felt his approach. And he felt it not only from the sound of the tramping hoofs of the approaching cavalcade, he felt it because as the Tsar came nearer everything grew brighter, more joyful and significant and more festive. Nearer and nearer moved this sun, as he seemed to Rostov, shedding around him rays of mild and majestic light, and now he felt himself enfolded in that radiance, he heard his voice — that voice caressing, calm, majestic, and yet so simple . . . and Rostov got up and went out to wander about among the campfires, dreaming of what happiness it would be to die — not saving the Emperor's life — (of that he did not dare to dream), but simply to die before the Emperor's eyes. He really was in love with the Tsar and the glory of the Russian arms and the hope of coming victory. And he was not the only man who felt thus in those memorable days that preceded the battle of Austerlitz: nine-tenths of the men in the Russian army were at that moment in love, though less ecstatically, with their Tsar and the glory of the Russian arms.

In some cases, the idealizing patient will go to great lengths to keep consistent his perception of the therapist as one who does not make mistakes. It is often too threatening for the idealizing patient to see the therapist as one who has faults. This is also manifested in the patient's relationships outside of group. For instance, this is why these patients frequently choose as a marriage partner someone who is entirely "wrong" for them. They have the propensity to only perceive the idealized good qualities of their partners, failing to see the more negative aspects of the person's personality. Once the realization of what the person is really like begins to "sink in," over time, they feel disillusioned and betrayed. A case vignette will help illustrate the lengths that an idealizing patient will go to keep their image of the "idealized other" intact.

Fred, a thirty-six year old accountant, had an intense idealizing transference for his group leader and would fiercely defend him against criticism by the other group members. He would also inevitably look to the leader for approval whenever he spoke in group. During moments of confusion, Fred would actually ask the group leader, "What am I feeling now?" Finally, after a painful empathic failure by the group leader,

Fred finally exploded angrily at him for failing to understand the nature of his discomfort. Unable to tolerate the realization that the group leader had faults or could err, Fred was overcome by his disappointment and responded in an uncharacteristic rage. After Fred's outburst had subsided, the other group members eventually congratulated him for his assertiveness, as this was the first time the other group members had not witnessed him readily complying to the demands of the group leader's wishes. Towards the end of the group, the leader also voiced his support of Fred's uncharacteristic challenge of him. In the next session, Fred announced to the leader that he had thought about the incident over the week and concluded that the leader had actually made the blunder on purpose. Fred said that he discovered, after "thinking about it carefully," that the group leader had actually done this in order to invoke him to react in an angry manner because the leader knew it would be good for him to do so. Fred promptly thanked the leader for his skill and foresight in utilizing such a creative strategy. So strong was Fred's need to keep his image of the leader as an idealized other, that he went through elaborate intellectual somersaults to insure that the leader's mistake was perceived as a well-planned-out and calculated strategy. This was also Fred's dilemma outside of group. He had been repeatedly passed over for promotion at his job because of his tendency to turn over his good ideas to his boss, who was extremely exploitive of him. Fred could not tolerate seeing his boss as someone other than what he wanted him to be.

Mirror hungry transference. If the child is not given the unconditional admiration and recognition of an uncritical mother while he is developing emotionally, he will seek this confirmation constantly in his adult life. These individuals will require a relationship with another who will be an agreeing and reflecting mirror. They will demand that others constantly respond to them, admire, and confirm them. They will be forced to seek externally in their adult life what they lacked internally as a child. Others become for them what Kohut calls self-objects. They will often be very successful people who will be obsessively driven to be recognized, acknowledged and admired by others. They will thrive on recognition and will feel deprived, empty and depleted if recognition and admiration is not forthcoming. If their sense of entitlement is challenged or not immediately gratified, they will be narcissistically injured and fly into a rage or become extremely depressed.

A case vignette will illustrate this transference problem:

> Tom, a 30-year-old cocaine addict was being seen simultaneously in both individual and group psychotherapy. He flourished in the individual sessions because all the time and energy was focused exclusively on him. He would literally start each individual session by asking the therapist how he looked today. He sought and needed confirmation from the therapist that he was all right. Much like someone standing in front of a mirror to make sure his tie was straight, Tom would pose in the same manner in front of the therapist. While he was able to get the mirroring he needed in individual therapy, he experienced much more difficulty with the group. The other group members began to tire of his insistence on talking about himself each week. Tom was reluctant to share the group spotlight and this eventually reached a crisis one week when it became blatantly obvious to the rest of the group that Tom was unwilling to give up "his time" in group, despite the acute emotional discomfort of two of the group's most supportive members. Since it was uncharacteristic of these two women to be so visibly upset, or to ask for group time, the other group members were enraged at Tom's insensitivity. Tom's behavior was especially provocative to the group, since both of these women had been consistently supportive of him in the past. Tom was unable to tolerate the group's reaction and eventually refused to return to the group, stating "I don't want to be part of any group that is not going to be supportive of me. I get too much of that in the real world."

Merger transference. Another variant of the narcissistic transference is referred to as the twinship, alter-ego, or merger transference. It is characterized by the patient's assumption that everyone in the group is either like him or similar to him. In some cases, the group members will expect the group leader's psychological makeup to be just like or very similar to his own. This phenomenon explains the uncomfortable feelings all of us experience in a strange surrounding, like when we visit a foreign city for the first time. In contrast, the merger transference explains the comfort we experience when we are in the presence of others whom we perceive to be like us.

In the most developmentally arrested group member, this will manifest in his refusal to see others in the group as different. He will protest at any attempts to differentiate between group members, insisting that "we are all just alike" or "I like everyone equally here in group." If this transference distortion is not challenged by the group leader, the members of the group will continue to hide their individual differences behind a facade of forced compliance and feigned similarity. They will never learn whether they can risk truly being themselves with others. Unless this is altered, the group will become a shared illusion, in which everyone will be squeezed into a mold of sameness and equality. The group leader's task is to contrast the individual group members' personal histories and repeatedly point out their differences. The aim is to get the group members to gradually move from the "we" to the "I." Each individual member must eventually come to recognize there is no threat in individuation and separation.

REPETITION COMPULSION

The repetition compulsion is the transference phenomenon most likely to occur first in group (Rutan, 1983); and it will manifest itself in the here and now of the group interaction. Through its manifestation, the group member will attempt to undo what has been done and is left uncompleted from his past. It involves the repetition of an experience. There is a general tendency in all human behavior to repeat painful experiences and to be haunted by an experience which is unfinished or incomplete. The repetition act, in adult experience, is usually self-defeating; but the underlying motive is assumed to be that the action seeks to redo the original trauma in the hopes that it will be mastered.

In an extreme case, this is the occurrence which takes place with children who grow up in an alcoholic home. An example will help clarify this point.

As a doctoral student completing my graduate work, I was employed part time as an intake counselor at a local alcoholism treatment center. Late one evening, around midnight, as I sat alone in my office catching up on my progress notes, the telephone rang. It was unusual that the phone should ring that late in the evening, as the agency had an answering service that took all incoming calls after midnight. As the telephone continued to ring repeatedly, some inquisitive impulse prompted me to answer the call. This was very uncharacteristic of me, but I felt compelled to discover what would lead a person on the other end to insistently pursue a call that went unanswered for such a long time. Since I expected to hear an intoxicated individual on the other end, I was somewhat startled by the gentle, soft and meek query of a woman's troubled voice. There was a profound sadness to her as she spoke; the type of sadness that grows out of an awareness which emerges after a person has struggled and discovered some unpleasant truth about herself. I politely informed her that the agency was closed for the evening, but that I would be happy to refer her to another number if it was an emergency. She kindly agreed that she could wait until morning and politely informed me that she would call back the next day. As I was about to hang up the receiver, she wondered if I would be so kind as to possibly answer one question that was presently plaguing her. Since her voice had the sound of a troubled soul who was struggling silently with a very personal and crucial issue, I quickly agreed that I would try. She paused, then asked in complete sincerity, "My present husband is an alcoholic, my first husband was an alcoholic, and my father was an alcoholic. Is there anything wrong with me?" I was deeply moved by the sincere inquisitiveness of her question. Unable to answer immediately, I sat silently with her as my mind conjured up the image of a troubled young woman sitting alone at her kitchen table after midnight, begging for an answer to a troubling question. No answer was necessary, as the full impact of her past had already come barreling down on her with the stark realization that the repetitive nature of her unconscious compulsions had already traced out a definable and painful pattern to her life.

This woman, like so many other adult children of alcoholics, is a perfect example of someone caught up in the throes of a repetition compulsion. This is why so many children who grew up with an alcoholic parent defy logic and continue as adults to marry or choose partners who are alcoholic. On an emotionally developmentally arrested level, they feel responsible for the family chaos. If only they had gotten daddy to stop drinking, everything would be all right. Since they couldn't fix daddy, maybe they can redo it differently this time with their spouse. The original traumatic experience (father's alcoholism) leads them to redo the experience in their adult life in the hope that this time it will be mastered. The awareness of this process remains buried, because the repetition compulsion, like most transference phenomena, is unconscious. Many adult children who "end up" married to alcoholics will protest that their spouses didn't even start to drink until they had been married for years. It is the personal characteristics of the spouse that they are drawn to alter, rather than the drinking, itself.

Since the repetition compulsion will manifest in the here and now of the group interaction, the group leader only has to observe the group members' interaction to decipher each member's personal history. Each member will manifest his particular idiosyncratic transference distortion in group. Those who have difficulties with anger in their life will have difficulties with anger in the group. Those who are taken advantage of by others in their life will be taken advantage of by members of the group. Each member will play out their uncompleted trauma of the past in the present. The group leader's task is to repeatedly point out each member's distortion as it occurs in the present and force each group member to examine in detail the many ways he keeps repeating his past in the present.

ABUSE OF TRANSFERENCE

The group leader had to keep a careful watch on the way he deals with transference in group. Interpretations can often be used as a means for the group leader to defend and distance himself from the group. Transference interpretations are only helpful if they come from empathic ties to group. Freud wrote of the danger of hurling interpretations in the patient's face if interpretations are used as a way for the therapist to defend against his own feelings of discomfort. Interpretations should never be used by the leader to give the impression of superiority. Once the leader tries to get himself in a one-up position, he has abandoned the group.

The group leader has to insure that he is not hiding behind the safety of his therapeutic technique when he elects to demonstrate to the group his awareness of transference phenomena. His own fear, anxiety, anger or need for recognition can color his therapeutic objectivity. A case vignette will demonstrate this potential problem:

During the tenth hour of a group psychotherapy training experience, a young woman angrily confronted the group leader, stating he was arbitrary, indifferent and aloof. The group stopped in its tracks and the group members all sat poised on the end of their chairs, for this was the first confrontation of the leader and the group was eager to see how he would respond. Finally, after a very agonizing few seconds, the group leader replied, "Do I remind you of your father?" The woman, relieved at the opportunity to move the exchange from the heat of the here and now encounter to the safety of the there and then, quickly agreed that this was indeed so and proceeded to explore the more familiar terrain of her relationship with her father. The initial crisis of the confrontation had been watered down and the rest of the group sat back comfortably in their chairs, relieved on some level that this issue could be dealt with on less threatening ground. Although the group members were relieved to be allowed to moved away from the overt expression of anger in the group, they had been cheated out of a valuable therapeutic experience. They were, in fact, given a demonstration on how to avoid direct confrontations. The issue between this woman and the group leader was unresolved. In fact, it remained unresolved for the rest of the group members during the remainder of the group experience, for her accusation was very true. The group leader was, indeed, arbitrary, indifferent and aloof. His urgency to move into the woman's there and then relationship with her father was reflective of his own need to avoid facing the painful accuracy of this woman's accusations, more so than out of an attempt to understand her transference distortions. Remember, transference is only transference if it is inappropriate to the present.

COUNTERTRANSFERENCE

Group leaders, like all therapists, remain human and are more similar to their patients than they are different. Consequently, they suffer their own transference reactions. In addition, the patient's intense transference towards the therapist may evoke in the therapist many unconscious responses which can interfere with his ability to respond therapeutically. This is technically referred to as countertransference. As the term is classically used, it refers to the total emotional reaction of the therapist to the patient with full consideration of the entire range of conscious, preconscious, and unconscious attitudes, beliefs and feelings in the therapist as a result of his contact with the patient.

While countertransference is an important concern for all therapists, it is frequently more of an issue for those who work with alcoholics and addicts because of the intense hostility, anger, disrespect, and distrust these patients commonly provoke in others. While countertransference can manifest itself in the therapist who uses a patient as a source of his own gratification or pleasure, it is likely to be the negative emotions that give the group leader the most difficulty. Imhof et al. (1984) agrees and cautions those who work with these patients to be careful of the intense feelings that alcoholics and addicts are likely to evoke in the course of treatment.

Imhof writes:

> The drug-abusing patient, with his sense of worthlessness, self-hate, and destructive rage, now meets his obverse – the "good" therapist, a "paragon of virtue," and essentially everything the patient is not. The resultant good-bad dichotomy is a serious threat to the ego identity of the patient, and the first order of psychic business for the patient is to reverse the imbalance. More specifically, the patient (unconsciously) begins to employ any strategy available to provoke, cajole, humiliate, and deceive the therapist – in essence to make the therapist more like himself, or worse than himself. Without the concurrent presence of the therapist's skill and understanding of the dynamics at work, including his own countertransferential and attitudinal postures, the proposed treatment may be short-lived, and the probable negative results all too frequently ascribed to the patient alone. (1984, p. 26)

Without an accurate awareness of possible countertransferential responses, the therapist will find that the clinical management of the alcohol or drug dependent patient to be virtually impossible. In addition, negative countertransference attitudes can be acted out in derivative forms. The therapist who is chronically late, cuts short his sessions, fantasizes during the treatment hour, becomes drowsy or refuses to return phone calls to patients within a reasonable amount of time may need to carefully assess his reasons for these

actions as chances are great that he is being influenced by unconscious feelings towards his patients.

Imhof (1984) lists six common countertransferential reactions
stimulated by alcoholic or drug dependent patients. He points out
that these reactions may be overt or transparent, and at other times
quite camouflaged.

1. The therapist can assume the role of the good parent who res-
   cues the bad impulsive child. The therapist may become over-
   involved, protective, maternal, permissive and overly nurturing, hoping that his outpouring of "love" and "goodness"
   will cure them of their drug and alcohol use. Much like the
   typical untreated Al-Anon member, he may believe that if he
   tries hard enough and gives his all to the alcoholic or addict,
   he will get them to stop their drug use and drinking because of
   their love for him.

2. The physician can inadvertently contribute to the patient's addiction by overprescribing medication. Misdiagnosis or failure
   of the physician to appreciate the drug abuse potential of his
   prescriptions can contribute significantly to the addict or alcoholic's problems. The addict's or alcoholic's own sense of futility may stir in the doctor his own countertransference need
   to do something for the patient. To not respond with something concrete that can help the patient immediately may be
   tied into the doctor's own need to be valued as one who brings
   relief to another's suffering. Such a countertransference need
   to be valued may result in the physician prescribing drugs even
   when his judgment tells him it may not be best for the patient.

3. The therapist can be captured by the remarkable and quick
   recovery of the addicted patient. He can be led to believe in
   the illusion of the dramatic cure which has taken place due to
   the effectiveness of his therapeutic skill. In the extreme, the
   therapist can come to hold the belief that the patient is "well
   enough" to try controlled drinking. The inevitable relapse can
   lead the therapist to feel deceived, resentful, angry, or that he
   is a "bad therapist" who has failed the impulsive child.

4. The therapist can get vicarious satisfaction from the patient's
   acting out and establish an alliance built on "you and me
   against the world." The therapist who is struggling from his
   own unresolved unconscious impulse fantasies can overly
   identify with the patient. He can develop the attitude of "only

I really understand you," which frequently leads the patient and the therapist to "play off" of each other.

5. The therapist can develop the commonly referred to syndrome of "burn out." He can become callous and indifferent to his patients. Instead of caring, the therapist employs difference defense mechanisms of which withdrawal, narcissistic distancing, boredom or anger are the most common.

6. Stereotypical classification by the therapist of his alcohol and drug dependent patients can lead to an attitude that his patients are nothing more than "junkies," "drunks" or "addicts" who will never change.

Self-reflection and self-analysis into one's participation and impact on the therapeutic relationship and treatment outcome is necessary if the group leader is to enhance his effectiveness in group. The cause of the alcoholic's and addict's failure in treatment is too often attributed to the patient's own psychopathology rather than the negative derivatives of the patient-therapist interaction. If the group leader is going to be able to avoid his own destructive countertransference influences, he must be emotionally and cognitively receptive to receiving, recognizing and analyzing the intense feelings generated by most chemically dependent patients.

Imhof makes five recommendations that the group leader follow so that the potential for destructive countertransference derivatives is minimized.

1. The field of addiction treatment is unique in its use of former patients (i.e., recovering alcoholics and addicts) as treatment providers. In many cases, this has numerous advantages to treatment (i.e., identification, alliance, altruism, etc.). In other instances, it can have detrimental effects. A recovering alcoholic or addict might be inclined to use the exact identical format for treatment that the therapist himself experienced. In such cases, a "what worked for me will work for you" attitude may result in unreasonable therapeutic expectations. In some cases, more emphasis can be placed on prior personal experience in relation to clinical training. It is important to realize that nothing can substitute for good sound clinical skills, whether the therapist is recovering or has never suffered from an addiction problem. The recovering person who has gotten himself well-trained clinically has much more to offer

than a therapist who is either just recovering or well-trained clinically.

2. One's own personal therapy is a very important asset to providing quality therapy. This is especially important in the field of group therapy. The group leader who knows what it is like, from personal experience, to be on the other side of the therapy group encounter, will be more sensitive to the issues that are likely to manifest in group. Yalom (1985) writes about the importance of a group training experience:

> Such an experience may offer many types of learning not elsewhere available. The student is able to learn at an emotional level what he may previously have known only intellectually: he experiences the power of the group, its power to wound or heal; he learns how important it is to be accepted by the group; he learns what self-disclosure really entails, how difficult it is to reveal one's secret world, one's fantasies, one's feelings of vulnerability, hostility, and tenderness; he appreciates his own strengths as well as his weaknesses; he learns about his own preferred role in the group; and perhaps most striking of all, he learns about the role of the leader as he becomes aware of his own dependency and his own unrealistic appraisal of the leader's power and knowledge. (1985, p. 523)

Imhof shares a similar opinion about personal therapy when he writes:

> We maintain that only through an examination of one's own emotional development can the therapist most effectively recognize, tolerate, and begin to sort out the infinite range of countertransferential and attitudinal considerations inherent in the treatment of such patients. (1984, p. 29)

3. Clinical supervision, especially in the field of alcohol and drug abuse, is essential if one is to successfully manage all of their countertransferential considerations which are likely to be evoked by these patients.

4. Continual education is required. The group leader must continue to familiarize himself with an ever-greater understanding of the multifactorial influences of alcoholism and drug dependence.

5. A constant evaluation of one's own personal values and attitudes towards individuals who abuse or are addicted to chemi-

cals is required. This also means the therapist has to carefully monitor his own attitudes toward his own personal alcohol or drug use. A therapist who is "recreationally" using marijuana or cocaine is ill-suited to treat someone who has an alcohol or drug problem. This is made more problematic by the fact that cocaine and marijuana are illegal. The moral and ethical stance of such a position has important ramifications for treatment. At the other extreme, the therapist who, for religious reasons, perceives drug or alcohol use as a moral issue needs to carefully assess whether working with alcohol or drug dependent patients is in his best interest, not to mention the detrimental effects this attitude can have on his patients.

If a group leader can discipline himself to follow these principles in the course of his work with addicted patients, it will enhance his chances of having a successful therapy group. Awareness of one's own countertransferential influences and reactions is essential while working with alcoholics and addicts in a group setting. A group leader who is finely tuned into himself has a valuable diagnostic tool at his disposal. How is each patient affecting him? What are the feelings he is having at this moment in regards to the group and its members? Constantly monitoring questions like these can give the group leader much valuable information about his group and its members. Each group member reacts differently to the group leader. Studying their individual reactions not only teaches the group leader about the individual members in the group, but it also gives the group leader an opportunity to understand himself better. Individual members often pick up on reactions, feelings and attitudes of the group leader that he may not be aware of in himself. An openness to self-reflection and a willingness to critically examine one's contributions to the group and its individual members reactions can give the group leader a valuable therapeutic tool if he has the courage to honestly monitor himself. Like Socrates urged, the group leader must "Know thyself."

REFERENCES

Alonso, A. (1981). Lecture given at Harvard Medical School course entitled Group Psychotherapy, Boston, Mass. Nov., 1981.
Blanc, G. & Blanc, R. (1974). *Ego psychology. Theory and practice*. New York: Columbia University Press.
Imhof, J., Hirsch, R., & Terenzi, R. (1984). Countertransferential and attitudinal consider-

ations in the treatment of drug abuse and addiction. *Journal of Substance Abuse Treatment, 1*, 21–30.

Kernberg, O. (1975). *Borderline conditions and pathological narcissism.* New York: Jason Aronson.

Kernberg, O. (1984). The couch at sea: Psychoanalytic studies of group and organizational leadership. *International Journal of Group Psychotherapy, 34*(1), 5–23.

Kohut, H. (1977). *The restoration of the self.* New York: International Universities Press.

Levy, S. (1984). *Principles of interpretation.* New York: Jason Aronson.

Rutan, S. (1983). Presented at Transference in Group lecture at the American Group Psychotherapy Association in Toronto, Canada, February.

Yalom, I. (1985). *The theory and practice of group psychotherapy.* New York: Basic Books.

Chapter 12

Resistance in Group

One of the most difficult technical problems confronting the group leader is the recognition and resolution of group resistance. The extent to which the group leader is successful in helping the group members deal with their individual and colluded efforts at avoiding emotionally charged issues determines to a large degree the success or failure of the group therapy experience. The group leader must not only manage the different individual resistances in group, but he must be able to identity the phenomena of a unified group resistance and successfully resolve the simultaneous resistance of each and all of the members in group. His handling of the group resistance is crucial. Unless he successfully develops strategies for coping with it, the group may remain at an impasse indefinitely, become fragmented, or dissolve totally.

In working with a unified group resistance, the group leader's previous experience of dealing with individual resistances in individual therapy will be of little use to him in the group setting. It is essential that the group leader develop special skills for detecting its occurrence in group and working resistance through on a group level. The group leader must learn to gauge the group's characteristic operating efficiency by noting the extent to which the group and its members contribute or detract from the group goals. The success or failure of a therapy group is determined to a large degree by how group resistances are managed by the group leader. Successfully negotiating its resolution requires that two important principles of group resistance be addressed before the group can be a true working group.

The first required principle, which must be established for dealing with group resistance, is to be able to recognize it when it occurs. It is impossible to cope with group resistance successfully if the group leader cannot see it or feel it. This requires that the group leader understand the different forms which resistance can take in group and how his reaction or inaction contributes to its duration, intensity and resolution. The group leader must help the group members come to recognize when they are being resistive. It is necessary to call their attention to the resistive pull of the group process. However, just calling this to their attention should not be expected to be enough to resolve its occurrence. Resistance is always there for a reason, and the group members should not be expected to give it up until the emotional forces held in check by it are sufficiently discharged or converted, so that they are no longer a danger to the safety of the group or its members. Each group member has to be able to come to understand the meaning of resistance in terms of his own life history and experience.

The second principle for dealing with group resistance requires that the group leader clearly understand the part he plays in the establishment and maintenance of resistance in his group. Resistance is always a product of the interaction between the patient and the therapist. In group, resistance can be induced by the leader who is passive, hostile, ineffective, guarded, weak, or in need of constant admiration and excessive friendliness. The group leader must be able to differentiate between the part he plays in this process and the part the individual group members play within the context of the group's regressive pull. If the leader does not establish a cohesive, safe atmosphere for his group members, resistance will be promoted by the very nature of its inherent threat to the safety of its individual members. Any group approach or technique which is applied without the careful evaluation of these principles is apt to decrease the chances of therapeutic success in group treatment.

RESISTANCE: A DEFINITION

There are a variety of definitions for resistance. Two simple definitions which best capture its favor are:

1. Resistance is a force that prevents the freeing of unconscious material.
2. Resistance is the avoidance of feelings and the denial of emotions.

The first definition reflects a more classical psychodynamic definition of resistance. Psychodynamic oriented group therapists define resistance as any force which opposes the patient's primary task to make conscious his repressed unconscious feelings. Resistance prevents the individual from freely conveying to the group leader all his thoughts and feelings. Until this is accomplished, the patient will remain unaware of the unconscious motives which continue to compel him to act in a self-defeating manner. The second definition is a more generalized one which pertains to an individual's tendency to avoid presenting any material which is emotionally meaningful to the therapist. The patient does this despite the fact that it is emotionally charged conflicts in his relationships with meaningful others, both in his past and present, that have led him to enter therapy in the first place. The patient's affect and the content of his verbalizations will remain inappropriate to the material and consequently work against the primary goals of therapy.

Resistance can take many forms in groups. It can manifest as silence, anger, excessive intellectualization, compliance, indifference, or even boredom. Boredom is an especially troublesome form of resistance because many group leaders fail to identify it as resistance. It is a commonly accepted fact that groups promote regression. Every group member is forced to deal with emotionally arousing issues related to survival, acceptance, rejection, and closeness. Boredom is literally not feeling one's emotions. If someone feels bored in group or starts to doze off as other group members speak, the group leader can feel confident that the bored individual is keeping powerful emotions out of his awareness. It is the group leader's task to bring such repressed feelings to the surface, where they can be examined and altered.

Nowhere is the principle of boredom as resistance more dramatically applied than in a therapy group conducted by Erv Polster. The group member can count on attracting Erv Polster's attention by just appearing bored in his group. In fact, the surest way to attract Erv Polster's interest is for the group member to announce in group that he is, in fact, bored. Nothing stimulates Erv's interest as much as a group member who can be in a close intimate setting with six to eight other people and not feel some emotional stirrings within himself. Erv's eyes will light up in his own unique penetrating fashion; and he will lean forward with sincere inquisitiveness and ask, "Now, that is interesting! Would you please tell me and the rest of the group how you manage to keep yourself bored in such an intimate gathering as this?"

Erv Polster (1980) also has his own unique definition of resistance. He views resistance as that which occurs when the patient doesn't do what the therapist wants him to do. Resistance does not exist for Erv Polster. For Erv, resistance is "the stuff" that therapy is made of. Operating from a classical Gestalt perspective, Erv Polster "goes with" the patient's resistance. Utilizing a Zen-typed martial arts stance when exploring resistance, Erv Polster moves in to use the resistance to his advantage. He magnifies the resistance because this is where the patient's energy is frequently blocked. Exploring and expanding the resistance will usually lead to a release of the repressed material.

Heinz Kohut (1977), coming from a more classical psychoanalytic point of view, expresses similar sentiments to those of Erv Polster when he writes about resistance. Kohut views resistance as being enhanced by the iatrogenic effects of an unempathic therapist. Resistance is lessened either by the group leader's empathic understanding or by another group member's sympathy and shared similar experience. If the group leader is vicariously introspective and remains empathically in tune with the patient, resistance will be greatly diminished.

Robert Goulding (1979) sees resistance somewhat differently, yet he agrees that its resolution is one of the most important ingredients to successful therapy. For Goulding, therapy with the patient is much like a chess match. A part of the patient wants to change and get better. This is the part that brings the patient to the therapy session. However, there is an equally strong part in the patient that wants things to remain as they are. This is the part that is resistant and tries to defeat the therapist. This is why Goulding cautions the therapist to watch for the first con. The first con will usually manifest itself in the patient's initial statement (i.e., "I don't think this will help, but . . .") or in other key words like can't need, should, or try (see Chapter 9).

While Kohut, Goulding and Polster each view resistance somewhat differently, they agree on the significance it plays in a person's psychological functioning. The group leader must never lose sight of the understanding that resistance is part of an individual's defensive system and that defenses are always there for good reason. As Scott Rutan said (1981), "Patients come to us with solutions, not problems." By this, he meant that resistance must be recognized as a defensive maneuver constructed by patients to protect themselves against painful emotional experiences, usually of a long-standing nature. The only problem is that the defenses they have erected to protect themselves are often worse than the original emotional trauma which led to its establishment. Their defensive operations usually end up more disruptive than the feelings or thoughts they were originally intended to protect them from. In dealing with resistance of this nature, the group leader must remember a simple principle about resistance. The more guarded and defended the person, the more pain, hurt and fear that is hidden behind the guardedness. Anger is almost always an emotion that is erected in direct proposition to the amount of hurt that a person has experienced in his life. The more angry the group member appears, the greater the likelihood that he is protecting himself from the exposure of powerful negative emotions like shame, guilt, hurt and self-loathing. Therefore, defenses must not be stripped away too quickly. Defenses must never be exposed just for the sake of their exposure. They must be slowly and carefully removed or altered as the person gradually develops new and healthier methods for protecting himself.

GROUP RESISTANCE AND THE WORK OF WILFRED BION

Wilfred Bion is one of the most influential figures in psychoanalytic group psychotherapy. He earned his reputation and fame in group therapy without the benefit of working with therapy groups himself. This makes his contributions all the more remarkable since his book *Experiences in Groups* (1961) continues to have a powerful effect on psychodynamic approaches to group therapy.

The most widely known aspect of Bion's work is his basic assumption theory. Bion drew a distinction between the basic assumption group and the work group. Within Bion's perspective, there were always two groups present in every group setting the overt or work group and the covert or basic assumption group. While the work group is always established to accomplish an overt task, a covert group exists alongside the overt group and often operates out of its own unspoken rules. Bion asserted that the primitive states of mind operating covertly in the basic assumption group tended to dominate the work group and would come to interfere with the declared task of the group. The emotional attitudes organized in these basic assumption states were described as unconscious processes and were differentiated into three categories. Each category possessed an as-if quality and were identified as dependency, fight-flight, and pairing.

I. Work Group   II. Basic Assumption Group
-----------   -------------------------
   A. Overt   A. Covert
   B. Task Oriented Activity   B. Hatred of Learning by
                                               Experience
   C. Readiness to Cooperate   C. Opposition to
                                               Development
   D. Ego Activity, Reality   D. Preferring the Comfort
      Testing and   of Magical Ideas Rather
      Responsibility   Than Ego Ideas Which
                                               Require Work
   E. Composed of Individuals   E. Group Mind
   F. Real and Quantitative   F. "As If" Quality

Dependency

The group will behave "as if" satisfaction, safety and the future of the group depends on a strong leader. The aim of the group is to obtain security by seeking the protection of a leader who can be seen as all powerful and all wonderful. The aim of the group is to find someone who will take care of them.

BASIC ASSUMPTION OF DEPENDENCY

1. Leader Idealized as Omnipotent and Wonderful
2. Helpless Dependency on Leader
3. Attempts to Extract Power from the Leader

Fight-Flight

The group acts "as if" there is an internal or external threat that must be challenged or from which they must escape. Action is essential within the fight-flight basic assumption. The group can flee into the abstract dialogue of the there and then or the group members can fight with each other, often giving the illusion that their fighting is doing "real work" in group. In actuality, their fighting is a defense against the real overt task of the group. If the group leader cannot tolerate internal strife, the group will direct its anger outward and find a cause, ideology, or other group to hate.

BASIC ASSUMPTION OF FIGHT/FLIGHT

1. Outfighting: Group Unites Against Foe
2. Infighting: Between Sub-groups
3. Flight from Task

Pairing

The group acts "as if" assertive feelings of anger or depressive feelings of despair do not exist. Passive contemplation is maintained through idealization through which the mood of hopefulness prevents the emergency of destructive rage or persecutory anxiety and depressions. The group lives in a state of hope that the intimacy of the group members may give birth to a new idea or a Messiah who will save them.

BASIC ASSUMPTION OF PAIRING

1. Intimacy of Pairing Sub-group
2. Tolerance Of and Collusion with the Pair
3. Hopeful Expectation of Salvation of Conflict by the Pair

Fusion

A fourth common basic assumption which Bion did not identify is that of fusion. The group acts "as if" all the members of the group were the same. The group and its members retreat into we-ness. This is represented by the group members who comment that they see everyone equally in the group. "I trust everyone here equally. I care equally for everyone in the group" are examples of how group members will go to great lengths to deny their individuality. It is a defensive reaction brought upon by the regressive pull of their need to be part of and included in a group, society or family. Bion asserts that we are forever social animals (see Figure 1).

Bion used the term valency to describe an individual's tendency

FIGURE I

PAIRING

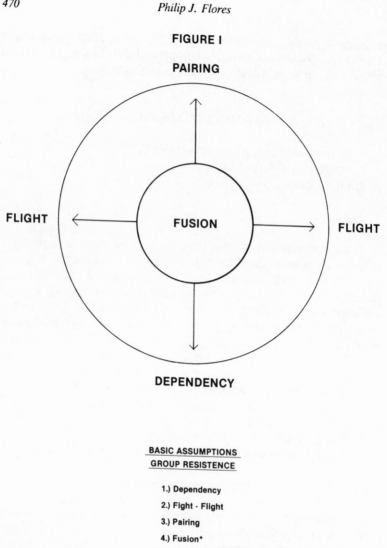

DEPENDENCY

BASIC ASSUMPTIONS
GROUP RESISTENCE

1.) Dependency
2.) Fight - Flight
3.) Pairing
4.) Fusion*

to be attracted to others with similar underlying motives, values and propensities. These valencies can exercise a powerful regressive pull and lead to the activation of basic assumptions when the group is faced with the frustration entailed in sustaining the requirements of the group work. Basic assumptions are primitive states of mind generated by the dilemma which is created by the dual pull of the group. Each member wants to be part of the group and yet they want to maintain their individuality. As Bion wrote, "The individual is a group animal at war, not simply with the group, but with himself for being a group animal and with those aspects of his personality that constitute his groupishness" (1961, p. 131).

While it is true that basic assumptions exist in group, it is important for the group leader to be aware that basic assumptions are stage specific and can be induced by the behavior of the group leader.

Stage Specific Basic Assumptions

1. Early phase of group development is marked by the dependency group. The group expects magical solutions will be bestowed upon them by the group leader. The emotional state is one of dependency and awe.
2. Middle phase of group development is marked by flight from tasks or engagement of battles within or outside of the group. The emotional state is one of hostility and fear.
3. Late phase of group is marked by state of hope. The group possesses the curative fantasy and hopes the intimacy of the group will give birth to ideas or a person who can bring about an ultimate answer to the group's dilemma. Pairing carries an emotional state of optimism and hopefulness. The group waits for the birth of a Messiah which must never be born because it would end hope.

The Leader's Influence on the Basic Assumptions

Otto Kernberg (1984), writing about the leader's influence on group development, emphasizes the important effect that the leader's personality has on the group's development. He has correctly pointed out that a passive, inactive and quiet group leader is more likely to provoke Bion's basic assumptions. Basic assumption states owe their existence, therefore, in a large part to the conditions imposed by the group leader himself upon the group. Brown (1985) takes a very similar stance and questions whether many followers of Bion have taken his basic assumption theory too literally and suggests that they have applied his ideas incorrectly to group therapy. Brown writes, "For some of his ideas are, I think, ultimately inadequate and misleading as a basis for therapy, particularly the unmodified concept of basic assumptions" (1981, p. 192). Brown further states that Bion ignores the more mature ego states in his work and is preoccupied with primitive processes. His viewpoint, Brown feels, is "based on a Kleinian approach to mental functioning that is preoccupied with primitive processes to the neglect of more mature ego functions" (1985, p. 215). This is why Bion overemphasized the basic assumption group. The work group is not opposed to the more primitive functions; rather it develops out of them and eventually supercedes them unless the group leader fails to guide the group through this process. Basic assumptions are, therefore, indications that the group is struggling unsuccessfully against resistance. Resolution of resistance, however, does not require that the basic assumption states be the focus of therapeutic interventions.

The group leader's attempt to resolve the basic assumption is a misdirected effort. This is where most psychodynamic group leader's fail to appreciate the impact that they make in inducing a basic assumption emotional state. Unmodified basic assumptions arise as a result of avoidances of genuine personal encounters. Difficult feelings in relationships are thereby disavowed and repressed. Repression and denial leads to basic assumption states.

It is with the choice of the intervention that the group leader is most likely to misdirect his efforts. Unmodified basic assumptions arise as a result of a situation which prevents genuine personal encounters. Difficult feelings in relationships are disavowed either through dependency, fusion, fight-flight or pairing. Any gathering of three or more people that does not permit true intimate contact is likely to induce a basic assumption emotional state. Group members must be encouraged to deal honestly with all feelings that emerge in the group climate. Negative as well as positive feeling must be expressed and acknowledged or else the group will stay stuck in a basic assumption state. Basic assumption states reflect ways that group members try to cope and rid themselves of dangerous feelings and impulses. Group members will attempt to engage the group leader on the basis of wishes and fantasies, which will protect them from their prohibited emotions. Ezriel (1952) states that group members will first try to establish three types of relationships with the group leader in their attempt to defend themselves:

1. Each group member will first try to establish the *required* relationship since he requires it in order to protect himself from the second relationship.

2. The second relationship is called the *avoided* relationship which the group member attempts to establish in order to avoid external reality because he is convinced that if he gave into his secret desire to enter into the avoided relationship, it would result in the third relationship.
3. The third relationship is not a relationship at all, but an expected result of the avoided relationship which is *calamity.*

Calamity is the feared result that must be avoided at all costs by each group member. Ezriel describes this process:

1. Required relationship: Idealization of therapist.
2. Avoided relationship: If established, it would result in the group member attacking the therapist.
3. Calamity: Based on the group member's fear that he would either harm the therapist or the therapist would retaliate and in turn destroy him.

During treatment, as the group leader induces more reality testing, the expected unconscious calamity does not occur. The need for the required relationship is removed and the avoided relationship and its related behavior pattern emerges. Both negative and positive emotions are experienced and expressed. True intimacy is established in group. In the basic assumption group, the leader of the dependency group has to be omnipotent, the fight-leader has to be unbeatable and the flight-leader uncatchable; the leader of the pairing group must be marvelous but unborn. As the expected calamity is corrected, the group members learn that they need not resist their true feelings towards the group leader. In the mature work group, which makes a more adaptive use of appropriate assumptions, the leader of the dependency group is dependable, the leader of the fight-flight group is courageous, and the leader of the pairing group is creative.

The group leader plays a very significant part in determining whether the group makes the transition from the basic assumption group to the work group. The group leader who needs to be idealized keeps the group dependent. Bad feelings are subsequently split off and projected onto other group members. The possibility of scapegoating is subsequently increased. The scapegoat serves an important function for the group. He is the container for the frustrations the group members have but cannot express toward the group leader. In every group, there will usually be one or two volunteers for the role of the group scapegoat. The group will eventually choose from the list of volunteers to determine who is to serve the capacity of the container for their anger.

The group leader who requires that the group be highly cohesive so that negative feelings cannot be directed between group members contributes to the group directing their negative feelings to the there and then outside of group. The group leader who encourages pairing in group allows the group members to use their need for hope to prevent the emergency of negative feelings like anger and despair.

However, pairing, like the other basic assumptions, can be viewed as a testing of the group leader. Pairing will continue if assertive feelings cannot be mobilized in a way that makes the defeat of rage and despair less dependent upon a leader who continues to foster a hopeful situation. If the group leader can help the group members accept his limitations and the rage or disappointment this realization produces, he will lead the group to become more autonomous. The negative forces of fight-flight won't be split off. In pairing, the group has the chance to accept and realize their fantasy wish. Pairing in group is really an experiment by the group in their effort to determine if it is safe to be intimate in group. Fantasy or illusion is not always defensive. It can be a creative adaptive response. It allows the group to perceive and imagine what doesn't exist and create it. The group will eventually learn that it can establish intimate relationships without sacrificing hope. More importantly, it can eventually learn to accept relationships, even if they aren't perfect, without becoming depressed, enraged or losing hope.

This is where Bion's original concept of basic assumptions has to be carefully evaluated and modified. Basic assumptions are not the result of the group's attempt to avoid intimacy as much as it is a reaction to a leader or a situation which prohibits and prevents intimacy. As Brown writes, " basic assumptions result in groups from avoidance of genuine personal encounter, so that difficult feelings in relationships are disavowed" (1985, p. 216). Basic assumption states are more likely, therefore, in settings where personal contact is forbidden, inappropriate or best avoided (i.e., disturbed families, large groups, work situations or therapy groups run on strict Bionian lines). In situations like these, it is easy to understand how a strong leader, an enemy, or a utopian idea can appear as a viable and entertaining alternative to all the group's problems.

Brown suggests that settings which promote genuine contact, such as in a well-functioning therapy group, will reduce the emergence of basic assumption states. A therapy group that faces up to its problems and differences and allows the full expression of all emotions, be they awkward, negative or positive, will prevent the emergence and persistence of basic assumptions. The group leader's task is not to promote basic assumptions in order to analyze or study their occurrence; rather it should insure that they do not manifest or persist in group.

In those group settings which are not intended to be therapeutic, basic assumptions serve important functions. The basic assumption states can be recognized in society through the institutions of the church, army and aristocracy. The function of the church is to organize dependency on a deity; the army is to defense the realm; and the aristocracy is to insure the next generation of superior leaders.

If Bion's and Ezriel's interpretations of the basic assumption phenomena are correct, their analysis of this process has two important implications for group therapy. First, their work implies that the basic assumptions are the result, not the cause of a group setting, where true intimate dialogue is prohibited. Secondly, as Brown clearly states, the group leader's task is not to analyze or heighten the basic assumptions, but facilitate intimate interaction between group members, thus minimizing and eventually eliminating the destructive forces which prevent the emergences of the overt tasks of the work group.

RESISTANCE OF INTIMACY IN GROUPS

However, the group leader will soon discover that facilitating intimacy in group is no easy task. While everyone desires intimacy, they fear it at the same time. Each group member will reveal his own particular strategies for systematically sabotaging intimacy. This is particularly true for recovering alcoholics and addicts. The group leader's task is to identify how each member of his group will erect elaborate precautions to prevent true intimacy. The group member's resistance is most strongly tied into their fear of intimacy. If the alcoholic or addict can find ways of preventing its occurrence, they will feel vindicated. "See, I was right, you can't really trust people."

If the group leader can discipline himself to watch closely for the different ways that the group members resist intimacy, he will help each identify their own particular idiosyncratic style. For instance, a group member may have the knack for saying the wrong thing at the wrong time in the wrong way to the wrong person. Sometimes, a group member will do all four at the same time.

Group therapy is the treatment of choice for resolving problems with intimacy. Resistance to intimacy is there because all addicts and alcoholics fear that if they risk being open to another, they will be rejected. Fears behind their resistance to intimacy must be resolved if a person is to be able to get close to another on a mature level. Childhood fears of intimacy must be dispelled and replaced with mature intimate feelings.

Steve, a thirty-nine-year old sales manager, had entered group therapy at the request of his family therapist. His wife and he had been married over fifteen years and had sought couples therapy because their sex life was unsatisfactory. After more than six months of couples therapy, it became obvious that their difficulty with their sexual relationship was the result of their difficulty with emotional closeness. They had been separated for nearly a year prior to entering couples therapy and their relationship had been marked by vacillating periods of closeness and emotional distancing. Steve complained that his wife kept him at a distance, was withholding and uninterested in him sexually. She countered that every time she got close to him, he would do something to push her away and she was no longer willing to trust him because of his inconsistency. Because they had become locked into a power struggle around this issue, it was judged to be best for them to deal with their fears of intimacy individually. After a month of group therapy, Steve's pattern of vacillating between closeness and distancing became apparent to the group. While such an observation by his wife led to denial and anger, he found himself more open to the consensual observation of the other group members. Steve also talked freely about his occasional sexual affairs and consistent marijuana smoking. Since his wife grew up in a home with an alcoholic father and was a recovering alcoholic herself with more than eight years of sobriety through AA, she reacted strongly to this inconsistent behavior Steve demonstrated when he was stoned. He objected to her accusations, saying that she just had been brain-washed by AA. However, as the rest of the group, many of them recovering alcoholics, began to voice similar concerns, Steve began to admit that his marijuana use had indeed concerned him for some time, but that he was reluctant to admit it to his wife because this would be admitting she was right. As Steve's contradictory messages were challenged by the other group members, he started to question his own motives about his marijuana smoking and affairs. Every time he would get angry about his wife's coldness, he would get stoned in an effort to stuff his anger because he "did not want to make matters worse." As she continued to pull away from him further as a result of his marijuana use he felt justified in his getting his sexual needs met elsewhere. After a sexual liaison with another woman, his guilt would compel him to undo his anger and he would once again make an effort to get close to her. She would start to respond to his efforts, but was weary of his motives. As she withheld, the pattern would be repeated as it had been for the last ten years.

As the group began to point out Steve's uncomfortableness with closeness and his mixed messages, he came to identify his fears of intimacy. Finally, one evening in group, Steve admitted he was afraid to get close to his wife or commit himself to the marriage. "I have one foot in and one foot out." "I'm scared that if I go ahead and do make a consistent effort with her, she might still reject me. I don't want to take that risk." Steve was not willing to face the possibility that he might be rejected if he got close. Like the pairing assumption state in Bion's schema, Steve did not want to risk true intimacy because it would require he give up the hope of intimacy. His idealized fantasy must forever remain unborn. This was exactly his issue with his mother. She was cold, distant and unwilling to accept Steve as he really was. True intimacy had always been absent from their relationship and Steve did not want to risk being rejected by another woman whom he cared for deeply. Steve's fear of intimacy was played out with his wife. If he risked being himself with her, he expected to be rejected. Since his own mother would only accept him if he met her wishes and expectations, he rebelled at complying with her wishes. Yet, he feared openly expressing his anger toward his mother because this would only lead to her pushing him away further. As he does with his wife, Steve kept one foot in the relationship (i.e., wanting closeness) and one foot out of the relationship (fears rejection if he were to be truly intimate with her, because she would only accept him if he met her expectations).

Resistance to intimacy in group will always emerge if the group members are given enough time together. The group leader must allow each member's resistance to manifest before their fears of intimacy can be observed and resolved. Observation of resistance in group will give the group leader much information about each member's fears of intimacy. As Freud once stated, "What people avoid telling you is more important than the content of their message of what they say they fear." Oscar Wilde expressed similar sentiments when he said, "People's masks tell you more than their faces."

Louis Ormont (1985) lists four major fears to intimacy in groups.

1. Fear of impulsivity
2. Fear of merger
3. Fear of abandonment
4. Fear of vulnerability

Fear of impulsivity. Group members, especially alcoholics and addicts, possess tremendous fears of their impulsivity. If they feel and show it, they fear it will get out of hand. Such fears are not limited to their anger or hostility, it also is manifest in their caring for others, which frequently gets confused with sexuality. One male group member in particular would stiffen noticeably whenever he spoke to other men in the group. He feared that if he showed warm feelings to other men, he would be viewed as a homosexual. Many men and women struggle with issues of intimacy because they do not know how to be close without turning it into a sexual encounter. Sex and closeness are often mutually exclusive. They fear if they get close to another, it will mean that they will have to act on their sexual feelings.

Fear of merger. Many individuals, especially those who have grown up in a home with a controlling and intrusive parent, will possess strong fears of merger. They fear they will be taken over by the other person if they get close. They must remain separate or else they will lose themselves in the other. Steve's wife in the earlier reported case vignette experienced such fears. She grew up in a home with a mother who tried very hard to control her because the mother was unable in any way to control her alcoholic husband. Steve's wife saw such efforts on his part to get close as an attempt to control her, since her mother used intimacy and closeness as a means of control.

Fear of abandonment. Each person usually possesses tremendous fears of abandonment. This is especially true for those who have been abandoned previously by another whom they deeply loved. Since everyone wants closeness and love, it would seem that the answer to their dilemma would be simple. Love and intimacy provides a rich source of gratification for both their instinctual and reality needs. The only problem with intimacy and closeness as a solution to a person's isolation, is that it puts the person at the mercy of his love object. Love, closeness and intimacy leaves a person extremely vulnerable to its loss or rejection. As Freud said, "we are never so defenseless against suffering as when we love, never so helplessly unhappy as when we have lost our love object or its love." People who have already experienced rejection are usually very reluctant to once again choose closeness and intimacy as a path to happiness.

This point was clearly demonstrated by Mary, a thirty-six-year old secretary who entered group because of her depression and lack of friends. She could never please her mother and father, as they were extremely critical of her appearance, intelligence and even her gender. Her older brother, who was much preferred because he was a male, was an extremely successful student, athlete and business man. Mary would be extremely sensitive to any remarks that the group members made which could be interpreted, even in the slightest fashion, to be critical of her. She would also constantly put herself down, saying that no one in the group really liked her and she understood why. Anytime the group leader directed any of his attention towards another group member, she would attack that group member and accuse the group leader of not showing the same degree of concern for her problems. Her behavior drove the group to distraction. Their protests to her accusations were futile and led many of the members to avoid her because of their frustration at her behavior. Her fear of rejection compelled her to test everyone she came in contact with. Finally, one evening during group, she stated her fear directly to the group leader. "I know I'm worthless and I'd rather have you reject me now before I start to care for you too much." Once the motive behind her behavior became obvious to the group and its members, the group leader would constantly interpret her actions to her and the other group members. Eventually, the group took over this confrontive process and did not "play out" their part in Mary's self-fulfilled prophecy. As they refused to succumb to her constant testing, they also began to show their concern for her. A repetitive pattern in Mary's life was consequently altered.

Fear of vulnerability. Fear of vulnerability is the most common fear of intimacy. Each group member fears that if he becomes truly intimate with another, he will be exposed as unworthy, undeserving or lacking. He fears that the other group members will discover that he is really inept. Avoidance of vulnerability will take many forms. Some group members will avoid intimacy by fact seeking ("What do you exactly mean by warmth?") or fault finding ("Thank you for your concern, but do you have to keep repeating it?"). Others will set unrealistic conditions for intimacy ("Could you say that more softly?") or take another's intimate statement away ("That reminds me of my friend at work and how he has the same difficulty."). Sometimes the group member will turn off another's intimacy by anger ("You are here now, but where were you last week?").

The group leader's task is to help his group members work through each of their fears of intimacy. At first, the members of the group will be puzzled by the leader's efforts because it will be contrary to all that they have learned about physical survival. Their early experiences have taught them it is not safe to be intimate, close and open with another. Don't expect them to discard their old though maladaptive, ways of coping. They must come to learn their fears were unrealistic as children, but their ways of relating need not continue to color their experiences as adults. As Shakespeare wrote, "What we cannot throw away, we must embrace." Each group member must be encouraged to face their fears. They must experience it and know it completely. They must learn it is a signal based on their childhood expectations. Keep pointing out what they are doing and constantly call it to the other group members' attention.

Show them and the other group members how their behavior is an attempt on their part to ward off the fear of intimacy.

Each group member possesses his own early form of intimacy fears. In the initial stages of group, he will continue to harbor childhood fears and fantasies about intimacy. As he begins to talk about his fears in group, his positions against intimacy will begin to soften. He will learn that his fears are grounded in his early bonding difficulties with his parents. These fears will get played out in group and he will come to learn about more mature forms of intimacy. He will eventually come to realize that his childhood expectations about intimacy are unfounded. One common fear is that his needs are bottomless. He feels ashamed if he needs, and his neediness usually frightens him because his needs were never appropriately met as a child. He was taught that it was dangerous to expect from others. He no longer has to deny his needs because of fears that it will leave him vulnerable. This is why he does not let others know he needs. He fears that if they know, he will be seen as needy and rejected. Other members will learn his fears of intimacy are related to his fear of indebtedness. If he takes from others, he fears that he will be indebted and must give back to them. If he gives to other members, he fears it will be expected of him in the future and that giving comes at a personal price.

As these issues and fears are resolved in group, the mature desires for intimacy will be experienced by each of the group members. Intimacy and closeness will carry a vital sense of experience for them. It will be an experience that sustains and not just be a happening. It will become embedded in their character and incorporated into their being. The group will come to share a common intimacy where the full range of emotions will have permission to be expressed and experienced. The whole group is always alive during an intimate moment.

Resistance to Feelings in Group

Group therapy must be a place where all feelings, anger as well as happiness, can be expressed. The full range of feelings must be presentable in group. However, there will be both individual and group resistance to the expression and recognition of feelings. The group leader must deal with the group resistance first before he tackles the individual resistances in group. Resistance is diminished whenever the feelings that get stirred up in group are appropriately dealt with. However, when feelings are too powerful, unconscious or disavowed, the group and its members can become stuck in Bion's basic assumptions. Every resistance in group can be traced to a feeling which was triggered by other members in the group. The group leader has to be able to trace the resistance to a place and time when the group stopped being effective. While the group and its members will often be aware of their resistance, their awareness is usually superficial and poorly integrated with the rest of their experience. It is the leader's task to bring to their awareness the unconscious feelings that led to their resistance. Fancher (1973) addresses this issue succinctly when he writes about Freud's early discoveries concerning resistance.

> Freud was forced to the conclusion that the most important part of the resistance was not the most obvious part. The conscious distress and disgust experienced by a patient was only the most superficial manifestation of his resistance. His deepest resistance was embodied in his transference neurosis, which was a replica of his real neurosis, and of which he was completely unconscious. This suggested to Freud that at the most significant level an individual is unaware of his own resistance and of the real nature of his conflicts. That is, he is as unconscious of the process of repression, itself as he is of the content of his repressions. (p. 200-201, 1973)

Dealing with resistance and the obstacles to emotional feelings is one primary task of the group leader. The leader must get the group and its members to be aware of the way in which they are resisting and blocking emotions. Since the group members do this to avoid pain and the unpleasantness of emotions, they must come to realize that there is no danger in feeling. They must come to recognize that their faulty maneuvers at protecting themselves are no longer necessary.

It is the alleviation of the disturbance of a person's emotional life that constitutes the primary function of psychotherapy. There are limits to what psychotherapy can or cannot do. The primary effectiveness of therapy is achieved within the realm of the many ways in which an individual's subjective emotional experiences interferes with their ability to function interpersonally and intellectually. In order to accomplish this task in group, the group leader must have access to each group member's feelings. This requires that there be an activation of their feelings in group. Each group member must come to experience the wide range of their emotions in group since feelings cannot be changed or learned about by just talking about them. They must be experienced and observed in group. There is always an element of risk involved in the activation of feelings. However, the group leader and the person experiencing the emotions never know exactly where the feelings will go. Since feelings are often contagious, there is no way to predict the emotional responses of the other group members to their interactions in group. This reflects the advantage as well as the disadvantage of emotional expression in group. It is this risk and the fear of the unpredictability of emotions that leads members to resist the expression of feelings.

Feelings do not usually occur in a vacuum. It requires an activation from another to energize feelings. The group leader needs to know how to facilitate the experience of emotions without interfering with the group members' experience. If the group and its members are working, it is best for the group leader to be quiet. When the person or the group is stuck, this is when the group leader must activate responses from other group members. It is often the interaction between the group members that evokes affect.

The belief that a person must be engaged on a real emotional level in order to get at repressed feelings in a relatively new belief which reflects a shift from the intrapsychic model to one based on interaction and object relations. The old analytic belief of Freud's was that it was only necessary to focus on feelings and the reasons (defenses) why a person blocked their feelings. Strict adherence to this model does not focus enough emphasis on feelings which are evoked in response to exchanges that occur within the interpersonal context. Feelings have an adaptive significance and always serve a problem solving function. It is within the interpersonal exchanges in the group that the group leader will learn how each group member has adapted to the feelings which are evoked by intimacy or anger.

Mental health is determined by the interplay between the individual and his feelings. The ability to experience one's feelings without resisting or running from them determines to a large degree whether a person is healthy or ill (see Figure II).

Illness is usually the result of an individual's blockage of his feelings. It is the unhealthy person who remains unconnected with his emotions and out of touch with his feelings. Contrary to the popular belief held by most group members, the healthy individual

FIGURE II

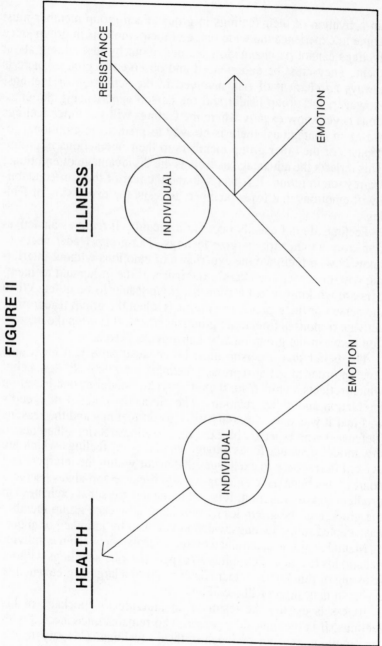

is the person who can experience his negative feelings like sadness, anger, envy and anxiety. Many alcoholics and addicts attempt to reach an erroneous ideal state where they believe they will never have to experience negative emotions again. Alcohol and drugs temporarily confirm their illusion. However, the negative feelings which they fear and resist constantly push for expression. Resistance of negative feelings is not as selective as the alcoholic and addict would like to believe. As negative feelings are denied and repressed, so are the positive feelings. The group leader must set the group in motion towards the expression of all repressed feelings. He must establish a climate in group of working towards health and away from illness.

It is when the group members direct their efforts towards the blocking and resistance of their feelings that problems arise. It is the healthy group member who can explore his feelings and the reasons which led him to feel as he does. When anger is too frightening or pain too overwhelming, the individual defenses become too rigid. The group member needs the encouragement and the safety of the group before he will risk getting his impounded feelings out. Only after the feelings have been expressed can the person then come to a proper understanding of what has happened to him. Cognitive distortions will be eliminated and there will be a greater chance for reflection on the experience so that the present does not remain tied to or determined by the past. This requires feelings to come through to a completion. If the person is angry, it must be expressed. Once an emotion has been given its full expression, it will often be a freeing experience for the individual. Ward (1984) expresses the importance of this principle when he spoke of the necessity of completing an experience before it can be understood. "After buying the sports car you always wanted, you then, in reflection, will understand why it was so important for you to have it in the first place." The understanding of the sequence of events that led to the expression of the anger or the purchase of the sports car will then bring the experience to a close. An emotional expression not understood only leads to increased resistance of that emotion in the future.

The group leader will discover that some group members organize themselves to protect themselves against feelings. Spontaneity is resisted and rigidity is embraced. They become all form and no spirit. Conventionality rules their lives and this keeps them away from the spontaneous expression of anger and intimacy. It is the group member who has ease in his interpersonal exchanges and emotional expressions that possesses good mental health.

Emotions can also interfere with a person's intellectual functioning. Not only does he lose spontaneity in his intimate interactions, he becomes rigid in his thinking and problem solving. Actively explaining a problem to another involves putting his difficulty in some order and thus removes it far enough away from his emotional or mental set, which frequently frees the person from his stuck position. If a person is frozen with anxiety and resistant to explore alternatives, he sometimes cannot literally think. A person needs the ability to shift mental sets. The person trapped into one mental set or emotional response can literally remain stuck. Ward (1984) gives an excellent example of such a condition.

> Company engineers had tried unsuccessfully for years to find the proper kind of solvent to dissolve the ink on newspapers so that the newspapers could be recycled for use at a savings of millions of dollars. Finally, distraught at their repeated failure, they sought the advice of an outside consultant. He rejected their initial requests to lead one of their research teams with the statement, "No, you have already thought about all the possible solvents. I doubt I would be able to find a new one. Instead, let's look for an ink which will dissolve in one of the solvents you already have."

Rigid mental sets, as this illustration suggests, can freeze an individual's thinking process. Psychotherapy should be directed towards unfreezing and reframing a person's experience. Often just talking about a feeling will allow the person to reorganize his conceptual understanding of the experience. Emotions can be like maps which freeze each person in the center of their universe. As the person gets "the big picture," he will come to realize that his perception of the problem has exaggerated its magnitude. The person will literally not be able to see the forest for the trees. Things that are closer to a person often look bigger than things which are far away. If the individual can put things in their proper historical and temporal arrangement, it will help reduce them to their proper size.

In interpersonal interactions, like those that occur in group, group members will evoke emotions in each other. The stronger the feelings produced, the more primitive the understanding of these emotions will be. If a person is very angry or hurt by another, it will seem as if the other did what he did only to anger or hurt him. In childhood, everything is emotional. Through the child's developmental process, he learns to understand his emotions more. Understanding helps reduce the intensity of the emotions and helps facilitate their proper expression. In group therapy, the group member must learn the proper sequence of experiencing emotions and the understanding of his emotions. If he doesn't, he will either remain a victim of his emotions or be emotionless. Understanding of feelings leads to less resistance to feelings and gives the person fuller expression to his feelings. This will allow him to modulate the appropriate expression of emotions rather than remain controlled or out of touch with his feelings.

The Group Leader's Effect on Group Resistance

The importance of leadership style and the personality of the leader is often ignored in assessing resistance in group. As Brown (1985) stated, the basic assumption states which Bion wrote about "may owe their existence in a large part to the conditions imposed on by the group by Bion, himself." Kernberg (1984) expressed similar sentiments when he asserted that both Bion and Freud's explanations of group dynamics were observations determined to a large degree by their own influences upon the dynamics of the group. Kernberg goes on to state that there is a common and erroneously held belief that the leader has no quality which affects a group, an organization, or an institution. This is a result, Kernberg contends, of an organization's need to negate the personality of its leader. The point which Kernberg wishes to make is that the leader cannot help but affect the group. More importantly, there are aspects of the leader which contribute and add to the resistance of the group.

While there are a number of treatment-destructive resistances which emerge in group, the attitude and the countertransference of the leader plays a critical part in this resistance pattern. Many a group member has been allowed to act out his tendency in this direction because the group leader has either ignored their behavior or only made half-hearted attempts at its resolution. Because the individual group member's resistance may evoke unacceptable feelings in the group leader, the group leader may try to circumvent his own anger, indifference, or anxiety instead of using it to confront the group member. Consequently, the group member's resistance never gets a chance to be completely aired and explored in group. The feeling behind the resistance remains shrouded in vagueness and denial and subsequently gets acted out by the group member. What is of critical importance is that once the resistance is sensed, it must be explored. Not to respond may contribute to the group member's destructive pattern and his eventual fleeing from treatment. Everything should take a back seat to resistance once it is observed. It must become the first order of business. There is never any therapeutic justification for postponing the confrontation of a treatment-destructive resistance. The group leader's primary objective must be to preserve the group and its existence for each of the group members.

While the group leader's countertransference issues may contribute to his reluctance to deal with individual resistances in group, there are certain characteristics of the leader that are certain to increase resistance in group.

1. Lack of empathy on the leader's part.
2. Failure to respond appropriately to group members at the right time.
3. Premature and incorrect interpretations to members of the group.
4. Hostile confrontation at an inappropriate time in group.

On the other hand, there are important qualities which a group leader must possess if he is going to minimize resistance in group. The group leader must be:

1. Intelligent,
2. Honest and non-corruptible,
3. A little narcissistic,
4. A little paranoid.

If the group leader is not a little narcissistic, he will not possess the charisma and energy needed to keep a group viable and alive. If he is not a little paranoid, he will be easily fooled or misled by his group members. However, the group leader has to have the ability to tone down his personality so as not to dominate the group and its members. He must be able, though, to use his personality and its effect on the group members to resolve resistances in group.

Resistance is never resolved if it is viewed as pathology. Focusing on it as pathology moves resistance from the realm of communication and puts it on the patient. Only when the group leader is able to ask himself, "What is this patient communicating to me with his resistance," will he be able to translate this back to the patient. This is what constitutes the essence of resolving resistance in treatment. The group leader must first understand what the group member is conveying by his resistance and then he must explain it in a way that the group member will understand. Many group leaders have been taught that silence is neutral. Frequently, silence as neutrality is the therapist's intent. However, patients do not usually perceive silence as an act of neutrality. They perceive it as indifference or rejection. Just because the group leader cares, he cannot expect his group members to know he cares; that he is benevolent and listening unless the group leader conveys this information back to his group members in a way they each understands.

The aim of psychotherapy is to experience what the patient experiences and convey this understanding back to them. If the individual is not understood, he will withdraw even farther. Each group member must be given the power to agree, disagree or change what the leader thinks he hears. If each group member does not feel he has the right to correct the leader's comments, he will resist sharing more information. The curative process emerges out of the communication between the group members and their leader. Three things must occur if resistance is to be minimized and resolved:

1. The group member must feel safe enough to allow repressed material into their awareness.
2. The expressed feelings associated with this material must be accepted by the group leader and its members.
3. This material must be integrated into the group member's personality.

All individuals have a desire to experience a continuity in their lives. As sense of safety is crucial for the sharing of repressed or disavowed aspects of the self with others in a group setting. If this can be accomplished in group, the members will give way to their powerful needs to be understood and accepted as real by others. Empathic understanding and acceptance helps restore meaning and continuity to their lives. Empathic connections with others in group increase deeper introspection. Feeling understood by another as an adult is experienced by them as being held as a child. It firms up the person's sense of self. It is the consolidation of the self which leads to the capacity to change and diminish the need to be resistant. There will no longer be a need for old defensive operations as the person feels more understood. If the group leader can avoid the pitfalls of focusing on resistance as defensive pathology, and instead focuses on the reasons why the resistances have emerged, he will enhance the effectiveness of his group and the health of its members.

REFERENCES

Bion, W. R. (1961). *Experiences in groups & other papers.* London: Tavistock.

Brown, D. G., Bion, W. R., & Foulkes. (1985). In M. Pines (Ed.), *Bion and group psychotherapy.* London: Routledge & Kegan Paul Ltd.

Fancher, R. E. (1973). *Psychoanalytic psychology. The development of Freud's thought.* New York: W. W. Norton.

Goulding, M. & Goulding, R. (1979). *Changing lives through redecision therapy.* New York: Brunner/Mazel.

Kernberg, O. (1984). The couch at sea: Psychoanalytic studies of group and organizational leadership. *International Journal of Group Psychotherapy, 34*(1), 5–24.

Kohut, H. (1977). *The restoration of self.* New York: International Universities Press.

Ormont, L. Lecture given at Harvard Medical School Seminar on Group Psychotherapy, Nov. 22–24, 1985.

Polster, E. Lecture given at the Gestalt Institute of San Diego, July, 1980.

Word, R. (1984). Lecture given at Atlanta Psychoanalytic Interest Group.

Chapter 13

Preparing the Chemically Dependent Person for Group

Once it is determined that the chemically dependent individual is in need of treatment, it is assumed he or she will be placed in a psychotherapy group. This is an assumption that is rarely, if ever, questioned in the alcohol and drug treatment field. Group psychotherapy, for reasons which are not always clearly articulated, is the prominent mode of treatment in all alcohol and drug treatment programs. Every inpatient unit, day hospital and aftercare program has group psychotherapy as an integral part of its treatment regimen. Other than the patient's involvement in Alcoholics Anonymous, it is hard to identify another treatment modality used more frequently in the treatment of addiction. Despite the prominence of its use, little effort is paid to the importance of preparing patients for entry into a psychotherapy group. This is unfortunate because entry into a psychotherapy group can be quite difficult and anxiety provoking for the prospective patient. Many addicted patients, who would otherwise profit from group psychotherapy, are unable to benefit more completely from treatment because they cannot manage the initial anxiety which group psychotherapy always triggers. Because AA is viewed by some as a form of a group therapy in which its members enter without preparation, many treatment personnel in the alcohol and drug field do not appreciate the importance of pre-group preparation for their prospective group members.

Fortunately, the importance of preparing patients for entry into other contemporary forms of group psychotherapy has not been overlooked by Yalom (1967) and others (Stone & Rutan, 1984; Agazarian & Peters, 1981). While the issue of patient preparation is a controversial subject, there has been substantial research in this area. It is important to understand the implications of this research and how pre-group preparation affects group members who are entering a group for the first time. The results from Yalom's and others' experiences in this area yields important information that can be helpful for the group leader who is about to embark on the difficult task of leading a group consisting entirely of alcoholics and addicts.

RECOMMENDATIONS FOR ENTRY INTO A THERAPY GROUP

While no one method has been universally accepted, Stone and Rutan (1984) recommend that preparation must accomplish the following:

1. Establish a preliminary alliance between patient and clinician,
2. Gain a clear consensus about the patient's therapeutic hopes,
3. Offer information and instruction about group psychotherapy,
4. Deal with the initial anxiety about joining a group,
5. Present and gain acceptance of a contract.

Establish a Preliminary Alliance

Entering a group is stressful and it is very helpful for new group members to have at least a minimal alliance with the group leader. Most patients will experience group therapy as the most difficult form of psychotherapy to begin. Having an alliance with the group leader, however brief this alliance may be, will minimize the impact of this difficulty.

As Sigmund Freud (1921) succinctly pointed out many years ago, groups promote regression. Members entering group for the first time are forced to experience and handle powerful emotions triggered by issues related to survival, rejection and acceptance. Each member must determine how they are to survive in the group and discover who is likely to attack or support him. Group members must adapt to the unknown demands of the group and learn which behavior will lead to acceptance and which behavior will lead to rejection. If the group is a particularly unstructured situation, as it is in dynamic group psychotherapy, clues regarding how to proceed are minimal. Through trial and error, members have to orient themselves to discover what behavior or interactions will work and what will not work. The ambiguity of such a situation produces regression and the degree of regression is idiosyncratic to each particular member. While the group leader can expect group members to regress in such an unstructured situation, the way the group members respond to this regression is unpredictable.

With a group of alcoholics and addicts in the early stages of their withdrawal from chemicals, techniques which promote regression can have detrimental and, in some cases, even catastrophic consequences. Alcoholics and addicts handle stress poorly. They rely on their previously maladaptive styles of coping—namely the ingesting of chemicals into their body—if they are forced to deal with ambiguity too early in their recovery. Only after they have learned more adaptive ways of coping should they be required to handle regression in group. The group leader must understand and appreciate that a relapse can sometimes be fatal for a group member. All interventions which have a potential to increase the likelihood of drug and alcohol use should therefore be used sparingly. Consequently, any measures which the group leader can take which will prevent regression during the early stages of recovery should be initiated and maintained.

One method for minimizing regression in group is to establish an alliance with the group member before they enter group. An alliance with the group leader will decrease the likelihood of a relapse occurring because of the intensity of the feelings which are triggered by the regressive pull of the group. An alliance is especially important if the group member has had no prior psychotherapy experience. It is the patient who has never been exposed to individual or group psychotherapy that is most likely to prematurely drop out of treatment.

Implications for Research Findings

A study conducted at a major university reported that 70 of 198 patients dropped out of therapy after less than five visits, even though their therapists felt they could benefit from further treatment (MacLeod, 1968). Yalom reports similar findings in another study which found one third of all patients beginning group therapy dropped out unimproved after the first dozen meetings (1966). This was contrasted to another study which found those patients who stayed in a group for 50 meetings were more likely to show clinical improvement. All of this suggests the importance of managing the first few initial meetings with newly acquired group members. It has been reasoned by MacLeod (1968) that the awkwardness of the management of the early hours of treatment were the most significant factors contributing to premature dropouts and treatment failures. If you cannot keep the patient in treatment, there is little chance they will have the opportunity to improve. He further suggests that

> the best technique for avoiding unfortunate instability in the treatment situation has always been focus on the development of a therapeutic alliance or relationship as promptly as possible, that is immediately. The focus on the development of a therapeutic alliance means that the patient and the therapist become acquainted actively as real people in a real current experience. The therapist should not attempt to present himself energetically as a transference object, such as by adopting a blank screen model. (1968, p. 402)

MacLeod concludes that any technique which is going to interfere with the development of the alliance or create undue additional significant frustration or anxiety in the early stages of treatment should therefore be used sparingly.

GAIN A CLEAR CONSENSUS ABOUT THE PATIENT'S THERAPEUTIC HOPES

Anybody who has worked with alcoholics or addicts on a sustained basis knows that they all possess a much desired but equally unreachable goal. Each wishes to be able to take drugs recreationally and to drink normally. This is a goal they can never attain and the sooner each addict and alcoholic realizes and accepts the limits of this goal, the less progress will be impeded in treatment. Admittance and acceptance of this limitation is in fact the first step of Alcoholics Anonymous. While some may argue that controlled drinking is a feasible option (Sobell & Sobell, 1973) for some alcoholics, research in this area is certainly inconclusive. The risk of relapse and the associated possible consequence of death is too important an issue to be debated academically. Within Alcoholics Anonymous, an alcoholic is somebody, who by definition of their alcoholism, cannot drink normally. Tell a group of eight alcoholics that there is a statistical probability that one of them may return to normal drinking and each alcoholic in that group will believe they are the one exception.

While abstinence should be the primary goal of treatment, especially for an alcoholic just beginning treatment, this does not imply other goals should be ignored. Vernon Johnson (1976), in his classic book, *I'll Quit Tomorrow*, outlines two explicit goals of alcoholics entering psychotherapy groups.

The purpose of this paper is to discuss the assumptions and techniques we are using in conducting group therapy. To begin with, let's look at some of the similarities within our group. In addition to our alcoholism we all have two things in common. First, before we came to the point of seeking outside help, we each tried our own *do it yourself* program in an effort to change ourselves. The second similarity is that we all failed. A basic assumption of group therapy is that a major reason for this failure is that our most determined efforts can't change what we can't see, and that there is a great deal that we are not seeing clearly.

For this reason our *goal* in group therapy is:

To discover ourselves and others as feeling persons, and
To identify *the defenses that prevent this discovery.*

While change is the ultimate goal, our immediate purpose is to see more accurately what needs change. This requires seeing ourselves — *discovering ourselves* — at a feeling level.

In examining our purpose one of the things that stands out is our emphasis on feelings. We stress feelings for several reasons. First of all, our behavior in the past has been so opposed to our value system that considerable feelings of remorse and self-loathing have been built up. It appears that we have accumulated a pool of negative feelings and walled them off with a variety of masks or *defenses that prevent this discovery*. This began with mild disapproval of ourself, then growing remorse, and finally a deep self-loathing. Statements such as: "I'm no damn good!" or "The world would be better off without me," reflect these negative feelings and attitudes. It is important to be in touch with these in order to take the First Step of the Alcoholics Anonymous Program where: "We admitted that we were powerless over alcohol — that our lives had become unmanageable."

> Being in touch with the hostile feelings we have toward our-
> selves and the sense of helplessness and hopelessness that ac-
> company them, make the First Step a moving description in-
> stead of simply an abstract theory. We *feel* the *powerlessness*
> and the *unmanageability*. One of the important functions of
> the group is to help us identify the defenses that prevent this
> discovery. (Johnson, 1976, p. 118–119)

Group psychotherapy from this perspective requires a focus on
feelings. Unlike groups with nonaddictive patients, the group leader
will soon learn that the chemically dependent individual is completely out of touch with his feelings. A seemingly simplistic intervention like, "What are you feeling right now?" will produce a
startling effect. As a group leader, you will soon discover that these
addicted individuals do not know how to identify and interpret feelings. They must learn how to accomplish this task, because an addict and alcoholic who does not learn to understand their feelings
will undoubtedly relapse. The chemically dependent individual
must be led to understand that the management of their feelings is
an essential requirement for the attainment of abstinence and recovery.

Ernest Kurtz views Alcoholics Anonymous as teaching the alcoholic that they cannot attain what all alcoholics unrealistically strive
for and that is unlimited control of their feelings (1979). The alcoholic's addiction to alcohol is for Kurtz related to the alcoholic's
misunderstanding and denial of the spiritual. "The active alcoholic
was attempting to attain the spiritual, the unlimited, by means of the
material. He was trying to achieve a *quality* of living by the mere
adding up of quantities of or experiences with alcohol" (p. 208).
The quality of living which the alcoholic pursued was confused with
the spiritual because it involved a claim to the absolute. Complete
control of feelings which is a striving to reach beyond the limits of
human finiteness. Only God or the absolute has absolute control of
feelings and AA set as its task to teach the alcoholic that he was
Not-God.

> The alcoholic attempted to achieve by the drinking of alcohol
> what reality would give only by living as fully human. Reality
> does not grant to humans *absolute* control over moods and
> feelings; emotions are meant to be a *response* to reality, and
> mainly to realities outside the self. *Absolute control* over emo-

tion, in the sense of absolutely autonomous self-determination of moods and feelings, involved a claim to unlimitedness, and so a claim beyond any human. (Kurtz, 1976, p. 209)

Treatment from this perspective requires the alcoholic learn how to identify and accept the limitation of his feelings if he wishes to maintain true sobriety. Consequently, the group leader has to gently encourage the alcoholic, and the addict, to understand the futility of a position that demands they either feel good all the time or avoid feeling bad at any time. Feelings are there for a reason. As Kurtz indicates, emotions allow us to judge reality and our relation to reality. Emotions tell us when we are really happy and when we are acting against the values we truly hold internally.

Once abstinence is maintained for at least a year, more explicit personal goals can be established by the patient. AA encourages its members not to make any significant changes (i.e., divorces, job transfers, etc.) until their first year of sobriety is achieved. AA intuitively knows what neuropsychological research has just begun to prove empirically. Alcoholics and addicts, because of their drinking and drug use, suffer from deficits in their cognitive processes that make abstract reasoning difficult. While their level of impairment is subtle, it is detectable with tests sensitive to its assessment. Chapter Eight will deal with this issue in more detail. For now, it will suffice to say that once sobriety is maintained for a least a year, many of the goals that are desired by nonaddictive patients can be initiated and negotiated with less danger of relapse.

OFFER INFORMATION AND INSTRUCTION ABOUT GROUP PSYCHOTHERAPY

Because a group will rapidly evoke intense feelings in the chemically dependent person, it will be important to help them feel grounded by giving them specific and concrete information about how groups work. Once they know what to expect, group members will be able to respond to the group more appropriately. There are a number of ways this can be accomplished.

A. Give the new group members reading material which explains the structure and rationales of group psychotherapy (Gauron & Rawlings, 1975).

B. Didactically explain to them what they can expect in group and how best to put the group to their advantage (Wogan et al., 1977).
C. Some group leaders have presented group members with an opportunity to view a group session behind a one-way mirror (Wogan et al., 1977).
D. In some cases, prospective group members have been given audio tapes of a "good patient's" participation in group. This was done in the hopes that new members would model their behavior after the "good patient" (Truax & Wargo, 1969).

All studies cited here showed a consensus on their results which suggests greater improvement after three months than those patients who entered a control group without preparation. While there was no evidence which suggested that any format led to fewer dropouts, there is a general agreement which indicates that group norms are shaped more quickly in the direction of a therapeutic group environment as a result of group member preparation.

Yalom sought to answer the question concerning the benefits of preparing group members for group. His query was prompted by his understanding of the crucial importance of early meetings in shaping the future course of group. Yalom had discovered that group norms established early in the life of a group tended to persist, outliving even a complete turnover in the group population. Consequently, Yalom reasoned that the establishment of healthy group norms early in group would be beneficial to the functioning of the group. Yalom was also aware that there was a cost involved in preparing members for group. Arguments, especially by psychodynamic oriented group therapists, suggested that any technique which interfered with the development and resolution of transference and transference distortions should be used sparingly. Since preparing members for group might interfere with this process, it was judged that group treatment would be impaired. It was essential that the group leader enhance the development of transference in group. Enigma and ambiguity on the leader's part would facilitate transference and the therapist should do nothing, like preparing group members, to interfere with this process.

Yalom's answer to this argument was that the benefits of preparing patients for group far outweigh the costs. Primarily, preparing group members enhanced the development of the other important curative factors operating in group. Yalom also felt that transference is a healthy organism; it will still manifest itself despite the organizational activity involved in the group members' preparation.

YALOM'S CONTROLLED STUDY FOR PREPARING PATIENTS FOR GROUP THERAPY

Yalom's 1967 study required a twenty-five minute preparatory meeting for new group members. Subjects for this study were randomly assigned to one of two conditions. Those prepared for group in the manner to be discussed and those randomly assigned to groups without preparation. The twenty-five minute preparatory meeting was designed to attain three goals.

1. Enhance the new group members' faith in group therapy and increase the positive expectancy that group would be helpful.
2. Enhance the attractiveness of group and develop cohesion.
3. Direct the group members towards the confrontive, here and now interaction within the group. Yalom placed the greatest emphasis on this topic during the preparatory session.

In order to accomplish these three goals, Yalom had each of the new group members presented with five sources of specific instructions.

1. A theoretical basis of group therapy was discussed with an emphasis placed on the interpersonal theory of psychiatry.
2. A rational description of group was presented.
3. The expected effectiveness and results of group treatment were outlined.
4. Sources of possible stress within group were identified.
5. Members were instructed to discuss their feelings with other group members in the group.

Theoretical Basis of Group Psychotherapy

Each perspective group member was presented with a brief history of the evolution of group therapy. It was explained that group first gained value because of economics. More people could be treated at less expense. However, group members were clearly told that group therapy had now evolved to the point that it was a very sophisticated and unique form of treatment that could justify itself on its own merit. In fact, group therapy is often the treatment of choice. In many cases, it has been found to be more effective than individual treatment. The remarks during this introduction were aimed to instill faith in group therapy as a mode of treatment and dispel any notions of group therapy being an inferior or a second class approach to treatment.

Rational Description for Group

Sullivan's interpersonal theory of psychiatry was briefly presented. Everyone was reminded that a universal concern for people was their difficulty establishing and maintaining close, gratifying relationships with others. Members were reminded that they may have wished many times to clarify a relationship, to be honest with another about their feelings, both positive and negative, which being able to get honest feedback on how others perceive them. Group therapy was described as a hall of mirrors; a place where they could discover how they affect others, how others perceive them and how they, in turn, are affected by others. Since the general structure of society does not permit such interactions to occur, group could be viewed as a social microcosm where honest interpersonal interaction was not only permitted but encouraged.

Effectiveness of Group Psychotherapy

Group members were cautioned that group therapy could be a difficult endeavor for them to initiate. While starting in a group was not often easy, in fact they were warned that it could be quite stressful working directly on their relationships with other members in the group, they were assured there would be tremendous carryover to the "real world." Each member was instructed that if they were willing to honestly work through, resolve and clarify their relationships with other group members, this would lead them to discover more pathways to more rewarding relationships with others outside of group.

Sources of Possible Stress Within the Group

All prospective group members were reminded how stressful and difficult it could be to be honest with others in the group. They were forewarned that at times, especially during the beginning of group, that feelings of puzzlement and discouragement could be expected. Each was warned that they might question how the group could possibly help them or their situation. At other times, it might not be apparent to them how working on group problems and their interpersonal relationships with the other group members could be of value in solving problems that led them to join the group in the first place. Puzzlement and discouragement should be expected and they were urged not to follow through with their inclinations to drop out of group. It was often difficult for people to risk revealing themselves honestly and they should be aware of their tendency to withdraw emotionally. Each was told that they may want to hide their feelings or may allow others to express their feelings for them. This, in turn, could lead to concealing their alliances with others from the group and its leader. There were a number of different emotions which they might expect to occur. Annoyance and frustration at the group leader for not giving more direction to the group was common. Many members might direct this frustration towards the other members and wonder, as Yalom says, "How can the blind lead the blind?" (1967, p. 418). Even when the group member is unaware of anxiety and nervousness, they are told these are common emotions during the beginning of group. While everyone fears attack and rejection for appearing foolish, it is essential that these fears be gradually worked through. On the other hand, each member is given the reassurance that group is not a forced confessional and that they can set their own pace in self-disclosing.

The Encouragement of Group Member Interaction

Group members were repeatedly instructed that the way group would be most helpful for them if they would be honest and direct with the other members and the group leader. The open sharing of feelings as it was occurring at this moment was emphasized continually by Yalom. This, the members were instructed, was the core of group therapy. Trust often took time to develop in group and they were reminded that people have different rates of developing trust.

While it was essential that trust, safety and cohesiveness be established, they were encouraged to view group as a form for risk taking. As learning and risk taking progressed, they were encouraged that new types of behavior could be tried.

Results of Preparing Group Members for Group

Yalom's 1967 study failed to have any significant effect on group members terminating therapy early or dropping out prematurely. A number of studies since that time have generally supported Yalom's findings indicating the pre-group preparation has little effect on group members staying in group. However, Yalom's study does show evidence that preparation of group members does enhance the member's faith in group and that those groups with prepared members engaged in interaction more quickly. Consequently, groups composed of prepared members are spared the initial stages of uncertainty and move more quickly into the basic task of group. Personal benefit and improvement is attained more quickly when compared to groups composed of unprepared group members.

Special Problems in the Preparation of the Chemically Dependent Individual

There is one unique aspect involved in preparing the chemically dependent person for outpatient group therapy that is usually not necessary for the nonaddicted members. Most alcoholics and addicts have at some time during their addiction attended meetings of Alcoholics Anonymous, Cocaine Anonymous or Narcotics Anonymous. In some cases, prospective members may be very active currently in AA, CA, or NA. These individuals should be encouraged to continue their participation in these organizations. It would be important to inform them that the psychotherapy group is not designed to treat their addiction or be a substitute for the peer-oriented (AA, CA & NA) program. Rather, the group can support or complement such peer-oriented programs. In some cases, if the person does not have enough sobriety, group therapy may be contraindicated, especially if the group leader is unfamiliar with the treatment format of these programs.

If it is judged that the prospective group member can benefit from group therapy, the group leader will have to give clear instructions that the therapy group does not operate like an AA, NA or CA meeting. This is especially important if the group member has never been in a therapy group previously and has been active in AA, NA or CA for years. Confusion between the AA format and group therapy can hinder both forms of treatment. Understanding the difference between peer groups and professional therapy groups is not as crucial for the member who has three years of sobriety as it is for the newly recovering individual with only two weeks of sobriety. The individual with a few years of recovery under his belt is usually more equipped to handle the adjustment to the change in treatment format. The newly recovering addict or alcoholic is in a highly charged emotional state and more easily confused and threatened by their misunderstanding of the differing demands each modality makes upon them. Transmitting this information can be helpful and in some cases crucial.

The peer-oriented and professionally oriented group (Alcoholics Anonymous, Narcotics Anonymous, Cocaine Anonymous) should both be considered to be active treatment groups designed to facilitate recovery and abstinence from alcohol. A critical difference exists between the professional-oriented and peer-oriented group. The professionally led therapy group emphasizes the use of specific behavioral and psychological prescriptions and techniques that are applied to a global generalized symptom reduction effort. In comparison, the AA format focuses on a specific regimented approach addressing one specific component of recovery (i.e., abstinence).

The core content in the professionally oriented group should consist of the attempt to facilitate increased gradual introspection and compliance through the use of group confrontation, discussion and education. In contrast the peer-oriented group is almost entirely supportive fostering a degree of dependence on the acceptance of a specific and limited treatment approach focused entirely on compliance and abstinence from alcohol and drugs.

TREATMENT CHARACTERISTICS

In order to gain a more comprehensive overview of the content of each treatment group, a projected list of similarities and differences between the two treatment groups is presented. Common and divergent elements are listed below:

Divergent Elements

Peer-Oriented Group (AA, NA, CA)	Professional-Oriented Group
1. Treatment goal will focus specifically on abstinence.	1. Treatment goals will be individually determined by the person which requires social, psychological, physical, and drinking related behavior be examined and evaluated.
2. Emphasis on the "how" of abstinence and recovery.	2. Emphasis on the "why" of abstinence and recovery.
3. Opening of group with readings of the AA "Big Book" and the Twelve Steps of Recovery.	3. Development of group cohesiveness and traditional group processes.
4. Structured use of life histories dealing specifically with personal history of alcoholism and recovery.	4. Verbal reports of general progress without notation and rigid format.
5. Didactic format by group leaders to impart AA principles.	5. Mobilization of group support and feedback.
6. Emphasis on the first four steps of AA's traditional twelve steps with less emphasis on feelings and emotions.	6. More emphasis on group discussion of feelings and emotions.
7. More democratic group leadership with members taking a more active role in the group discussion.	7. More traditional role of group leader in the group process.
8. Group discussion focused on ways to remain abstinent.	8. More confrontation and exploration of resistance.

Common Elements

1. Group discussion.
2. Correct misconceptions about addiction.
3. Impart information on addiction and need for compliance.
4. Formulation of treatment issues.
5. Group support at beginning.
6. Aim to reduce patient complaints and behavior that interfere with alcohol and drug abstinence.
7. Attempt to involve and change family environment.
8. Search for continuing causes of abstinence difficulties.

These specific treatment procedures should be developed and monitored in their application throughout the course of treatment in order to insure the treatments offered (professional vs. peer [AA]) are both clinically meaningful and discriminately different. In this way maximal benefit can be realized by the individual by contrasting different types of therapy with the identifiable characteristics of certain alcoholics and addicts.

Deal With the Initial Anxiety About Joining the Group

Most people are quite anxious about joining a group. The group leader should encourage the prospective members to talk about their anxiety in group and reassure them that all individuals entering group will be sharing these feelings. Instruction should be given that it will be helpful to discuss such feelings during the initial start of the group.

However, alcoholics and addicts pose some unique problems for the group leader when it comes to the issue of pre-group anxiety. The group leader will find that pre-group preparation with this population will result in anxiety being manifested in one of two extremes. For alcoholics who have a propensity for more acting out behavior (i.e., sociopathic features, repeated difficulty with the law, etc.) and more illicit drug abuse (i.e., cocaine, heroin, marijuana, amphetamines, etc.), the group leader will find that their anxiety is usually kept out of their awareness. With those alcoholics and addicts who have a propensity for a more isolated existence (i.e., agoraphobic features, fear of crowds, etc.) and more licit drug abuse (i.e., prescription medications like Valium and Librium), the group leader will find that their anxiety is much more in their awareness because it is extremely high and often incapacitating. Each particular set of patients has to be approached differently when preparing them for group.

With the group member who has more characterological features and whose anxiety is more unconscious, it would behoove the group leader to raise the anxiety to their awareness before they enter group. If their anxiety remains unconscious, there is a greater chance that they will react in group in the way they deal with all situations that produce anxiety in the "real world" — namely by acting out. Such group members must learn that membership in a group means expressing feelings verbally and not behaviorally. Once they become aware of their anxiety and agree to express such feelings verbally, they must be encouraged to realize that anxiety is universal. Such an awareness will reassure them that they are not less of a person just because they experience fear or discomfort.

Group members who have less characterological features accompanying their addiction are more likely to have a history of anxiety disorders (i.e., panic attacks, phobias). Their use of drugs and alcohol is often an attempt at self-medication. As they become increasingly alcohol and drug free, their anxiety may actually increase. Entry into a group will be especially difficult for this population of addicted individuals. Reassurance, support and enhancement of their inadequate defensive process is a must if they are to enter and survive the initial entry into a therapy group.

Research and clinical opinion about the allayment of initial anxiety during pre-group preparation with prospective group members who are not addicted sheds some light on issues that should be addressed with the chemically dependent individual. Agazarian and Peters (1981) list four common fears that may be stimulated by entry into a therapy group:

1. Confidentiality of personal information.
2. Rejection by the group.
3. Embarrassment over revealing intimate information to other group members.
4. Pathology of others.

CONFIDENTIALITY OF PERSONAL INFORMATION

Agazarian and Peters (1981) write,

Prospective group patients often worry that information presented in group sessions will "leak" and get back to someone who knows them in the outside world. They can be assured that this has not proved the case in the past and that such an event is not expected to occur in the future. If time permits associations to this worry can be explored with the patient. Most important is to encourage the patient to raise this concern with the group where it is always a therapeutically productive issue. (p. 189)

Confidentiality is always a concern for alcoholics and addicts. Many who enter an aftercare group or outpatient group may not feel it necessary to discuss it as an important issue because of their exposure to the required anonymity of Alcoholics Anonymous. However, this issue needs to be addressed even if the group leader has to force the topic into discussion. Confidentiality cannot be assumed because many alcoholics and addicts have engaged in embarrassing, humiliating and, in some cases, even illegal behavior while intoxicated. Confidentiality needs to be assured. Members should be told that they will undoubtedly talk about their experiences in group with friends and family, but that they should do so in a manner that the other members aren't talked about specifically or that their identities are revealed.

WORRIES ABOUT REJECTION BY GROUP MEMBERS

Worries about rejection by group members are best dealt with by helping the worrier to link up his present fear with the painful experiences in the past via his associations. Again, the patient should be reminded that this may be a useful group-related issue for him to discuss with the group. (Agazarian & Peters, 1981, p. 189)

The issues raised by Agazarian and Peters will be similar with a chemically dependent population. Despite the fact that an addict or alcoholic, while drinking or taking drugs, might act in a way that indicates that rejection is of little concern to them, they have a tremendous need to be accepted and approved of by others.

FEAR OF BEING EMBARRASSED

Agazarian and Peters (1981) suggest,

Fear of being embarrassed in front of group members should

be handled in much the same way as fear of rejection. In addition, the information already given about the way a group operates through sharing and honest feedback is helpful in letting the person know that he will not be alone in revealing his intimate thoughts and feelings. (p. 189)

Embarrassment and shame are crucial issues for addicts and alcoholics. As Kurtz (1976) suggests, the chemically dependent individual suffers from tremendous feelings of shame. Their self-esteem is very tenuous and, as a rule, they possess extremely intropunitive superegos. Consequently, even the smallest discretion will drive them to punish themselves in an overly sadistic and harsh manner. On the other hand, any indications that others may perceive them as loathsome or shameful will lead them to act out in a defensive and provocative manner. They cannot tolerate others perceiving them as they feel or perceive themselves. Many alcoholics and addicts need and require confirmation and gradification from the painful feelings of shame and embarrassment.

FEARS CONCERNING THE IMAGINED
PATHOLOGY OF OTHERS

Fears concerning the imagined pathology of as-yet-unseen fellow group members are quite likely to be projections, the defensive nature of which is not conscious to the patient. Such fears may be expressed as fear of mental contamination (Foulkes and Anthony, 1973) or as doubts about what "a bunch of sickies" can do for the patient. Exploration of free associations is one avenue of relieving this kind of concern. Another is by telling the patient that these are people like himself who share many of his anxieties and concerns; such information helps him to approach the projective nature of his fear. (Agazarian & Peters, 1981, p. 186)

Usually, alcoholics and addicts are much more accepting of others' shortcomings and limitations. Because they have experienced such dreadful feelings and emotions during their numerous intoxications and withdrawals, they can readily accept such conditions in others. However, most alcoholics and addicts have tremendous fears that underneath their addiction, others may discover that they are either "crazy," perverted or loathsome. They fear the truth will finally emerge and people will see them as they truly are. Consequently, it will be important to reframe any of their concerns about their pathology and place it within the disease model. This will bolster their self-image until they are able to identify with the other members in the group and learn their fears are universally shared.

PRESENT AND GAIN ACCEPTANCE OF THE CONTRACT

Presenting and having a group member accept a contract before entering a therapy group is the most crucial contributing factor to a successful outpatient therapy group. Unfortunately, its importance is often ignored and too little time is spent on training group leaders in this preparation process. For many addicts and alcoholics entering an inpatient treatment program under coercion or distress, it is impractical, and in some cases impossible, to get a working contract established. Since it is not feasible nor desirable to adjust treatment goals for the state of the art, abstinence should always be the primary goal of treatment. Newly entering inpatients are rarely asked, or in any condition to decide, if they will agree with the goal of the treatment unit at the hospital. Most would prefer to receive treatment without having to go through the difficulties which a therapy group demands. Consequently, they have little choice in their contract at this time. This is the way it should be. Nevertheless, it would still benefit the group leader to actively engage the new group members in the process of understanding the requirements and demands which the therapy group will impose upon them.

Inpatient and outpatient therapy groups pose different and unique problems for the group leader. Chapter 8 will address the differences that a group leader will have to negotiate when conducting an inpatient group. The suggestions to be presented here are most suitable for an aftercare group or an ongoing outpatient group.

Stone and Rutan (1984) outline seven elements which they feel are essential in the contract for an ongoing, open-ended therapy group. They feel the group members should agree:

1. To be present each week, to be on time and to remain throughout the meeting
2. To work actively on the problems that brought them to group.
3. To put feelings in words, not actions.

4. To use the relationships in group therapeutically, not socially.
5. To remain in the group until the problems that brought them to the group have been resolved.
6. To be responsible for their bills.
7. To protect the names and identities of fellow group members (Stone & Rutan, 1984, p. 114-115).

Stone and Rutan view the contract not so much as a formal written document, but rather a verbal agreement regarding the ground rules for group. The ground rules provide the foundation for a productive and safe therapeutic environment and should be mutually agreed upon before a member enters an outpatient or aftercare group. In order to insure an understanding of the group rules, I give each incoming member a written description of my seven ground rules for group. Figure 1 is a copy of these ground rules.

The group leader will learn that the establishment of a clear contract and the understanding of the ground rules of group will prevent many of the difficulties which usually emerge in group. Managing the boundaries of group is one of the most important elements of an effective group. It helps establish the therapeutic environment (cohesion) and allows the other curative factors to be set in motion. Furthermore, the contract allows the group leader to use its violations as a way to understand the various resistances, character traits, and transferences that take place in group.

FIGURE I

These seven ground rules and accompanying notes have been prepared to help new members in a psychotherapy group understand how a group works.

1) Confidentiality. The members of the group each agree that they will not reveal the identity of any other member of the group either by name or identifying material. Group members would not feel free to be completely open with their most intimate feelings if they thought they would be talked about outside the group.

2) Contact between group members outside of group. There is no ground rule prohibiting such contact; however, any contact should be shareable within the group. This keeps cliques from forming which, if they did, could damage the integrity of the group as a working unit.

3) No sexual contact between group members. The members agree that during their membership in group no sexual liaisons will be formed. This freedom from sexual liaisons facilitates an intimacy between group members which, in turn, provides a basis for growth and change. Thus, the trust necessary for openness and problem solving can develop.

4) No hitting or damage to the office. Anger is to be expressed verbally rather than physically. Anger freely expressed can form the basis for insight and growth just as affection freely expressed.

FIGURE I (continued)

5) <u>Graduation versus termination from group.</u> When members begin thinking about discontinuing psychotherapy, they are expected to discuss this in group as freely as they have discussed other feelings. <u>Graduation</u> from group therapy is a time of joy and sharing and invariably has been thought out and discussed with the group. On the other hand, a group member may make a decision to <u>terminate</u> at a point in therapy where he or she is beginning to face some critical issues. The input of other members in group can be valuable at this point. While no one needs the permission of the group to discontinue psychotherapy, it is in the spirit of growth that leaving the group be discussed in group--not just on the telephone with the therapist.

6) <u>Charges.</u> The rate for group psychotherapy is on a per-session basis. If the group member does not give twenty-four hours notice that they will be absent from group, he or she will be charged for the session. The reasoning is that members are being charged for slots that are reserved for them. It is their responsibility as to whether and how they choose to use this time.

7) <u>Attendance.</u> Regular attendance and punctuality enhances the value of the group for each member. In the event of a member's inability to or decision not to attend a session, a telephone call to this effect is expected. Members are allowed to join the psychotherapy group only if they are willing to commit to twelve sessions. This agreement assures that the group process will not be disrupted by members "dropping in" for one or two sessions and then dropping out of group. This agreement also ensures that the person who joins the group will make enough of a commitment to benefit from the group.

REFERENCES

Agazarian, Y. & Peters, R. (1981). *The visible and invisible group*. London: Routledge & Kegan Paul.

Foulks, S. H. & Anthony, E. J. (1973). *Group psychotherapy. The psychoanalytic approach*. (2nd ed.). Harmondsworth: Penguin.

Freud, S. (1921). *Group psychology and the analysis of the ego*. Complete psychological works of Sigmund Freud. London: Hogarth Press.

Gauron, E. F. & Rawlings, E. I. (1975). Procedure for orienting new members to group psychotherapy. *Small Group Behavior, 6,* 293-307.

Johnson, V. (1976). *I'll quit tomorrow*. (2nd ed.). New York: Holt, Rinehart & Winston.

Kurtz, E. (1979). *Not God, a history of Alcoholics Anonymous*. Center City: Hazelton Educational Services.

MacLeod, J. A. (1968). Management of the initial phase of psychotherapy: Optimal frustration as a guide to technique in psychotherapy. *Comprehensive Psychiatry, 9*(4), 400-406.

Sobell, M. B. & Sobell, L. C. (1973). Alcoholics treated by individualized behavior therapy: One-year treatment outcome. *Behavior Research and Therapy, 11,* 599-618.

Stone, W. & Rutan, S. (1984). *Psychodynamic group therapy*. Lexington: Callamore Press.

Truax, C. B. & Wargo, D. G. (1969). Effects of vicarious therapy pretraining and alternative sessions on outcome in group psychotherapy with outpatients. *Journal of Consulting Clinical Psychology, 33,* 440-447.

Wogan, M., Getter, H., Anidur, M. J., Nichols, M. F. & Okman, G. (1977). Influencing interaction and outcome in group psychotherapy. *Small Group Behavior, 8,* 26-46.

Yalom, I. D. & Rank, K. (1966). Compatibility and cohesiveness in therapy groups. *Archives of General Psychiatry, 15,* 267-276.

Yalom, I., Houts, P. S., Newell, A. B. & Rand, K. H. (1967). Preparation of patients for group therapy. *Archives of General Psychiatry, 17,* 416-428.

Chapter 14

The Curative Process
in Group Therapy

Heinz Kohut, in a book published after his death, asked the important question of how does analysis cure (1984): While Kohut responded to this question from a self-psychology perspective, his answer needs to be extended because his formula does not take into consideration the special curative forces which exist in group therapy. Psychological cure is both a process and an event that is influenced by many different factors. Group therapy differs from individual therapy in that the circumstances which influence its occurrence is a process unique to group. However, as an event or goal, cure remains very similar for both individual and group therapy. Cure, from Kohut's perspective, is accomplished when a person can develop healthy object relationships. By this, he means that a psychologically healthy individual is one who possesses the capacity to engage in healthy interpersonal relationships with other healthy individuals. Interpersonal distortions, manipulations, pathological dependency and unrealistic expectancies are all minimized. Most importantly, the person who has obtained a healthy respect for themselves will be drawn to and choose others who are as healthy as they are. Kohut is operating on the principle that sick people attract sick people and healthy people are drawn to healthy people. Kohut is therefore suggesting that a person who is "cured" in therapy is one who develops the ability to pick and choose better friends, lovers, and partners. Kohut also challenges the erroneous belief that healthy or "cured" people no longer have the need for others and that they can operate completely independent of others' opinions, actions, or confirmations. Mental health, for Kohut, is not so much determined by complete autonomy from others as it is determined by a person's ability to trade archaic and childish ways of getting their needs met for more mature ways of obtaining gratification in their adult relationships. As Kohut writes,

> Self-psychology holds that self-selfobject relationships form the essence of psychological life from birth to death, that a move from dependence (symbiosis) to independence (autonomy) in the psychological sphere is no more possible, let alone desirable, than a corresponding move from a life dependent on oxygen to a life independent of it in the biological sphere. The developments that characterized normal psychological life must, in our view, be seen in the changing nature of the relationship between the self and its selfobjects, but not in the self's relinquishment of selfobjects. In particular, developmental advances cannot be understood in terms of the replacement of the selfobjects by love objects or as steps in the move from narcissism to object love. (Kohut, 1984, p. 47)

If one agrees with Kohut's description about the nature of cure and the definition of mental health, how is this to be obtained in group therapy? Kohut defines this process in individual therapy as being accomplished by the laying down of psychological structure. Kohut asks the question of "How does this accretion of psychological structure take place?" (1984, p. 98). He then answers his own question from a self-psychology perspective. Psychological structure is laid down via 1. optimal frustration and 2. in consequence of optimal frustration, via transmuting internalization (see Chapter 6). Cure is obtained when the person, through a good-enough relationship with an appropriate mirroring and caring other, learns how to honor, accept, and take care of themselves while not allowing themselves to be treated with disrespect, harm, or injustice.

Group therapy parallels Kohut's description of cure in that it helps lay down psychic structure. The question which remains to be answered is how group therapy helps the individual obtain a firm sense of self through optimal frustration via transmuting internalization. Kohut is suggesting a firm sense of self is established as the group members work through their individual differences in group and learn more adaptive ways of resolving interpersonal and intrapersonal conflicts. The group enhances this process because it supplies each member with a source of support, identification, and acceptance while at the same time giving each individual a set of healthy values that can be internalized and incorporated. Eventually, each member's substitution of the group's healthy norms for their individual destructive norms are reinforced by the group until these values become part of their individual psychic structure.

To properly understand how cure is obtained in a therapy group, it involves the investigation of two related, but distinctly different aspects of the curative forces which operate in group. First, there are the identified curative factors which enhance a person's move from pathological behavior to psychological health. There is also a curative process in group which moves the individual through progressive and separate stages of increasing health, cure, and recovery. Yalom (1985) has done extensive research in identifying the curative factors in group and Stone and Rutan (1984) have done a comprehensive analysis of the curative process which exists in group. Each of their respective positions will be described in relation to Kohut's formula for the attainment of a healthy cohesive self.

YALOM'S CURATIVE FACTORS

Cure for Yalom is an enormously complex process which "occurs through an intricate interplay of various guided human experiences" that he refers to as curative factors. This complex process of cure is intricately tied up with what Yalom comes to identify as therapeutic change. Cure cannot be achieved unless a group member changes. To accomplish therapeutic change, the group leader must develop strategies and tactics which will enhance the curative process.

The effectiveness of a therapy group has been evaluated extensively by Yalom (1985). He has gained valuable information by asking group members and group leaders to identify qualities that they found helpful in a therapy group. While Yalom acknowledges that the process of cure in a therapy group is an intricate process and that different people in group respond differently to the many varying influences of group, he feels that even at the risk of oversimplifying these complicated processes, much can be gained by attempting to identify and categorize these varying curative factors. Numerous studies (see Yalom, 1985, pp. 71–112) have been conducted over the years in an attempt to identify the rank ordered importance of these curative forces. In most of the studies, group members have been asked to rank order statements describing twelve potential helpful attributes of their group experience from most to least helpful. The twelve curative factors are summarized in Table I.

To help understand the implications that these curative factors have on an alcoholic's and addict's recovery, each will be explored in relation to the special circumstances that are created when the addicted patient is treated in a therapy group.

TABLE I

Curative factors Operating in Psychotherapy Group

1) Altruism   The feeling that a member is helping others and is important in their lives.   Patients forget themselves momentarily, at least, and focus on helping others.   People need to feel they are needed.

2) Catharsis   Expressing negative and positive feelings toward other members and the group leader.   Acceptance for openness and personal change as a result of trying out new behavior begins to emerge.   Feelings are no longer held inside.   The process of learning how to express one's feelings emerges.

3) Existential Factors   Individual learns there are limits in the world and that they alone are responsible for their life.

4) Group Cohesiveness   Emotional sharing and acceptance.   A feeling of belonging and approval, with a feeling of warmth and closeness.   There is mutual support and then heightened self-esteem.   A sense of "We-ness" is established.   This is a precondition for effective therapy.

5) Guidance   The imparting of information (i.e., "Why don't you try this?", advice giving).   Early Group Stage.

6) Identification   Individual learns vicariously by listening and watching others in group.

7) Instillation of Hope   Seeing others getting better, knowing that the group has helped others gives members faith in the treatment mode.   The expectation of effectiveness is established.

8) Interpersonal Input   Seeing how one relates to others and they to him, and then working on achieving more satisfying interpersonal relationships.

9) Interpersonal Output   Patient expresses feelings openly and the group is supportive.   The group allows the patient to examine the incident with the consensual validation from others.

10) Insight   Patients gain a more objective perspective regarding interpersonal behavior.   Patients gain some understanding into what they are doing to and with other people.   There is an understanding as to why.

11) Recapitulation of the Primary Family   The group resembles the family in many aspects.   Unresolved family issues are recapitulated and corrected.

12) Universality   Feeling that I am not that different from others.   "We're all in the same boat."   As common denominators emerge, support occurs.

CURATIVE FACTORS IN GROUP

Cohesiveness

Group cohesiveness is more likely to be an important factor with alcoholics than with nonalcoholics because of the dependency conflicts typically associated with alcoholism. As Brown and Yalom (1977) suggest, cohesiveness is not of itself a curative factor but is instead a necessary precondition for effective therapy. Brown and Yalom have shown that, early in the life of the group, the issue of drinking serves as a unifying theme and members are often held together by this common bond until other sources of cohesion develop. It is essential that the therapist take advantage of this bond. Later, as Yalom showed, it is possible to differentiate each patient, by examining with the group the different defensive functions each person's drinking has played in his or her life. The support and reinforcement of the group can serve as a powerful incentive for the primary goal of sobriety. Interpersonal and intrapersonal changes can then be facilitated, after a supportive and caring atmosphere has been established.

Universality

Considering the evidence for a post-alcoholic personality, the concept of universality is even more curative for alcoholics than for nonalcoholics. Brown and Yalom (1977) found that alcoholics generally had difficulty in distinguishing between thought and action; many would respond to fantasies with the same guilt and fear that would accompany actual behavior. While this eliminates fantasy work as a therapeutic option in group, it does indicate the importance that universality can play in quieting the alcoholic's thoughts that they are unique in their wretchedness. This sense of uniqueness is heightened for alcoholics by their social isolation and the guilt feelings associated with their drinking behavior. The phenomenon which Yalom describes as a process of "being welcomed back" to the human race results from sharing similar concerns and experiences and is an important curative factor in the early stages of the alcoholic's recovery. Often, for the first time in his life, the alcoholic will realize that he is not a loner with his own personal and unique hell. The understanding that there are others who share his plight can serve as a powerful incentive to recovery, forgiveness and acceptance of self.

Instillation of Hope

Group members often remark at the end of therapy how important it was for them to have observed the improvement of others (Yalom, 1985). A group therapist should by no means be above exploiting this factor by periodically calling attention to the improvement that members have shown. As matter of fact, one of the great strengths of Alcoholics Anonymous is that each recovering alcoholic is a living inspiration to others. It is more than a mere coincidence that AA meetings involve members telling of their downfall and salvation.

Equally important is the fact that, at the beginning of therapy, alcoholics are usually in a crisis. They have attempted to control their drinking numerous times in the past and have failed. This, plus the dependency and passivity characteristics typical of alcoholic patients, requires that the therapist be directive and convey the message that he knows he can be of help. In fact, it may often be beneficial to state openly that, if the patient chooses to follow the recommendations of both AA and the therapist, chances are excellent that the client will remain sober and be abstinent at the end of treatment two years later. This is especially important considering that 90% of relapses occur during the first year of sobriety (Chalmers & Wallace, 1979).

Imparting of Information

The imparting of information is generally not highly valued as a curative mode in most therapy groups (Yalom, 1985). However, this situation is probably reversed in alcoholism treatment. If not highly valued, it is at least highly important that the array of information about alcoholism be conveyed to recovering alcoholics. The disease concept, tolerance, physiological complications, and the addiction process are all simple, but crucial matters of which all alcoholics should be aware. Alcoholics who come to construe their alcoholism as a physiological disorder complicated by psychological, sociological and cultural factors show the best chances of recovery (Wallace, 1978).

In the early stages of sobriety, because guilt is counterproductive to both treatment and the acceptance of the disease concept of alcoholism, the patient should not be encouraged to delve deeply (beyond superficial drinking experiences) into prior life problems.

Therapy time should be spent, instead, on the imparting of information on what alcoholism is and how to avoid drinking. This fulfills the alcoholic's need for structure and direction while, at the same time, helping him interpret his alcoholic behavior within the confines of what Wallace and Yalom call respectively the "exotic belief" and "vital lies." Fehr (1976) agrees that, in the early stages of treatment, when the therapist works individually with each patient, interaction between members of the group should be limited. This beginning part of therapy is described as the diagnostic-teaching phase wherein the patient explores those problems which contribute to and are associated with excessive alcohol consumption. In this process, alcoholics can learn how to become agents for themselves and other group members. Thus, in the early stages of treatment, the group therapy time is utilized more efficiently in individual diagnostic work with each patient.

Existential Factors

Yalom (1975) emphasizes a crucial principle for interpersonal change: "This principle — that change is preceded by a state of dissonance or incongruity — has considerable clinical and social psychological research backing" (p. 263). This is especially true for alcoholics, who, through their excessive drinking, have created a deep rift between their sober values and their alcoholic behavior. Unlike the typical neurotic patient, alcoholics have experienced "a stay in their own personal underworld, an experience which AA members refer to as hitting bottom. Some alcoholics emerge from this experience with an increased degree of integration. Many do not, however" (Brown & Yalom, 1977, p. 447).

Hitting bottom has a dual meaning for therapy; it is at once an impediment and a potentially invaluable reference point. An urgent experience (or in Jasper's phrase, a "boundary situation") can, if properly integrated, lead to growth (Friedman, 1964). "As patients face their limits, their symbolic deaths, they are often able to make some massive shifts in their life perspective. They may rearrange their priority of needs and trivialize the trivia in life" (Brown & Yalom, 1977, p. 448).

It is Yalom's experience that neurotics in therapy frequently avoid religious and existential factors in group, even though they are of great concern to them. Yalom feels that therapy groups with neurotics often tend to water down the tragedy of life, but that members who plunge deeply into themselves, who confront their fate most openly and resolutely, pass into a mode of existence which is richer than prior to their illness. Never is this more applicable than with alcoholic patients, who recognize and share a common theme which is widely addressed by the AA philosophy (AA, 1955). The development of authenticity of character after being pushed to the edge of the psychic abyss is a theme that is also expressed by the most popular existential writers (Buber, 1960; Camus, 1960; Heidegger, 1963; Sartre, 1956). Yalom agrees with Camus when he expresses the idea that no one considers his life with absolute seriousness until he comes fully to terms with his power to end his life.

Such themes as suicide, hitting bottom, and the tragedy of life are far more meaningful in alcoholic groups than they normally are in nonalcoholic groups. The therapist, if he or she is to help patients integrate their experience in a healthy fashion, must not be frightened away by the patient's dread, but must gently and repeatedly lead the alcoholic back to his experience. "Any horror revisited long enough becomes detoxicated" (Brown & Yalom, 1977, p. 477).

Altruism

Although the alcoholic's behavior while drinking may suggest otherwise, alcoholics do not like interpersonal conflict, nor do they handle it well. They will support each other emotionally in group, and if they sense that another is experiencing too much discomfort, they will rescue him, often interfering with important and necessary therapeutic catharsis. The therapist will soon discover alcoholics do best in relationships characterized by complimentary rather than competitive interactions. Brown and Yalom describe the alcoholics in their study as unusually conscientious and, rather than happy-go-lucky, "they were exceedingly prone to assume blame and guilt for dysphoric events in the group or distress suffered by others" (p. 450). These patients were inordinately cautious and generally experienced a deep sense of responsibility for others. Above all they avoided any behavior which might cause pain to another. This deep feeling of caring and support, evident in alcoholic groups, can be a powerful therapeutic asset. Yalom explained that this hypervigilance resulted in a constant surveying for signs of disturbance; group members would frequently submerge their own needs in an effort to be helpful to others. It was evident to Yalom that this was part of a deeper and shared character structure common to all the subjects in his study.

Identification, Interpersonal Input and Output

Through interaction with the therapist and the group, the alcoholic will often learn for the first time how to relate with others in a meaningful and sober manner. Usually all socializing in the past was either influenced by or a product of alcoholic consumption. For some individuals lacking intimate relationships, the group can represent the first opportunity for accurate interpersonal feedback. The alcoholic's general feeling of separateness and isolation must give way to the feeling of being a part of, and in some kind of harmony with, what is going on around him/her. In many cases the group can fulfill the need quite inadequately.

Catharsis

As Yalom illustrates, the intensity of the emotional expression is highly relativistic. Consequently, the expression of emotion must be appreciated from the perspective of the individual. A seemingly muted expression of emotion, for an alcoholic or addict, may represent an event of considerable intensity. Contrary to what many people think, alcoholics and addicts do not handle the expression of emotion well. They are usually incapable of modulating the expression of their own feelings. Part of this problem is related to the fact that alcoholics and addicts have usually had poor and inadequate models for the appropriate demonstration of affect. An alcoholic and addict is usually adept at the suppression of an uncomfortable feeling and frequently keeps the recognition of the true affective state far from their conscious awareness. An often unrecognized fear is that once they start to express emotion, they will either be overwhelmed or explosive. However, if the alcoholic or addict does not get in touch with his or her own feelings and if they fail to learn to master these impulses treatment is likely to be impaired. Consequently, a group therapist has to constantly monitor his group and guide them between what Wallace cautions as too little emotional expression and too much emotional expression. The basic task of the group therapist therefore involves the choosing of a safe course between two equally hazardous alternatives. It is important to lessen denial and encourage increased self-awareness and the affective arousal associated with self-disclosure while simultaneously keeping anxiety at a minimal level (Wallace, 1978). This means that the group therapist must be content with the gradual deepening of self-disclosure rather than demanding dramatic breakthroughs.

Unlike neurotics, whose defenses are usually inadequate, alcoholics and addicts are adept at keeping troublesome feelings out of their awareness. However, if a group therapist pushes an alcoholic or addict to feel and express their emotions too quickly, the consequence is usually an overwhelming flooding of emotions. During the early stages of recovery, such an occurrence must be avoided. It is this author's experience, that many of the early and premature cathartic experiences in group often have long-term detrimental results. While it is often self-satisfying for the therapist to get past the defenses of the alcoholic and addict, so that they get in touch with feelings that have been long buried, the usual result is a person avoiding treatment. Therefore, the work of a group therapist with this population is what many psychodynamics theorists refer to as the building of ego-strength.

As Erv and Miriam Polster write, an individual's defenses are there for a reason and the defenses must not be stripped away too quickly (1973). Wallace agrees and points out "that denial is there for a purpose, it is the glue that holds an already shattered self-esteem system together. And it is a tactic through which otherwise overwhelming anxiety can be contained" (Wallace, 1978, p. 15). On the other hand as Yalom writes, there is little chance that permanent change will occur unless there is an affective arousal state accompanying the self-understanding. Self-understanding by itself only feeds the alcoholic's and addict's defensive system and makes treatment more difficult. The consequence of insight without catharsis results in an alcoholic or addict who can tell you all the reasons why they drink and do drugs while at the same time continuing to drink and do drugs. Certainly, the alcoholic and addict needs little help in that area of their recovery.

Family Reenactment

As Yalom illustrates, and research addressing the importance of different cultural factors substantiates, the recapitulation of the primary family experience is usually not ranked as helpful by group members. However, as Yalom points out, only successful encounter group's members cited this factor as important. Yalom thus implies that the issue of family reenactment is important even though group members may not identify it as such. I believe this is also true with addictive patients in group. One of the best predictors of alcoholism is the kind of home alcoholics come from. A broken home is the background for 40% of alcoholics, and 40% (some overlapping) report problem drinking in at least one parent (Ray, 1972). Group therapy therefore allows group members to understand their own attitudes and defenses about drinking by observing those same attitudes and defenses in others who are struggling with similar problems.

However, as Yalom suggests, even though the specter of early family experiences often haunts the members of the group, it is generally unproductive to focus explicitly on this subject. Rather, the shift in perspective about the past and the understanding of the influence of the early family experience will occur because of the vitality of the work that the alcoholic or addict does in the present. Change is less likely to occur through a direct summons and inquiry of the experiences with the family in the past. Talking about the parents in the past can also become a defense against exploring the feelings and issues that the members have towards each other and their current struggles to remain abstinent from alcohol and drugs. Addicts and alcoholics are usually adept at "playing the psychotherapy game" and discover early that this is a topic that professionals usually love to "jump on because it is such a hot item." Consequently, focusing directly on the parental influences and experiences often leads to a discussion which only feeds the alcoholic and addict's defensive system and impedes productive group work in the present.

Self-Understanding

Yalom criticizes the naive and popular conceptualization which views psychotherapy as a "detective search . . . a digging or a stripping away" of defenses until a person discovers and identifies the true negative aspects of themselves. Self-understanding as it was ranked in importance by group members in Yalom's original study, referred instead to self-understanding as "discovery and accepting previously unknown or unacceptable parts of myself" (Yalom, 1975, p. 92). Therefore, self-understanding as it is intended here, refers to group members discovering previously unknown and unidentified positive aspect of themselves. Group therapy with alcoholics and addicts must be run on this principle. Because addicted individuals generally possess such strong feelings of shame, embarrassment and self-loathing, it is extremely curative when they learn that they can be viewed by others in a positive manner. As Kurtz (1982) writes, the alcoholic suffers from deep feelings of shame. In fact, Kurtz views Alcoholics Anonymous as a program for the treatment of shame. While most contemporary forms of Western-based psychotherapy are directed toward the treatment of guilt, Alcoholics Anonymous directs its healing towards a more primitive emotional arrestment. Guilt, according to Kurtz, implies "I feel bad for something I have done." Shame, a more profound feeling all alcoholics and addicts struggle with, implies "I feel bad because of what I am." Addiction from this view implies that group therapy must enhance the self-understanding and the acceptance that one is worthwhile despite their strong feelings of self-loathing and self-hatred. As Kurtz suggests, the healing of shame requires more than talking about shame. It requires the alcoholic and addict identify those aspects in another and eventually accepting the other who share what the alcoholic and addict shares. This principle — before a person can be healed, they have to know they can heal another — is what Searles (1972) identifies as the "therapeutic symbiosis." While Searles was referring to the therapist in his description, this principle also applies to group members. It is this opportunity to learn that one has the ability to help another in being a healer which supports the use of group psychotherapy. In fact, this is the very same principle which AA applies within the Twelfth Step of its Twelve-Step Program for recovery. The alcoholic and addict maintains their own sobriety by helping another alcoholic or addict get sober.

CURATIVE FACTORS IN AA

It is important to remember that Yalom's curative factors not only operate in therapy groups, but they exist as well in AA. While the conditions for change and the therapeutic mechanisms of change may differ in each group, the process of cure is similar even though each may place more emphasis or value on different curative factors. Emrick (1977) investigated this possibility and searched through the literature on AA for direct or indirect reference to Yalom's twelve curative factors. Emrick's research showed that ten of Yalom's twelve curative factors were operating in AA groups. Table II lists Emrick's findings and the ranked ordered importance of each curative factor.

As Emrick (1977) concluded, "If the factors more frequently mentioned play more central roles in AA, then the composition for and mechanisms of change operating in AA is reflected in the ranking of the factors" (p. 130). Comparing these rankings with those of Yalom (1985), Emrick hypothesized that AA groups were different in the centrality and importance of these curative factors. Apparently AA groups place more emphasis on guidance, identification and instillation of hope, while professional group therapy relies more on interpersonal learning, catharsis, insight and existential awareness. In order to determine the degree of similarity between the two, Emrick felt it would be valuable to explore this comparison by randomly assigning alcoholics to psychotherapy groups and AA groups and later administering Yalom's instrument for measuring, members' perceptions of the curative factors. Further, it may be important to explore the possible matching and differentiation of treatment effects based on the personality characteristics that Emrick et al. (1977) have identified as being differentially suited either to AA or to professional care.

Emrick maintains that

> clients appropriate for AA seem to be those who are responsive to peers, drawn towards a spiritually oriented approach, comfortable talking about their alcoholism in front of large groups and enjoy socializing with reformed alcoholics. Uniquely suited for professional care seem to be those alcoholics who . . . are responsive to professionals, are strongly invested in introspection, view alcoholism as a psychological problem, wish to talk at most to a few people. . . . (p. 138)

Curative Factors Operating in Different Types of Therapy Groups

Kanas and Barr (1982) sought to answer the question of how an outpatient therapy group for alcoholics might differ from therapy groups with alcoholic inpatients. They also compared the rankings of these curative factors with non-alcoholic outpatients and inpatients. Table III lists the results of their study.

Table II and Table III reveal the importance which cohesion has

TABLE II

FREQUENCY OF PUBLICATIONS (N = 26) REFERRING TO CURATIVE FACTORS OPERATIVE IN AA GROUPS.

Curative factor	Number of Publications
Altruism	21
Group cohesiveness	20
Identification	14
Instillation of hope	12
Guidance	12
Universality	10
Catharsis	8
"Insight"	6
Interpersonal learning, "output"	2
Family reenactment	1
Interpersonal learning, "input"	0
Existential awareness	0

Source: Emrick, et al (1977)

TABLE III

Group Therapy Curative Factors in Different Populations

Study	Yalom (1975)	Maxmen (1973)	Feeney & Dranger (1976)	Kanas & Barr (1981)	
Population	20 psychiatric outpatients	100 psychiatric inpatients	20 alcoholic inpatients	8 alcoholic outpatients	
# Hourly sessions	64 (approx.)	9	35 (approx.)	36.8	
Mean duration	16 months	18 days	49 days	25.9 weeks	
Ranking method	Q-sort	Questionnaire	Q-sort	Questionnaire	
Ranking order					Composit Ranks
Interpersonal input	1	5	3	7	3.7 (2)
Catharsis	2	8	1	6	5.7 (6)
Group cohesiveness	3	2	4	3	3.0 (1)
Insight	4	9	2	8	5.7 (6)
Interpersonal output	5	7	7	4	5.0 (5)
Existential factors	6	6	6	9	4.2 (4)
Universality	7	4	8	5	4.0 (3)
Instillation of hope	8	1	5	1	5.7 (6)
Altruism	9	3	9	2	6.7 (7)
Family reenactment	10	11	10	11	10.4 (10)
Guidance	11	10	11	10	11.0 (11)
Identification	12	12	12	12	12.0 (12)

Source: Kamas & Barr (1981)

in a therapy group. Although none of the individual studies specifically ranked cohesiveness as the number one curative factor, a composite rank of the individual curative factors reveals the universal importance of cohesion in groups. As Yalom repeatedly states, "group cohesiveness is the *sine qua non* of effective long-term group therapy, and the effective group therapist must direct his or her efforts towards maximal development of these therapeutic resources" (p. 111, 1985). In describing the curative factors which exist in groups, Yalom draws the distinction between those curative factors which are mechanisms of change and those curative factors which are conditions for change. The importance of the attainment of cohesion in group cannot be overstated. Repeated studies and Yalom's own clinical opinion continually point to the necessity of first establishing an atmosphere of safety and trust before the group's curative forces can be activated. While cohesiveness itself may not be more important than any of the other curative factors, it is an essential and crucial condition which allows the other mechanisms of change and cure to be set in motion.

Mechanisms of Change and Cure in Group Therapy

Yalom's interactional group therapy model provides the group leader with a unique opportunity to assess his group members' capacity to engage in healthy or destructive interpersonal relationships. In light of Kohut's description of cure which was given earlier in this chapter, it is vitally important that the interpersonal and intrapersonal distortions which a group member possesses be modified if they are to attain psychological health. This is important for two reasons. First, as Carl Rogers, Heinz Kohut and other object relations theorists have emphasized, to have the potential to engage in healthy authentic human relationships is in itself a powerful ongoing curative process. Secondly, people generally treat and relate to others as they treat and relate to themselves. For instance, critical punishing people are usually critical and punishing of themselves. Forgiving, caring and honest people are more likely to treat themselves in a like manner. External exchanges with others are usually clear representations of a person's internal reality. There are a variety of windows into the world of the unconscious. Transference, free associations, slips of the tongue, body language, character styles, dreams, compulsions and resistances are other examples of ways of getting through to a person's internal world. Watching their object-relations and interpersonal exchanges with other members in the group is just another excellent avenue for understanding the individual's internal unconscious process.

Group leaders working in the Sullivanian, Rogerian or Object-relations tradition stress the here-and-now relationships and the corrective emotional experience over classical insight as a major curative force. As Stone and Rutan write, "In group therapy the presence of a network of human relationships, rather than just the single relationship to the analyst, increases the opportunities for multiple experiences that can produce change" (p. 53, 1984).

Stone and Rutan also state that in order to achieve the structural changes needed in rebuilding a person's fragmented or flawed ego, a safe, trusting and cohesive atmosphere must first be established in group. They also feel that an unintrusive group leader is required if the group members are going to let down their defenses long enough to allow their parataxic distortions and fragmented selves emerge so that they can ultimately be examined and altered.

Stone and Rutan outline the three mechanisms of change which are required if people are to be cured in group. These mechanisms are:

1. Imitation
2. Identification
3. Internalization

Imitation

As members of a group watch others benefit from the open sharing and expression of emotions, they will be encouraged to do the same because of their desire to gain symptom relief and their need to belong and be accepted by others in the group. Rutan and Stone write:

> In therapy groups individuals have the opportunity to observe many interactions, styles of relating, and problem-solving techniques. Much of the early learning in groups is imitative. Patients who have difficulty tolerating and sharing strong emotions can first observe as other members interact intensely. As they learn that members are not harmed, but rather are typically drawn closer by such exchanges, such patients see some hope for change and, as a consequence, can begin to share feelings by imitating those who are more successful in that task. Though primarily used early in group membership, imitation remains one of the ways in which members gain new behavioral options throughout their treatment. The successes following imitative behavior make the group more attractive, enhance a wish to belong, and increase cohesiveness. This furthers identifications among the members. The use of imitation is both a result of feeling that others have been successful and a means of discovering alternative ways of thinking, expressing, or behaving. It is by no means limited to group therapy; but group therapy, by virtue of the multiple interactions and relationships, expands the opportunities for change through imitative learning. (p. 54, 1984)

Identification

Identification has long been a favorite theoretical mechanism to explain how children develop broad attributes and generalized behavior patterns similar to those of their parents. Classically, identification is the unconscious process through which an individual comes to emulate or model another whom they admire, respect, or wish to be like. As the members in the therapy group and the group itself becomes cohesive and attractive, this furthers identifications among the members. Rutan and Stone described the importance of this process in stimulating the curative forces in group.

> Identifications arise not only from the content of the memories, associations, and feelings, but with the process of telling about them as well. Consciously these identifications may be expressed as feelings of attraction, belonging, and attachment to the members and the group. These are the building blocks from which group cohesiveness develops. Similarly, universalization, the development of the sense that one is not alone in his or her feelings, furthers group attraction and identifications among members. A circular process begins that enhances these powerful influences members have upon one another. In turn the resultant identifications alter fundamental ways in which the members perceive and respond. The incremental building of identifications forms the base for lasting change. (p. 56, 1984)

Internalization

The third and final stage of change and cure culminates in the group members internalizing the values, norms and behavior of other members in the group. This signals a true independent move to psychological health and cure. Group members no longer have to rely on more primitive external sources of identification or imitation to produce change in themselves. Through the resolution of conflicts and continual examination of emotionally laden interactions in group, psychic structure has been slowly and methodically laid. Rutan and Stone summarized the importance of this change.

> Internalization produces greater flexibility in handling both internal and interactive states and is the result of working through conflicts or building new psychic structure to handle previously disruptive anxiety. The therapist can facilitate healthy internalization by detailed examination and reexamination of emotionally laden interactions. Through identification, clarification, and interpretation, individuals integrate

knowledge gained in the here-and-now transactions with their sources and prior assumptions. This results in an increased integration of affects and object relationships as well as diminished inner conflict. The outcome can be observed in the therapy setting where a patient might indicate a new way of behaving to recurrent stimuli. (p. 57, 1984)

The mechanisms of change which Rutan and Stone described as occurring in group are also active in AA. As the alcoholic proceeds through the initial stages of his recovery, he begins with the first stage in which he imitates the behavior of other alcoholics by stating "I can't drink." Attending numerous AA meetings, the newly recovering alcoholic realizes that if he is to stay sober he must imitate the behavior of his fellow AA members. This is the initial stage where a great deal of external control is necessary (i.e., hospitalization, detoxification, Antabuse, etc.). At this stage, the alcoholic needs protection against his own impulses to drink. The second phase is what Wallace (1978) calls the "I won't drink" stage and the alcoholic now identifies with his fellow AA members. His desire to remain abstinent is not determined by external pressures, but more by his own desire to remain sober and active in AA. The third and final stage is the stage of internalization which Wallace calls the "I don't have to drink stage." Conflict resolution is obtained. The alcoholic has successfully worked the twelve steps of the AA program and has obtained a high degree of serenity in his recovery. While the danger of a relapse is never completely eradicated in any alcoholic, the alcoholic's recovery is much more stabilized than at any other stage of his recovery. (See Table IV, adapted from Wallace, 1978.)

THE CURATIVE PROCESS

Rutan and Stone believe that the mechanisms of change inherent in imitation, identification, and internalization are enhanced by a curative process that requires confrontation, clarification, interpretation, and working through. Each of these factors is stage specific to the curative process.

Confrontation

In treating the addicted patient in a group setting, confrontation is essential at the beginning of treatment. The focus should not be on

TABLE IV

STAGES OF TREATMENT

STAGES	PATIENT STATUS	TREATMENT
Stage I	"I can't drink" (Need for external control) Imitation	Detoxification Antabuse AA (1st 4 steps) Directive Psychotherapy Hospitalization Education
Stage II	"I won't drink" Identification	Supportive Psychotherapy AA (All 12 steps)
Stage III	"I don't have to drink." Internalization	AA=Sponsorship & 12th Step work Insight Oriented Psychotherapy

the alcoholic's or addict's unconscious assumptions; rather the group leader must constantly point out to them the external aspects of their behavior. The purpose of treatment during the initial stages of recovery is to do for the alcoholic or addict what they are unable to do for themselves. Because their denial is so strong and their pathological defenses so rigid, they require a strong caring relationship with a group leader who will serve as a container for their anger and anxiety while pointing out, in a nonpunitive manner, the destructive patterns of their behavior.

Learning to confront successfully requires 1. timing, 2. the capacity to form an alliance and 3. empathy. If these skills are not adequately developed, group members will respond defensively, withdraw emotionally, attack the group and its members because of their own fears, or drop out of treatment.

Confrontations can take many forms, however. Rutan and Stone point out the many ways confrontation can be manifested in group. Confrontations in group can be contagious and can affect each group member differently.

Most confrontations take place among members or between therapists and members. However, one form of confrontation in groups is distinct. Looking into the hall of mirrors, patients might observe others involving themselves in unproductive and pathological behavior and begin to be curious about the extent to which they too engage in identical or similar behaviors. This is a form of self-confrontation. In a therapy group no confrontation is given in isolation. Every member of the group hears and is affected, even though the confrontation may have been directed primarily at another member. Thus interventions must take into account more than an appreciation of the openness of a particular individual to hear them: they must include an awareness that the other members will have their own responses. (p. 61, 1984)

Clarification

Clarifications in group follow from interactions and confrontations. They serve the purpose of placing the individual interactions and exchanges in sharp focus. Clarifications help group members see repeated patterns in their behavior. As the group progresses in its development, the varied patterns of each individual member will begin to emerge. This is a middle phase process of group therapy in which each group member's behavioral constellation is brought to their and the rest of the group members' attention. A cold distant group member might be told, "This is a common complaint of your wife and is the reason you find yourself without friends. It might be helpful for you to explore in group what it is that leads you to affect others in the way you do."

Interpretations

Interpretations differ from clarifications in that they are aimed at the unconscious in an attempt to get the group members' repressed unconscious material to their awareness by helping them gain an understanding of their hidden motives and conflicts. A later stage process of group therapy, successful interpretations require an emotional and cognitive component to their delivery. However, the timing of an interpretation is crucial. If given in the midst of an emotional storm or too intellectually derived, they will fail to have an impact on a group member's understanding and behavior.

Working Through

Confrontation, clarification, and interpretation help group members become aware of their patterns of behavior and unconscious conflicts, but they alone are insufficient to bring about deep and lasting change. In working through, the emphasis is on increasing the person's capacity to examine themselves and understand their areas of conflict and vulnerability. As they develop the capacity to interpret their own behavior, they will also develop a more varied and flexible defensive system which will protect them more adequately from undue anxieties while allowing more authentic intimacy with others.

Working through consumes the major portion of time in an ongoing therapy group. As each group member comes to understand and identify disturbing self-defeating behavior, the associated thoughts and feelings are worked on and resolved. However, the consolidation of these thoughts, feelings, and behavior will continue to emerge in a slightly disguised form repeatedly throughout the person's treatment in group. An example will help clarify this point.

> Martha, a thirty-two-year-old, freelance photographer sought psychotherapy because of her severe depression and suicidal ideation. Two weeks into individual therapy, it was discovered her depression was closely related to her excessive alcohol consumption. When encouraged to stop drinking and enter AA, Martha quickly complied. In fact, as therapy progressed, Martha readily complied to all the therapist's numerous requests. She had developed an acute idealizing transference in which she perceived her therapist to be "just perfect." Since the symptoms which had originally brought her to psychotherapy had quickly subsided, her therapist did not want to challenge her description of him as perfect too quickly for fear it would either prompt her to relapse or trigger a recurrence of her depression. As Martha's psychotherapy progressed, it became more apparent that she had at times gotten dangerously close to withdrawing into her own fantasy world where everything was perfect. She related that as a child, she had been sent by her school to see a psychiatrist because of her autistic-like self-absorption. Her early family life was marred by a distant father and a hostile, intrusive mother who demanded that Martha be perfect in her behavior, appearance and school work. At the age of thirteen, Martha discovered, through a reading of her sister's diary and some documents she found hidden in a closet, that she had been adopted. When she confronted her mother with her concerns, her mother exploded and denied all

the evidence to the contrary. This only drove Martha to pursue her perfect fantasy world with more determination since her reality-based world was too chaotic, threatening and erratic.

After six months of individual therapy, Martha continued to insist that she had made the perfect choice in her therapist and believe that through his guidance in therapy everything would be perfect. All she had to do in order to be perfect was to perfectly perform all his requests since she sincerely believed he was perfect. After three more months of behaving perfectly, Martha began to realize that things weren't turning out perfectly. She still felt angry, sad, and upset at varying times. Finally, she confronted her therapist, stating angrily that she was doing all he wanted, but that she still wasn't perfectly happy. Assured by him that he had not given her any formulation or suggestions, Martha confessed that she had inferred these formulas from their conversations. He then pointed out to her how she was attempting to create in the therapy situation the same circumstances which had existed in her early home life with her parents. Specifically, she believed if she did all things perfectly, the end result would turn out perfectly.

Encouraged by this insight, Martha proceeded to progress in therapy and began to make plans for termination. However, as she came closer to the termination date, her despair once again returned. Eventually, Martha came to realize that her despair was triggered by her realization that as she came closer to ending therapy, she had to face the realization that she was not yet perfect. She had held on to the fantasy that somehow, she would be perfect when therapy ended. Encouraged further by this insight, Martha decided to continue therapy to insure that she was not fooling herself once again.

However, her need for perfection surfaced again in another form. After two difficult sessions in which she left the therapist's office feeling worse than when she had entered, Martha was struck by another important realization. Her therapist had twice made comments that had hurt her. She could not understand why he had done that. Since she still continued to perceive him as perfect, he must have hurt her on purpose. When she learned that her therapist had not hurt her intentionally, but apparently had made a mistake in his understanding of her feelings, she was forced once again to deal with the despair that this realization produced.

Transferred to a therapy group after another few months of individual therapy, her perfection fantasy resurfaced again. She had secretly bargained with herself that this time things would indeed really be perfect. Again, this was worked through only to have it resurface in another form. Two years after entering therapy, Martha's constant retreat into her perfect fantasy was rekindled by a new relationship with a man. The same theme emerged. She held on to the belief that this man and this relationship would now be perfect. After each progressive stage was worked through in therapy, Martha's reliance on her perfect fantasy diminished in the intensity and length of duration.

Taken in the proper sequence, confrontation, clarification and interpretation can help the group members work through their various conflicts, resistances, and self-defeating repetitive patterns. To enhance this process in its correct sequence, the group leader must:

1. *Confront the defense first.* For example, a withdrawn group member might be confronted with the following observation. "You deny your need for people. But, it is obvious to all of us in group that you are easily upset when people don't respond favorably to you. It is also obvious that you take great joy in the attention that others give you."
2. *Clarify the defense.* "There, you are doing it again. Every time someone reaches out to you, you do something to push them away."
3. *Interpretation.* "You keep denying your need for others because you are so frightened that they will get close to you and then reject you just as your mother did repeatedly when you were growing up."
4. *Working through.* The pattern will emerge again and again in varying forms. The group leader's task is to keep pointing out its occurrence in a nonjudgmental manner and help the group member come to a personal resolution about his fears, fantasies and catastrophic expectations.

Working Through With the Addicted Patient

In working through with the typical addicted patient, the group leader must accomplish a sequence of tasks if he is to keep his group members sober. First, he must get them to stop using chemicals. Through coercion, confrontation, encouragement or appeal, this must be the first goal of treatment.

Secondly, the group leader must guide each member through a corrective emotional experience. The purpose of group treatment at this point is not insight — to make the unconscious conscious — but rather to promote the reliving of old experiences in group so that they can be reexperienced by a sober and more mature psyche. The alcoholic and addict must come to discharge his old pent-up emotions in a safe and constructive way so that he can work through the depression and hurt which is always buried underneath the anger. The individual must then come to identify and break the cycle of "The world and everyone in it is terrible. I am also terrible." Destructive relationships must be altered or severed and healthy relationships with healthy people must be substituted. Self-esteem, which is always negatively affected by this cycle, is eventually restored. The grandiose false self-organization which has been erected as a defensive facade must be given over to the true self so that authentic relationships can be established. As the sense-of-self is firmly established, the person will then develop the capacity to make more autonomous decisions and healthy choices. Destructive dependencies will be altered and the person will be free to engage in true intimate relationships without losing themselves in old archaic needs and expectancies.

Stages of Cure in a Therapy Group

Cure in group therapy requires that the group leader carefully monitor the stage specific behavior of the group. Do not expect the group to say goodbye before they say hello. Don't expect the group to share true intimacy before trust has been established. The group leader who is finely tuned to the stage consistent behavior of the group is more likely to have a successful group experience for his group members. An understanding of group development and the curative process will help the group leader guide his group successfully through the difficult and different developmental stages which are sure to confront the group.

In the pages that follow, the six different phases of group development will be presented and discussed. The first two phases of group must be resolved before the group will be ready to move on to the more intimate phases of interpersonal interaction (see Table V).

TABLE V

PHASE OF GROUP DEVELOPMENT

I. DEPENDENCE

    A. Each member enters group with the curative fantasy
    B. Flight from intimacy and the here and now is prominent
    C. Parallel talk is pronounced
    D. Pseudo-cohesion develops

II. COUNTER-DEPENDENCE

    A. Rebellion dominates
    B. Scapegoating
    C. Intimacy is avoided by fighting

III. RESOLUTION OF POWER/AUTHORITY ISSUES

    A. Pairing and fusion is pronounced
    B. Disappointment and disillusionment
    C. The group and the leader is found to be lacking

IV. STAGE OF REAL COHESION

    A. Deeper intimacy develops after anger and disappointment is resolved

V. INTERDEPENDENCE

    A. Consensual validation of ambiguity
    B. Group maturity and true intimacy

VI. TERMINATION

    A. Separation/individuation

1. Dependence

Safety and trust are crucial during this phase. Like the chatter which occurs at a cocktail party, the group members' exchanges will be directed more at their desire to be accepted. What they have to say at this phase isn't as meaningful as their interest in presenting themself as a valuable and important asset to the group. Like the conversation at a cocktail party, after the person has worked through their initial anxiety they will then say, "Oh! What did you say your name was?" Now, they are ready to engage each other on a more meaningful level.

The group members rely on the group leader extensively during this phase. As they enter the group, they have a vague expectation that the group will somehow magically help them. But they also fear they will be traumatized and defeated by the group as they were by their parents. Their curative fantasy will be pronounced as they try to get from the group leader what they had wanted from their parents in the past. Many members hope they will be accepted, affirmed and will not be rejected by the group. This is often all they want. Just to be told by the group that they are okay will often confirm their sense of self and for many will be initially therapeutic.

Group will be used frequently by the members to strengthen certain deficient parts of themselves. Kohut, in particular, placed extensive emphasis on the individual's intuitive drive to repair fragmented egos and defective selves. Their intuitive fantasy is that their sense of self will be mended and strengthened through their interaction and acceptance by the group.

2. Counter-Dependence

Although the group may shift its focus to more affective arousing issues, their fears of intimacy are still dominant. Each group member will test the leader and the group to insure they are safe from humiliation and threat. Their basic question remains. Will I and whatever I say be accepted here? They must come to realize that the boundaries of the group are clearly set and safely managed.

3. Resolution of Power/Authority Issues

After anger is finally expressed and worked through in group, a stage of pseudo-cohesion develops. Hope is prominent in group and Bion's basic assumption of pairing is central to this phase of the group's development (see Chapter Eleven).

4. Stage of Real Cohesion

This is a phase that the group strives to attain but unfortunately is only temporary. However, while it lasts, it is warm, genuine, and authentic. But just when the group begins to feel as if it will be more cohesive, it falls apart. This is to be expected. If the group leader needs to have and believe in a continual, safe, trusting group, he will be disappointed. This is much like the mother who during the child's separation/individuation stage of development requires the child to stay in her lap and behave. The group leader must not interfere with this developmental stage, but must be able to contain the group's aggression and anger without allowing it to turn into harmful scapegoating.

5. Interdependence

This is the phase that Alonso (1985) refers to as the borderline existence of the group. Splitting and projective identification occurs repeatedly among the group members. The group and the leader is found lacking. People threaten to leave. Competition and fighting among group members emerges. The group members change and their working through the group conflicts occurs in a helix during this phase. The same issues emerge and reemerge. As each issue is worked through in group, the members progress to a deeper stage each time until their conflicts are resolved.

The group enters the final stage of maturity. Each member has the opportunity to learn that they are independent and separate from the group. The principle of "I must learn that I can live without you before I can be intimate with you" is experienced on more deepening levels. Separation is the key. This is a process of reparation and forgiveness. They realize that "No one, not you or myself is perfect." However, the group and its members eventually acknowledge that although they are not perfect they are good enough.

6. Termination

Termination is then addressed in group. The group must allow each person to leave, even if the person hasn't changed in the way that the group thinks they should have changed. The group members must be able to depart autonomously. The process of termination in groups often requires an active group leader who will not allow the terminating group member to depart inconspicuously. It is a rare event in our society when termination can be completed publicly. Many group members will avoid addressing termination because of the array of emotions it will trigger. However, there are many advantages to the termination process. Hope is gained by all the members. They learn that others can and do get better. It also allows each to deal with their unresolved feelings of abandonment and loss. For many people, experiencing a successful goodbye can be a new and corrective experience in their lives.

CONCLUSION

It should be fitting to end this book with a chapter that ends with the topic of termination in group. I hope I have been able to leave

Philip J. Flores   541

the reader with the same message and feeling that I would like the group leader to leave his group members with when they terminate and depart from their therapy group. Specifically, I hope the reader and group members leave with a better understanding of addiction, less confusion about group therapy, some direction and specific guidelines for their recovery and, most importantly, some hope for their future. Despite all our efforts to give, guide, and support, each of us is ultimately alone when it comes to our life, recovery, and growth. This is the inevitable plight of the human condition. As the existentialists repeatedly say, we are ultimately alone and solely responsible for our fates. Nevertheless, while we are individually alone and responsible, this does not imply we cannot be helped, supported, and encouraged by others in our life and in our community.

As group leaders, while we have our group members in our therapy groups, we can hopefully give them something that they will be able to carry with them after group ends. Specifically, we can give them what everyone wants—an experience and a sense of community where they feel they are accepted and belong. Feeling alienated, empty, and not understood is a struggle which every chemically dependent person experiences. The therapy group gives them this sense of belonging and being understood at a very basic level. This is why the theme of cohesion, trust, and safety has been such a prominent one throughout this book. While everyone wants to be accepted, loved, and recognized, they want it unconditionally. The primary conflict for us all, the addicted as well as the nonaddicted, is to belong and be connected to something larger than ourselves without losing ourselves. Alcoholics and addicts perhaps feel this a little more intensely and this may be why their demand for autonomy and independence takes on such rebellious, self-centered, and demanding properties. They fear that belonging to someone or something will cost them their individuality. This is a constant theme for all of us. Can I be close and truly intimate without losing myself or my separateness coming at a cost to my independence? Can I tolerate being alone without giving up my autonomy to get my need for human closeness met?

Group therapy, directed along the lines prescribed in this book, can meet the needs of both poles of this human dilemma. It first allows the chemically dependent person to get close and be intimate with others who are accepting of him without cost to his identity and autonomy. It then encourages his individuality while giving him the tools to get close to others without compromising his separateness. Ultimately, it allows the alcoholic and addict to deal with the emotions triggered by all intimate encounters without relying on alcohol and drugs to sedate, buffer, or alter their feelings.

In many ways group therapy, much like Alcoholics Anonymous, can be viewed as a holding environment—a cohesive, safe community where people can get at the depth of understanding the relationship between their private and public selves. At the same time, they can be encouraged and allowed to evolve in separate ways at their own pace. As suggested by Wallace earlier in this book, recovery is a time-dependent process. During the early stages of recovery, the alcoholic and addict needs to be welcome to join a safe, trusting, and healing culture. Later, as they gradually evolve through different stages, they will then be encouraged to separate while learning how to be close without losing their identity or isolating themselves from others. As AA so correctly points out, the AA member is a recovering alcoholic. He or she is never recovered. Our growth and evolution continues throughout life. Group therapy, as a part of an alcoholic's or addict's recovery, helps propel this process. It is a process that doesn't end once the person leaves group therapy or gets sober, for the issues of belonging and being alone remain constant themes in our lives. Group therapy helps the recovering person learn ways to successfully adapt to this very central human process.

REFERENCES

A.A. World Services, Inc. (1955). *The story of how many thousands of men and women have recovered from alcoholism*. New York: Author.

Alonso, A. (1985). Lecture given at Harvard Medical School Seminar on Group Psychotherapy. Nov. 22-24.

Brown, S. & Yalom, I. (1977). Interactional group therapy with alcoholics. *Quarterly Journal of Studies on Alcohol. 38*, 426-456.

Buber, M. (1960). *I and thou*. New York: Charles Scribners Sons.

Camus, A. (1960). *The myth of sisyphus, and other essays*. New York: Vintage.

Chalmers, D. & Wallace, J. (1978). Evaluation of patient progress. In S. Zimberg, J. Wallace & S. Blume (Eds.), *Practical approaches to alcoholism psychotherapy* (pp. 255-277). New York: Plenum.

Emrick, C. D., Lassen, C. L. & Edwards, M. T. (1977). Nonprofessional peers as therapeutic agents in effective psychotherapies. In G. E. German & A. Rozin (Eds.), *The therapist contribution to effective psychotherapy: An empirical assessment*. Elmsford, NY: Pergamon Press.

Heidegger, M. (1963). *Being and time*. New York: Harper & Row.

Kanas, N. & Barr, M. A. (1982). Outpatient alcoholics view group therapy. *Group, the Journal of the Eastern Group Psychotherapy Society. 6*(1), 17-20.

Kohut, H. (1984). *How does analysis cure?* Chicago: University of Chicago Press.

Kurtz, E. (1982). Why AA works. The intellectual significance of Alcoholics Anonymous. *Journal of Studies on Alcohol*. *43*(1), 38-80.

Polster, E. & Polster, M. (1973). *Gestalt therapy integrated*. New York: Brunner/Mazel.

Ray, O. (1972). *Drugs, society & human behavior*. St. Louis: C. V. Mosby Co.

Rutan, J. S., Stone, W. N. (1984). *Psychodynamic group therapy*. Lexington, Mass: The Collamore Press.

Sartre, J. P. (1956). *Being and nothingness*. New York: Philosophical Library.

Searles, (1973). Concerning therapeutic symbiosis. *Annals of Psychoanalysis*. *1*, 247-262.

Wallace, J. (1978). In S. Zimberg, J. Wallace & S. Blume (Eds.), *Practical approaches to alcoholism psychotherapy*. New York: Plenum Press.

Yalom, I. (1975). *The theory & practice of group psychotherapy* (2nd ed.). New York: Basic Books.

Yalom, I. (1985). *The theory & practice of group psychotherapy* (3rd ed.). New York: Basic Books.

Index